Europe at the end of the twelfth century

Latin Christian state
Byzantine Christian state
Muslim state

0   500

Miles

REP. OF
NOVGOROD
Novgorod

RUSSIA

Kiev

CUMANS

BLACK SEA

EMPIRE

GEORGIA

CASPIAN SEA

GARIA

TINE

Constant-
inople

SHAH
OF
ARMEN

SELJUK
KINGDOM OF RUM

AEGEAN SEA

DOM. OF
SALADIN

ARMENIA

Antioch

CRETE

CYPRUS

Tripoli

Bagdad

Damascus

SEA

Jerusalem

PERSIAN
GULF

Alexandria

The Emergence
of the
European World

The Emergence

of the

European World

JEROME BLUM
Princeton University

RONDO CAMERON
University of Wisconsin

THOMAS G. BARNES
University of California, Berkeley

LITTLE, BROWN AND COMPANY   BOSTON / TORONTO

Published simultaneously in Canada by Little, Brown & Company (Canada) Limited
Printed in the United States of America

Preface

THE INTERMIXTURE IN OUR OWN TIME of European, or Western, civilization
with non-Western civilizations and cultures is producing a new, global
civilization. It is the purpose of this book to tell the story of Western civilization from the "Dark Ages" when Europe emerged as a cultural entity up
to the early part of the nineteenth century when political, intellectual, and
economic changes of enormous consequence were laying down new patterns
for European development. These new patterns, whose roots reached far
back into the European past, were destined to have great influence in the
development of the rest of the world, too. The history that is recounted in
these pages, then, is an integral and important part of the heritage not only of
Western civilization but also of the global civilization that is now emerging.

We owe many acknowledgments for help that we have received in the
writing of this book; so many, indeed, that we cannot name them all. A
complete listing would have to begin with the teachers who introduced us
to the study of history, would include the many historians whose works we
have used, and would end with the students in the classes that we ourselves
have taught who did much to shape our conception of the kind of book
we wanted to write. We are especially indebted to Professors William J.
Bouwsma, University of California, Berkeley; Roderic H. Davison, George
Washington University; Charles F. Delzell, Vanderbilt University; Klaus

Epstein, Brown University; Franklin L. Ford, Harvard University; Leonard Krieger, University of Chicago; George L. Mosse, Robert L. Reynolds, and Philip D. Curtin, all of the University of Wisconsin; and Herbert H. Rowen, Rutgers University. Each of these men read portions of our manuscript. Their careful criticisms and suggestions proved of great value to us. Professor Robert Lindsay of Ohio University aided in the preparation of the bibliography. Mr. Reese Jenkins and Mr. James Sturm, of the University of Wisconsin, were helpful at many points. Finally, we are grateful to the editorial staff of our publisher, and particularly to Donald Hammonds, David Giele, and David Lynch for their skilful assistance and their often-tried patience.

Jerome Blum
Rondo Cameron
Thomas G. Barnes

Table of Contents

List of Maps and Charts

Illustrations

Chapter opening illustrations from: The Bettmann Archive, Inc.; Culver Pictures, Inc.; Charles Phelps Cushing; Visual Services, Inc.

The Emergence
of the
European World

PART ONE

The Emergence of the
European World

EUROPE is the smallest of the five major continents, contains less than 10 per cent of the world's land area and, in the mid-twentieth century, had slightly more than 20 per cent of the world's population. In quantitative terms Europe may appear of slight importance in our global age.

The "European world," however, is more than a matter of numbers and geography. It is a concept of civilization. It includes European culture in the Western Hemisphere and also outposts of European culture in Asia, Africa, and Australasia. The history of the European world, in short, is the history of Western civilization.

As a distinctly human attribute culture is as old as man himself, but the earliest civilizations for which we have evidence apparently originated in the fourth or fifth millennium before Christ, in association with the development of settled agriculture and the domestication of animals. This occurred first in western Asia, perhaps along the "fertile crescent," the semicircle stretching from Egypt to the Persian Gulf. The early civilizations of Babylonia, Egypt, and probably that of the Indus valley in India, were offshoots of this "cradle of civilization." The only other known civilization with definitely independent origins was that of the pre-Columbian inhabitants of America that evolved in the first millennium after Christ, although the origins of Chinese civilization (second or third millennium B.C.) may have been mostly independent of the original center in western Asia. All other civilizations were, in some measure, derived from these first civilizations.

As a social phenomenon, civilization grows and is transmitted by means of social processes. The growth of civilization is essentially the proliferation and elaboration of all the elements of which civilization is composed. New elements enter the stream by means of chance discovery, and even more by novel combinations of existing elements. These discoveries or new combinations are usually the result of social interaction, as is the transmission of civilization from one generation to another.

The diffusion of civilization is also the result of social interaction, especially through trade, conquest, and mass migration. The confrontation of a relatively primitive society by an advanced or "civilized" society usually results in at least a partial adoption by the former of the civilization of the latter. If, however, the civilized society is feeble it may succumb and its civilization may expire. A civilization is seldom completely obliterated; some of its elements are incorporated into the culture of the more primitive society and help bring about the evolution of a new civilization.

In a very real sense all civilization is a single entity, the civilization of man. But civilization is in a constant state of change and is never quite the same from place to place or at successive points in time, so that it is customary to speak of "civilizations" as well as "civilization." European, or Western, civilization originated from the fusion of German ("Barbarian") culture and Roman civilization during the so-called Dark Ages from the fifth to the tenth century A.D. Roman civilization, in turn, was descended from the earliest civilizations of western Asia and Egypt by way of the Greeks. Since the process of civilization is cumulative, each of these predecessors contributed important elements to the European heritage.

From the beginning of their civilization Europeans have been aggressive and expansionist, conquering, colonizing, trading, proselytizing, and ultimately spreading their culture to every part of the world. Initially this cultural expansion owed much to the vigorous propagation of the Christian faith. Christianization gave to the European world a unity and cultural cohesiveness that was the ideological foundation of its civilization. The first phase of expansion reached its apogee in the period from the beginning of the tenth to the beginning of the fourteenth century. During those centuries European culture spread from its initial centers between the Loire and Rhine rivers in present-day northern France, Belgium, and western Germany throughout the continent, from Spain to Scandinavia, from Iceland to southern Italy, from England to Russia, and even briefly, during the Crusades, to Palestine. The central political fact of European expansion in this early phase was the system of interdependence called feudalism, which knitted diverse and often discordant petty political entities into a defensive posture sufficiently strong to preserve internal order and to withstand threats from without. Economic growth was part of the expansion and the twelfth and thirteenth centuries witnessed the crest of a wave of material prosperity of the European world with burgeoning towns and cities as the centers of trade.

In the fourteenth century Europe descended into an era of crisis and contraction that lasted more than a hundred years. Economic life was overcome by stagnation and decline. Population declined and great stretches of land lay empty and untilled Civil wars among ruling cliques of feudal lords and petty princes proved the beginning of the end of the old political structure; feudalism, which in preceding centuries had been the bulwark of internal order had become the greatest threat to order. Mass insurrections of discontented peasants and urban workers broke out in every part of Europe. Civil commotion was joined by a grass-roots protest against the increasing materialism and decreasing spirituality of the Roman Catholic Church. The papacy, at the pinnacle of its power in the twelfth and thirteenth centuries, now reached the low ebb of its fortunes, and the pope himself for a time became a tool of the French king.

The way out of the morass of decay was indicated by emerging national monarchies, by a new wave of economic expansion, and by a revitalization of European intellectual life. At the expense of the political power of the old aristocracy, kings succeeded in the fifteenth and sixteenth centuries in fashioning nation-states, challenging the interference of both Church and lords in internal affairs and each other in state rivalries productive of wars. Economic revival, buttressed by increasing population, began in the latter part of the fifteenth century. Demand grew, commerce and industry expanded, gold and silver poured into Europe from the New World, prices rose, and there began to emerge a worldwide pattern of trade with Europe as its center. Starting in the fourteenth century in the Italian city-states the intellectual and artistic revival of the Renaissance spread to northwestern Europe in the fifteenth and sixteenth centuries and touched every institution and facet of contemporary Europe. It was much more than a new conception of man, a revival of classical learning, and an artistic flowering without parallel in history. It was the expression of a confident civilization prepared for change and demanding expansion.

The confidence of the European world as it broadened its horizons found new outlets beyond the frontiers of Europe. Bold and skilful navigators journeyed to far-off places. Their discoveries, followed by colonization and exploitation, gave a stake in the greater, once unknown, world to the maritime states of the Atlantic seaboard of Europe and confirmed the shift in the focal point of the European world from the Mediterranean to Western Europe.

The unified Christian faith of Western Europe fell victim to the new confidence. Beginning with Martin Luther's challenge in 1517 to abuses long evident in the Roman Catholic Church, the Protestant Reformation soon became a revolt against ecclesiastical authority, producing theological variety and denominational atomism and ultimately assuring the triumph of secularism. The key to the success of the Protestant reformers lay in the leverage that their revolt presented to secular rulers for aggrandizement of their power and property. The net gain of the age of the Reformation went to the rulers of the emerging nation-states, whether Protestant or Catholic, who were already fashioning the absolutism that would dominate the European world from the mid-seventeenth to the end of the eighteenth century.

Finally, in perhaps the supreme achievement of the epoch, European man evolved a new way of looking at himself, the world, and the universe. New attitudes of secularism and individualism produced new patterns of thought that made possible new approaches to old problems. Above all, a great outburst of scientific speculation in the sixteenth century heralded the beginning of the revolution in science that is still not ended.

The attainments of the European world during this great age of expansion have about them the aura of modernity. So, too, has the sense of crisis which dominated the first six decades of the seventeenth century. A series of destructive wars, compounded of religious motives and dynastic ambitions, filled most of that period and brought in its wake civil commotion and revolution. The simple confidence of the Renaissance and the spiritual exhilaration of the Reformation evaporated. The beneficiaries were the new absolutist monarchs under whose rule order was once more regained.

---- CHAPTER ONE ----

The Heritage of the European World

EUROPE is as much a geographical as a historical fact, and its history has been conditioned by the physical theater in which it has unfolded. Europe forms the westernmost fifth of Eurasia, the greatest land mass on earth, and no definite boundary marks it off from Asia. In contrast to the rest of Eurasia, Europe resembles a peninsula. The Atlantic Ocean on its west, connecting four continents—Europe, North America, South America, and Africa—provided the avenue for the political, cultural, and economic expansion of Europe from the fifteenth century onward. Bays and inlets cut deep incisions into the seacoasts of Europe, and it has many straits, such as those commanding the entrances to the Mediterranean, the Baltic Sea, the Black Sea, and the North Sea. In the power struggles of the European states the straits and narrow seas have been of major strategic importance.

A mountain spine, dominated by the Alps, separates the Mediterranean region from the great plain that extends from the Atlantic coast of France through the Low Countries (Belgium and Holland) across northern Germany and Poland, into Russia as far as the Ural Mountains, and merges with the Great Siberian Plain at the southern end of the Urals. This fertile plain with its many gentle hills has simplified the movements of armies bent on conquest in the wars that have marred Europe's history.

The navigable rivers that lace the continent had much to do with the

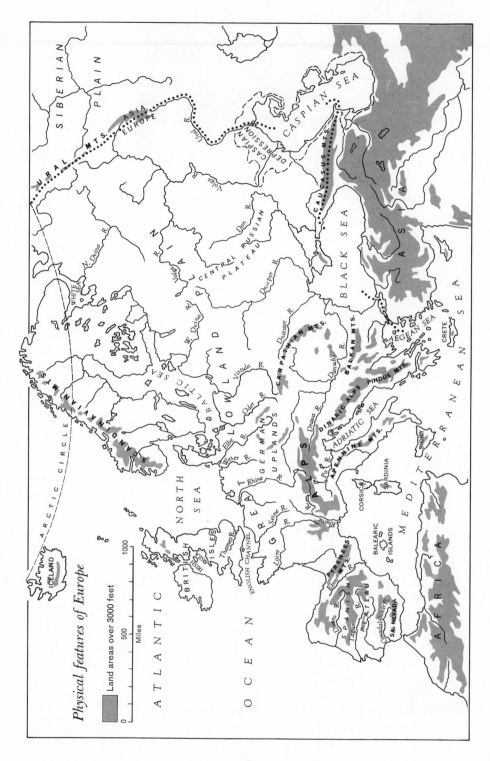

Physical features of Europe

Land areas over 3000 feet

growth of trade and communications, the establishment of cities, and the formation of the states of modern Europe. In northwestern and Central Europe they flow northward into the Atlantic and its subsidiary seas, except for the Danube which runs into the Black Sea. In Eastern Europe the great plainland is drained by rivers flowing into the Black and Caspian seas. In Southern Europe, because of the sharp change in elevation, there are few navigable streams.

The Legacy of Ancient Civilization

Western civilization claims a distinguished lineage. Its immediate forerunners were the civilizations of classical Greece and Rome. These, in turn, were built on the achievements of Egypt, Mesopotamia, and other ancient civilizations of the Near East, or southwestern Asia. Prior to the emergence of the first civilization, however, mankind had undergone a long civilizing process of perhaps a million years.

One of the distinctive features of human culture is the use of tools; man is sometimes called, in fact, a tool-using animal. Since tools are usually made of durable materials, it is possible to trace the development of culture by means of those which have survived. The earliest recognizable tools (as distinguished from sticks and stones appropriated from nature on the occasion of their use) are chipped flints and other stones in a variety of sizes and shapes, used as crude axes, knives, scrapers, and so forth. The period in which they constituted the most important tools of man is called the Paleolithic or Old Stone Age. It lasted roughly a million years, until about 8000 B.C. in southwestern Asia, and even longer in other parts of the world. Paleolithic man undoubtedly developed other elements of culture that entered into our heritage, such as primitive notions of art, religion, and social organization (the family and the tribe, for instance), but apart from a few rare specimens of cave paintings in France and Spain there is little direct evidence of them.

THE BIRTH OF CIVILIZATION

Between about 8000 B.C. and about 4000 B.C. men in various parts of the world gradually perfected the technique of making stone tools by polishing instead of chipping them. This period of prehistory is called the Neolithic or New Stone Age. People in the region between the Tigris and Euphrates rivers and the Mediterranean developed settled agriculture (wheat or barley), domesticated animals (pigs, goats, and sheep), and invented pottery. They probably also invented textiles, since basket weaving almost certainly preceded pottery, but no material evidence survives. These various developments are sometimes referred to collectively as the Neolithic Revolution.

9

By permitting the regular production and accumulation of food, they made possible the growth of permanent urban settlements or cities and a more complex social organization and culture.

During the next four thousand years the region west of the Indus River, including the Mediterranean basin, produced other major elements of civilization that entered into the heritage of the European world. These included the development of new varieties of plants and domesticated animals, fermented beverages, metallurgy (especially the use of copper, bronze, and iron), and architecture, as well as the invention of the wheel, the sailing ship, and money. It is not possible to say precisely when or where most of them were invented or discovered, much less who was responsible. In only a few instances can one link special achievements with particular peoples.

Empires rose and fell in Egypt and Mesopotamia, Persia (modern Iran), Syria, Asia Minor, and the islands of the eastern Mediterranean. The arts of government, including terrorism and torture as well as codified civil law, were refined. Not all improvements in civilization came from the great and powerful. The Phoenicians, a seafaring people from the region of modern Lebanon, ranged from the eastern Mediterranean to modern Britain, where they traded Eastern manufactures for the tin of Cornwall. They also colonized extensively in the western Mediterranean at Carthage (modern Tunisia), Marseilles, and the Iberian peninsula. Their most important contribution to civilization, which grew out of their trading habits, was the invention of the first alphabet. Another Semitic people from the eastern Mediterranean who enjoyed a brief period of earthly glory in the tenth century B.C. made a far more lasting contribution to civilization than the fabulous temple of their King Solomon. The monotheistic religion of the ancient Hebrews provided the foundation for Christianity and Islam as well as modern Judaism.

CLASSICAL GREECE

Greece was the earliest direct ancestor of European civilization. Springing from an earlier non-Greek civilization, it developed rapidly between about 800 and 600 B.C. This was the great period of maritime and colonial expansion of the Greek city-states, which ultimately numbered over one hundred autonomous units located on the Grecian peninsula, nearby islands, and other Mediterranean shores.

Small, independent, and vigorous, the city-states defy generalization. Sparta and Athens, the two most important, represent the extremes. Sparta was militaristic and autocratic in social and political structure. In contrast, Athens developed a system of government that was broadly based on consent, and during its Golden Age, 600–400 B.C., it introduced a rational legal system, representative assemblies, the election of military leaders, and other features of an open society. Both city-states produced leaders of great capacity; but there is historic irony in the fact that Pericles of Athens (d. 429 B.C.), who presided over the period of greatest democracy and cultural vitality in Athens, was also the leader who provoked the strife between Athens and Sparta that led to the Peloponnesian Wars (431–404 B.C.), a general Greek conflagration. The Greek city-states were so weakened that a half-century later Philip of Macedon and his son Alexander the Great could erect a huge, if short-lived, empire on their remains.

Greece's glory was her culture. Her architecture, sculpture, and crafts have been imitated but seldom equaled. Her tragedians—Aeschylus, Sophocles, and Euripides—cast the bravery of the human spirit, the dilemma of power, and the destructiveness of self-consuming arrogance in terms that still move men. The satirical drama of Aristophanes, pillorying contemporary mores, and the histories of Herodotus and Thucydides are brilliant facets of literary genius. Greek scientific genius remained unequaled for two thousand years and Socrates, Plato, and Aristotle erected the framework of philosophy in its principal branches that has remained to this day.

The Macedonian Empire of Alexander the Great and its successors passed on Greek culture to Rome. From there Greek culture, especially Plato's philosophy, passed into early Christianity. The rediscovery of Aristotle in the twelfth century led to his dominance in the theology and philosophy of the later Middle Ages. The Renaissance recovered the bulk of Greek culture and passionately sought to fashion European civilization on it. Ever since, the classical glory of Greece has had a hold on European man's sensibilities unmatched by any other cultural influence except the Judaeo–Christian religious tradition. The glory that was Greece has proven to be the European world's richest intellectual inheritance.

ROMAN CIVILIZATION

In 509 B.C., in the middle of Greece's Golden Age, a small city-state in Italy established its independence from militaristic northerners who had ruled it for a century. Within 250 years Rome became master of all Italy and within another 250 years of the whole of the Mediterranean world and nearly all of Europe west of the Rhine and south of the Danube. For nearly 500 years more the Roman Empire constituted a monument to military prowess, statesmanship, administrative capacity, and engineering skill.

The Roman heritage has survived because of the solidity and durability with which the Romans built. Aqueducts, straight roads, and domed and barrel-vaulted buildings of towns and villas still exist. More subtle were the grammatical foundations, which enabled Latin to survive, to be parent to five modern languages, and to condition the crude language of our Anglo-

Saxon linguistic forebears. Roman law was a masterful combination of precedent, decrees, and scholarly creation, informed by equitable practice and rationalized and codified by the Eastern Emperor Justinian in the sixth century. Roman law became the basis of the Church's canon law, the handmaiden of early modern absolutism, and ultimately the basis of the law of most European nations from France to Russia, of international law, and one of the founts of our own Anglo-American law. The Roman *jus naturale* (natural or fundamental law) nurtured the constitutionalism of European civilization; its concern with right and justice as practical and attainable objects, not abstract ideals, has been one of the great civilizing influences of all time. Roman law served to keep alive the memory of the Roman genius for good government and contributed to Europe's nostalgia for Rome's order and grandeur.

THE ADVENT AND RISE OF CHRISTIANITY

During the five centuries from the ministry of Christ to the fall of Rome, Christianity grew from a small band of persecuted followers of a publicly executed and repudiated messiah of the Jewish people to become the great unifying force in Western society. Christianity derived from its Judaic origins the idea of one universal God and the law of Moses. The unique contribution of the New Testament, and the foundation of Christianity, was the idea of the redemption of mankind from sin to life everlasting through the love of God in Christ's sacrifice. The Christians' claim of Christ's divinity put them outside the pale of Judaism, but it did not alter the basic contribution of Judaism to the new faith.

Decisive to the future success of Christianity was the work of Saul of Tarsus, or St. Paul, a Jew and a Roman citizen, who had never known Christ personally but who, following a miraculous conversion, broadened the new faith to attract non-Jews. Propagandist, organizer, and mediator, Paul's zeal and common sense, his mysticism and practicality, won converts and created cells of believers throughout the eastern part of the empire and in Rome itself. The promise of a better life in the next world, the equality of all men in the sight of God, and the expression of love in Christ's sacrifice appealed strongly to the poor, whose lives were hard and empty of hope.

Harsh, though sporadic, persecution did much to strengthen Christianity. Alone among the popular religions Christianity forbade emperor worship, even to the point of death. This rigidity won admiration and respect. It also held tremendous attraction for responsible Romans who were shocked by the declining morality of the later empire. The last major phase of persecution, under Emperor Diocletian (A.D. 285–305), was followed in 319 by the conversion to Christianity of his successor, Constantine, and toleration of the faith. By A.D. 400 Christianity was the official religion of the empire; no other religions were tolerated.

Great variety existed in the Church's organization in the first century, with major responsibilities resting in the hands of laymen. As communication between the cells increased, episcopacy (the institution in which bishops claim spiritual descent from the original Apostles) and a professional priesthood developed. Episcopacy followed the Roman administrative pattern: bishops exercised authority over a city and its environs (a "see") and archbishops oversaw a number of bishops (a "province"), usually from the capital of a Roman province. The greatest prestige attached to the bishop of Rome, although the growing claim of Rome to authority over all other bishops was resisted by the great Eastern bishoprics of Jerusalem, Alexandria, Antioch, and eventually by the imperial city of the East, Constantinople.

The fourth and fifth centuries were the great formative era of Christian doctrine. Authority was dispersed over an episcopate wherein no bishop exercised primacy over the others. The Church was indeed universal and included different cultures and areas with vastly different problems. The complexity and subtlety of the New Testament invited numerous definitions, and for every doctrinal position there were respectable and responsible supporters. Thus arose the great heresies of those centuries: Gnosticism, Manichaeism, Donatism, monophytism, Pelagianism, and above all, Arianism. The heresies were never completely destroyed. Behind them were reasonable questions and doubts, which the tendency of orthodoxy to counter by appeals to mysticism did not satisfy, and most of the heresies arose later in new and different garb.

The fourth and fifth centuries were also the era of the Fathers of the Church. Basil formulated the rule of Eastern monasticism and gave to the Eastern Church the most commanding of its liturgies or order of worship. Jerome translated the New Testament into Latin; his work has remained the authoritative translation for Roman Catholicism to this day. Ambrose Christianized much of the ethical content of the classics, especially Cicero's works, and along with the Eastern fathers brought the speculative power of Greek philosophy into Christian doctrinal definition. Augustine of Hippo (354–430), the most original of the Western fathers, fought heresy by stressing the fundamental importance of God's grace in strengthening the imperfect human will. Borrowing greatly from Plato, he held up the objective of making the city on earth as much like the City of God as human weakness would permit, and urged the Christian to seek in faith rather than reason the explanation of the otherwise inexplicable. Augustine's influence on Christian dogma was pervasive. It moved materialists and mystics, popes and the opponents of the papacy.

By 476, when the barbarian Odoacer deposed the last Western emperor in Rome, Christianity in the West possessed the institutions, the doctrine, the clergy, the unity, the discipline, and the zeal to bridge the wide gulf that opened between Greco–Roman civilization and the unknown new world that was to be European civilization.

The Birth of Europe

Prior to the collapse of the Roman Empire in the West there had been no "Europe" except in a shadowy geographical sense. The frontiers of the empire had indeed extended to the highlands of Scotland, the mouths of the Rhine, and even across the Danube into what is now Rumania, whose name and language are indicative of its origins. But the empire also included large areas of North Africa and western Asia; the Mediterranean did not so much divide Europe from Africa as it united the disparate, far-flung provinces of the empire about the capital. As long as Rome remained the center of the ancient world, a truly European civilization could not emerge.

THE FALL OF ROME

The empire reached its peak of power and prosperity under Emperor Marcus Aurelius, who died in 180. Thereafter its western portions underwent a gradual decline, politically, economically, and culturally. The removal of the capital to Constantinople (330) constituted a major watershed in the development of European civilization. It began the separation of the empire into East and West, with the East being the wealthier, more advanced area and the West being increasingly subject to incursions of barbarians from both within and without the empire. What remained of the empire in the West was a hollow shell, which simply crumbled under its own weight.

Insofar as there is any point in trying to arrive at a "cause" of the fall of Rome, and of classical civilization in general, one must say that it was the failure of the Romans to maintain, much less to improve upon, the institutions and organizations that had made them great. The Roman world paid a price for peace and order in the form of taxation to maintain the army and the imperial bureaucracy; it exchanged its economic surplus for stable government. With the growth of corruption and inefficiency in the central government, the price became too high. The always increasing burden of taxation varied inversely with the benefits that government conferred. The result was inability to collect sufficient revenue to maintain essential services and order. With the decay of Roman power, transportation and trade became more hazardous and costly; pirates infested the Mediterranean and robber bands controlled the mountain passes. The great Roman roads fell into disrepair, and in some areas the pavement was even dug up for use as building material. Long-distance trade fell to a mere trickle.

Because of the decline in trade, the *latifundia* (large estates) that had once produced surpluses for urban markets became more self-sufficient, and cities dwindled in size. Rome itself, which had exceeded one million inhabitants at its height in the second century, fell to but a few thousand at its nadir in the tenth. In northwestern Europe a manorial system of economy characterized by self-sufficient villages began to take shape. Thus a major feature of the decline of ancient civilization was the gradual reversion of economic life to a primitive subsistence basis.

THE GERMANIC INVASIONS

North of the Rhine and the Danube lived numerous Germanic tribes. Although the Romans called these peoples barbarians, the Germans were by no means naked savages. They practiced settled agriculture and had an intricate system of social organization based on kinship and personal loyalty. They were also effective warriors. The defeat that they inflicted on Roman legions at the battle of Teutoberg Forest in A.D. 9 was so decisive as to cause the Emperor Augustus to give up permanently the idea of extending the boundaries of the empire beyond the Rhine.

In time the Romans and the immediately neighboring Germans settled down to generally peaceful relations. They traded with one another, and some German tribes moved inside the empire or settled down along its borders as allies (foederati) and border guards. The Romans also employed Germans as mercenaries in their legions, so that by the third century most of the soldiers and many of the generals were of German origin. In this way many Germans became partly Romanized, although they did not give up entirely their barbarian ways, such as an abhorrence of urban life. By the same token the empire became increasingly barbarized.

The gradual Germanic penetration of the empire was transformed into a mass movement by the sudden invasion of Europe by the Huns in the last quarter of the fourth century. These nomads poured out of central Asia and fell upon the Germanic tribes, thereby starting a great wave of migration from one end of Europe to the other. Many Germans looked for refuge behind the fortified frontiers of the empire. The Romans, unable to hold back the human flood, decided to admit the Germans as allies. This served only to hasten the disintegration of Rome, for the barbarian tribesmen swept through the empire, sacking Rome itself on several occasions. The various tribes finally settled in different sections of the empire, which they took over for themselves—the Visigoths in Spain, the Vandals in North Africa, the Franks in Gaul, the Burgundians in southeastern France, and the Angles and Saxons in Britain. In Italy German mercenaries under Odoacer deposed the Western Emperor and set up their own king in 476—a year that is often given as the traditional date for the end of the Western Empire. The emperor in Constantinople sent the Ostrogoths, another Germanic people, to win back Italy for him, but the victorious Ostrogoth leader Theodoric took over Italy as his own kingdom. Emperor Justinian (527–565) made a last desperate bid to win back the West and restore the unity of the

Mediterranean world. Although he at first enjoyed success, a new wave of barbarians, the Lombards, swept into the Italian peninsula, conquered most of it, and left only a few areas still under the rule of the emperor in Constantinople.

The ease with which the German invaders carved out kingdoms for themselves demonstrates the extent to which the empire had decayed. The invaders formed a minority—often a very small minority—in the lands they conquered; yet the Roman citizens who lived there offered little resistance. Apparently they had become so alienated from the Roman imperial government, and the conditions under which they lived had deteriorated so badly, that they saw no purpose in struggling to preserve the empire. Coming as warriors and frequently as conquerors, the Germans imposed themselves on the native inhabitants, dispossessed and sometimes intermarried with the old Roman aristocracy, and exploited the common people, most of whom had already been reduced to serfdom.

The Germans had no purposeful intention of destroying Roman civilization. Even after the final overthrow of the Western Empire they continued to acknowledge a vague allegiance to the emperor in Constantinople. Nevertheless, their triumph brought classical civilization in the West to an end. The German rulers lacked the political experience and the trained bureaucracy to preserve the Roman form of centralized government. Since German society was based upon tradition and custom, the conquerors would not accept the Roman system of written laws, courts, and administrative decisions; they supplanted Roman legal procedures with their own crude practices. The individual German was bound by ties of blood to a "folk" and considered himself responsible only to the customs and laws of his tribe, no matter where he went. He gave unpaid service to his king in war and peace out of personal loyalty. He also saw no reason for taxation, so that the kings found it almost impossible to raise the money needed to run governments, and administration remained rudimentary.

The decline in economic life that had begun in imperial times continued. Similarly, the downward trend in intellectual activity was accelerated by the Germanic conquests. The Romans themselves showed little interest in the enrichment or even the survival of their own literature and art, while the Germans rarely even mastered Latin, and added nothing to the cultural legacy of the ancient civilization. By the end of the fifth century the Roman Empire was no more than a vague memory in Western Europe. Classical civilization was dead; Europe had begun to emerge.

CAROLINGIAN EUROPE

Of all the Germanic tribes the Franks created the strongest state. Led from the fifth to the early seventh centuries by a series of strong rulers of the Merovingian dynasty, they conquered much of France. Later Merovingian rulers were weaklings, but fortunately for the Franks a new line took power in the eighth century. This dynasty came to be called Carolingian from its greatest member, Charlemagne or Charles the Great. Charlemagne, fourth ruler of his line, set out to create a European empire that would rival that of ancient Rome. He pushed beyond the Frankish frontiers to make himself ruler of what are today the Low Countries, Switzerland, western Germany, Bohemia, Austria, and parts of Denmark and northern Spain; he overthrew the Lombard kings of Italy and conquered the peninsula down to and including Rome. His empire thus became the first broad-based European state. Europe as a political and cultural entity came into being. This fact received symbolic recognition when, on Christmas Day in 800, Pope Leo III crowned Charlemagne in St. Peter's Cathedral as Emperor of the Romans. The so-called "Holy Roman Empire" was, as Voltaire maliciously described it in the eighteenth century, neither holy, nor Roman, nor an empire; but far outlasting Charlemagne's own Frankish territorial empire, it gave Europeans a sense of unity and coherence. Its final dissolution occurred at the hands of Napoleon in 1806, after an existence of more than a thousand years.

Charlemagne's policies encouraged the sense of European unity in other respects. A devout Christian, he supported the pope's claims to spiritual leadership over the entire Christian community, even though he insisted on maintaining personal control over the dispensation of churchly patronage. He subsidized scholars and artists and strongly supported the Church's efforts to maintain classical learning. On the other hand he continued the Germanic tradition of division of inheritance. Only the fact that two of his three sons predeceased him saved his empire from immediate breakup, and civil war broke out during the reign of his only surviving son and successor, Louis the Pious (814–840). In 843 the empire disintegrated into three main parts, one approximating modern France, another western Germany, and the third an uncertain borderland between them. Charlemagne's ambiguous legacy to Europe thus contained the seeds of both unity and strife.

THE THREAT OF ISLAM

The unity of fledgling Europe was endangered by the rapid advance of another new and even more vigorous civilization in the seventh century. Islamic or Moslem civilization, based on the religious teachings of the prophet Mohammed, exploded with the fury of a desert whirlwind from its home in the Arabian peninsula. Mohammed, who was a merchant before he became a religious leader, borrowed heavily from Judaism and early Christianity. Although he denied the divinity of Christ, he accepted Jesus and the ancient Hebrew prophets as spokesmen of the one true god, Allah. Mohammed regarded himself as the last and greatest of the prophets. In the Koran, the holy book of the Islamic religion, he stressed not only monothe-

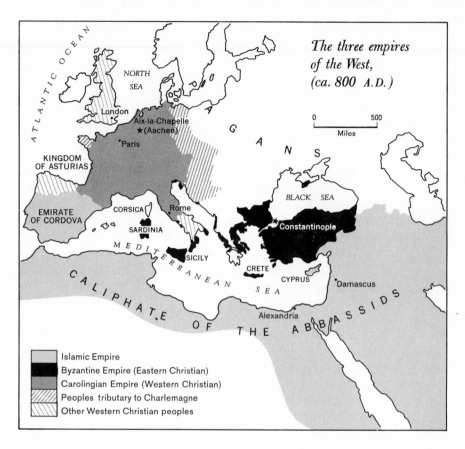

The three empires of the West, (ca. 800 A.D.)

- Islamic Empire
- Byzantine Empire (Eastern Christian)
- Carolingian Empire (Western Christian)
- Peoples tributary to Charlemagne
- Other Western Christian peoples

ism but also life after death, including the rewards of heaven and the punishment of hell. Another principle of Islam required the faithful to engage in the *jihad* or holy war against unbelievers.

Mohammed believed in the union of religious, civil, and military authority. By the time of his death in 632, only ten years after the beginning of his rise to power, he had established control over the principal cities of Arabia. The most spectacular phase in the expansion of Islam came immediately after his death. In less than two decades a few hundred thousand desert nomads from Arabia, proud and fanatical, wrested control of Syria, Egypt, and Libya from the Byzantine (Eastern Roman) Empire and overran the once formidable Persian Empire. Civil wars among rival Arab leaders slowed the pace of conquest for a time, but it accelerated again at the end of the seventh century, spreading Islam to the banks of the Indus River, central Asia, and along the shore of North Africa.

In the year 711 a mixed force of Arabs and Berbers crossed the Strait of Gibraltar and invaded Visigothic Spain. It proved an easy conquest. In less than two years the Moslem forces extended their control to all but the most northern mountain fringes of the Iberian peninsula, from which they did not finally withdraw for more than seven centuries—until 1492. Islamic armies also crossed the Pyrenees and invaded Frankish Gaul. Although turned back at Tours in 732 by Charles Martel, grandfather of Charlemagne, they continued to menace the Frankish state for many years.

As a result of their conquests in the Greek-speaking Eastern Empire, the Arabs took over much of the learning of classical Greece. They drew great wealth from the control of trade routes between East and West, built great cities with spectacular palaces and mosques, and founded important universities. Moslems became the world's leaders in scientific and philosophic thought—a position that they held for several centuries. During the intellectual revival of Western Europe in the eleventh and twelfth centuries many Christian scholars went to Moslem Spain to study classical philosophy and science. Modern mathematics is based upon the Arabic system of notation; algebra was an Arabic invention. Many ancient Greek texts are known to us today only through Arabic translations. Western civilization owes a large debt to Islam.

VIKINGS AND MAGYARS

While the Christians of Western Europe were still defending themselves from Arab attacks in the south, another fierce breed set upon them from the north. The Vikings or Northmen in Scandinavia were distant relatives of the Germanic tribes who had taken over the legacy of Rome. Late in the eighth century they began to pour out of their northern homeland.

Unlike other Germanic migrations, those of the Vikings took place by sea and were connected with both trade and piracy. They expanded in many directions, sometimes to make sudden piratical forays and return to their homeland, sometimes to settle permanently in distant lands. When they discovered uninhabited islands in the North Atlantic, including Iceland and Greenland, they colonized them, preserving their own language and customs in the new environment. Elsewhere they settled as conquerors over native populations and soon adopted the native culture. Vikings became rulers in Scotland, England, Ireland, France, and Russia. The province of Normandy in western France was named for the Northmen (Normans) who settled there in the tenth century, and in the next century their descendants established new Norman kingdoms in Sicily and England.

The Viking invasions began to taper off in the tenth century, and political conditions became more stable in both Scandinavia and Western Europe. Christian missionaries penetrated the northern countries and by the year 1000 had made many converts. Scandinavia entered the mainstream of the European world.

In the ninth century a nomadic horde from central Asia, called Magyars or Hungarians, rode into the Danube valley and established themselves in what is now Hungary. From there they loosed raids against neighboring Germany and Italy and even went as far as eastern France. By the year 1000 they, like the Vikings, had accepted Christianity and were incorporated into European civilization.

Medieval Civilization in Its Prime

At the beginning of the second millennium of the Christian era three competing civilizations occupied Europe and the Mediterranean basin: Islamic, Byzantine, and Western European. Of the three, the European was the most backward. The Arabs took over and built upon the civilizations of the lands that they conquered. The Byzantine or old Eastern Roman Empire had lost some of its former power and glory but remained an impressive center of culture. Its influence extended far beyond the contracted boundaries of the empire into Slavic lands and the Near East as well as Western Europe. The emperor was universally regarded as pre-eminent among the world's rulers, and Byzantium itself (or Constantinople) was deemed to be the greatest, most brilliant city in the world. Western Europe, however, was on the eve of its first great age of expansion. Over the next three centuries it grew in population, wealth, and the arts of civilization and expanded territorially in both the south and east. Before the end of this age of expansion Western civilization equaled if it did not surpass its rivals in culture as well as in political and military power.

FEUDALISM

The political basis of medieval civilization was feudalism. Although historians and anthropologists have discovered similar systems of sociopolitical organization in many different parts of the world, to which they have extended the name feudalism, the feudalism of medieval Western Europe was distinctive in both its origins and its manifestations.

Feudalism developed as a response to the peculiar conditions of Western Europe from the fifth to the ninth centuries—specifically, to the breakdown of central authority, the increasing self-sufficiency of the economy, the ties of personal loyalty and dependence of the Germanic tribes, and the necessity for defense against invaders from all directions. Under feudalism a mounted fighting man, the knight, held a grant of land, called a fief or *beneficium,* from his superior or feudal lord. The grant gave him the right to receive an income from a particular estate or manor. In return he became the lord's vassal and had to swear oaths of homage and fealty, which implied that he would at the lord's command present himself for military service, perhaps with a number of retainers, and provide his lord with certain other services. He had the duty of maintaining order on his

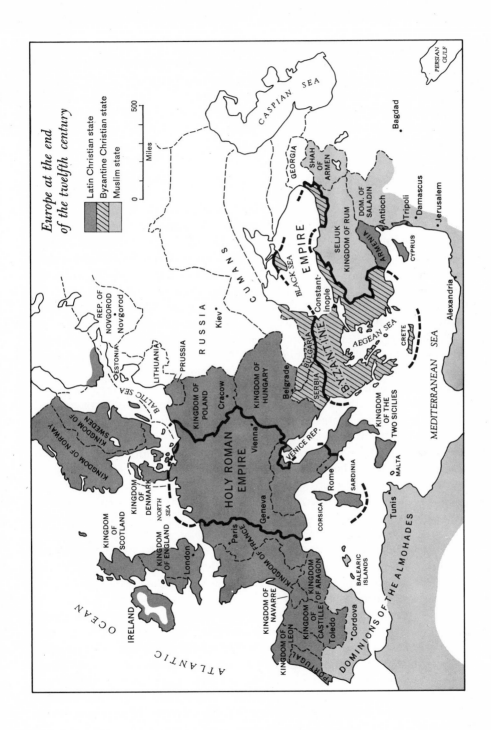

Europe at the end of the twelfth century

Latin Christian state
Byzantine Christian state
Muslim state

estate and collecting various fees or feudal dues from his dependents. Sub-infeudation was permitted; that is, a vassal could grant similar rights and privileges to those below him in the social scale.

Two points about feudalism are of particular importance. In the first place, feudalism applied only to the ruling (and fighting) classes of medieval society—perhaps 5 per cent of the population. Although the common man, typically a peasant, was affected by the feudal system, he was not a part of it. Second, feudalism must be distinguished from manorialism, a closely related but different institution.

ECONOMIC ORGANIZATION: THE MANORIAL SYSTEM

Throughout the Middle Ages—indeed, throughout the history of Europe until very recent times—most of the people obtained their basic subsistence from agriculture or related occupations. Therefore climate and geography exercised a profound influence on individuals, communities, and entire societies. The characteristics of the terrain, the fertility of the soil, the amount of rain all combined to dictate the kinds of crops that could be grown. Along with the level of technology, they also dictated the productivity of the soil and thus the maximum density of the population.

The characteristic unit of settlement, especially in northwestern Europe, was the peasant village; the characteristic form of economic and social organization was the manorial system. This system began to take shape in the last centuries of the Roman Empire. It represented a remarkably successful adaptation of social and economic institutions to the peculiarities of soil and climate in a period characterized by local self-sufficiency. A typical village might contain from 20 to 200 households (perhaps 80 to 1,000 inhabitants). The majority of villagers were normally in a state of serfdom, that is, bound to the lord on whose land they lived and subject to him. Whether they were serf or freeman (and there were numerous gradations within and between these two categories), the external features of their lives differed little. The houses were usually rude, one-room structures made of mud and wattle, thatched with straw, having a single low doorway, no windows, and a hole in the roof that served as a chimney. There were no barns, and in winter the livestock shared quarters with the family. The pace of life was determined by the rhythm of the seasons—punctuated, on occasion, by periods of famine, epidemic, and enemy invasion.

The villages usually lay in the midst of huge open fields. Within each field a peasant household cultivated a number of strips in common with other households with adjoining strips. The size of the strips varied greatly within villages or regions. A normal peasant holding was about thirty acres in dozens or scores of strips, though here again great variation occurred. In addition to cultivated fields, each village possessed common pastureland and woodlands or forests. The church was the center of social life, and usually a crude mill, a smithy, a community oven, and a wine press supplied community necessities. Cloth was woven from yarn spun at home by women from local wool or flax by means of a distaff (hence the "distaff side"; the spinning wheel was a comparatively late invention). Most other commodities in common use were produced locally in household or village.

The relationship of villagers to the feudal nobility, their superiors in the social hierarchy, varied from place to place and time to time. Usually each village had near it a castle or manor house, in which the feudal lord or his representative lived. In principle the lord's function was to provide protection and enforce justice among the villagers. In return the villagers had to cultivate the "demesne," the lord's land, give him various labor services and other dues, and be subject to his discipline. In practice such a relationship frequently degenerated into a system of outright exploitation. On some estates—especially in the vicinity of towns after the revival of commerce, where markets offered peasants the opportunity to sell surplus produce for money—the peasants gradually emancipated themselves from direct subservience, substituting payment of money rents for labor services or dues paid in produce.

ECONOMIC REVIVAL AND THE GROWTH OF TOWNS

In the second half of the eleventh century Europe entered upon an era of economic growth marked by improvements in farming techniques, a rise in population, the clearing of much new land for the production of food, an increase in the size and number of towns, and an expansion in trade, both local and international. Heavy wheeled plows drawn by teams of as many as eight oxen came into wide use to turn over the heavy soils of Western Europe. Three-field rotation replaced the long-practiced two-field system. Instead of planting a field one year and letting it lie fallow the next, the villagers planted a field for two years in succession and then fallowed it for a year to allow it to regain its fertility. The resulting increase in output and expansion of agriculture into newly cleared areas helped increase the population. The surplus production was exchanged for manufactures of the growing towns, breaking down the tendency toward manorial self-sufficiency.

New towns sprang up and old ones grew nearly everywhere in Western and Central Europe, but most strikingly in Flanders and northern Italy. The Flemish centers specialized in the manufacture of woolen cloth, while the town economy of Italy depended mainly on international trade, particularly the importation of silks, spices, and other expensive wares from the Orient. Trade relations were soon established between Flanders and northern Italy, at first overland via the fairs of Champagne in northern France, later by sea through the Strait of Gibraltar. For three hundred years or so after 1050 trade continued to spread through Western Europe,

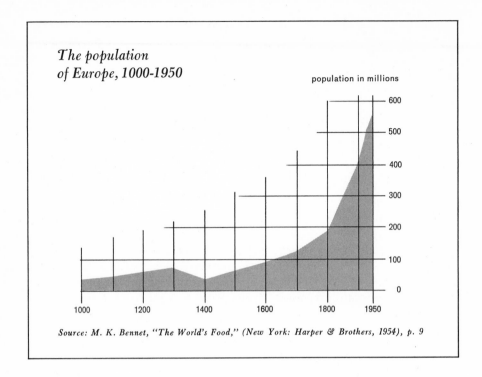

*The population
of Europe, 1000-1950*

population in millions

Source: M. K. Bennet, "The World's Food," (New York: Harper & Brothers, 1954), p. 9

permitting greater local and regional specialization in production and larger accumulations of wealth.

The growth of towns and trade created a new element in European society. The people of the towns—the "bourgeoisie" (from *bourg*, "town")—stood outside the existing social patterns. Feudal lords did not understand or have sympathy with the needs of townspeople, feudal law was inadequate for handling commercial litigation, and the bonds of serfdom clashed with the personal freedom that townsmen needed to go about their business. Everywhere in Western Europe the towns struggled to gain local autonomy and personal freedom for their citizens. Most of them succeeded, though some were more successful than others, depending upon the strength of their rulers; thus, the towns of France and England gained less autonomy than those of Germany and Italy. This difference turned out to be of much importance to later political development, for it allowed the monarchs of France and England to draw upon the wealth of the townspeople and build up centralized states, in contrast to the rulers of Germany and Italy.

THE CRUSADES

Between 1095 and 1270 the West launched a succession of expeditions to wrest the Holy Land from the Turkish Moslems. The Crusades were inspired by the popes, most of them were led by kings, and engaged the best of Europe's nobility. They represented the first era of European expansion, a forerunner of the outward thrust of Europe in the fifteenth and sixteenth centuries.

Although ultimately unsuccessful in their primary aim, the Crusades affected most aspects of medieval civilization. Two major developments resulted. The first was increased trade between the East and Europe in luxury commodities, raising the standard of living in Europe and contributing to a more civilized life among its aristocrats. Carried on by such cities as Venice, Genoa, and Pisa, the trade stimulated navigation, cartography, and the new techniques of ship construction, and spurred manufacturing and banking in Italy, Flanders, and other parts of northern Europe. No less significant was the broadening of the West's horizons. European man came into contact with civilizations different from and even superior to his own. The Crusades perceptibly shifted European attention from its northern preoccupation, dating from Charlemagne's era, to a Mediterranean focus, restoring the Mediterranean world to a major creative role in Europe. From these developments sprang the great cultural and intellectual flowerings of the High Middle Ages and the Renaissance.

THE ROLE OF THE CHURCH

The Crusades illustrate only one facet of the Church in the Middle Ages. The Church provided the framework for medieval life. It was a pervasive, continually civilizing influence. It anointed the king at his coronation, sanctified the feudal contract in the vassal's oath to the lord, and blessed the fields of the manor. Its holy days provided the peasant respite from a hard life. To the castle it added the church as the dominant monuments of civilized man in an imperfectly civilized landscape. Its sacraments prepared king and cottager alike for salvation. It attempted to govern the rules of warfare and impose the Peace of God on earth. It provided resorts of spiritual rest and mills of spiritual exertion in monasteries and nunneries. It controlled a large part of the economy by its vast landed estates. Most of the art, literature, and music of the age awaited its inspiration and throve on its patronage. All knowledge was subject to its approval, and truth was its sole preserve. Its clergy was a privileged order, and the service of God was an avenue for social advancement, wealth, and power in both Church and state.

From the middle of the ninth century to the beginning of the eleventh the Church passed through an eclipse. The papacy was a pawn in German imperial politics, the bishops were adjuncts to vigorous lay noblemen, and the monasteries and parish churches were dominated by lay patrons. Clerical immorality, sale of church offices, and inattention to clerical responsibilities were rife. In a little over a century the situation was dramatically altered. From a monastery founded at Cluny in France in 910 there emanated a movement for reform of the Church that in the last half of the eleventh century "captured" the papacy itself in the person of Pope Gregory VII. He was the first of a line of great medieval popes who brought the Church to the peak of its power. The Gregorian reforms removed the election of the pope from the German Emperor and Roman nobility to a college of cardinals, wrested the appointment of bishops from lay hands by a compromise in which appointment was shared by pope and lay ruler, and thoroughly purged the Church of most of the abuses that had reduced its effectiveness.

In the process of reform, the seeds of a greater papal ambition were planted. The papacy emerged as a territorial power in Italy and became involved in German imperial politics in a way that was eventually more corrosive of its authority than its old subservience had been. Pope Innocent III (1198–1216) humbled the kings of France and England and emerged the arbiter of European politics. He bequeathed to his successors in the thirteenth century a constant struggle, first with the emperor and then with the emerging monarchies. The pontificate of Boniface VIII (1294–1303) witnessed the extreme claim of the papacy to control over lay monarchs, but the king of France shortly afterwards gained control over the papacy and made it a tool of French interests for seventy years.

At the same time the church reforms revitalized European intellectual life so that the twelfth and thirteenth centuries became a golden age of learning and spirituality. The revival of learning was closely associated with the method of reasoning known as "scholasticism." Centered in the recently founded universities, scholasticism resulted from the rediscovery of Aristotle by way of the Moslems in Spain, who had preserved and studied the Aristotelian texts. In the hands of Thomas Aquinas (1225?–1274) Aristotelian philosophy was intermeshed with Christian doctrine. Aquinas's *Summa Theologica* was the sum of all knowledge, logically ordered in a hierarchy of values with theology at the top. He asserted that there were two ways of knowing truth. One source, revelation, presents man with mystery, which he accepts on faith; Scripture and the teaching of the Church are the channels of this knowledge. The other source is reason, which reveals the truth of nature; the channel for this is philosophy, especially Aristotle's. The portions of knowledge derived by revelation and reason are never in conflict because both come from the sole fount of truth—God. Aquinas's marriage of faith and reason was the glory of scholasticism.

Scholasticism did not win an easy victory, for parallel to the intellectual revival occurred a spiritual revival that was antagonistic to it until Aquinas accomplished the ultimate synthesis. In Western Christendom the new pietism created an emotional fervor that found outlets in an emphasis on love, devotional practices, and adoration of the Virgin Mary. Two great

orders of begging friars, the Dominicans and the Franciscans, were founded
on its principles. Dominic (1170–1221) and his friars turned to the towns,
largely neglected by the existing church organization, to preach redemption.
Francis of Assisi (1182–1226) embraced poverty in order to minister to
all needs of all men in total self-effacing love, teaching men of God's love
by example. The friars represented the opposite of scholasticism in motivation. Yet Aquinas was a Dominican, and by the end of the thirteenth century
the Dominicans and Franciscans dominated the universities. Aquinas had
successfully knit together revelation (the pietist's way to truth) and reason
(the rationalist's way to truth). He not only reconciled pagan philosophy
with the Christian faith, but also reconciled devotion and learning—two
strains of twelfth- and thirteenth-century Christianity that might have torn
faith asunder without him.

MEDIEVAL CULTURE

Medieval culture appears at first sight to have been wholly dominated by
the religious concerns of Western man. Cathedrals and abbeys are the material vestiges of medieval man's other-worldliness. Most of the music of
the Middle Ages that has come to us had a liturgical use, either as the music
of the Mass or as hymns of devotion. Sculpture and painting have survived
as incidental decoration to a harmonious whole: statues of Christ, the saints,
and the prophets graced the façades of churches; illumination of the initial
letters of manuscripts graced the Word of God or books of devotion. Although much of the literature of the High Middle Ages is written in the vernacular (instead of Latin), it is generally moralistic and didactic. Whether
in the popular passion and morality plays, Chaucer's *Canterbury Tales*,
Joinville's *History of St. Louis*, or above all Dante's *Divine Comedy*, the
impression is overwhelmingly one of faith.

In both music and literature a strong undercurrent of secularism was
present. Yet the lyric poetry of the troubadours, the chivalric epic *Song of
Roland*, and the chivalric romances—Chrétien de Troyes' *Lancelot*, Eschen-
bach's *Parzival*, and Malory's *Morte d'Arthur*—also represented ideals encompassed in the Church's faith: chivalry, feudal honor, and loyalty. Even carnal
love was increasingly recognized by the Church as a human attribute derived
from God's perfect love. Nor did the cruder Goliard poetry—doggerel composed by vagabond scholars and renegade priests mocking virtue, the pope,
the clergy, even Scripture, and extolling vice—or the light Latin poetry of
university students incur much wrath. The medieval Church, while it felt
compelled to correct error and extirpate heresy, was not overly concerned
with the vanities and verbal licentiousness of the orthodox.

The medieval church building can be seen as a symbolic reaching heavenward—especially the towering Gothic cathedral, which had been released
from the more massive and fortresslike Romanesque by technical advances

in the twelfth century. The history of Gothic architecture is marked by the use of more and more glass, fewer walls, richer colors, and increasing un-conventionality of decorative forms. The asceticism and martial discipline of a civilization embattled by barbarians to the north, Moslems to the south, and the devil everywhere in the early Middle Ages gave way in the twelfth century to a society more sure of itself, less concerned with mere survival, and having greater room for love, compassion, lightness, and joy. Gothic architecture, the literature of romance, the growth of melody and poly-phonic harmony in music following the earlier Gregorian chant—all testify to a civilization that had passed through the smoke and din of battle to the sights and sounds of joy.

The Crisis of the Medieval Order

From the thirteenth to the end of the fifteenth century the history of medieval Europe was dominated by three major developments. The first was the destruction of Byzantium, the rise of its successors, and the impact that this had on Western Europe. The second was the rise of national mon-archies at the expense of the feudal lords and feudal system. The third was the progressive decline of the papacy's temporal influence over the emerg-ing national monarchies and the reduction of its spiritual authority over in-dividual Christians. These three developments amounted to a crisis of the established order of medieval Europe. They presaged the Renaissance, the Protestant Reformation, and the emergence of absolutism in early modern Europe.

THE ECLIPSE OF BYZANTIUM

As the twelfth century witnessed medieval civilization at its prime in the West, it also witnessed the beginning of the decline of Byzantium. The causes of decline stemmed from six centuries of almost continuous hostile invasions. The demands made by this long confrontation weakened the economy, induced corruption, and brought about political instability.

The Crusades accelerated the decline. The West's intervention did not seriously reduce Turkish pressure on Byzantium, and it introduced a dis-cordant Western element in the persons of the ambitious feudal lords who seized and held Byzantium from 1204 to 1261. Even after the Byzantine Greeks had regained the Empire, remnants of the Western lords retained control of a number of key regions of the Empire. The Crusades also put Byzantium's trade in the hands of the northern Italian port cities.

In the mid-thirteenth century the Seljuk Turks, who had long mounted the Islamic attack on Byzantium and against whom the Crusades had been raised, were themselves defeated by the last great wave of barbarians, the

Mongols. The Seljuk dynasty disintegrated, but over the next century the Ottoman dynasty organized a new Turkish empire which attacked Byzantium with new vigor. The Ottoman Turks absorbed the outer regions of Byzantium by a brilliant policy of aggression and conciliation. In 1453 they took Constantinople itself and the Byzantine Empire disappeared.

Politically the Ottoman Empire was the successor of Byzantium, but in a more subtle way Byzantium's successor was a people who, though never colonized by Byzantium, accepted the Christian faith of Constantinople. Russia, in the centuries after the fall of Constantinople, exerted the formative influence on Slavic peoples and emerged as a major power in Eastern Europe.

KIEVAN RUSSIA

Early in the first millennium of the Christian era nomadic Slavic tribes settled down in the valley of the Dnieper River. In time the tribes formed federations, each with a city as its center. In the eighth century Northmen—called Varangians in Russia—came down the Russian rivers from their northern homeland and hired themselves out to the cities as mercenaries. In time chieftains of the Varangian bands took over as rulers of the cities that had hired them. Early in the ninth century the Varangian ruler of Kiev succeeded in establishing his supremacy over the rulers of the other cities. Thus was created the loose union of semiautonomous city-states called the Kievan federation.

The Kievan state lay along one of Europe's most important trade routes —the river network that runs from Scandinavia to Constantinople and the East. Just as in the West, economic activity expanded, population rose, wealth increased, towns grew in size and importance, improvements were introduced into agriculture, and much new land was taken under the plow. As in Western Europe, too, religion played an important part in the evolution of social and political life. The Russians became Christians late in the tenth century. Linked both economically and culturally to Constantinople, they chose to embrace the Eastern or Greek Church rather than Latin Christianity. This was a major determinant of future Russian history, for the split between the Greek and Latin Churches helped to alienate Russia from the intellectual and social currents of Western lands for centuries.

The growth and prosperity of Kievan Russia continued into the last part of the twelfth century. Then waves of nomad invaders from the Asian steppes, climaxed in the thirteenth century by a great invasion of the Mongols or Tatars, destroyed the Kievan federation. The great mass of the Russian people fled to the northeast into what is now the north-central part of European Russia. There, cut off almost entirely from Western contact, the Russians lived for the next two centuries in small principalities whose rulers constantly warred with one another. The principalities paid tribute to the Mongol conquerors, who ruled loosely over Russia from their headquarters in the southern steppe. During the "Tatar Yoke," Russian political, economic, and intellectual life suffered a nearly disastrous decline.

In the fourteenth century the frontier principality of Moscow emerged as the dominant power in northern Russia. As the Mongol hegemony disintegrated, Moscow, supported by the Russian Orthodox Church, extended its power over the other principalities. Late in the fifteenth century the Muscovite ruler adopted the title "tsar" (caesar) of "all the Russias," began to assume Byzantine-like control over the Church in Russia, and autocratically began the destruction of the old nobility's power from his seat in the Kremlin, a chilly bastion in the heart of Moscow.

THE EMERGENCE OF NATIONAL MONARCHIES

The king in feudal society was an anomaly, a leftover from an older tradition of centralization, such as that of the Carolingian Empire or of tribal chieftainship. Certain regalia and panoply surrounded him, he was solemnly anointed at his coronation, and his title "emperor" or "king" denoted a lord who knew no lord on earth. His authority was limited, however, by the large areas of political, administrative, judicial, military, and economic power that both his vassals and the vassals of his vassals held.

During the eleventh century in France and England there began a surge of kingly power at the expense of the great feudal nobles that by the end of the Middle Ages saw these two countries emerge as unified nation-states, with the monarchy as the unifying force. In Germany and Italy during the same period exactly the opposite occurred, although in Germany the monarch enjoyed initially a position more favorable than that of the king of France.

Prior to the eleventh century Anglo-Saxon England was incompletely feudalized, and kingship was infused with characteristics of tribal chieftainship. When William, Duke of Normandy conquered England from its last Anglo-Saxon king in 1066, he instituted full-fledged feudalism with three significant limitations: all land was held ultimately from him and military service was owed only to him; bishops and abbots were no different from lay nobles in their feudal obligations to him; and the assets of the Anglo-Saxon king were retained by the Conqueror. The latter included direct taxation, militia service outside the feudal web, communal courts of justice, and the office of the sheriff, a local official responsible solely to the king. From this advantageous position William and his successors for the next 150 years built up a bureaucracy, central and local, for the collection of taxes, defense, and preservation of order or the "king's peace." Relying upon their feudal responsibility to do justice to their vassals and their regal responsibility to dispense justice in the old communal courts, the Norman kings evolved a common law—common to all England—and developed the use of juries. Litigants, seeking a more equitable justice, flocked to the king's courts—to the ultimate eclipse of the feudal courts of his vassals, to his own profit, and to the enfeebling of the feudal nobles. By commuting feudal services due in kind into money, the monarch was strengthened fiscally. Despite occasional collisions with the assertive twelfth-century papacy, the Norman kings generally had the support of the Church. They also forged an alliance with London and the other developing towns of England, who depended upon the king for their liberties, the preservation of order, and the expansion of trade.

In the thirteenth century baronial reaction set in. The barons wrested Magna Carta from King John in 1215, reforming specific abuses of royal power but not retracting the extensions of royal power that were already part of the fabric of government. A baronial rebellion placed John's successor under baronial control from 1258 to 1265 and resulted in the transformation of the feudal right of a vassal to be consulted in extraordinary circumstances into a parliament, a meeting of the king with the bishops, the barons, and representatives of the towns and the countryside. Both Magna Carta and Parliament had future potentialities for withstanding royal aggrandizement, but they did not check the centralizing tendency of English monarchy. In the last quarter of the thirteenth century Edward I (1272–1307) brought English medieval monarchy to the apex of power and, in turning Parliament into a tool of the monarchy, further reduced the nobles' strength. As a tool of baronial faction Parliament played its part in the deposition and murder of four English monarchs during the fourteenth and fifteenth centuries, but to no avail, for by the beginning of the fourteenth century the English monarchy had already undermined feudalism as an institution capable of preventing the emergence of the monarchic nation-state.

The French kings of the Capetian dynasty between 987 and 1314 evolved many of the same institutions and methods as William the Conqueror and his successors had used to reduce the independence of the great feudal barons. The Capetians had further to go, however, and started from a smaller and feebler base. In 987 the domain of the king of France was a small nucleus of the whole kingdom, centered on Paris; he had vassals with domains many times greater than his own. By skilfully playing feudal politics, the Capetians advanced their regal power and expanded their domain.

The French development of centralized monarchy was slightly behind that of England, since it started from less favorable foundations and necessitated the acquisition of domain, unlike England, where William took his domain entire at the Conquest. By the end of the Middle Ages, however, the French monarchy was in almost as favorable a position as the English, for in France there was no central focus for feudal opposition to the centralizing tendency of the monarchy. French feudal opposition was based on provincial autonomy. It was not coordinated in the Estates-General, which did not gain the indispensability for legislation and extraordinary financing that the English Parliament had obtained by the fifteenth century. Thus the Hundred Years' War, 1338–1453, between English monarchs who claimed the throne of France and the Valois dynasty, successors of the Capetians, ultimately strengthened the hand of the French king by making him the center of patriotic resistance to English invasion. After Jeanne d'Arc rallied the French monarchy and people to ultimate victory, the French monarchy was more powerful than ever. England's defeat helped to plunge that land into a civil war, the War of the Roses from 1455 to 1485, that was the last disruptive shudder of the English feudal nobility.

The political development of Germany offers a striking contrast to that of England and France. In Germany the central power had to retreat before the demands and pressures of local lords and the Church. This withdrawal represented a reversal of the trend that had started in the tenth century when the Saxon dynasty established itself as ruler over a great part of Germany and managed to gain a large measure of control over the feudal nobility. Encouraged by their success in Germany, the Saxon kings tried to extend their rule to neighboring lands and succeeded in making themselves kings of Italy. In 962 Otto I was crowned emperor by the pope as the successor to Charlemagne, and the title lodged with German rulers for the next 850 years. The revival of the title of emperor gave a psychological lift to many people by providing a badly needed symbol of continuity and Christian unity in a perilous time.

Otto's intervention in Italy proved a heavy burden on his successors, for they found themselves constantly involved in Italian and papal political conflicts and wars. Moreover, the emperor's power depended upon the continued support of the Church. As long as the Church had no quarrel with him, things went well. When the Church under the leadership of Gregory VII won out over Emperor Henry IV (1050–1106) in the struggle to free the papacy from imperial authority, the power of the emperor began to ebb. The rivalry between the Hohenstaufen and Welf families for the imperial throne in the twelfth century brought chaos, and feudalism took deeper root in Germany; the great lords assumed local authority and became almost independent princes. During the twelfth century the emperors somehow managed to keep their German realm from complete disintegration, but by the outset of the thirteenth century all effective power in Germany was in the hands of the great lords and powerful churchmen. Germany, where the trend in the tenth century had been toward unification, had broken down into a land of independent principalities and cities and was destined to remain disunited for another six hundred years.

Meanwhile in Italy the growing strength of the towns, prospering from the expansion in economic life, offered a serious threat to the emperor's claims to dominate that land. In 1176 the cities of the Lombard plain in northern Italy, supported by the pope, defeated the emperor's army and won near-independence. In the first part of the thirteenth century Emperor Frederick II (1194–1250) seemed for a time on the verge of reestablishing imperial control over Italy. His ambitions ran counter to the wishes of the papacy, however, for Rome was determined that no secular ruler should be master of the whole peninsula. The pope rallied Frederick's enemies, made the war against him a holy crusade, summoned a council that deposed Frederick, and constantly stirred up public opinion against him. Frederick was never decisively defeated, but after his death the towns of northern and central Italy became completely independent of imperial authority. Sicily and Naples, acquired by the emperors through marriage, also were lost to them when at the pope's invitation Charles of Anjou, brother of France's King Louis IX, invaded Sicily and made himself ruler. The papacy's victory over the emperors meant that Italy became a land divided among many independent city-states in the north and center, the papacy at Rome, and the Angevin kingdom in the south. Like Germany, Italy was destined to remain disunited for another six hundred years.

DECLINE OF THE PAPACY

A head-on collision between the papacy and a French monarch of the new style resulted in the humiliation of Pope Boniface VIII in 1303 and the removal of the papacy to Avignon in the south of France in 1305. The issue was the right of the king to tax the clergy of his kingdom. The king won and the papacy lost. From 1305 to 1378 seven popes resided in Avignon, the "Babylonian Captivity" of the papacy, where the pontiff was a tool of the French throne's secular ambitions and an object of contempt to France's enemies, England and the Holy Roman emperor. From 1378 to 1409 two popes presided simultaneously, and from 1409 to 1417 three popes vied for authority—the pawns of power politics, hurling anathemas at each other. The Great Schism was healed only by a return to the device that had brought unity to the early Church, the great council. The Council of Constance (1414–17), comprising all the bishops of the Western Church, restored the unity of the Church by electing a single new pope. Reform was postponed, but the council asserted that a council was superior to the pope and provided for regular councils. Successive popes stood in fear of great councils, with their reforming zeal and their representation of secular national interests in the persons of bishops who were dependent upon their kings and princes. In the early fifteenth century the pope and councils effectively canceled each other out, and none of the reforms of the Church and its clergy that had been moved by the councils were implemented. After 1450 there were no more councils for a century—the next one was called to attempt to heal the breach known as the Protestant Reformation, which was provoked in part by the earlier failure to reform.

The era of the Babylonian captivity and the Great Schism seriously weakened the prestige and authority of the papacy, and gave national monarchs the opportunity to erode the power of the Church as they had eroded the power of the feudal nobility. A more fundamental erosion was that of the allegiance of individual Christians to the Church of the papacy. The last quarter of the fourteenth century witnessed two heretical movements in two countries. In England the Oxford theologian John Wyclif attacked clerical abuses, argued for a Church without property, asserted that the Church should not stand between the individual and God, and called for a reduction of the importance of the sacraments in Christian life. He enjoyed royal protection, although in the years following his death in 1384 his followers—called Lollards—were heavily persecuted. Wyclif's doctrines reached Bohemia and moved a professor–priest there, Jan Hus, to mount a similar attack. His movement was nationalistic, aimed at severing Bohemia's connection with the German emperor. Despite the burning of Hus as a heretic at the Council of Constance, his movement continued and fought the king of Bohemia and the papacy to a compromise, which recognized certain practices as orthodox in Bohemia that were condemned as heresy everywhere else. In common with the earlier Albigensian and Waldensian heresies of the thirteenth century in the south of France, the Lollards and Hussites advanced anticlericalism or opposition to the priest and his power as an intermediary between man and God. The heresies were popular, enjoying large followings. Moreover, the Hussite heresy was national, giving clear evidence of how far the Church had grown from lay sentiments and aspirations. When popular anticlericalism, patriotism, and the ambitions of kings and princes coalesced, the stage was set for the Protestant Reformation of the sixteenth century.

CHAPTER TWO

Economic Change and the Expansion of Europe

THE ECONOMIC EXPANSION of the twelfth and thirteenth centuries slowed down or leveled off in the first half of the fourteenth century and about the middle of the century gave way to a long depression, lasting in most parts of Europe approximately one hundred years. In spite of the depressed conditions, the period witnessed continued changes in economic organization and commercial institutions in the direction of modern capitalism. Meanwhile improvements in the techniques of shipbuilding and navigation facilitated a renewed interest in oceanic exploration and overseas trade. Toward the middle of the fifteenth century economic activity picked up and, reinforced by the progress of exploration and discovery, began a sustained expansion that carried on into the seventeenth century.

The Great Depression of the Later Middle Ages

Evidence of the great depression that began in the middle of the fourteenth century can be found in the movement of population and prices, in the changes in agriculture, commerce, and industry, and in social unrest and political disturbances. Although the depression varied in intensity in different parts of Europe and was broken by minor fluctuations, it was sufficiently general to be considered a European phenomenon. The evidence is not yet complete enough to establish with certainty the causes of the depression, but one of the most obvious symptoms (and a possible cause) was the great decline in population.

FAMINE, PLAGUE, AND WAR

The population expansion of the eleventh, twelfth, and thirteenth centuries had already begun to level off by 1300. The simplest explanation is that the society had expanded to the limits of its food supply provided by the available technology. In the first half of the fourteenth century local famines became more and more frequent. Then came the greatest natural disaster of the Middle Ages—indeed, one of the greatest of all times—the Black Death or bubonic plague (although it may not have been the bubonic plague exclusively). It carried away as much as one-third of the total population and an even larger proportion of some local populations.

The plague apparently reached Europe from central Asia, possibly even from China, but it spread first through the Genoese. Genoa had a colony on the Crimean peninsula in the Black Sea, which the Mongols besieged in 1347. Siege conditions alone would have been conducive to an epidemic; but there is a story that the Mongols, who were themselves afflicted by the plague, catapulted the bodies of men who had died of it into the fortress of the Genoese: an early form of biological warfare. Some of the survivors returned to Europe as unsuspecting carriers of the disease. It spread first along the main routes of communication and trade, afflicting mostly the thickly settled, highly urban areas of Europe. Italy, France, and England each apparently lost between one-third and one-half of its population in a very few years. The Italian city of Siena lost 70 per cent of its population in a single year; neighboring Florence lost 50 per cent. Peripheral areas of Europe off the main trade routes escaped the worst ravages of the plague. No area, however—from the Mediterranean to the Arctic, from Constantinople to Iceland—escaped it entirely. The disease became more or less endemic, breaking out again every ten or fifteen years for the remainder of the century.

Wars both civil and international added to the effects of plague and famine, further reducing population and causing disorganization and dislocation. Wars were standard in medieval Europe, but they increased in intensity in the fourteenth and fifteenth centuries. Domestic strife further weakened the already staggering economy and brought other social and political changes. The strife took two principal forms: civil war between rival ruling groups or cliques, chiefly nobles and other aristocrats, such as the War of the Roses in England; and genuine social revolt in which the mass of the people rose against their rulers. The first type resembled a war between independent states (to which it was often related) and usually affected only those directly involved either as participants or as peasants whose land was fought over and ravaged. The social revolts, however, profoundly influenced the lives of the masses. They, in turn, broke down into two main varieties: peasant revolts and risings of urban workers.

In the 1320's the weavers of Ghent and other Flemish cities rose against their merchant employers and feudal lords, temporarily controlled the countryside, provoked the enmity of the peasants, and even formed an alliance with the English king. In 1358 the peasants of northern France, burdened with oppressive taxation by the Hundred Years' War, rose in a "Jacquerie" (from the name Jacques Bonhomme, meaning a common fellow, and applied to peasants indiscriminately). They burned chateaus and murdered feudal lords and royal officials. In Florence in 1378 the *ciompi*, workers in the woolen industry, waged a full-fledged class war against their masters and temporarily gained control of the city. Peasant unrest in England flamed into revolt in 1381, merging with the religious protest of the Lollards.

These are but a few examples of the social discontent that boiled over into rebellion and class war. The majority were brought on by economic distress caused by the plague or declining markets and production and aggravated by oppressive taxation and other restrictions or regulations of the ruling classes. They resulted in arson, murder, pillage, and indiscriminate slaughter. Without exception avenging nobles or masters eventually put them down with equal or greater ferocity.

AGRARIAN CRISIS

The reduction in population and the dislocations caused by the wars resulted in a shortage of labor to till the soil and the resulting abandonment of much land. The labor shortage produced a rise in money wage rates and made it easier for the peasants to secure better terms from their lords, either by deserting their original holdings and going to another area, or by threatening to do so. Thus the labor shortage led both to the emancipation of serfs and to the commutation of traditional labor services and payments in kind into payments in money. Peasants rented the land for a fixed payment of money instead of giving labor service and a share of their produce to the lord. This process had already taken place to some extent in Western Europe, but the depression following 1350 greatly hastened it throughout the area of manorial economy.

Some lords who had formerly engaged in demesne farming—that is, who had cultivated their own demesne either for subsistence or for a marketable surplus—found it so difficult and expensive to get labor that they rented out their demesnes and became *rentiers* or rent receivers. In contrast, some of the more enterprising peasants became capitalistic exploiters of the soil, or farmers in the modern sense. These developments contributed in Western Europe to liberation of the serfs and gradual decay of the institution of serfdom.

In Eastern Europe a very different process took place. While the serfs in Western Europe were being freed, the peasants in Eastern Europe, who had been relatively free, were subjected to a process of enserfment that eventually developed into its worst form—that found in Poland and Russia in the eighteenth and early nineteenth centuries. Such town life as had existed in the past died out in Eastern Europe. The lords became more powerful in society, at the expense of both the townsmen and their nominal sovereigns, and had a free hand to exploit the peasants. Although there were other factors, the growing political power of the lords was the main reason for the paradox that serfdom in Eastern Europe increased at the very time that serfdom in Western Europe declined.

COMMERCIAL AND INDUSTRIAL DEPRESSION

With the agrarian crisis and the decline in population went a commercial and industrial depression. The demand for merchandise declined. Manufacturing became more expensive because of the shortage of labor and rising wage rates. The combination of these two factors led in the late fourteenth and early fifteenth centuries to increased regimentation and regulation of commerce and industry, as merchants and manufacturers sought to protect their shrunken markets and get the most from their expensive labor. The regimentation and regulation operated at both the local and the regional or international levels. At the local level the rules of the artisan associations, called "gilds," became more restrictive as opportunities diminished. The gilds limited the number of master craftsmen who might belong; they exacted higher entrance fees, limited output (no master might produce more than a certain quota of goods), enforced strict working rules (no master might hire more than a given number of apprentices or do night work), and limited new members to the sons or relatives of deceased masters.

At the regional and international levels shrinking markets and declining profits produced a rivalry approaching open warfare, such as that between Venice and Genoa or Florence and Pisa. Florence increased its importance in this period of depression by crushing its rivals with superior political and military force and reducing them to the status of satellites.

Another result of the depression in industry was an attempt by manufacturers, especially those who were not among the favored few, to escape from the higher labor costs and restrictive regulations of the gilds by moving their workshops to the countryside. There they obtained cheaper labor and could regulate industrial processes as they chose. This movement was most successful in England, where the gilds and master manufacturers were not as powerful as elsewhere. They were powerful enough to regulate

TABLE 1

AGE OF ECONOMIC DECLINE, 1300–1475
GRAIN PRICES IN ENGLAND, FRANCE, AND ALSACE
(1351–1375 = 100)

Period	England	France	Alsace
1351–1375	100	100	100
1376–1400	71	48	71
1401–1425	70	55	64
1426–1450	70	74	74
1451–1475	54	33	49

Source: W. Abel, *Agrarkrisen und Agrarkonjunktur in Mitteleuropa* (Berlin, 1935), p. 34.

the trade in the city, but they could not prevent the development of industry in the countryside. A great woolen industry began to develop in England when the industrialists set up fulling mills on the streams in the west of England and in Yorkshire and induced the peasants to take up spinning and weaving in their cottages.

THE HANSEATIC LEAGUE

There were also attempts to regulate international trade. The Hanseatic League, the most famous attempt, was composed of German trading cities such as Lübeck, Hamburg, Bremen, Cologne, Danzig, Magdeburg, and Leipzig. The League grew out of the cooperation of merchants from these cities in foreign trading centers. In London all German traders lived together in the *Stalhof* or "Steelyard," where they had special trading privileges and a certain amount of self-government free from the interference of the English king. They had a similar settlement in Bruges. In Venice at the *Fondaco dei Tedeschi,* the German factory or foundation, German merchants could get board and room in addition to special trading privileges. Bergen, Norway, was in effect a German city, as was Wisby on the island of Gothland in the Baltic. German colonies existed in several Russian cities. As a result of the increasing pressure on markets after the Black Death and the attempts of the Danish king to drive the German merchants out of Denmark, the cities from which the merchants came banded together in 1370 to establish the Hanseatic League as a formal political framework, although it was never more than a loose federation of independent towns.

The success of the League aroused the antagonism of other merchant groups, who eventually persuaded their governments to take positive action to break the League's power. With the return of prosperity in the latter half of the fifteenth century the component cities of the League, feeling that

39

they had less to gain by subordinating their activities to group policy, began to break away and follow their individual interests. By the beginning of the sixteenth century the League had ceased to play an important role in European commercial affairs.

The Rise of Modern Capitalism

It is impossible to give a precise definition of capitalism. Capitalism is a historical phenomenon, and historical phenomena do not have the neat precision of logical postulates or mathematical formulas. Without attempting a precise definition, therefore, we will simply list some of the distinguishing features of modern capitalism.

BASIC CHARACTERISTICS OF CAPITALIST ECONOMY

Capitalism's most fundamental feature is private ownership of the means of production, or private property. In this characteristic it differs from collective or public ownership in the various forms of socialism and from the extremely diffuse rights in property found in medieval Europe in the period of manorial economy. Also significant is that capitalism produces goods for sale on the market: it is an exchange economy, not a subsistence economy. Private property and market-oriented production bring out a third characteristic: economic decisions are in the hands of private individuals who are primarily concerned with their own economic welfare. In this feature it differs from the centralized, comprehensive planning of production of socialism, and from the reliance of pre-capitalistic society upon custom or tradition for economic guidance.

Fourth, capitalism's market orientation leads to extensive use of money and credit and a system of prices. They are needed not only to facilitate exchange but also to quantify economic values and permit rational calculation. Such calculation—for example, of prospective profits and losses from alternative types of investment—is necessary to make the economy flexible and responsive to changes in consumer demand and the conditions of supply, as well as to stimulate the introduction of technological improvements. Although credit may not be strictly necessary to a capitalist economy, it is in fact an almost invariable accompaniment. It is usually by means of credit that the capitalistic entrepreneur (that is, the organizer of production) gains control over the resources, including labor, necessary for production.

Some authorities assert that a rational or predictable legal framework—a "government of laws, not of men"—is a prerequisite for the operation of capitalism. It is necessary, they maintain, in order to have laws that define and protect property, enforce contracts, settle disputes equitably, and prevent arbitrary interferences in private relationships by the sovereign power (whether he is a monarch or the head of a republican form of government). Such a legal framework greatly facilitates the operation of a capitalist system, and all fully developed capitalist systems operate in such an environment. A strong argument can be made from historical evidence, however, that capitalism contributed as much or more to the development of such a legal framework as the latter contributed to the growth of capitalism.

One aspect of a rational legal framework is a certain measure of equality before the law. This implies neither equality of economic circumstance nor political equality. It does mean, however, that if the greatest noble in the land owes a legally incurred debt to a petty tradesman and refuses to discharge it properly, the tradesman can force the noble to defend himself in a court of law. If this were not possible, capitalists would be wary of doing business with nobles—as, indeed, they have been throughout history, when political inequality has overridden legal equality.

Closely related to a rational legal framework is yet another characteristic, which is easily misunderstood: the necessity for at least a limited amount of personal freedom. This necessity raises certain questions in the study of capitalism: how much freedom is required, and what kind of freedom? Whose freedom? Need the workers be free? Is capitalism compatible with slavery? Obviously it is, for the American South before the Civil War was a capitalistic area, engaged in capitalistic agriculture, selling on a world market, and employing slaves. Nevertheless, for a capitalist system to operate there must be certain specific freedoms. Individuals must be free to dispose of their property; if a person owns property but is not free to sell it, he does not really have control of it. The freedom to enter into contracts—to agree to do certain things in return for certain considerations or rewards—is another essential freedom of the capitalist type of organization. Substantial numbers of individuals must be legally free to go into any occupation or profession they choose. They must be free to undertake production—that is, to become entrepreneurs—if they can gain control of the necessary capital; and they must be legally free to seek employment from others. Geographical and social mobility—the freedom to move up (or down) through the various social ranks—are essential and are related to the concept of equality before the law. On the other hand, democracy or political freedom—the freedom of the masses to participate in elections and government—is not a necessary part of capitalism. Only very recently have the masses been able to participate in the process of government; and when they have, there have been frequent departures from the capitalist system.

These are a few of the distinguishing features of capitalism. They do not exhaust the list, nor can they be accepted without qualifications. Like civilization itself (and capitalism, as well as other forms of economic organization, is a part of modern civilization), they did not all come into existence at any one time and place. They developed gradually, piecemeal, along with the system itself.

HISTORICAL STAGES OF CAPITALISM

If the distinguishing features of capitalism did not all arise at once, can it be said when the system began? Certainly some of the features existed in the ancient world. The Greeks and other ancient peoples used money, possessed private property, and had an elaborate network of trade and markets. Roman law contained many of the concepts basic to modern capitalist legal doctrines. It might be claimed that capitalism has existed since the beginning of human history, or at least since the beginning of civilization. Such a statement is meaningless, however. Modern capitalism differs profoundly from the forms of economic organization of the ancient world and from those of the non-Western world in modern times. Modern capitalism is, in fact, a distinctive contribution of the Western world to modern civilization.

One historical description of modern capitalism is that it is a form of economic organization that developed gradually in Europe in the later Middle Ages, spread to the Western Hemisphere and other parts of the world in early modern times, and reached its peak development late in the nineteenth century. The rise of modern capitalism was not a specific episode in world history, for it had been rising more or less continuously—at least until the early twentieth century—since the early Middle Ages. Nevertheless, certain periods of history stand out as especially important for its development. One was the period of economic expansion of the twelfth and thirteenth centuries, which witnessed the birth of modern capitalism. The cities of northern Italy were its cradle. Another extremely important period lasted from the end of the eighteenth century to the beginning of the twentieth century, when capitalism became the dominant form of economic organization throughout the Western world and made significant penetrations into the non-Western world. A third period of crucial importance lasted roughly from the mid-fourteenth to the early or mid-seventeenth centuries, the era with which this chapter is concerned.

Although the great depression of the fourteenth century served in some ways as a check on the development of capitalism, in other respects it stimulated its development in Western Europe. Under the pressure of increased competition the capitalistic entrepreneurs further refined, rationalized, and elaborated the techniques and institutions that they had inherited from their Italian and Flemish predecessors of the twelfth and thirteenth centuries. Sometime in the fifteenth century a new period of expansion began. It is difficult to give the exact date of the revival because it varied from one region to another. The year 1475 might be used as an average date for the beginning of the upswing. This second great expansion of the economy, enormously stimulated by geographical discovery and overseas exploration, carried on through the sixteenth and into the seventeenth centuries, petering out at different times in different parts of Europe.

The growth of population provides the clearest evidence of the economic expansion of the early modern period. After the Black Death the population continued to decline until near the end of the fourteenth century, when it finally stabilized at about 60 per cent of its maximum in the first half of the century. It began to grow again near the middle of the fifteenth century, surpassing its previous maximum early in the sixteenth century and pushing on to about one hundred million at the beginning of the seventeenth century, when it leveled off again. At mid-century the population of Europe was about twice as large as it had been at its low point in the beginning of the fifteenth century.

THE ELABORATION OF CAPITALIST TECHNIQUE

All sectors of the economy—agriculture, industry, commerce, and finance—benefited from the general economic expansion, but commercial and financial developments were most significant for the progress of capitalism. As in the period of depression, merchants and financiers continued to improve and refine their techniques of doing business and introduced new institutions. Double-entry bookkeeping, introduced in the early fourteenth century, probably in Venice, gave businessmen a method of keeping closer check on the status of their affairs and permitted them to calculate more accurately the possible outcomes of their ventures. Maritime insurance, utilized in a rudimentary fashion as early as the twelfth century, greatly reduced the hazards of loss faced by individual businessmen. Soon after the invention of printing in about 1450 merchants' newsletters—embryonic *Wall Street Journals*—appeared, helping merchants to keep abreast of prices in distant ports and of commercial and political developments that might have a bearing on their business.

As the scope of commerce widened and the volume of transactions increased, the business organizations themselves became larger and more complex. During the expansion of trade in the twelfth and thirteenth centuries the typical merchant had been a traveling merchant, working on his own account and carrying his goods with him. The principal exception was a simple form of limited partnership, the *commenda*, in which a wealthy merchant or capitalist who did not travel provided the capital for a junior partner who did. Usually such partnerships were limited to a single voyage, although they could be renewed frequently. Even before the great depression a significant change in the organization of business had taken place, with the rise of the resident or "sedentary" merchant, who conducted his business from a central office by means of numerous traveling employees, agents, and partners located in distant centers of commerce. In the course of the fourteenth and fifteenth centuries this form of organization became even more elaborate. The *commenda* took on new and more complex forms,

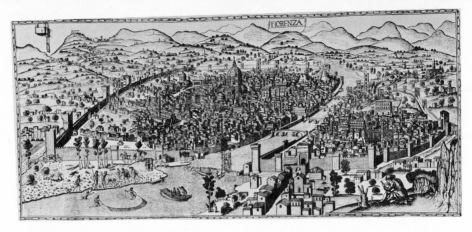

Florence in the Late Fifteenth Century

*"Our beautiful Florence contains 270 shops belonging to the wool merchants' guild . . .
also 83 rich and splendid warehouses of the silk merchants' guild. . . . The number
of banks amounts to 33; the shops of the cabinetmakers . . . to 84; and the
workshops of the stonecutters and marble workers . . . to 54. There are 44 goldsmiths'
and jewelers' shops, 30 gold-beaters, silver wire-drawers, and a wax-figure maker . . .
Sixty-six is the number of the apothecaries' and grocer shops; 70 that of the butchers,
besides 8 large shops in which are sold fowl of all kind, as well as game and also the
native wine called Trebbiano . . . ; it would awaken the dead in its praise."* From
a letter of Benedetto Dei to a Venetian (1472), in G. R. B. Richards, ed., FLORENTINE
MERCHANTS IN THE AGE OF THE MEDICI (Cambridge, 1932).

Courtesy of Staatliche Museen, Berlin and Prints Division, New York Public Library

and the "true company" (*vera societas*), a forerunner of the modern corpora-
tion or joint-stock company, came into existence.

The sedentary merchant, unlike his peripatetic forebear, was in a position
to extend his financial control over the processes of production as well as
of distribution. The woolen industry of Florence, for example, employed
as many as thirty thousand workers, mostly under the control of the great
merchants. In some cases merchants accumulated so much wealth that they
could no longer employ it themselves in their own businesses. They became
bankers and financiers, financing the business of others, including that of
popes, kings, and emperors. The famous Medici family of Florence was
one example; the Fuggers of Augsburg in southern Germany were another.

The decline of the Champagne fairs in northeastern France in the early
fourteenth century and the rise of Bruges in Flanders as the principal
entrepôt for the Italian trade with northern Europe marked another stage
in the development of capitalism. The city fathers of Bruges established
a permanent, continuous *bourse* or market in place of periodic, temporary
fairs. Other mercantile cities soon adopted this institution, notably Antwerp
on the Scheldt River, which replaced Bruges as the major northern entrepôt
near the end of the fifteenth century. The bankers of important commercial
cities also established clearing houses to facilitate the payments of their
clients, eliminating the need for coin in many transactions. Most bankers
were private individuals or family firms that combined banking with money

changing or mercantile operations, but in 1401 the city of Barcelona established the first public bank. It was followed by another in Genoa in 1407. The bankers also developed credit instruments, such as letters of credit and bills of exchange.

One of the factors contributing to economic expansion was an increase in the money supply. The output of the silver mines of central Europe declined in the fourteenth century, at first because the richest veins of ore had been worked out, then because of the ravages of the plague and the population decline. With the development of new mining techniques and the increasing demand for silver for both monetary and artistic uses, output increased once again after about 1450. The Portuguese brought back driblets of gold among the early fruits of their exploration of the African coast. The consequence of the increased supply of money, together with the continual debasement of coinage by sovereign rulers, was a gentle rise in prices. The largest increase in the money supply came in the sixteenth century, when an inflow of precious metals resulted from the discovery of the New World.

The Great Discoveries

The world in the second half of the twentieth century stands on the verge of a great age of exploration, the exploration of space. Five hundred years

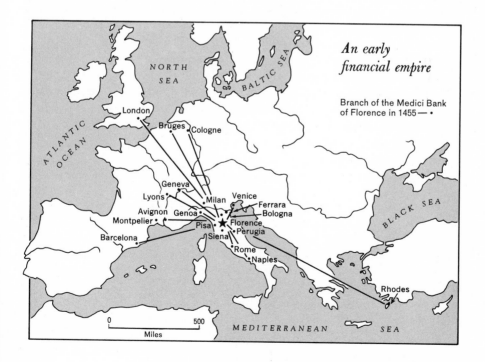

An early financial empire

Branch of the Medici Bank of Florence in 1455 — •

ago, in the second half of the fifteenth century, Europe stood on the verge of a great age of exploration also. The comparison presents some interesting parallels and contrasts.

Today it is a rare person who is not aware that great new discoveries are soon to be made in space. In the fifteenth century educated persons at least were aware of and curious about the possibility of discoveries of lands and peoples unknown to them or that they knew only through shadowy myths and legends. That is the principal similarity between the times; the differences are great. It is unlikely that astronautical explorers will discover new, hitherto unsuspected worlds in space that will compare in importance for us with the discovery of the Western Hemisphere, a new world for Europeans.

The risks involved for the men who made the first daring sea voyages into the unknown were much greater than for the first astronauts, brave though the latter may be. Magellan's expedition (1519–22) set out with five ships and 243 men; three years later it returned without its commander—one ship and 18 half-starved, disease-ridden men. Nor was this an isolated example. Many expeditions did not return at all. If the expected losses in the exploration of space were anywhere near as great proportionately, it is most unlikely that the exploration would be undertaken.

Although the techniques were different and the risks were greater, the motives behind the explorations were quite similar to those of today. The rulers and statesmen who financed the explorations—then as now the cost was so great that only the resources of governments could suffice—sought wealth, power, and prestige for themselves and their countries. They were also moved by religious zeal, similar to the ideological zeal that animates the race for space today, and by scientific curiosity. The brave but not necessarily virtuous men who actually made the discoveries were inspired by much the same motives. They also possessed the psychological trait essential to any hazardous undertaking, the spirit of adventure. Whatever the mixture of motives, the immediate goal of the early explorations was to find a sea route to the East.

EARLY CONTACTS WITH THE FAR EAST

In the thirteenth century, at the very time that the commercial revival reached its peak in Europe, the conquests of the Mongols created the largest empire thitherto recorded, stretching from Korea in the east to Poland and Hungary in the west. The pope and several European rulers sent emissaries to the court of the Great Khan, as the Mongol ruler was known, hoping to effect an alliance against the Moslems in the Near East. Although these attempts were fruitless, the Mongols willingly received European missionaries, craftsmen, and merchants. In 1289 the pope sent an Italian friar to assume the post of archbishop of Peking, where he built a flourishing Christian community and remained till his death in 1328. The Mongol rulers sent ambassadors to the kings of France and England and other European courts.

Conditions were therefore propitious for the establishment of direct contact with China, the heartland of the Mongol Empire. Among the earliest and most famous European merchants and travelers in China were members of the Polo family of Venice. In 1255 two brothers, Nicolo and Maffeo Polo, who had traded in the Black Sea area, traveled across central Asia, reaching China itself after several years and numerous adventures. They returned to Europe in 1269 but two years later again set out for China, this time accompanied by Nicolo's young son Marco. When they reached Peking in 1275, they received a gracious welcome from Kublai Khan (1214–1294), who proved to be a humane and enlightened ruler. For fifteen years Marco traveled throughout eastern Asia in the service of the Khan, returning to Italy in 1295. His book relating his adventures provided much information about Asia in that period. Meanwhile a lively trade had grown up between Europe and China, so that it became profitable to write and sell merchants' handbooks and travel guides describing the best routes, the chief commercial cities, and the principal goods in demand.

After about 1340 the Mongol Empire began to break up, and in 1368 a native, antiforeign dynasty, the Ming, overthrew the Mongols in China itself. The new dynasty excluded Europeans from China. Eastern products, especially pepper, cinnamon, and other spices from the Indies, continued to come into Europe, but at the eastern end of the route the trade was controlled by Arab merchants in the Indian Ocean, and at the western end by Venetians and Genoese in the Mediterranean. The trade was extremely lucrative, especially since the Venetians and Genoese followed monopolistic policies and excluded other Europeans from the eastern Mediterranean by diplomacy and force. Consequently, there was a persistent search for alternative routes to the East by land and sea. In the end the Portuguese finally achieved the breakthrough by finding an all-water route to the Indies.

BY SEA TO THE EAST

Notable technological developments in ship design, shipbuilding, and navigation took place in the later Middle Ages. The Mediterranean ships of Greco-Roman times had been mainly oared galleys with auxiliary sails. They were still a great factor in the Mediterranean commerce of the thirteenth and early fourteenth centuries, but their limitations for oceanic navigation are obvious, quite apart from the lack of navigational devices to enable mariners to determine their position and bearings in the open sea. The early Norsemen performed heroic feats in similar, even smaller oar-propelled boats when they discovered and settled Iceland, Greenland, and even (briefly) North America; but as events proved, their ships were quite incapable of sustaining large-scale overseas commerce.

Foremost among the improvements in ship design and shipbuilding, the hinged sternpost rudder replaced the steering oar, and lateen (fore-and-aft) sails with a deep keel permitted tacking into the wind. Together, these devices gave greater maneuverability and directional control and dispensed with the oarsmen. Ships became larger, more manageable, more seaworthy, and had greater cargo capacity, enabling them to make longer voyages. At about the same time a rudimentary magnetic compass, probably introduced from China, reduced significantly the large element of guesswork involved in navigation. Similar developments took place in cartography. Most medieval maps were highly stylized, not giving a true representation of distance and direction. Practical seamen began compiling books of sailing instructions, called *portolanos,* including greatly improved maps and charts.

The Italians had been leaders in the art of navigation. As early as 1291 the Vivaldi brothers of Genoa sailed down the Atlantic coast of Africa in an effort to reach India by sea, never to be seen again. In the thirteenth century Genoese and Venetian galleys began to make annual voyages through the Atlantic to Bruges and London. The Italians were conservative in ship design, however, and the lead was taken by seamen who sailed the open seas, especially the Flemish, Dutch, and Portuguese. The Portuguese, in particular, seized the initiative in all aspects of the sailor's art: ship design, navigation, and exploration. The vision and energy of one man, Prince Henry, called the Navigator, were chiefly responsible for the great progress in geographical knowledge and discovery made by Europeans in the fifteenth century.

Henry (1394–1460), a younger son of the king of Portugal, devoted himself to encouraging the exploration of the African coast with the ultimate object of reaching the Indian Ocean. At his castle on the promontory of Sagres at the southern tip of Portugal he established a sort of institute for advanced study to which he brought astronomers, geographers, cartographers, and navigators of all nationalities. From 1418 until the end of his life he sent out expeditions almost annually. Carefully and patiently his sailors charted the coast and currents, discovered or rediscovered and colonized the islands of the Atlantic, and established trade relations with the native chiefs of the African coast. Henry did not live to realize his greatest ambition. In fact, at the time of his death his sailors had gone little farther than Cape Verde; but the scientific and exploratory work carried out under his patronage laid the foundation for subsequent discoveries.

After Henry's death exploratory activity slackened somewhat for lack of royal patronage and because of the lucrative trade in ivory, gold, and slaves that Portuguese merchants carried on with the native kingdom of Ghana. King John II, who came to the throne in 1481, renewed the explorations at an accelerated pace. Within a few years his navigators pushed almost to the tip of Africa. Realizing that he was on the verge of success, John sent out two expeditions in 1487. Down the coast went Bartholomew Diaz, who rounded the Cape of Good Hope (which he at first named the Cape of Storms) in 1488; through the Mediterranean and overland to the Red Sea went Pedro de Covilhão, who reconnoitered the western edges of the Indian Ocean from Mozambique in Africa to the Malabar coast of India. The way was paved for the next and greatest voyage, that of Vasco da Gama in 1497–99, around Africa to Calicut in India. As a result of disease, mutiny, storms, and difficulties with both his Hindu hosts and the numerous Arab merchants whom he encountered, da Gama lost two of his four ships and almost two-thirds of his crew. Nevertheless, the cargo of spices with which he returned sufficed to pay the cost of his voyage many times over, and was tangible proof of his success.

Seeing such profits the Portuguese lost no time in capitalizing on their advantage. Within a dozen years they had swept the Arabs off the Indian Ocean and established fortified trading posts from Mozambique and the Persian Gulf to the fabled Spice Islands or Moluccas. In 1513 one of their ships put in at Canton in South China, and by mid-century they had opened trading and diplomatic relations with Japan.

THE NEW WORLD

In 1483 or 1484, while the crews of John II were still working their way down the African coast, a Genoan who had sailed in Portuguese service and married a Portuguese presented himself at the Portuguese court. He came to ask the king to finance a voyage across the Atlantic in order to reach the East by sailing west. Such a proposal was not entirely novel. There was a general belief that the earth was a sphere. But was the plan feasible? Christopher Columbus, the Genoan, thought it was, although the weight of opinion was against him. John's advisers had a more nearly correct impression of the size of the globe than did Columbus, however, who thought that the distance from the Azores to the Spice Islands was little greater than the length of the Mediterranean. Although John had authorized privately financed expeditions west of the Azores, he concentrated his own resources on the more likely project of rounding Africa. His answer to Columbus was No!

Columbus persevered. He appealed to the Spanish monarchs, Ferdinand and Isabella. Although he impressed Isabella with his manner, his personality, and his ambitious ideas, she and her husband were engaged at the time in the last crusade, a war against the Moorish kingdom of Granada, and had no money to spare for such an unlikely scheme. Columbus tried to interest the realistic and parsimonious King Henry VII of England, as well as the king of France, but in vain. At length, in 1492, Ferdinand and

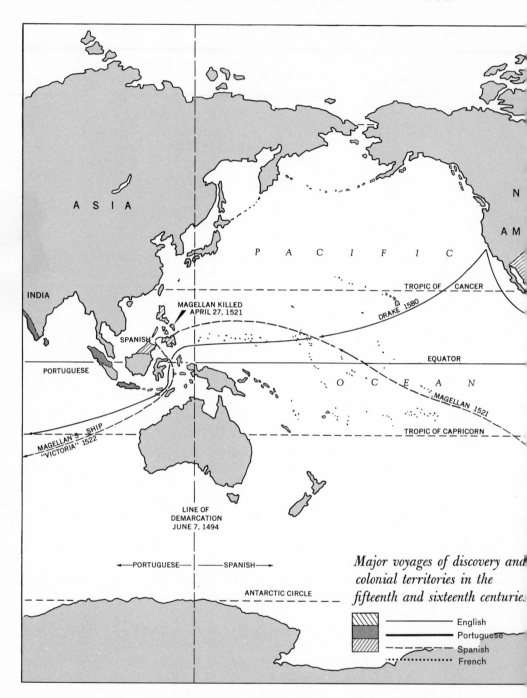

ASIA

INDIA

PORTUGUESE

SPANISH

MAGELLAN KILLED
APRIL 27, 1521

P A C I F I C

TROPIC OF CANCER

DRAKE 1580

EQUATOR

O C E A N

MAGELLAN 1521

TROPIC OF CAPRICORN

MAGELLAN'S SHIP
"VICTORIA" 1522

N

AM

LINE OF
DEMARCATION
JUNE 7, 1494

←PORTUGUESE | SPANISH→

ANTARCTIC CIRCLE

Major voyages of discovery and
colonial territories in the
fifteenth and sixteenth centuries

English
Portuguese
Spanish
French

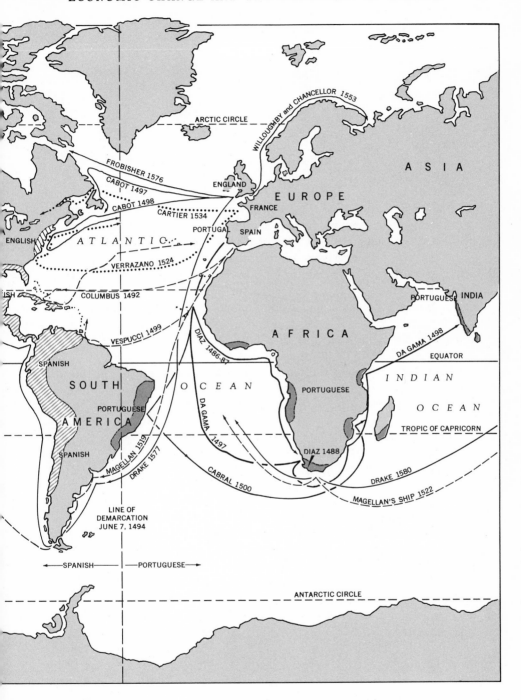

Isabella conquered the Moors. As a sort of victory celebration, and in hopes of scoring a triumph over their fellow monarch in Portugal, whose successes were becoming the envy of Europe, Isabella agreed to underwrite an expedition. In five small ships, by no means the equal of their Portuguese counterparts, Columbus and his crew set sail on August 3, 1492. After spending a month in the Canaries for repairs and losing two of its ships, the tiny fleet sailed westerly for five weeks before sighting land on October 12.

For Columbus it was the culmination of a life's ambition. He thought he had reached the Indies. Though dismayed at their obvious poverty, he dubbed the inhabitants Indians. After a few weeks of reconnoitering amongst the islands, later called the West Indies, he returned to Spain to spread the joyful tidings. Since he had lost his flagship, the *Santa Maria*, by shipwreck in the islands, Columbus left some of his men in a fortified post on Santo Domingo. The following year he returned with 17 ships, 1,500 men, and enough equipment (including cattle and other livestock) to establish a permanent settlement. Within a few years the Spanish had several flourishing colonies. Altogether Columbus made four voyages to the western seas. He discovered the coasts of Central America and northern South America in addition to the islands, and persisted until the end of his days in believing that he had discovered a direct route to Asia.

Immediately following the return of the first expedition, Ferdinand and Isabella applied to the pope for a "line of demarcation" to confirm Spanish title to the newly discovered lands. This line, running from pole to pole at a longitude 100 leagues (about 350 miles) west of the Azores and Cape Verde islands, divided the non-Christian world into two halves for purposes of further exploration, with the western half reserved for the Spanish and the eastern half reserved for the Portuguese. The next year, 1494, the Portuguese king in the Treaty of Tordesillas persuaded the Spanish rulers to set the line 370 leagues west of the islands. This suggests that the Portuguese may have already known of the existence of the New World, for the new line placed the hump of South America—the beachhead that later became Brazil—in the Portuguese hemisphere. In 1500, on the first major Portuguese trading voyage after da Gama's return, Pedro de Cabral sailed directly for the hump and claimed it for Portugal before proceeding to India.

Cabral was not the first European to discover South America. Besides possible unidentified predecessors, Columbus himself had discovered it in 1498, and several other explorers did likewise between 1498 and 1500. One of them, a Florentine agent of the Medici bank who resided in Seville, gave the new world his name. Amerigo Vespucci explored the northeast coast of South America in 1499 and discovered the mouth of the Amazon River. On subsequent voyages he concluded from studies of the flora and fauna that the continent could not be Asia. In letters to Europe he referred to it as the *Mundus Novus*, the "New World." In 1507 a German geographer,

Martin Waldseemüller, labeled it America in honor of Vespucci. At first the name referred only to South America. Both the Spanish and the Portuguese refused to use it, but the name caught on and was eventually applied to both continents of the Western Hemisphere.

Meanwhile explorers of other nations followed up the news of Columbus' discovery. In 1498 John Cabot, an Italian sailor who lived in England, secured the backing of Bristol merchants for a voyage on which he discovered Newfoundland and Nova Scotia. The following year he and his son Sebastian led a larger expedition to explore the northern coast of North America, but since they brought back no spices, precious metals, or other marketable commodities, their commercial backers lost interest. Cabot also failed to persuade Henry VII to provide financial support, though the king did give him a modest reward of ten pounds for planting the English flag in the New World. French merchants sent another Italian, Verrazano, to discover a western passage to India in the 1520's. A decade later the Frenchman Jacques Cartier made the first of three voyages that resulted in the discovery and exploration of the St. Lawrence River. Cartier also claimed for France the area later known as Canada; but, failing to find the hoped-for passage to India, the French, like the English, evinced no further immediate interest in the New World except for fishing on the Grand Banks of Newfoundland.

In 1513 the Spaniard Balboa discovered the "South Sea," as he called the Pacific Ocean, beyond the Isthmus of Panama. By the 1520's Spanish and other navigators had explored the entire eastern coast of the two Americas from Labrador to Rio de la Plata. It became increasingly clear not only that Columbus had not discovered the Indies but that there was no easy passage through the center of the new continent. In 1519 Ferdinand Magellan, a Portuguese who had sailed in the Indian Ocean, persuaded the king of Spain to let him lead an expedition to the Spice Islands by way of the "South Sea." Magellan had no thought of circumnavigating the globe, for he expected to find Asia a few days' sailing beyond Panama, within the Spanish orbit as determined by the Tordesillas Treaty. His main problem, as he saw it, was to find a passage through or around South America. This he did, and the stormy treacherous straits he discovered still bear his name. The "peaceful sea" (*Mare Pacificum*) into which he emerged, however, yielded not riches but long months of starvation, disease, and eventually death for him and most of his crew. The remnants of his fleet wandered aimlessly in the East Indies for several months. At length one of Magellan's lieutenants, Sebastian del Cano, took the one surviving ship and its skeleton crew through the Indian Ocean and home to Spain after three years—the first men to sail entirely around the earth.

Overseas Expansion and the Feedback to Europe

The first century of European overseas expansion and colonial conquest—that is, the sixteenth century—belonged almost exclusively to Spain and Portugal. For Spain it was the *Siglo de Oro,* the "golden century." The eminence that these two nations have achieved in history is due mainly to their pioneering in the discovery, exploration, and exploitation of the non-European world. Prior to the sixteenth century they had been backward, semi-feudal kingdoms on the periphery of European civilization; afterward their power and prestige declined rapidly until by the beginning of the nineteenth century they had sunk into a state of somnolence approaching suspended animation, from which they have not yet fully recovered. In the sixteenth century, however, their dominions were the most extensive and they were the wealthiest and most powerful nations in the world.

THE STAKES OF EMPIRE

By 1515 the Portuguese had made themselves masters of the Indian Ocean. Vasco da Gama returned to India in 1501 with instructions to halt the Arab trade to the Red Sea and Egypt, by which the Venetians had obtained spices for distribution in Europe. In 1505 Francisco de Almeida went out as first Portuguese viceroy of India. He captured or established several cities and forts on the East African and Indian coasts and in 1509 completely destroyed a large Moselm fleet in the battle of Diu. In the same year Alfonso de Albuquerque, greatest of the Portuguese viceroys, assumed his duties and completed the subjugation of the Indian Ocean. He captured Ormuz at the entrance to the Persian Gulf and established a fort at Malacca on the narrow strait between the Malay Peninsula and Sumatra, a post that controlled the passage to the Celebes and Moluccas islands from which the most valuable spices came. Finally in 1515 he captured Ceylon, the key to mastery of the Indian Ocean. His attempt to capture Aden at the entrance to the Red Sea was repulsed, and a small trickle of trade continued to take this old route, but it did not effectively interfere with the Portuguese monopoly. Albuquerque established his capital at Goa on the Malabar Coast; Goa and Diu remained Portuguese possessions until 1961. The Portuguese also established trade relations with Siam and Japan. In 1557 they established themselves at Macao on the south coast of China, which they still hold. Because of their small population they did not attempt to conquer or colonize the interior of India, Africa, or the islands but contented themselves with controlling the sea lanes from strategic forts and trading posts.

Although at first it looked less promising, the Spanish Empire eventually proved to be even more profitable than the Portuguese. Disappointed in their quest for spices and stimulated by a few trinkets plundered from the savages in the islands of the Caribbean, the Spanish quickly turned to a search for gold and silver. Their continued efforts to find a passage to India soon revealed the existence of wealthy civilizations on the mainland of Mexico and northern South America. In 1519–21 Hernando Cortez effected the conquest of the Aztec Empire in Mexico. Francisco Pizarro conquered the Inca Empire in Peru in the 1530's. By the end of the sixteenth century the Spanish wielded effective power over the entire hemisphere from Florida and southern California in the north to Chile and the Rio de la Plata in the south (with the exception of Brazil). At first they merely plundered the original inhabitants of their existing movable wealth; when this source was quickly exhausted, they introduced European mining methods to the rich silver mines of Mexico and the Andes.

The Spanish, unlike the Portuguese, undertook from the beginning to colonize and settle the areas that they conquered. They brought European techniques, equipment, and institutions (including their religion) which they imposed by force upon the Indian population. Besides European culture and manufactures, the Spanish introduced many natural products that were previously unknown to the Western Hemisphere but soon became naturalized. These included wheat and other cereal grains (except corn, which traveled in the opposite direction), sugar cane, coffee, most common vegetables and fruits (including citrus fruits), and many other forms of plant life. The pre-Columbian Indians of America had no domesticated animals except dogs and the llama. The Spanish introduced horses, cattle, sheep, donkeys, goats, pigs, and most domesticated fowls.

Among the other features of European civilization that were introduced into America, some spread with great rapidity and lethal effect, such as firearms, alcoholic liquors, and the European diseases of smallpox, measles, and typhus. The native population may have numbered as many as ten or twelve million at the time of Columbus, but by the end of the century these killers had reduced it by half or more. To remedy the shortage of labor and because Indians did not make good slaves, the Spanish introduced African slaves as early as 1501. By 1600 a majority of the population of the West Indies was composed of Negroes and mixed breeds; Negroes were not so important on the mainland, except in Brazil and northern South America.

ECONOMIC CONSEQUENCES

The transplantation of European culture, together with the modification and occasional extinction of non-Western cultures, were the most dramatic and important aspects of the expansion of Europe. Expansion also had a feedback. European culture itself underwent substantial modification as a result of expansion.

On the economic side expansion resulted in a great increase in volume

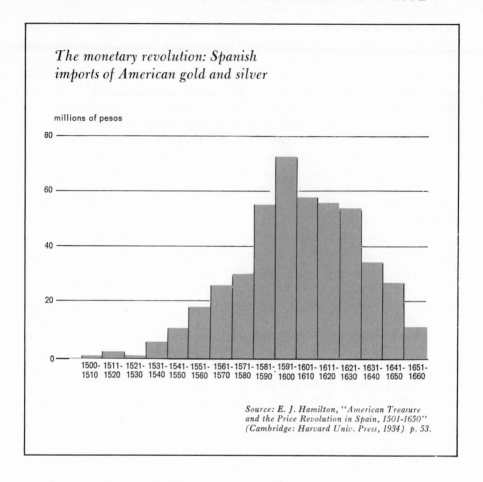

The monetary revolution: Spanish
imports of American gold and silver

millions of pesos

Source: E. J. Hamilton, "American Treasure
and the Price Revolution in Spain, 1501-1650"
(Cambridge: Harvard Univ. Press, 1934) p. 53.

and variety of goods traded. In the sixteenth century spices from the East and bullion from the West accounted for an overwhelming proportion of imports from the colonial world. As late as 1594, for example, 95 per cent of the value of legal exports from the Spanish colonies in the New World consisted of gold and silver bullion. Nevertheless, other commodities entered the stream of trade, gradually expanded in volume, and by the seventeenth and eighteenth centuries overshadowed the original overseas exports to Europe. Exotic dyestuffs such as indigo and cochineal added color to European fabrics and made them gayer and more salable both in Europe and overseas. Coffee from Africa, cocoa from America, and tea from Asia became staple European beverages. Cotton and sugar, although they were known earlier in Europe, had never been produced or traded on a large scale. When sugar cane was transplanted to America, the production of sugar increased enormously and brought that delicacy within the budget of ordinary Europeans. The introduction of cotton goods from India, at first a luxury reserved for the wealthy, led eventually to the establishment of one of Europe's largest industries, dependent upon a raw material imported from America and catering especially to the masses. Chinese porcelain had a similar history. Tobacco, one of America's most celebrated and controversial contributions to civilization, grew rapidly in popularity in Europe in spite of determined efforts by both Church and state to stamp it out. In later years tropical fruits and nuts supplemented European diets, and furs, hides, exotic woods, and new fibers constituted important additions to European supplies.

One very special branch of commerce dealt in human beings: the slave trade. It was dominated at first by the Portuguese, then in turn by the Dutch, the French, and the English. Although the Spanish colonies were among the largest purchasers of slaves, the Spanish themselves did not engage in the trade to any great extent but granted it by contract, or *asiento*, to the traders of other nations. Usually the trade was triangular in nature. A European ship carrying firearms, knives, other metalwares, beads and similar cheap trinkets, gaily colored cloth, and liquor would sail for the West African coast, where it exchanged its cargo with local African chieftains for slaves, either war captives or the chief's own people. When the slave trader had loaded as many chained and manacled Africans as his ship would carry, he sailed for the West Indies or the mainland of North or South America. There he exchanged his human cargo for one of sugar, tobacco, or other products of the Western Hemisphere, with which he returned to Europe. Although the death rate for slaves in transit from disease and other causes was dreadfully high (frequently 50 per cent and sometimes more), the profits of the slave trade were extraordinary. European governments took no effective steps to prohibit it until the nineteenth century.

Many foodstuffs previously unknown in Europe, although not imported in large quantities, were introduced and naturalized, eventually becoming important staples of diet. From America came potatoes, tomatoes, beans, squash, pumpkins, and corn (called maize by most Europeans), as well as the domesticated turkey, which in spite of its name reached the Mediterranean from Mexico. Rice, originally from Asia, became naturalized in Europe and America.

Trade within Europe also grew. For example, the Portuguese brought spices back to Lisbon and sold them to merchants from other countries for distribution throughout Europe. Moreover, the Portuguese and Spanish, concentrating on the exploitation of their overseas empires, could not produce all the manufactured goods that were in demand there. They purchased the goods from other European countries, stimulating industry and commerce even in countries without colonies of their own. Shipbuilding and the production of naval stores, firearms, and munitions were among the most important industries involved. The textile industries found new outlets and in turn borrowed new techniques and materials from the textile industries of Asia. Metalware for use as tools and implements and glass-ware in the form of mirrors, bottles, and scientific instruments were in great demand in Europe and overseas. The brewing and distilling industries created new products such as rum and gin and increased their output to supply both markets. New industries, including sugar refining, tobacco processing, and cotton textile manufacture, that depended on imported raw materials, grew in importance. Other manufactures ranging from porcelain to snuff boxes developed to satisfy newly created tastes.

Along with the increase in trade and industry there was an increase in the number of merchants, shippers, manufacturers, wage laborers, and others involved in the market economy, as well as an increase in the number, variety, and strength of trading, or capitalistic, institutions, such as stock exchanges, warehouses, banks, and the like. Capitalism, already well established in northern Italy and the Low Countries, took in a larger and larger fraction of the European population in the course of the sixteenth century. One important reason was the phenomenon known as the "price revolution."

TABLE 2

THE PRICE REVOLUTION
GRAIN PRICES IN ENGLAND, FRANCE, AND ALSACE, 1451–1600
(1451–1500 = 100)

Period	England	France	Alsace
1451–1500	100	100	100
1501–1525	108	118	96
1526–1550	113	172	146
1551–1575	173	335	275
1576–1600	275	572	347

Source: W. Abel, *Agrarkrisen und Agrarkonjunktur in Mitteleuropa* (Berlin, 1935), p. 60.

As a result of the flow of gold and silver from the Spanish colonies, the stock of money metals roughly trebled in the course of the sixteenth century. As the quantity of money increased, its buying power decreased, so that the price of goods rose. The rise in prices was roughly proportional to the increase in the quantity of money. The effect of this inflation on commerce and industry was even more striking than the rise in prices itself. A businessman buys merchandise at one price, and after processing or transporting it or performing some other service, he expects to sell it at a somewhat higher price. If the value of the merchandise increases during the time that it is in his possession because of continued price inflation, he makes a double profit, the one he expected plus the windfall gain. During the period of the price revolution the windfall gain was often as great as, at times even greater than, the expected normal profit. In many countries wages and rents rose much more slowly than prices, favoring merchants and manufacturers at the expense of wage earners and landowners. The combination of these factors led to greatly increased economic activity and the accumulation of capital (wealth) in the hands of the commercial and manufacturing classes.

A SHIFT IN EUROPE'S CENTER OF GRAVITY

A final major economic consequence of the expansion of Europe—in a sense, the sum and culmination of all the other changes—was a pronounced shift in the location of the principal centers of economic activity within Europe. During the fifteenth century the cities of northern Italy retained the leadership in economic affairs that they had exercised throughout the Middle Ages. The Portuguese discoveries, however, deprived them of their monopoly of the spice trade. A series of wars involving invasion and occupation of Italy by foreign armies further disrupted commerce and finance. The decline of Italy was not immediate or drastic, for the Italians had reservoirs of capital, entrepreneurial talent, and highly refined economic institutions to carry them through for several generations. Italy's decline was probably more relative than absolute, because of the great increase in the volume of European commerce. Nevertheless, the Venetians' famous Flanders fleet made its last voyage in 1532, and in the latter part of the century Venetian ambassadors complained of competition from cheaper French and English woolens in the markets of the Near East, which the Italians had regarded as their exclusive domain. By the early seventeenth century Italy had fallen into the backwaters of economic life, from which it did not emerge until the twentieth century.

Spain and Portugal enjoyed a fleeting glory as the leading economic powers of Europe. Lisbon replaced Venice as the great entrepôt of the spice trade. In 1521 the Portuguese king haughtily refused an offer of the Venetian Republic to purchase the entire annual import of spices, but the Portuguese did not develop their commercial or capitalistic institutions. Instead, all trade with the East became a royal monopoly, strictly regulated for the benefit of the crown and royal favorites. Distribution of the spices and other exotic products in Europe was handled by the Dutch and Flemish in the north and by Italians in the Mediterranean. Their ships and merchants flocked to the harbor of Lisbon, sharing in the wealth of the Indies and building up stores of capital in their own countries. Thus, although the Portuguese monopoly was extremely lucrative for a time, in the long run it strengthened the capitalistic institutions of Portugal's trading partners more than those of Portugal itself. Both industry and agriculture declined in Portugal. Finally in 1580 the Portuguese crown fell to Philip II of Spain, who was less interested in protecting the Portuguese Empire than the

Spanish. By the end of the sixteenth century Dutch and English interlopers, who had been kept from trading with Portugal itself because of their hostility to Spain, began trading directly with the Orient—a portent of the imminent decline of the Portuguese Empire.

Spain, to which the American treasure first came, was the first to feel the effects of the price revolution, and its wealth and power were such that the legend of Spanish might did not die for more than two hundred years. Ironically, the seeds of its decline were sown by the same phenomenon that brought it wealth. The Spanish crown instituted a state monopoly over all trade in precious metals and foolishly tried to prevent their export from Spain to the rest of Europe. The state was, however, the worst offender. Most of its expenditures went for war and war preparations or subsidies to idle aristocrats, who spent their incomes on luxurious consumption, including products purchased abroad. Much of the young manhood of Spain was recruited to fight dynastic wars in Europe or control the natives and direct mining operations in the New World. The merchant class never had the opportunity to develop that it had in other countries, and Spain did not become an important nation commercially or industrially. Although it retained its extensive colonial empire until the early nineteenth century, it was already in full decline economically, politically, and militarily by the middle of the seventeenth century.

Central, Eastern, and Northern Europe did not participate significantly in the commercial prosperity of the sixteenth century. The Hanseatic League flourished in the fifteenth century but declined thereafter. Although the main causes of its decline were independent of the great discoveries, the latter probably hastened the decline by strengthening the commercial power of Dutch and English cities. Southern Germany and Switzerland, which had also become commercially prominent in the fifteenth century, retained their prosperity for a time; but since they were no longer on the most important trade routes and had no ports to benefit from the increase in seaborne trade, they slipped backward along with the rest of Central and Eastern Europe. All of Central Europe soon plunged into religious and dynastic wars, which sapped its energy for economic activity.

The area that gained most from the economic changes associated with the great discoveries was the region bordering on the North Sea and the English Channel: the Low Countries, England, and northern France. This area, opening on the Atlantic and lying midway between northern and southern Europe, was clearly destined geographically for great prosperity in an age of worldwide oceanic commerce, especially after the economic decline of Spain and Portugal. The political development of these countries also contributed to making the area the focal point of capitalist economy—a position that it had distinctly gained by the end of the sixteenth century and held continuously until the twentieth.

France, geographically contiguous with Spain, initially obtained Spanish gold and silver through the hands of merchants. Throughout the sixteenth century, however, France, too, engaged in dynastic and religious wars, and for the most part its government followed policies unfavorable to business interests. Therefore France did not gain as much as did the Netherlands and England, which benefited most from the increase in trade and the influx of precious metals.

Although Flanders never fully recovered from the great depression of the late Middle Ages, its neighboring provinces continued to prosper. With the gradual decline of Bruges as the principal entrepôt for trade with southern Europe, Antwerp arose to take its place. All seventeen provinces of the Low Countries, from Flanders and Luxembourg in the south to Holland and Groningen in the north, fell to the crown of Spain early in the sixteenth century. They were therefore in an excellent position to capitalize on the trading opportunities of the Spanish Empire. In the second half of the sixteenth century the Netherlands revolted against Spanish domination. Although Spain repressed the revolt in the southern Netherlands (modern Belgium), the northern Netherlands won their independence. Economically this episode resulted in the decline of the southern provinces because Spain enacted so many harsh punitive measures. Trade shifted to the north, and Amsterdam became the great commercial and financial center of the seventeenth century.

England at the time of the great discoveries was just emerging from the status of a backward, raw materials-producing area into something of a manufacturing country. Its agriculture was also becoming more capitalistic and market-oriented. The War of the Roses decimated the ranks of the great nobility but left the urban middle classes and peasants almost untouched. The new Tudor dynasty, which came to the throne in 1485, depended heavily on middle-class support and gave favors to it in return. The price revolution had its greatest effect in England. England gained gold and silver as a result of mercantile activities, and the rise in prices benefited English merchants, manufacturers, and progressive agriculturists at the expense of wage earners and small peasant farmers. Although these factors produced a certain amount of social unrest, they also made the English social structure more fluid and flexible than that on the Continent and contributed to the strength of the institutions of capitalism.

POLITICAL, SOCIAL, AND CULTURAL CONSEQUENCES OF THE EXPANSION OF EUROPE

In hundreds of ways important and trivial, obvious and subtle, the great discoveries and overseas expansion of European civilization influenced the lives of Europeans. The shift in the center of economic activity entailed a shift in the locus of political power. In the sixteenth century the Hapsburgs, who ruled in Spain, central Europe, the Low Countries, and Spanish

America, constituted the greatest concentration of political power that Europe had seen since Roman times. Portugal had more political power than ever before or afterward. With the decline of Spain and Portugal in the seventeenth century, the balance of power swung northward to countries with good harbors, large navies, and flourishing commerce: the United Netherlands, France, and England.

Among the social consequences of European expansion were an increase in wealth, luxury, patronage of the arts, and the political power and social influence of merchants and financiers. The discoveries provided new themes for art, new forms of luxury, and new areas for the exercise of wealth and power. Changes in diet and dress were brought on by products imported from overseas. For the first time such things as sugar, spice, rum, and tobacco entered the diets of ordinary Europeans. The wealthy decked themselves in silks, exotic furs, and ostrich plumes, weighted their fingers with precious stones, doused themselves with strong new perfumes, and consumed their highly spiced foods from utensils of silver and gold.

In the long run intellectual influences had the greatest impact. The discoveries introduced new words into European vocabularies and provided new themes for literature. It is more than mere chance that the great achievements in the national literatures of Spain, Portugal, the Netherlands, and England coincided with the period of rapid overseas expansion and commercial prosperity. In Spain it was the Golden Age; in England, the Elizabethan Age. The greatest epic poem in the Portuguese language, *The Lusiads* ("The Portuguese") of Luiz de Camoëns (1524–1580), celebrates the achievement of Vasco da Gama.

In science, affected even more than literature, knowledge of the world overseas provided facts to verify or refute existing theories and insights from which new theories grew. It revolutionized the study of geography. When Gerardus Mercator (1512–1594), inventor of the famous Mercator projection for showing the earth on a flat map, drew his map of the world less than fifty years after the first circumnavigation, he could present a reasonably accurate picture of at least the major continental outlines as we know them today. Astronomy, zoology, botany, and geology all received new data to digest and rationalize. The practice of medicine benefited directly from the introduction of new drugs such as quinine and camphor, as well as being misled by the introduction of many spurious ones.

In religion the immediate effect of the discoveries was to summon forth a vigorous missionary effort that ultimately carried Christianity to far corners of the world. A less obvious but ultimately deeply significant effect was the impetus the discoveries gave to the study of comparative religions and the challenge to long-accepted Christian dogma that resulted from this study. The institutions and behavior of hundreds of peoples who were previously unknown or slightly known to Europeans, from the most primitive and cannibalistic West Indians to the highly civilized Hindus and

Chinese, provided food for thought for moralists, political philosophers, and proto-anthropologists. For at least three centuries the "noble savage" or "man in the state of nature" was used as the starting point for both democratic and authoritarian political theories. Those who dreamed of more nearly perfect societies, such as Thomas More in *Utopia* in the sixteenth century and Francis Bacon in *The New Atlantis* in the seventeenth, placed them in the newly discovered regions overseas.

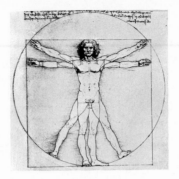

CHAPTER THREE

The Renaissance

FOR MOST of us the word "Renaissance" conjures up a vision of the magnificent art produced in northern Italy from the late fourteenth to the early sixteenth century. Actually artistic creativity was only one, albeit a major, aspect of the history of the era, and the Renaissance was not limited to Italy, though it began there. If the later fourteenth century is accepted as an arbitrary starting point for the Renaissance, and 1520 as an even more arbitrary finishing point, a greatly heightened interest in and knowledge of Greek and Roman classics is apparent as an outstanding characteristic of the era. The new-found enthusiasm for antiquity had a profound influence on every aspect of intellectual and cultural life, affected religion, and brought about changes in man's attitude toward government. Above all, there appeared a new emphasis on the power of human creativity, a heady compound of individualism and secularism, which underlay all intellectual and aesthetic achievements of the era.

The Renaissance in Italy

People in northern Italy during these years were certain that they were living in a time of intellectual revolution, marked by a rebirth (the meaning of *renaissance*) of the values of classical, Greco-Roman civilization. They scorned the thousand years that separated them from the end of classical antiquity as the "dark ages," in which they were convinced there had been no great cultural achievements. They were confident that the "dark ages" had ended and that they were living in a "golden age." In the 1430's a Florentine named Matteo Palmieri wrote: "It is but in our own days that men dare boast they see the dawn of better things. . . . Now, indeed, may every thoughtful spirit thank God that it has been permitted him to be born in this new age, so full of hope and promise, which already rejoices in a greater array of nobly-gifted souls than the world has seen in the thousand years that preceded it." Palmieri's braggadocio was common currency among his contemporaries.

Historians have long debated whether the Italians of the Renaissance were right in their boast that their age broke abruptly with the immediately preceding centuries, or whether the Renaissance only continued trends that had already been much in evidence during the preceding three centuries of medieval civilization. It is now generally agreed that the Renaissance had its roots firmly sunk in the Middle Ages. At the same time, most historians recognize the Renaissance as an age of transition in which individualism and secularism began to erode the corporate and religious world view that characterized the Middle Ages. In this sense the Renaissance in Italy marked the onset of the modern world.

The real problem in dealing with the Renaissance is to analyze the proportion of "modern individualism" to "medieval corporateness" or of "modern secularism" to "medieval religiosity" at any one point, and even to determine exactly what is meant by key concepts such as "modern individualism." The Swiss historian Jacob Burckhardt, in *The Civilization of the Renaissance in Italy* (1860), the foundation of modern histories of the subject, described the Italian Renaissance man as

> the first born among the sons of modern Europe. In the Middle Ages both sides of human consciousness—that which was turned within and that which was turned without—lay dreaming or half awake beneath a common veil. The veil was woven of faith, illusion, and childish prepossession, through which the world and history was seen clad in strange hues. Man was conscious of himself only as a member of a race, people, party, family, or corporate body—only through some general category. In Italy this veil first melted into air; an *objective* treatment and consideration of the state and of all things of this world became possible. The *subjective* side at the same time asserted itself with corresponding emphasis; man became a spiritual *individual,* and recognized himself as such.

The school of "Renaissance" historians that evolved from Burckhardt's theories provoked a controversy with the "medievalists" that is still alive. The Dutch scholar Johan Huizinga, in *The Waning of the Middle Ages*

(1919), argued that although the fourteenth and fifteenth centuries may for convenience's sake be called the "Renaissance," they were the terminal centuries of the Middle Ages for Europe outside Italy. The exponents of these two points of view have sought either to extend Burckhardt to the north or to extend Huizinga to Italy, with the result that all of the hitherto vivid contrasts between "Renaissance" and "medieval" have tended to become blurred. As the "Renaissance" advocates have underestimated the importance of the survival of fundamental institutions and governmental practices from the Middle Ages, so the "medievalists" have strained to find "Renaissance" attributes in the twelfth century. As in any controversy, sound research has sometimes been overinflated and men have seemed to take extreme positions. The conflict might be resolved by a more vigorous investigation of how the Renaissance differed from "modern times" rather than from the Middle Ages. Then its transitional quality—the only point of agreement among most of the contestants—would perhaps be made more apparent.

The Italian Renaissance had substantial foundations. Political and social developments in northern Italy were among the most important. During the Middle Ages feudal lords held political and military leadership in most parts of Europe. In northern and central Italy, however, the long contest for power between papal and imperial forces promoted the emergence of independent city-states or communes. These small states were ruled by oligarchies composed of rich merchants and nobles from the surrounding countryside who had been compelled to move into the cities. The fusion of the wealthy burghers and the nobility within the cities created a new social and political milieu, which was completely different from the feudal society dominant elsewhere in Europe. In this new milieu people had a civic consciousness, a pride in their city's particular qualities, and conceived of their city's glory as concrete and material. In this new milieu secular interests were paramount. The city-states engaged in an intense rivalry with one another. Their competitiveness extended into the realm of culture. Rulers sought to exalt themselves and their states, and men of private means wanted to call attention to themselves. As a result they eagerly sponsored artists and scholars whose works were to enshrine for posterity the merits and glories of their patrons.

The competition in patronage presupposed the existence of surplus capital. Here again circumstances favored northern Italy. Although most of Europe had experienced an economic decline, hard times, and a fall in population during the century from about 1350 to 1450, Italians had amassed great riches during the preceding era of economic growth. They continued to be active in banking, trade, industry, and agriculture and, despite the depression, continued to pile up wealth, though probably at a slower rate. The decline in economic activity, however, meant that there were fewer opportunities for profitable investment in business enterprise. Consequently, wealthy men turned more of their surplus capital into works of art, handsome buildings, and the support of men of letters.

The political, social, and economic foundations of the Renaissance exhibited the elitist nature of the age. Political power, social prestige, and wealth were limited to the upper echelons of society—although these were a larger proportion of the whole population in northern Italian city-states than in most other areas of Europe—and there was nothing egalitarian about society. In every facet of the Renaissance, from humanism to art, the social presupposition of inequality was present. The Renaissance was a spiritual and aesthetic experience only for those who had arrived materially. It bore less relation to the real condition of most men than did the all-embracing order of medieval religion it scorned.

Italian Humanism

The first historians of the Renaissance treated the "revival of antiquity" as a new phenomenon. Actually, many of the classical authors were known and read in medieval times. There was an important qualitative distinction, however, in the way a scholastic of the High Middle Ages and a scholar of the Renaissance used the ancient writings. Medieval scholastics tried to reconcile them with Christian theology and blend them with Christian ideals. To the scholars of the Renaissance, classical times seemed a golden age in which people, untroubled by concerns about salvation, were interested in man for man's sake alone. The secular and individualistic attitude that they found in the classics coincided with, and seemed to justify, their own conception of how men should live and act.

The study of the classics came to be known as "humanism," from *studia humanitatis,* the Latin term for studies that give man the understanding to express his own individuality in his conduct, speech, and writing. Most of the humanists, as the men who pursued the classical studies were called, were laymen. Some were clerics, however, and included men who held high Church office. Other important churchmen gave their patronage to humanists. Thus, the secular influence of humanism was often sponsored and advanced by men of the Church.

PETRARCH

The first of the Renaissance humanists was Francesco Petrarca (1304–1374), or Petrarch as he is called in English. While still a boy, Petrarch became enamored of the classics, particularly the rhetorical works of Cicero. Compelled by his father to become a lawyer, Petrarch called his time at law school seven wasted years. After his father's death he gladly gave up his practice for the study of Latin classics. The great figures of antiquity became so real to him that he called Cicero his "father" and the poet Virgil his "brother." He wrote extensively in classical Latin, searched tirelessly for classical Latin manuscripts, and spent long hours editing and ridding them of the errors of copyists. He could not read Greek—to his great sorrow —but he collected and preserved classical writings in that language, too. In his own Latin writings he did not slavishly imitate the ancients but developed his own flowing style.

Although he was happiest when he was working at his desk, Petrarch did not spend his life in the scholar's traditional ivory tower. He traveled widely and knew many of the important men of his time. Imitating his "brother" Virgil, he loved nature and wrote lyrically about rural sights and sounds. He eagerly sought personal glory and fame, and while still in his thirties won recognition throughout Italy and elsewhere in Europe as the foremost literary figure of the time.

Petrarch was the first to call the period since classical times the "dark ages." He was certain that a new age of glory and light was dawning in which, he said, men "will be able to walk back into the pure radiance of the past." His enthusiasm and fame inspired others to seek out old manuscripts in monasteries and other repositories, to write treatises in Ciceronian Latin, and to sing the praises of classical antiquity. Many of these humanists were employed by rulers, popes, and men of wealth as secretaries, government officials, or teachers. Through such positions of influence they transmitted to others the view of life and the secularism that they found in the classics.

At the end of the fourteenth century a number of Greek scholars settled in Italy to teach classical Greek. Eager Italians soon learned to read and prize the writings of Greek antiquity. After the fall of Constantinople to the Turks in 1453, exiled Byzantines swelled the tide, bringing with them a number of new texts. In the second half of the fifteenth century a few humanists began to study Hebrew and other Oriental tongues. During this period printing was introduced into Italy from Rhineland Germany, where it had just been invented. Until then, copyists had laboriously transcribed the ancient writings. The printed editions of the Greek and Roman classics greatly stimulated their circulation.

HUMANIST TECHNIQUES OF SCHOLARSHIP

As they continued their intensive study of the ancient writings, the humanists developed new scholarly techniques that laid the foundation for modern methods of historical and literary analysis. They became skilled in the art of textual criticism and learned how to examine sources in order to make sure that they were genuine or were accurate copies. The most famous triumph of the new scholarly methods came in 1440 when Lorenzo Valla, one of the greatest Latinists of his day, proved spurious a document called the Donation of Constantine, which had long served as one of the main supports for the papacy's claim to spiritual and temporal sovereignty. The Church maintained that shortly after Emperor Constantine's conversion to Christianity in the fourth century he had in a charter, the Donation, given to the bishop of Rome spiritual supremacy over the other patriarchates of the Church and temporal dominion over Italy and Western Europe. On the basis of the language and anachronistic historical references in the charter, Valla proved that it was a forgery, probably written in the eighth century by someone in the papal chancery.

The humanists' enthusiasm for antiquity was also responsible for the development of the study of archaeology. People had used the ruins of ancient Rome as stone quarries and had stripped marble from the classical monuments to burn for lime. Humanists lamented the destruction of these ancient glories and wrote treatises on classical archaeology and epigraphy (the deciphering and interpretation of ancient inscriptions). In the second half of the fifteenth century the popes forbad further depredations and sponsored excavations that recovered ancient works of art, including such masterpieces as the Apollo Belvedere and the Laocoön statues of the Hellenistic period. In other cities of Italy wealthy men and scholars built up their own private collections of classical works of art and ancient objects.

HUMANIST EDUCATION

The achievements of the humanists included an almost total reconstruction of the theory and practice of education. In medieval Europe formal education had been limited mainly to the training of clergymen and had been capped by the rigorous disciplines studied in the universities. In the fifteenth century humanists, inspired by classical ideals, argued that the aim of education should be to produce men whose every action expresses their own individuality and who lead good and useful lives no matter what career they follow. They set up curricula to include the classics, mathematics, music, religion, and some science, in order to teach the student intellectual discipline, stimulate his imagination, and provide him with guides to moral conduct. They maintained, however, that education was more than just book learning. They insisted on training in good manners. They also added athletics and outdoor activity in imitation of Greek educational philosophy, which held that both mind and body must be developed in harmony.

Only the sons of the rich could afford to attend the new schools, save for a few scholarship students. Nevertheless, the educational innovations lived on far beyond the era of the Renaissance. They persist today in our effort to give students a liberal education that will broaden their perspective, deepen their understanding, and develop their sense of civic responsibility.

The humanists did not restrict their educational work to youths. Many gave public lectures before large and appreciative audiences, often delivering a series of talks in one city and then moving on to another town. This method of adult education popularized the ideals of humanism. Humanists also taught one another by forming academies, supported by wealthy patrons, to discuss scholarly and philosophical problems. By the end of the fifteenth century nearly every Italian cultural center had its own academy. The Platonic Academy at Florence, founded by Cosimo de' Medici, was the most famous, especially during the reign of Lorenzo the Magnificent. As its name indicates, this academy devoted itself especially to the study of Plato and tried, among other things, to reconcile the tenets of Platonism with the theology of Christianity.

THE ITALIAN HUMANIST IMAGE OF MAN

The intellectual and political ferment of the Renaissance convinced men that they lived in a new era and gave them a feeling of freedom from traditional restraints and the old concern that life was only a preparation for salvation. Above all, it encouraged them to believe that man is the master of his own destiny, that there need be no limit to his ambitions and virtuosity, and that his purpose on earth is to develop himself to his fullest capacities.

A new, humanistic image of man is to be found in the writings of many men of the Italian Renaissance. In 1434 Leon Battista Alberti wrote, "If anyone wishes to investigate carefully what it is that exalts and increases . . . honor and felicity, he will clearly see that men are themselves the source of their own fortune and misfortune." Fifty years later Giovanni Pico della Mirandola explained in an essay, *The Dignity of Man,* that God had put man in the center of the universe and said to him, "We have made you neither heavenly nor earthly, neither mortal nor immortal, so that, more freely and more honorably the molder and maker of yourself, you may fashion yourself in whatever form you shall prefer. . . . [T]o man it has been granted to have what he chooses, to be what he wills."

The emphasis upon man as his own master resulted in a revision of the old scale of social values. Success and fame no longer needed to depend upon birth and social status but upon a man's native abilities. The man who began life as a peasant or worker could rise to the heights if he had talent, imagination, intelligence, self-reliance, and ambition. The men of the Renaissance summed up in one word the qualities that enabled the outstanding individual to shape his own destiny and achieve greatness in whatever field he chose. That word was *virtù,* from the Latin word for "man" (*vir*). It had nothing to do with "virtue" in the modern sense of moral rectitude, which was not considered necessary for the possession of *virtù*.

The new emphasis upon individuality also produced an intense self-consciousness. Renaissance men sought ceaselessly to prove themselves men of *virtù* in the eyes of their fellows. The rulers and the rich spent mightily on ostentatious display, on great public and private entertainments, and on works of art and buildings, to call attention to their generosity and achievements. Men showed scant modesty in telling about their abilities and boasted publicly about their exploits. Their ideal was the "universal man" (*uomo universale*), that is, the man who excelled in many different fields.

The most famous of the universal men were Michelangelo (1475–1564), Leonardo da Vinci (1452–1519), and Leon Battista Alberti (1404–1472). Michelangelo's sculptures and frescoes are among the world's greatest artistic creations. He was also an architect, a military engineer and, when he was past the age of seventy, the author of beautiful sonnets. Leonardo distinguished himself as painter, architect, anatomist, scientist, inventor, and engineer. Alberti commanded four skills—painting, architecture, poetry, and music—and was master of the traditional disciplines of mathematics, philosophy, and law. He wrote treatises on all of these subjects in pure and elegant prose.

Although these three men and a few others stand out as giants, many lesser men passed easily from one artistic or intellectual field to another—perhaps too easily. There was much superficial dazzle in the *universali* because many of the skills were highly related and based upon specific (classical) models that were limited in number and variety. Few of the universal men felt under any compunction to command the more profound and intricate disciplines of either medieval learning, which they rejected, or of classical philosophy, which was in Italy hardly yet a subject of learned controversy. Men believed that they could master many fields, and if their grasp outreached their capacity, their universality of interest produced the richness and excitement of Renaissance culture.

The self-confidence of these men and their conviction that a man should be judged by his accomplishments rather than his birth had practical limitations. Low-born and newly risen men successful in politics or business in the Italian city-states were stalked by a sense of inferiority to the more established feudal aristocracies in the north. In search of recognition as aristocrats, they sought to acquire the courtliness and fine manners of the natural born noble. Manuals on etiquette appeared in the late fifteenth and early sixteenth centuries to meet the demand. They analyzed proper behavior and laid down rules to transform the soldier of fortune or the newly rich merchant into a man of breeding and a connoisseur of taste. Some manuals contained elementary instructions, for their readers often started from scratch: for instance, a gentleman should not thrust a stinking thing under another man's nose to show him how bad it smells; nor should he spit, nor pare his nails in public.

A book called *The Courtier*, begun in 1510 and published in 1528, was the most famous of the manuals of etiquette. Its author, Baldassare Castiglione, belonged to an ancient but impoverished noble family. Having spent several years at the court of Urbino in northern Italy, he cast his book in the form of conversations among the highly cultivated members of that court. He pointed out that it was easier to become a gentleman if one was born into the nobility, but conceded that high birth was not essential. Despite his aristocratic bias, his conception of the gentleman corresponded with the Renaissance ideal of the well-rounded individual. The true gentleman had to have courage, skill in outdoor sports, knowledge of the classics, and eloquence in his speech. He must have polish and wit, grace and nonchalance. He must know something about the arts, especially music, and be adept in the social graces and the pursuit of love. He must wear his learning and his accomplishments lightly, as if they were perfectly natural to him, and must avoid pedantry and pomposity. Castiglione's book enjoyed great success in Italy and soon appeared in a number of foreign translations. It had an enormous and lasting influence in shaping the social behavior of Western man. Gross manners and vulgarity, of course, did not disappear, but *The Courtier* and its many imitators established the pattern for gentlemanly behavior.

The Courtier marked a peak in Italian Renaissance humanism; indeed, it marked the onset of a decline for the humanist man. Harking back to the feudal chivalric ideal of the High Middle Ages, it testified to the waning of the old civic pride that had nurtured the early humanism of Petrarch two centuries before in favor of a would-be *uomo universale*, who was more surface than substance, more manner than man.

Italian Art

If Italians had done nothing else during the Renaissance, their painting, sculpture, and architecture would alone have made it one of the most brilliant epochs in the history of human achievement. Probably no other age has produced so much artistic genius. Their works, their techniques, and their themes set the standards for the art of the Western world until very recent times, and they provide the models to which modern art is invidiously compared.

The artists of the Renaissance shared to the full the self-confidence and egoism that typified the era. They were not content to be anonymous craftsmen, as most of their medieval predecessors had been. They passionately sought recognition, vied openly with fellow artists, and were often intensely

Perseus, by Benvenuto Cellini
"Now it pleased God that, on the instant of [the statue's] exposure to view, a shout of boundless enthusiasm went up in commendation of my work, which consoled me not a little. The folk kept on attaching sonnets to the posts of the door, which was protected with a curtain while I gave the last touches to the statue. . . . At last I brought the whole work to completion: and on a certain Thursday morning I exposed it to the public gaze. Immediately, before the sun was fully in the heavens, there assembled such a multitude of people that no words could describe them. All with one voice contended which should praise it most." From Cellini's autobiography, THE LIFE OF BENVENUTO CELLINI, tr. J. A. Symonds (New York, 1926).

Brogi—Art Reference Bureau

jealous of one another. They demanded that their patrons accord them respect and honor and took quick offense if they felt that they had been slighted. The patrons readily acquiesced to the demands and accepted affronts from artists that they would not have taken from others. Patrons competed with one another for the services of artists, paid them extravagantly, and accepted them as equals. As Cosimo de' Medici said, "One must treat these people of extraordinary genius as if they were celestial spirits, and not like beasts of burden."

The artists shared the conviction that their era represented a complete break with the immediate past. They had utter contempt for the art of the Middle Ages (though they readily adopted techniques that had been developed by their "brutish predecessors") and admired only the art of classical antiquity. Their fondest hope was to equal and, if possible, to exceed the accomplishments of the ancients. In their self-conscious imitativeness and their aspiration to excel the imitated, the artists of the Italian Renaissance revealed both their power and their limitations.

PAINTING

Giotto di Bondone (*c.* 1270–1337) was the transitional figure in the passage from medieval to Renaissance art. Until his time Italian painting, dominated by Byzantine influences, had been flat and two-dimensional, though it was far more ambitious and highly developed than art elsewhere in Europe. Giotto broke away from this style and produced much more realistic paintings. Although his work seems primitive compared to later Renaissance art, his successful attempts to provide an illusion of depth by contrasting light and shade (*chiaroscuro*) and by varying the brightness of colors made him a revolutionary figure in the history of art.

For nearly a century after Giotto, Italian artists seemed content to imitate his techniques and little advance was made. Then suddenly in Florence a great new wave of innovation and progress began. Masaccio (*c.* 1401–1429) was the first great figure of the outburst. Taking up where Giotto had left off, he produced in a brief career works that were exceptional in their physical realism, organic unity, and portrayal of character and emotion. Their precise anatomical detail, representation of movement, and perspective and foreshortening set the pattern for Italian painting. After Masaccio's death artists traveled to Florence to study his murals and draw inspiration from them.

Painters conceived their problem to be the combination of a faithful portrayal of what they saw with beauty. To achieve realism, they made careful studies of nature. They also sought, and attained, technical mastery. They worked out theories of perspective based on experimentation and mathematical principles. They studied anatomy, botany, and zoology. They filled their sketchbooks with drawings of faces and the human figure, as well as with sketches and diagrams to illustrate perspective. Insisting that every part of a painting had to be in harmonious relation with every other part, they made systematic studies of relations such as the length of the hand, the width of the foot, or the thickness of the waist to the whole figure.

Despite the differences between Italian Renaissance and medieval art, the new artists remained closely linked to their predecessors in one very important respect: the choice of themes. Italian Renaissance art, like the medieval, was above all a religious art. By far the majority of the subjects selected came from the Bible. Traditional scenes of Christianity predominated—the Nativity, the Crucifixion, the Stations of the Cross, or the miracles of the saints. Renaissance artists, too, did much of their work for churches and monasteries. While retaining some of the religious symbols that had been so important in medieval art, they added their own genius and worldly outlook. The saints are recognizable human beings, the Madonnas are beautiful young women, the faces of patrons or of the artist and his friends often appear, and the Biblical scenes somehow never seem far from scenes of contemporary Italian life.

With the notable exception of Michelangelo, the greatest artists engaged in portraiture. Their brushes were able to produce more than just the features of the subjects. They knew how to penetrate to the innermost qualities of personality. "Paint the face," urged Leonardo, "in such a way that it will be easy to understand what is going on in the mind." Their portraits are dramatic character studies that reflect the Renaissance conception of man as an individual, noble, dignified, and free to make of himself what he wishes.

Landscape painting was another major innovation of Renaissance art. At first, landscapes were used as symbols. Forbidding rocks and mountains were meant to symbolize hell or terror; gardens represented paradise. As men became increasingly interested in the world in which they lived, painters introduced local Italian landscapes as background, even in paintings of Biblical subjects. The revival of interest in Latin authors who proclaimed the beauties of country life, especially Virgil, also drew the attention of artists to rural scenes. Usually artists included landscape to give a painting the illusion of depth, and the landscape formed a minor part of the picture. Then, as they learned more about color, light, shadow, and perspective, they became ever more entranced with scenery, and landscapes began to dominate many paintings. Landscape emerged as a distinctive artistic genre, far removed from the original pictorial representations of sacred themes.

As artists grew more interested in portraying reality and learned more about the techniques of their craft, they made increasing use of the nude in their work. This was another great innovation. Like the ancient artists whom they admired, they realized that clothing masks the human form and prevents the artist from conveying to the observer the full sense of life and movement and energy. Above all others, Michelangelo mastered the nude as a medium of expression. His towering genius enabled him to make the male form seem almost superhuman as in the heroic figures in the Biblical scenes that he painted on the ceiling of the Sistine Chapel in the Vatican.

In the latter part of the fourteenth and early fifteenth centuries—the era that is often termed the High Renaissance—classical allegories became fashionable in art. They were essentially pagan in origin, drawn from classical mythology. Influenced by the metaphysical teachings of the Neo-Platonists in the Florentine Academy and by a renewal of interest in such esoteric studies as astrology, artists often intended several layers of meaning in their paintings. For example, Raphael (1483–1520) in a painting of Cupid and Psyche told the well-known story and also tried to show the ascent and ultimate deification of the human soul. Bandinelli portrayed the struggle between lust and reason by painting a battle scene between one group of gods, including Venus, Cupid, and Vulcan, who represented the baser instincts and another group of gods, led by Jupiter, Minerva, and Mercury, who symbolized man's higher nature. The use of this pictorial language, which was comprehensible to only a few, contributed to intellectual snobbery. Those who knew enough to understand what the artist meant felt

The Creation of Man, detail from ceiling of Sistine Chapel, by Michelangelo

"Thus, singlehanded, he completed the work in twenty months, aided only by his mixer of colors. . . . He used no perspective or foreshortening, or any fixed point of view, devoting his energies rather to adapting the figures to the disposition than the disposition to the figures, contenting himself with the perfection of his nude and draped figures, which are of unsurpassed design and excellence. . . . The venerable majesty of God with the motion as He surrounds some of the cherubs with one arm and stretches the other to an Adam of marvellous beauty of attitude and outline, seem a new creation of the Maker rather than one of the brush and design of a man." G. Vasari (1511–1574), in THE LIVES OF THE PAINTERS, SCULPTORS AND ARCHITECTS, W. Gaunt, ed. (London, 1963).

superior to the many who did not share their knowledge and who saw only the literal meaning. The pious might justly fear that the ignorant would be seduced from faith by the pagan figures.

SCULPTURE

Sculpture bore a close relationship to painting and followed a parallel course in its development. Many artists, including Giotto, Leonardo, and Michelangelo, excelled in both art forms. Like the painters, the sculptors carefully studied human anatomy, experimented with new techniques, used the nude, chose many of their themes from the Bible and classical literature, and developed the art of portraiture.

Donatello (*c.* 1386–1466) was the first major Renaissance sculptor. His work opened a new chapter in the history of sculpture, just as the work of his contemporary and fellow Florentine, Masaccio, started a new era in painting. Donatello freed sculpture from its medieval function of serving only to embellish architecture; it became an independent art. Donatello's sculptures combined realism, classical proportions, and harmony and had a dramatic and emotional effect.

Renaissance sculpture reached its zenith with the work of Michelangelo. He produced statues that many critics think have never been equaled. He began by conscious imitation of the classical style and succeeded so well that a Roman art dealer buried one of his pieces, a sleeping Cupid, then dug it up and sold it as an antique. He soon passed through this imitative stage and at the age of twenty-three did the "Pietà." In this work he first demonstrated his full powers. Soon after its completion Michelangelo carved a gigantic nude of David out of a single block of marble that was sixteen feet in length. The statue of the young shepherd who had just slain Goliath was the embodiment of the daring, power, and confidence of youth. As Michelangelo grew older, a consciousness of man's struggle to free himself from sin and achieve immortality dominated his work. In his sculpture, as in his painting, he sought to harmonize the physical and the spiritual in order to show the indivisibility of body and soul.

ARCHITECTURE

In architecture, as in painting and sculpture, the Renaissance broke with medieval ideals and, even more than in the other arts, with the style of the Middle Ages. The Gothic was abandoned in favor of classical forms and classical decoration. Renaissance architects, however, did not raise servile imitations of ancient buildings. They adapted the domes, columns, rounded arches, and symmetry of classical architecture to their own purposes. This adaptation was necessary, since the city patronage that supported them required compact buildings in a limited space (often side by side, as along Venice's Grand Canal) in contrast to the more ample landscaping of the classical monuments that were their models. In an age of universal skills many architects were also painters or sculptors, and in their architecture they pursued the same goals of harmony and beauty that inspired the other arts. They insisted that each part of a building harmonize with every other part. If the parts were related so intimately that nothing could be added or taken away from the building without destroying its harmony, beauty was achieved. One of their greatest accomplishments was church architecture. Like the ancients, they considered the circle to be a symbol of God because it had neither beginning nor end. Therefore, they built churches with the altar at or near the center of the building and crowned them with circular domes. They intended that everything in the church should be in perfect mathematical proportion in order to represent the closest human approximation of divine order and harmony. Not limiting themselves to religious buildings, they also designed lavish palaces, private homes, and country villas for the rich and powerful.

Filippo Brunelleschi (1377–1446), a Florentine contemporary of Masaccio and Donatello, was the pioneer of the Renaissance architectural style. He went to Rome to study the ancient ruins and learn the techniques of classical Roman architecture. When he returned to Florence, he received a commission to build a dome for the cathedral. His creation became a model for many later domes, among them St. Peter's in Rome and the Capitol dome in Washington.

Florence remained the great center of architecture and the other arts until the end of the fifteenth century. Then artistic and cultural supremacy shifted to Rome. As far as architecture was concerned, one reason for the transfer was the fact that in 1499 Pope Julius II persuaded an architect named Bramante to move to Rome. Bramante's work in the capital of Christendom led Renaissance architecture into its greatest phase. His own greatest work, and the culmination of Renaissance architecture, was the basilica of St. Peter's. Bramante's plan called for a church in the shape of a huge Greek cross having arms of equal length and crowned with a vast dome. It would have covered an area nearly twelve thousand square yards larger than that covered by St. Peter's today, which is still the largest church in Christendom. After his death in 1515 a series of other men took over and altered Bramante's plans. In 1546 Michelangelo, who was seventy-one years old, agreed to take charge. He returned to the main outlines of Bramante's plan but added many features of his own, including a new design for the dome. He died long before the building was completed and many of the details of his plan were changed, but the great dome that dominates the skyline of Rome followed his design.

The Northern Renaissance

To fifteenth-century Italians the culture of the North seemed so far behind theirs that when the French king invaded Italy in 1494, they regarded the attack as a new barbarian invasion. One reason for the lag was the economic and political chaos of the late fourteenth and the fifteenth centuries. Princes and nobles lacked the time and money needed to patronize artists and scholars. The disruption of wars, brigandage, want, misery, social strife, and pestilence made men pessimistic and insecure, in striking contrast to the optimism of Italians of the Renaissance. In Italy the fusion of the nobility and the upper bourgeoisie in the cities produced a changed milieu in which new ideas could flourish. In the North the nobility still dominated with its traditional value system, and tales of chivalry remained the favorite form of literature even among members of the merchant class. In Italy classical writings served as the inspiration for a new world view. In the North stories of ancient Troy, Greece, and Rome were woven into fanciful tales of chivalric derring-do. A deliberate effort was made to keep alive the exaggerated glories of the knightly past by the introduction of elaborate court ceremonials, royal sponsorship of chivalric love and poetry, tournaments, and the creation of new knightly orders, such as the English Order of the Garter and the Burgundian Order of the Golden Fleece.

The French invasion of Italy in 1494 permanently established Northern Europe's connection with Italian culture. The invasion accelerated immeasurably the process of cultural interchange that had already begun with traveling scholars and artists, students, clergymen, and merchants. By the beginning of the sixteenth century Italian culture exercised an unprecedented and almost hypnotic influence over European cultural life. Princes sought the services of Italian scholars and artists, and the monarchs of France, England, and Spain, secure on their thrones and having large revenues at their disposal, could afford lavish patronage. Even the miserly Henry VII of England (1485–1509) had a tomb made for himself and his wife by a Florentine artist, Torrigiano, which was so elaborate that a century later Francis Bacon said of Henry that he "dwelleth more richly dead than he did alive in any of his palaces." The much more extravagant Francis I of France (1515–47) persuaded Leonardo da Vinci to come to France by offering him 7,000 gold florins and a palace of his own choosing.

NORTHERN ART AND ARCHITECTURE

Northern artists combined the artistic traditions of their own lands with the style and techniques that they learned from the Italians. This was done most successfully by Albrecht Dürer (1471–1528). While he was still an apprentice painter in Germany being trained in the Gothic style, he saw some engravings of Italian paintings and copied them in an attempt to learn how to draw the human form. Later he traveled to Italy to study and do research in artistic techniques. Influenced by the Italians, he used classical themes, studied mathematics and art theory, and wrote treatises on perspective and proportion. Yet he remained faithful to his own German tradition. His works have an intensity and air of mysticism, as well as sometimes a gaunt, inhuman, allegorical terror, that clearly distinguish them from Italian works of art.

Dürer was the leading figure among the artists who made the era from the 1490's to the 1520's the greatest in the history of German creative art. Another major artist of the period, Hans Holbein the Younger (1497–1543), stands out as one of the greatest portrait painters of all time. In his early years he painted religious subjects, but later he devoted himself completely to the portrayal of secular society. The meticulous detail, simplicity of composition, and complete frankness of his portraits reveal the intermingling of the German and Italian elements, an amalgam of the two traditions, which can be seen in the work of other important German painters of the era. For three-quarters of a century painting in England was conditioned by the impact that Holbein made on aristocratic taste during his two long sojourns there. He died in England while serving as court painter to Henry VIII.

The Germans had no rivals in their mastery of woodcuts and copper engravings. Dürer above all others excelled in these media; indeed, he owed his greatest fame to his graphic art. His prints and those of other German artists served as powerful weapons of propaganda in the Protestant Reformation. A plate or woodcut could turn out thousands of copies of a drawing of a religious subject illustrating a theme of the reformers, or it could reproduce a caricature satirizing the Roman Catholic priesthood.

In the late thirteenth and the fourteenth centuries Flanders, which was then a part of the Duke of Burgundy's possessions, was the scene of a great artistic outburst. Flemish painting alone in all of Europe rivaled that of the Italian Renaissance. The Flemings, unlike the Italians, made no conscious effort to break with the medieval past. Instead, they moved easily and gradually from the medieval toward a modern style, and their painting remained deeply spiritual and symbolic in the medieval manner. They differed from the Italians, too, in that they did not develop systematic and scientific studies of anatomy, perspective, and composition. They arrived at technical mastery by practice and, later, by heavy borrowing from the Italians.

Flanders, like northern Italy, was a land of cities with a rich urban patriciate. The great Flemish artists, however, did not paint primarily for these people. Many of their major works were done for the court of the Burgundian dukes, which more than any other court in Europe retained the medieval traditions of chivalry. In their art the Flemings reflected these two currents—the urban milieu from which they sprang and the chivalric trappings of court life.

The van Eyck brothers, Hubert (c. 1370–1426) and Jan (c. 1390–1440), were the first great figures of the Flemish school. Their painting "The Adoration of the Lamb," covering both sides of six wooden panels, became the inspiration and model for other Flemish artists, just as the paintings of their Italian contemporary Masaccio inspired Italian artists. It was painted in oils and established the superiority of that medium for portraying colors and color depth. Until then artists had preferred to mix colors with egg yolk thinned with water (tempera), though the use of oil as a binding fluid for colors had been known for centuries.[1] Improvements in the refine-

---

[1] Italian artists also practiced fresco painting, in which the pigments were mixed with water only. The artist painted on wet lime-plaster walls, and the colors dried and set with the plaster to become a permanent part of the wall. The Sistine Chapel ceiling, painted by Michelangelo, is the most famous example of this technique.

Adoration of the Lamb, by Jan van Eyck

"This belief [that Jan van Eyck was the inventor of oil painting] can no longer be maintained. Yet the fact remains that he must have devised certain improvements unknown before—improvements which enabled him to surpass both in minuteness and in luminosity whatever was achieved by his predecessors, contemporaries and followers. Whether he distilled new varnishes, driers and diluents . . . or merely applied the processes of the nouvelle pratique *with greater sophistication, it is difficult to say. Certain it is, however, that in his pictures the oil technique, though not invented by him, first revealed itself in its full glory. . . ."* E. Panofsky, EARLY NETHERLANDISH PAINTING (Cambridge, 1953).

A. C. L.—Art Reference Bureau

ment of linseed oil and in solvents and thinners after 1400 made it possible for the van Eycks to perfect the use of oil paints.

Contact between Italy and Flanders greatly increased in the sixteenth century. Flemish artists came more under Italian influence, as evidenced by better composition and the introduction of nudes into painting. The overall quality of their work, however, declined.

France's invasion of Italy in 1494 also introduced the north to Renaissance architecture. The architectural theories that came to the north in the first quarter of the sixteenth century, however, were already obsolete in Italy, and this cultural lag enabled northern craftsmen to absorb the new forms into the older local tradition and thoroughly domesticate the first stage of Italian architectural influence. The early sixteenth-century Renaissance buildings in France, the Low Countries, and Germany show a compromise between late Gothic structure and Renaissance proportions, with a tendency to use Renaissance decoration to give an overall effect of the new. In England the Renaissance made slight impact on building until the last half of the sixteenth century, when much of the fantastic decorativeness was derived from the Low Countries and obtained from design handbooks or "do-it-yourself" manuals for English gentlemen.

THE NATURE OF NORTHERN HUMANISM

Italian humanists held a fundamentally secular outlook; they rejected the medieval past and studied the classics to find models for the worldly life that they thought men should live. Like the Italians, the humanists of England, France, Germany, the Low Countries, and Spain believed that man as a rational being had the capacity to lead a good life, but unlike the Italians, they had a profoundly religious world view. They wanted to integrate the new learning with the whole Christian heritage, including the best of medieval scholarship. They believed that the literature of classical antiquity together with the literature of Christian antiquity (the writings of the early Church Fathers and the New Testament) contained a wisdom that would improve individual man and, far more important, revitalize the Christian society of their own time. Their intention to reconcile the new wave of classical heritage and Christianity was similar in motivation though not in method to that of Aquinas in the thirteenth century during the first revival of classical learning. Their religious orientation gained for them the name of "Christian humanists."

A new pietism, which originated in a movement called *Devotio moderna* and centered in the Low Countries and Germany during the fifteenth century, put its religious stamp on Christian humanism. The movement had its immediate cause in the deep distaste felt by many devout Christians for the worldly preoccupations of the people and the clergy. The *Devotio moderna* pietists skirted heresy, but their quietism and social respectability allowed them to avoid provocation of Church or state. The movement comprised communities of laymen and laywomen, called Brethren of the Common Life, who lived according to ascetic discipline but not under monastic vows or organization. They emphasized the direct relationship of the individual to God and thereby lessened the importance of the priesthood as an intermediary between man and his Creator. Study of the Bible and other religious texts and a love of learning were important features. Above all, they were interested in education and became associated with schools run by men who had studied in Italy and returned filled with humanist zeal. Through their influence the schools combined religious earnestness and discipline with a humanist education and came to be recognized as the best of the day. The most famous one, at Deventer in the Netherlands, had 2,000 students.

THE SPREAD OF HUMANISM IN THE NORTH

During the last quarter of the fifteenth century and the first decades of the sixteenth, the impact of Italian humanism on Northern Europe made itself felt through many channels. Monarchs and princes, impressed by the elegance of Italian courts, decided that they must have secretaries and diplomats who could write and speak polished Latin. The Italian humanists whom they named to these offices served as transmitters of humanist culture. Other Italians took posts at universities to teach Greek and Latin and classical literature. Northerners went to Italy to study in increasing numbers and returned home to write about and teach the new learning. Historians applied the critical methods of humanist scholarship to historical sources and repudiated long-believed legends. Schools and universities introduced humanist studies into their curricula—though not without bitter controversy with traditionalists—and new universities were founded in which the humanities held a central position. By 1520 most of the German universities, Oxford and Cambridge in England, Alcalá in Spain, Louvain in Brabant, and the University of Paris had introduced the teaching of Greek and the study of Greek texts.

The invention of printing from movable type in the Rhineland in the middle of the fifteenth century contributed greatly to the rapid spread of humanism in the North. This technological innovation reduced drastically the cost of books. Wood-block printing, invented by the Chinese, had reached the West by the early fifteenth century, when books of crude pictures and short texts began to appear, although Chinese experiments with movable type do not seem to have been known in the West. The Chinese had also invented paper made of fiber or rags, and by the twelfth century some paper was being made in Europe, but it did not displace parchment (made from thinly sliced animal skin) until the printing press replaced the medieval copyist. Traditionally the credit for the first printing by movable type goes to Johann Gutenberg of Mainz in the 1440's. The process spread rapidly, and by 1500 thousands of books had been issued by printers all over Europe. During the last half of the fifteenth century a growing proportion of printed books were classical texts, grammars, and humanist writings. The press immeasurably hastened humanism's conquest of learning in the North.

The early printers tried to make their books look like medieval manuscripts. They modeled type faces on the heavy black letters of the scribes, sometimes used hand-painted decorations and initial letters, and occasionally printed on vellum. By the early decades of the sixteenth century, however, leading Italian printers, influenced by the handwriting developed by the humanists, adopted the Roman and italic types that are familiar today. The new typography soon spread to Northern Europe.

THREE CHRISTIAN HUMANISTS

The Christian humanists hoped that their study of the early texts of Christianity, particularly the Bible, based on the humanist techniques of textual criticism and philology, would enable them to purge Christian doctrine of the obscurities and errors added through the centuries by theologians who had not read the original texts. They argued that once the texts were published, they would reveal Christianity in its purest form. The abuses and materialism that had turned men from the Church and saddened the faithful would disappear, and the Church would gain renewed strength, vitality, and inspiration. They believed, too, that secular learning would increase the piety of the individual and enable him by the use of reason to improve his nature because, as the English humanist Thomas More put it, education in Latin and Greek "doth train the soul in virtue."

Learned men in all the lands of Europe shared these opinions to a greater or lesser degree. They motivated the Christian humanist movement in Spain, centering on the newly founded university of Alcalá, where the first translation of the New Testament drawn from Greek manuscripts was completed in 1514, known as the Complutensian Bible. They also motivated the work of three outstanding Christian humanists, who also illustrated the similarities and differences among Christian humanists generally.

Lefèvre d'Étaples (c. 1450–1536), the most brilliant French thinker of his time, studied in Italy and then lectured on classical philosophy at the University of Paris. He was an intensely religious man with strong mystical leanings, who put less emphasis upon human reason and more upon divine intercession than did most of his fellow Christian humanists. He wrote many treatises on religious philosophy, published commentaries on Biblical texts, and in 1523 put out a French translation of the Bible. His views anticipated principles that were soon to be enunciated by the Protestant reformers, particularly the doctrine of justification by faith. Yet, like other Christian humanists, Lefèvre repudiated the reformers and remained loyal to Catholicism, even though the theological faculty of the University of Paris condemned him as a heretic.

Thomas More (1478–1535), the most prominent figure in English humanism, was the only one of the great humanists who was not a professional scholar or teacher. He had a brilliant career as a lawyer, diplomat, and politician, rising to the high office of Lord Chancellor of England. He was almost unique among humanists in that he never studied in Italy. His brilliance won him the attention of his elders, and he advanced rapidly. Despite worldly success he practiced a rigorous medieval piety. He long wore a hair shirt next to his skin, and sometimes the blood that it drew stained his outer clothing. As Lord Chancellor, he repressed Protestants as heretics. Later he himself died on the scaffold for his Roman faith.

More wrote somber devotional works that warned of the need to prepare for death, but his most famous book was in a very different vein. Called *Utopia*, the Greek word for "nowhere," the book was first printed in Latin in 1516 and was soon translated into other languages. More wrote it to criticize the evils of contemporary society and show men the way things might be if they lived according to the social and political ideals of Christianity and followed the counsels of reason. Utopia was a mythical island in the New

World where property was held communally and each individual received as many goods as he needed. The government regulated economic life, education, and public health. There were only a few simple laws, the work day was limited to six hours, and every religious creed was tolerated except atheism. Everyone on the happy island lived in peace and prosperity—in contrast to contemporary Europe.

Of all the Christian humanists, none had greater influence and fame than Desiderius Erasmus (1466–1536). He dominated the intellectual life of Northern Europe to an extent unequaled by any man until Voltaire in the eighteenth century. He had disciples in every land of Europe, was on intimate terms with nearly all the great men of his time, and maintained a voluminous correspondence. He owed his reputation to his prodigious literary output, his vast erudition, his polished and persuasive literary style, his clarity and wit, his moderation, and his abundant common sense. He loved learning for its own sake but felt it must be used to combat ignorance, superstition, corruption, and violence. His books had enormous popularity; they were the first best sellers in the history of printing.

Erasmus was born in Rotterdam, the younger of two sons of a Catholic priest. He received his education at the famous Brethren of the Common Life school at Deventer and then was persuaded to accept ordination as a priest. He soon regretted this decision and set forth as a free-lance scholar and writer on travels that carried him through many lands. His distaste for clerical life and his love for the classics did not diminish his deep piety and devotion to Christianity. He believed that Christianity, stripped of the gloss and interpretations of theologians and restored to its original form, offered the perfect guide for both the individual and society. He wrote for the general reader in the hope of spreading this message, and he longed for the day when the Bible would be translated into every language, so that everyone could read and understand it for himself. He had nothing but contempt for the people and practices that he felt perverted the true nature of Christianity. He poured ridicule and scorn on the ignorance and venality of priests, the worship of relics, the exaggerated veneration of saints, and many other abuses in the Catholic Church.

Erasmus' views and influence made him a leader in the movement for reform of the Catholic Church. For a time he went along with Martin Luther, the great German reformer, but he could not go all the way. He wanted to reform the Church from within, not break away and start a new church. Erasmus and the other great Christian humanists treasured the unity of Christendom above any difference of opinion about doctrine. When Europe finally split between Catholic and Protestant, Erasmus and most of the other Christian humanists remained within the Catholic fold. The irony was that in their efforts to reform the Church they loved, they unwittingly helped to undermine it and to bring about a revolution.

Renaissance Science

One of the current battlegrounds for Renaissance historians is this question: was the Renaissance era productive of scientific advance? Historians usually have drawn a clear distinction between Aristotelian metaphysics, which was the science of the Middle Ages, and the experimentally oriented natural philosophy of the late sixteenth and seventeenth centuries, which was basic to the development of modern science. The Renaissance seems to have little or no place in this pattern. Caught between two eras of science, it was neither the culmination of one nor the origin of the other. Copernicus (1473–1543), the greatest scientific figure of the era, exemplifies the problem. He was not an experimental scientist, but he was the point of origin for the great revolution on which modern science is founded. (See pp. 187–200.) He was very much a Renaissance humanist, yet he is most meaningfully treated in relation to the scientists of the late sixteenth and seventeenth centuries. Here again the Renaissance manifested itself as an age of transition.

In the Middle Ages the study of the physical world was dictated by the categories laid down centuries before by Aristotle. Such was the authority of Aristotle that data derived empirically, by experimentation, was neither needed nor sought. This does not mean that the Middle Ages were scientifically sterile. Outside the scholastic-dominated universities, alchemy, the attempted transmutation of base metals into gold, and astrology were practically motivated studies of the physical world. These studies grew rapidly in the fifteenth century, but it is difficult to assess precisely their contribution to modern science. Humanism acted as a powerful solvent of Aristotelianism by re-establishing the classical tension between Aristotle's materialism and Plato's idealism. This resulted in the growth of a Neo-Platonic movement in Italian humanism, which was associated with Marsilio Ficino (1433–1499) and Cosimo de' Medici's Platonic Academy in Florence. The Neo-Platonists reintroduced Plato's passion for numbers and harmonics, which probably contributed to awakening an interest in geometry and higher mathematics.

Renaissance humanists contributed to later scientific advances by uncovering and editing previously unknown works of classical science and making accurate translations from the original Greek of texts that had been known only from Arabic or Hebrew translations. Admiration for antiquity and philological scholarship, rather than scientific curiosity, inspired this work. Yet it made available ancient scientific knowledge that might otherwise have taken European scientists a long time to rediscover. In addition, the humanists' intensive examination of the original classical texts produced an intimate knowledge of ancient science that led ultimately to the recognition by scientists of both the truth and the errors of ancient science and that suggested new avenues of scientific investigation.

The interest of Renaissance artists in the human body, which resulted from their efforts to achieve naturalistic portraiture, encouraged anatomical research. Anatomical study and dissection became accepted parts of the artist's training. The most famous and skilled of the artist-anatomists was Leonardo da Vinci. His notebooks contain hundreds of drawings and comments based upon his careful dissections of human and animal cadavers (they also include designs for submarines, airplanes, machine guns, and other modern inventions). Leonardo never published his anatomical investigations; they remained unknown until the end of the eighteenth century. His findings, therefore, had no influence on subsequent anatomical study.

The credit for the pioneering work in anatomy goes to Andreas Vesalius (1514–1564), a Fleming who taught anatomy at the University of Padua in Italy. His university became the chief center of scientific study, especially of medical science. Vesalius, like all medical men of that era, followed the teachings of Galen, who around A.D. 150 had summed up most of ancient Greek medical knowledge in several treatises. Galen had long been considered the final authority in medical science just as Aristotle was in physical science. When Vesalius's dissections showed that Galen's work contained many errors, he decided to write his own textbook. Called *On the Structure of the Human Body*, it appeared in 1543—the same year that saw the publication of Copernicus's book on the heliocentric theory. Vesalius illustrated his findings with beautifully executed woodcuts in which the anatomical drawings stood out against a background of Renaissance landscapes.

The book dealt with the relationship between the individual organ and the body as a whole. Vesalius showed that anatomy could be learned only by actual dissection, not by reading Galen. Although some scholars refused to be convinced, in time more open-minded men realized that Vesalius made Galen obsolete. They followed his technique of meticulous observation, and as a result a stream of important discoveries in human anatomy were made.

The very elusiveness of Renaissance science affords insight into some of the limitations of the period. For all its glory, the Renaissance did better in heralding the brave new world than in determining its course. Petrarch's words, "that to things transitory things eternal should succeed," seemed almost prophetic of the Renaissance's fate. Renaissance endeavor was too diffuse to be systematic; Renaissance man was too enamored of classical beauty to look beyond it. The high level at which the Renaissance operated, its preoccupation with a classical ideal that had only limited relevance to the contemporary condition of man, and the narrowness of its social base divorced it from reality. For historians, the unrealistic quality of so much of the Renaissance makes the age elusive, transitional, even transitory.

CHAPTER FOUR

The Politics of the Renaissance

Politica est res dura (politics is a hard business) was a Roman maxim rediscovered by the Renaissance and much favored in discussion of contemporary politics. Medieval politics, of course, had not been "soft," as the feudal lords in France and England discovered, as King John realized when forced to accept the humiliation of Magna Carta, and as Pope Boniface VIII learned when agents of the French king burst in upon him in his residence and put him under arrest. Yet in politics, as in art and letters, the Renaissance image of man brought about a changed emphasis and a new departure in theory and practice, both domestic and international. *Virtù* was not confined to artists—indeed, it was most clearly enunciated in the Renaissance conception of the statesman. Italian politics of the fourteenth and fifteenth centuries was dominated by men of *virtù* who with brutal realism consciously fashioned the techniques of statecraft and raised it to an art. As one would expect of the Renaissance, practice begot theory.

Political Theory

Theoretical politics in the Middle Ages had no existence separate from the synthesis of learning that was capped by theology. John of Salisbury in

Policraticus (1159), the first systematic work on political philosophy in the Middle Ages, argued that God must be preferred before any man on earth and that the ruler must exercise his power in subjection to God and God's will. This view remained basic to medieval political philosophy, being embellished by later authors but not changed in substance. The tendency was to justify a hierarchic order of society that assured stability, and to give to that order divine sanction under the surveillance of God. Political theory existed within this framework as a minor branch of philosophy, which in turn was the servant of theology.

In the last part of the Middle Ages there was a discernible shift away from this position to a conception of politics as having more than subordinate importance to the conduct of man's affairs. In the fifteenth century men began to write of politics in real rather than theoretical terms and to regard politics not as a branch of philosophy, not as a human activity subject to an ultimate theologically derived good, but as a study of practical importance based on practical experience.

NICCOLÒ MACHIAVELLI

Niccolò Machiavelli (1469–1527) was the greatest of the new political philosophers. It is accurate to credit him with the founding of modern political theory, based on his observations of Italian Renaissance politics in action. Machiavelli served from 1498 to 1512 as an official and diplomat of the republican government of Florence. The work provided him with a close knowledge of the operation of government and the whole spectrum of attitudes and activities of contemporary Italian politicians at a time of great vitality and stress. In 1512 the overthrow of the republican government by the Medici cost him his post, and for the remaining fourteen years of his life he tried unsuccessfully to get back into government. He filled his years of involuntary retirement with study and writing. In the breadth of his literary accomplishments—political and military treatises, histories, plays, poems, and stories—he demonstrated the proper Renaissance versatility.

Machiavelli was a child of the Italian Renaissance at its peak. Italian politics was one foundation of his political education; the other was a classicist's knowledge of the political history of Rome, especially under the republic. The long treatise called *Discourses on the First Ten Books of Livy* (a Roman historian) was based upon Roman history and less explicitly related to practical experience than to classical times. In the *Discourses* he attempted a systematic analysis of six specific forms of government, which he argued followed one another in cyclical order: monarchy, tyranny, aristocracy, oligarchy, democracy, and mob rule.

Machiavelli owed his undying fame to his pamphlet *The Prince*, written in 1513 and addressed to Lorenzo de' Medici in 1515 in the hope that the prince would recognize and employ his talent. The success of *The Prince* was not what its author had hoped, but it long outlived his ambitions and became the guidebook to power politics for future centuries. Because of it, Machiavelli's name became a synonym for political cunning and unscrupulous behavior—an identification that does less than justice to the man and the subtlety of his argument.

Machiavelli conceived of the state as a work of art, the creation of a leader who by the imposition of his *virtù* on the state and society increased the *virtù* of the mass of the people. *The Prince* has as its theme the doctrine that the ruler should use any means, however unprincipled, to win and hold power, to create a strong central government, and to preserve the state. The prince should keep his word or break it, be just or unjust, reward his supporters or sacrifice them, depending upon whichever action best suits the interests of the state. Men in general are "ungrateful, fickle, false, cowards, and covetous" and will not keep faith with the ruler, so that he need not keep faith with them. "The experience of our times," Machiavelli wrote, "shows those princes to have done great things who have no regard for their promises, who have been able by craftiness to confuse men's brains, and who have conquered over those who put their reliance on good faith." Machiavelli's cynicism and low opinion of mankind grew out of his own experiences in the world of Italian politics. Yet he had an idealistic end in view. He hoped that a ruler who followed his advice would be able to unite all Italy and drive out the foreign armies that had invaded the peninsula. He believed that good could come out of evil: the unprincipled despot could achieve desirable social ends more easily than could a just ruler.

Machiavelli placed the state and its preservation in the center of political theory, by which he ensured that political theory would never again take second place in the concerns of men. Machiavelli's empiricism—that the prince should do what he has learned by experience is best—was a powerful solvent to the accepted, static, hierarchic pattern of medieval thinking about political order. Since the exact structure of the state was secondary and its preservation primary, Machiavelli's argument fitted the whole gambit of political systems that he had dealt with in the *Discourses. Raison d'état,* reason of state as the justification for any course of action no matter how immoral, was just around the corner once Machiavelli had postulated necessity as the governing cause of political action.

Italian Politics

In Machiavelli were present most of the theoretical ingredients for the best and the worst in European politics. The first manifestation of both ingredients was in the Italian politics of the Renaissance that schooled Machiavelli. This brand of politics stemmed principally from the growth of the city-states of northern Italy in the late Middle Ages. The conflict rising out of German imperial attempts to control Italy and the papacy's moves to counter them gave the city-states the opportunity to emerge in the thirteenth century as independent political entities. Their near-monopoly of trade with the East provided the economic base for independence and determined the social composition of the oligarchies that ruled them.

In most of the city-states factionalism was endemic, splitting the oligarchies and nurturing a constant struggle for power. The factions first grew out of the political alignments within each city, by which one side supported the Hohenstauffen imperial claim and the other the Welf. The "Ghibelline" (Hohenstauffen) and "Guelph" (Welf) labels were increasingly applied to factions that were divided over more basic and less exalted causes. Class distinctions dividing the wealthy merchants and bankers from the shopkeepers, craftsmen, and professional men who made up the lesser bourgeoisie, as well as from the wage earners who formed the mass of the city population, added to the internal strife. Each class suspected the other and wanted to gain control of the government. Most of the time the wealthy oligarchs (in Florence they were called *popolo grosso*, "fat people") managed to keep control. However, the unceasing social and political discord persuaded many city dwellers by the end of the thirteenth century that the only way to achieve internal order was by one-man rule. Sometimes this was done by turning the government over to the head of a political faction or the leader of a social class. In other cases an ambitious man assumed dictatorial power by a coup d'état. Sometimes an outsider was asked to take over in the hope that he would not be tied to any of the contesting groups within the city. In still other instances a mercenary captain hired to defend the city seized power for himself.

In this way, many of the northern Italian cities came under the rule of despots. The circumstances by which the despots came to power made their tenure insecure. They could not depend upon the traditional loyalty of their subjects, as legitimate monarchs could in other lands. Rivals never ceased plotting to overthrow them; they lived in the shadow of assassination and revolution. They had to be ruthless, cunning, and coldly rational to win and hold power. The stories of their atrocities and their craftiness are legion. To give only two examples, in 1409 Giovanni Maria Visconti, ruler of Milan, loosed mercenaries against his subjects, massacring two hundred Milanese, because people cried out to him in the streets to end the war that he was waging. Again in another city, a soldier of fortune named Oliverotto invited all the leading men, including the uncle who had raised him, to a banquet. After a sumptuous dinner and elaborate entertainment, he gave a signal to hidden confederates to rush out and kill the guests. He then made himself dictator.

RENAISSANCE DESPOTISM

Despite the constant wars among the city-states, the rulers, whether oligarchs or despots, were afraid to arm their subjects lest they be overthrown. The people, for their part, had no desire to fight for rulers whom they distrusted or despised. Therefore the rulers hired mercenary captains, called *condottieri* (singular, *condottiere*), who had their own bands of troops. The mercenaries had no loyalty to their employer, fighting for the highest bidder and changing sides without compunction. They preferred long wars to ensure their employment; the consequences were indecisive battles and prolonged sieges. Since his soldiers were his capital assets, the condottiere avoided wasting them in frontal assaults. Nor did he want to kill the opposing mercenaries, preferring to capture them for ransom. To minimize the loss of personnel, the mercenaries developed a code of military etiquette that disapproved of such practices as night battles or the use of artillery.

Sometimes the condottieri seized power from their employers and established themselves as tyrants. Some of these men had begun life as the sons of humble peasants or tradesmen. Not all of them, however, had lowly origins. Some came from backgrounds of wealth and culture, and a few were actually rulers of petty city-states seeking greater fortunes. Among the aristocratic condottieri was Federigo da Montefeltro (1422–1482), Duke of Urbino, who was one of the most cultured and admired men of his time.

The crimes and immoral lives of the despots set an evil example for the rest of society. Violence and treason became commonplace in Italian life. Yet the record of the despots was not all black. They were aware that ruthlessness alone would not keep them in power and that they must satisfy the demands of their subjects or be overthrown. They often improved methods of taxation, ordered the construction of public works and buildings to give people employment and beautify the city, built canals, promoted irrigation projects to increase farm production in the countryside around the city, enforced impartial justice (except where their own interests were involved), and followed policies to encourage business enterprise.

They made a major and lasting contribution in the inspiration that their success provided to other men. Their careers represented a triumph of individualism—of *virtù*. They demonstrated that a man of ability and determination could win fame, power, and wealth regardless of birth or social status. The more intelligent despots surrounded themselves with men of their own stamp, with whom they could establish rapport, rather than with simpering courtiers. Thus the intellectual and social climate of the despot's entourage proved highly favorable to the advancement of creativity and individual ability.

Finally, the despots distinguished themselves as patrons of art and culture. Many of them possessed a genuine appreciation of beauty and learning.

Italian States in 1494

1 Asti, Montferrat
2 Benevento
3 States of the Church
4 Duchy of Ferrara
5 Republic of Florence
6 Republic of Genoa
7 Republic of Lucca
8 Marquisate of Mantua
9 Duchy of Milan
10 Duchy of Modena
11 Kingdom of Naples
12 Duchy of Piombino
13 Marquisate of Saluzzo
14 Republic of San Marino
15 Duchy of Savoy
16 Republic of Siena
17 Republic of Venice

All craved lasting fame and knew that they could gain it by commissioning magnificent buildings, pictures, and other artistic works as perpetual monuments to their greatness. They hoped to win the respect and support of their subjects by surrounding themselves with the luxury and glamor expected of a prince. Their sponsorship of art and learning brought fame to the state and appealed to civic pride and loyalty. Without them, the Renaissance in culture was inconceivable.

Though the future of most Italian city-states lay with the despots, the civic consciousness of the cities must not be overlooked. There was explicit in the invitation to the despot, and implicit in the coup d'état of a condottiere, a commitment to rule the city-state for the benefit of the city. Machiavelli presupposed this commitment in his prince—and it was a quality usually to be found in the despots, whatever their faults.

ITALIAN POLITICS IN THE FIFTEENTH CENTURY

By the fifteenth century five states had emerged as the dominant powers of the peninsula. They were Milan, Florence, and Venice in the north, the Papal States in the center, and the kingdom of Naples in the south. Almost unconsciously the five developed a balance of power principle among themselves, by which they tacitly agreed that no one state would gain a preponderance of power and, if one tried, the others would war against it. This was the first example in modern times of a group of states using the balance of power principle as a guide in mutual relations. They maintained permanent ambassadors at one another's capitals so that each ruler could keep in constant touch with what was happening in the other states. They also employed secret agents and depended upon merchants and bankers to gather information. Several states, notably Venice, drew up regulations for the training of diplomats and their conduct abroad. The Italian system of diplomacy became the norm for all of Europe in the sixteenth century.

Milan, which had long been an important economic center with territory covering a large part of Lombardy, was one of the first to succumb to despotism. In 1277 the Visconti, a noble Milanese family, seized power and ruled arbitrarily for almost two hundred years. Around 1400 Gian Galeazzo Visconti tried to unite northern and central Italy in an absolute monarchy under his scepter. The determined resistance of Florence and Venice shattered his plans, and the Milanese state was restricted to Lombardy. When the direct Visconti line ran out in 1447, the Milanese tried to regain their freedom by establishing a republic. The new government hired Francesco Sforza (1402–1466), a condottiere, to defend it. Sforza, the illegitimate son of a condottiere, had married the illegitimate daughter of the last Visconti ruler. In 1450 he overthrew the republic and made himself despot. His dynasty lasted fifty years. Ludovico, last of the Sforza rulers, was one of the most famous princes of his time. Called the Moor, probably because of his dark complexion, he won renown for his intelligence, political acumen, and sponsorship of the arts and learning. During his reign (1479–1500) he surrounded himself with scholars and artists, including the famous Leonardo da Vinci. His court was one of the most brilliant and luxurious in Europe.

Florence was the chief city of Tuscany and, until the end of the fifteenth century, the great center of Renaissance culture. It lay on the banks of the Arno halfway between Milan and Rome. The city owed its economic strength to banking families and manufacturers, especially the woolen cloth industry. From the thirteenth century on, the Florentine Republic was torn by struggles between political parties and between social and economic classes. After long years of struggle and experiment with different kinds of governments, ranging from radical democracy to dictatorship, Cosimo de' Medici (1389–1464) took over power. Cosimo was the head of the Medici banking and mercantile clan, the wealthiest family in Italy and probably in Europe. He kept himself in the background and seldom took public office. Instead, like a modern American political boss, he ruled the city by controlling the elections, so that only men who took orders from him were chosen for public office. He gained and kept power by the typical political boss tactic of siding with the poor against the rich. He showed great skill in conducting the foreign affairs of his state, and he was a great patron of culture. When he died in 1464, the grateful Florentines inscribed on his tomb the title *Pater Patriae*, "Father of the Country."

Cosimo's son, who succeeded to the rule of Florence, reigned for only five years. In 1469 Cosimo's grandson, the twenty-year-old Lorenzo (1449–1492), took over power. Lorenzo, known as the Magnificent, became the most famous of all the Medicis. In 1478 his rule was challenged by a powerful conspiracy led by the Pazzi, one of the great families of Florence. He overcame the threat and, to prevent its recurrence, adopted despotic measures. He tightened his control over the state by making the councils that governed the city responsible to him alone, and he cruelly punished those who plotted against him. Once he had established despotic rule, he devoted himself to his great passion—patronage of arts and letters. His great liberality, his intellectual interests, and his excellent taste did much to make Florence one of the greatest centers of arts and letters known to history.

During Lorenzo's reign expensive wars, heavy taxation, lavish spending, and new and vigorous foreign competition brought on a serious decline in Florence's economic life. Lorenzo, who lacked the business acumen of his forebears, made matters worse by using state money for his own business purposes. His reputation became tarnished, and the Florentines began to turn against him and his family. A Dominican friar named Girolamo Savonarola (1452–1498) entranced great crowds with denunciations of Lorenzo's corruption, preached against the luxury and paganism of the Renaissance, and prophesied the ruin of Italy unless people mended their ways. After Lorenzo's death in 1492 Savonarola won a wide following that included some of the greatest figures of the Renaissance. In 1496 Lorenzo's son, who had succeeded him as head of state, was driven into exile and Savonarola became virtual dictator of Florence. Under the spell of his sermons huge bonfires were fed with things that he called "vanities"—such as books, paintings, luxurious clothes, and wigs—and laws were passed to forbid gambling, horse racing, profanity, and coarse songs. Savonarola bitterly attacked the pope, Alexander VI, for his immoral life and the corruption at Rome. Alexander replied by excommunicating him.

The Florentines soon found that the rigors of puritanism were ill-suited to their tastes. Political factions who were hostile to Savonarola, Franciscan monks who opposed him because of the old rivalry between their order and the Dominicans, and pressure from the papacy succeeded in bringing about the friar's downfall. In 1498 he was arrested, tortured, and burned at the stake in the great square of Florence. After a period of internal strife the Medicis returned to power in 1512.

The political history of Venice, or the Republic of St. Mark as it was called, stood in sharp contrast to the internal turmoil of Milan and Florence. An oligarchy of merchant aristocrats gained control of the state in the thirteenth century and retained power almost without challenge. The aristocrats, who formed about 2 per cent of the republic's population, transformed the general assembly of all citizens into a Great Council and restricted membership to their own group. The doge, the nominal head of state, who formerly had been elected by popular vote, was named by the Council and became a figurehead. Smaller councils, of which the Council of Ten was the most important, handled the actual affairs of government.

Although they allowed no opposition, the Venetian oligarchs ruled wisely and did much to improve the economic welfare of the people. Venice, long one of the great trading centers of the world, continued to gain most of its wealth from sea commerce. All merchant galleys belonged to the state, which built the ships in the Arsenal, a huge shipyard that was probably the largest industrial establishment in Europe.

Until the fifteenth century the Venetians showed little interest in Italian politics. They directed their statecraft to the extension of maritime trade and to the conquest of territory in the eastern Mediterranean. The Venetians looked upon their policy of isolation from the rest of Italy as the foundation of their strength. The advances of the Ottoman Turks in the Mediterranean region, however, made it more difficult to trade with the East and cost the Venetians some of their overseas possessions, while the growing power of Milan and Florence seemed to threaten Venetian overland trade routes into Italy and Europe. These developments persuaded the oligarchs that their state must plunge into Italian affairs. As a result, Venice pushed out her frontiers, became one of the largest of the city-states, and played a major role in the wars and politics of the peninsula.

The Papal States, the fourth of the chief powers of Italy, almost disintegrated as a political unit during the Babylonian Captivity and Great Schism (1305–1417). The accession of Martin V to the throne of St. Peter in 1417 marked the beginning of the restoration of papal sovereignty. His successors re-established papal control over central Italy and took an active part in Italian political life. They also distinguished themselves as patrons of art and learning and once again made Rome a renowned center of culture. In their concern with power politics, art, and learning the Renaissance popes —as the pontiffs from Nicholas V (1447–55) to Clement VII (1523–34) are sometimes called—relegated their religious duties to second place. Their worldliness and the flagrant immorality of some of them occasioned criticism throughout Europe.

The kingdom of Naples-Sicily (later the kingdom of the Two Sicilies) comprised the southernmost parts of Italy and the islands of Sicily. In the thirteenth century the realm had been divided, Sicily under the ruler of Aragon (Spain) and the mainland under a prince of Anjou (French). From 1435 to 1458 the two parts were reunited under a single monarch, only to be divided again, then finally reconstituted as one by Spain in 1504. The kingdom never regained the political importance and prosperity that it had known in its medieval period of glory, and it lagged far behind the rest of Italy in culture.

The success of Renaissance politics in forging a balance of power that prevented the ascendancy of any single state preserved the territorial integrity of the major Italian states almost to the end of the fifteenth century. Then in 1494 Ludovico Sforza of Milan invited French assistance to counter an expected attack from Naples. The need to preserve the Italian balance of power became the excuse for a northern European monarchic nation-state to plunge Europe into its first general war, with Italy as the battlefield.

The Rise of the Nation-States

The emergence of strong monarchies in medieval France and England centralized government at the expense of the feudal nobility. During the troubled times of the fourteenth and fifteenth centuries, when economic decline, wars, rebellions, and social unrest racked most of Europe, the chances for continued evolution of strong centralized states seemed doomed. Central governments became powerless, or nearly so, as feudal lords contested with their kings and with one another for domination. Then in the second half of the fifteenth century the trend toward decentralization was dramatically reversed. Strong kings in France, England, and Spain, who are sometimes referred to collectively as the New Monarchs, put an end to the internal disorders in their lands, restrained the power of the feudal nobility, extended the royal power and domain, and gained a wider sphere of action and greater control over their subjects. Their achievements led to the establishment of the national territorial state as we know it today.

Behind the success of these monarchs was the realization by most of their subjects that internal order depended upon the curbing of feudal power. This feeling was strongest in the middle classes in the towns. The growth of trade in the fifteenth century strengthened their position and encouraged them to supply the taxes to support monarchic power. The taxes enabled the monarchs to dispense with armies that had been based on feudal military service by armed retainers of the great feudatories. As tactical developments reduced the military necessity for mounted knights and castles, it became feasible to destroy the feudatories' castles. Many of the nobility, particularly the smaller landed proprietors, concluded that the authority of the monarch was not easily withstood and that cooperation with him might secure lucrative offices and honors and preserve their privileges and immunities. The kings drew strong support from lawyers who were trained in the Roman law and held posts in the government. They argued that the king incorporated within himself the will of the people and that he had the power to enact laws by his own authority. Their argument provided legal justification for the monarch to disregard the feudal and customary laws that had protected the rights of the nobility and other special groups against royal encroachment. Now the will of the king was regarded as the law.

The monarchs of the new nation-states did not consciously intend to create anything like a modern national territorial state. They were motivated by dynastic ambitions, wanting to build up the power, glory, and continuation of their families. Their states differed greatly from the states of today. Much that was medieval still remained, and they had only begun to evolve the administrative techniques and trained bureaucracy that characterize the modern state. Their claims to supremacy had not yet won universal acceptance; the Church, feudal lords, and other privileged groups still enjoyed special powers and immunities. Nonetheless, one clearly sees the outlines of the modern state in the governmental structure of these monarchies. In fact, the word *state* in its modern sense of a land, its people, and its government first came into use in the first half of the sixteenth century. The transition from medieval to modern political organization that began in this era presents one of the most significant evidences that Europe had entered into a new stage of its history.

The final stages of the transition from feudal monarchy to the monarchic nation-state in France and England and the first stages in Spain occurred during the reigns of Louis XI, Henry VII, and Ferdinand of Aragon, respectively. A century later Francis Bacon, English philosopher and statesman, called these monarchs the "Three Magi" among the kings of their time.

LOUIS XI OF FRANCE

Louis XI inherited the throne of France in 1461. He was a cynical, brutal, and suspicious man, meticulously scrupulous in religious observances, but with absolutely no moral sensibilities. People were pawns to him, to be used to serve his own ends. His craftiness and intrigues won him the nickname "the Spider." Shabbily dressed and miserly, he shunned ceremony. At the same time he was highly intelligent, imaginative, and alert, and he never lost sight of the ambitious goals he set for himself and his country. He was a skilled negotiator and outstanding administrator, and he learned from his mistakes. Perhaps most important, fortune favored him. His opponents could not compare in ability, his feudal enemies died without heirs, so that their lands reverted to him, and his people craved a strong king who could keep peace and order.

The provincial autonomy retained by the greater feudal lords within the kingdom posed a constant threat to Louis's authority. Their connection with him was still feudal, excluding him from direct governance of their provinces. Only by bringing their provinces within his own domain could he exercise effective sovereignty over all of France. The opportunity presented itself when the Duke of Burgundy, his most unmanageable and dangerous vassal, made a vigorous bid for complete independence.

In the fourteenth century the Dukes of Burgundy had begun to acquire territory and to create a centralized state, at the expense of the French mon-

Louis XI of France, by Lugardon
"I knew him, and was entertained in his service in the flower of his age, and at the height of his prosperity, yet I never saw him free from labor and care. . . . When his body was at rest his mind was at work, for he had affairs at several places at once, and would concern himself as much with those of his neighbors as in his own, putting officers of his own over all the great families, and endeavoring to divide their authority as much as possible. When he was at war he labored for a peace or truce, and when he had obtained it, he was impatient for war again. He troubled himself with many trifles in his government, which he had better have left alone: but it was his temper, and he could not help it. . . ."
Philip de Commines (1447?–?1511), in his MEMOIRS (London, 1856).

Courtesy of The Louvre

arch, from their base in Franche-Comté between France and Switzerland. Through marriages, treaties, and conquests they gained control of most of the Low Countries. By 1450 the Duke of Burgundy, who was nominally a vassal of both the king of France and the Holy Roman Emperor, had become one of Europe's most powerful rulers. Duke Charles the Bold (1467–1477) dreamed of adding more territory to link up the Low Countries and Franche-Comté, thereby creating a "middle kingdom" between France and Germany. Charles's dream came to nothing in 1477 when he died in battle against the Swiss, who were threatened by Charles's ambitions and were subsidized by Louis. Since Charles left no male heirs, all of his possessions except the Low Countries (which went to his daughter Mary) reverted to the French throne. A few years later the lands of the house of Anjou came to Louis when the last of that line died. By the time of his death in 1484 Louis had nearly doubled the size of his kingdom; its boundaries approximated those of modern France. Of the great feudal domains, only Brittany remained outside his sovereignty, and he prepared the way for its absorption by arranging a marriage between his son and the heiress of that duchy.

To win and hold the support of the middle class, and at the same time to increase the prosperity of the realm so that he could get more tax revenues, Louis promoted the economic interests of the upper bourgeoisie.

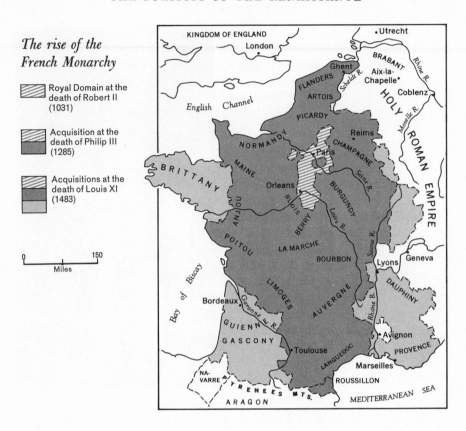

The rise of the French Monarchy

Royal Domain at the death of Robert II (1031)

Acquisition at the death of Philip III (1285)

Acquisitions at the death of Louis XI (1483)

He regulated trade and industry to their advantage, encouraged the development of new manufactures, improved harbors and river channels, and took an active part in restoring and expanding French foreign trade and shipping. He chose many advisors and officials from the bourgeoisie.

He permitted the provincial estates and the Estates-General to remain in existence but paid little attention to them. The Estates-General, the chief parliamentary body of France, met only once in 1468, and then only to give formal approval to certain decisions Louis had already made. He restricted the power of the *parlements*, the high courts of justice. He held the clergy in check by intimidation and made himself master of the distribution of high clerical offices. He extracted ever-increasing amounts of money from his subjects to pay the costs of government and the army. When he ascended the throne, the government's regular revenues amounted to 1.8 million livres; at the time of his death they had risen to 4.5 million livres. In addition to the regular revenues, he raised large sums by special subsidies, forced loans from townspeople, and the sale of offices.

During the reign of his son and heir, Charles VIII (1483–98), who was a far less able man, the feudal nobility tried to regain some of its lost powers, but Louis had built so well that the nobles could not organize effectively against the throne. The long French involvement in war in Italy, which began in 1494, also served to hold down feudal unrest, for the military campaigns drained off their energies. The royal bureaucracy continued to grow and took over more and more of the functions of local government, the fiscal system became more efficient, and taxes kept rising. By the Concordat of Bologna in 1516 King Francis I won recognition from Pope Leo X of the throne's almost complete control of Church wealth in France and the appointment of bishops and abbots. The French clergy became in effect a national clergy principally controlled by the king.

HENRY VII OF ENGLAND

From 1455 to 1485 two rival dynasties, York and Lancaster, did battle for the throne of England in a disruptive civil war. The Wars of the Roses—the emblem of the Yorkists was a white rose, that of the Lancastrians was a red rose—seemed to result in 1483 in a clear Yorkist victory under the Duke of Gloucester, who reputedly murdered his youthful nephew, King Edward V, and usurped power as Richard III. Two years later Richard III was killed in battle in a military invasion mounted by the Welsh Duke of Richmond, Henry Tudor, the Lancastrian claimant. Henry assumed the throne as Henry VII, the first of an able dynasty that ruled England for almost a century and a quarter.

Displaying characteristic political acumen, Henry reinforced his conquest by marrying Elizabeth, heiress of the York dynasty, thereby uniting the Lancaster and York claims. Some of the Yorkists continued to oppose him and rebelled several times during the first half of his reign. Henry moved ruthlessly against his foes and in 1497 smashed the last armed challenge to his supremacy.

He took other firm measures to break the power of the barons. During the Hundred Years' War and the troubles of the fifteenth century English lords had almost of necessity kept armed forces, sometimes numbering several thousand men who wore the livery (coat of arms) of their employers. These private armies made it impossible to preserve internal order and the rule of law. Earlier kings had passed legislation against the practice, but when offending barons were brought into court for trial, judges were over-awed, witnesses feared to testify, and juries were afraid to convict. By legislation and the use of every instrument of law. Henry repressed abuses of the legal system by his "overmighty subjects" and effectively re-established public peace and royal authority. Because many noble families had been wiped out in the Wars of the Roses or their lands had been seized for treason, his position was further strengthened by the opportunity to reduce the estates of his enemies. A thoroughgoing pragmatist and legalist, Henry recognized that rebellion could be avoided by moving disputes from the field of battle into the courtroom. In this he was no innovator: as in most other aspects of government, his contribution rested in using to the full the institutions and procedures that were already in existence. His emphasis on making court cases out of what might otherwise have become private wars and his assurance of the integrity of the courts and the enforcement of their decisions established a rule of law that was the Tudor dynasty's firmest support.

Henry leaned heavily for support on the upper middle class and the untitled, landed lesser nobility or "gentry," as they were called in England. He chose most of his counselors from these groups instead of from the great nobility, as earlier rulers had done. He used them in the increasingly efficient central bureaucracy, which he oversaw personally. He depended upon unpaid justices of the peace, chosen from the gentry, to represent the royal power in local government, and he began the process that placed nearly all local administration in their hands. The institution of justice of the peace dated back to earlier centuries, but under Henry and his Tudor successors the office gained new powers and importance. A paid, professional, local bureaucracy such as France's might have been more efficient, but the justices of the peace, who were loyal servants of the king as long as their interests coincided, admirably suited Henry's purpose.

In the first half of his reign Henry summoned Parliament ten times to provide legislation to establish his supremacy and to grant the extraordinary revenue required to withstand the threats to his throne. After 1497 he convened it only once. He felt strong enough to rule alone, and his remarkable financial talents enabled him to meet the costs of government without new taxes voted by Parliament. When he mounted the throne, he had an empty treasury. Knowing that as long as he lacked money or had to depend upon others for it he would not have his own way, he economized, took back royal lands that had passed to others, confiscated the land and wealth of his enemies, enforced taxes, levied heavy fines and forced loans, set up a more efficient government revenue office, and carefully checked the accounts himself. When he died, it was said that he had "the richest treasury in Christendom."

One reason he could amass so much wealth was that he did not have to support a standing army. Except for the 250 or so men in the Yeomen of the Guard (which he established) and a few small garrisons scattered throughout his possessions, Henry had no professional soldiers. He depended upon the patriotic support of his subjects, for every able-bodied Englishman was supposed to fight for the king when called.

Henry knew that it served his interests to promote the prosperity of the people, especially the merchant class. He encouraged foreign trade with continental Europe by treaties that afforded more favorable conditions for English merchants and the export of English wool and woolen cloth. He protected home industry by import and export restrictions. To promote

English shipping, he restricted the importation of certain goods to English ships.

Through his forcefulness and wise policies, Henry ended a century of strife. Under his rule Englishmen enjoyed peace, confidence, and a growing prosperity. To his young son, Henry VIII, he left a united country, a degree of control over the people and Parliament that no other English king had ever had, and a full treasury. Henry VIII would soon dissipate the latter, but he never wasted the royal control and the unity of the nation.

FERDINAND AND ISABELLA OF SPAIN

By the fifteenth century the Christian kingdoms of the Iberian peninsula had been consolidated into four monarchies: Castile in the center and northwest, Aragon in the east, Portugal in the west, and the tiny mountain kingdom of Navarre in the north. Castile was by far the largest; it held two-thirds of the peninsula. The Moorish (Islamic) kingdom of Granada on the southern tip of the peninsula was all that remained of the Moslem Empire that had once held most of Spain.

In 1469 a marriage was arranged between Isabella, heiress of Castile, and Ferdinand, heir of Aragon. The marriage proved to be a turning point in the history of the Spanish state. Yet it did not by itself create a unified monarchy. Though both kingdoms accepted the two monarchs as their rulers, each kingdom kept its own laws, courts, parliaments, army, taxation, coinage, and tariff barriers, and the citizens of one kingdom were considered aliens in the other. Spanish nationalism scarcely existed. At most, people identified themselves with their kingdom.

In view of these circumstances the establishment of a unified national state seemed unlikely, but Ferdinand and Isabella had one extremely important factor that worked in their favor: the deep and traditional loyalty of the Spanish to the Church. The Church was the one institution common to, and venerated by, all Christian Spaniards. The new monarchs, who were themselves so devout that the pope gave them the title "the Catholic Sovereigns," deliberately built their policy of unification around the Church. To do so, they had to control the Church in Spain. Despite papal objections, they successfully asserted their right to appoint prelates, tax the Church, rid it of abuses, and curtail the right of ecclesiastical appeal to Rome.

As part of the policy of identification of loyalty to the throne with loyalty to Catholicism, the monarchs insisted upon religious uniformity among their subjects. The first victims were the Jews. During the Moorish era and for some time thereafter Jews had lived happily in Spain. In the fourteenth century anti-Semitism took on new proportions, and in 1391 Christian mobs in Castile murdered thousands of Jews. To save themselves, some of the survivors became Catholics: they were called *conversos* (converts) or *Maranos*. A number of the converts secretly remained Jews. In 1478 the

The Christian re-conquest of the Iberian peninsula

Early 10th century
Mid-11th century
Mid-12th century
End of 15th century

Christian state
Muslim state

Key to
map numbers

1 Dominion of Almohades
2 Kingdom of Aragon
3 County of Barcelona
4 K. of Castile and Leon
5 Caliphate of Cordova
6 Emirate of Cordova
7 Kingdom of Granada
8 Kingdom of Leon
9 Ks. of Leon and Castile
10 Independent Moorish States
11 Kingdom of Navarre
12 Kingdom of Portugal

monarchs received permission from the pope to establish a special Church court called the Inquisition to ferret out, punish, and confiscate the property of these people. In earlier times courts of Inquisition had been subject to the ecclesiastical authorities; this one was established by Ferdinand "according to my pleasure and will in this kingdom and my lands." It represented the union of political and religious power in the hands of the throne and became a powerful instrument of the monarchs in their drive to gain control of the Church and exercise authority over their lay subjects. The throne appointed its officials and drafted its instructions, and for many years it remained the only royal institution that had equal power in both Aragon and Castile. The fanaticism and tortures of the Spanish Inquisition gave it an undying notoriety, and its name became a synonym for unfair and cruel judicial bodies. The zeal of its officers arose in part from the fact that one-third of the property confiscated from its victims went to the inquisitors and two-thirds to the king.

Many of Spain's Jews refused to be cowed into conversion and remained openly loyal to their faith. In 1492 the throne issued an ultimatum that offered Jews the choice of Christian baptism or exile and confiscation of their property. An estimated 150,000 to 200,000 people chose exile, depriving Spain of many of its leaders in the professions, learning, and economic life. Most of the refugees settled in the Near East, where they called themselves Sephardim and down to very recent times retained the language and customs of Spain.

The other victims were the Moors. In 1492 the kingdom of Granada fell to the armies of Ferdinand and Isabella, bringing to an end the Christian reconquest of Spain that had started four hundred years before. The treaty of annexation guaranteed the Moslem Moors freedom of religion, but very soon pressure was exerted on them to become Catholics. Some Moors revolted, whereupon the government decided that their action nullified the treaty. In 1502 a royal decree ordered all Moslems to become Catholics or leave Spain. Those who forsook Mohammedanism for Christianity were called Moriscos and came under the supervision of the Inquisition.

Like the other monarchs of nation-states, Ferdinand and Isabella faced the problem of controlling an unruly nobility. By skilful manipulation and the judicious use of force they regained much land for the crown. They outlawed private wars, destroyed many castles, forbade the building of new ones, and appointed men of middle-class origin to high government posts.

To aid in the restoration of internal order, the throne in 1476 revived an old institution called the Hermandad (Brotherhood). This was an association of cities to maintain a constabulary and courts to preserve internal order. The new Hermandad, financed by the cities but under royal control and outside the regular legal system, dealt ruthlessly with rebels and lawbreakers. In twenty years it achieved the aim of restoring internal order and gaining universal respect for the authority of the throne, whereupon its powers were greatly reduced to prevent it from becoming a new threat to the throne.

The sovereigns established control over the cities by naming their own men to the once autonomous city councils and appointing an inspector, called a *corregidor*, to keep close watch on town governments in the interest of the throne. They paid little attention to the once-powerful *cortes* (parliamentary assemblies), summoning them irregularly and only to give approval to proposed royal actions.

GERMANY AND THE HAPSBURG DYNASTY

The contrast between the development of the monarchic nation-state in France, England, and Spain and the continuing princely particularism in Germany was marked. There was, however, a growing nationalist sentiment in Germany, which tended to identify the empire and the emperor with Germany. The new nationalist sentiment could not overcome the forces of disunity. The emperor, from 1438 on always the head of the House of Hapsburg, was chosen by majority vote of seven electors, the count palatine of the Rhine, the margrave of Brandenburg, the king of Bohemia, the elector of Saxony, and the archbishops of Mainz, Trier, and Cologne, and had little real authority. Actual power resided in the hands of about 2,500 local and regional authorities. They included 50 ecclesiastical princes, 30 secular princes, over 100 counts, about 70 prelates, 66 imperial cities, and about 2,000 imperial knights who together owned less than 250 square miles of land. The emperor could levy a very limited amount of taxes, and his title carried with it no land from which to draw revenues. He therefore had to pay most of the costs of the imperial government from his own possessions. The other chief central authority of the empire, the Imperial Diet (Reichstag), represented the electors, the princes, and the cities. These groups knew that any increase in the central power would be at their expense, so they adamantly opposed any efforts in that direction.

Though German nationalist sentiment could identify the empire with Germany, it could not identify Germany with the empire, for the empire included non-Germanic peoples, such as the Czechs of Bohemia-Moravia and the Swiss. The religious movement led by Jan Hus in Bohemia in the early fifteenth century was nationalistic as well as heretical, and it left a legacy of Bohemian national separatism that the incorporation of Bohemia into the Hapsburg domain in the early sixteenth century did not immediately destroy. The Swiss also champed at the imperial bit. Resenting increased imperial taxes to strengthen the emperor's administration over them, they rebelled. They defeated the imperial army in 1499 and declared their independence although they did not win formal recognition by the empire of their independence until 1648. Each of the thirteen cantons that made up the confederation was itself an almost independent state. Each sent two delegates to a federal diet that met regularly to decide matters affecting the confederation as a whole. All acts of the diet had to have unanimous approval. Even when such unanimity was achieved, a canton could refuse to implement the legislation because there was no central executive authority to enforce the diet's decisions.

The general feudal disorder in fifteenth-century Europe was especially severe in Germany. For a time it seemed as if the individual German states of the empire would themselves fall apart. By the latter part of the century the rulers of Brandenburg, Bavaria, Saxony, and a few other princedoms overcame these dangers. On a small scale they emulated the accomplishments of the centralizing monarchs, restoring internal order, increasing revenues, and gaining recognition of their sovereignty. With their positions strengthened, the princes opposed even more strongly any increase in the power of the imperial government. Emperor Maximilian (1486–1519), who seemed to many Germans the ideal monarch, met with rebuffs in his efforts to unite the empire and build up the central power. He had to yield to a group that demanded constitutional changes to weaken still more the power of the emperor.

In contrast to his failure to win greater power for the emperor, Maximilian enjoyed spectacular success in establishing the fortunes of his family, the Hapsburgs. Their possessions already included much of modern Austria. By a series of marriages Maximilian vastly increased the territories of his house and created a new family empire for his descendants. He himself married Mary of Burgundy, by which he won the Netherlands for his dynasty. His greatest coup came when he arranged a marriage between his son, Philip, and Joanna, heiress of Ferdinand and Isabella. The son of the marriage, Charles V, ultimately inherited the Austrian, Burgundian, and Spanish possessions, including Spain's enormous empire in the New World. Maximilian also arranged marriages between others of his progeny and the ruling family of Hungary and Bohemia, thereby securing the thrones of those lands for his dynasty. The Hapsburgs gained far more power and fame by nuptial diplomacy than they ever won in battle. A famous Latin couplet put it well:

> Bella gerant alii, tu felix Austria nube
> Nam quae Mars aliis dat tibi dona Venus.

(Others may wage war, you happy Austria marry;
What Mars gives others, Venus gives to you.)

The new Hapsburg empire, built on marriages and family alliances, was a purely dynastic state. A common ruler provided the only bond that held together the scattered territories and heterogeneous peoples who made up the realm. It differed radically from the national territorial states established by the centralizing monarchs. The latter, motivated in their state-making policies by the desire to increase the power and glory of their dynasties, built on the foundation of a homogeneous population and compact territory. Their national territorial states—France, England, and Spain—rather than the supranational state of the Hapsburgs set the pattern for the future evolution of the European state system. With the emergence of the monarchic nation-states and the dynastic power of the Hapsburg emperor, the prerequisites were present for a new kind of statecraft: general European war.

The Italian Wars

In 1494 Charles VIII of France led his army across the Alps into Italy. Charles had a tenuous hereditary claim to the throne of Naples, which he used as the pretext for his invasion. His plans went far beyond the conquest of Naples. He hoped to establish domination over all of Italy and then lead a crusade against the Turks, recapture the Holy Sepulcher in Jerusalem, and win the imperial crown for himself. The turmoil of Italian domestic politics gave him the opportunity for invasion. Ludovico Sforza of Milan had reason to believe that Naples would lead a coalition of Italian states against Milan. To ward off this threat, Sforza invited Charles to invade Italy and claim the crown of Naples. At the start of the campaign Charles won easy victories. An alliance called the Holy League quickly formed against him. Its members included Spain, the empire, Venice, Milan, the Papacy, and ultimately England. Each of the states felt its interests involved and damaged by the French conquests.

The Holy League was the first of the great coalitions of states that have become standard features of international relations. The allies drove Charles out of Italy in 1495. The French, however, would not give up their dream of domination in Italy and returned again and again to the attack. Each time they were rebuffed by a coalition in which Spain usually took the lead. States entered and withdrew from the conflict, changed sides without compunction, and sought allies wherever they could find them; the French even leagued with the Turks, who until then had been regarded as the common enemy of all Christian states. Italy became a battleground for foreign armies and the war spread into France and Germany. Periods of uneasy truce punctuated the long struggle, but the conflict ended only in 1559 when by the Treaty of Cateau-Cambrésis the French finally abandoned their Italian ambitions and Spain (by this time ruled by the Hapsburgs) emerged as the dominant power in Italy.

RESULTS OF THE ITALIAN WARS

The Italian wars disrupted Italy economically and politically. The most notable victim was the Italian Renaissance. By the mid-sixteenth century, when Spain gained ascendancy in Italy and rigorous Catholic orthodoxy stifled the secular spirit of the Italian Renaissance, Italian creativity was already in sharp decline.

The Italian wars also completed a revolution in military tactics. For five hundred years heavily armored cavalrymen had dominated the battlefields of Europe. That predominance was ended not by firearms but by a new kind of infantry tactic. The revolution began in 1476 and 1477 when in three successive battles Swiss infantrymen, armed with eighteen-foot pikes, halberds (ax-head pikes), and broadswords, smashed the charge of the knights of Burgundy. The Swiss fought in compact squares of about 6,000 men, 85 men across and 75 ranks deep. Their success depended upon strict discipline. They had to ignore their wounded and close up the gaps caused by enemy action, since their strength lay in their massed impact. Bowmen and gunners preceded them in the attack to harass the enemy, then fell back to let through the pikemen and halberdiers.

The military prowess of Swiss infantrymen made them the most respected fighting men in Europe. Monarchs eagerly sought Swiss soldiers to fight for them. Providing mercenaries became a sort of state monopoly, in which the diet of the Swiss Confederation or the government of one of the cantons gave outsiders permission to recruit soldiers in return for cash, commercial privileges, shipments of grain, or other forms of payment. The Swiss Guards, who have patrolled the Vatican since 1510 in the brilliantly colored uniforms designed by Michelangelo, are the last reminders of the days when soldiers were Switzerland's chief export. Other armies soon copied the Swiss tactics, and by 1560 formations of massed pikemen surrounded by men armed with muskets were standard. The day of the mounted soldier, however, was not yet over. Heavy cavalry, charging in groups of 400 to 500, lances at tilt, and supported by armed crossbowmen, still presented a formidable fighting force, while light cavalry was indispensable for raiding and foraging.

During this era firearms underwent important changes. In artillery attention was drawn away from huge pieces to the development of readily portable, accurate cannon and improved gun carriages to transport them. In musketry, the invention of the matchlock and the wheel lock—firing mechanisms that did away with the need to hold a match to a touchhole to fire the weapon—and new designs in gun stocks improved efficiency. The musket displaced the bow as the chief battle weapon. Curiously enough, the spread of firearms reduced firepower. The longbowman could get off six arrows a minute, and the crossbowman, one a minute, but it took the musketeer several minutes to load and fire his weapon, and accuracy was considerably less than with a bow. Nevertheless, the heavy ball that the gun fired made it a much more effective and brutal weapon, especially in the close-in, massed fighting which made accuracy irrelevant.

Charles VIII began his invasion in 1494 in a medieval spirit—as the first step in a chivalric crusade against the infidel. Instead, his invasion marked the opening of the modern era of international relations. In previous conflicts only immediate neighbors had usually been involved, such as the English and the French, the Florentines and the Milanese. The various disputes and wars among states had few cross-relations with one another. It was almost as if they were shut up in so many watertight compartments. Now for the first time all the major states found that their interests were enmeshed in a single issue of international relations: the French scheme to dominate Italy. Combinations of powers emerged that had not been known before. The balance of power concept, by which states combine to check the ambitions of the most powerful among them, came into operation among the major European powers. The price for the preservation of that balance would be recurrent wars. The Italian wars established the basic pattern of European alignments for centuries, pivoting on a dynastic rivalry between the Hapsburgs and the ruling house of France. All that was lacking to give the Italian wars the full flavor of modernity was an ideological conflict. The Protestant Reformation and the Catholic reaction would supply it.

CHAPTER FIVE ————

Reformations, Protestant and Catholic

In 1520 the Church of Rome commanded the allegiance of practically everyone in Western and Central Europe. All except the small Jewish minority worshiped according to the same basic rites, accepted the Church's claim that it alone held the keys to salvation, and recognized the pope as the final authority on matters of faith and church organization. Within a generation that religious unity had vanished as a result of the great movement called the Protestant Reformation. Northern Germany, parts of Switzerland, the Dutch Netherlands, Sweden, Denmark, Norway, Iceland, England, and Scotland had permanently seceded from the Church; for a time Poland and Hungary seemed ready to break away; and large groups in France and Bohemia subscribed to the new creeds of Protestantism.

The medieval Church can be likened to a monolith. Its unity and hierarchic structure capped by papal authority were indeed the Rock of Peter. Yet it was a rock incised everywhere by particularism. There were local variations in the details of liturgical practice, significant differences in ecclesiastical organization, and restrictions on the exercise of papal authority over clergy and laity of varying force from one region to another. Areas farthest from Rome were least susceptible to continuous papal influence; for example, clerical incelibacy was still a major problem in Ireland in the fifteenth century, whereas it had long since disappeared elsewhere in

Europe. The more highly developed medieval monarchies had wrested control from the papacy over many facets of ecclesiastical government. By 1520 most of the countries of Western Europe and Bohemia had witnessed outraged reactions to abuses within the Church. The virulence, even the success, of movements demanding reform of the Church in the late Middle Ages were conditioned by the strength of local particularism. A reformer such as the Oxford theologian John Wyclif (who died in 1384) escaped condemnation as a heretic—although his theological position was in advance of Luther's of a century and a half later—because he enjoyed the protection of the king of England. The Bohemian heretic Jan Hus, burned at the stake at Constance in 1415, enjoyed such a popular following in Bohemia and Moravia that neither his execution by the emperor nor repression of his movement sufficed to extinguish Hussitism for two centuries. The depth of the incisions varied, but where they were deepest, the monolith gradually crumbled away.

The Eleventh Hour of the Medieval Church

Abuses in the Church had long been evident, and the Protestant Reformation was hardly unheralded. For several centuries devout churchmen had attacked corruption within the Church and the loss of spirituality among the clergy. Although many clerics led devoted and religious lives, too many others forgot their high calling and abused their position and power. The sale of important and profitable Church offices, including bishoprics, was one such abuse. The practice was called simony after the Bible's Simon Magus, who offered money to purchase the power of bestowing the Holy Spirit (Acts 8:9–24). Pluralism, by which one man held several major ecclesiastical offices, made the proper fulfillment of duties impossible; many bishops never even visited their dioceses. Lucrative and powerful offices went to relatives of princes, popes, and bishops. This practice was called nepotism from *nepos*, Latin for "nephew," and a euphemism for the illegitimate children of prelates.

Many high clerics had little interest in their posts except for the revenues they produced and the prestige and political advantages they offered. Some were involved in affairs of the secular state, subsidized by the faithful to do the work of princes; this kept them from the cure of souls and identified them in the popular mind as power-hungry, puffed-up prelates, monopolizing the functions of both Church and state. Churchmen from the highest rank to the lowest frequently led immoral lives. Among the parochial clergy widespread ignorance and indolence incurred the contempt of the laity. In some monasteries monks and nuns forgot their vows of poverty, chastity, and obedience and lived for worldly pleasure. The great mendicant orders, the Dominicans and Franciscans, betrayed their missions: the silver-tongued preaching of the former was committed to ecclesiastical politics, and the humility of the latter was sometimes displaced by sloth and arrogance.

The faithful resented the heavy expenditures of the Church and its constant pressure on them for more money. Popes needed great sums to support their political ambitions, maintain a luxurious court, and pay the costs of an elaborate and inefficient administrative organization. Bishops needed money to meet the expenses of their own costly style of living. Resentment of the Church's fiscal demands merged with the growing contempt for the clergy and bordered on anticlericalism.

Since the early twelfth century the abuses had brought denouncements and pleas for reform in every generation. The need for reform was no greater in the sixteenth century than in the preceding centuries—in fact, the evidence indicates some improvement—yet all the earlier attempts at change failed, whereas the movement started by Martin Luther in 1517 surprised even him by the extent of its success. Luther offered few startlingly new theological ideas; earlier reformers had preached many of the same doctrines and many had gone further in theological innovations. Luther's success was attributable to a combination of religious, political, and social circumstances, which in his day favored the propagation of new doctrines and a revolt against papal power.

THE PIETIST REVIVAL

A widespread religious revival that began in the fifteenth century explains in part the heightened discontent with the Church. Pious and thoughtful Christians, including both clergy and laity, organized movements such as the Brethren of the Common Life in the Rhineland and the Low Countries to revitalize popular interest in faith and salvation. The new printing presses turned out thousands of devotional books written for popular consumption as guides to pious living. A new interest appeared in mysticism—the belief that by giving up all earthly desires and yielding completely to God, man could commune directly with the Creator. Intellectuals played a part in the religious ferment. Christian humanists used their scholarly and literary talents in the attempt to restore the Church to its original purity.

Those who were caught up in the wave of popular pietism considered themselves devout communicants of the Church, but because of the worldliness of the Church they began to feel that they knew better than Church officials how to lead Christian lives and attain eternal salvation. This presumption was close to heresy in the eyes of the authorities. From it emerged a way of spiritual life that was increasingly independent of the organized Church and prepared many people for Luther's message, especially in Germany, England, the Low Countries, and France.

DECLINE OF THE PAPACY

A decline in the power and prestige of the papacy contributed to the weakened hold of Catholicism on many people and their readiness to accept Protestantism. The prestige of the papacy never recovered fully either from the "Babylonian captivity," when the popes lived in Avignon and were subservient to the king of France, or from the even more damaging Great Schism (1378–1417), when first two and then three men claimed the papal throne. The Schism was a mockery of papal authority; three sets of keys to the Kingdom of God was an impossible situation that shocked the devout and appeared ridiculous to the less devout.

The popes who ruled after the Schism ended did little to restore the tarnished prestige of the throne of St. Peter. The Renaissance popes were far more concerned with establishing the papacy as an Italian political power, patronizing arts and learning, living in splendor, and enriching their relatives and favorites than they were with improving their role as religious leaders. Nicholas V (1447–55), first of the Renaissance popes, loved books so much that he spent great sums for ancient and modern works and offered 10,000 gold pieces for a translation of Homer. Sixtus IV (1471–84) showered wealth and power on his nephews and lived in sensuous luxury. The deeds of Rodrigo Borgia, who ruled as Alexander VI (1492–03), made his name a byword for lust and cruelty. During his pontificate the immorality and venality of the papacy knew no bounds. Much of the money that poured into Rome from Catholic Christendom was spent on an attempt to create an Italian kingdom for his beloved son Cesare. Julius II (1503–13) was the favorite nephew of Pope Sixtus IV. His doting uncle made him a cardinal at twenty-eight and endowed him with twelve bishoprics, one archbishopric, and three abbeys. As pope, Julius made his chief task the expansion of the temporal power of the papacy. In pursuit of this ambition he engaged in a number of wars and sometimes personally led his troops into combat, thereby winning the nickname, the Warrior Pope. Leo X (1513–21), son of Lorenzo de' Medici, used the wealth of the Church for magnificent pageantry and patronage of the arts. The ever-increasing demands of the popes for money, their worldliness, and their immorality aggravated the resentment, the doubts, and the sense of alienation already felt by many Christians.

STATE AND CHURCH

The loss of the pope's prestige contributed to the decline in the power and authority of the Church, but the prime cause of decline was the rise of the new monarchs. They wanted to extend their domination over everything in their realms, including the Church. Ferdinand and Isabella in effect controlled appointments to Church office in Spain, taxation by the Church, and ecclesiastical jurisdiction. In France King Francis I gained almost the same powers by the Concordat of Bologna in 1516, in return for his renunciation of the once popular doctrine of the supremacy of a Church council over the pope. The English Parliament in the mid-fourteenth century passed laws limiting the papal power of appointment to Church offices in England and restricting the legal jurisdiction of the Church. The statutes were not vigorously enforced, and the pope exercised somewhat more influence in England than he did in Spain and France until Henry VIII demonstrated the power of the monarchy by reviving the statutes and reducing the English clergy to obedience.

In Germany, where a strong central power did not emerge, there were fewer limitations on papal powers of appointment, ecclesiastical jurisdiction, and taxation. Rome drew enormous sums of money from Germany. The situation aroused the envy and cupidity of minor German rulers. This fact, together with the low moral prestige of the Church, made the German people and their rulers more receptive to the idea of revolt.

The signal for revolt came in 1517 from the small university town of Wittenberg in Saxony. Following a standard academic practice, a monk named Martin Luther posted on a church door a challenge to other scholars to debate certain theological propositions. This seemingly unimportant act triggered the forces that wrecked the unity of Western Christendom, generated bitter religious enmities, and brought on war and suffering whose results have not yet entirely disappeared.

Luther and the German Reformation

Luther (1483–1546) came from a moderately prosperous family of peasant origin and received a university education. His father wanted him to become a lawyer, but after a mystical religious experience Luther decided to become a friar of the Augustinian order. He dedicated himself to theological studies and in a few years became professor of Biblical exegesis at the University of Wittenberg. He held a number of other responsible offices, including that of district vicar of his religious order.

Luther could have congratulated himself on a modestly successful career; instead, terrible doubts about his worthiness gnawed at his conscience and an unshakable burden of guilt overwhelmed his spirit. He prayed, fasted, scourged himself, and confessed for as much as six hours at a time, and still he could not free himself from his spiritual agony. He could not see how man, abject creature that he is, could overcome by his own efforts his inherent sinfulness. Through constant study of the Bible, Luther finally found an answer. Man must throw himself on God's mercy and accept His grace, realizing that he is too sinful to merit it by his own acts. Only then can man be saved. Good works, such as prayers, fasts, pilgrimages, reciting the rosary, veneration of relics, and the asceticism of the monastery, will avail him nothing. God gives His grace as a reward for faith alone, and man must rejoice in God's mercy and love, gratefully do His will, and follow His commandments.

The doctrine of "justification by faith" struck at the heart of the Catholic belief that man is saved by faith *and* good works. If faith alone saves, and if man himself can do nothing to merit salvation, he does not need the mediation of the Church and its priests between himself and God. All man needs is faith in God and the Bible to give him God's word so that he can live according to God's will. Yet Luther did not at first realize the revolutionary nature of his teaching. He did not criticize or deride the Church, as many of his contemporaries did, and in fact wanted only to give the Bible a larger place in the theological curriculum of his university. Then in 1517 a Dominican friar named Johann Tetzel appeared in the neighborhood to sell papal indulgences.

According to the accepted doctrine most men were so sinful that they could not do penance for all their transgressions during their lifetime. After death they had to spend time in purgatory, a temporary place of punishment, to atone for their sins before they could go to heaven. However, the saints had done good works far in excess of the amount they needed to expiate their sins, and above all Christ by His sacrifice had amassed an infinity of good works. The Church taught that the pope could draw upon this Treasury of Merits, as the storehouse of good works was called, for the benefit of both the living and the dead by granting indulgences for their sins. The pope had the power to transfer credits in the Treasury of Merits so that the person receiving the indulgence would escape a specified amount of time in purgatory or, if he received a plenary indulgence, would escape all the time he would have had to spend there to complete penance for his earthly sins. It was even possible to get indulgences for people who were already dead and thereby reduce their time in purgatory. Theoretically the Church freely gave the indulgence and the grateful recipient made a voluntary contribution, but the issuance of indulgences frequently coincided with a drive to raise additional money for the papacy.

The indulgences that Tetzel sold were nominally intended to raise money to build St. Peter's in Rome. In fact, Pope Leo X had arranged for young Albert of Hohenzollern, who already held two bishoprics, to be archbishop of Mainz in return for a heavy fee. Albert borrowed from the Fugger banking firm to pay Leo. The pope then offered to help Albert pay back the Fuggers by letting him have half the income from the sale of the indulgences in Albert's three bishoprics; the rest was to be used for St. Peter's.

RELIGIOUS REVOLT

Luther knew nothing of these behind-the-scene arrangements, but he had strong doubts about the efficacy of indulgences. As a professor, he decided that the problem should be discussed in proper academic fashion by writing a statement in Latin of his views and inviting other scholars to debate with him. On October 31, 1517, he posted ninety-five "theses" on the Wittenberg church door, which served as the university's bulletin board. Three basic points underlay his ninety-five propositions. First, the pope should not take money from Germany to build St. Peter's; second, the pope did not control purgatory, and if he did, he should release everyone from it; and third, the Treasury of Merits did not exist, so that the pope did not have any superfluous good works at his disposal.

Luther had not expected any reaction outside the university community. To his great astonishment his theses, printed in Latin and German, spread rapidly throughout Germany. The sale of indulgences fell off. Albert of Hohenzollern and the Dominican Order to which Tetzel belonged pressed the pope to discipline Luther. Luther had a powerful protector in his prince, Elector Frederick the Wise of Saxony. For political reasons Pope Leo did not want to antagonize Frederick and delayed taking punitive action. Meanwhile, the attacks leveled at Luther by defenders of the Church compelled him to work out the implications of his theological position. In doing so, he moved further and further away from orthodox doctrine. In a public debate at Leipzig in 1519 with Johann Eck, a German theologian of renown, he denied the divine origin of papal supremacy, asserting that the bishop of Rome had not been recognized as head of the Church in the early days of Christianity. Eck compelled Luther to admit to sympathy with some of the doctrines of Jan Hus, burned as a heretic a century before. By that admission Luther identified himself as a heretic.

In the face of Luther's avowal of heresy and his growing popular following Pope Leo could delay no longer. In 1520 he issued a bull (letter) that gave Luther sixty days to recant. Luther replied by burning the document in public, together with the books of the Church's canon law, and by writing three pamphlets on his program of religious revolution. The first pamphlet, *Address to the Christian Nobility of the German Nation*, advanced his thesis of the "priesthood of all believers." The priesthood was no more sacred in the eyes of God than any other occupation or "calling." There was no real difference between priest and layman. Every Christian had the right to interpret the Bible according to his own lights rather than having to accept the Church's interpretation; the Bible, not the Church, was the final authority on doctrine. Since the Church had failed to reform itself, the secular government had to do it. Luther called upon the German nobility to take part in establishing a national church, free of

Luther, by Lucas Cranach

"And so it will profit nothing that the body should be adorned with sacred vestments, or dwell in holy places, or be occupied in sacred offices, or pray, fast, and abstain from certain meats, or do whatever works can be done through the body and in the body. Something widely different will be necessary for the justification and liberty of the soul, since the things I have spoken of can be done by an impious person, and only hypocrites are produced by devotion to these things. . . . One thing, and one alone, is necessary for life, justification, and Christian liberty; and that is the most holy word of God, the Gospel of Christ. . . . For the word of God cannot be received and honored by any works, but by faith alone." From Luther, *On Christian Liberty* (1520).

Courtesy of the Fogg Art Museum, Harvard University, Meta and Paul J. Sachs Collection

abuses and severed from Rome. In the second treatise, *The Babylonian Captivity of the Church,* he denied the authority of the priesthood to mediate between the individual and God, asserting that the sacraments are useful only as *aids* to faith rather than the means of grace and the way to salvation. In the tract *On Christian Liberty* he restated his basic tenet that faith alone makes the true Christian. If a man has faith, he will do good works automatically, for as Luther quoted from the Bible, "a good tree bringeth not forth corrupt fruit, neither doth a corrupt tree bring forth good fruit."

The pope had no choice but to excommunicate Luther and request the civil authority to punish him as a heretic. Luther had become a national figure, however, and the religious issues he raised had become national issues. Elector Frederick of Saxony and other German princes insisted that he could not be condemned without a hearing by the civil authority. In 1521 they persuaded Emperor Charles V to summon Luther before the Imperial Diet at Worms and to promise that the reformer would not be harmed while he was there. When Luther appeared before the Diet, he refused to repudiate a word of what he had written or said. He explained that only the "Scriptures or right reason" could convince him that he was wrong. "I trust neither popes nor councils," he said, "since they have often erred and contradicted themselves." He ended his speech with the famous words, "On this I stand, I can do no other. God help me. Amen."

After discussion the Diet issued an edict that declared Luther a heretic and outlaw. Elector Frederick once more came to his aid and hid him in Wartburg Castle. Luther spent much of his time there translating the New Testament into German and writing religious tracts. After almost a year in Wartburg he decided to take his chances in the world. He returned to Wittenberg, and gathering together a band of followers including a number of fellow priests, he established the first Protestant church.

SOCIAL AND ECONOMIC REVOLT

As Luther's doctrines swept across Germany, they became intertwined with revolutionary social and economic ideas. Minor nobles saw in the religious confusions a chance to improve their economic position and increase their political importance. In 1522 under the leadership of Franz von Sickingen and the humanist Ulrich von Hutten they started a conflict, called the Knights' War, against the Catholic ecclesiastical princes in the hope of winning more land and power for themselves. The rulers of the larger states quickly joined forces and crushed the rising.

In 1524 a peasants' revolt provoked a far more serious and bitter struggle. A deterioration in their social and economic position during the generation before the Reformation had produced unrest among the peasants. The new Lutheran ideas appealed strongly to them on religious grounds and had the additional merit of affording them the opportunity to make their economic and social demands part of the national movement for religious reform. In the most widely accepted statement of their program, called *Twelve Articles*, they utilized the teachings of religion to support their demands. They asked for the abolition of serfdom where it still existed, limitations on the tithes paid to the Church and the rents and services paid to the lords, an end to seizure of common land by the nobles, and an extension of their traditional right to hunt, fish, and cut wood in the forests for their own use. They were the first, but not the last, to attempt to forge a bond between Protestantism and social amelioration.

At the start of the revolt the peasants looked to Luther for sympathy and support. His neutrality vanished when the peasants employed violence against constituted authority; Luther passionately denounced them. In his view, civil government must always be obeyed. In the pamphlet *Against the Thieving and Murderous Peasants* he urged the princes to wipe out the rebels as if they were mad dogs. His advice was superfluous. The princes suppressed the revolt with barbarity; an estimated 100,000 peasants lost their lives in battle and on the scaffold. Luther's recommendation for mercy after the revolt went unheeded. Luther's attitude toward the revolt cost him the support of many of the common people. The Lutheran Reformation ceased to be a truly national movement based on broad class support as Luther relied increasingly upon the princes and subordinated his church to the temporal power.

THE RELIGIOUS RADICALS

Some of Luther's followers wanted to carry reform much further. Radical sects, called Anabaptists (re-baptizers), believed that infant baptism had no scriptural warrant and that the true Christian must be baptized as an adult, just as early Christians had been. They argued that both Luther and the Catholics erred in having the Church include all believers, since the Church should be a "company of saints" with strict requirements for membership. It should be limited to Christians who had experienced a spiritual regeneration and received baptism as adults. The Church should be independent of the state and the government should have no power over religion.

The radical sects drew most of their members from the peasantry and the urban artisans. These pious, hard-working people listened with wonderment to the preachers who came among them and told them that the end of the world was at hand and that God had selected them for His people. Most of them believed that God had chosen them for suffering and martyrdom, but a few believed that they as God's instruments must enforce His will, by violence if necessary. They followed democratic procedure in the administration of their churches, and some of them advocated communal ownership in accordance with the Biblical description of the earliest Christians.[1]

The Anabaptists offered both a religious and a political threat to established society. Catholic and Protestant governments alike persecuted them. In 1535 rulers of the two faiths joined forces to besiege the town of Münster, where some of the more fanatical Anabaptists had taken over, abolished private property, and introduced polygamy on Biblical authority. The besiegers showed no mercy when they finally captured the city. In succeeding years thousands of Anabaptists died for their faith. The remnants of the movement lived on, stripped of its violent elements, under the leadership of Menno Simons (died 1561). The people today called Mennonites still live in simple Biblical piety and reject worldly concerns, as urged by the original Anabaptists. Though stoutly condemned, the Anabaptist doctrines did in some instances creep into Protestant theology, most notably in the exclusive notion of the "company of saints" in English puritanism in the seventeenth century.

THE SPREAD OF LUTHERANISM

In contrast to the failures of the knights, the peasants, and the religious radicals, the secular rulers of Germany succeeded in drawing great advantage from the religious revolt. They looked upon the efforts of the emperor

---

[1] "All whose faith had drawn them together held everything in common; they would sell their property and possessions and make a general distribution as the need of each required." Acts 2:44–45.

to restrain Luther as an infringement upon their own freedom. They insisted that they and not the emperor had the right to decide the religion of their states. They saw a chance to end the power of the Church in their territories, stop the flow of gold to Rome, and enrich themselves by confiscating Church property. In addition, Luther's social conservatism and his great respect for civil authority appealed strongly to them. The free cities of West Germany became Lutheran within a few months after Luther's appearance at the Diet of Worms in 1521, and soon a number of secular principalities followed their example. Catholicism persisted in most of the principalities ruled by churchmen, but even in them there were desertions, above all in Prussia, the territory of the Order of the Teutonic Knights. In 1525 Albert of Hohenzollern, Grand Master of the Order, left his clerical calling to become a Lutheran, secularized the domain of the order, and declared himself Duke of Prussia. By the time Luther died in 1546, most of northern Germany had become Lutheran.

The new religion spread to the Scandinavian countries. The monarchs there, like the German princes, saw in Lutheranism the chance to enrich themselves at the expense of the Church and to control religion in their own countries. The Swedish king Gustavus Vasa became a convert, and the national assembly declared Lutheranism the state religion and placed all Church property at the disposal of the king. In Denmark Frederick I adopted Lutheranism in 1527, making it the official religion of his state as well as of Norway and Iceland, then possessions of the Danish crown.

Lutheranism suffered a serious intellectual loss in the defection of many of the Christian humanists. In the first years of the revolt the humanists, led by Erasmus, hailed Luther for his efforts to reform the abuses in the Church and return Christianity to its original principles. As time went on, they found themselves repelled by Luther's dogmatism, his intolerance of any views other than his own, his violent and often vulgar language, and his sweeping denunciations of the Church and the pope. Erasmus tried for several years to mediate between Luther and Rome. He avoided commitment to either side and suffered the disfavor of both. In 1524 he openly broke with Luther, and most of the other Christian humanists followed his lead.

During the years of gains and setbacks Luther continued the work of establishing his new church. He replaced the Latin liturgy with a service in German, consisting mainly of preaching, Bible reading, and hymn singing. Luther himself wrote a number of hymns, among which was the stirring "A Mighty Fortress Is Our God," sometimes called "the *Marseillaise* of the Reformation." Of the seven sacraments he retained only baptism and communion. He published a long and a short catechism to indoctrinate church members in Lutheran doctrine (they proved so successful that the Church of Rome soon imitated them and put out its own catechism), and he wrote many Biblical commentaries. He made Lutheranism a state church, in which the government had supreme power over the church except in matters of doctrine. Monasticism was abolished, and the state supported the church with income from the monastic and other confiscated property. The state appointed ministers and certified their competence. Luther ended clerical celibacy and in 1525 married a former nun.

The Swiss Reformation and the Rise of Calvinism

As early as 1519 an independent Protestant movement arose in Zurich, Switzerland. Its leader, Ulrich Zwingli, was a priest who had been deeply influenced by the writings of the Christian humanists. He started on his career as a reformer before he knew of Luther. When he did read Luther's writings, he found himself in close agreement except on the issue of the "real presence." Luther maintained that in the Holy Communion the bread and wine remained bread and wine but Christ was present in them. This doctrine, known as "consubstantiation" (united in one common substance), differed from the orthodox Catholic doctrine called "transubstantiation" (changed into another substance), which held that the bread and wine became in substance the flesh and blood of Christ. Zwingli took a third position, namely, that the bread and wine served merely as symbols of Christ's flesh and blood and as a commemoration of the Last Supper.

In 1529 Zwingli met with Luther to try to iron out doctrinal differences. Because they could not reach a common ground, two separate branches of Protestantism developed: the Lutheran and the Reformed. Their failure to agree was the first in the long series of schisms productive of so many different denominations in Protestantism. The name "Protestant" itself did not come into general use until 1529, when it was applied to a group of Lutheran German princes who presented a protest at the Imperial Diet against a new law that they thought operated against the further growth of their religion.

Reformed Protestantism spread into other parts of Switzerland until the country was divided between Catholic and Protestant. War broke out between the two camps, and Zwingli lost his life in battle in 1531. Soon after his death the combatants made a peace agreement that allowed each Swiss canton to choose its own religion. Protestantism made no further gains, and Switzerland settled into the division that for the most part still exists, with Catholicism dominant in the more mountainous regions and Protestantism in the cities and more fertile parts of the country.

CALVIN AND GENEVA

The city of Geneva, not then part of the Swiss Confederation, adopted Protestantism in the 1530's, largely as a political expedient to rid itself of the domination of the neighboring Catholic state of Savoy. Most of the 13,000 Genevans remained Catholics, and many of those who chose Protestantism saw no necessity for basic theological changes. William Farel, chief Protestant preacher of the city, was outraged at this attitude but was unable to cope with it. In 1536 he called on Jean Calvin, a young French scholar who had already achieved modest fame as a Protestant theologian, to help him enforce the new orthodoxy in Geneva.

Calvin (1509–1564), son of a prosperous French lawyer, first studied for the priesthood, but at his father's insistence he turned from theology to law. While he was a student, he became interested in humanist learning and steeped himself in the writings of the early Church Fathers, especially St. Augustine. To his humanist and legal education he owed a mastery of Latin and French prose, an interest in ethical problems, and the legalistic cast of his thought.

In 1533 Calvin converted to Protestantism and decided to spend his life as a scholar and writer. He lived for a time in Basel, a sanctuary for Protestants and an intellectual center of the new faith. There in 1536 he published in six chapters the first version of his great work, *Institutes of the Christian Religion,* a treatise on the principles of Christianity. In later editions Calvin expanded the book until the last edition in 1559 had eighty chapters. The book's merits hardly lay in its originality. Calvin drew heavily from other reformers, particularly Luther, from the Church Fathers, especially St. Augustine, and from the Bible itself. Calvin's great contribution was his synthesis and logical presentation of hitherto unsystematized doctrines. Calvin's role in Protestant theology can be justly compared to that of Thomas Aquinas, who three centuries before had performed much the same service for Catholic theology.

Although Calvin, like Luther, insisted that man is saved by faith alone, he shifted emphasis from God's love and the saving power of man's faith to the omnipotence of God. As punishment for Adam and Eve's transgression in the Garden of Eden, God condemned man to live in perpetual sin; no one deserves to be saved. Yet God in His infinite mercy decreed that He would save some men for eternal life. Calvin called these fortunate people "the elect." The rest of mankind was condemned to eternal damnation. Since past, present, and future are one to God, His decree had always existed; everyone was foreordained to heaven or hell from the beginning of time. This was the doctrine of "predestination." Although Luther and other reformers had professed this fatalistic and awesome doctrine, which originated with St. Augustine in the fifth century, Calvin made it dominate his entire theology.

In answer to the objection that by human standards it seemed unjust for God to save or condemn without regard to merit, Calvin explained that whatever God does is the highest form of justice. It might be thought that acceptance of the doctrine of predestination would have made men immoral, since whatever they did could have no effect on their salvation or damnation. Instead, Calvin's followers believed that the ability to live by a strict moral and religious code is a "sign of election"; as Calvin said, "Who are 'chosen unto eternal life are chosen unto good works." Even if a pious life does not guarantee membership in the elect, an immoral life certainly proves that one is not among the chosen. Acceptance of the doctrine thus operated in favor of a sober, industrious, and upright life. In an era when anxiety about salvation pressed heavily on most men, Calvin's theology had an enormous appeal. It relieved believers of concern about their eternal destiny. Assuming that they were among the elect, they gained an unbounded self-confidence and self-righteousness that won them the dislike as well as the grudging admiration of men less certain of salvation.

Calvin also differed from Luther in the emphasis he put on Scripture. To Luther the Bible was the vehicle for the teachings of Christ. To Calvin it served as the supreme authority in every aspect of life; man must live in strict obedience to its precepts. He differed even more markedly from Luther on the relations between church and state. Luther accepted the supremacy of the state. Calvin asserted that the church, or more precisely its ministers, must dominate, for the sovereignty of God comes before the sovereignty of man. Unlike Lutheranism and Zwinglianism, Calvinism provided—in principle at least—for relatively broad-based lay participation in church government. It had no place for prelates, and its government by both ministers and lay elders gave some measure of reality to the "priesthood of all believers." Among later generations of Calvinists this democratic orientation and the emphasis on God's sovereignty led to defiance of political-ecclesiastical despotism in Scotland, England, the Netherlands, and North America and contributed significantly to the development of constitutional government.

When Calvin took over Protestant leadership in Geneva, he applied his ideas to the government of the city and organized it as a theocracy. The chief governing body, called the Consistory or Presbytery, consisted of six (later twelve) ministers and twelve laymen or "elders." The Consistory both made and enforced the laws, which regulated with severity every aspect of human conduct including speech, dress, and manners. Calvin literally had a captive audience for his sermons, for failure to attend services (as well as sleeping or laughing in church) was punishable by a jail sentence. Calvin's powerful personality dominated the Consistory and made him virtual dictator of the city during his lifetime (except for a short period when a revolt against the severity of his rule drove him from the city). He enforced his stern moral code with the assistance of gossips, informers, and spies, and he did not hesitate to use torture, exile, and execution to compel adherence to the new orthodoxy. In 1553 Michael Servetus, a Spanish scholar fleeing Catholic persecution for denying the doctrine of the Trinity, sought refuge in Geneva. Instead of giving him sanctuary, Calvin had him arrested, tried, and burned at the stake for heresy.

THE SPREAD OF CALVINISM

The close relationship of Lutheranism with German nationalism and the political ambitions of German princes made Lutheranism a national faith confined to Teutonic lands. Calvinism was not associated with the political ambitions of rulers and was related to only a slight extent with the nationalist strivings of peoples. It became the international form of Protestantism, leaping over national boundaries and spreading throughout the Western world, impelled by the militancy, dedication, and sense of destiny of its adherents. As long as Calvin lived, Calvinists looked to Geneva for guidance and kept in constant touch with each other through the agency of Geneva. The Genevan Church, which was organized according to the constitution drawn up by Calvin, served as the model for Calvinist churches everywhere long after Calvin's death.

Calvin himself hoped to achieve the greatest success in his own country, France. The first French edition (1541) of the *Institutes* was dedicated to Francis I, king of France, in the hope of converting that monarch. Although unsuccessful in this ambition, Calvin wielded enormous influence over the Huguenots, as French Protestants were called, and was the principal architect of the French Reformed Church. During his brief exile from Geneva (1538–41) Calvin resided in Strasbourg, where he planted the seeds of the new faith. It soon spread throughout the Rhineland and to other parts of Germany. It also spread to the Netherlands, superseding Lutheranism, which had made earlier inroads, and proved a potent weapon in the Dutch struggle for independence from Catholic Spain.

Calvinism achieved two of its most notable triumphs in English-speaking countries. In the sixteenth century Scotland went through a long period of political turmoil in which Protestantism became an ally of the nobles opposed to French influence, exercised notably by Mary of Lorraine, widowed mother of and regent for the infant Mary Queen of Scots. In 1559 John Knox, a former priest who had converted to Protestantism and spent several years in exile studying under Calvin in Geneva, returned to Scotland just as the anti-French party gained the upper hand. He was a powerful speaker and in 1560 persuaded the Scottish Parliament to sever all ties with Rome and set up the Church of Scotland according to the Calvinist, or Presbyterian, model. Although Calvinism gained many converts in England, it never became the dominant sect there, except for a brief period in the seventeenth century. In New England, on the other hand, several colonial settlements began as Calvinist theocracies.

The Reformation in England

In the 1520's Luther's movement won a small following in Oxford and Cambridge, the two English universities. Yet curiously the Reformation in England in its first stage had little to do with religion as such and was not anti-Catholic. It aimed for "Catholicism without the pope." The explanation for the anomaly lay principally in the character and ambitions of England's king, Henry VIII of the House of Tudor. In 1521 Henry, who had received training in theology, wrote a refutation of Luther in Latin. Pope Leo X rewarded him with the title "Defender of the Faith," still borne by England's monarchs. According to his own definition Henry remained a Catholic to his death. He broke with Rome not because of theological differences but because the pope would not grant him a divorce.

HENRY'S DIVORCE

Soon after ascending the throne in 1509, Henry married Catherine of Aragon, his brother's widow, for dynastic purposes. Canon law, based on Scripture (Lev. 20:21), forbade marriage to the widow of a brother, but Pope Julius II granted a dispensation for the marriage for political reasons. In eighteen years of married life Catherine bore one surviving child, her daughter Mary. Henry wanted a male heir to ensure the stability of his dynasty. He had also fallen in love with a young lady, Anne Boleyn. In 1527 he petitioned Pope Clement VII to annul his marriage to Catherine on the grounds that Julius II had exceeded his authority in granting the dispensation.

Under ordinary circumstances the pope probably would have obliged. He had recently granted similar favors for two of Henry's kin. Catherine of Aragon, however, happened to be the aunt of Emperor Charles V, who held Rome at the time and controlled the papacy. If Clement agreed to Henry's request he would incur Charles's wrath. On the other hand Henry's chief minister, Cardinal Wolsey, warned the pope that if he turned Henry down England might defect from Rome. Faced with this dilemma, Clement resorted to evasion and even suggested that Henry follow Old Testament practice and take two wives.

During the negotiations from 1527 to 1529 Henry never wavered in his religious orthodoxy, but in 1529 he decided upon a course of action that ultimately made his orthodoxy irrelevant. He summoned Parliament and kept it in session for seven years passing the statutes needed to make England independent of Rome. It is unlikely that Henry had a definite plan other than to pressure the pope into granting the annulment by progressively drying up the flow of papal revenue from England, subjugating the English clergy, and reducing papal power over the English church. When these tactics failed, Henry had the spiritual and legal responsibilities of the pope transferred to his pliant new Archbishop of Canterbury, Thomas Cranmer, who in 1533 annulled the marriage of Henry to Catherine and declared valid his earlier, secret marriage to an already pregnant Anne Boleyn. In 1534 Henry and Parliament took the decisive step with the Act of Supremacy, which declared that the king, not the pope, was supreme head of the Church of England.

Most Englishmen, confused by the course of events and moved by patriotism, dynastic loyalty, or fear, accepted the break without protest. A few stalwarts refused to renounce their allegiance to Rome and to take the oath required by the Act of Supremacy. Among them was Sir Thomas More, humanist luminary and formerly Henry's chief minister. He was beheaded for treason in 1535.

THE HENRICIAN REFORMATION

Henry moved next against England's eight hundred monasteries and nunneries. In 1536 and 1539 Parliament passed acts of dissolution, allowing Henry to close the religious houses and confiscate their lands. Henry explained publicly that this was done because a survey made by his officials revealed that the monks and nuns led sinful and useless lives, but Henry had other, more pressing reasons. As long as the monasteries existed, they would serve as centers of propaganda for Rome. Most important, Henry sought the property of the monasteries. He needed money badly to pay off debts and finance his policies. The lands he seized and sold ultimately came to rest in the hands of the rising landed gentry, who became stout defenders of Henry, his Protestant successors, and the Anglican Church, for fear that if Roman Catholicism came back they would lose their newly acquired properties.

None of these actions made Henry or his subjects feel any less orthodox than they had always been. Although the king rather than the pope headed the Anglican Church, doctrine and practice remained unchanged. At one time Henry moved cautiously toward Protestantism, but when a Catholic uprising called the Pilgrimage of Grace broke out in the north of England in 1536, he retreated. To make certain that England would remain Catholic, Parliament passed the Act of the Six Articles in 1539 at Henry's behest. It reaffirmed the orthodox doctrines of the sacraments, the mass, auricular confession, and clerical celibacy, and it decreed the death penalty for those who did not abide by these articles.

Anne Boleyn had one daughter, Elizabeth, born in 1533. Henry soon wearied of Anne and accused her, probably unjustly, of adultery. He had her tried and beheaded in 1536. The day after her execution Henry married Jane Seymour, one of Anne's maids-in-waiting, who died the following year after giving birth to a son, the future Edward VI. In quick succession Henry took three more wives: Anne of Cleves, a pawn in an abortive Protestant alliance against the emperor and whom Henry soon divorced; Catherine Howard, beheaded on charges of adultery when Henry thought his dynasty threatened by her powerful noble family; and Catherine Parr, a twice-widowed gentle lady, who was widowed a third time by Henry's death.

PROTESTANTISM IN ENGLAND

Despite Henry's determination to keep Protestantism out of England, a small but influential group of Protestants formed, led by Thomas Cranmer, Archbishop of Canterbury. The reformers had their chance when Henry died in 1547 and was succeeded by his ten-year-old son Edward VI. They dominated the council of regency that ruled for Edward. Under their influence the new government repealed the Act of the Six Articles, made English the language of religious services in place of Latin, abolished many Catholic ceremonies and practices, and allowed clergymen to marry. In 1549 Archbishop Cranmer composed the Book of Common Prayer to replace the Catholic orders of worship. After approving the book, Parliament ordered its use in every church in the kingdom. In its first edition the Book of Common Prayer contained much that was Catholic, but a new edition issued three years later emphasized Protestant doctrine. The eloquence and solemn beauty of the Book of Common Prayer gave added strength to the cause of Anglicanism.

THE BRIEF RETURN TO ROME

Protestantism received a severe setback in 1553 when Edward died and was succeeded by his half-sister Mary. A plot to exclude Mary and give the crown to the Protestant Lady Jane Grey, grand-niece of Henry VIII, met with failure. The majority of the people of England still looked upon Mary Tudor as their rightful sovereign despite her religion. Mary's fondest ambition was to return England to the old faith and eradicate Protestantism. She pushed legislation through Parliament to repeal all the religious changes of Henry VIII and Edward VI. In theory England was once more Roman Catholic.

The queen and her advisers made no attempt at a genuine spiritual revival of Catholicism, however. Theirs was an archaic Catholicism, unaffected by the still nascent Catholic Reformation, which twenty years later would vigorously regain areas all over Europe for Rome and contain Protestantism. All moves to reclaim the confiscated monastic lands and other Church endowments that had been settled in the gentry's hands met with strong opposition. Mary did not have the money to re-establish medieval

Catholicism in its full panoply, nor did she have the foresight to establish the new reformed Catholicism. In her determination to suppress heresy Mary executed hundreds of Protestants, most of them obscure artisans and many of them women. Her efforts gained her the name of "Bloody Mary" and an abiding hatred for Roman Catholicism among the English as a cruel and oppressive faith; the persecutions accomplished little else.

Mary forfeited much of the popular support for Tudor monarchs when she married Philip, son of Emperor Charles V and soon to be king of Spain. Mary hoped to gain the emperor's support in the drive to re-establish Catholicism in England. Charles welcomed the marriage, seeing it as an opportunity to make England a part of the empire that the Hapsburgs had acquired through marriage. The English, moved both by the fear that their country would lose its independence and by a growing patriotism that included suspicion of all foreigners, especially those who were Roman Catholics, despised the marriage. From then on the national church became identified with national independence. The marriage itself was not successful. Mary, eleven years older than Philip, was in love with her husband, but he did not return her affection and spent as little time with her as possible. When she failed to produce an heir Roman Catholicism in England was doomed.

THE ELIZABETHAN SETTLEMENT

When Mary died in 1558 the majority of Englishmen were actively hostile to Catholicism. They welcomed with relief her successor, Elizabeth, the daughter of Anne Boleyn and the last of Henry's children. Elizabeth had no strong religious convictions, but she saw which way the wind blew. Under her guidance Parliament repealed the religious legislation of Mary's reign. England again broke with Rome and re-established the independent Church of England with supreme control in the monarch's hands. In 1563 the queen and the church promulgated the Thirty-Nine Articles, an ambiguous and avowedly comprehensive formulation of England's religion. The articles were strongly Protestant in such matters as the rejection of papal supremacy, the right of the clergy to marry, and the use of English instead of Latin in church services; but they avoided commitment on such critical Lutheran doctrines as the priesthood of all believers and justification by faith, the Calvinist doctrine of predestination, and Catholic doctrines of the efficacy of the sacraments and the validity of good works. Elizabeth and her advisers hoped to make the Anglican Church as inclusive as possible, so that it might contribute to national unity rather than becoming a source of denominational discord. Before the end of her long reign it was evident that her settlement in religion had failed to satisfy those of her subjects who wanted a more Protestant Anglican Church.

The Catholic Reformation

Not all of those who wanted to end the abuses in the Roman Catholic Church left that Church to become Protestants. Many remained loyal to the old faith and continued to press for changes from within. Their efforts were by no means in vain. In fact, the first successful Catholic reform began in Spain over twenty years before Luther posted his theses on the church door at Wittenberg. It furnished many of the most zealous combatants in the war against Protestantism in the sixteenth century.

Ferdinand and Isabella resolved to establish control over the Church in Spain and to weed out corruption in it. They turned the task over to Cardinal Francisco Ximenes de Cisneros, Archbishop of Toledo, Grand Inquisitor, and their confessor and closest adviser. An investigation of conditions in the monasteries and nunneries, which had been done at royal behest, persuaded Ximenes that drastic action was needed. In 1494 he obtained a papal order empowering him to regulate all Spanish monasteries. He instituted stern disciplinary measures, reintroduced the ascetic rules of the religious orders, and exiled to Morocco monks who seemed incorrigible.

Ximenes had a more difficult time in reforming the secular clergy, but as head of the Inquisition he exercised general supervision over the Spanish Church and succeeded in rooting out many evils. As a result of his reforms the moral condition of the Spanish clergy was much superior to that of most of Europe's clergy. Attacks made by Protestant reformers on the corruption of the priesthood in other countries had little pertinence to Spain.

Ximenes realized that the educational level of the clergy, particularly of those in higher posts, had to be raised. In 1508 he established a university at Alcalá which served as the training ground for many of the next generation of bishops and made an important contribution to the overall improvement in the scholarly standards of the Spanish Church. Reflecting the humanist interests of its founder, the new university had chairs in Greek and Hebrew in addition to the more traditional subjects.

ROMAN CATHOLIC REACTION TO THE
PROTESTANT REFORMATION

The reform movement in Spain was not an isolated phenomenon. Elsewhere such movements as Christian humanism and a revival of piety among laymen and priests gave evidence of a demand for reform that predated the Protestant revolt and arose spontaneously within the Church. Nevertheless, the amazing speed with which Protestantism won converts put the Church very much on the defensive. At first many Catholic leaders felt that the way to handle the revolt was to suppress the Protestants by force. As time went on more and more leaders realized that if the Church was to check the further expansion of Protestantism, it would have to remove the abuses that offended so many of the communicants and, above all, it would have to develop and strengthen its spiritual resources. In this way the reform movement in the Catholic Church became a counterreformation, designed to counteract the Protestant Reformation.

Shortly before 1517 several prominent churchmen and laymen in Rome formed a group called the Oratory of the Divine Love. Though not numerous, they and their successors through example and exhortation wielded enormous influence in reducing clerical abuses and monastic corruption throughout Italy. Stimulated by these developments, the papacy began to direct serious attention to reform. The era of the Renaissance papacy ended; from the time of Paul III (1534–49) men of higher moral and religious standards were elevated to the throne of St. Peter and took the lead in reforming the Church "in head and members."

In its drive to revive Catholicism and repress Protestantism the Church received invaluable assistance from a new kind of religious order. In the new orders the members lived out in the world and were freed of the time-consuming communal obligations of monastic clergy, while discipline and education enabled them to resist the temptations of worldly life that beset ordinary pastoral clergy. They served the Church and the papacy with untiring devotion and unquestioning obedience. The new orders included the Capuchins, the Theatines, the Ursuline nuns, and most important the Jesuits, founded in 1540 by Ignatius Loyola.

LOYOLA AND THE SOCIETY OF JESUS

Loyola (1491–1556), of a noble Spanish family, was raised to be a soldier and in his youth showed little interest in religion and learning. In 1531 he received a serious wound in battle against the French, and during a long and painful convalescence his thoughts turned to religion. After a period of agonized soul-searching he emerged with the conviction that he must give up his career as a soldier of the king of Spain and become a soldier of Christ. He decided that first he must drive sin out of his mind and body, and so lived nearly a year in rigorous asceticism in the town of Manresa. After a pilgrimage to Jerusalem, he next decided to train his mind. He entered the University of Alcalá to study philosophy and theology and then studied for seven years at the University of Paris.

While living at Manresa, Loyola began to work out a manual for those who wanted to share his experience. He called it *The Spiritual Exercises*, explaining that just as physical exercises develop the body, spiritual exercises like prayer, meditation, and examination of conscience "prepare and dispose the soul to rid itself of all inordinate attachments . . . and to seek and find the will of God." Loyola's manual demanded complete obedience to the Roman Catholic Church as God's representative on earth: "To attain the truth in all things, we ought always to hold that we believe what seems to be white to be black, if the Hierarchal Church so defines it."

At Paris Loyola attracted a small group of disciples. Intent upon forming a religious order they offered themselves to the pope for any service he might assign them. In 1540 Pope Paul gave his approval for the establishment of the order. From the beginning Loyola, the old soldier, insisted upon a military form of organization, with a general as commander. He gave a martial name to the band, the Company of Jesus, though it soon came to be called the Society of Jesus. He required from members the unhesitating obedience that is demanded of soldiers.

The new order grew quickly from the nine disciples who had made up the original group. Organized "to employ itself in the defense of the Holy Catholic faith," the Jesuit order threw itself into the struggle to stem Protestantism and win converts to Catholicism. Jesuit schools were founded to train the young in the traditional religion as well as in secular subjects; they dominated the educational system of Catholic Europe for the next two centuries. Cognizant of the importance of influence, the Jesuits managed to become the confessors for men of the ruling elite and mingled actively with the great of the world. Through their foreign missions they won thousands of converts in lands across the sea: a year after the order was founded, Francis Xavier sailed to the Orient to blaze the way for Jesuit missionaries. Within Europe they took their place in the front line of the Catholic counterattack against Protestantism. Through their fervor, diplomacy, and flexibility they played a major role in holding southern Germany, Austria, and France for Catholicism and winning back Poland and much of Hungary to the old religion, and they spearheaded a valiant if unsuccessful attempt to regain England for Catholicism.

THE COUNCIL OF TRENT (1545–1563)

Long before Luther mounted his attack, Christians who were disturbed by deterioration in the Church had called for a general council that could order and carry through needed reforms. The demands grew in intensity after the Protestant revolt began. Emperor Charles V, one of the strongest advocates of such a meeting, hoped not only for reform but also for the Protestants to attend so that an arrangement could be worked out to reunite Christendom. The papacy opposed a council in the fear that it would reduce Rome's power and that the council would reach a compromise with Protestantism.

Time and time again Rome postponed decisive action. Finally Charles prevailed, aided by powerful churchmen, and Pope Paul III summoned a council to meet in Trent, an Austrian city just across the border from Italy. The council met in three sessions, in 1545–47, 1551–52, and 1562–63. The number who attended fluctuated but was never large. The Italian delegates,

Council of Trent in Session

*"If anyone says that the sinner is justified by faith alone, meaning that nothing else is
required to cooperate in order to obtain the grace of justification, and that it is not
in any way necessary that he be prepared and disposed by the action of his own will, let
him be anathema."* CANONS AND DECREES OF THE COUNCIL OF TRENT, tr. Rev. H. J.
Schroeder, O.P. (St. Louis, 1941).

Courtesy of The Metropolitan Museum of Art, Dick Fund, 1941

who had a short distance to travel, always held the majority; the cost of
travel, wars, and other difficulties prevented representatives from other lands
from attending in large numbers. The Italian majority enabled the pope to
keep control of the council, for most of the Italian prelates were dependent
upon him. In addition, the popes had the invaluable aid of a group of skilful Jesuits, whose erudition and orthodoxy gave them much influence in
the discussions in the lobbies and won over many delegates to the papal point
of view.

Guided by the papal party, the council rejected all compromise with
Protestantism and denounced the theology of the reformers. The tenets of
Catholic dogma that the reformers challenged were tightly defined. The
council declared that salvation was achieved not by faith alone but by faith
and good works. It reaffirmed the seven sacraments and the doctrine of
transubstantiation, denied the Protestant claim that the believer could find
the guide to salvation in the Bible alone, and stated that the Bible as interpreted by the Church and the traditions preserved in the Church were the

true sources of authority. It declared the Vulgate, the Latin translation of the Bible that had been made by St. Jerome in the late fourth century, to be the only authoritative version of Scripture, ordered that only Latin be used in the mass, and gave approval to the veneration of saints and relics, the use of images, the cult of the Virgin, pilgrimages, and indulgences as spiritually rewarding acts. It revised the Index, the list of books that Catholics were forbidden to read, and drafted rules by which to judge books in the future. Subsequently the Index was kept up to date by a special Congregation of the Index, composed of cardinals and formed in 1571.

The council found it easier to refute Protestant and define Catholic theology than to root out the many abuses within the Church. Still, it accomplished much. It prescribed drastic reform of the monastic orders, directed that bishops reside in their dioceses and have more control over the clergy within their dioceses, denounced the appointment of immoral and incompetent men to high church office, decreed the elimination of abuses in the granting of indulgences, enacted a series of measures to improve the morals and discipline of the clergy, and ordered the establishment of a seminary in every diocese to train priests.

The council itself did not enforce its decrees; that was left to the pope. Throughout its deliberations the council, dominated by the papal majority, acknowledged subordination to the pope, left the final decisions in difficult matters to him, and agreed that he was not bound by a majority vote of the delegates. Thus the council provided the papacy with a further opportunity to extend its influence and domination. Fortunately for Catholicism the men who occupied the papal throne were equal to the task assigned them. Under their leadership the Roman Catholic Church regenerated itself and carried through moral and administrative reforms. Instead of continuing the retreat before Protestantism, it took the offensive and not only stopped the further expansion of Protestantism but won back lands that had seemed irretrievably lost.

THE CONFRONTATION OF TWO REFORMATIONS

Max Weber, a German sociologist, has argued that Protestantism, especially Calvinism, stimulated the development of capitalism because of its emphasis on serving God in a secular occupation and on the virtues of sobriety, hard work, and thrift as signs of election. The "Protestant ethic" provided the religious justification for the "spirit of capitalism." According to R. H. Tawney's elaboration of Weber's thesis, "the tonic that braced" the new capitalists for the conflict with the entrenched aristocracy "was a new conception of religion, which taught them to regard the pursuit of wealth as, not merely an advantage, but a duty." The controversy over Weber's thesis has been considerable, and his most trenchant critics have pointed to the existence of the spirit of capitalism in Europe before Calvin

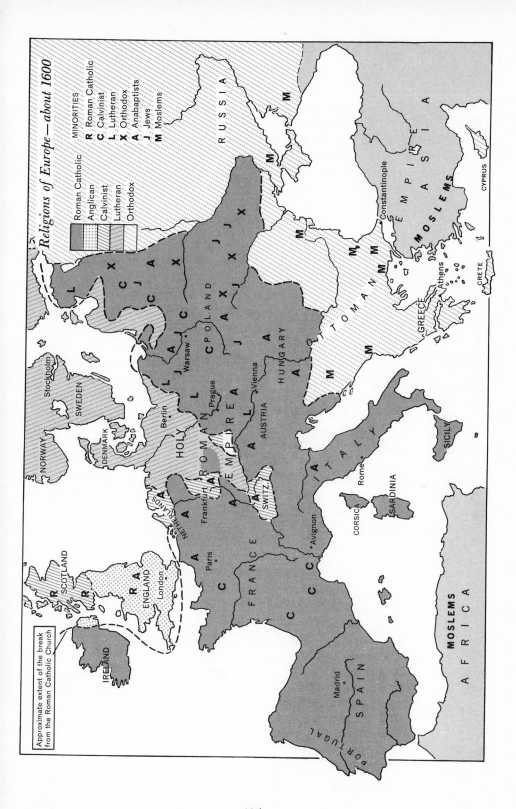

Religions of Europe—about 1600

Roman Catholic
Anglican
Calvinist
Lutheran
Orthodox

MINORITIES
R Roman Catholic
C Calvinist
L Lutheran
X Orthodox
A Anabaptists
J Jews
M Moslems

Approximate extent of the break
from the Roman Catholic Church

and in Catholic societies after him. Yet the connection between English and Dutch economic vitality and Calvinism, and between the French Huguenots' prosperity and Calvinism, seems more than coincidental. Perhaps the Weber thesis makes more sense when stood on its head: many aspiring capitalists of Europe may have found Calvinism congenial, thus accounting for its widespread acceptance in the economically more progressive societies.

Nevertheless, the principal factor in determining whether or not Protestantism took root in a country seems to have been the attitude of the country's ruler. Where the monarch favored Protestantism, the country became Protestant, as in northern Germany, Scandinavia, and England. Where the monarch opposed Protestantism, as in Spain, Italy, Austria, and France, the country remained Catholic. Rulers frequently identified religion with the state and felt that all subjects should embrace the same faith. Those of a different creed were deemed guilty of disloyalty and even of treason. The government took upon itself the enforcement of religious uniformity, and the religion it enforced was that of the ruler. The most important converts to Protestantism were the rulers, for their conversion led to the establishment of Protestantism as the religion of their subjects. Often genuine religious sentiments drew rulers to the reform movement. More commonly, the prospect of confiscation of Church lands, the desire to curb the power of the Church and establish their own full control of their states, and resistance to papal and imperial demands proved stronger attractions and helped persuade them to break the connection with Rome.

Popular pressure became critical only in the few instances when the prince remained Catholic but extended a measure of toleration to Protestants, or when he embraced a conservative Protestantism and then attempted to hold the line against further reform. In these situations Calvinism in particular proved destructive of continued monarchic determination to preserve uniformity. Such cases occurred in certain German principalities in the sixteenth century and in England, Scotland, and France in the seventeenth century.

Calvinism provided a continuing provocation to Catholicism of a kind not offered by Lutheranism and Anglicanism after the mid-sixteenth century. A Roman Catholicism refurbished, rigidified, and armed by the Council of Trent conceived its prime enemy to be Calvinism. The confrontation of the two disciplined and ideologically zealous antagonists was evident by the second half of the sixteenth century. It merged with the dynastic and political ambitions of princes and nationalist loyalties to keep Europe in turmoil for a century and nurtured a seemingly endless series of international wars and civil conflicts.

CHAPTER SIX

The Age of the Reformation

THE impact of the Protestant and Catholic Reformations was political as much as religious; the division of Europe into two ideological camps affected domestic politics in the northern European countries and international politics everywhere. Inevitably the division threatened established rulers. The monarchs of the nation-states found it difficult to control segments of their populace who opposed them on grounds of conscience. The dynastic conglomeration known as the Holy Roman Empire and its dynastic ally, Spain, could not prevent the establishment of Protestant states in northern Germany and the Low Countries. To the foreign policy considerations of the Italian wars was added the religious antagonism among the powers. Religious differences were not as strong a determinant of foreign policy as dynastic considerations, but they did serve to make diplomacy more complex and war more horrible.

The Empire of Charles V

In 1519 the seven electors of the Holy Roman Empire unanimously chose Charles I of Spain and Burgundy as successor to Emperor Maximilian. Charles spent 850,000 florins in bribes to the electors to persuade them to vote for him rather than the other candidates, who were not able or willing to spend as much. He borrowed more than half of this money from the Fugger banking house. When he delayed in repaying the loan, Jakob Fugger sent him a sharp reminder: "It is well known that without me Your Majesty could never have won the Imperial crown, as I can prove with written statements of all the delegates."

The nineteen-year-old victor became Emperor Charles V. The imperial honor that he sought at such heavy expense represented only a part of his power, for Charles's father was the heir of Emperor Maximilian and Mary of Burgundy, and his mother was the heiress of Ferdinand and Isabella. While he was still a boy, his father had died and his mother, known as Joanna the Mad (*la Loca*), had to be confined. From his father's side the youthful Charles inherited the Hapsburg possessions in Central Europe and the Burgundian domains of the Low Countries and Franche-Comté; through his mother he inherited Spain, its dominions in Italy, and its vast new possessions in America. The marriage alliances that had been so skilfully negotiated by his grandfather Maximilian had paid off handsomely.

With all this, the most richly endowed monarch of Europe was not satisfied. Throughout his career he sought to enhance his power and enlarge the territories ruled by the House of Hapsburg. His plans went beyond mere dynastic ambitions, for his ultimate aim was the medieval ideal of the unification of all Christendom under one scepter.

Charles was a man of great perseverance, patience, and common sense, but the obstacles were too formidable to admit of success. He could not even mobilize for a common policy all of the lands over which he already ruled. One reason was that his empire was a purely dynastic creation, a group of states held together not by any common interests but by the single fact that all of them had the same ruler. In addition, he was plagued by three great problems: the religious revolt in Germany and the German princes' opposition to Hapsburg domination; a seemingly endless war with France; and the threat of Turkish aggression. Perhaps Charles could have handled any one of these three successfully, but throughout his reign these and many lesser problems competed for his attention—and for his limited resources. Although the gold streamed into his treasury from the New World, there was never enough to cover all the expenses of a man who, in the words of one of his enemies, wanted "to be master everywhere."

LUTHERANISM AND THE GERMAN PRINCES

In a famous example of Monday morning quarterbacking, Napoleon Bonaparte once remarked that if Charles had allied himself with Lutheranism instead of combating it, he could have created a united Germany that included Austria and the Netherlands and could have conquered Europe.

Instead, during the decade of the 1520's when the Lutheran movement took shape Charles, preoccupied with other matters, did not spare the time even to visit Germany, much less take an active personal part in German religious problems. He made his brother Ferdinand his regent. But Ferdinand was otherwise occupied, too. He became king of Hungary and Bohemia in 1526 after their ruler, his father-in-law, had died in battle with the Turks. The defense of his new possessions against the Turks became Ferdinand's main concern. Thus, neither of the Hapsburg brothers could give concentrated attention to the religious revolt and the no less serious social and political problems that accompanied it.

In 1530 Charles finally found himself free to visit Germany for the first time in ten years. He summoned the Imperial Diet to meet at Augsburg to discuss the religious problem. Luther, who was still under imperial ban, could not attend. Philip Melanchthon, a close associate of his, acted in his place as chief defender of the new faith. Melanchthon, who was more of a conciliator than Luther, drew up a statement of Lutheran beliefs. In the hope of reaching a compromise he toned down or omitted any mention of certain key features of Lutheranism, including the priesthood of all believers, the denial of papal supremacy, and the denial of the existence of purgatory. His statement, known as the Augsburg Confession, became and still remains the official credo of orthodox Lutheranism. Melanchthon's efforts at compromise failed. The Catholic theologians demanded complete surrender, and the Protestant princes left the diet. The Catholics, who then had uncontested control, passed decrees aimed at the extirpation of Protestantism in Germany.

The Lutheran rulers replied by drawing together for mutual defense into a coalition called the League of Schmalkalden (from the town where the allies met for discussion). For a time it appeared as if Charles would attack the Protestants, but new Turkish aggression distracted his attention and in 1532 he was compelled to agree to a truce, called the Nuremberg Standstill. In return the Protestant princes agreed to send troops to help Charles against the Turks.

The truce lasted almost fifteen years. Protestantism continued to make great gains in Germany and even made inroads into Austria. In 1545 the emperor returned to Germany determined to smash the Protestant League, and the next year he began the conflict known as the Schmalkaldic War. Though the Protestant forces outnumbered the imperial troops, the League lacked strong leadership and unity of purpose. Charles soon triumphed, but it proved easier to win the war than to convert Lutherans back to Catholicism. Charles tried to make it easier for Protestants to forsake their religion by promising them small concessions, such as the right of their priests to marry. His efforts at religious compromise pleased neither Protestants nor Catholics. More important, the German princes, Catholic as well as Protestant, looked with much concern on the great increase in the emperor's power that had resulted from his victory over the Schmalkaldic League.

Within a few years the Protestant princes allied themselves with Charles's perennial enemy, France, and in 1552 war broke out again. This time it went badly for the imperial cause. Charles realized at last that he could neither crush the Protestants nor make himself supreme in Germany. In 1555 the Imperial Diet met again at Augsburg and agreed to the Religious Peace of Augsburg. This provided that each ruler could choose for himself whether he wanted his state to be Catholic or Lutheran, whereupon his subjects had to adopt the religion he selected. Other Protestant sects, notably Calvinism and Anabaptism, were specifically excluded from the arrangement. In later years jurists summed up the settlement in the maxim *cuius regio, eius religio,* "whose territory, his religion." This principle was a commonplace in an age when men believed that everyone in a state had to be of the same religion. Lutherans and Catholics who did not want to give up their religion had the right to migrate to a princedom of their own faith.

The Peace of Augsburg included provisions for further efforts to restore religious unity to Germany, but no better solution was found, and the 1555 agreement remained the basis for settlement of religious conflicts. It therefore determined that Germany would remain divided between Lutheranism and Catholicism. Its significance went beyond the religious question; by recognizing the right of the princes to choose their religion, the Peace signified the defeat of Charles in his bid to dominate Germany and the victory of the princes in their struggle for sovereignty.

The Holy Roman Empire lived on for another 250 years, but Charles's failure to establish his supremacy in Germany marked the true end of the imperial idea. The empire existed only as a meaningless shadow. Germany's disintegration was complete: it was a conglomeration of independent states that rarely joined together in any common policy.

For a time after 1555 Protestantism, especially Calvinism, made new gains within the empire. Then Catholicism, stimulated by the decrees of the Council of Trent and the activities of the Jesuits, took on new vigor and won back many Protestants in Austria, southern Germany, and Bohemia. The Protestants were concerned about this resurgence, but no serious conflicts broke out between the two faiths. Early in the seventeenth century Protestant rulers, worried by Catholic attacks on the Religious Peace of Augsburg, formed a Protestant Union, whereupon their Catholic counterparts banded together into a Catholic League. For a time the two groups seemed ready to clash in a territorial dispute about Cleves-Jülich in northwestern Germany. The controversy was settled in 1610 without resort to arms, but within a few years the disputants found themselves involved in the ruinous Thirty Years' War.

HAPSBURG VERSUS VALOIS

The Italian wars, which began when France invaded the peninsula in 1494, broke off temporarily in 1516. Then Charles V was able to encircle France by means of his control of Spain, the Netherlands, and Germany. France, like every other encircled nation in history, did not accept containment readily. Moreover, the kings of the Valois dynasty, who had ruled France since 1328, had their own imperial ambitions that conflicted with Hapsburg aspirations not only in Italy but also in the Netherlands, northern Spain, and even Germany. In fact, Francis I of France (1515–47) had been Charles's chief rival for election as Holy Roman Emperor. The many clashes of interest between Hapsburg and Valois made war inevitable. The other states, recognizing that the victor in this battle of giants would dominate Europe, entered the struggle first on one side and then on the other in hopes of maintaining the balance of power, so that neither Hapsburg nor Valois would crush the other.

In Francis I Charles had a formidable foe. Brilliant, learned, artistic, witty, Francis was also capricious, inconsistent, and extravagant. Yet he was masterful in furthering monarchic supremacy within France. He won from the papacy the appointment of French bishops. He further restricted the political powers of the *parlements,* the law courts that were bulwarks of the power of the nobility. He refined and strengthened the central bureaucracy, broadened its base of recruitment, centralized finance, and built a first-class war machine. He absorbed the nobility into a splendid court and occupied them with the externals of government—a policy that was the keystone of French absolutism until the French Revolution. In 1515 he reconquered Milan in a glorious victory over the Swiss mercenaries; by 1520 he had diplomatically outmaneuvered Cardinal Wolsey, the capable viceroy of England's Henry VIII.

War between Francis and Charles began in 1522. In 1525 imperial troops destroyed the French army at the battle of Pavia in Italy, and Francis himself was taken prisoner. He was held in a Spanish prison until he agreed by the Treaty of Madrid in 1526 to renounce his claims in Italy, Burgundy, and the Netherlands.

Instead of ending the war, Charles's victory at Pavia only served to renew it. Francis never intended to keep the pledges forced from him in the Madrid treaty, even though the Spanish retained his two sons as hostages. He found it easy to win allies against Charles, for other states feared that the Hapsburgs had grown too strong. Charles, who had to divert many of his resources to meet renewed Turkish aggression in central Europe, found himself hard pressed both militarily and financially. In 1527 his unpaid troops in Italy mutinied; forty thousand of them descended upon Rome and sacked it. The Eternal City has fallen to invaders many times in its long history, but never has it suffered a worse fate. For eight days the imperial soldiers murdered, looted, and destroyed. Four thousand people perished and two-thirds of the city was left in ruins. The sack of Rome ended the artistic and cultural pre-eminence of the city, firmly established Spanish control over the papacy, and ended forever the political independence of the popes.

Charles, enraged by Francis's failure to keep the promises made in the Treaty of Madrid, called the king of France "a coward and a rogue" and challenged him to a duel. Francis accepted, and for a while it seemed as if for the first time a European war would be settled by personal combat of the opposing leaders. The negotiations broke down and the two never met on the field of honor. By 1529 the French had suffered so many reverses that they were ready for peace. The Treaty of Cambrai, called the Ladies' Peace because it was negotiated by Louise, mother of Francis, and Margaret, aunt of Charles, repeated most of the terms of the Treaty of Madrid. In addition, Francis agreed to pay an enormous ransom for the two sons he had left as hostages in Spain.

Still the war did not end. It erupted intermittently, interfering with Charles's attempts to deal with his German and Turkish problems. In his diplomatic policies Francis never ceased trying to make the emperor's tasks more difficult, allying himself at different times with Protestant German princes and even with the Turks, whom most Europeans considered the common enemy of all Christians. When Francis died in 1547, his son, Henry II, continued his policies and in 1552 started a new war against Charles. The conflict dragged on until 1558, by which time both sides were exhausted. In 1557 the Spanish and French governments had in effect declared themselves bankrupt and repudiated a large part of their debts, so that financial as well as military necessity dictated the end of the war. In the spring of 1559 they signed the Treaty of Cateau-Cambrésis. France gave up its claims in Italy, the Low Countries, and Spain but retained some small pieces of territory on its northeastern frontier and in northern Italy and also kept the city of Calais, captured from the English in 1558.

The Hapsburgs had finally triumphed over the Valois. After long years of war they had won domination of Italy and kept France out of the Low Countries and the Empire. Spain emerged as the dominant power of Europe, while France sank into thirty years of anarchy and civil war. Under the Spanish yoke Italy exchanged the intellectual excitement and freedom of the Renaissance for rigorous Catholic orthodoxy, intellectual degeneration, and thought control. Of the once independent Italian states only the Republic of Venice preserved its freedom; all the others were under Spanish suzerainty.

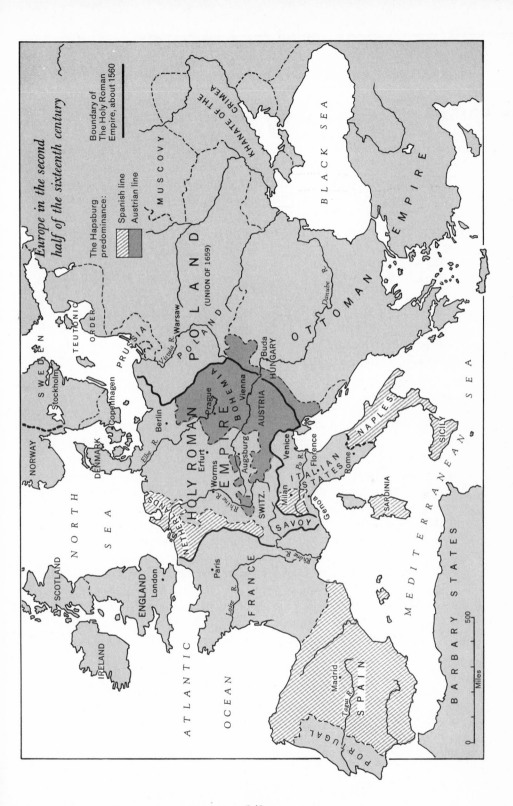

Europe in the second half of the sixteenth century

Boundary of
The Holy Roman
Empire, about 1560

The Hapsburg
predominance:
Spanish line
Austrian line

NORWAY

SWEDEN

Stockholm

TEUTONIC

ORDER

PRUSSIA

Warsaw

P O L A N D
(UNION OF 1569)

M U S C O V Y

KHANATE OF THE
CRIMEA

B L A C K   S E A

O T T O M A N   E M P I R E

Danube R.

DENMARK
Copenhagen

Berlin

Elbe R.

HOLY ROMAN

EMPIRE

Erfurt

Worms

Rhine R.

Augsburg

SWITZ.

Vistula R.

Prague

BOHEMIA

Vienna

AUSTRIA

Buda

HUNGARY

Venice

Milan

SAVOY

Genoa

Po R.

Florence

Rome

I T A L I A N
S T A T E S

NAPLES

SARDINIA

SICILY

M E D I T E R R A N E A N   S E A

SCOTLAND

IRELAND

ENGLAND
London

NORTH
SEA

A T L A N T I C

O C E A N

Paris

Loire R.

F R A N C E

NETHERLANDS

Rhône R.

Madrid

Tagus R.

S P A I N

PORTUGAL

B A R B A R Y   S T A T E S

0   500

Miles

THE TURKISH MENACE

In 1520 the Turks under the leadership of a new sultan, Suleiman II "the Magnificent," launched an advance along the Danube. In 1526 at Mohács in southern Hungary they routed the Hungarians. Three years later they stood at the gates of Vienna. Charles, who till then had left the defense of Central Europe to his brother Ferdinand, had to shift troops from the west to repulse this threat. In 1532 the Turks again invaded Austria and again they were pushed back. Other troubles drew Charles away from the conflict and Ferdinand, who was then king of Hungary, carried on alone. Attempting to drive the Turks out of Hungary, he was defeated by Suleiman, who occupied most of the country. Finally in 1547 Ferdinand had to sign a truce recognizing the Turkish conquest of Hungary and agreeing to pay the Turks tribute for the small western strip that he still held. Meanwhile pirate chiefs who ruled in Algiers and Tunis and were under the protection of Turkey made the waters of the western Mediterranean unsafe for European shipping. Charles, who in his war against the Turk called himself "God's standard bearer," made two campaigns to northern Africa in an unsuccessful attempt to stamp out the pirates.

DIVISION OF THE HAPSBURG DOMAIN

In 1555 Charles, tired, discouraged, and prematurely aged, decided that the time had come to rid himself of his responsibilities. He wanted his son Philip to succeed him as ruler of both the Hapsburg and the Spanish possessions, but Charles's brother Ferdinand would not agree. After bitter discussions the emperor divided his realm. He turned over the Hapsburg patrimony in Central Europe to Ferdinand, who was elected emperor, and to Philip he gave Spain, the Low Countries, and the Spanish possessions in Italy and the New World. After his abdication Charles retired to luxurious quarters that he had built as an annex to a Spanish monastery. There he spent the two remaining years of his life in offering gratuitous advice to his son Philip, performing religious devotions, strolling in his gardens, and in the rather unusual activity of rehearsing his own funeral. He died in 1558. His will provided that thirty thousand masses should be said for the repose of his soul.

The Wars of Religion in France

The kings of France had wasted much blood and treasure in their long and futile effort to win domination over Italy. More than anything else the country needed peace and unity of purpose to recuperate. Instead, an even more costly and far more damaging civil war broke out that nearly destroyed France. Towns, villages, even families, split and fought one another, and assassinations, wanton destruction, and armed raids became part of everyday life in many areas. Historians count eight separate civil wars, the first beginning in 1562 and the last ending in 1593. These conflicts can be viewed as one war that lasted for thirty years broken by periods of truce.

The enmity between Catholic and Protestant bore the largest share of responsibility for the war, and religious fanaticism explained the special ferocity of the combatants. Despite harsh persecutions, including torture and burning, many Frenchmen were attracted by the doctrines of their countryman Jean Calvin. By 1559 the Calvinists felt strong enough to convene a synod in Paris, at which seventy-two individual congregations were said to have been represented. They drew up the *Confession of Faith of the Reformed Churches of France*. The rapid diffusion of the new creed astonished their contemporaries, including even Jean Calvin, who followed events in his homeland closely and sent a stream of counsel from his stronghold across the border in Geneva. The Calvinists were very much in the minority. Out of a population of sixteen million they numbered only about 1.2 million; the rest were Catholic. Calvinism, however, won many converts from the nobility: between 40 and 50 per cent of the French nobility were at one time Protestant. The movement drew its rank-and-file membership from among the urban merchant and artisan classes, making it strong in the towns. For these reasons the sect had a strength out of proportion to its numbers.

More than religion was at stake in the conflict. The ambitious feudal nobility saw the opportunity to use religious controversy as a vehicle to win back its old dominance. The wars of religion were also wars of political factions headed by powerful noble families. If strong and wise kings had led France during those years, the country might have escaped its long agony. Instead, three of the weakest kings in French history followed one another on the throne. They were the sons of Henry II (1547–59) and Catherine de' Medici. For years Henry, infatuated with his mistress, Diane de Poitiers, had neglected his wife, a daughter of the Florentine Medici family whom he had married for her money. When Henry perished in a jousting accident in 1559, Catherine as queen mother came into her own, for her sons were incapable of ruling. The eldest, Francis II, was a youthful invalid who soon died; the second, Charles IX (1560–74), was more than half-demented; the third, Henry III (1574–89), was an effeminate degenerate. Catherine, who held the real power, was an ambitious and scheming woman. Unfortunately for France her talent for intrigue, cruelty, and duplicity far exceeded her not inconsiderable statesmanship.

Three groups of great aristocrats vied for control of the state. The Catholic party was headed at first by Francis, Duke of Guise. His family held great stretches of land, were related to kings, and considered themselves on a par with royalty. The Huguenot party was led by Bourbon princes, one of whom was king of Navarre (on the French–Spanish border) and another the Duke of Condé. The Bourbons were a junior branch of the French royal family. Ultimately a third party developed, whose partisans believed that the political unity of France was more important than its religion and wanted to end the senseless civil war by having the state tolerate both religions. They were called the *politiques.*

Open warfare began in 1562 when soldiers of the Duke of Guise massacred a Huguenot congregation of three hundred at Vassy. In 1570 the Huguenot forces, led by Admiral Gaspard de Coligny, defeated the royal troops, and Queen Catherine had to promise freedom of worship to the Huguenots and turn over four important fortified towns to them for two years as a guarantee that she would fulfill her promises. To seal the agreement Catherine gave her daughter Margaret in marriage to the youthful Protestant leader, Henry Bourbon, king of Navarre.

Catherine soon regretted her concessions and arranged to have Coligny assassinated. The attempt failed. She decided to try again and this time to include as victims the many Huguenot nobles who flocked to Paris for the wedding of Henry of Navarre and Margaret, thereby obliterating the Protestant leadership with one savage blow. Early in the morning of St. Bartholomew's Day, August 24, 1572, armed Catholic bands under Guise leadership fell on the sleeping Huguenots and murdered them. The massacre quickly spread from Paris to other cities. Before the slaughter ended, ten thousand Huguenots had been killed. Coligny's head was sent to the pope, and the Supreme Pontiff had a special medal struck to commemorate the massacre and commissioned the artist Vasari to paint the scenes in Paris when the Protestants fell. The unsmiling Philip II of Spain is said to have laughed aloud when he heard the news and ordered his clergy to sing a *Te Deum,* the triumphant hymn of thanks to God for victory.

The Huguenots reacted violently to the St. Bartholomew's Day Massacre, and the civil war was renewed. The Catholic party, led now by Henry, Duke of Guise, formed the Catholic League. Supported by Spain, the league became the dominant power in the government. Henry III, the last of Catherine de' Medici's sons, sought to escape from its domination by ordering the assassination of Henry of Guise in 1588. When the League rose in fury against the king, Henry allied himself with the Protestant leader, Henry of Navarre, and together they besieged Paris, the stronghold of the League. Henry III's murder in 1589 by a Dominican friar ended the Valois line. Henry of Navarre became king of France as Henry IV, first monarch of the Bourbon dynasty.

Five years passed before Henry could win recognition of his title from all of his subjects and take possession of his capital, Paris. He had to abjure

Protestantism and become a Catholic before the majority of his subjects would accept him. Henry did not find that too great a sacrifice; he is supposed to have said "Paris is well worth a mass." In reality, Henry was a *politique*. "We are born not only for ourselves," he said, "but above all to serve our country." He felt that conversion was a small price to pay for the restoration of peace to the realm. Most of his countrymen agreed.

Henry realized, however, that the Huguenots had to be placated if internal order was to be maintained. The country had reached a religious stalemate. Compromise offered the only way out, and Henry, with wisdom and tolerance, devoted his efforts to a solution. After long and difficult negotiations with religious and political leaders he issued the Edict of Nantes in 1598. This decree granted Huguenots liberty of conscience and freedom to worship in two places in every district except large towns, where they had to hold their services outside the walls. It gave them civil and legal rights equal to those of Catholics, set up mixed tribunals of Catholic and Protestant judges to hear cases in which Protestants were involved, and turned two hundred fortified towns over to Huguenot governors and garrisons so that they could protect themselves if the need arose.

This famous edict stands as a landmark in the history of religious toleration. For the first time the government of a major European state recognized that two religions could coexist without destroying the state. On the other hand, the edict created a potentially dangerous political situation. By allowing the Huguenots to control fortified places, Henry unwittingly created a "state within the state" that could become a serious threat to the supremacy of the central government.

The Spanish Predominance

When Charles V, who had been born in the Netherlands, came to Spain for the first time twenty months after he had inherited its throne, he did not like his new subjects, and they returned his antipathy with interest. The youthful Fleming who could not speak their language and who gave high offices in the Spanish government and Church to fellow Flemings was not to their taste. In 1520 open rebellion against his rule broke out and was put down only with difficulty. After this bad beginning Charles and the Spaniards began to be drawn to one another. The devoutly Catholic Spaniards admired his staunch defense of Catholicism and were proud of his vast dominions and imperial title. Charles, for his part, surrounded himself with Spanish grandees, appointed Spaniards to high office, and learned the language. He flattered all Spaniards when he remarked that Italian was the proper language to use when speaking with women, German with enemies, French with friends, and Spanish with God. More important, he made Spain

View of the Escorial

"The Escorial engrossed the leisure of more than thirty years of [Philip II's] life: it reflects in a peculiar manner his tastes, and the austere character of his mind. . . . The traveller who gazes on its long lines of cold gray stone, scarcely broken by any ornament, feels a dreary sensation creeping over him. . . . But he may read in this the true expression of the founder's character. Philip did not aim at the beautiful, much less at the festive and cheerful. The feelings which he desired to raise in the spectator were of that solemn, indeed sombre complexion, which corresponded best with his own religious faith." W. H. Prescott, HISTORY OF THE REIGN OF PHILIP THE SECOND (Boston, 1858).

Photograph from FPG

the fulcrum of his empire, the "fortress, strength, treasure, and sword," as he himself put it, of his effort to defeat the enemies of Catholic Christendom, whether Turk or Lutheran.

He passed on the concept of Spain as the bulwark of Catholicism to his son Philip II (1556–98). Under Philip's rule this idea was fused with a nationalistic fervor. The Spanish began to feel that God had given Spain the mission to save Catholicism in the Old World and to spread it in the New. This sense of messianic mission, buttressed by the vast resources Philip had at his command, made Spain the greatest world power in the second half of the sixteenth century.

The new king was Spanish to the core. Although his realm stretched far beyond the Spanish frontiers, he never left his homeland after 1559. He was a cold, reserved, and cruelly arrogant man. He lived in the Escorial, a magnificent but gloomy palace that he built near Madrid, separated from contact with human reality by the grotesquely elaborate court ceremonial that he himself devised. His policies and personality made him highly unpopular with most Europeans, and historians have often depicted him as a morose, fanatical tyrant. Spaniards, however, admired him, and today they count him as one of their greatest rulers—the one who led them to the highest pinnacle of power in their entire history.

PHILIP AND CATHOLICISM

Philip, like his predecessors Ferdinand and Isabella and Charles V, identified the interest of Spain with the interest of Catholicism. He was an especially devout man and consciously tried to adjust his own policies and actions to the teachings of his church. In his determination to maintain the supremacy of Catholicism he allowed harsh persecution of non-Catholics and gave a free hand to the Inquisition. Nevertheless, when Spanish national interests or political necessity clashed with religious concerns, the former always triumphed; Philip rationalized the conflict by persuading himself that what was best for Spain was best for Catholicism. For instance, as long as the pope agreed with his policies, Philip was loyal and submissive, but when the pope disagreed with him, he did not hesitate to show his anger and oppose him. Indeed, Philip's actions made him seem in some ways almost as antipapal as Henry VIII of England. He all but extinguished Rome's jurisdiction in ecclesiastical disputes in Spain, forbade the publication of papal decrees without prior approval of Spanish officials, disregarded the decrees that did not suit him (such as the one excommunicating anyone who took part in a bullfight), and deprived the pope of any voice in Church appointments. He regarded the Spanish Church as a branch of his government, demanding that it assist him both politically and financially at any time. The papacy paid a price for Spain's orthodoxy.

Like other rulers of his time, Philip viewed as a threat to his power the existence in his state of any religion other than his own. The Inquisition ruthlessly ferreted out the members of the small Spanish Protestant community. After a number had been burned alive and others had been meted out less horrible punishments, the movement collapsed.

The Moriscos, or converted Moors, offered a more serious problem. When in 1502 the Moors of Granada had been offered the choice of conversion or exile, most had chosen conversion. The Moriscos, however, retained their own language, dress, and customs, and many of them were suspected of being secret Moslems. Their nonconformity was intolerable to the government and the Catholic Church, which subjected them to constant harassment. In 1567 Philip issued a decree outlawing their distinctive practices and turned a deaf ear to their complaint that the forbidden practices had no religious significance. Goaded beyond endurance, the Moriscos rose in revolt in 1569. Government forces triumphed in 1570 after a conflict marked by atrocities on both sides. The government then moved the entire Morisco population to other parts of Spain and repopulated Granada with Spaniards of old Catholic stock. The persecution of the Moriscos did not end in their new homes. Finally in a series of decrees issued between 1609 and 1614 Philip's successor ordered their expulsion from Spain. There is reason to believe that many of them evaded these orders and remained in Spain, shielded by large landowners who found them more docile farm workers than the Spanish peasants.

TRIUMPH OVER THE TURKS

The Ottomans, who had given so much trouble to Philip's father, continued their westward push in the Mediterranean. By 1560 they had expelled the Christians from most of their outposts in northern Africa, and in 1570 they took the Venetian island of Cyprus, the easternmost Christian possession in the Mediterranean. At the pope's urging, Spain and Venice joined naval forces to stop the Turks. On October 7, 1571, Don John of Austria, Philip's half-brother, commanding an allied fleet of over 200 vessels, engaged the Turkish fleet of 250 vessels (almost the entire Ottoman naval force) at Lepanto in the Gulf of Corinth in Greece. In three hours of fierce fighting the allies destroyed 80 Turkish galleys, captured 130 others, killed or captured thousands of the enemy, and freed 10,000 Christian galley slaves.

Christian Europe went wild with joy at the news of the great victory, but because of an excess of caution and dissension among their leaders, the allies did not follow up their victory with further action against the enemy; they failed even to recover Cyprus. The Turks quickly built a new fleet and continued to ravage the coasts of the western Mediterranean. Nonetheless, Lepanto ended the threat of Turkish domination over the Mediterranean. For the first time the Turks had suffered an overwhelming defeat at the hands of Europeans, and the Christian world began to lose some of the terror long inspired by the Ottomans. The decline in Turkish power allowed Philip to turn his full attention northward, where serious trouble had broken out in the Netherlands.

THE REVOLT OF THE NETHERLANDS, 1568–1609

The seventeen provinces that made up the Netherlands or Low Countries, corresponding roughly to modern Holland, Belgium, and Luxembourg, formed Europe's wealthiest area. For centuries the southern provinces had been centers of trade, finance, and industry. The northern provinces first amassed wealth through fishing and then shifted to commerce and shipping. The tenor of life was predominantly urban, and though the cities of the Low Countries were not independent city-states as in Italy, they were the centers of economic and political power. The provinces had no special ties with one another, and there was no unified system of central administration. Each province had its own special privileges that dated back to medieval times, its own nobility, its own law courts, and its own parliamentary estates. The only bond that held them all together was their common sovereign.

When Charles V ruled over the Low Countries, they were satisfied, for he had been born among them and they thought of him as one of their own. On the other hand, Philip II of Spain was a foreigner, who could speak neither Dutch nor French. He never visited them after 1559, he levied heavy taxes, he kept Spanish troops among them, and he used Spaniards as his officials. In addition, Calvinism had won many converts, and when Philip ordered strict enforcement of the laws designed to repress the new faith, he incurred the hatred of the growing number of Protestants. He antagonized the nobility, too, by excluding them from his administration or giving them only unimportant posts. The nobles not only resented this but feared, with reason, that Philip planned to make himself absolute ruler and deprive the Low Countries of the special political and legal privileges they enjoyed. Several hundred nobles banded together to resist this development. One of Philip's officials contemptuously referred to them as "beggars," and they proudly adopted the name as their designation. In time it became the nickname for all Low Countrymen who opposed Philip.

Matters reached a crisis in 1566 when the Calvinists, who had been stirred up by the preachers, descended upon Catholic churches and monasteries in a frenzy of destruction. In their hatred of the symbols of "popery" they smashed images and stained glass windows and defaced paintings and tapestries. The disturbances confirmed Philip in his determination to root out Protestantism in the Low Countries, break the power of the nobility, and make himself absolute ruler. He sent in an army of ten thousand under the Duke of Alva to carry out these aims. Alva's brutality united nearly all Netherlanders in a common effort against the Spanish oppressor. In a land that till then had known no sentiment of national unity a new feeling of national consciousness arose, and in 1568 there was an open revolt.

Hatred for the Spanish reached a peak in 1576 when long-unpaid Spanish troops stationed in and around Antwerp sacked the city with dreadful ferocity. After this disaster, called the "Spanish Fury," Antwerp, formerly the chief business center of the Low Countries, never recovered its eminence. Infuriated Catholics and Protestants joined together in 1576 in an agreement called the Pacification of Ghent to drive out the Spaniards; but religious suspicions and Spanish arms and diplomacy soon broke up the alliance. Calvinists in the southern provinces sought refuge in the north (modern Holland), which strengthened Protestantism there and left the southern provinces (modern Belgium) in the hands of the Catholics.

In 1579 the ten southern provinces, under Spanish auspices, formed the League of Arras to defend Catholicism. The seven northern provinces, where the rebels had established their control, countered with the Union of Utrecht in which they bound themselves in a common effort against Spain. From that time, the north and south went their separate ways. In 1581 the United Provinces, as the northern provinces were called, declared their independence from Spain in the Act of Abjuration, whose words foreshadowed later declarations of independence in other lands. The document asserted that the ruler of a nation existed for the welfare of his subjects, rather than the people existing only to serve his purposes, and declared that a ruler who destroyed the liberties of his subjects could lawfully be deposed.

The new state chose William of Orange to occupy the office of chief executive or stadholder. William, a Protestant noble, had won the nickname of "the Silent" (*le Taciturne*) as a young man because of his reserve in diplomatic negotiations with the French, though actually he was an eloquent and affable person. He had led the rebels from the beginning and emerged during the struggle as one of the great leaders of Europe. His patience, tolerance, determination, concern for his people, and belief in government by consent held his followers together and kept alive their spirit of revolt. Philip recognized William's unique importance by offering the huge bounty of 25,000 gold crowns for his assassination, in the hope that the revolt would collapse with William's death. After several unsuccessful attempts had been made on his life, William fell in 1584 before the bullets of a young Catholic fanatic.

Although the revolt faltered, new leaders quickly took over in the persons of William's son and successor, Maurice of Nassau, who proved himself a skilled military tactician, and Jan van Oldenbarneveldt, who handled political and diplomatic affairs. The rebels continued to fight with the aid of English troops. After Philip's death in 1598 peace negotiations started. They dragged on until 1609, when the weary combatants agreed upon a truce of twelve years. For all practical purposes the seven United Provinces of the north, commonly called the Dutch Republic or Holland (from its largest province), had won independence, though the Spanish refused to acknowledge the fact for another forty years. The ten southern provinces, called the Spanish Netherlands, remained under Spanish rule.

THE ANNEXATION OF PORTUGAL

Spain gained temporary compensation for the setbacks in the Netherlands by Philip's acquisition of Portugal. In 1580 the Portuguese ruling line died out. Philip claimed the throne through his mother, eldest daughter of King Manuel (1495–1521). Although others had better claims, Philip used diplomacy and threats to gain official approval for his succession. The Portuguese people, who harbored a traditional hatred for Spain, took up arms in support of another candidate, but Spanish troops easily put down the rising and Philip had himself crowned. He thereby united the Iberian peninsula under one scepter for the first time in nine centuries and acquired the vast Portuguese overseas possessions in South America, Africa, and Asia. Sixty years later in 1640 the Spanish lost these gains when the Portuguese won back their independence.

THE ANGLO-SPANISH RIVALRY

The open aid that England gave to the rebellious United Provinces after prolonged surreptitious assistance was one more in a long series of provocations that Spain suffered from the island kingdom. During the reign of Mary Tudor, the second of Philip's four wives, England had been in the Spanish camp. When Elizabeth came to the throne in 1558, she retained the Spanish alliance—in fact, she let Philip think that she might accept the marriage proposal he made to her. Soon, however, relations between the two nations became strained. English merchant ships boldly traded with the Spanish colonies in the New World despite Spanish efforts to keep foreigners out of the trade. English pirates and adventurous "sea dogs," such as Sir John Hawkins and Sir Francis Drake, preyed on Spanish shipping, made daring raids on coastal towns in Spanish America, and carried slaves from Africa to the Spanish colonies in the New World.

Philip had to endure these aggravations because of his involvement in the Netherlands and because his lack of sea power made it impossible for him to invade England. Instead, he gave his support to intrigues to make Mary Stuart, former Queen of Scots and a Catholic, the ruler of England in place of Elizabeth, and thereby to re-establish Catholicism and amity with Spain. Mary, whose great-grandfather was Henry VII, was heir to the unmarried Elizabeth. She had inherited the throne of Scotland from her father and also reigned as queen of France for a year before the premature death of her husband, Francis II (1560). Her religion, her politics, and her immoral personal life enraged her subjects, who in 1567 forced her to abdicate in favor of her infant son, James VI. She fled to England, where Elizabeth decided that prison was the safest place for an exile who was a Catholic rival for the English throne.

Meanwhile, the English watched closely the course of events in the Netherlands, fearing that if Spain triumphed, it could easily mount an invasion of England from the Low Countries. Since the reign of Henry VII, England had been sensitive to the presence of a major power in the Low Countries. When the murder of William the Silent weakened the rebels, Elizabeth sent six thousand English soldiers to help them. Then in 1587, when a new Catholic plot to assassinate Elizabeth and give the throne to Mary Stuart was uncovered, Elizabeth reluctantly sent Mary to the block. Mary's execution persuaded Philip that he had to invade England to win it for Catholicism and for himself. He declared himself a claimant to England's throne. Indeed, Mary's death freed him from the anxiety that if she had become queen of England, France might have benefited more than Spain, since Mary, whose mother was a Guise and who had herself been raised in France, had strong ties with that land.

In 1587 he started to assemble his invasion fleet. Officially called the "Most Fortunate Armada," it soon won the popular name of "Invincible Armada" in tribute to its might. In May, 1588, 130 vessels manned by 8,000 sailors and carrying 19,000 soldiers and several hundred priests (including the head of the Inquisition) who were to aid in the re-Catholicizing of England, sailed from Lisbon. The fleet's mission was to establish a beachhead on the English coast, then cross back to the Continent to escort 30,000 Spanish troops from the Netherlands under the command of the Duke of Parma. Thus reinforced, the invaders would march on London.

Philip's carefully laid plans took insufficient account of the ineptitude of his commanders, the seamanship and gunnery of the English, and the vagaries of the weather in the English Channel. In July, 1588, in one of the most famous naval battles in history the smaller English fleet harried the lumbering ships of the Armada, broke up the Spaniards' formations, cut out individual ships, and destroyed them one by one. The Spaniards tried to regroup in the harbor of Calais, where they planned to rendezvous with Parma's troops, but a Dutch fleet kept Parma bottled up many miles away at Bruges. The English set fire to eight small vessels and let them drift into the Spanish fleet, driving it out to sea. Once again the English attacked, and the Spaniards, hopelessly beaten, decided to sail for home. A violent storm, famed as the "Protestant wind," blew the hapless remnants of the Armada around the northern tip of Scotland. Many ships came to grief on its rugged shores, as well as off northern Ireland. Of the 130 vessels that had sailed out of Lisbon, a third never returned, and most of the ones that limped back suffered severe damage and heavy casualties. English losses totaled 60 men, with not one ship lost or even seriously damaged.

The rout of the Armada did not end the war. The conflict dragged on until 1604 and ended in a draw, with neither side able to claim victory. Nor did the battle mark the decline of Spanish naval power and the beginning of English maritime supremacy, as is sometimes claimed. English sea power had surpassed that of Spain for some time; in fact, the Spanish strengthened their navy and increased their sea power after the Armada's defeat. The English were never able to blockade Spain or to cut off the Spanish treasure fleets from the New World. Between 1588 and 1603 the treasure fleets brought more American gold and silver into Spain than during any other fifteen-year period in Spanish history. Popular misconception has it that English, Dutch, and French raiders captured vast amounts of Spanish treasure. Actually, during the many years in which the Spanish treasure fleets regularly crossed the Atlantic, raiders captured significant portions of the fleet only twice: the Dutch in 1628 and the British in 1656.

The Armada's most important effect seems to have been psychological.

The English triumph gave great encouragement to Protestants everywhere, who took it as a sign that God was on their side. The Catholics hardly shared this interpretation, of course, but the defeat made them realize that Spain, the wealthiest and strongest power in the world, was not invincible. Although Spain continued to dominate Europe for another generation, other nations no longer stood in quite the same awe of it. In England the story of the Armada became part of the national legend, as a symbol of the victory of free men over tyranny and of youthful vigor and daring over cautious and bumbling old age. It also served to obscure the vacillation of so much of Queen Elizabeth's diplomacy and war policy.

Philip tried to regain some of his prestige by intervention in the religious wars of France in the hope that he could establish domination of that country. He sent troops to aid the Catholic League. His plans came to nothing when Henry of Navarre became a Catholic, for it was no longer possible for Philip to claim that he was in France to defend it from Protestantism and he had to withdraw.

FINANCIAL TROUBLES AND BANKRUPTCY

Vast sums poured into Spain each year from the seemingly inexhaustible gold and silver mines of Mexico and Peru. Yet there never seemed to be enough to cover the costs of Philip's wars and domestic expenditures. He started his reign under the handicap of an enormous debt inherited from Charles V, and within little more than a year he had to make a declaration of bankruptcy. He never afterward managed to achieve financial solvency, despite desperate expedients. He wrung every penny out of the old taxes and imposed so many new and oppressive ones that the country groaned under the burden and economic life was seriously handicapped. He sold titles of nobility and high offices, established government monopolies on important commodities, forced contributions from the clergy, and borrowed heavily and at high interest rates. Still he could not make ends meet, and in 1575 the government again declared it could not pay its creditors. A composition of the debts by which the creditors suffered heavy losses was agreed upon, and the government staggered along for a few more years. Then the tremendous expenditures on the Armada threw the state once more into hopeless financial difficulties. Finally in 1596 the bankers refused to lend any more money, and for the third time Philip had to declare his state bankrupt. When he died in 1598, he left his successor an enormous and unpayable debt.

During Philip's long reign Spain reached the peak of its power and greatness—and also began the descent from its high point. Philip tried to do too much at one time. He attempted simultaneously to develop, colonize, and protect a world empire, fight the Turks, retain mastery over the Netherlands, dominate Italy, France, and England, and always and everywhere defend Catholicism and crush Protestantism. This impossible program impoverished his country and gained it the enmity of other countries. The wonder is not that Philip failed to reach his goals but that he accomplished as much as he did.

Elizabethan England

Not the least of the obstacles that prevented Philip from realizing his ambitions was the woman who sat on England's throne. Elizabeth I (1558–1603), daughter of Henry VIII and Anne Boleyn and last ruler of the Tudor line, proved to be even more able than her father or her grandfather. When she came to the throne, she found her country on the brink of anarchy. Under her inspired leadership the nation rallied and reached new heights of power and prosperity. Before she became queen Elizabeth had known adversity and humiliation; she had even faced the danger of execution during the reign of her Catholic half-sister Mary Tudor. These experiences disciplined her in self-reliance and taught her to be crafty and to dissemble. She had a keen mind, a good education, and a natural aptitude for politics, diplomacy, and intrigue. Above all, she loved her people and her country—an affection that her subjects returned many times over. Few rulers have been blessed with the devotion given this lonely woman. It was no boast when she said in a speech to her last Parliament in 1601, "And though God has raised us high, yet this I count the glory of my crown, that I have reigned with your loves. . . . And though you have had and may have mightier and wiser princes sitting in this seat, yet you never had, nor shall have, any love you better."

Following the pattern set by her father and grandfather, Elizabeth ruled with a strong and sometimes despotic hand. Her instinct for absolutism was, of necessity, conditioned by her need of Parliament's cooperation for legislation and taxes. She knew the importance of able and devoted counselors, and she chose her advisers wisely and well (mostly from the gentry) and retained them long. Her principal minister for forty years was a commoner named William Cecil, whom Elizabeth later raised to the peerage as Lord Burghley. His detailed knowledge of the workings of government, his enormous capacity for work, his moderation, his interest in economic growth, his sound common sense, and his obedience to the royal will made him an invaluable instrument of the great queen; to him belongs much of the credit for the success of her reign.

Despite her penchant for absolutism, Elizabeth's technique in ruling was to proceed with caution, to compromise, and never to be so committed to a policy that retreat was impossible. She demonstrated these qualities at the very outset of her reign when she was confronted with the legacy of religious strife and near bankruptcy left by her predecessor Mary Tudor.

Since she had no strong religious feelings herself, the national interest rather than religious conviction dictated the course of her policies. In France she would have been called a *politique*. Though she had no intention of re-establishing papal authority in England, she sought to placate English Catholics and attempted to beguile the Continental Catholic powers into thinking that she might return to Rome in order to reduce their hostility to England. At the same time, she resented the pressure of the extreme English Calvinists, or Puritans as they came to be called, for further religious reform. She chose to steer between the two extremes by attempting to create a national church that offered a compromise in theology and worship, which she hoped would hold the loyalty of the mass of her subjects. Adherence to the state religion became synonymous with patriotism.

ECONOMIC EXPANSION

The economic policies of the government did much to promote the economic growth of the country. By prudent management and economies Elizabeth reduced the indebtedness she had inherited with the throne and restored confidence in England's financial position. As a result, her government could borrow money at low rates of interest from European bankers at a time when other monarchs, such as Philip II, had to pay high rates because they repeatedly declared themselves unable to meet their financial obligations. As part of her economic program Elizabeth ordered a reform of English money. So many coins of doubtful value or short weight were in circulation that people had no confidence in the currency. During 1560–61 the government called in the old money and issued new coins whose face value corresponded to their intrinsic worth. The restoration of public confidence in the coinage proved a boon to business activity.

To encourage the growth of foreign commerce, the government gave monopolies to joint-stock companies that were established by English merchants to trade with new overseas areas. The Muscovy Company trading with Russia, the Eastland Company in the Baltic, the Levant Company in the Mediterranean, and the East India Company (1600), destined to become the greatest of all, were among the trading companies founded during Elizabeth's reign. The activities of these companies, as well as of the bold and sometimes piratical English seamen who cut in on the trading monopolies that Spain and Portugal tried to maintain in their overseas possessions, brought new wealth to England. They also served to advance English sea power by training men in seamanship and by providing a merchant fleet that could be armed when needed to reinforce the royal navy.

Industry and agriculture prospered, too. A rise in population created a heightened demand for manufactured goods and foodstuffs, and this demand, together with the additional gold and silver brought into the country by increased foreign trade, caused a steady rise in prices. The price rise produced an optimistic attitude among businessmen and enabled them to make large profits, which they reinvested in productive business or agricultural enterprise. The increase in foreign trade gave a special boost to industrial production, especially the manufacture of woolen cloth, which was England's most important industry and chief export. The woolen industry benefited, too, from the migration into England of Calvinists from France and the southern Netherlands who had fled their native lands to escape persecution. They introduced new ideas and techniques that proved of value to English industrial development.

Shipbuilding and coal mining also underwent major expansion during this era. The growth of sea commerce and the needs of the royal navy provided the stimulus for shipbuilding. The growth of coal mining was due to the general increase in industrial activity. Expanding industries such as iron production, glassmaking, and the manufacture of salt by evaporation of sea water found it cheaper and more efficient to use coal for fuel than to depend upon England's still plentiful but dwindling timber supply. In London people began to burn coal instead of wood for cooking and heating. Much of the coal was shipped by sea to London from Newcastle, a port on the Tyne River, and was therefore called sea coal. Some of the coal mines and the new industrial plants were large enterprises with much capital invested in them and hundreds of workers.

In its eagerness to support economic development the government tried to mobilize the labor resources of the nation in the interest of the employers. The Statute of Artificers of 1563, which brought together many existing laws and practices, sought to increase the size of the labor force by ordering all able-bodied men except scholars, gentlemen, and landowners to follow a trade or work in agriculture. To make sure that they were trained in the skills needed to produce goods of high quality, the statute fixed the period of apprenticeship at seven years. It empowered the justices of the peace to fix maximum wages in their districts and ordered punishment for employers who paid above the maximum. This statute with some modifications remained in force until the early nineteenth century. It was supplemented in 1601 by the Poor Law, which like the Statute of Artificers codified existing laws and practices. It required local authorities to levy a tax to provide relief money for unemployable indigents, and to establish workhouses and houses of correction for "sturdy beggars," the indigents who could work.

FOREIGN AFFAIRS

On her accession the chief threat to Elizabeth's rule came from France and, more specifically, from French influence in Scotland. Mary Stuart, Queen of Scots, claimant to the English throne, and wife of the youthful king of France, lived in France. Her mother, Mary of Lorraine, sister of the

Guises who had great power in the French government, ruled as regent in Scotland in her stead with the support of French troops. For a time a French invasion of England from Scotland seemed imminent. A religious-nationalist revolution in Scotland under the leadership of the fiery and austere Calvinist reformer John Knox saved England from that threat. The French were forced to withdraw in 1560. The Scottish Parliament abolished papal power in Scotland and established a Calvinist presbyterianism as the official religion of the country. The danger to England of a French attack through Scotland was gone forever. Queen Mary returned to Scotland, only to flee to Elizabeth's less than tender refuge in 1567.

For the rest of Elizabeth's reign France, torn by civil war, no longer offered a serious threat to England. In fact, for brief periods the two ancient enemies were allied with one another. Spain became the chief enemy. England remained at peace from 1560 to 1585, the longest period without war that England had known since the thirteenth century, but Elizabeth did everything she could short of war to harass and inconvenience Spain. In 1585 Elizabeth sent troops to help the Dutch, thereby starting the war with Spain that lasted until 1604.

For years Elizabeth used the question of her marriage as an instrument of diplomacy in her relations with other powers. Everyone assumed that she would wed, and nearly every eligible ruler in Europe proposed to her at one time or other. As many as twelve representatives of willing royal suitors were at her court at a time. As she grew older, the applicants for her hand were sometimes years younger than the Virgin Queen, but this did not deter them from the pursuit. Elizabeth always seemed ready to accept whichever proposal seemed politically most valuable at a given time, but then always found good reasons that made her change her mind. She never married.

The defeat of the Spanish Armada in 1588 climaxed Elizabeth's reign. In the remaining years of her life the people grew increasingly restive under her strong rule. The war with Spain cost much in men and money and seemed to achieve nothing. A famine occurred in the late 1590's. Trade declined during the war years. Her trusted counselors died, and she could not find suitable replacements. Parts of Ireland were in open rebellion in support of the Catholic faith. The Puritans continually pressed for reforms that would move the English church in the direction of Calvinism. Elizabeth was dependent upon Parliament for taxes to carry on the war, but she found it increasingly difficult to manage the House of Commons, which had a strong Puritan element in it. These adverse developments only slightly tarnished the glory of her long reign. When she died in 1603, at the age of seventy, she left England immeasurably stronger, wealthier, more united, and prouder than she had found it at her accession forty-five years earlier.

CHAPTER SEVEN

The Borderlands of Europe

So FAR we have dealt almost exclusively with the countries of Western Europe—Italy, Spain, France, England, Germany, and the Netherlands. These countries take up a relatively small area: it is only 800 miles from Rome to Amsterdam, and 600 miles from London to Prague. Yet they formed the heartland of Western civilization. Most of the institutions, ideas, and techniques that characterize Western society and that have spread to all parts of the globe had their origins in these countries.

On the north this heartland was bordered by the Scandinavian kingdoms and on the east by the Slavic lands and the Ottoman Empire. At one time or another through the centuries each of these borderlands played an important part in the course of general Western history. The Ottoman Turks during the fifteenth and sixteenth centuries were the most feared people of Europe. In the sixteenth century Poland, which was far larger than it is today, seemed destined to become a great power. Russia emerged as the chief Slavic state in the seventeenth century, though its time of greatest power and influence has come only recently. In the sixteenth and seventeenth centuries Denmark and Sweden became important powers.

The Creation of the Russian State

First place among the royal statemakers of Europe belongs to the men who ruled over Muscovy in the fifteenth and sixteenth centuries. No other European monarch equaled their success in establishing absolute rule over their subjects. The process started with Ivan the Great (1462–1505), who transformed the grand duchy of Moscow into an all-Russian national state. His autocratic, centralizing policies and the pomp and ceremony with which he surrounded himself set the pattern for the men who followed on the Russian throne.

Many of the high nobility, especially the princes who had once ruled over lands absorbed by Muscovy and the descendants of the former rulers, resented the efforts of the Muscovite grand dukes to establish themselves as absolute monarchs. The princes had to accept unification under the leadership of the grand duchy, but they wanted to share in the rule of the new state. Instead, Ivan III and his successor, Vasilii III (1505–33), did everything possible to curb their power and privileges. They were allowed to enter Muscovy's service but were not used as chief officials or advisers. When the princes protested, they were exiled, forced to become monks, or even executed.

Vasilii's death in 1533 gave the aristocracy its chance to seize power, for Vasilii's heir, Ivan IV, was an infant of three. Instead of uniting in a common cause against the throne, the great princely families vied with one another for control of the state, resorted to violence and murder, and threw the country into anarchy. In public the great nobles showed respect for the youthful monarch, but inside the Kremlin they treated him with contempt, looted his treasury, and committed acts of violence in his presence.

IVAN IV

Ivan suffered these affronts with the resolve that when he grew up, he would show the aristocrats that he was indeed their master. He took his first step at the age of thirteen when he suddenly ordered the arrest of a prince who had offended him and had him strangled and thrown to the dogs in the kennels. Three years later he announced that he would hold his coronation and take a wife. He had himself crowned with the title of tsar in 1547 and assumed personal rule of the country. He chose his tsaritsa from more than a thousand girls who are said to have appeared in answer to his summons to the Russian aristocracy to present their daughters to him. He picked the daughter of a noble family, against the wishes of the princes, who wanted him to marry into a princely family.

During the first thirteen years of his personal rule Ivan instituted a series of administrative and military reforms of major importance. A new law code modernized court procedure and improved administrative practices. Local government was reorganized to allow greater power to locally elected officials. A manual for the Church was drawn up that dealt with Church administration as well as religious and moral questions. In 1556 he established a ratio between the amount of land that a noble held and the number of soldiers that the noble had to provide for the tsar's army. Failure to meet this quota, or to pay a cash sum in lieu of soldiers, was punishable by loss of land. The noble himself had to serve in the tsar's forces from the age of fifteen until death, or until illness or old age incapacitated him. Ivan's record of domestic accomplishment was paralleled by his accomplishments in foreign affairs. Military campaigns against the Tatars of Kazan and Astrakhan brought the entire basin of the Volga River down to the Caspian Sea under his rule. This fertile territory of thousands of square miles was opened up to Russian colonization, and the Volga itself became a chief artery of expanding Russian commerce.

Friction grew between Ivan and the great aristocrats, although until the 1560's he remained on good terms with them and chose his closest friends and advisers from their number. Then he turned on them, arresting, exiling, or executing high nobles and their families on the slightest pretext. In 1564 he embarked on a policy designed to end forever the power of the aristocracy. He suddenly left Moscow with a great retinue and threatened to abdicate because of what he called the treasonous conduct of the aristocracy and clergy. He remained away until his subjects invited him back on his own conditions, which were that the realm be divided into two segments. In one segment, the existing governmental machinery continued to operate and the landowners remained undisturbed. In the other, called the *Oprichnina*, a new administrative organization was set up and the tsar confiscated all private property. Ivan revealed his purpose by choosing to include in the Oprichnina that part of his realm containing the properties of the princes and the old high nobility. He kept about one-fourth of the confiscated lands for himself and gave the rest to the *oprichniki*, the men of the Oprichnina organization, who held the lands they received on condition of military service to Ivan. He executed many of the former proprietors (estimates of the number executed run from 400 to 10,000); the rest he settled on the frontiers, far from their old homes, on service tenure, transforming them from private proprietors to men who held their land in return for military service to the tsar.

The ostensible purpose of the Oprichnina was to root out treason. It was symbolized by the oprichniki's black uniforms, black horses, and the dog's head and broom attached to their saddles. In fact, Ivan used the oprichniki to terrorize his subjects into accepting his will without question. The oprichniki murdered, tortured, and pillaged not only the aristocracy but also the plain people. In 1570, when a rumor reached him that citizens of

Novgorod planned to put their city under Polish rule, Ivan, without bothering to check the story, ordered the oprichniki to sack the city and harry the entire region. In Novgorod itself the slaughter of more than 60,000 people irreparably destroyed the city's prosperity and prestige. Similar episodes, though not as bloody, took place in other parts of the realm. Ivan disbanded the Oprichnina in 1572, deciding that it had accomplished its purpose. The power of the aristocracy had been smashed and everyone in the realm had been forced to recognize that "the great and the small live by the favor of the sovereign." But the violence of the Oprichnina upset social and economic life and left a legacy of suffering and discontent that was not erased for many years.

The damage done to the Russian social fabric by the Oprichnina was compounded by the long and unsuccessful Livonian War, which dragged on from 1558 to 1583. The conflict began when Ivan invaded neighboring Livonia (comprising present-day Estonia and parts of Latvia). He hoped to gain access to the Baltic by taking Livonia from the Knights of the Teutonic Order, military monks who had held it since the Middle Ages. The Knights turned for help to their other neighbors, and Russia soon found itself fighting against Lithuania, Poland, and Sweden. The war brought much sacrifice and suffering to the Russian people, and in the end Ivan had to relinquish his ambitions for Livonian territory and also lost some of his own realm to Sweden.

The rebuff to Russian ambitions of westward expansion was balanced by successes in the east. During the sixteenth century Russian merchants, especially the Stroganov family, penetrated into Siberia in search of furs, other forest products, and metals. In 1583 a band of nearly a thousand Cossacks from the steppes of southern Russia sponsored by the Stroganovs conquered western Siberia for Russia.

Even as a child Ivan IV had evidenced the extremes of cruelty that marked him as a man. As he grew older his name became a byword for savagery and bloodlust. His subjects, who stood in dread and awe of him, dubbed him Ivan the Terrible. In one of his fits of ungovernable rage he killed his eldest son with a blow of his staff. Periods of vice-ridden dissipation alternated with seizures of remorse, when the frantically religious Ivan would prostrate himself with wild fervor before his icons. He kept lists of the people murdered at his command and paid priests to pray for their souls. He held the unshakable conviction that his sovereign power came from God, that he represented God on earth, and that those who resisted his power resisted God. By the time of his death in 1584, Ivan had established unchallenged authority in a vast realm that reached from the Polish frontiers far into Asia and from the Arctic Ocean to the Caspian Sea, but his subjects paid a heavy price in human suffering and degradation during and for many years after his reign.

THE TIME OF TROUBLES

On Ivan's death his eldest surviving son Fedor became tsar. Weak in mind and body, Fedor gladly allowed his wife's brother, Boris Godunov, to run the country. Boris was a keen, vigorous man of noble but not princely birth. He followed Ivan's centralizing and autocratic policies without the use of terror and established himself so securely that, when Fedor died childless in 1598, he easily gained the throne for himself. He soon encountered grave troubles. A series of crop failures brought on famine, brigandage, and widespread unrest; the peasantry, who formed the great mass of the population, resisted the new authority over them that had been given to the lords; and nobles and princes who were Boris' social equals or superiors considered him a usurper and intrigued against him. Boris' difficulties reached their climax when a pretender to the throne claiming to be Dmitrii, a son of Ivan IV who had died as a child, invaded Russia in 1604 with Polish aid and won a large following. His appearance ushered in the decade known as the Time of Troubles, during which the country was torn by civil war, social disorder, brigandage, and foreign invasion.

The unsettled state of the country following Boris' death and the murder of his son and successor by the false Dmitrii in 1605 gave the aristocrats a chance to realize their old ambition. A group led by Prince Vasilii Shuiskii murdered Dmitrii and proclaimed Shuiskii tsar. Risings of the peasants, a new false Dmitrii, and an invasion by Poland and Sweden induced a coup d'état that overthrew Shuiskii in 1610. The aristocrats offered the throne to the Roman Catholic son of the king of Poland on condition that he govern with the aid of the nobles.

The Catholic Polish occupation of Moscow evoked a national liberation movement, led by Orthodox priests and a meat dealer named Kuzma Minin. A militia of 100,000 came into being, composed mainly of lesser nobles and city people; joined by Cossack forces, they drove out the Poles in 1612. The victors summoned a national assembly (*zemskii sobor*) to meet in the city of Moscow in January, 1613, to elect a new tsar. The assembly's choice, after heated debate and much behind-the-scenes negotiation, fell on Michael Romanov, sixteen-year-old scion of a noble family. The assembly made Michael the absolute ruler of Russia with all the powers that Ivan IV had exercised.

The election of Michael marked the end of the Time of Troubles. The state that emerged from those difficult years was unlike any Western state, and far more absolute. It was a "service state," in which every subject from the greatest noble to the humblest peasant had to perform specific functions designed to preserve and aggrandize the powers of the state. In return for the right to hold land and rule over their peasants, the nobles had to serve in the tsar's army and bureaucracy. In turn, the peasants had to work for their lords and pay them dues in cash and kind, so that the lords had the means to perform their state service.

THE RUSSIAN CHURCH

In their drive to gain autocratic power the Muscovite rulers had an invaluable ally in the Russian Church. Following the example set by the Church in the defunct Byzantine Empire, the Orthodox Church considered itself subservient to the ruler. It preached submission to the throne and glorified the ruler's absolutism by declaring that he had Godlike powers. In support of the claims of the throne to autocratic power, theologians advanced the theory that the city of Moscow was the "third Rome." According to this theory, the first Rome, in Italy, and the second Rome, Constantinople, had both fallen for their sins; Moscow succeeded Constantinople as the center of the true faith and the capital of the Christian world.

A serious threat to the power of the Church—and thus of the tsar—was raised in the sixteenth century by a group of churchmen who held that the acquisition of material goods undermined the ascetic ideals of monastic life. They urged that the monasteries rid themselves of wealth and land. The reformers had the support of secular landlords who, as in other European lands, yearned to acquire Church property. The throne finally confirmed the monasteries' right to keep their riches and to add to them. The support given to the throne's claim of absolutism by the Church leaders opposing monastic reform doubtless helped persuade the throne to decide against the reformers. By the second half of the sixteenth century certain monasteries owned huge complexes of property and, after the tsar, were the greatest landlords of Muscovy.

ECONOMIC CHANGES

In the latter part of the fifteenth and for much of the sixteenth centuries, while the rulers of Muscovy laid the foundations of absolutism, Russia experienced an era of economic growth. Money came increasingly into use, much new land was taken under the plow, population grew, internal trade flourished, and cities grew in size and took on new importance as centers of trade and industry and markets for farm goods. Foreign trade increased with both the East and the West. Trade with the West received an important stimulus when English seamen, in search of a northeast passage to the Indies, sailed above Scandinavia into the White Sea and in 1553 landed on the shores of northern Russia. Although the route was open for only three summer months (ice and storms made it unnavigable for the rest of the year), a lively trade with England sprang up, and then with the Netherlands.

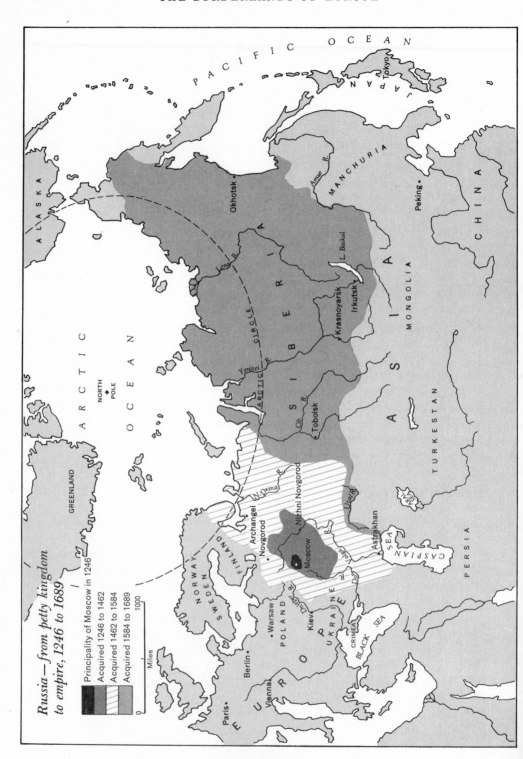

PACIFIC OCEAN

ALASKA

ARCTIC OCEAN

NORTH
POLE

GREENLAND

ARCTIC CIRCLE

S I B E R I A

Okhotsk

Lena R.

Yenisei R.

Ob R.

Tobolsk

Krasnoyarsk

Irkutsk

L. Baikal

Amur R.

MANCHURIA

Peking •

CHINA

MONGOLIA

A S I A

TURKESTAN

PERSIA

CASPIAN SEA

Astrakhan

Ural R.

Volga R.

Nizhni Novgorod

Don R.

Moscow

Novgorod

Archangel

N. Dvina R.

FINLAND

NORWAY

SWEDEN

Berlin •

Warsaw •

POLAND

Kiev •

UKRAINE

Dnieper R.

CRIMEA

BLACK SEA

E U R O P E

Vienna •

Paris •

*Russia—from petty kingdom
to empire, 1246 to 1689*

Principality of Moscow in 1246
Acquired 1246 to 1462
Acquired 1462 to 1584
Acquired 1584 to 1689

Miles
0   1000

JAPAN

Tokyo •

166

The economic upswing continued until the last third of the sixteenth century, when a catastrophic depression swept the country. A mass flight of population from the most populous and economically important parts of Russia, especially the Moscow region and the northwest, reached its height in the 1570's and 1580's. In some districts as many as 97 per cent of the farm homesteads were empty, and great expanses of land lay untilled. Most of the migrants fled east and south into the regions that Ivan IV's conquests had opened up to Russian settlement. A much smaller number went into the far less hospitable districts of northern Russia. Still others fled into the "untamed steppe," the no-man's land beyond Russia's southern frontiers, to join the Cossack bands that roamed its open plains. The great depopulation of the economic centers had serious repercussions on economic life. Agriculture, by far the chief industry of the country, suffered from the withdrawal of so much land from cultivation and the flight of so many farm workers. Trade and industry suffered from the sharp decline in both supply and demand.

The most important cause of the mass flight seems to have been the series of natural and man-made calamities that engulfed the most populous parts of the country in the latter half of Ivan IV's reign: the long Livonian War bringing heavy taxation and enemy invasion in the northwest; devastating Tatar raids; at least two plague epidemics and several years of famine; above all, the Oprichnina, with its violence, plundering, and heavy exactions. Recovery began in the late 1580's. People drifted back to their old homes, deserted land was once more cultivated, and agricultural production increased. The recovery continued until the beginning of the next century when a series of crop failures brought on famine and unrest, which was aggravated by the other miseries of the Time of Troubles. Once again, thousands fled their homes and economic life came to a standstill.

THE ENSERFMENT OF THE PEASANTRY

At the insistence of landlords in the fifteenth century, rulers began to impose restrictions on the right of peasants to move freely from one place to another and permitted lords to have legal jurisdiction over their peasant tenants. Until the economic upswing of the late fifteenth and sixteenth centuries, however, the landlords usually demanded only payments in cash and kind from their peasant renters and only exceptionally required the peasants to work for them. The economic expansion provided an opportunity for the lords to profit from producing for the market on their own account. To get the necessary labor, they increased their demands for labor rent from the peasants. The lords also raised the money rents, for they needed more money to meet the costs of the service the government now required of them and to cover the rise in living costs accompanying the economic expansion. In addition to the increased demands of their lords, the peasants' taxes rose, for the government needed more money to pay for its policies of war and expansion.

In order to meet these financial demands, many peasants borrowed from their lords at extortionate rates of interest. The loan agreement required the peasant to pay the interest by working full-time for the lord, and the law forbade the peasant to leave until he had paid his debt. Since the peasant was unable to amass enough cash to pay the principal of the loan, he became a permanent peon of the lord, bound by his indebtedness. The economic downturn in the latter part of the sixteenth century forced more of the peasantry into debt servitude. Even those who managed to stay out of debt lost their freedom: the labor shortage caused by the mass migrations impelled the lords to persuade the government to issue laws in the 1580's and 1590's forbidding peasants to move and compelling those who had moved to come back. Thus, the peasant lost his right of freedom of movement and became legally bound to the lord on whose land he lived. Not all the peasants who fled during the great migration returned home, but even they did not escape the new restrictions (except the small number who went north or joined the Cossacks), for the lands on which they settled belonged to nobles and the laws bound them to their new lords.

The peasants' resentment of these restrictions set off peasant uprisings in every part of Russia, but their efforts came to nothing. They had lost their freedom of movement and were subject to the will of their lord, having to work for him, make him payments in cash and kind, hold land at his pleasure, and accept his legal jurisdiction over them. In other words, by the seventeenth century the once-free Russian peasant had become a serf.

THE ROMANOVS, 1613–1682

Michael, first tsar of the Romanov dynasty that ruled Russia for the next three hundred years, was a weak and self-effacing man. First his mother and her greedy kinsmen dominated the state, then his father Filaret, whom Michael had made patriarch (head) of the Russian Church, made himself coruler and ran the state until his death in 1633. On Michael's death in 1645 his sixteen-year-old son Alexis succeeded. Like his father, Alexis lacked qualities of leadership and allowed a succession of royal favorites to run the state for their personal gain. Alexis was succeeded in 1676 by his son Feodor, a sickly lad of fourteen, whose reign of six years was also dominated by grasping favorites.

Under these inept rulers Russia's economic structure recovered only slowly from the severe blows it had previously received. In the 1620's a very gradual upturn began. During the succeeding decades new crises, new wars, new uprisings, and misgovernment acted as brakes to economic improvement, but by the end of the seventeenth century the Russian economy had made up most of the ground it had lost.

Nearly all the great aristocratic families who had been so important in preceding centuries had been wiped out by the policy of extermination mounted by Ivan IV and by the disorders of the Time of Troubles. The few families that survived still kept some of their prestige, either because they were kinsmen of the Romanovs or had proved their loyalty to the new dynasty. The lesser nobility had also suffered in former times, especially during the Time of Troubles. Many had been killed; others had lost everything and sunk into the peasantry. Yet, as a class, they triumphed. They had been loyal partisans of the tsars in their struggle in the sixteenth century against the great nobility, leaders in the national revival of the Time of Troubles, and electors of Michael. They were rewarded by becoming the ruling class in place of the old aristocracy. They received land grants, serfs, and high posts in government from their grateful sovereign, in return for service in the army and the bureaucracy.

During the second half of the seventeenth century the status of the serfs deteriorated still further. In the absence of government restrictions the serf owners bought and sold peasants like so many cattle. They even killed them without fear of punishment. The least oppressed were the 10 per cent of the peasantry who were not serfs but who lived on land that belonged to the state, mainly in the infertile regions of northern Russia. These people, who were supposed to pay taxes and quitrents to the state, were theoretically restricted in their ability to move about, but were in practice relatively free. Still other peasants fled from the settled regions to join Cossack bands that roamed the Black Sea steppes. In the course of time the Cossack bands had formed loose, semimilitary, autonomous federations along the chief rivers of the southern steppes—the Dnieper, the Don, and the Volga. Hardened by their rough lives, they included in their ranks cutthroats capable of barbaric atrocities. The Cossacks won a reputation for military prowess both in the service of Russia and in the Polish army.

The increased restrictions on personal liberty, the misrule by favorites, the wars that filled thirty of the seventy years between Michael's accession and Feodor's death, the heavy tax burden resulting from these conflicts, and the harsh punishments meted out to those who tried to escape their military or tax obligations, all served to stir up discontent and unrest among the masses. A number of uprisings in the chief cities were harshly repressed. In rural areas the peasants usually expressed their discontent by running away. Sometimes they turned to violence, bursting into disorganized local outbreaks. In 1670 there was a mass rural uprising that for a few months threatened the survival of the government. Stenka Razin, a Cossack who had won notoriety as a freebooter along the shores of the Caspian, led his gang along the Volga, burning, looting, and killing as they moved northward. He urged the peasants to turn against their masters and free themselves. Thousands heeded his call, and within a few months he had control of 800 miles along the Volga. In August, 1670, he was defeated by the tsar's troops, his revolt collapsed, and Razin himself (betrayed by some of his fellow Cossacks) was executed after excruciating tortures. His name lived on among the peasantry, long celebrated in their poems and songs as a champion of freedom.

Religious controversy added to the discontent of the people. Although the Russians were deeply attached to Christianity, many identified true religion with a superstitious veneration of external forms and the repetition of traditional prayers. The liturgy and sacred writings of the Russian Church had come from the Greek Church, and when learned priests tried to correct errors in the liturgy or mistranslations in the writings, they were bitterly resisted. In 1652 a reforming priest named Nikon, who had won the favor of Tsar Alexis, was elected patriarch. He ordered corrections in the religious manuals and liturgies to bring them into line with the original Greek practices. Many of the changes were petty, such as directing that the priests make the sign of the cross with three fingers instead of two. The innovations raised violent opposition from clergy and people alike. Nikon, who was politically ambitious and offended the tsar by his pretensions, was deposed as patriarch in 1666, but his reform movement was upheld by Church and state, and its opponents were labeled heretics.

The dissenters formed a schismatic group called the Old Believers. They won a wide following among the masses, who were always ready to believe the worst of their rulers and saw the reform movement as a diabolical plot to deprive them of a chance for eternal salvation. Viciously persecuted by the authorities, thousands of Old Believers burned themselves alive in mass holocausts to save themselves from forced conversion to the abominated new practices. The extreme fanaticism subsided in the 1690's when the government's persecution became less violent, but the Old Believers retained their separate identity. Strongest in the backwoods of the north and northeast and in the southern steppe frontier, where they gained many adherents among the Cossacks, they often joined revolts against the government. Like so many other persecuted minorities, they also distinguished themselves by their industrious habits, and in the eighteenth and nineteenth centuries many became leaders in Russian economic life.

Poland to 1660

Poland in the first centuries of the modern era included large parts of today's Russia and Germany, stretching from the Baltic to the Black Sea. Much of this territory was Lithuanian, but after 1386 Poland and Lithuania had the same king. The two countries maintained separate governments until they were merged by the Union of Lublin in 1569. Under the union each partner kept its own administration and laws but had a common diet, currency, and system of land tenure.

The king of this vast realm was elected by the noblemen. To win and hold the throne, the monarchs made many concessions to the nobility: the nobility formed the army, filled most government offices, comprised the national and provincial diets, and helped the king to rule by means of representatives. They used their political power to transform the once-free peasantry into serfs and to pass legislation in the interests of the landowners that crippled the economy of the towns and thereby prevented the development of a prosperous middle class. The nobles, extremely proud of their privileges, successfully resisted all efforts by the throne to centralize the state. Although they constituted less than 10 per cent of the population, they considered themselves "the nation," referred to their country as a Republic of Noblemen, and looked upon the king they elected as merely the titular head of their republic.

THE GOLDEN AGE

In time this semianarchic political arrangement led to the disappearance of the Polish state. For a few decades in the sixteenth century, however, during the reigns of Sigismund I (1508–48) and Sigismund II (1548–72), Poland seemed about to become a major European power. During this Golden Age of Poland's history, the country achieved relative political stability and made important territorial acquisitions. It also made significant cultural advances, stimulated in large part by Queen Bona, a Sforza of Milan and wife of Sigismund I. Bona made the Polish court a center of Italian Renaissance culture.

The Protestant Reformation made great headway in Poland, and for a time it looked as if Protestantism might establish itself permanently. The lure of Church property and the chance to assert the power and privileges of their class against the authority of the Catholic Church and the throne attracted many noblemen to Protestantism. Sigismund II, whose wife was a Calvinist, showed much sympathy for Protestant teachings. In 1555 he granted freedom of worship to all Protestants, and in 1573 the national diet, in which Protestants held a majority, passed the Compact of Warsaw, which affirmed the principle of religious liberty. Protestantism, however, lacked roots among the masses, and the many Protestant sects opposed one another as vigorously as they opposed Catholicism. When in the latter part of the sixteenth century the Jesuits led a determined counteroffensive, Catholicism was easily re-established and Protestantism suppressed.

THE BEGINNING OF THE DECLINE

Sigismund II's death in 1572 ended the dynasty that had been continuously in power since 1386. The field was open and foreign princes eagerly sought election, handing out bribes and favors to win support. Fifty thousand nobles met outside Warsaw and chose as their monarch the French candidate, Henry of Anjou, degenerate younger brother of King Charles IX of France. The noble electors required him to accept certain provisions (called the Henrician Articles), which all kings after Henry had to accept. The Articles, a written summation of the privileges of the nobility, required the king to summon the national diet every two years, forbade him to marry without the diet's approval, allowed him no voice in the designation of his successor, prohibited him from leading his troops across the frontier without the diet's consent or for more than three months at a time, required him to accept the Compact of Warsaw guaranteeing religious freedom, and established a council of sixteen nobles who, in relays of four, resided at court for six months to advise the king. The monarch's failure to carry out any part of the Articles released his subjects from their oath of allegiance to him.

When Henry inherited the French throne after only a few months on the Polish throne, he returned home with alacrity. His successor, Stephen Bathory, prince of Transylvania, was elected after near civil war and proved himself one of Poland's ablest kings. Unfortunately, his achievements were canceled out during the long reign of his successor, the Swedish Sigismund III (1587–1632). Because Sigismund was heir to the Swedish throne, Polish leaders hoped that the union of Sweden and Poland under one ruler would create a great new power that would dominate Eastern Europe. But Sigismund's Catholicism cost him the Swedish throne, while in Poland his ineptness, bigotry, endless machinations to win the Swedish throne, and intervention in Russia during the Time of Troubles brought his country continuous war and much domestic suffering and discontent.

The recovery of Russia and the growth of Swedish power produced increased external pressures on Poland. The country's internal weaknesses prevented it from defending its vast territories from greedy neighbors, nor was it able to preserve internal order. Beginning in 1648, a series of catastrophes called the "deluge" by Polish historians overwhelmed the country. During the previous decades there had been frequent risings of the bitterly oppressed serfs against their masters; and the Cossacks, who lived in the Ukraine (on Poland's southeastern frontier) and resented the efforts of Polish nobles to settle there and impose serfdom and Roman Catholicism on them, had risen frequently in protest. In 1648 the current of revolt came to a climax in a great rising under Bohdan Khmelnitskii, who proclaimed himself *hetman* (leader), of the Cossacks. In 1654 Khmelnitskii induced Russia to go to war against Poland for possession of the Ukraine. In the next year Sweden took advantage of Poland's troubles by invading. Only a wave of religious zeal and patriotic ardor that swept Poland saved it from partition between Lutheran Sweden and Orthodox Russia. Peace with Sweden in 1660 cost Poland Livonia, and peace with Russia in 1667 cost it the eastern Ukraine and Smolensk. Although Poland had survived the Deluge, her only hope for the future depended upon the nobility agreeing to constitutional reforms to limit their power. Instead, they became even more selfish and irresponsible, and a little over a century later, independent Poland disappeared.

POLISH JEWRY

By the mid-seventeenth century Poland, with about a half-million Jews, had the largest Jewish community in Europe. Most of the Jews earned their living from small trades and crafts. A few became wealthy and served the government as fiscal agents or tax farmers; others were employed by rich nobles to manage their property or run the inns and distilleries on their estates. A much smaller number were moneylenders, and a few became doctors and apothecaries. Polish Jews spoke a German dialect that they had brought with them into Poland, called Yiddish (from the German word *jüdisch*, "Jewish"). It was written with Hebrew characters and contained many words from Hebrew and other languages.

The Polish government in the sixteenth century allowed the Jews a remarkable degree of self-government. They had their own courts, where they were judged according to Jewish law based upon the Bible and rabbinical commentaries. A council made up of twenty-four Jewish laymen and six rabbis acted as an overall supervisory agency for Polish Jewry. It assisted in enforcing government edicts, acted as a court of appeal for disputes among Jews, passed laws concerning dress and social life, supervised education, and apportioned taxation.

In the seventeenth century calamities overwhelmed Polish Jewry. The Cossacks who rose under Khmelnitskii made the Jews their special target. Between 1648 and 1658 they massacred 100,000 Polish Jews. In the years that followed continued waves of anti-Semitic violence engulfed the country. Some Polish Jews, in search of a haven, began to move westward to new Jewish communities in the countries from which their ancestors had fled.

Scandinavia to 1660

In Scandinavia, as in Russia and most of the rest of Europe, the struggle for supremacy between throne and nobility dominated the course of events during the first two centuries of the modern era. In the Scandinavian lands the nobles held an important advantage in the conflict because the throne remained an elective office, not a hereditary one. The nobles demanded increased privileges as a price for their vote and continued support.

DENMARK

Until the fifteenth century any Dane could become a noble, which would exempt him from taxes, simply by equipping himself at his own expense for military service. Then, in order to make itself an exclusive caste, the nobility arranged that no one could claim nobility unless he showed that his ancestors for three generations had been exempted from taxes. When old noble families died out, they could not be replaced by new ones, so that the nobility was almost halved between the fifteenth and mid-seventeenth centuries. The nobility expanded their powers over the peasants, who made up the greatest part of the population, and by the end of the fifteenth century most of the peasants had been reduced to serfdom. The nobility also broke the legal monopoly held by town merchants on foreign trade by selling their produce directly to foreign buyers instead of through the middlemen of the cities.

For a few years during the early sixteenth century it seemed as if the throne might succeed in gaining the upper hand over the nobility. Christian II, who was elected king in 1513, tried to follow the model of the "new monarchs" and establish royal supremacy. With the support of the townspeople he attempted to reduce the power of the nobility and great churchmen, protect the rights of the merchants, abolish the worst abuses of serfdom, and make the crown hereditary. The nobility rose in revolt and in 1523 drove Christian from the throne and elected his uncle to succeed him. The power of the nobility stood at its zenith. They ruled the state in alliance with the king, exercised still greater control over the peasants, gained a monopoly of all high government posts, and were exempted from tithes to the Church. They profited even more in 1536 when Lutheranism was adopted as the state religion, for the king confiscated the property of the Catholic Church and divided it between himself and the nobility.

As a result of the power vacuum left by the decline of the Hanseatic League, Denmark and Sweden frequently engaged during the sixteenth century in furious wars that centered on the control of the Baltic. Although Denmark never succeeded in decisively defeating Sweden, it managed to establish its hegemony in the Baltic, increasing Denmark's international prestige and bringing new wealth by trade. The upswing in his country's fortunes persuaded King Christian IV (1588–1648) that he could make Denmark the chief power of Northern Europe. He badly overestimated the strength of his country. He was soundly defeated in the Thirty Years' War (see Chapter Nine) and in a war with Sweden in the 1640's. When he died in 1648, whatever ascendancy and prestige Denmark had once enjoyed had disappeared.

SWEDEN

During the fifteenth and early sixteenth centuries the Danes engaged in endless intrigues and wars to re-establish the domination over Sweden that they had held briefly after the Union of Kalmar in 1397. In 1520 Christian II of Denmark had himself crowned in Stockholm as king of Sweden, but soon a revolt led by Gustavus Eriksson drove out the Danes. In 1523 a national assembly (*Riksdag*) of the four estates—nobility, clergy, townspeople, and peasantry—chose Gustavus as their monarch.

The new king, who ruled as Gustavus Vasa, faced a difficult task. Sweden was poor and thinly populated, an unruly nobility and the powerful Church posed threats to internal order, and the country was surrounded by foreign enemies. Gustavus proved equal to the problems. His technique of rule resembled that of the Tudors of England; like them he carefully cultivated good relations with the Riksdag. In 1527 he summoned the Riksdag in order to take possession of Church property, counting on the nobles' envy of Church wealth (the Church owned more land than all the nobles put together) and the growing religious discontent with Catholicism. A sizable proportion of the confiscated land went to the nobility. In the succeeding years under Gustavus' guidance Lutheranism became Sweden's state religion, with the Church firmly under the control of the king.

He extended his power over local government by replacing noble provincial governors with his own appointees. He introduced reforms into government administration and personally supervised all government activities, built up a strong army and navy, regulated and encouraged trade and industry, and operated a profitable business in goods he received as taxes or produced on his own properties. In 1544 the Riksdag, at his suggestion, repealed the old law that made the throne elective and declared it hereditary in Gustavus' line.

After Gustavus' death in 1560 the nobles made gains at the expense of his weak successors. Then in 1599 Charles IX, youngest of Gustavus' sons, took the throne. The new king, supported by the middle class and the peasantry, repressed the nobility and re-established the supremacy of the royal power. During these years Sweden took the first steps in the creation of a Baltic empire for itself. Sweden entered the Livonian War between Russia and the Teutonic Order and made large territorial gains. Early in the seventeenth century Charles IX saw an opportunity to gain more power and land at the expense of Russia, then going through the Time of Troubles, and he invaded that country. He also became involved in wars with Poland and Denmark. When he died in 1611, he passed on all three wars to his sixteen-year-old son and successor, Gustavus Adolphus.

The new king proved to be the greatest ruler in Swedish history. At thirteen he was negotiating with ambassadors from foreign lands, and his proud father used him as an assistant in matters of state. Despite his early education in statecraft, the three unfinished wars that he inherited from his father placed him in a desperate position. The nobles took advantage of his difficulties and his youth to renew their demands for more power.

Gustavus' forceful personality, unusual intellectual abilities, and great military skill enabled him quickly to establish himself as leader of the country and to undermine concessions that he had earlier made to the nobles. He maintained control over the aristocrats by converting them into a service nobility whose task was to serve the state as government bureaucrats and army officers, and he placated them by creating a House of the Nobility as the upper house of the Riksdag and by giving them large tax exemptions. He reorganized the government by adopting the collegial method of administration, by which each government department was run by a board or "college" of officials. He improved the military administration and built up an exceptionally strong army, based originally on conscripts, though later reinforced by mercenaries. He converted the noble-dominated Council of State into a cabinet of heads of his administrative departments. In these and other reforms he had the invaluable assistance of Axel Oxenstierna, chief minister throughout his reign.

Gustavus Adolphus owed his international fame to his prowess as a war leader. The Lion of the North, as he came to be called, fought many wars and lost only one—the conflict with Denmark that he inherited from his father. His many victories, and above all his successful intervention in the Thirty Years' War, raised Sweden to the status of a great power and won it much new territory and domination over the Baltic. His last victory, at Lützen in 1634, cost him his life.

Gustavus Adolphus left his throne to his only child, a six-year-old girl named Christina. A regency council headed by Oxenstierna and made up of the heads of the chief government departments, all of whom were noblemen, ruled the country. The nobility took advantage of the situation to win extensions of its privileges and to gain additional property for itself at the expense of lands belonging to the crown. Christina took over personal rule in 1644 but failed to reassert the supremacy of the throne. A person of much learning, she lacked the ability to rule, squandered money on a luxurious court, and gave away or sold great stretches of crown land. The country's internal political and economic situation began to deteriorate, and unrest appeared among the peasantry and townspeople. Weary of her duties and attracted to Catholicism, Christina abdicated in 1654 in favor of her cousin, who ruled as Charles X. A few days after her abdication Christina left Sweden dressed as a man, became a Catholic, and spent most of the rest of her life in Rome, supported by the charity of the pope.

The new king was able to restore some of the damage done to the throne's prestige during Christina's reign by persuading the nobility to return a large proportion of the crown lands she had given them and to accept taxation on one-fourth of their property. Noble opposition to these measures was stilled by the outbreak of a new war brought on by Charles's ambition to win territory at the expense of Poland. In the First Northern War, which lasted from 1655 to 1660, Sweden faced Poland, Russia, Denmark, Brandenburg, and Holland. If all of these states had cooperated, Sweden would have faced certain defeat; fortunately for Sweden, its enemies could not agree among themselves. Charles died before the war had ended, but a council of regency took over for his infant son and successor and succeeded in making a peace by which Sweden gained more territory and retained its leading position in Northern Europe.

The Ottoman Empire to 1656

The Ottoman Turks stood at the zenith of their fortunes in the century after the fall of Constantinople, especially during the long reign of Sultan Suleiman the Magnificent (1520–66). They continued their conquests until their empire extended to the Persian Gulf, across North Africa almost to the Atlantic, and deep into Central Europe. Approximately fifty million people of many nationalities, languages, and religions lived within their sprawling realm.

SLAVES IN THE GOVERNMENT

In the course of their amazing ascent from obscurity during the thirteenth century the Turks developed a system of administration unlike that of any other major state. Its most striking feature was the part played by slaves who belonged to the sultan. They were members of the ruling elite of the empire, holding high office in government, in the sultan's court, and in the army. No social opprobrium was attached to slavery, and many of the most powerful and wealthiest men of the empire were slaves. The sultan himself was born of a slave mother, for all the women in his father's harem were slaves. The use of slaves in government did not originate with the Ottomans. From ancient times despots had preferred to be served by men who owed everything to them, including their lives, but the Ottomans developed the practice to a point never reached before or since.

In the mid-sixteenth century the sultan owned about eighty thousand slaves. The law entitled him to take one-fifth of all prisoners of war as bondsmen, and his agents carefully selected the captives who best suited his purposes. He acquired others by purchase and by a periodic levy of male children between the ages of ten and twenty in the Christian provinces of the empire. Taken from their homes, screened for their abilities, converted to Islam, and given intensive training for the posts for which they seemed best suited, the young slaves began their careers at a low level. Advancement depended upon ability; they could rise to the highest offices

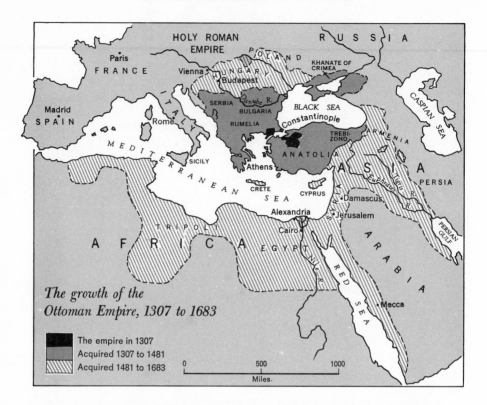

The growth of the Ottoman Empire, 1307 to 1683

The empire in 1307
Acquired 1307 to 1481
Acquired 1481 to 1683

0   500   1000
Miles.

in the empire, including that of grand vizier. The use of merit as the criterion for promotion stood in sharp contrast to Christian Europe, where theoretically birth, not ability, determined advancement. Since Islamic law prohibited the enslavement of born Moslems, the Ottoman Empire, hated foe of Christendom, depended heavily upon men of Christian origin for its administrators and soldiers.

Many Christian parents dreaded the conscription, and to avoid it they sometimes married off their sons as children, for married boys were ineligible for the child tribute. On the other hand, the system was not without its compensations. The boy who became a slave of the sultan had a chance to acquire wealth and power far beyond what he could hope for if he stayed in his native village, so that ambitious Christian parents sought to have their sons chosen, and Moslem parents sometimes paid Christian families to take their sons and pass them off as their own in the hope that they would be taken into the sultan's service.

A special group of slave soldiers, the Janissaries, formed the elite corps of the sultan's standing army, numbering about twelve thousand in the early sixteenth century. In peace as well as in war they lived in barracks under rigorous discipline, and until the late sixteenth century they were forbidden to marry. They were the sultan's shock troops and personal body-guard.

The reigning sultan named his own successor from among the many sons born to him by his harem women. To prevent civil war among rival sons, it became customary for the designated heir to have all his brothers killed. This brutal practice became law in the late fifteenth century and continued in use for the next hundred years.

MOSLEM PARTICIPATION IN GOVERNMENT

The sultan had unlimited power over his slaves. In contrast, his power over his free subjects was limited by the sacred law of Islam, based upon the Koran and the teachings of Mohammed and applicable to secular as well as to religious matters. The sultan could not alter the Mohammedan law, for it was believed to be of divine origin. In order to adapt it to changed circumstances brought about by time, he could supplement it by issuing new regulations or interpretations, called *kanuns*. Since the chief religious and legal leaders of the Moslem population had to approve the kanuns before they became effective, there was a check on the absolutism of the sultan.

The men who passed on the sultan's decrees were part of a hierarchy of consultants, judges, and teachers known as the *ulema* (learned ones). It controlled the legal, religious, and educational systems of the empire. Rank in the ulema depended upon education (which was nearly free) and ability. The most important members were the *muftis*. Each major administrative division of the empire and each large city had a mufti assigned to it to hear appeals under Islamic law and to provide expert opinions on all legal and religious problems. The mufti of Constantinople, whom the sultan himself consulted, was known as the *Sheikh-ul-Islam*, the "Elder of Islam." He was the empire's chief religious and legal authority. In this sense he stood over the sultan, for he could pass judgment on the sultan's actions or legislation, declare them illegal under the sacred law, and even call upon the people to depose the sultan.

TREATMENT OF MINORITIES

The Christians of the West considered the Turks cruel and uncultured barbarians who tyrannized the peoples they conquered. Actually, Turkish atrocities were no worse than the horrors perpetrated by Christians on fellow Christians, such as the Sack of Rome in 1527, the holocaust loosed by Ivan IV in Novgorod in 1570, or the St. Bartholomew's Day massacre in France in 1572. Moreover, Turkish culture compared favorably with that of the contemporary West. Although their religion forbade representations of the human form in painting and sculpture, the Turks stood at a high level of achievement in architecture, poetry, and decorative design. Most important, far from oppressing the peoples that they conquered, they allowed them a degree of freedom and toleration unparalleled in the Christian world of that day. In the Ottoman Empire no one suffered because of his religion or nationality. Each non-Moslem group was given official status, had its own ecclesiastical hierarchy, practiced its faith without molestation, provided its own education, and settled civil law disputes by its own religion and customs. Turkish courts exercised jurisdiction only in criminal matters.

Most of the Christian peasants of the Balkans enjoyed under the Ottomans a degree of peace and security that they had not known before. They were not taxed beyond their capacity to pay, and they were not brought under the yoke of serfdom that weighed so heavily on peasants in Central and Eastern Europe. Thousands of persecuted Jews streamed into the empire, where they could live and work without fear. When Ferdinand, who had a reputation for political wisdom, expelled the Jews from Spain in 1492 and they emigrated to the empire, the sultan is supposed to have said, "How can you call this Ferdinand wise—he who has impoverished his dominions to enrich mine?"

BEGINNING OF THE OTTOMAN DECLINE

The reign of Suleiman the Magnificent marked the end of a long, uninterrupted record of Ottoman victories and expansion. After his death in 1566 the empire began a gradual decline, punctuated by brief periods of recovery, which continued for centuries. The decline was attributable in large part to internal decay and demoralization. The first great setback came in 1571 when the Spanish-Venetian fleet defeated the Turkish navy at Lepanto. Thereafter the Turks were on the defensive although the Thirty Years' War, which preoccupied the European powers, gave them a respite from Western aggression during the first half of the seventeenth century.

CHAPTER EIGHT

Social, Intellectual, and Cultural Dynamism, 1500–1660

THE FIRST ONE AND ONE-HALF CENTURIES of modern Europe were characterized by ferment in areas other than politics and religion, though all the
developments were closely linked. Nowhere was the ferment more apparent
than in the social structure, where classes were regrouping; in science,
where new, empirically oriented methods were beginning to attain preponderance; and in the arts, where the "baroque" expressed a new extravagance and passion in the wake of the troubles of the sixteenth century.

Society and Social Dynamics

Princes, popes, protestors, politicians, and painters have commanded our
attention so far. In their distinctive ways they constituted a creative elite in
early modern Europe, and the history of the European world is peculiarly
their own. Though their dominance makes the historian's task easier, it
tends to obscure the mass of people whose lives they ordered but of whose
existence they were aware only in a general way. It also obscures the fact
that the medieval hierarchic order of society survived unquestioned long

181

after its ideals and institutions had been undermined or destroyed outright. The elite conceived of the masses as their servants at best, and as a police problem at worst. Yet in the sixteenth and early seventeenth centuries forces were at work in Europe that were rapidly smudging the neat medieval picture and creating new dynamics, with which statesmen and theorists in the late seventeenth and eighteenth centuries would have to grapple. Some of the results of these forces have already been described: the decline of the feudal nobility, the destruction of the authority of the universal Church, and the unleashing of new religious aspirations by men who saw no necessity for a hierarchy between themselves and God. Other forces varied greatly in their incidence in any one part of Europe, but one or more of them were increasingly evident everywhere.

THE TRADITIONAL ORDER

> The prince exalted above all his subjects, whose majesty does not admit of any division, represents the principle of unity, from which all the rest derive their force and cohesion. Below him are the three estates. . . . The estate of the clergy is placed first because of its dignity in ministering to religion. It includes both nobles [bishops] and commoners [priests]. Next comes the military estate, which also includes nobles and commoners [mere soldiers]. Last there is the third estate of scholars, merchants, craftsmen, and peasants.
>
> JEAN BODIN (French, 1576)

> Shepherds of people had need know the calendars of tempests in state, which are commonly greatest when things grow to equality. . . .
>
> FRANCIS BACON (English, c. 1610)

These two quotations, though not wholly representative and wrenched from context, sum up the traditional notion of social order. The "estates" were the major groupings of society (not to be confused with political estates, such as the Estates-General in France), and Bodin arranged them in hierarchic order under the prince. He made clear the functional distinctions that determined the groupings: the cure of souls, the defense of society, and the remaining—inferior—occupations. Any twelfth-century commentator could have written this, although he might not have spoken of the prince in such terms and he would not have included "mere soldiers." Bacon reflected the contemporary horror of equality and its supposed connection with civil disorder. The hint of social dynamics in Bacon's words was also in Bodin's words and is a clue to the necessity felt by both men to reassert vehemently the validity of the old order. In their countries, as elsewhere in Europe, there was a great deal of social movement within the existing framework—so much that the whole order seemed threatened by the dilution of the distinctive characteristics of each grouping and the blurring of the lines between them. Neither man was arguing that the movement should not occur, but only that the individual who had gone up (or down) the social ladder should accept the fact of his status. What worried them deeply was the possibility that the various levels in the hierarchy were becoming reversed, particularly the chance that the "lowest" estate was advancing at the expense of the second estate. Their anxiety was not unfounded.

For the clergy in Western and Central Europe, Catholic and Protestant, the Reformation era was socially damaging and sometimes disastrous. In some countries Protestantism's fundamental anticlericalism largely wiped out the privileged status of clergymen and eliminated the monastic clergy. The seizure of Church lands undermined the economic independence of the clergy. In England, where the Reformation was most conservative, the clergy retained more privileges, but symptomatic of their downgrading was the fact that they were no longer accorded the old honorific title "Sir." Ecclesiastical predominance in the House of Lords was ended when the dissolution of the monasteries removed the abbots from that assembly and left only the bishops. In the Catholic countries of France and Spain, the monarchs had subverted the clerical establishments to their own ends, although in general the clergy remained more influential than in Protestant states. With the exception of the papal state, nowhere in Western Europe in the seventeenth century was the Church the means to wealth and power that it had been in the sixteenth. The secularization of bureaucracy was nearly complete, even in France, where the two most prominent chief ministers of the early seventeenth century were cardinals. Indeed, in the Catholic Church itself after the Council of Trent the bishops were subjected to almost total papal control in areas where they were not firmly subject to monarchic power.

Everywhere but in Poland the "old" nobility suffered a loss of power, if not of prestige, in the sixteenth and early seventeenth centuries. Their titles of honor remained as long as the families survived, but their status was diluted by the rise of the "new" nobility—those who had been ennobled for service to the monarch. The new nobility often lived sumptuously, as befitted noblemen; they gained the wherewithal to do so from service to the monarch or from fortunes made initially in commerce. The sale of offices was common practice in most of the states of Europe, and merchants and lawyers found it relatively easy to purchase office and nobility. Nobility everywhere had the right either to exemption from taxation or to some control over the assessment of taxes. The mark of the nobleman was a landed estate, and the return to the land of the new nobility in an era when prices rose faster than rents meant that the nobility had to increase rents, improve production, or both, in order to survive. In the seventeenth century the economically least viable element of the landed nobility became increasingly impoverished, and the poverty-stricken hidalgos of Spain, *hobereaux* of France, lesser gentry of England, and petty nobles of Poland and Russia formed pockets of discontent.

THE DYNAMICS OF CHANGE

In 1500 Europe had about 69,000,000 people; by 1600 it had about 89,000,000. Every country apparently experienced the increase in population. Few people had yet migrated from Europe. Within Europe the population increase stimulated internal migration. Since more food was needed, people brought new areas of farmland into cultivation. Others were drawn to the cities by the increased demand for labor to produce goods and services; urban population, though still a small proportion of the total population, rose steadily. The volume and value of commerce and manufacturing within Europe grew enormously, and overseas expansion brought in goods from every quarter of the world. Although the total amount of imports from other continents was tiny in comparison with imports today, Europe's role— or more precisely Northern Europe's role—as the organizer and center of a world-wide economy had begun.

Between 1600 and 1620 the long wave of economic expansion that had begun in the fifteenth century came to its end in most of Europe. International trade declined. Imports of bullion from America fell steadily and by 1660 had shrunk to a fraction of what they were a century before. Prices dropped, reaching a low point between 1660 and 1680, and the profits of business declined. The overseas expansion of Europe slowed up, a number of overseas trading companies collapsed, and efforts to establish new ones often proved unsuccessful. Despite this retardation, the gains that had been made during the sixteenth-century expansion were retained. The European economy in 1660 was greatly advanced over what it had been two hundred years before.

BUSINESSMEN

*The expansion of economic activity that began in the late fifteenth century provided a literally golden opportunity for a relatively few clever and enterprising men to build up large fortunes. Most of these outstandingly successful capitalistic entrepreneurs came from the middle class, although some belonged to the nobility or gentry and others rose from the ranks of the peasantry or the urban working class. Usually they did not restrict themselves to one line of business but operated simultaneously in a number of fields; often they took an important part in politics. The Fuggers of Augsburg, Germany, had widespread textile and mining interests as well as their banking house, which had branches and agents throughout Europe and had made Jacob Fugger (1459–1529) the creditor of emperors, popes, and princes. The Russian Stroganovs dealt in salt, iron, furs, fish, grain, and other metals that were produced in their lands on the border of Siberia. They traded throughout Muscovy and had much to do with the Russian conquest of Siberia. Thomas Gresham (1519-1579), member of a wealthy English family of merchants and landowners, dealt in English woolen cloth, iron, paper, and finance. Financial agent to Queen Elizabeth and an important political figure, he founded the Royal Exchange in London as an arena for business transactions between merchants and bankers, modeled on the bourse of Antwerp, the most commercially advanced city of the century.

Not many businessmen amassed large fortunes. In business, as in every other field of human activity, only a few people had the imagination, ability, persistence, and luck needed to become outstandingly successful. Most businessmen were small merchants, shopkeepers, and peddlers. Many benefited from the price rise and the economic expansion, but only on a modest scale.

WAGE EARNERS AND PEASANTS

The great mass of Europeans—the workers and the peasants—did not share even moderately in the material benefits of the economic expansion. The scanty data on the wages of labor show that although wages went up, their increase lagged behind the increase in prices. As a result, the purchasing power of the workers' wages (their "real" wages) declined; workers could buy less with the amount of money they earned. Their standard of living fell. The wage data are based upon the actual amount of money paid workers. Wages, however, did not represent the wage earner's entire income. Many—perhaps most—workers were fed by their employers during working hours or received a cash allowance to buy food. In addition, many laborers had a small plot of land or a garden that furnished them with part of their food needs. The data on prices show that the prices of a number of items bought by workers, such as low-quality textile wares and certain other manufactured goods, did not go up as steeply as food prices; in fact, the price of certain of these manufactured commodities did not increase as much as wages. The worker could therefore buy more of these limited wares. Nonetheless, it seems probable that the worker's standard of living did decline.

The economic condition of most of the peasantry of Europe also deteriorated during the first two centuries of the modern era. A very small minority who owned their own holdings and had enough land to produce a surplus to sell, and who also had some business ability, benefited from the economic expansion. By far the greatest number of peasants rented the land that they tilled from landowners who belonged to the upper classes. Landlords in many parts of Europe took advantage of the opportunity that the price rise gave them to increase their incomes by engaging directly in the production of farm products. They believed that they could make more money from direct production than from the rental of their land. In England the fields and common pastures that the peasants had used were consolidated or "enclosed" into large units on which proprietors raised sheep to meet the increased demand for wool from England's textile industry or grew foodstuffs to sell to the growing population of the towns. By the beginning of the seventeenth century between 10 to 20 per cent of all the farmland in England had been enclosed. Thousands of peasants had to give up their holdings. Some took jobs as farmhands or shepherds on the enclosed lands, others worked for more prosperous peasants who had not been dispossessed, and still others eked out a living by weaving cloth in their cottages. Some left their native villages and went to the cities to find work as unskilled laborers, or became vagabonds, roaming the roads of England and making their meager livings as best they could by begging and stealing.

In Spain the peasants suffered not only from the increased demands of the landlords but also from the heavy taxation levied by the government. They were also oppressed by the special privileges held by a great gild of sheep raisers called the Mesta. The Spanish crown granted the Mesta the right to graze its flocks, totaling several million sheep, over a large area of Spain, allowed it to take over private pastures for grazing, and forbade the planting of crops in lands through which the sheep of the Mesta passed. Spanish agriculture decayed, and the poverty-stricken peasantry barely managed to keep alive. Peasants in other parts of Europe suffered similarly from the increased demands of the lords and the state. In addition, they were hit harder than any other group by the destructive wars that filled the era. In those days armies lived off the land, and friend and foe alike stripped the peasants of whatever they had.

TECHNOLOGY AND INNOVATION

It may seem paradoxical that impoverishment of the masses should have accompanied economic expansion. In our industrial age the long-term upward movement of economic growth has produced a higher, rather than a lower, standard of living. The reason that this did not happen in the economic upswing of the sixteenth century lay primarily in the fact that technology, above all in agriculture, did not keep pace with the increase in population, so that the amount of goods produced was not enough to feed, clothe, and house adequately the growing number of people. Most Europeans lived on the margin of subsistence, and when crops failed, as they did with terrible frequency, famines swept the country and thousands died of starvation or, weakened by undernourishment, fell easy prey to disease. In a few regions of Europe, particularly in Holland, farmers began to employ more intensive methods of cultivation. They planted clover and turnips, which restored fertility to the soil and at the same time provided food for animals; and they used fertilizer. Nearly everywhere else the peasants continued to use the traditional methods of tillage.

Although some technical innovations were made in industry, particularly in certain aspects of textile and metal manufacturing, new techniques remained very much the exception. Important changes did take place, however, in manufacturing organization. In preceding centuries the artisan gilds in the towns had usually controlled the manufacture, and even the sale, of many wares. As trade grew, merchants and gild members who had become discontented with the restrictive practices of the gilds distributed raw materials or semifinished goods to peasants in the countryside, in the so-called "domestic" or "putting-out" system. The peasants worked on these goods in their own homes at piece rates, usually performing just one stage in the manufacturing process.

In contrast to the dispersion of industry represented by the domestic system, centralized large-scale factories were also being established in this era, especially in England, where some of the new plants employed hundreds of workers. The factories did not use the special kinds of power-driven machinery that we associate with factory industry today. Factory workers used the same hand methods and simple tools and machines that small producers used in their shops and homes. The factories did offer important advantages in that the activities of the workers could be organized and coordinated to increase output per worker.

The leveling-off of economic expansion in the early seventeenth century coincided with the growth of the joint-stock company, in which a group of merchants, each with limited capital, pooled their resources, invited investment, and usually obtained a royal charter of monopoly for a prescribed area of trade. The social consequences of this development were most pronounced in England, where landed proprietors often invested in the companies, and in Holland. Since the fortunes of the state were intimately connected with these ventures, a premium was placed on cooperation and mutual support between the ruler and the merchants. Joint-stock investment did not smooth over but rather increased the economic discrepancies between big merchants and small merchants, who tended to remain craftsmen as much as merchants.

The Scientific Revolution

Greek science, particularly Aristotelian science, accepted as valid for nearly two thousand years, presupposed that nature works in an orderly fashion according to laws that are discoverable by reason alone. Experimentation and observation had little place in this process. Significantly, the Greek scientist was not so much concerned with *how* nature works as with *why* it works, raising questions more moral and aesthetic than mechanical.

Those who in the sixteenth century first achieved radical breakthroughs in science did not reject Greek science, but they asked new questions of the Greek material. In the late sixteenth and early seventeenth centuries there was a shift toward gathering new data—data derived from observation and finally experimentation. The latter development was the beginning of empiricism. From that point the scientist's major question became not *why* but *how* nature works. The sum total of the scientific achievements in this century and a half comprised the Scientific Revolution.

THE OLD COSMOLOGY

The most dramatic and revolutionary advances were made in the study of physics and astronomy. For centuries Western man had accepted the Greek view of the cosmos, which was in agreement with appearances. Men could plainly see the celestial bodies move each day in a circular path around the earth; consequently, they constructed a geocentric or earth-centered cosmology. The earth stood unmoving at the center of a series of hollow transparent spheres that daily rotated around the earth. Each of the crystalline spheres had imbedded in it one of the heavenly bodies—the sun, the moon, and the five known planets (Mercury, Venus, Mars, Jupiter, Saturn). Next came the sphere of the fixed stars, holding the stars that move about the earth but seem to be motionless with respect to one another. Finally there was an outermost sphere, the *primum mobile* or "first mover," which provided spin to the spheres nested within it. Beyond lay the "empyrean," where God dwelt. The heavenly bodies, glowing like great luminous jewels in their marvelously clear spheres, were thought to be made of a pure and immortal substance, entirely different from the corrupt and mortal matter that made up the earth. Men believed, too, that they followed natural laws different from those of earthly phenomena.

This tidy arrangement of the cosmos satisfied everyone but the astronomers, who had difficulties with it from the very outset. The planets (from the Greek word for "wanderer") presented an especially difficult problem. Instead of moving steadily in one direction from east to west, they seemed at times to stop briefly, then move in a backward or retrograde path for a while. They appeared brighter at some times than at others, and they did not seem to move at a uniform rate of speed. Yet astronomers assumed axiomatically that the planets follow circular orbits, for since ancient times the circle had been considered the perfect form of motion.

Claudius Ptolemy, the Alexandrian Greek astronomer and geographer of the second century A.D., modified the geocentric system so that the earth was not exactly in the center. The celestial bodies moved along an eccentric path with reference to the earth. This provided an explanation for the change in brightness of the planets: at certain parts of their eccentric orbit they were farther from the earth than at other times. Ptolemy created a

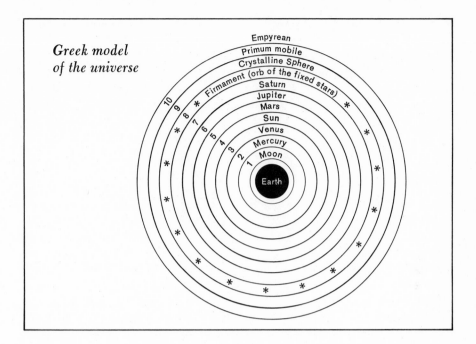

Greek model of the universe

system of epicycles to explain the retrograde motion of the planets. The heavenly bodies were said to move in a small circle whose center in turn moved in a large circle around the earth. He explained the apparent lack of uniformity in the planets' speed of movement by demonstrating geometrically that the velocity was uniform with respect to one point, called the equant, and circular with respect to another point. Ptolemy's work was translated into Arabic and honored by the Moslems with the title "Almagest" (a contraction of "the greatest of books"). It was transmitted to the West through translation from the Arabic in the twelfth century and became the fountainhead of Western astronomical science. It was supported by common sense, reason, and superficial observation. Moreover, the system worked well enough, and even today navigation is predicated on the earth standing still at the center of the constantly revolving heavens.

The growth of data on celestial movements, however, entailed constant modifications of the Ptolemaic model. By the middle of the sixteenth century over seventy simultaneous circular motions were required to explain the motions of the heavenly bodies. Astronomers, beset by the discrepancies between the theory and their own observations, found that they could not accurately predict the future positions of the planets. Imbued with the humanist spirit of the Renaissance, they turned to Ptolemy in the original Greek in the thought that perhaps errors and inaccuracies had accumulated in the process of translation from Greek to Arabic to Latin. They did find errors of translation, but these did not alter the basic theory. In search of

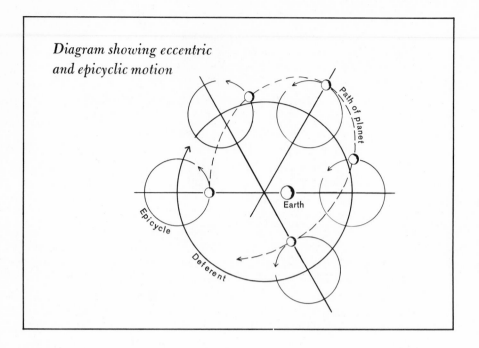

Diagram showing eccentric and epicyclic motion

further guidance they studied the works of Ptolemy's predecessors in Greece. There they found the inspiration to create an entirely new concept of the universe, marking the start of the scientific revolution.

COPERNICUS AND THE HELIOCENTRIC THEORY

The book with which the revolution began appeared in 1543. Written in Latin, it was entitled *Six Books Concerning the Revolution of the Heavenly Spheres.* Its author was a Pole named Nikolaus Koppernigk (Copernicus in Latin), born in Cracow in 1473. After study at the University of Cracow he spent ten years at Italian universities, where he immersed himself in humanist and medical studies. Through an uncle who was a bishop, he received an appointment as a canon of the cathedral at Frauenburg, a provincial town in East Prussia. There he spent the rest of his life busily occupied in church administration, the practice of medicine, and study of the classics and astronomy.

Copernicus, who was not an outstanding observer of the celestial bodies, relied upon the recorded observation of others. He was drawn to the study of astronomy by a feeling of concern about the discrepancies in the Ptolemaic system. In addition, he had a curiously conservative—even reactionary—reason, which was his conviction that the ancient Greeks had been right in their belief that the planets follow perfect circular orbits at uniform velocities. The intellect, he wrote, "recoils in horror" from the thought that any other form of motion is possible for the heavenly bodies; "it would be unworthy to suppose such a thing in a universe constituted in the best possible way."

A well-trained humanist, Copernicus decided to study all the ancient writings he could find in order to work out "a more reasonable arrangement of circles." He found that ancient Greek scientists had suggested that the sun, not the earth, stands immobile at the center of the cosmos, and that the earth and the other planets rotate about the sun in concentric circles. Inspired by this discovery, he showed by brilliant calculations that the motions of the heavenly bodies can all be explained by assuming a sun-centered or heliocentric universe.

Copernicus' model of the universe had many shortcomings. Like Ptolemy he had to use epicycles to explain planetary orbits, although he did reduce their number from 80 to 34. He did not need Ptolemy's equant, but he had to use the eccentric path of motion, for the common center of the concentric circles of his system fell a little to one side of the sun. He retained the old belief that the planets were firmly imbedded in crystalline spheres. His insistence upon perfect circular motion proved wrong, and his explanation for the rotation of the earth and the other planets—that "rotation is natural to a sphere and by that very act is its shape expressed"—begged the question.

Copernicus belonged more to ancient than to modern science, yet his work had enormous consequences. His rearrangement of the solar system

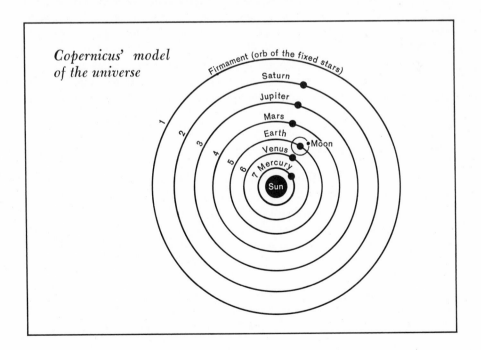

Copernicus' model of the universe

provided the stimulus for later scientists to complete the demolition of the old cosmology. By removing the earth from the center of the cosmos and placing it among the other planets, he struck the first great blow at the ancient belief in the distinction between base earth and pure celestial bodies. Earth and its companion planets were found to follow the same physical laws.

Catholic and Protestant religious leaders alike denounced Copernicus' book as being opposed to Holy Scripture. Scientists were less vehement, but it took over a century for them finally to give up the earth-centered cosmology. Even Tycho Brahe (1546–1601), the Danish scientist who was the ablest astronomer in the generation after Copernicus, did not accept the heliocentric theory. He developed an hypothesis in which the earth remained immobile at the center of the cosmos with the sun and moon revolving about it, but with the other five planets revolving about the sun. His theory appealed to many astronomers, for it had the simplicity of the Copernican system without its assertion of an orbiting and rotating earth, which was so contradictory to human experience and common sense. The traditional belief in the revolving crystalline spheres was shaken in 1577 when a new comet in the upper sky and raced straight through what were supposed to be the impenetrable spheres. Although Tycho could offer no substitute for the spheres to explain how the planets stay in their orbits, most astronomers followed him in rejecting their existence.

Tycho's skill in astronomical observation won him the patronage of the king of Denmark. He was given a small island that lay between Sweden and Denmark, where he built a fantastic castle-observatory called Uraniborg, the "Castle of Heaven." He designed measuring instruments of great size rigidly mounted on solid foundations to gain the highest possible accuracy for the unaided human eye. He was the first man since the Greeks to introduce major improvements into astronomical observation, and he attained an accuracy of measurement far beyond that of any previous astronomer.

KEPLER, "LEGISLATOR OF THE SKY"

In his last years Tycho quarreled with the king and lived for a time in Prague. There he engaged a young German assistant named Johannes Kepler (1571–1630). Tycho recognized that Kepler had great intellectual powers and gave him access to his vast collection of observations in the hope that the younger man would firmly establish the truth of Tycho's geocentric theory. Instead, Kepler used Tycho's data to support the Copernican system.

More than any other astronomer up to his time Kepler insisted on the closest possible agreement between theory and observation. After four years of computations on the orbit of Mars he found a small discrepancy (not

Johannes Kepler, by Jan van der Heyden

"His life work was possible only when he succeeded in freeing himself to a large extent from the spiritual tradition in which he was born. . . . He had to free himself from an animistic, teleologically oriented manner of thinking in scientific research. He had to realize clearly that logical-mathematical theorizing, no matter how lucid, could not guarantee truth by itself; that the most beautiful logical theory means nothing in natural science without comparison with the exactest experience. Without this philosophic attitude, his work would not have been possible."
From Albert Einstein's introduction to C. Baumgardt, JOHANNES KEPLER: LIFE AND LETTERS (New York, 1951).
Courtesy of Prints Division, New York Public Library

more than one-fourth of 1 per cent) between Tycho's observations, which he knew to be accurate, and the uniform and circular orbit required by Copernicus' theory. Other scientists might have explained away this seemingly insignificant discrepancy by making convenient assumptions. Kepler, with the integrity characteristic of great scientists, was not content, and back he went to his computations. After more years of work he reached the epochal conclusion that each planet moves not in a circular but in a slightly elliptical orbit, with the sun at one of the two foci of the ellipse. This was Kepler's first law, the law of elliptical motion. He also determined that the planets do not move at a uniform velocity, as men had always thought. They move faster as they near the sun and slow down as they go away from it. This rule, Kepler's second law, the law of equal areas, stated that a line joining the sun to a planet sweeps out equal areas in equal times.

All the data of observation fitted the new theory. The epicycles and eccentrics were gone forever. Gone, too, was the obsession of astronomers since Grecian times with the circle as the basis of cosmic order. Still, Kepler, who had published his first two laws in 1609, remained unsatisfied. His belief in the simplicity and harmony of nature—a conviction that has run through the entire history of science—persuaded him that an overall relationship of order and regularity exists among the motions of the different planets. After more years of seemingly endless calculations, in 1619 he announced with enormous and justified pride his third great principle, the harmonic law of planetary motion. It declared that the time a planet takes to orbit around the sun varies proportionately with its distance from the sun: the square of the time is proportional to the cube of the distance.

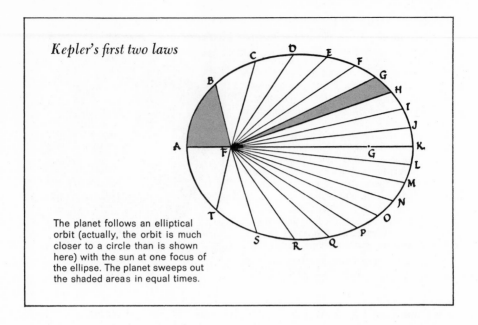

Kepler's first two laws

The planet follows an elliptical orbit (actually, the orbit is much closer to a circle than is shown here) with the sun at one focus of the ellipse. The planet sweeps out the shaded areas in equal times.

Astronomical observations made since Kepler's time have borne out the accuracy of his laws. In addition, modern physicists have found that they can use his laws to describe the motions of electrons around nuclei under the action of electrical forces. Kepler's contributions, however, went beyond astronomy and physics. He demonstrated to scientists the supreme importance of precise data. His use of mathematical relationships to explain planetary motion helped to establish the mathematical equation as the means of expressing laws of physical science. Above all, he was the first to seek a universal physical law to explain the motions of the universe in quantitative detail. Earlier astronomers had either held that the celestial bodies followed their orbits because of their special or even divine qualities or, like Copernicus, maintained that it was the nature of a sphere to go in circles. Kepler set out to prove, as he wrote in a letter in 1605, "that the celestial machine is to be likened not to a divine organism but rather to a clockwork," with all its motions caused by a single force, just as a simple weight causes all the motions of a clock.

Kepler hit on what he thought was the all-powerful single force after reading a book called *De Magnete* (*On the Magnet*), published in 1600 by William Gilbert, an English physician. After much experimentation with compasses and lodestones, Gilbert had arrived at the conclusion that the interior of the earth was a huge magnet. This theory led Kepler to decide that a magnetic force emanating from the sun drove the planets in their courses. It was an imaginative answer to the question of what was the physical cause of planetary motion, but it was wrong. Before the right answer could be found, scientists had to gain a greater understanding of the laws governing the mechanics of motion. That understanding came through the work of the Italian scientist Galileo Galilei (1564–1642).

GALILEO

Before Galileo even the boldest scientists had not broken completely with the old Greek ways of thought. They still looked for meaning in natural phenomena, and they considered it their obligation to seek out final causes. Galileo concentrated on describing how natural phenomena operated and expressing his descriptions and observations in mathematical terms. He believed that the scientist could describe all natural phenomena mathematically. Science, he wrote, "is written in that great book which ever lies before our eyes—I mean the universe—but we cannot understand it if we do not learn the language and grasp the symbols in which it is written." His insistence on observation, on quantification, and on mathematics as the best methods for ordering and understanding nature made his work the watershed between the old and the new in science. Since his day science has been pointed in the direction he defined and away from the metaphysical speculations about first causes that had formerly preoccupied scientists. Galileo well merits the title Father of Modern Physical Science.

Although Kepler had discovered the mathematical laws for the movement of the planets, Galileo found the laws for the movement of bodies on earth. Since the days of Aristotle it had been accepted that a heavier body falls more rapidly than a light one. A few men had questioned the maxim, but Galileo was the first to test and disprove it experimentally. The famous story that he simultaneously dropped two iron balls from the Leaning Tower of Pisa is now regarded as a legend, but he did prove that bodies of different weight fall at the same rate of speed (when allowance is made for wind resistance owing to difference in size and shape). Since the timing mechanisms available to him were not accurate enough to measure the speed of freely falling bodies, Galileo experimented with balls that were rolled down inclined boards. He thereby discovered the principle of uniform acceleration, by which the velocity of a freely falling body increases at a uniform rate. Continued researches led him in his last years to the monumental discovery of the law of inertia, by which a moving body will continue forever in a straight line and at the same speed unless acted upon by an outside force. A modern astronomer has written that this discovery was "one for which the world had waited two thousand years. From now on the science of dynamics could make progress at breakneck speed."

In 1609 Galileo heard that lens makers in the Netherlands had recently constructed a practical telescope. Inspired by this report and aided by his own knowledge of optics, Galileo built himself a telescope that magnified objects by thirty diameters. He turned his instrument heavenward, becoming the first man to so employ the telescope. His observations dispelled the widely accepted belief in the unblemished and unchanging nature of celestial bodies. He saw that the sun has spots, that Saturn bulges instead of being perfectly spherical, that Venus goes through phases like the moon, and that the moon itself has a rough surface with mountains, valleys, and plains like the earth and, like earth, reflects the light of the sun. Most surprisingly he discovered that Jupiter has moons revolving around it (he saw four of the twelve known satellites).

Galileo, who had long been convinced of the accuracy of Copernicus' cosmology, believed that his own observations supported the accuracy of that theory. He published his first findings in 1610 in a book called *The Sidereal Messenger*. He soon discovered, however, that scholars, philosophers, and churchmen who opposed the Copernican system because they felt that it flew in the face of theology and common sense not only refused to accept his findings, but would not even look through his telescope to see what he saw. Undaunted, Galileo continued to lecture and write in defense of the heliocentric theory until 1616, when the Catholic Church declared that it was contrary to the teachings of the Bible and ordered him neither to hold nor to defend it.

With the election of Pope Urban VIII, who was reputed to be a humanist, Galileo felt encouraged to write again about the heliocentric theory. The pope agreed that he could write a comprehensive treatise on cosmology, provided he treated the Copernican system as an hypothesis and not as a proven fact. In 1632 Galileo published the *Dialogue on the Two Chief Systems of the World,* which purported to be an impartial discussion among three men of the relative merits of the Aristotelian-Ptolemaic and Copernican systems. In reality, it ardently defended the latter hypothesis, with the anti-Copernican defeated at every turn. Outraged, the pope ordered Galileo to come to Rome, where the Inquisition tried him and in 1633 ordered him to make a formal renunciation of the Copernican theory. Galileo complied. His book was placed on the Index of Prohibited Books where it remained until 1835. A sentence of imprisonment was immediately commuted to house arrest, which lasted for the remaining eight years of his life.

The trial of Galileo is one of the most famous episodes in the long struggle between freedom of thought and authoritarianism. In his case freedom won, for despite the Church's efforts Galileo's influence made itself felt throughout Europe. Even in Catholic lands scholars and churchmen read and accepted his arguments for the Copernican system. It was impossible for a serious scientist to continue to support the geocentric theory.

Instead of choosing martyrdom Galileo continued his researches in the years after his trial. One of his contemporaries, Giordano Bruno (1548–

1600), made a different choice. Bruno had asserted that the stars were like the sun and were at an enormous distance from earth, and that space was infinite and the universe eternal, without beginning or end. These startlingly modern views brought him to trial for heresy. Bruno refused to renounce his beliefs, and after years of confinement in a dungeon he was burned at the stake in Rome in 1600 as a martyr not to religion but to a new cosmology which the old faith could not yet reconcile with its traditional order.

THE LIFE SCIENCES

The core of the scientific revolution was physics and astronomy. In other branches of science progress was less spectacular. The discovery of mathematics as a language of explanation of physical phenomena—not so readily applicable to the life sciences—probably contributed most to the discrepancy between physics and physiology.

Vesalius' pioneering work in anatomy in the early sixteenth century established the University of Padua as the center of medical study. Vesalius changed the basis of anatomy by exposing Galen's errors, but he continued to accept Galen's physiology, which maintained that air passes directly from the lungs to the heart and that the blood flows to the heart from the liver and passes from one side of the heart to the other through invisible pores in the thick tissue dividing the heart. These theories became increasingly suspect, and in 1628 William Harvey, a Padua-trained English physician, published an *Essay on the Motion of the Heart and the Blood,* which established that the heart is a pump circulating the blood through veins, lungs, and arteries. It remained for Marcello Malpighi, an Italian, to discover in 1661 (with the aid of the newly invented microscope) that tiny capillaries connect the arteries and the veins.

SCIENTIFIC METHOD

Seventeenth-century scientists had not yet broken with the mysticism and metaphysics that had surrounded the study of nature since Grecian times. They continued to seek the final causes of phenomena and believed that their discoveries showed that everything in nature fitted into a divine and harmonious plan. A few men, however, began to argue for the separation of the study of nature from metaphysical preoccupations. They saw no need to search for final causes and felt that empirical observation and mathematical measurement were all that were necessary in scientific investigation. They attacked the deductive method, in which for centuries scientists had deduced natural phenomena by reasoning from the general to the particular or from the abstract to the concrete, as when Copernicus said that the earth rotates because it is the nature of a sphere to rotate. They urged the use of the inductive method, in which one proceeds from the particular to the general and from the concrete to the abstract, so that theoretical propositions are derived by observing and comparing large amounts of data. Two men stand out as the prophets of this "scientific method": Francis Bacon and René Descartes.

FRANCIS BACON

Francis Bacon (1561–1626), who was not a scientist but a distinguished English lawyer and statesman, was a man of sweeping philosophical interests. He planned to write a great work covering all knowledge, to be called the *Instauratio Magna* (The Great Renewal), but he published only two parts of the projected study—*The New Organon* and *The Advancement of Learning*. In *The New Organon* he argued that the inductive method should replace the deductive logic that had been taught in the original *Organon*, written many centuries before by Aristotle. He urged men to put aside false beliefs and prejudices, to which he gave the Platonic name of "idols." The "idols of the tribe" are the fallacies common to human nature and shared by all men. The "idols of the cave" are fallacies peculiar to an individual, since each man dwells in his own cave. The "idols of the market place" represent errors that arise from the imprecise use of words when men consort with one another. The "idols of the theater" are faulty philosophical dogmas, which are as unrepresentative of reality as a stage play.

In *The Advancement of Learning* Bacon offered a detailed criticism of medieval science, tried to classify the sciences in a logical order, and called for larger expenditures on science and increased educational and research facilities. Making no distinction between pure science and applied science or technology, he argued that all science should be applied to raising the material welfare of mankind. "Knowledge itself is power," he wrote, and should be sought not for understanding but for use.

Bacon's ideas made a lasting impression. His vision of scientific knowledge as the means to material improvement was the forefather of the idea of "progress" that has played so great a role in modern history. His emphasis on the importance of experiment gave wider currency to empiricism. His insistence upon the importance of precise terminology has become a characteristic of the scientist. Nevertheless, Bacon himself had only a limited understanding of science and made no contribution to actual scientific investigation. His advice to abandon old dogmas had much merit, but his overemphasis on the collection of data was inimical to generalization and the use of intuition and imagination, which are •s important as data in the scientific process. Most of all, he failed to recognize the supreme importance of mathematics as a scientific tool. The abstractness of mathematics and the use of deduction in mathematical manipulations did not fit into his notion of experimentation.

CARTESIANISM

René Descartes (1596–1650) appreciated the importance of mathematics. He was one of the greatest figures in the development of that branch of learning, besides making important contributions to astronomy and physics. His invention of analytical or coordinate geometry allowed the union of algebra and geometry. He showed that a curve in space can be expressed as an algebraic formula and can thus be handled mathematically. The application of algebra to spatial relationships proved an enormously valuable tool for scientific research, particularly in the study of motion.

Descartes' work in mathematics and other branches of science was part of his plan to construct a systematic scientific philosophy that could be applied everywhere and that would enable man to achieve certainty in his knowledge of the universe. In 1637 he published a number of scientific essays, including the *Discourse on Method*, to illustrate what he considered the successful application of his system of analysis. The *Discourse*, written in the form of an intellectual autobiography, contained the essentials of his philosophy and explained how he arrived at it. He said that he began by doubting the truth of everything in order to rid himself of erroneous philosophical beliefs. One fact alone remained beyond doubt—his own existence. His explanation was, "I think, therefore I exist" (*cogito ergo sum*). From this fundamental axiom he set out to deduce a system of universal philosophy predicated upon four rules: (1) to accept as true nothing that is not self-evident, (2) to break each problem into as many parts as possible, (3) to reason always from the simple to the complex, and (4) to make exhaustive notes of all the data to make sure that nothing is omitted.

The old metaphysical concern was not dead in Descartes. The fact that he could conceive of God as a perfect being seemed to him to prove the existence of God, for he did not know how else man could have gotten the idea of perfection, since man himself is imperfect. "God necessarily exists," he argued, "as the origin of the idea I have of him." As he proceeded further, he developed the theory, famed as Cartesian dualism, according to which there are two forms of reality, mind and matter, with God as the creator of both forms and the connecting medium between them. Mind and matter have separate existences; mind, the "thinking substance," exists in ourselves as our own self-consciousness, whereas matter, the "extended substance," occupies a portion of space.

Much of Descartes' scientific speculation turned out to be wrong, in great part because he failed to practice the scientific method that he preached. He succumbed to the seduction of deductive reasoning, starting from principles that he considered to be self-evident. He did not bother to make experimental verifications of his conclusions. His philosophy, however, made a profound and enduring impact, and the *Discourse on Method* stands out as one of the most influential books in Western intellectual history.

Descartes' effort to prove that the universe is a perfect mechanism that runs according to mechanical laws, his conviction that mathematics provides the key to the operations of nature, and his belief that all knowledge can be unified into a single universal science influenced not only scientists but all of literate society. His faith in reason and his insistence upon clarity and simplicity were guides for the rationalists who dominated Western thought during the period of the Enlightenment in the eighteenth century.

Most important, Cartesianism proved of decisive importance in completing the break between ancient and modern thought. By urging men to doubt all old authorities and to use their reason to arrive at truth, Descartes made it seem natural for those who followed him to appeal to reason, that is, to use their own independent judgment, instead of appealing to some traditional, external authority. By demonstrating that man can start with the single premise of his own existence and, by unaided reason, work out the nature of the universe and the existence of God, Descartes fostered a new feeling of man's dignity and importance and an unlimited confidence in the possibilities open to human reason.

Political Theory

The most immediate impact of the scientific revolution was on political theory. The introduction of the scientific method gave political theorists a sounder base from which to work. The cosmological revolution shattered the God-centered nature of the universe, divorcing the age-old search for natural law from dependence on God and throwing the full burden of discovery on man's unaided reason based on experimentation or at least observation. All that man needed was to apply the scientific method to political observations and from the data he collected deduce universal laws.

THOMAS HOBBES

Thomas Hobbes (1588–1679) set out to do just that. He was over forty when he became fascinated by the new natural science and immersed himself in its study. He was convinced that social relationships could be described with as much precision and accuracy as the relationships among physical phenomena, and adopted a materialistic view of the universe, believing that man himself is nothing more than a machine in motion. He had planned to develop his theories in three long treatises but political unrest in England interfered with his plans. Faced with the civil disruption in England in the 1640's, he fled to the Continent, where he lived from 1640 to 1651. While abroad he wrote several treatises in support of absolutist government, including *Leviathan,* his masterpiece, published in 1651. He

chose the name because he compared the sovereign power of the state
the great sea monster mentioned in the Book of Job of which the Bible sa
"Upon earth there is not his like."

In *Leviathan* Hobbes argued that all men possess instinctive feelings
of fear and self-preservation. These instincts, he said, provide the underlying motivation for social organization. Human life in the "state of nature,"
that is, in the absence of all government and with all men equal, was
unendurable. There was a "war of all against all," constant fear reigned,
and life was "solitary, poor, nasty, brutish, and short." Hobbes, like Machiavelli, held a low opinion of the human race. Driven by the instinct of self-
preservation, men decided to leave the state of nature and made a contract
with each other by which they agreed to transfer all their rights to a
sovereign, to whom they gave unlimited power. The only rights they retained
were those allowed them by the sovereign, who used his unlimited power
to enforce obedience and unity. The government—the sovereign power—did
not have to be a monarchy, but Hobbes favored kingship as the form of rule
best suited to absolutism.

Hobbes's political theory based its demand for the total subjugation of
the individual to the sovereign on enlightened self-interest. The assertion
that absolute power came initially from the consent of the governed offended those who held that royal power came from God, and also raised
the question as to what would happen if the governed took back their
consent. Hobbes said that this was impossible because the contract, once
entered into, was unbreakable. In a society whose legal system enshrined
the contract as a reciprocal agreement, the argument was feeble, for if the
sovereign did not deliver his part of the bargain (security and peace of
mind), the subjects might justly argue that they could take back their part
(absolute obedience). Hobbes not only failed to satisfy the absolutists with
his contract, but he could not win the adherence of their opponents, who
saw his argument as a bulwark for absolutism. His materialism cost him all
religious support. Consequently, his influence was limited in his own time,
but *Leviathan* became the classic theoretical statement of absolutism and
served as the starting point for much of later political theory.

The Baroque

The Renaissance exhausted itself in Italy by the second quarter of the
sixteenth century. Other nations took over leadership in the arts, but they
continued to look to Italy for instruction and inspiration. Many of their
artists studied in Italy, and the Italian influence showed strongly in the
works that they produced. New forces, however, such as the Protestant and
Catholic Reformations, economic changes, and the emergence of the cen-

tralized national states, produced a society that differed in many ways from the society of Renaissance Italy. Artists sought to express the temper of the changed times, and their efforts brought on a new era in art history.

THE NEW STYLE

The transition from the Renaissance style took place gradually. Art historians generally agree that in their movement away from the Renaissance, artists first developed a style called "mannerism." The mannerists rejected the Renaissance canons of proportion, perspective, and harmony. They painted subjective pictures, portraying scenes and people as they saw them in their inner vision rather than as they saw them with the eye, so that their paintings have abnormal perspectives and distorted figures. For example, the Spanish painter El Greco, the greatest of the mannerists, is said to have refused to go out into the streets of the city of Toledo when he was painting it because that would have dispelled his inner vision of the way Toledo looked.

Mannerism was too subjective to win wide acceptance. Artists in revolt against its principles developed a new style, the "baroque." The word was coined by art critics of the eighteenth century who considered the style in bad taste; thus, the word came to mean "extravagant" or "bizarre." The baroque emerged around the middle of the sixteenth century and reached its height around 1660. The new style was a general European phenomenon, but it was strongest in Catholic countries, from southern Germany to Italy and Spain. In fact, some have termed it the art of the Catholic Reformation, in that it expressed the religious ideas of the Council of Trent; Jesuits and other churchmen who had attended the Council were responsible for spreading it through Catholic Europe. This seems too narrow an interpretation, for the baroque style also found its way into Protestant lands. Moreover, not all baroque art was religious art; much of it was worldly and sensuous.

Baroque is difficult to define. One art historian has said that a single baroque style does not exist, and that the very diversity of styles was one of the distinguishing features of the seventeenth century. It is possible, however, to describe the essential characteristics or common denominators of baroque art. It aimed at grandeur, extravagance, and decorativeness. Baroque artists wanted to make things seem larger than life; they used elaborate theatrical effects to magnify the impressiveness of their work. Baroque art has been called "a grandiose make-believe." At the same time baroque painters rejected the fantasies and strange proportions and perspectives of mannerism. They believed that the artist should paint things as they really are. "Imitate natural things well," was the way one of the greatest baroque painters put it. Many artists had a passion for representations of everyday life, and landscapes and still-lifes became more important and more common than ever before. Space and light held a special fascina-

View of Toledo, by El Greco

"Greco was never tired of painting this rock city . . . Toledo became Gethsemane. Clouds hover above the ash-grey stony land, slashed like the curtain of which it is written that at the hour of Christ's death it was rent in twain; grey storm light lies on the meadows, which tumble down to the Tagus; the dust, driven by the breath of the storm, is laid on the green earth like the dust of the charnel house. In the greyness of this menacing, rocky wilderness Greco found himself. . . ." L. Goldscheider, EL GRECO (London, 1954).

Courtesy of The Metropolitan Museum of Art, Bequest of Mrs. H. O. Havemeyer, 1929, The H. O. Havemeyer Collection

tion. Painters tried to give the illusion of boundless space, to convey a sense of the infinite to the viewer. Renaissance artists had learned how to give the illusion of depth. Baroque artists managed to give the illusion of infinite prolongation of the space confined within the canvas by means of lines reaching out from the front of the picture, by devices such as mirrors in the painting that reflected things not shown in the painting itself, or by including passageways that led to the end of the painting. They used light for this purpose, too; for example, they painted light coming into the picture from a source not shown in the picture.

The Flemish artist Peter Paul Rubens (1577–1640) has been called the most representative of the baroque style. He filled his pictures with a ferment of vitality, richness, excitement, dynamism, and sheer joy of life. They have an extravagance and grandiosity that seems to transcend reality. The people appear as demigods. Although he modeled his lusty, bulging nudes after the Flamandes (Flemish women) that he knew, they have been justly termed "cosmic Flamandes."

Baroque architects built lavishly ornamented churches and other buildings, replete with cherubs and angels, gilt and colored marbles, intricate designs, curved lines, and twisted and bent columns. Their buildings have a theatrical quality; they seem almost like scenery for the stage. They give the impression of tension and of a great mass in movement. Most of the important works were animated by a strong moral, religious, or political purpose. For example, the magnificent piazza in front of St. Peter's in Rome, designed by Giovanni Bernini (1598–1680) with two great semicircles of colonnades, presents a magnificently theatrical setting for the vast church, and overwhelms the viewer with the realization that he stands at the center of a great and powerful world religion.

In music, the baroque era ended the longest musical tradition in the West. Polyphony had originated in the twelfth century. It was the structuring of music from equal and independent parallel elements. No one strand of music was significantly more important than another. In contrast, baroque music was characterized by a single element, the melody, supported by harmony. The human voice dominated polyphony; a significant development in the baroque change from polyphony to harmony was the beginning of instrumental dominance. Giovanni Palestrina (c. 1525–1594) represented the high point of polyphony with his mastery of an intricate vocal web of choral patterns. The Italian composer Claudio Monteverdi (1567–1643) represented the new departure into harmony and instrumental accompaniment. He and his disciples found in opera the perfect expression for the baroque passion for pageantry and exaggerated emotion.

Baroque characteristics marked the work of many of the writers of Western and Central Europe during the years from the mid-sixteenth to the mid-seventeenth centuries. Like their fellow artists in other fields of creative activity, the writers of the baroque age took delight in exaggeration and overemphasis. They used ornate language, rich in adjectives and exclamatory expressions, and they piled up similes and metaphors. Their writing was filled with tension, struggle, and movement. They cherished the dramatic and theatrical, and they tried to achieve contrast and surprise. Violence attracted them; they were inclined to linger over scenes of horror and carnage. Above all, they tried to capture in their prose and poetry the deepest human emotions and to convey a sense of the supernatural forces that they believed control the destinies of men.

THE DYNAMISM OF THE AGE

New-risen noblemen, aspiring merchants, astronomers, physicists, baroque writers and artists, had in common a sense of dynamism, of power in motion. The depiction of supernatural forces sought by the baroque was most often cast in religious form, but its abiding attribute was its dynamism. Dynamism was no less the abiding attribute of Kepler's laws of motion, Galileo's postulates of terrestrial bodies in motion, Harvey's pumping heart coursing blood through the circulatory system, Descartes' brilliant construct of the dynamic act of thought as the proof of existence, and the inexorable and irresistible *Leviathan* of Hobbes. Society itself was dynamic in a way that it had not been before, as the old social order gave way before the new.

Yet European man's new sense of dynamism had about it a strange quality of fear and foreboding, almost as if there had opened a door on terrors which in the centuries before had been locked up. The wars and insurrections, the violence, destruction, and hard times of the first six decades of the seventeenth century justified this fear and foreboding.

CHAPTER NINE

Age of Crisis, 1600–1660: Absolutist Solution

THE FIRST SIX DECADES of the seventeenth century have no universally recognized label, such as the Renaissance or the Reformation. It was an age of crisis, filled with uncertainty, confusion, civil conflict, and seemingly endless war. Economic difficulties multiplied, the vigorous demographic expansion of the sixteenth century leveled off and in some areas population actually declined, trade fell off, unemployment was widespread, periodic visits of the plague were particularly virulent, and crop failures occurred with destructive regularity. Above all, it was a time of crisis in relations between monarchs and their subjects, particularly the nobility, with revolutions against monarchic authority breaking out in France, the Netherlands, Spain, Portugal, Naples, England, Scotland, and Russia.

It was also an articulate age, filled with theoretical controversy about the nature of government and the role of the sovereign. Participants in the debate ranged from monarchs, leading statesmen, and high churchmen down to humble cobblers and tailors. Missing from the controversial literature of the age was the Renaissance's boundless enthusiasm for the "new man." Men were disturbed by what seemed to be the forces of evil and the conditions of decay surrounding them, and their sense of foreboding was articulated in violence, both verbal and physical.

The outlets were as various as men: masses and mysticism, the baroque yearning for cosmic unity in Catholic countries, the assurance of the salvation of the faithful or the elect in Protestant countries in passionate, interminable sermons, and everywhere the fearful and implacable pursuit of heterodoxy, of witches, heretics, sinners. Astrology served for the more pagan spirits— the young imperial freebooter, Wallenstein, had his horoscope cast by Kepler. The solace of cynicism seemed to transcend faith and unfaith alike. War was almost a palliative to the lower orders when to stay at home might just as well mean starvation, beggary, or death of the plague.

Though the three greatest developments on the Continent in this age—the Thirty Years' War, the decline of Spain, the reconstruction of France—were all intimately linked politically, not least they were also ingredients of the common crisis. The emergence of absolutism, which was both a cause and the ultimate effect of the crisis, seemed to most Europeans the only way out of crisis, the only escape from uncertainty, confusion, civil conflict, and hard times.

The Thirty Years' War

The Religious Peace of Augsburg in 1555 had established a precarious religious and political balance between Protestants and Catholics in the Holy Roman Empire. The two camps had managed to avoid all-out war but, as incidents of conflict multiplied, they began to prepare for an inevitable armed clash. The spark that set off the war could have come from any part of the empire; it happened to come from Bohemia.

Bohemia had long been in name an elective monarchy. The estates, assembled in a diet, were supposed to choose a monarch, but for nearly a century they had always found it politically expedient to elect a member of the Hapsburg family. Most Bohemians were Protestant and all were proud of their nation's past glories and independence. Increasingly, they feared the efforts of the Hapsburgs to expand the power of the central government and strengthen the position of the Catholic Church in Bohemia. Their fears reached a peak in 1617 when the childless Emperor Mathias had his cousin Ferdinand elected king of Bohemia and designated as successor to the imperial crown. Ferdinand had a reputation for extreme piety and intolerance. When he became king of Bohemia he swore to uphold the right of the Bohemian Protestants to practice their religion, but his actions soon belied his words. In 1618 a group of Protestant Bohemian nobles decided to rebel.

The first overt act of rebellion came in Prague on a bright day in May, 1618, when a mob of Bohemian Protestants burst into a room high up in Hradschin Castle and threw three Catholic officials out of the window. The trio dropped nearly fifty feet but only one suffered injuries. Catholics claimed that angels had supported the men in their descent to save them from bodily harm, but Protestants noted that the three had landed in a pile of manure that happened to be under the window. Whether miracle or comic accident, the event, known by the imposing name of the Defenestration of Prague, signaled the beginning of a war lasting thirty years, in which nearly every European state became involved and which brought horror and misery to many of the common people of Germany and Bohemia.

THE HAPSBURG ASCENDANCY, 1618–1629

The Bohemian estates announced the deposition of Ferdinand and offered the crown to the youthful Frederick, imperial elector of the Rhineland Palatinate in western Germany, a staunch Calvinist, and leader of the Protestant Union of German princes. When Frederick and his wife, the daughter of King James I of England, came to Prague for his coronation late in 1619, the Jesuits mockingly prophesied, "He will be a winter king. When summer comes he will be driven from the field." Events soon proved them correct. Frederick failed to obtain hoped-for aid from his English father-in-law, the Dutch, and his fellow princes of the Protestant Union. At the same time Spain rallied to the aid of Ferdinand (who in 1619 succeeded Mathias as emperor), the pope sent him money and, most important, the ruler of Bavaria, who was head of the Catholic League of German princes, sent an army under the command of Count Tilly. In 1620 at the Battle of White Mountain not far from Prague, Frederick's army was crushed and the "winter king" fled with his wife to Holland.

Emperor Ferdinand followed up his victory with ruthless repression and established an Austrian and Catholic domination of Bohemia that lasted for three hundred years. The Jesuits vigorously forced Catholicism upon the people; those who tried to keep their Protestant faith had to pay special heavy taxes and have soldiers quartered in their homes. An estimated 150,000 people fled the country, among whom were most of Bohemia's leading intellectuals. Ferdinand confiscated all or part of the lands of the rebel nobles and gained possession of half of Bohemia. He sold or gave away the confiscated lands to Catholics, many of whom came from other parts of the empire or abroad. In this manner the old Bohemian Protestant nobility was largely supplanted by a Catholic nobility who had no sentimental or historical attachments to Bohemia and who owed their position and their loyalty to the Hapsburg emperor.

The imperial forces followed up their easy victory over the Bohemians with the conquest of the Palatinate and the deposition of Frederick. Other Protestant princes in Germany, fearing that a similar fate would befall them, sought a leader. In 1625 Christian IV of Denmark, who as Duke of Holstein was also a prince of the empire, decided to champion the Protestant cause. Concern about the fate of Lutheranism in Germany doubtless helped to inspire Christian's intervention, but the main impetus came from his desire to maintain and increase the German possessions of his dynasty. England offered to subsidize him heavily to help cover the cost of his campaign, in the hope that he might restore Frederick in the Palatinate and harry Spain, England's prime enemy.

In search of additional military support, Emperor Ferdinand accepted an unusual offer from Albert von Wallenstein, Duke of Friedland, to provide and lead an army of twenty thousand at no cost to the emperor. Wallenstein, a Catholic Bohemian landowner, was a lonely and sinister man, loving no one and loved by no one, driven by unfathomable ambition, believing in nothing except astrology and his own destiny. Through skilful management he greatly increased the fortune left him by his wealthy wife. When the Bohemian revolt broke out in 1618, he led local levies against the rebels and lent large sums to the emperor. After White Mountain he bought many of the confiscated lands of the Bohemian nobility at bargain prices. By the time he made the offer to the emperor, he owned one-quarter of all the land in Bohemia.

In his campaigns against the Danes Wallenstein showed himself to be a consummate general. By 1629 Christian had acknowledged defeat and withdrawn from battle, ending the first phase of the war. Hapsburg power stood at its zenith, while the Protestant cause in Germany was apparently doomed. In the elation of victory the emperor issued the Edict of Restitution in 1629, decreeing the return to the Catholic Church of all lands taken from it by Protestants since 1552. The edict enraged Protestant rulers, who had profited from the lands, and convinced them that the emperor intended to destroy both Protestantism and princely independence. Catholic princes also became anxious when the emperor named his relatives to recovered bishoprics and when the Jesuits, who were so close to the emperor, took over some of the recovered monasteries. It seemed that Ferdinand planned to use the victory they had helped him win to increase Hapsburg control over Germany. They also feared Wallenstein, who with his own army and his great wealth appeared to be the emperor's tool in establishing imperial control over Germany, as well as being an unscrupulous adventurer carving out a new kingdom for himself at their expense. Filled with suspicions, leading Catholic princes refused to name Ferdinand's son "King of the Romans" (traditional title of the heir-apparent of the emperor) and demanded the dismissal of Wallenstein and the dissolution of his army. Against his wishes, Ferdinand gave in.

SWEDEN AND THE RESTORATION OF PROTESTANTISM, 1631–1635

Ferdinand received a much harder blow to his plans when in 1631 King Gustavus Adolphus of Sweden invaded Germany. Gustavus—statesman, military genius, and devout Lutheran—entered the war to save German Protestantism, but like Christian of Denmark he had ulterior motives. The "Lion of the North" feared that too much power for the Hapsburgs in Germany would endanger Sweden and interfere with Swedish trade on the Baltic. He also had ambitions for territorial acquisitions on Germany's Baltic coast.

Part of the money that Gustavus Adolphus needed for his crusade to save Protestantism came from a Catholic country and a cardinal of the Church. The French government, under the guidance of Cardinal Richelieu, was alarmed at the growing power of the Hapsburgs, its traditional enemy. Already ringed by Spain, the southern Netherlands, and Italy, all under Hapsburg control, France wanted to prevent the Hapsburgs from closing the circle by gaining domination of Germany. "If Germany is lost," said Cardinal Richelieu, "France cannot exist." In 1631 France agreed to subsidize the Swedish fight against the Hapsburgs in the cause of Protestantism. In return, Gustavus Adolphus promised not to interfere with the practice of the Catholic religion in the regions that his armies freed from Hapsburg control.

In a series of brilliant campaigns over less than two years Gustavus Adolphus reversed the fortunes of the two faiths in Germany, placing the Protestant princes in the ascendancy. In desperation Emperor Ferdinand turned to Wallenstein for help. Before that irascible genius would consent to raise an army, he demanded many concessions, including full charge of the army and large financial guarantees.

Wallenstein's enormous prestige and good pay attracted men to his regiments, and he soon had a powerful force of 40,000. In September, 1632, he faced Gustavus Adolphus for the first time, and the Swede tasted his first defeat on German soil. The two titans met again a few weeks later at Lützen, near Leipzig. Although the Protestants routed the imperial army, the Protestant cause suffered the irreparable loss of Gustavus Adolphus, who was killed in action. There is a story that as Gustavus lay dying on the battlefield, the enemy soldiers around him asked his name. "I am the King of Sweden," he replied, "who do seal the religion and liberty of the German nation with my blood." His intervention had indeed saved Protestantism in Germany from the annihilation that it suffered in Bohemia, and he had frustrated the Hapsburg attempt to establish imperial supremacy.

The war continued as even more of a struggle for political power. Wallenstein intrigued with Protestant leaders and Cardinal Richelieu, apparently planned to seize political power and perhaps make himself dictator of

Germany or king of Bohemia. When the emperor and his counselors decided to relieve him of command, Wallenstein ordered his army to desert to the enemy. Only a thousand followed him. While in flight, he and four of his closest associates were murdered by officers loyal to the emperor and anxious for reward.

Both sides now made serious efforts to end the war. In 1635 the emperor and all but one of the German princes opposing him reached an agreement on peace terms that was highly favorable to the Hapsburgs. The settlement was never effected, however, for at this juncture Cardinal Richelieu decided that France should actively enter the war on the Protestant side to smash the Hapsburg power. The French intervention prolonged the conflict for another thirteen years.

THE LAST PHASE, 1635–1648

With the entry of France the war lost nearly all connection with religious issues and became a dynastic struggle between Bourbon France on the one side and Hapsburg Austria and Spain on the other. The conflict went badly for the French until superior resources and the brilliant leadership of two young generals, Condé and Turenne, turned the tide in France's favor. Peace negotiations began in 1641. Three years later the representatives of the warring powers met in the towns of Münster and Osnabrück in Westphalia, northwest Germany, in the first peace congress of modern history. The delegates took four more years to agree on terms. Finally in 1648 they signed a series of treaties known collectively as the Peace of Westphalia.

The terrible war had ended. It had reduced large tracts of Germany to ruins. The competing armies lived off the land, and the soldiers, most of whom were mercenaries, had no pity on those they looted: civilians were considered legitimate prey. Soldiers stripped the countryside bare, brutally sacked the cities, and for amusement raped, burned, and tortured. In many regions farming came to a standstill. Germany's population, racked by famine and disease as well as war, fell drastically. Impoverished and torn by these disasters, the country suffered a severe economic setback. Another crippling effect of the war was the stimulation that it gave to princely particularism, preventing the cooperation of German states. The war did not "destroy" Germany, because there was no national entity to destroy, but it did fix on Germany the atomization into many independent sovereignties that was the enemy of German unity and vitality.

THE PEACE OF WESTPHALIA, 1648

The Peace of Westphalia represented a victory for German Protestantism and the sovereignty of German princes, and a defeat for the Catholic

The Peace of Westphalia

This contemporary print celebrates the signing of the Peace of Westphalia on October 24, 1648. The central figures are the boy king Louis XIV, Emperor Ferdinand III, and Queen Christina of Sweden. All three succeeded their fathers who had reigned at the beginning of the war. Kneeling are clergy and laity (D), a Catholic bishop to the left, a Protestant minister to the right. Peace (A) is seated on her throne and before her stands figures representing Fear of God (F) and Penance (G). On the right stands War (I) faced by a general (L) and a cavalier (M). An angel (H) praises Peace, and another angel (K) bearing a tattered flag and broken sword warns War to leave Germany. E. A. Beller, PROPAGANDA IN GERMANY DURING THE THIRTY YEARS' WAR (Princeton, 1940).

Reformation and the imperial ambitions in Germany of the Hapsburgs. It confirmed the Religious Peace of Augsburg, which had given each German prince the right to determine the religion of his subjects, and it placed Calvinism on a par with Lutheranism and Catholicism. It allowed the Protestants to keep the lands they had taken from the Catholic Church after 1624. It gave recognition to each German state as a sovereign power with the right to govern itself and conduct its own foreign affairs. It directed that the emperor gain the consent of the diet of the empire, formed of representatives of the 350 princedoms, bishoprics, and free cities of Germany, before he could issue laws, levy taxes, recruit soldiers, or make war or peace in the name of the empire. Since the ambitions, jealousies, and pettinesses of the many German rulers made agreement on such matters impossible, these provisions ended any possibility of imperial control over Germany and doomed German unification. As signatories of the treaties, France and Sweden became guarantors of the peace terms, which meant they could legally intervene in German affairs as protectors of the provisions of the treaty. France used this pretext time and again during the next 150 years to keep Germany disunited.

The territorial arrangements of the peace confirmed the disintegration of the Empire. France received three bishoprics in Lorraine and extensive rights in Alsace. Sweden gained western Pomerania on the Baltic shores and the bishopric of Bremen, thereby gaining control of the mouths of the Weser, Elbe, and Oder rivers, the three most important commercial water routes of Germany. The emperor recognized the independence of the Swiss, which had actually been won long before. (See p. 106.) Spain agreed to recognize Dutch independence and to end its war with the United Provinces.

Neither Spain nor France, however, was ready to end its war with the other. Spain foolishly hoped to recoup some of its losses, and France dared not pass up the opportunity to complete the ruin of its old foe. Only the outbreak of civil commotion in France kept Spain from certain disaster. The war continued until 1659, when Spain had to accept defeat. In the Peace of the Pyrenees, signed that year, Spain recognized French conquests on the Spanish–French frontier that made the Pyrenees France's southern boundary, ceded some land to France in the Netherlands and, to seal the treaty, agreed to a marriage between the youthful French king, Louis XIV, and the daughter of the Spanish king.

The Peace of Westphalia settled religious and political issues that had long kept Europe in turmoil. Catholic and Protestant finally realized that neither was strong enough to destroy the other and that they must learn to live together. Out of the forced compromise a spirit of toleration slowly grew. Religious conflict continued as an important issue in the domestic politics of several nations, but never again did the enmity between Catholic and Protestant become a major issue in European international politics.

In politics the peace confirmed the end of Hapsburg dreams of domination in Germany, and also marked the end of Hapsburg supremacy in Europe. The once-powerful Hapsburg family alliance—the Madrid-Vienna axis—went down in defeat. The Austrian Hapsburgs turned their attention to the construction of a new domain in southeastern Europe. Hapsburg Spain dwindled in power and was replaced by France as Europe's greatest power. In rejecting the old imperial idea, the Peace of Westphalia recognized the fact that Europe had become organized into a system of independent sovereign states, each unabashedly following its own interests. The concept of a supranational unity based upon religion or politics vanished.

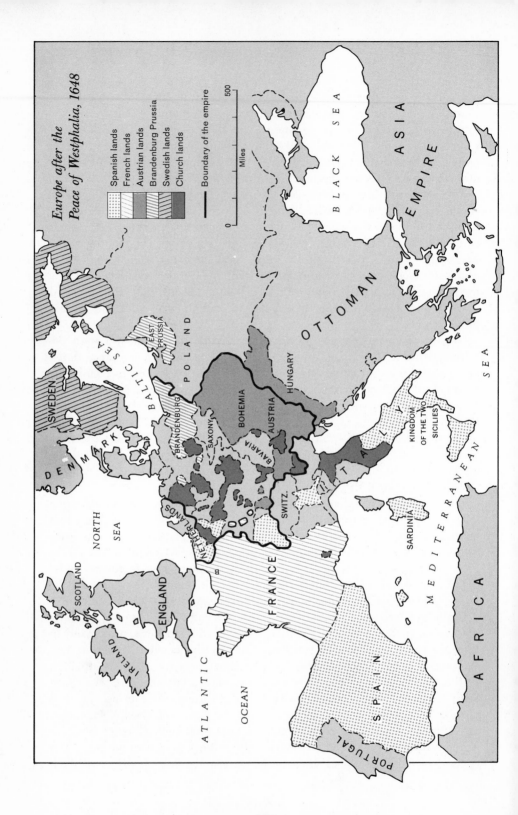

Europe after the
Peace of Westphalia, 1648

Spanish lands
French lands
Austrian lands
Brandenburg Prussia
Swedish lands
Church lands

Boundary of the empire

500

Miles

0

BLACK SEA

ASIA

OTTOMAN EMPIRE

SWEDEN

BALTIC SEA

DENMARK

EAST PRUSSIA

POLAND

BRANDENBURG

SAXONY

BOHEMIA

AUSTRIA

HUNGARY

BAVARIA

SWITZ.

ITALY

KINGDOM OF THE TWO SICILIES

SARDINIA

MEDITERRANEAN SEA

AFRICA

NETHERLANDS

FRANCE

SPAIN

PORTUGAL

NORTH SEA

SCOTLAND

ENGLAND

IRELAND

ATLANTIC OCEAN

The Decline of Spain, 1598–1665

Shortly before his death in 1598, Philip II of Spain remarked sadly, "God, who has given me so many kingdoms, has not given me a son able to govern them." Philip III (1598–1621), known as the Pious, inherited the religious ardor of his father but none of his other qualities. Lazy, pleasure-loving, and unbelievably extravagant, he gave control of the government to ill-chosen favorites who used their power to enrich themselves and their families. Court and government were shot through with corruption and graft.

ECONOMIC DETERIORATION

The misrule of Philip's reign hastened the economic as well as the political decay of Spain. During the sixteenth century economic life had advanced in Spain, albeit less rapidly than in England, France, or the Netherlands. Toward the end of the reign of Philip II the trend turned markedly downward. The economic crisis was above all a crisis for Castile, the central kingdom under the Spanish crown. Castile supported the Spanish economy in the sixteenth century with its agricultural production, mercantile activities, and territories in the New World. From Castile came the bulk of the government's revenue and most of the manpower for the armies: approximately 80 per cent of the population of the Iberian peninsula was Castilian, and nearly one-half of the Castilians were located in the plateau country of central Castile within a one-hundred-mile radius of Madrid.

In the middle of the sixteenth century the expansion of the Castilian economy stopped. Foreign goods displaced Spanish-made wares, and Castile's trade and industry dwindled. Castilian manufactures were increasingly luxury goods, for which there was no mass market. The privileges of the Mesta (see p. 186) held back the raising of crops, drove up food prices and made Spain dependent upon Northern and Eastern Europe for grain. The agrarian depression in Castile caused extensive depopulation. Castile became less and less able to supply the men and the money upon which Spanish power rested.

To the crisis in the internal economy was added a crisis in the colonial economy. As long as silver imports were maintained at a high level, the effects of the Castilian economic crisis were moderated. After 1600 the flow of silver from America began to taper off, and by 1660 it had dropped to less than one-tenth of its amount in 1600. Exhaustion of mines, smuggling of bullion, and increasing shipments of precious metals from Spanish America to Asia were the chief causes of the silver decline. The Spanish government had long depended upon the stream of bullion from the New World to subsidize its power; the diminution in this stream after 1600 signaled the decline of Spain in general.

A large measure of responsibility for the economic deterioration belonged to the inordinate ambitions and misguided policies of the government. The heavy cost of war, the crushing burden of taxation, the drain of the king's ornate court, and the inefficiency and corruption of the bureaucracy, placed heavy demands upon the economy and stifled economic advance. In particular, the government's credit policy had ill effects on the economy. To raise money for war, the government borrowed at such high rates of interest that private investment in economically productive areas was discouraged. The government encouraged foreign merchants in return for their advance of credit to the government, resulting in a drain of bullion from Spain and increasing foreign encroachments on the colonial market. Finally, the government turned to a dangerous fiscal device, which has been used by other hard-pressed governments: cheapening the value of money to make it easier to pay the debts. The government debased its coinage by substituting copper for silver. Inevitably prices rose sharply. The overall rise in prices served to reduce the purchasing power of taxes, which added to the government's fiscal problems.

Paradoxically, the same nation that was retreating from reality into super-Catholicism, mysticism, and baroque fantasy also produced in the early seventeenth century a native school of economic theorists, the *arbitristas* (projectors), who called attention to the problems of the economy and suggested remedies. They urged that royal expenditures be curbed, the parasitic growth of the Church halted, the sale of government offices ended, the tax system reformed, the currency stabilized, inducements offered to keep labor on the land, and technological advances applied in irrigation and making rivers navigable. Nothing was done by Philip III and his extravagant ministers to implement the proposals, but in his successor, Philip IV, a Spanish statesman emerged who intended such reforms.

THE COUNT-DUKE OLIVARES

Philip IV (1621–1665), who was only sixteen when he succeeded his father, turned the rule of the country over to the Count-Duke Olivares. The new chief minister had for years intrigued to reach this eminence; when at last he attained his ambition, he exulted, "All is mine!" He was no more reluctant than his predecessors to use his power for selfish ends, but unlike them, he had loftier goals. He meant to return his country to the glorious days of Philip II, when it had been the colossus of the world. What Olivares did not sufficiently appreciate was that Spain could not recapture its past glory without an economic revival. More than anything else Spain needed a long period of peace and retrenchment. Instead, Olivares involved his country in disastrous wars.

The renewal of the war with the Dutch in 1621 and the precipitate intervention in the Thirty Years' War, which after 1635 meant war with France, postponed his proposed renewal of the economy. The heavy exactions of men and money that were imposed to continue the war effort deepened the economic crisis and met with resistance. In 1640 open revolt broke out, first in Catalonia and then in Portugal. The Catalans established a republic and put themselves under French protection. They held out until 1652, when a domestic crisis in France compelled the French to reduce their support and allowed Spain to reconquer the province. The Portuguese, who had been ruled by Spain since 1580, took advantage of the Catalan revolt to declare their independence. In a rising that lasted only three hours they overthrew the Spanish government in Lisbon. The Portuguese gave the crown to the Duke of Braganza, who ruled as John IV and founded a dynasty that reigned until 1910. In 1647 a wild and bloody revolt flared out in Naples, which had been a Spanish dependency since 1504. The revolt continued for over six months before the Spanish re-established their control.

Failure to defeat the Dutch and the French, the revolts of 1640, and the heavy attrition of war cost Olivares his office in 1643 and ended Spain's hope of regaining its former position. In the war with the Dutch, which lasted until 1648, Dutch naval victories destroyed Spanish sea power and enabled the Dutch to consolidate their dominance in the East Indies and make extensive inroads in Brazil. The war with France dragged on until 1659, ending with the humiliating Peace of the Pyrenees. The final result of the long years of war was defeat on every front, economic ruin, and the fall of Spain to the status of a second-class power.

THE GOLDEN AGE OF SPANISH CULTURE

In the latter part of the sixteenth century Spain entered its greatest period of artistic creativity. Painting and literature were the glories of this golden age of culture, although other branches of the arts also flourished. All aspects of creativity were informed by the manneristic or baroque styles.

Among the painters of Spain three names stand out: El Greco, Velasquez, and Murillo. El Greco (c. 1547–1614), whose real name was Domenicos Theotocopoulos, came from Crete; the Spaniards called him "the Greek." He had studied in Venice with the great Renaissance artists Titian and Tintoretto, from whom he derived a manneristic use of light and color. He settled in Toledo, where he painted the pictures that have won him immortality. He developed a distinctive style by which he conveyed to the viewer mystical and visionary experiences. Although a foreigner, he instinctively assimilated the spirit and psychology of Catholic Spain and became completely Spanish, like that other famous foreigner, Charles V.

Velasquez (1599–1660), who also studied in Italy and greatly admired El Greco's work, painted in a very different style. He was interested in bringing out personalities rather than expressing ideas and mystical experiences. He penetrated to the essentials of what he saw, leaving out details, so that his paintings are impressionistic rather than photographic; the French impressionists of the late nineteenth century hailed him as one of their precursors. As painter to Philip IV's court for thirty-seven years, he produced forty portraits of the king as well as many portraits of the grandees of Spain and other personages. His portraits are psychological studies: when Pope Innocent X saw the one that Velasquez had done of him, he winced and said, "Too true!"

Velasquez painted relatively few religious works, in contrast to Murillo (1617–1682), who specialized in religious paintings. Murillo's pictures, although filled with warmth and gentleness, are sentimental and sometimes saccharine. He specialized in idealized portraits of saints with their eyes turned heavenward. He enjoyed great popularity during the eighteenth and nineteenth centuries, when he was regarded as one of the world's greatest masters.

In Spanish literature the great names are Cervantes, Lope de Vega, and Calderón. Cervantes (1547–1616) wrote many works, but he owes his fame to the prose epic *Don Quixote*, which appeared in two parts in 1605 and 1614. Some critics have called it the greatest novel ever written. It tells about a simple country gentleman who read so many stories about the days of chivalry that his brain became addled. He imagined that he was himself a knight-errant, dedicated himself to a lady named Dulcinea (whom he had never seen), and rode forth on his old nag to do battle against injustice, defend the innocent and virtuous, and conquer a realm. He had a series of ridiculous adventures, loyally attended by Sancho Panza, an illiterate peasant with much common sense. Sancho realized that his master was mad but quickly came to love and admire him—as does the reader of the book—for Quixote, despite his folly, was a man of saintly character, full of courage, sincerity, and goodness. His adventures took place within the everyday Spanish world, which Cervantes described with great artistry and in much detail, providing a vivid panorama of Spanish life from the nobility down to criminals on their way to the galleys. Above all, the tale is an allegory of the conflict between mystical idealism, exemplified by Quixote, and common-sense realism, exemplified by Sancho.

Lope de Vega (1562–1635), probably the most prolific writer of all times, was a dramatist and poet. In his later years he became the arbiter of Spanish letters and a national idol. Like Shakespeare, his contemporary, he was distinguished for ingenious plots of intrigue, patriotic and historical subject matter, archetypal characterization, and imaginative staging. Only a few of his many hundreds of plays and poems have great power, for he wrote too much and generally with too slight an intent.

Calderón (1600–1681) demonstrated both the strengths and the weaknesses of baroque drama in the many secular plays that he wrote in the first three decades of his career. They were dramatically effective, ingenious, and mystical, yet often shallow, precious, and stilted. It was in the short allegorical dramas on the sacrament of the Eucharist, following his ordination to the priesthood at the age of fifty-one, that he wrote most movingly and originally. His devotional fervor reflected both the passion and the abiding religiosity that ennobled so much of the baroque style in the golden age of Spanish culture.

The Reconstruction of France

The history of France in the seventeenth century presents a striking contrast to the story of Spain's decay. An upward surge after the dissolution of the Wars of Religion carried France by mid-century to the position of European leadership that Spain had occupied in the sixteenth century.

ACHIEVEMENTS OF HENRY IV

The great recovery began with the reign of Henry IV (1589–1610), first king of the Bourbon dynasty. When Henry ascended the throne, France was in a sad state after many years of civil war. Many districts had been devastated, fields lay untilled, roads and bridges were destroyed, navigable rivers had become silted, and economic life had suffered a severe setback. The kingdom was still plagued by political dissensions and religious hatreds, the throne had lost most of its prestige and was in danger of losing its power, and morale was at a dangerously low level. Henry was undaunted by the enormous task of reconstruction that faced him. By persuasion, bribes, pressure, and force he re-established royal authority over the great feudal lords, the parlements, and the governors of the provinces. He quieted religious discontent by becoming a Catholic himself, while issuing the Edict of Nantes to placate the Huguenots. He worked hard to improve the well-being of his people. Few monarchs have been so solicitous of the welfare of their subjects; when he became king, he said in a typically warm and homely manner, "I hope to make France so prosperous that every peasant will have a chicken in his pot on Sunday." His interest in the people's welfare stemmed not only from genuine love but from a realization that the prosperity of the country would strengthen the monarchy.

In his work of reconstruction, especially of economic life, Henry had the invaluable assistance of the Duke of Sully, an austere and methodical Calvinist. Sully introduced economies into the government, reduced corruption and inefficiency, and encouraged economic growth to increase tax revenues. When he took control of the finances, he found a debt of 300 million livres; when he left office in 1610, the treasury had a reserve of 13 million livres. He was responsible for the repair and construction of roads, canals, and bridges, the dredging of rivers, and improvements in the postal service. He did everything he could to encourage agriculture in the belief that it was the only true form of wealth. Under his guidance marshes were drained to increase the country's area of plowland and pasture, and improved techniques of tillage and animal husbandry were introduced.

Another of Henry's Protestant aides, Barthélemy de Laffemas, headed a Commission of Commerce to stimulate the growth of all aspects of French economic life. The commission encouraged the development of old industries and introduced new ones, including the culture of silkworms and the manufacture of silk. Several government-sponsored efforts to found overseas trading companies modeled after the highly successful Dutch and English ventures failed, but in 1608 Quebec, the first successful French overseas colony, was established by Samuel de Champlain. Under Henry's leadership France regained much lost ground. Yet much remained to be done when in 1610 a religious fanatic named Ravaillac, who was obsessed with the idea that Henry was the archenemy of Catholicism, leaped on the king's coach in a narrow Parisian street and plunged a dagger into his heart.

LOUIS XIII AND MARIE DE' MEDICI

Henry's son and successor, Louis XIII (1610–43), was only nine at his accession, and his mother, Marie de' Medici (whom Henry had married for her money in 1600 after divorcing his first wife, Margaret of Valois) became regent. Her misrule quickly threatened to undo all that Henry had accomplished. Lazy and slow-witted, she allowed Italian favorites to take power and enrich themselves, while Henry's wise, trusted, and disapproving counselors were turned out of office. Discontent appeared on every side and civil commotion again threatened France. In an effort to quiet the unrest the queen convened the Estates-General. The three orders—clergy, nobility, and commoners or Third Estate—met in 1614. Instead of addressing themselves to the problems that faced the country, they exchanged recriminations, accomplished nothing, and discredited the Estates-General as a representative assembly. Marie grew tired of the harangues and dismissed the meeting. One hundred and seventy-five years passed before the Estates-General met again.

The discord mounted until a palace revolution in 1617 drove the queen from the court, killed the chief Italian favorite, and gave power to the young king. Nothing really changed, however, for Louis was weak and uncertain and new favorites took over. Revolts broke out among feudal lords and among Protestants, who feared new oppression by the Catholic Church. The situation continued to deteriorate until 1624, when the king named Cardinal Richelieu as his chief minister.

Cardinal Richelieu, by Philippe de Champaigne

"Cardinal de Richelieu was a man of his word, unless great interests swayed him to the contrary, and in such cases he was very artful to preserve all the appearances of good faith. . . . He was more ambitious than was consistent with the rules of morality. . . . He distinguished more judiciously than any man in the world between bad and worse, good and better, which is a great qualification in a minister. . . . He had religion enough for this world. His own good sense, or else his inclination, always led him to the practice of virtue if his self-interest did not bias him to evil, which whenever he committed it he did so knowingly." Cardinal de Retz (1613–1679), in his MEMOIRS (London, 1896).

RICHELIEU AND THE REVIVAL OF FRANCE

The new minister had been born in 1585 of an old and noble family. Through family influence he became a bishop at twenty-two. Although he described his see as "the sorriest bishopric in the kingdom," he worked hard at the duties. In 1614 he attended the Estates-General, where his eloquence, his abilities, and his distinguished appearance won the attention of Marie de' Medici. She appointed him to the Council of State, where he served her faithfully. After her fall from power he effected a reconciliation between her and her son, the king. As a reward for his services, Louis persuaded the pope to make Richelieu a cardinal, appointed him to his council in 1622, and two years later made him chief minister.

From then until his death in 1642 Richelieu ruled France. Throughout his long tenure he pursued one supreme goal with inflexible determination—the increase of the power and glory of the French throne at home and abroad. To that end he undertook three programs: suppression of the political and military privileges of the Huguenots, reduction of the power and prerogatives of the nobility, and defeat of the Hapsburgs. He met with complete success in the first and third objectives, and almost complete success in the second.

Richelieu's hostility to the Huguenots did not come from any fanatical opposition to their religion. He considered the Huguenots a threat to the absolute power of the king and the security of the realm because of the special privileges and fortified places guaranteed to them by the Edict of Nantes. The fact that the most eminent of their leaders were noblemen increased his concern. The difficulties they made in the years of unrest following Henry IV's death persuaded Richelieu that their power had to be reduced. In 1627–28, after the Huguenots had once again risen against the government, royal forces besieged La Rochelle, their chief stronghold, and forced it to surrender. Soon other Protestant citadels capitulated. In 1629 in the Peace of Alais the government abolished the Huguenots' special military and political privileges but allowed them to keep their religious and civil freedom. Thereafter the Huguenots became loyal subjects, while Richelieu scrupulously respected their rights and exhibited no animosity toward them.

The cardinal moved with equal determination against the nobility, who had taken advantage of the disturbed times to resume many of their independent ways. The nobles resented his policies and constantly plotted his downfall. Richelieu, with spies everywhere, managed to outwit his enemies and to persuade the king to punish them severely. He sent a score of the highest aristocracy to the scaffold and drove others into exile. To reduce the nobles' power to wage local wars or terrorize the people of a rural district, he ordered the dismantling of all fortified castles except those on the frontiers. He sought to abolish dueling, the last vestige of the nobility's practice of waging private wars. Moreover, too many nobles were perishing in "affairs of honor"; in 1607, for example, four thousand nobles were said to have been killed in duels. Henry IV had tried without success to abolish the custom. Although Richelieu's efforts were more effective, they did not stop dueling altogether: in the twenty years following his death nine hundred nobles perished for the sake of their honor.

By completing the evolution of a sophisticated bureaucracy, Richelieu was able further to exclude the nobility from central government and to reduce their provincial power. Under him councils became the principal instruments of royal authority. Derived from the single council of the king in the Middle Ages, the councils permitted specialization and division of labor within the administration. The hierarchic and overlapping arrangement of responsibilities among the councils allowed for constant and effective control from the top. The High Council of State, presided over by the king and comprising his ministers of state, determined top-level policy in domestic and foreign affairs and supervised the other councils. The Council of Dispatches, including members of the High Council plus second-ranking officials, was an administrative body with oversight of police matters, power to imprison indefinitely by means of warrants called *lettres de cachet,* and responsibility for instructions to the *intendants,* the government's agents in the provinces. The Council of Finance, which was less august in membership, was responsible for fiscal policy and controlled the accounts. The Privy Council was the largest of the councils, in effect comprising the membership of all the other councils. It was essentially a court of justice with a wide appellate jurisdiction and power to review criminal judgments. In 1632 the councils were empowered to revoke any judicial decrees that contradicted royal authority, threatened the public interest, or abridged the king's rights.

There were twelve parlements; the oldest and most important one was at Paris. Their members, who inherited their posts, formed a special class among the nobility. In addition to serving as trial and appellate courts, they had the responsibility of recording royal legislation. Although the king alone legislated, the process of recording his acts gave the parlements the opportunity to petition for changes or to remonstrate against the royal legislation. The judicial autonomy of the parlements was severely limited by the 1632 edict empowering the councils to revoke judicial decrees. In 1641 their rights of protest when recording acts were drastically curtailed. With the Estates-General no longer convened, Richelieu was shutting off the last avenue of protest open to the nobility.

The intendants were the most effective means for reducing the provincial power of the nobility. Henry IV had begun the practice of sending out agents of the central government to attend to many of the duties of local administration. Richelieu developed the system, giving the administrators the titles of *intendant* (commissioner) of justice, police, and finance. Their powers involved inspection and supervision at the very minimum and could be instantly increased to meet any emergency. They became the chief administrative instruments for absolutist centralization.

Although certain places on the major councils were reserved for the nobility, Richelieu's policy was to staff the bureaucracy as much as possible from the middle rank of society, especially lawyers. Intendants came from this rank. In this way Richelieu depleted the power of the old nobility and furthered the growth of the "nobility of the robe." (See p. 262.) The new nobility's commitment to absolute monarchy was considered the safest counterpoise to the power of the old nobility.

In foreign policy Richelieu worked ceaselessly for the downfall of Hapsburg power in Spain, the Netherlands, and Germany in order to win security and international prestige for France. In the Thirty Years' War he subsidized the enemies of the Hapsburgs, and when in 1635 it looked as if the war might end, he intervened with French troops and prolonged the war another thirteen years. Although the cardinal died before the war ended, his plan was successful, for the House of Hapsburg was humbled and France stood supreme.

The French paid a heavy price for Richelieu's successes. Unlike Henry IV, he had no concern for the welfare of the people; he once compared them to mules who, "being used to burdens, are spoiled more by rest than by labor." He needed huge sums of money to carry out his programs, and so he taxed mercilessly. More than once the peasants in different parts of the country were driven to armed insurrections, which were put down with a cruel hand. The people hated and feared him. The week of mourning decreed by the king when Richelieu died in 1642 was in some places lit by bonfires to celebrate his passing.

MAZARIN AND THE FRONDE

Louis XIII died a few months after his great minister. Since the new king, Louis XIV, was only four, his mother, Anne of Austria, ruled as regent. The reins of power rested in the hands of an Italian-born cardinal named Jules Mazarin. The new chief minister had come to France as a papal legate, attracted the attention of Richelieu, become a French subject, and entered the king's service. Louis XIII had him elevated to the cardinalate (although he had never been ordained a priest) and, when Richelieu died, made him chief minister. Under the regent Mazarin's power greatly increased, for Anne conceived a strong affection for him and may even have secretly married him.

Mazarin, who came from a humble, middle-class background, was an avaricious and grasping man. He used his high position to gain enormous wealth for himself and the numerous relatives he brought to France, as well as to marry his nieces into the greatest families of the kingdom. He also had enormous ability and tried to continue Richelieu's policies, but he found it difficult to hold in check the forces that opposed those policies. The old nobility resented the effrontery of the foreign parvenu who dared to carry himself as their equal. The middle classes and the nobility of the robe were alarmed at his financial excesses, rapacity, and the increased taxation, which was even being exacted from the formerly tax-exempt new nobility.

In June, 1648, the discontent erupted into an open revolt led by the parlement of Paris and joined by many of the old nobility. This was the first of two risings known collectively as the *Fronde* (taken from the word for the slingshot used by Parisian boys at play, since some of the nobles gave the impression of merely playing at revolt). Amid much talk of constitutionalism, a great deal of selfish power politics took place among the *Frondeurs*, especially the old nobility who were fighting to preserve their archaic privileges. The first revolt quickly collapsed. In 1650 a new *Fronde* broke out, led by the old nobility and their private armies and involving a number of the nobility of the parlements as well. Devoid of any unifying principle beyond individual ambitions, the nobles shifted allegiance rapidly and conducted a series of private wars rather than a concerted campaign. By 1653 the movement had died out, after bloody skirmishes and a great deal of looting and devastation of the common people.

Mazarin weathered the storm by astute withdrawals at critical moments and the foresight not to wreak vengeance upon his enemies. He remained in power until his death in 1661. He passed on to his former charge, the young King Louis XIV, a country in which the nobility had been tamed and the parlements discredited, a position in international affairs that was second to none, and a people who were ready to support a strong, absolute monarch as the apparent alternative to feudal anarchy.

The Emergence of Absolutism

In the late Middle Ages the king ruled with the estates in a mixed monarchy in which the power of the king was shared with representatives of the clergy, the nobility, and the commoners—the orders or ranks of society that were privileged by law. Whether the institutional form of representation was called the Estates-General (France), Parliament (England), Riksdag (Sweden), Cortès (Spain), States (Netherlands), or Stati (Italy); whether the representatives met in one, two, or three chambers; whether the privileged orders excluded one or two of the ranks mentioned—whatever the differences in the extent of power and authority of the representatives, such mixed monarchy limited the exercise of royal power. The king and the estates were conceived of as separate but cooperating entities in a dualistic government.

In the second half of the fifteenth century strong kings emerged who were able to increase the power of the throne at the expense of the privileged orders. Monarchic power grew rapidly in the sixteenth century but was not yet able to eclipse completely the traditional institutions of the privileged orders. The climax of this royal struggle for freedom from the restrictions of mixed monarchy came in the first half of the seventeenth century. The crisis of that period was above all a crisis in the relations between monarchs and their privileged subjects, especially the nobility. It was a confrontation between the monarch who claimed to be the sole representative of the state and the traditional constitutional entities, the estates.

THE THEORETICAL FOUNDATIONS OF ABSOLUTISM

Usually, mixed monarchy is regarded as the national counterpart of the supranational church-state dualism of the Middle Ages. Therefore, it is argued, the destruction of the latter entailed the decline of mixed monarchy, a proposition that eludes proof. The Reformation did serve in two demonstrable ways to undermine mixed monarchy. First, it gave enormous vogue to Machiavelli's postulate of the preservation of the state as the transcendant morality in politics, for in the conflict with the Church the justification of the secular authority depended upon the moral primacy of the state. Second, striving to justify either the expulsion of papal authority or its reduction within their realms, princes made high claims to be under no sovereign power on earth: "this realm of England is an empire, and so hath been accepted in the world, governed by one supreme head and king." It was put thus in the preamble to an act of Henry VIII's reformation parliament in 1533 abolishing ecclesiastical court appeals to Rome. This kind of argument was easily domesticated into a weapon against the estates. It also slipped readily into an argument that the king ruled by divine right, as God's agent on earth, an argument that contradicted accepted medieval theory only in that it left out the pope as God's agent on earth in matters spiritual and the superiority of things spiritual to things secular. With the notion of the preservation of the state as the transcendant morality in politics and the divine right of kings, two essential ingredients of absolutist theory are already present.

Political theory in the late sixteenth and seventeenth centuries was concerned principally with sovereignty and where it was to be found: who has ultimate authority within the state? The quest for sovereignty strengthened the absolutist tendency in political theory, for in mixed monarchy by definition sovereignty was either dispersed and shared or else did not exist at all. The wars of religion and the crisis-ridden atmosphere of the early seventeenth century made men thirst for certainty, for a definition of the precise place where authority rested. Sovereignty came of age as a central concern in political theory with Jean Bodin (1530–1596), the French politique with whom we are already familiar and whose words we now repeat: "The prince exalted above all his subjects, whose majesty does not admit of any division, represents the principle of unity from which all the rest derive their force and cohesion." (See p. 182.) The vital phrase is that concerning the indivisibility of majesty. Bodin did not deny that sovereignty could rest in the people or an oligarchy, but his own predilection was for sovereignty being vested in the monarch. The title to Book VI, chapter 4, of his *Six Books of the Commonwealth* (1576) is, significantly, "A comparison of three legitimate types of commonwealth, popular, aristocratic, and monarchial, concluding in favor of monarchy." Monarchy was preferable because there must be some "head of state in whom sovereign power is vested, who can unite all the rest." It required greater perspicacity and a more noble view of human nature than men of those troubled times could afford to have in order to conceive of unity coming from any source other than the will of one man.

The great emphasis on "reason of state," implicit in Machiavelli and first treated systematically by the Italian Jesuit, Giovanni Botero (1540–1617), made its contribution to absolutist theory by inducing men to define the state, the actions of which depended upon the justification of "reason of state." In *Of the Reason of State* (1598), Botero argued that the state is an ethical entity which though it might use unethical means to attain its ends must never divest those ends of their ethical content. It was difficult to conceive of a conglomeration of persons—an estate—as one ethical entity, but not at all difficult to conceive of a single person—the monarch—as the personification of the ethical state.

There was no theoretical opposition to monarchic absolutism comparable in weight to absolutism's proponents in the early seventeenth century. The German theorist, Johannes Althusius (1557–1638), an orthodox Calvinist, attacked absolutism on behalf of theocracy, whose end, if not technically absolutism, could be a tyranny that would make monarchic absolutism seem tame in comparison. The Jesuit polemicists and theoreticians, Cardinal Robert Bellarmine (1542–1621) and Father Francisco Suarez (1548–1617), assailed the divine right of monarchs in defense of the divine right of the pope. They were, in one sense, merely exalting one absolutism to the detriment of many absolutisms. Thus the only theoretical opposition to monarchic absolutism came from the extremes of the Reformation and were directed in essence at the "blasphemous" nature of divine right monarchy.

THE NATURE OF ABSOLUTISM

Absolutism was monarchy with the restraining limitation of the estates removed; that is, it was unmixed monarchy, since one of the entities in the old dualism had disappeared. The king's authority was unbound by any higher authority on earth, particularly by any body of popular representation. Absolutism was not totalitarianism, for in the absolutist state vast areas of national life were practically, if not theoretically, outside the monarch's purview. The tendency in more recent times for government to expand its activities to the point of totalitarianism, beyond the traditional activities of preserving order, assuring defense, and conducting foreign relations, seems to have had little to do with absolutism in the seventeenth century. Neither was absolutism naked tyranny. It conceded limitations on *power* if not on *sovereign authority;* specifically, it recognized the law of God and the law of nature as limiting the absolute monarch's power. Though the absolute monarch could make law to govern his subjects, he could not change God's law or nature's law. In practice these unchangeable higher laws provided no guarantees to the subject, but they did remind the absolute monarch, as he recognized in his coronation oath, that his power was limited if uncontrolled. James I of England, the most articulate absolute monarch (and one of the least successful) put the case for absolutism as follows:

> Kings sit in the throne of God and they are called gods. Therefore they must imitate God and His Christ in justice and righteousness, David and Solomon in godliness and wisdom—wisdom to discern godliness as the

fountain from which wisdom floweth. Justice without righteousness were to no purpose. It must come from a clear heart, not for private ends. From this imitation all commonwealths, especially monarchies, are settled.

Clearly the king had to serve God's ends in his exercise of power; he had to approach as closely as possible the justice and righteousness of God. In the first sentence James struck the note of justification for absolutism: the divine right of kings. All seventeenth-century absolutists, with the significant exception of Thomas Hobbes (see pp. 200–201), founded absolutism on divine right. Only in the eighteenth century, when rationalism had banished that "infamous thing" religion, was absolutism justified as "enlightened despotism," that is, as rational despotism.

Absolute monarchs held sway over most of Europe by 1660, the principal exceptions being England and the Dutch Republic. Absolutism had received its theoretical framework and been given ample justification. As a matter of political practice, absolutism still placed a heavy reliance on the loyalty and commitment of the monarch's ministers. The first half of the seventeenth century was the age of the great ministers: Richelieu and Mazarin in France, Olivares in Spain, Laud and Strafford in England, Oxenstierna in Sweden. Although these men advanced the programs of their monarchs, the attributes of absolutism were in their hands. Such men of power were potentially as great a threat to absolute monarchs as were the feudal nobility—greater even, because they controlled states that had already routed the feudal nobility. This threat was not unrecognized. Louis XIV of France, whose youth had been spent in the shadow of Mazarin, was alive to the danger. His final contribution to the fashioning of absolutism was to rule from 1661 until his death in 1715 without a minister able to challenge his absolute authority.

CHAPTER TEN

Absolutism versus Oligarchy: England and the Dutch Republic

ABSOLUTISM'S PATTERN of success was broken in England and the Dutch Republic during the first half of the seventeenth century. The Wars of the Roses in the fifteenth century had so decimated the ranks of the English feudal nobility that Henry VII was able to build a more absolutist monarchy by 1500 than the French king was able to construct for another century. The chief beneficiaries of the decline of the old nobility, in addition to the king, were the people of middle rank, particularly the landed gentry. Because of the peculiar development of the medieval Parliament in England and the Tudors' own confidence that Parliament was a tool of monarchy, the House of Commons, the estate of the middle rank in England, was not destroyed and could serve as a stage from which to attack absolutism. As long as Tudor absolutism seemed the only alternative to chaos, the gentry cooperated with it, especially since the Tudors reciprocated by being solicitous of their interests. When Stuart absolutism threatened their interests, they had in Parliament the means to stem and ultimately to destroy absolutism.

In the case of the northern Netherlands, the revolt against Spain in the late sixteenth century enfeebled the old nobility by placing the preponderance of power in the middle-class oligarchy of Holland, who alone could finance the war of independence and who never lost control of the conduct of the war. The same oligarchy enfeebled the potentially strong monarchy of the House of Orange in the seventeenth century.

To other European states in the seventeenth century, England and the Dutch Republic were simply "the Protestant powers" or, between 1649 and 1660, "the Protestant republics." Contemporaries noted that parliamentary institutions remained vital and vigorous only in these two countries. They were also the rising colonial and naval powers, building commercial empires at the expense of the Spanish and in collision with each other. Trade and finance bound Amsterdam and London in the tightest economic web of Northern Europe. They commanded both sides of the narrow seas linking the North Sea with the Atlantic. At critical moments—whether they opposed Spain or France—the safety of one depended upon the survival of the other. Relations between the two countries were always complex: sometimes hostile, seldom affectionate, always respectful. They were more continuously and intimately involved with each other than with any other power. Once England intervened significantly in Dutch internal politics; once the Dutch intervened in English internal politics; and the two countries fought three wars with each other, largely because of commercial rivalry.

England's Constitutional Crisis, 1603–1640

"When I came into this land, though I were an old king (having governed a kingdom since I was twelve years old), yet I came a stranger hither in government though not in blood." Thus did James I of England sum up his unfamiliarity with English institutions, laws, and customs, and the fact that he was the great-great-grandson of Henry VII and a cousin to Queen Elizabeth, whom he succeeded. He had reigned for thirty-six years on the throne of Scotland as James VI before coming to England in 1603. He continued as king of Scotland, uniting the two crowns, although each country remained independent of the other.

James's background and personal qualities went far in explaining his lack of success as the first Stuart monarch of England. He had fixed ideas on almost every aspect of government, which had been born in the long struggle to curb the power of the nobility in Scotland and to establish independence of the theocratically oriented Calvinism of Scottish churchmen. His ideas bore but slight relevance to the country that he was to rule until his death in 1625. He was a learned man. Like most monarchs of the day he believed in the divine right of kings; he even wrote a theoretical treatise called *The Trew Law of Free Monarchies* (1598) to explain and justify his conviction. Unfortunately he overestimated his abilities, was an extremely bad judge of men and political possibilities, and never understood the traditions or the obstinacy of the people he ruled.

James inherited from Elizabeth a war with Spain, a rebellion in Ireland, a debt of £400,000 (about two years' revenue), an able chief minister in Robert Cecil, a somewhat antiquated bureaucracy (though as sound as any in Europe), an overwhelmingly Protestant populace, and a pattern of relatively frequent convocations of Parliament. By the end of 1605 James had ended the war with Spain, settled the Irish turmoil, and increased the debt by half by his courtly extravagance. He had also fallen afoul of the growing current for further reform of Protestantism in the Anglican Church and had come into head-on collision with Parliament.

PURITANISM

In 1603 puritanism was a perfectly respectable minority movement within the established Church of England, desirous of clarifying the ambiguous Elizabethan settlement in more rigidly Protestant terms and ending what the Puritans considered vestiges of Roman Catholic practice in the Anglican Church. Two things puritanism was not: it was not separatist, that is, it had no intention of leaving the established church; and it did not differ significantly in doctrine from the conservative majority group in control of the church. Where the Puritans parted company with the espiscopate, the bishops, was in the latter's refusal to draw certain logical conclusions from its doctrinal position. For instance, the Puritans felt that the sacramental forms of worship laid down in the Book of Common Prayer were irrelevant, and that clerical garments, the use of the ring in marriage, and bowing the knee at the name of Jesus were mere "popish remnants." The bishops feared that if these established forms were discarded, the whole order of state and church would be in jeopardy. They especially feared the possibility of the replacement of episcopacy as the governing institution of the church by "presbyteries," assemblies of ministers and lay elders of the various congregations.

Shortly after his accession James was presented with a petition supposedly representing the views of nearly a thousand Puritan ministers (therefore called the Millenary Petition) requesting in restrained language certain changes in church practices. The petition induced James to call a conference at Hampton Court Palace in 1604 between the bishops and some of the Puritan clergy, with the king presiding. The bishops attacked the Puritans, pushing them into a more extreme position than they meant to take. James, who had experienced presbyterianism in Scotland, angrily told the Puritans that presbyteries "agreeth as well with a monarchy as God and the Devil," delivered the maxim "no bishop no king" to express his conviction that espiscopacy and monarchy were interdependent, and threatened that if the Puritans did not conform, he would "harry them out of the land, or else do worse." Soon after the conference, rules compelling greater conformity to established church practices were promulgated, resulting in the expulsion of over two hundred Puritan ministers from their parishes. Puritanism began to take on a more radical hue, assuming more extreme positions against the worship of the church and against episcopacy as the governing institution of the church. The Hampton Court Conference had a happier result as well, in that James authorized a new translation of the Bible. Completed in 1611, the King James version took its place as one of the greatest works of English prose.

PARLIAMENT

Every Tudor monarch had used Parliament to undertake major programs of change: Henry VII for legislation to establish civil order, Henry VIII to accomplish the break with Rome, Edward VI to establish Protestantism, Mary to dismantle it, Elizabeth to reconstruct it. During the latter years of Elizabeth's reign there had been considerable continuity in the membership of the House of Commons, more frequent sessions to obtain parliamentary revenue for the war with Spain, and growing assertiveness by the Commons. The Spanish war dampened opposition during the 1590's, but in 1601 the old queen had to go personally to Parliament, concede to the vehement demand of the Commons for the suppression of royal monopolies, and smooth frayed tempers with her last great dulcet song of affection. Many members of the 1601 Parliament returned to sit in James's first Parliament in March, 1604.

The House of Commons was composed mostly of the landed gentry of England and Wales. Of the approximately five hundred members, there were two representatives from each English county (one from each Welsh county), and the rest were representatives of towns that happened to have sent members in the late Middle Ages or to have been enfranchised by the Tudors. The county members were elected on a fairly broad franchise, including most substantial farmers as well as the gentry, although election rigging was common practice. With few exceptions the town members were elected by the town merchant oligarchies. Only London and a few other major economic centers, however, consistently returned merchant members. Increasingly during the sixteenth century the towns returned neighboring gentlemen, often at the behest of a powerful patron—a councillor of the king, a nobleman, or a major gentleman of the county. A large number of lawyers were elected, who by status and inclination were as one with the gentry. Noblemen sat in the House of Lords, a body that could stop positive action taken by the Commons but could not prevent negative action taken by the Commons to impede the course of legislation or financial proposals.

The gentry who sat in the House of Commons were the masters of their counties. They held the reins of local administration as justices of the peace, sheriffs, and commanders of the militia, the only military force in England. Their economic dominance was built on the lands of the monasteries dissolved by Henry VIII and was constantly reinforced by wealth from trade, law, and royal service brought by new recruits to the class. They were educated well above the average of the period anywhere in Europe. They were jealous of their social position at home and assertive of their "privileges" as members of the House of Commons: immunity from arrest except for serious crimes during sessions of Parliament, the right to settle disputed elections, and the right to debate freely without fear of reprisal.

If James I and Charles I (1625–49) had been able to live within the limitations of the ordinary royal revenue, they need never have summoned Parliament. Indeed, twice (in 1614–21 and 1629–40) they attempted to get along without Parliament for long periods. Rising prices, extravagance, unforeseen circumstances (especially war), and inability to reorganise the bureaucratic structure to gain greater yield from existing sources of ordinary revenue compelled James and Charles to use extraordinary means to raise revenue and ultimately to fall back on Parliament. This gave Parliament the initiative. The House of Commons demanded the righting of "grievances"—including the abolition of extraordinary means of raising revenue—before granting money. The king, unable to manage the House, either had to consent to the abridgment of his power involved in the "grievances" or had to dissolve Parliament without obtaining the money needed. This dilemma arose time after time between 1604 and 1640, and in such a war of attrition the king was at a serious disadvantage.

THE GRIEVANCES, 1604–1621

In James's first Parliament the broader constitutional issues of grievances were joined with the Puritan desire for reform—a combination that became increasingly disruptive of relations between king and Parliament. The first grievances concerned the Commons' privileges of settling disputed elections and freedom from arrest. In both issues James acceded. Then the House, in an unprecedented document called the Apology of 1604, justified its privileges and informed the king that it would no longer disregard the incursions on its privileges that it had allowed during Elizabeth's reign out of respect for her age and sex. During the course of this first Parliament, the Commons raised again the issue of monopolies (which Elizabeth had barely managed to quiet in 1601), attacked the ancient right of the king to levy a sum of money for provisions for the royal household, attacked increased custom duties, and threw out legislation proposed by James that would unite his two realms, England and Scotland. Most significant, it complained of the Court of High Commission, the major ecclesiastical court, which was particularly zealous in making Puritans conform to the established order in the church.

An untoward incident during this first Parliament gave fresh impetus to an old fear. The number of Roman Catholics had decreased sharply during the last two decades of Elizabeth's reign. Unrelenting persecution by the government produced frustrations that found expression in extremism. In November, 1605, an elaborate plot was laid by a handful of Catholic terrorists to blow up king and Parliament in one blast of gunpowder hidden in the cellars of the Parliament building. It was foiled just in time. The Gunpowder Plot excited an almost psychotic fear of Catholicism, which gave the Puritans an opportunity to raise the specter of "popery" as the sole alternative to further reform of the English church.

Although it did not sit continuously, James's first Parliament remained in existence for seven years. It was dissolved in 1610. It had evidenced the complete breakdown of the king's ability to control the Commons by the presence of royal councillors exercising initiative in debate, the secret of Tudor parliamentary management. In the vacuum left, the Commons instituted a sophisticated system of committees, making the House more manageable by the leaders of the opposition. After three years of foundering with extraparliamentary financial expedients, James summoned a Parliament in 1614. Opposition of members to the king's demands led to its quick dissolution, and four members were imprisoned in direct defiance of the Commons' claim to freedom of speech in debate. Six more years of financial expedients followed, during which James initiated a foreign policy that seemed to threaten the future of Protestantism in England and to lend support to the Catholic Hapsburgs, who in 1618 had opened war against Protestantism on the Continent and whose first victim was James's own son-in-law, the Protestant king of Bohemia. James sought to marry his son and heir apparent, Charles, to the daughter of the king of Spain. Hatred of Spain and Catholicism made the "Spanish marriage" the prime grievance of the Parliament of 1621.

The Parliament began in a conciliatory mood. Money was granted readily on the understanding that the king would help his son-in-law and the Protestant cause on the Continent. Nonetheless, the old grievance against monopolies was raised immediately, and the Commons revived its long-disused power to impeach, that is, to put on trial before the House of Lords a person suspected of high crimes. The weapon was turned against two monopolists and two judges suspected of taking bribes, one of whom was no less a person than the Lord Chancellor, Francis Bacon. Convicted by the Lords, the defendants were heavily fined and dismissed from office. Then the Commons turned to the Spanish marriage, petitioning the king to extirpate Catholicism in England and marry his son to a Protestant princess.

James replied that foreign policy was his prerogative, not to be discussed without his leave. The Commons' remonstrance was torn from the record by the king's own hand, Parliament was dissolved, and the chief leaders of the opposition were sent to prison.

The Parliament of 1621 was the turning point in the constitutional confrontation. The Spanish marriage proposal raised the specter of Catholicism as could no domestic issue. The impeachment of the monopolists and Bacon produced a weapon that could be used against any of the king's ministers in the future. The opposition organization in the Commons reached maturity, and able leaders stepped forward to lead it.

THE CONSTITUTIONAL CONFRONTATION, 1624–1628

When James convoked his last Parliament in 1624, the Spanish marriage proposal had broken down; Prince Charles and James's young favorite, the Duke of Buckingham, had visited the prospective bride in Madrid and found neither the lady nor her countrymen to their liking. Parliament convened in high hopes of a war to retrieve Protestant fortunes on the Continent. It was not disappointed. James, having denied the Commons' competency to discuss foreign affairs in 1621, now gave over to it the direction of his foreign policy, entreating it to give "your good and sound advice." James declared war on Spain, and the Commons gave him greater support than at any other time in his reign. James died just at the outbreak of hostilities, with his sincerely pacifist policy of the previous twenty years in ruins and the political initiative in the hands of Parliament.

Charles I (1625–49), a youth of twenty-five, was as wholly under the influence of the Duke of Buckingham as had been his father. Buckingham was a capable but erratic, power-hungry, and arrogant man. In the last five years of James's reign he had built up a system of patronage that put every aspect of administration and policy into his hands. He thirsted for military glory, and the war offered him his chance.

The war went badly from the outset. A naval expedition to Cádiz was wholly mismanaged. The Commons impeached Buckingham, and except for Charles's timely dissolution of Parliament in 1626, his beloved lieutenant would have fallen. Troops were forcibly billeted on private persons. The dissolution left a shortage of money to carry on the war. In 1626 and 1627 Charles sent out writs to selected wealthy people, ordering them to lend money to the government. This forced loan met with stout resistance. Meanwhile, despite his marriage to the sister of King Louis XIII of France in 1625, Charles had drifted into war with France in 1627. Buckingham commanded an expedition to help the French Huguenots at La Rochelle. His utter defeat set the stage for the summoning of Parliament in 1628 to finance the woefully bungled war.

Charles I of England, by H. G. Pot

"His kingly virtues had some mixture and alloy, that hindered them from shining in full lustre, and from producing those fruits they should have been attended with. . . . He was very fearless in his person, but not very enterprising. He had an excellent understanding, but was not confident enough of it; which made him oftentimes change his opinion for the worse, and follow the advice of men who did not judge so well as himself. This made him more irresolute than the conjuncture of his affairs would admit: if he had been of a rougher and more imperious nature he would have found more respect and duty." Earl of Clarendon (1609–1674), HISTORY OF THE GREAT REBELLION (London, 1888).
Courtesy of The Louvre

THE PETITION OF RIGHT

The new Parliament directed an attack against the king's "prerogative," those powers which the king alone might exercise and for which he was not answerable to either Parliament or the law. Charles held that those who refused to pay the forced loan could be imprisoned by order of his council without cause being shown and that such imprisonment and the loan itself were justified by his prerogative. He also maintained that troops might be billeted on individuals in time of emergency for the defense of the realm. The Commons countered that these practices were against the liberties of the subject, which were assured by law. The issue was a constitutional one, in which both sides based their arguments on unclear history, ambiguous law, and arbitrarily chosen precedents. The issue was compromised when the king assented to a petition of the Parliament asking that the subject's liberties be confirmed—specifically, that no one be compelled to make a gift or loan without the consent of Parliament, that no man be imprisoned without cause being shown, and that troops not be billeted upon individuals against their will. The Petition of Right, as this was called, proved a landmark in assuring the liberties of Englishmen, although it was hardly honored by Charles in the next decade.

LAUDIANISM

Buckingham's assassination in 1628 by an officer whom he had failed to promote removed the most awkward grievance of the Commons, but a new one quickly took its place. It, too, was personified by an individual, William Laud (1573–1645), bishop of London. Laud represented a new generation of Elizabethan churchmen who were born in the 1570's and 1580's. These men had attended Oxford and Cambridge just as the Puritan tide in each university was turned by vigorous repression from Elizabeth's last archbishop of Canterbury, John Whitgift. Their idea of church order was derived from a comprehensive theological treatise published in the 1590's by Richard Hooker, an Oxford theologian. He wrote, "And that kings should be in such sort supreme commanders over all men, we hold it requisite as well for the ordering of spiritual as civil affairs." The Puritans' presbyterianism seemed to these men to threaten the king's supremacy; the Puritans' three-hour sermons, stark severity of dress, lack of church ornamentation, and distaste for the liturgical grandeur of the Book of Common Prayer did not reflect the "hidden dignity and glory" of the church in heaven.

To the Puritans it seemed that Laud and his adherents were bringing the Anglican Church back to Rome. Nothing was further from the Laudians' intention, but in the superheated atmosphere of virulent anti-Catholicism in early seventeenth-century England guilt by association stuck. Laudianism lacked the local roots that were the strength of puritanism and had few clerical adherents outside the church hierarchy and the universities. Laudians controlled the church organization, however, and could count on royal support and the assistance of the machinery of the state in their determination to break puritanism once and for all.

PERSONAL RULE, 1629–1640

In the second session of the 1628 Parliament the Puritan opposition to Laudianism was inextricably wedded to the constitutionalist opposition to unparliamentary financial exactions, inflation of the king's prerogative, and incursions on the Commons' privileges. A full-scale attack was mounted against both the Laudian bishops and the king's levying of customs duties without parliamentary consent. Charles dissolved the Parliament, but not before the opposition leaders had held the speaker of the House in the chair while the Commons in an uproar resolved that the Laudians and those who counseled such duties were "capital enemies to the kingdom and commonwealth." The opposition leaders went to prison, where the most outspoken of them, Sir John Eliot, died three years later. Charles resolved never to call another Parliament and to rule by prerogative alone. The next eleven years were the period of his "personal rule."

Charles managed to end the wars with Spain and France, which had been the largest drain on his resources. In Laud (whom he made archbishop of Canterbury in 1633) he had a prelate who was able to break the leadership of puritanism by means of the courts of High Commission and Star Chamber, and who repressed puritanism with enough vigor to people Massachusetts with its exiles. In Thomas Wentworth, later Earl of Strafford, Charles possessed an adviser who, having been one of the leaders of the opposition in the Commons in the 1620's, had an insider's knowledge of the opposition. Laud and Strafford worked in close harmony, strove for a thoroughgoing reassertion of royal authority, and managed to finance personal rule as long as peace lasted. Their ambition was considerable: the tightening of royal control of local government in England and the extortion of every possible revenue from England and Ireland. The former they accomplished through vigorous surveillance of the justices of the peace by the king's council and its agents, the circuit judges of assize. The latter they managed by exploiting every source of finance available through the king's prerogative. These included customs duties, ship money (a tax on the counties of England to support the navy), the sale of offices, honors, monopolies, and immunities, heavy fines in Star Chamber for all kinds of derelictions or payments to avoid punishment there, and large loans floated through the city of London. By 1637 the personal rule seemed secure.

In that year Charles and Laud attempted to impose the Anglican Book of Common Prayer on the Presbyterian Church in Scotland. The reaction was a national rebellion. Charles was forced to raise the militia in England to reassert royal authority in Scotland. In 1639 he suffered a humiliating defeat at the hands of the Scots and was forced to make concessions that required heavy financing. Laud and Strafford urged him to summon Parliament; there was no other way to raise the money needed.

"Another Protestant Republic"

In the summer of 1640 European statesmen feared that England was about to become "another Protestant republic." In April Charles had convened Parliament, only to be assailed by John Pym, leader of the opposition in Commons, for every act both secular and religious of his personal rule; the king dissolved Parliament after just three weeks. Charles's renewal of the attack against the Scots in the summer precipitated the disintegration of personal rule. The English militia was in mutiny, revenue was uncollectable, and sedition and civil commotion were rife. After the Scots had occupied the north of England and had only been halted by Charles's promise to buy them off, Charles convened his fifth (and last) Parliament in November. The "Long Parliament" (it did not formally dissolve until 1660) had Charles firmly in its grip, for if he could not get the money to pay the Scots, a Scots Presbyterian army might make common cause with the English Puritans and overthrow him altogether.

THE LONG PARLIAMENT

Between November, 1640, and September, 1641, under the able leadership of Pym the Long Parliament unanimously dismantled the personal rule.

Strafford was executed, Laud imprisoned for four years and then executed, other ministers driven into exile, the bishops reduced to obedience, the judges subdued, and Puritan prisoners of the previous decade released from jail. Ship money was declared illegal. The courts of High Commission and Star Chamber were abolished, and the king's power to commit persons to prison was made judicially reviewable. Statutes were passed requiring that Parliament be summoned at least every three years and that the existing Parliament not be dismissed without its consent. To all of this Charles assented; he had no choice.

The unanimity with which the members of the House of Commons carried through these measures continued until the late summer of 1641. Until then Pym had managed to curb the question of further reform of the Church, but he finally felt obliged to give in to a radical Puritan element in the Commons that sought to abolish episcopacy. An equally sizable element defended episcopacy. Those who believed that the king had conceded enough to safeguard the liberty of the subject attached themselves to this group. In November a massive catalogue of the government's misdeeds coupled with a demand for remedies that would clearly abridge the king's prerogative was adopted by the Commons by a majority of only eleven votes.

The initiative still rested with Pym. Rightly distrusting Charles's sincerity, he sought further safeguards in the coming months. An armed attempt by the king personally to arrest Pym and four other leaders in the Commons failed. Pym attempted to push through legislation that would transfer command of the militia—the nation's only army—from the king to Parliament. Charles refused to give his consent, retired to the north, and in August, 1642, called upon his loyal subjects to join him in suppression of the Parliament. About half the Commons rallied to his standard. The civil war had begun.

CIVIL WAR, 1642–1648

Most of those who chose sides in this conflict did so on the basis of political and religious scruples. Nevertheless, certain patterns appeared in the choice of allegiances in the conflict. There was no clear class distinction between the leaders of the Royalists and the Parliamentarians: they were all substantial landed gentlemen. Age and locale appear to have affected the commitment of the individual gentleman more than his wealth or social status. The gentlemen in the king's camp were by and large younger than those in Parliament's. Younger men were more susceptible to the color and dignity of the Laudian-influenced church, in reaction to the severity of their elders' puritanism. The majority of the Royalists came from the west and north, while those of the Parliamentarian cause came principally from the south and east, where puritanism had always been stronger. The people of the south and east were also more active in trade, industry, and finance, although this fact does not justify the frequently drawn inference that the Parliamentarians were the economically predominant element foreclosing on a bankrupt monarchy. Economic factors played a more important role in the choice of allegiances further down the social scale. The lesser gentry, those on the lower economic rungs, were jealous of the dominance of the greater gentry and saw a chance of increased power in the cause of Parliament. The nobility was overwhelmingly Royalist. The merchants (numerically many times greater than the nobility) were overwhelmingly Parliamentarian; most of the larger towns went Parliamentarian, even in areas that were Royalist. The rank and file of the two armies evidenced wide social differences. The king's army depended heavily on farmers and agrarian laborers; the Parliamentarian army included a large handicraft element, which provided it with capable noncommissioned officers. The mass of the population preferred neutrality, but this luxury was not long allowed them, for the war dragged on and both sides began conscripting troops.

The center of Parliamentarian power was London. The king's headquarters were in Oxford, sixty miles northwest of the metropolis. The navy went Parliamentarian at once and blocked assistance to Charles from Holland and France. The first two years of the war saw a great deal of skirmishing, culminating in a sizable advance by the king's forces toward London and the Parliamentarian perimeter in late 1643. To meet this threat the Parliamentarians had a bold new force, the "New Model Army," drawn from the militia of the eastern counties. It was well-disciplined, highly Puritan in ideology, and ably officered. The second-in-command was a masterful strategist, member of Parliament, and landed gentleman named Oliver Cromwell. In a series of bitter engagements in 1644–45 the New Model Army crushed the Royalists, forcing Charles to retreat northward. In 1646 Charles surrendered to the Scottish army. The Scots had come in on Parliament's side when Parliament agreed in the Solemn League and Covenant in 1643 to establish presbyterianism in England.

The victor was Cromwell and the New Model Army more than it was Parliament and the Scottish allies. The New Model Army had a strongly radical political and religious complexion. Some noncommissioned officers and enlisted men demanded a broader franchise that would in effect give the vote to handicraftsmen and small farmers (that is, to themselves). This won them the name Levellers. Others, called Independents, demanded congregationalism, that is, the autonomy of each church congregation. They opposed the presbyterian system supported by the majority in Parliament, in which individual congregations were grouped together and governed by elected courts or presbyteries made up of clerics and laymen. Cromwell and most of the officers of the army favored congregationalism, although they were more conservative than most of the rank and file.

After two years of negotiations with the Scots, Charles won them to his cause by promising to establish presbyterianism in England and started the

Oliver Cromwell, after S. Cooper
An Enemy Pays Tribute to Cromwell.
*"He was one of those men whose enemies
cannot curse him without at the same
time praising him; for he could never
have done half that mischief without
great parts of courage and industry and
judgement. And he must have had a
wonderful understanding in the natures
and humours of men, and as great a
dexterity in applying them, who from
a private and obscure birth (though of a
good family), without interest of estate,
alliance or friendships, could raise
himself to such a height. . . .
Wickedness as great as his could never
have accomplished those trophies
without the assistance of a great spirit,
and admirable circumspection and
sagacity, and a most magnanimous
resolution."* Earl of Clarendon, HISTORY
OF THE GREAT REBELLION
(London, 1888).
Courtesy of the National Portrait
Gallery, London

war again. A rapid defeat of the Scots by the New Model Army resulted in
the end of the presbyterian majority in the Commons—and the end of the
monarchy. In December, 1648, a detachment of New Model troops led by
Colonel Pride barred the presbyterian members from the Commons. The
"Rump"—what was left of the Commons after "Pride's Purge"—tried Charles
on the ground that he was an enemy of the people. In January, 1649, he was
publicly beheaded, monarchy was abolished, and "another Protestant republic" was indeed established, called by its founders the Commonwealth.

THE COMMONWEALTH, 1649–1653

The government of the Commonwealth consisted of the fewer than one
hundred members remaining in the Commons and a council of state elected
by them. The House of Lords was dissolved. There was no clear authority except in the army, where Cromwell was leader. The all-important
question of church organization was settled by having the church remain
subject to the authority of the state—a far cry from Calvinist theocracy.
Control over the church was in the hands of county committees, who also
controlled local government. To destroy royalism and episcopalianism, many
Royalists' lands were seized and the lands of the former church hierarchy
were confiscated. Royalists who wished to save their lands from confiscation
had to pay heavy fines, and in order to pay the fines, they often had to sell

much of their estate. The beneficiaries of the land grab were merchants, lawyers, speculators, army officers, bureaucrats, and lesser gentry. A new landowning element came into existence, and despite partial restitution of lands to their former owners when the monarchy was restored in 1660, this new landowning element remained.

Few Englishmen outside the ruling group cared for the new republican government. Radical agitation continued to disturb the army. In addition, the government had to put down revolts in Ireland and Scotland. During the reigns of James and Charles unrest had developed in Ireland over English efforts to convert the Catholic Irish to Protestantism, the settlement of English and Scottish Protestants in northern Ireland on land confiscated from Catholic Irish rebels, and the generally harsh rule of the English. Open revolt broke out in 1641, but neither the king nor Parliament could spare the soldiers to put down the rebellion. After the death of Charles, the Irish proclaimed his son, Charles II, their king. Late in 1649 Cromwell led an army across the Irish Channel and defeated the rebels. The savagery of his troops, who hated the Catholic Irish, and the extreme harshness of his settlement, by which thousands of rebels had to give up their lands to new English settlers, left a legacy of bitterness and hatred for England that has not yet disappeared. In 1651 Cromwell defeated a Scottish invasion that was also aimed at putting Charles II on the throne.

Meanwhile, Parliament was tied up in incessant wrangling over various constitutional proposals and reforms. Its strong civilian bias threatened the continued domination of the army. In April, 1653, Cromwell led soldiers into the Commons and drove out the members. Later that year he summoned a hand-picked Parliament of "godly men," derisively called the Barebones Parliament from one of its members who bore the name of Praisegod Barebones, but this assembly wanted more radical religious changes than suited the conservative leadership in the army. Cromwell's fellow officers convinced him to dismiss it and accept a new constitution called the Instrument of Government drawn up by them.

THE PROTECTORATE, 1653–1660

The new constitution of December, 1653, represented a form of quasi-monarchy. Cromwell was designated Lord Protector, ruling with a council and a Parliament composed of an "Other House" (similar to the old House of Lords) and a House of Commons, with which the Lord Protector was to share legislative power and the control of the army and navy. The franchise for election of members of the Commons was more restrictive than the old franchise. The Instrument, the first written constitution of the English-speaking peoples, was an attempt at legitimacy on Cromwell's part, but Parliament and Protector quickly found that they could not get along with one another. To suppress growing unrest, Cromwell imposed military rule on England. He purged the army of its more extremist elements and purged Parliament of the members who opposed him. Those who remained in the Commons offered to make him king. He refused the crown but accepted their offer to make the protectorship hereditary. The move cost him the allegiance of republicans. His support of religious toleration lost him the religious extremists. Burdensome taxes alienated everyone. He was forced to rely upon the army for the power to preserve order. As long as he lived, Cromwell never lost control of the army.

When Cromwell died in 1658, his son Richard succeeded to the Lord Protectorship. By 1659 Richard had lost control of the army. Political chaos resulted. The man who stepped forward to end it was George Monk, an ex-Royalist but loyal Cromwellian general. Resisting the temptation to establish a military dictatorship, he sought stability by recalling the Long Parliament just as it had been prior to the purge of the presbyterians in 1648. Behind Monk stood the navy, most of the army, the city of London, legitimists, presbyterians, and Anglicans—in short, all those who had tasted too much of political instability and feared military dictatorship.

Charles II, who had been in exile on the Continent, issued a conciliatory statement at Breda, a town in the Netherlands, expressing his willingness to accept parliamentary government. Reassured by the Declaration of Breda, Parliament invited Charles to take the throne. He returned unconditionally, leaving to Parliament the terms of the amnesty to be extended to his former opponents (except those who had signed his father's death warrant), the religious settlement by which to restore the Church of England, and the question of the disposal of confiscated lands. Parliament settled these questions with considerable moderation and substantial justice. All the acts that had been passed in the Long Parliament in 1640–42 and received Charles I's assent were held to be legally valid. The later ordinances of the Long Parliament and of the republican period were held to be null and void. Legally, it was as if the previous eighteen years had never occurred.

In other respects the previous years were not so easily eradicated. A king had been destroyed—not by covert murder following deposition, not on the field of battle, not by a mob, but by due process of law, even if the tribunal was illegal. In the last weeks of the king's life the House of Commons had declared "that the people are, under God, the original of all just power." Men could forget neither the action nor the words, and if in 1660 almost every Englishman viewed with horror the possible repetition of the execution of the king, the fact that institutionalized opposition had brought down a monarch in the name of the people made monarchy anything but absolute in England.

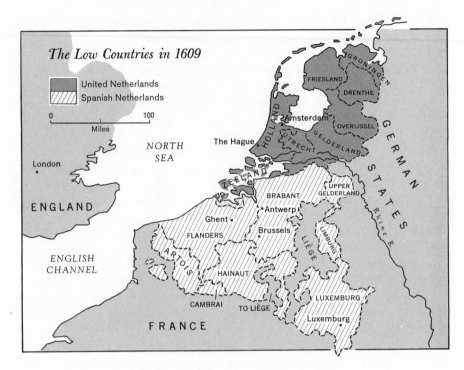

The Low Countries in 1609

United Netherlands
Spanish Netherlands

0   100
Miles

GRONINGEN
FRIESLAND
DRENTHE
NORTH SEA
Amsterdam
OVERIJSSEL
GERMAN STATES
The Hague
HOLLAND
UTRECHT
GELDERLAND
London
ZEELAND
UPPER GELDERLAND
BRABANT
Antwerp
ENGLAND
Ghent
Brussels
FLANDERS
LIÈGE
LIMBURG
ARTOIS
Rhine R
ENGLISH CHANNEL
HAINAUT
LUXEMBURG
CAMBRAI
TO LIÈGE
Luxemburg
FRANCE

The Rise of the Dutch Republic

Although in 1609 Spain agreed to a twelve-year truce with the States-General of the seven northern provinces of the Netherlands (see p. 152), it refused to recognize the legal independence of the rebel provinces. The truce left Spain in control of the ten southern provinces. The boundary between north and south did not correspond with the linguistic, cultural, or religious boundaries of the Low Countries. After the truce the ten southern provinces were thoroughly re-Catholicized by Spanish Jesuits. The United Provinces or Dutch republic to the north stood independent.

Dutch independence cut two ways. Each of the seven provinces retained a large measure of independence from the others. The Union of Utrecht of 1579 had established a loose confederation of the provinces with a national assembly, the States-General, composed of delegates from the provincial assembly or "States" of each province. The provincial assemblies were institutions of medieval origin representing the nobility and the various towns of the province. Each provincial States elected its own chief minister or "stadholder." The States-General had jurisdiction over foreign affairs and defense. Traditionally it chose as its executive officer or "captain general" the stadholder of the province of Holland, who was also stadholder of four other provinces. In this complex arrangement of authority sovereignty was ill-defined. The history of the Dutch republic between 1609 and 1660 was above all the history of the struggle between the proponents of provincial sovereignty, seeking to preserve the loose confederation and almost fanatically opposed to centralizing tendencies, and the adherents of the captain general, seeking to create a tighter federal union responsive to his authority.

PROVINCIAL DOMINANCE UNDER OLDENBARNEVELDT

Political and economic pre-eminence within the republic belonged to the province of Holland. It was the second largest, the most populous, and geographically the most commanding of the seven provinces. It was also the seat of government, and it contained Amsterdam, economic heart of the country. The States of Holland was led by Jan van Oldenbarneveldt (1547–1619). As holder of the appointive office of advocate, Oldenbarneveldt was nominally the servant of the States, but through his outstanding abilities and power of persuasion he became the commanding figure in the assembly. He headed the delegation of Holland to the States-General, and as chief representative of the most important province he dominated the States-General. For all practical purposes he determined the policies of the United Provinces. He overshadowed Maurice of Nassau (1587–1625), William the Silent's son and successor as captain general and stadholder of Holland. It was Oldenbarneveldt who had the political finesse to unite the seven provinces behind Maurice's brilliant war effort against the Spanish. It was also he who arranged the truce of 1609 against the will of Maurice.

Oldenbarneveldt's tenure marked one of the two periods of provincial dominance in the republic in the seventeenth century. The growing conflict between him and Maurice illustrated the conflict of sovereignty in the new republic between the provinces and the central government, represented by the captain general. The clash centered around a dispute between strict Calvinists and the Arminians, who were followers of Jacobus Arminius (1560–1609), a liberal Dutch theologian. Arminius challenged the rigid doctrine of predestination. He argued that by the exercise of will a man could condition his chance for eternal salvation or damnation. Oldenbarneveldt's sympathies were with the Arminians, while for political reasons Maurice declared himself a supporter of the strict Calvinists.

Oldenbarneveldt had also divided the merchants of Amsterdam, who controlled the pursestrings of the country. Some of them wanted to form a company that would challenge the lucrative monopoly of the Dutch East India Company, founded in 1602. Oldenbarneveldt, who was a key official of the East India Company, successfully opposed their plans, and the indignant merchants sided with Maurice and the orthodox Calvinists.

Continued religious disputes brought on civil disorder and a threatened break between the States-General and the province of Holland. The States of Holland raised a small army and took steps toward a declaration of independence from the States-General. Maurice and the States-General took up the challenge, and in 1618 Maurice marched into the province of Holland at the head of a body of troops. Not a hand was raised against him in defense of the position of the States of Holland, and Maurice took over undisputed control. Oldenbarneveldt was arrested, and after a trial before a special court, without legal jurisdiction, nearly all of whose members were his personal enemies, he was executed in 1619.

STADHOLDER VERSUS STATES-GENERAL

Maurice's victory allowed him to tighten the loose confederation into a closer union that was increasingly dependent upon the captain general. His brother and successor, Frederick Henry of Orange (1625–47), sought to centralize power still further. Persuaded by his brilliant generalship in the war with Spain (which began in 1621), the States of the five provinces of which he was stadholder agreed to settle the succession on his sons. This was a clear break with the elective principle of the stadholdership.

Frederick Henry made himself a monarch in all but name. At the Hague he maintained a court that rivaled the courts of kings in its splendor. By marrying William, his son and heir apparent, to the eldest daughter of Charles I of England, he added luster to his upstart dynasty. He played power politics in the grand manner, allying the republic to Richelieu's France in the 1630's. He staffed the council of state with his own nominees, had ambassadors abroad correspond directly with him, and in 1634 obtained the support of the States-General for establishing a standing committee of that body, called the Secret Council, under his control.

Frederick Henry's dynastic alliance with the Stuart monarchy in England was a major ingredient in the downfall of his ambitions. His involvement on the side of Charles I brought him into serious conflict with the Calvinist merchants of Holland, whose economic interests, religious predilections, and political views put them in complete sympathy with the English Parliamentarians. His alliance with France worked against him, too. In 1646 the Dutch discovered that Spain and France, who were at war with each other, were considering a deal by which France was to gain the neighboring Spanish Netherlands. Since France was considered a greater threat to Dutch independence than Spain, Frederick Henry was forced to begin peace negotiations with Spain. William II, who succeeded his father in 1647, wanted to continue the war, but Holland and the States-General wanted it to end. The latter prevailed with the signing of the Treaty of Münster in 1648.

William, who was blocked at every move by the supporters of provincial rights, planned a coup against the States of Holland, but he died in 1650 before he could carry through his plan. His only child was not yet born. The States of Holland, the only effective authority remaining, found itself in command of the republic. A great national assembly was convened in 1651 to re-establish the old provincial autonomy. In 1653 the States-General delivered such powers as Oldenbarneveldt had formerly held into the capable hands of Jan de Witt, the chief executive or grand pensionary of Holland. The second golden age of Dutch republicanism began. It lasted until the return to power of the Orange dynasty in the person of William III as stadholder in 1672.

THE FIRST ANGLO-DUTCH WAR

It is ironical that just as republicanism reasserted itself in the Netherlands upon the death of William II and triumphed in England with the execution of Charles I in 1649, the two Protestant republics drifted into war with one another. Behind the first Anglo-Dutch war of 1652–54 was a long commercial rivalry that had seen a number of tense and bloody confrontations in the East Indies, North America, and the West Indies. In what is today Indonesia, the English East India Company (founded in 1600) challenged its Dutch counterpart. In 1651 the English Parliament passed the Navigation Act, aimed at destroying the near-complete monopoly of the English carrying trade by Dutch shipping. The English demand to search Dutch ships suspected of carrying French goods (England and France were engaged in an undeclared maritime war) was resisted by the Dutch and triggered the war.

It was a maritime war of incredible feats of seamanship and valor on both sides. The Dutch admiral Tromp and the English admiral Blake were almost evenly matched as masters of naval tactics. England triumphed because of greater resources and a larger fleet of more heavily armed warships, built up during the civil war, whereas the Dutch relied mainly on armed merchantmen. The death of Tromp in action in July, 1653, while he was attempting to break the English blockade of the Dutch ports, helped to decide the outcome. The Dutch made peace overtures to Cromwell, who was in complete command of England. His reservations about war with a sister Protestant republic and hopes for a political union between the two induced him to meet the Dutch halfway. The treaty stipulated the expulsion of the exiled Stuarts from Holland and in a secret clause carried an ambiguous guarantee by the Dutch to exclude the house of Orange from the captain-generalship of the Dutch republic. This guarantee was meant to prevent assistance to the Stuarts from their Orange in-laws; it was repudiated on the restoration of the Stuart dynasty in England in 1660. The treaty was not harsh and did not seriously weaken the Dutch commercial dominance. Nevertheless, in two ways the war was decisive: it laid the foundation for English naval preponderance, which after 1688 was as much a bulwark to Dutch independence as before it had been a threat; and it determined the tactics of naval warfare for a century to come.

DUTCH DIVERSITY

To stress the political, religious, and constitutional struggles of the Dutch republic, its foreign entanglements, and its commercial dominance is to do less than justice to a nation whose diversity, like its resoluteness, was out of all proportion to its size. Nowhere else in Christian Europe was there such a large measure of toleration in religion in the early seventeenth century. Despite orthodox Calvinism's triumph within the state church after Oldenbarneveldt's death in 1619, there was little persecution of Roman Catholicism. A synagogue of Spanish Jews was publicly dedicated in Amsterdam in 1598, where Jews were readily accepted in the following years. The Dutch example persuaded Denmark, Savoy, Modena, and England under Cromwell to invite Jewish settlement. It was an Amsterdam Jew, Baruch Spinoza (1632–1677), who carried Cartesianism to its ultimate theological end by equating God and nature. It was an Arminian, Hugo Grotius (1583–1645), who laid the foundation for the rational and peaceable ordering of man's affairs on a global scale in the first systematic treatise on international law.

The Flowering of Dutch Culture

The first half of the seventeenth century was the great period of Dutch art. The arts expressed the diversity of Dutch society as well as the exhilarating sense of integrity that came from newly won independence. Commercial wealth created a patron class that supported and encouraged the arts.

The impact of diversity was most evident in the differences between Dutch architecture and painting. Architecture in the Netherlands (north and south) in the late sixteenth century was manneristic in the extreme. Flamboyant strapwork decoration overpowered the classical lines of the structure itself. In the seventeenth century the manneristic style remained highly favored in the republic, while it was replaced in the Spanish Netherlands by the baroque. Under the stadholdership of Frederick Henry the Dutch republic experienced a new elegance, in which the houses of the richer merchants and nobility expressed an absolutely correct and simple classicism.

In painting, on the other hand, Dutch artists created their own style. Their patrons were municipal councils, townsmen's clubs, and substantial merchants—but not the Calvinist Church, which called art "popish idolatry." Dutch patrons demanded portraits that depicted their own solid virtues and serenity, town scenes, seascapes, landscapes, animal pictures, and still lifes. The artists tried to capture quiet scenes of everyday life and objects that appealed to the material instincts of an affluent and comfortable people.

Each town, especially in Holland, produced coteries of artists supported locally. Specialization was rife: a patron might turn to three different artists for a portrait, a canal scene, and a still life of oysters on a pewter platter.

Dutch painting was by and large sober, unspectacular, patient, detailed, and soft in color. The artists were extremely sensitive to light and shade, which they used to achieve visual unity—unlike the baroque artists, who used light to create startling dramatic effects. Out of the very rich run of Dutch painters, three can be selected for special mention. Frans Hals of Mechlin (1580–1666) specialized in group portraiture. He was more successful in grouping and capturing the dynamics of individual figures in a mass than in portraying personal character. Jan Vermeer of Delft (1632–1675) was a master of the home scene, immortalizing the prosaic of life in incredibly still, hushed tones. Although his technique was extraordinary, his most compelling characteristic was his complete detachment from the scene. Under his flawless brushwork mirrors and musical instruments and even people were transformed into a still life.

Rembrandt van Rijn of Amsterdam (1606–1669) towered over all other Dutch painters. He dealt with the common stuff of his countrymen, seeking an unsmiling sobriety and somberness. He cannot be called baroque because his passion was internalized, unlike Rubens', yet he was as intense and masterful as Rubens. He brought enormous psychological insight to his portraits and religious scenes. Working from the restricted horizon of Dutch painters, he came close to expressing the full range of human experience. No human emotion was outside his grasp, except joy. He repressed gaiety for serenity. This one flaw, reflecting the solid virtues of republican Holland and the moral overtones of a Calvinist environment, robbed him of unquestioned supremacy in the European art of his century.

ENGLAND AND HOLLAND—A BACKWARD GLANCE

During the two generations when the dominant tide in the principal powers of Europe was toward royal absolutism, in England and Holland alone the flood tide was turned to ebb. There were certain common causes for the reversal. In both countries the challenge to the authority of the state inherent in Calvinism was a potent solvent of absolutist ideas and sentiments. Unified moneyed interests centered in London and Amsterdam provided counterpoises to the power of the state. If Frederick Henry had been able to subvert Amsterdam's oligarchy or Charles I had been able to take London, the history of the two countries might have been different. The continuing vitality of representative institutions provided a platform for opposition to absolutism in both nations. The representative institutions also determined the conservative cast of mind of the opposition. Those who struggled against absolutism in Holland and England based their opposition on backward-looking principles, such as the preservation of "provincial sovereignty" or the "liberties of the subject." Although this circumstance grew from their basic commitment to historical representative institutions, it was fortuitous that the two men who wielded greatest power were not subverted by triumph. Jan de Witt and Oliver Cromwell, unlike many liberators who have entered a revolutionary matrix only to leave the mold as despots, were men of rare moderation. Above all, they were children of the States and Parliament.

PART TWO

Absolutism, Enlightenment, and Revolution (1660–1815)

THE PERIOD from the mid-seventeenth to the early nineteenth century was one of the great transitional epochs in human history. Scientific breakthroughs made by men of immense creativity in the later seventeenth century established firmly the mechanistic interpretation of the physical universe. They also provided a foundation for the Enlightenment of the eighteenth century with its belief in the power of reason to uncover universal natural laws that govern social behavior, just as the great natural scientists had found out the laws that govern physical matter. Transformations in economic life increased man's efficiency in the production of goods, manufactured and grown, launching the European world on industrial and agricultural expansion that soon took on revolutionary proportions. During this epoch the political framework of our own times was established by the final triumph of the secular nation-state. The religious struggle that had kept Europe in turmoil for more than a century ended, and with it went the last hopes for a united Western Christendom. Religious disputes continued to disturb the internal peace of some countries and to affect relationships between nations, but religion no longer exercised the influence it once had in European affairs.

By 1660 the absolutist solution to the continuing problem posed by the efforts of the nobility to increase its power at the expense of the sovereign and to the problem of creating the modern nation-state had won wide acceptance. The personal rule of Louis XIV of France brought absolutism in that country to its pinnacle, provided it with enough momentum to last three-quarters of a century after his death, and spawned imitators all over Europe. Russia emerged as a European power under the rule of Peter the Great, whose conscious imitation of the practices of Western absolutist monarchs was a kind of technological borrowing no less important than the technicians and artisans he imported into Russia in his program of "europeanization." In the eighteenth century a new brand of absolutism known as "enlightened despotism" evolved. It used the doctrines of the Enlightenment to justify absolutism, as theorists had justified it by divine right in the sixteenth and seventeenth centuries. In three states absolutism was successfully resisted by oligarchies that won out over princely pretensions: England, the Dutch Republic, and Poland. Of these three, Poland did not survive the eighteenth century, the Dutch Republic declined economically and militarily, and England alone emerged as a first-rank power able to seize an empire and retain unimpaired its representative institutions.

Absolutism, though it differed from state to state, invariably comprised governmental centralization, both legal and administrative, and a consequent growth of a bureaucracy dependent upon the absolute monarch; subjugation of the Church within the monarch's domain and enforcement of religious uniformity as a facet of political loyalty; a standing army subject to the monarch's discipline; and an amalgam of economic policies (lumped together under the name mercantilism) aimed at building a strong national economy to make the state as self-sufficient as possible and thereby increase its capacity to wage successful wars. The prime victim of absolutism was everywhere the nobility. In the absolutisms of Western Europe the nobility's power was eroded by the loss of its traditional representative institutions, the process of centralization, and the rise through service to the monarch of a new nobility dependent upon the ruler's favor. In Central and Eastern Europe the absolutist monarch subjugated the nobility to his will by drawing them into state service and by allowing them greater privileges over their peasants. The object of absolutism everywhere was not domestic order and public welfare so much as the aggrandizement of the territory, the power, and the glory of the monarch and of his dynasty. Marriage alliances, contracted between royal dynasties, and wars were the accepted means to these ends. With the added dimension of the colonial dependencies of the powers, dynastic wars became in fact world wars.

In the last quarter of the eighteenth century the outbreak of revolution in the New World and the Old announced the end of absolutism and the dawn of a new democratic age. In the French Revolution wars were fought for the first time by mass mobilization of citizens in defense and furtherance of an ideology. And for the first time—though unhappily not the last—the European world witnessed the facility with which democratic ideology could be turned to serve the ambitions of a dictator and support the apparatus of a despotic state bent upon conquest abroad.

— CHAPTER ELEVEN —

The Pinnacle of French Absolutism

Absolutism reached its apogee during the long reign of Louis XIV. His France was consciously and sometimes slavishly imitated by monarchs of other lands in statecraft, bureaucracy, military organization, and the more ostentatious features of culture. There was certainly no more glittering model to follow. When Louis began his personal rule in 1661 his kingdom was the strongest in Europe. Spain was a defeated second-class power; the English king had just regained the throne; the Hapsburg Emperor's hegemony in Germany was shattered and he was struggling against the Turks on the eastern frontiers. Within France a discredited nobility, having had its fling in the Fronde, was softened for the servility offered by Louis. The French administrative structure was the most highly developed in Europe. The Church, the middle ranks of society, and the corporate towns of France were solidly behind the throne. Richelieu and Mazarin, who had run France for almost four decades, had done their work well.

"I Am the State"

As a youth, Louis gave little promise that he was to become one of the most renowned rulers of all time. Mazarin is supposed to have said, "There is stuff enough in him to make four kings and one honest man." His parents, Louis XIII and Anne of Austria, detested one another; they had been married for twenty-three years before Louis, their first child, was born in 1638. So surprised were the French at the unexpected event that they hailed the infant "Louis the Godgiven." Five years later Louis XIII died and the child became Louis XIV, the third Bourbon king of France. The direction of his education was entrusted to Cardinal Mazarin. Apparently the tutors appointed by the cardinal did only a mediocre job in instructing their royal pupil in the usual academic subjects, but to judge from his later career, his tutelage under the masterful cardinal provided a matchless training in the art of absolutist kingship.

When Cardinal Mazarin died in 1661, Frenchmen expected a new first minister to conduct the affairs of state while the handsome twenty-three-year-old king continued to content himself with the semblance of power. Instead, Louis called together his counselors and declared:

> I have summoned you the Chancellor, with my ministers and secretaries of state, to tell you that it has pleased me hitherto to permit my affairs to be governed by the late Cardinal. I shall in the future be my own first minister. You will aid me with your counsels when I ask you for them. I request and order you, Monsieur Chancellor, to seal no decree except by my command, and I order you, my Secretaries of State and you, Monsieur Superintendent of Finances, to sign nothing without my command.

In this injunction, never waived by Louis, he recaptured personal oversight of a bureaucracy that in its very complexity and efficiency threatened to serve its own interests rather than the king's. Louis believed himself to be by God's will the personification of the state and therefore the person best able to decide on the needs and interests of the realm. According to him, whatever aggrandized his own power and glory and that of his dynasty, aggrandized the power and glory of France. Although he never actually spoke the words, "L'état, c'est moi" (I am the State), which are almost universally attributed to him, he certainly reflected the sentiment that they expressed.

THE MAN

Louis, who set so high a value upon his person and opinions, was actually of little more than average intelligence and abilities, but he was supremely self-confident. He had a majestic appearance and great personal charm; in fact, he was courtliness personified. He was also blessed with robust good health. Always in complete control of himself, he never for a moment forgot his own place nor that of any of his subjects. Short on imagination but long on common sense, he knew how to conceal his true feelings and

Louis XIV of France,
by Hyacinthe Rigaud

"He was born prudent, temperate, discreet, master of his emotions and his tongue; can it be believed? he was born good and just, and God had endowed him with sufficient to become a good king and perhaps even a rather great one. . . . Glory was to him a weakness rather than an ambition. . . . Submissiveness, servility, an air of admiration combined with sycophancy, and above all, an air of being nothing without him, were the only ways to win his favor. If a man strayed from this path ever so little there was no return for him. . . ." MÉMOIRES DE SAINT-SIMON (1675–1755) (Paris, 1916), Vol. XVIII.

Alinari-Art Reference Bureau

intentions, and he trusted no one. He worked methodically and unceasingly, spent six to nine hours each day on the affairs of state, and permitted nothing to interfere with his daily work routine. He was not a great man, but he possessed a rare combination of talents and qualities that enabled him to play to perfection the role he assigned himself. He well merited the title sometimes given him, the Grand Monarch.

Louis's marriage in 1660 to Maria Theresa, his first cousin and daughter of Philip IV of Spain, was a state marriage for purely dynastic ends. He never loved her, and indeed he had earlier fallen in love with and hoped to marry Marie Mancini, Cardinal Mazarin's niece. Within a year of his marriage to Maria Theresa he took his first mistress, Louise de la Vallière. Royal mistresses had never been rare in European courts, but in the late seventeenth century they were kept more openly. They were, in effect, an institution of state, providing the monarch such companionship and loving solace as a wife married for reasons of state could not provide. Mistresses were generally reliable and at least initially grateful; queens were too often neither. La Vallière loved Louis, and her affection was requited until 1667, when she was forced to share the Grand Monarch with a haughty lady-in-waiting to the queen, the Marquise de Montespan. In 1674 La Vallière retired to a nunnery and Montespan held the field.

In 1669 the widow of the poet Paul Scarron had become the governess of the children of Louis and Montespan. Madame Scarron, who was then thirty-four, came from a famous Huguenot family but had herself become a Catholic, and a particularly devout one. Her new post brought her to the constant attention of the king, who found himself attracted by her intellectual and physical qualities as well as her piety and correctness of manner. In 1678 he created her Marquise de Maintenon. When Montespan's involvement with a notorious sorceress and purveyor of love potions and poisons became public knowledge in 1680, Louis dropped his old mistress and installed the ex-governess in her place. In July, 1683, Queen Maria Theresa died (she once said that in all her married life she had only twenty days of happiness). She bore Louis six children, only one of whom survived— Louis the Dauphin (heir apparent). Shortly after her death Louis wed de Maintenon in a private ceremony, but because of her nonroyal birth and previous marriage Louis never officially recognized her as queen. The marriage proved a turning point in his career. He abandoned his love affairs, settled down to a life of almost middle-class respectability and quickened piety, and found domestic happiness.

"NONE HIS EQUAL"

There was no power in the France of Louis XIV to challenge his unique authority within the state. His emblem was the sun, the center of the universe; from this he was sometimes called the Sun King. His motto was *Nec pluribus impar,* "None his equal." He liked to think—and panegyrists like Bossuet never tired of telling him—that the rays of glory and power descended from him to all his inferiors.

Louis made it a cardinal principle of administration to exclude men of high birth from the most important government offices. He chose his ministers from humbler backgrounds, so that they would owe their prominence to him alone. At first his principal counselors, whom he inherited from Mazarin, were Michel Le Tellier, secretary of state for war; Hugues de Lionne, in charge of foreign affairs; and Nicholas Fouquet, superintendent of finances. All three were from families of bourgeois origin. Fouquet quickly came under the suspicion of the young king as being overly ambitious. and in September, 1661, he was arrested on charges of high treason. His trial lasted three years; he was finally condemned to life imprisonment. His place was taken by Jean Baptiste Colbert, son of a merchant of Rheims who had entered government service under Mazarin.

For the next decade the "Triad"—Colbert, Le Tellier, and Lionne—were the king's closest advisers. Although Louis did not have a creative mind, he knew how to employ the talents of his counselors, and with their help he achieved the successes of the first part of his reign. It is not possible to determine how large a part the king himself played in framing the policies of state, but it is certain that he always made the final decision.

SUBJUGATION OF THE NOBILITY

Louis's exclusion of the old aristocracy from the innermost ruling circle was part of a deliberate plan to destroy once and for all the threat that the nobles as a class presented to the power of the monarch and to reduce them as individuals to a condition of subservience to him. He never convened the Estates-General of the kingdom, and his officials kept close scrutiny upon the provincial estates. Early in the reign he sent out special courts to hear complaints against nobles and to deal out punishments to those who abused their powers and mistreated their peasants. The most famous tribunal sat in the province of Auvergne in 1665–66, where it condemned several nobles to death. Although personal influence saved most of these men from the block, the nobility of France realized that the king was determined to make his law and his will supreme over the old feudal privileges.

Louis further diminished the status of the nobility by selling patents of nobility to wealthy commoners as a way of raising money and a reward for faithful service. Although earlier monarchs had done the same, the traffic in titles reached a new peak in Louis's reign. He further cheapened the value of a title by revoking all new grants of nobility nine times during his reign and then compelling the nobles to purchase them over again. He broke with precedent by imposing taxes on the nobility. Immunity from ordinary taxes had long been one of the most prized privileges of the aristocracy; their contribution was supposedly in the form of military and other governmental services of feudal origin. The great wars of the last half of Louis's reign created such a need for money that in 1695 the king decided to levy a head tax on the nobles as well as all his other subjects, and in 1710 he ordered them to pay an income tax of 10 per cent, called the *dixième* or "tenth."

Louis struck the most damaging blow at the nobility by making attendance at court and adulation of his person the price of favor. Those who would not live at court he would not favor: "He is a man I never see; I do not know him." If a noble wanted a pension or some ceremonial but lucrative post, if he wanted to maintain his standing among his peers, if he wanted his children to marry well—he had to live at court. The harshest punishment he could receive was to be banished from the king's presence. As a courtier once said to Louis, "Sire, away from Your Majesty one is not only miserable but ridiculous."

VERSAILLES AND THE COURT

When Louis began his reign, the court was at the Louvre in Paris. Louis disliked the city because it was the center of the Fronde and because the public came and went as it pleased at the Louvre, allowing the king little

Palace of Versailles

"Your Majesty knows that apart from brilliant exploits in war nothing testifies more to the grandeur and the character of princes than buildings; and all posterity measures them by the scale provided by the magnificent palaces they built during their lifetime." Colbert to Louis XIV, September 28, 1665, reprinted in LETTRES, INSTRUCTIONS ET MÉMOIRES (Paris, 1868), Vol. V.

Photograph from Brown Brothers

privacy. He knew that if he wanted to win and hold the awe of the masses he could not live too close to them. He decided to build a new residence that would surpass in splendor all the other palaces of the world. He selected Versailles, a few miles from Paris and already the site of a modest palace that had long been one of Louis's favorite rural retreats. In 1668 work began on new buildings. The court moved to Versailles in 1682, although the buildings were not all completed until 1710. In addition to Versailles, which was for the court, the king built two other palaces nearby: the Trianon for himself and his ladies, and Marly (destroyed during the French Revolution) for himself and his most favored friends. The cost was enormous: thirty thousand workers were employed just to dig the canals that brought in water for the many fountains. An elegant blend of architecture with magnificent formal landscaping, Versailles conveys the grandeur that Louis intended. It was justifiably imitated by monarchs of other lands who sought a monumental expression of power. Versailles became an institution of state, like the courtiers, the mistresses, and the Grand Monarch who inhabited it.

Under Louis the royal court became far more numerous and luxurious than it had ever been. There were several thousand noble courtiers and over four thousand servants, not including the military guards. The upkeep of the huge establishment was one of the chief expenses of the state. Life at court was regulated with fantastic precision, for Louis had a great fondness for ceremony and lavish display. The center around which everything orbited was the Sun King himself. The nobles were reduced to the level of minor actors and onlookers in a continuing pageant.

The court's day began when the king arose, and ended when he retired. These two events, known as the *lever* and the *coucher,* were public occasions. In between, the courtiers' time was occupied by attendance upon the king as he passed from one carefully planned activity to the next. The *lever* began when the king awakened around eight o'clock. Before that hour the courtiers had had to assemble in his anteroom. When the king gave the word, they were admitted to the bed chamber singly and according to their rank. For the king's close relatives both sides of the double door into the bedroom were opened; for all others, only one side. After each person had entered, the door was closed, and the next man had to scratch lightly on the panel to be admitted—knocking was forbidden. All told, 150 to 200 nobles watched Louis put on and take off his clothes every morning and night. Each step in the process was carried out ritually, and the whole procedure seemed like a preposterous ballet. For example, in the morning a valet handed the king's shirt to the grand chamberlain, who handed it to the heir apparent, the Dauphin, who handed it to the king. Each night the king graciously allowed a noble to hold a candlestick while he climbed into bed. Although the room was well lighted, so that this single candlestick added nothing, men of ancient and proud lineage vied with one another for the privilege of holding it.

About five thousand courtiers lived in apartments in the palace at Versailles and another five thousand lived nearby. They spent their lives in hunts, masquerades, concerts, plays, receptions, gambling, licentiousness, and above all, gossip. Boredom reigned supreme. Flattery and hypocrisy were the keys to success. It was inevitable that people who lived in such an artificial atmosphere and had no chance to occupy themselves in useful tasks should become demoralized. Louis indeed triumphed in his plan to reduce the nobility to impotency.

THE DECLINE OF THE NOBILITY AS A CLASS

The 10,000 who lived at or near Versailles were the pick of the aristocracy. Numerically they formed only a small part of the nobility. In 1715 an estimated 200,000 of France's 20,000,000 people were nobles. In France, as in other Continental lands, all the children of a noble were themselves nobles. The nobility ranged from the great lords who surrounded the king through provincial nobles who lived comfortable if undistinguished lives down to the minor nobility who owned tiny scraps of land and whose standard of living was hardly distinguishable from that of the more prosperous peasants. The impoverished squires were called *hobereaux,* "small hawks," by their contemptuous fellow nobles.

Financial difficulties were not restricted to the *hobereaux*. One of the most striking phenomena of French social history during the age of Louis XIV was the impoverishment of the nobility as a class. There was a general economic decline in France in the last decades of the seventeenth and first decades of the eighteenth centuries, so that the income of all the nobility fell. Matters were made worse for the great aristocrats by the high cost of court life. They resorted to various expedients, such as marrying into wealthy bourgeois or recently ennobled families, but they found that the easiest way to solve their money problems was by the sinecures and pensions that the king gave them in return for their constant attendance upon him. Economic pressure had much to do with transforming the once turbulent and independent French aristocracy into a parasitic court nobility.

Besides the economic differences among them, the nobles were stratified according to rank. At the top were the princes of the blood, who were the king's relatives outside of his immediate family; then came the select group of great lords called peers, who were honored by the appellation of "king's cousins"; last came the nobles of various other titles down to baron. Nobles were also divided according to origin. Those who traced their noble lineage back through many generations or who had won their titles through military service were called the *noblesse d'épée*, "nobility of the sword." They considered themselves socially superior to nobles who acquired their titles by purchase or by inheritance of certain offices. The latter were known as the *noblesse de robe*, "nobility of the robe," from the gown worn by lawyers.

PERFECTING THE ABSOLUTIST MACHINERY

Despite the centralizing activities of one and a half centuries, in 1661 France still comprised three hundred political and administrative areas, each with a measure of autonomy in functions and institutions. The provinces had distinctive legal and administrative institutions. Cities enjoyed special corporate privileges in the provincial estates, a sometimes assertive representative body. There were hundreds of internal tariffs and tolls. Louis was determined to supplant particularism with his own centralized administration in order that his will might penetrate into every corner of the kingdom.

Louis's approach to the problem of government represented a quest for orderliness and rationality that had spread from science and philosophy into the mainstream of political life. In some ways Louis was a good Cartesian, believing that he could create an administrative machinery that would automatically produce security, the welfare of his subjects, and the perpetuation of his own power. Although he fell short of the goal, he came as near to perfecting the machinery of absolutism as any monarch of the age.

Louis completed the sophistication of the numerous councils of Richelieu's day, adding new ones but reducing the initiative of all of them. Except in the most routine functions, each council had to wait upon the will of the king. No longer could the Council of Dispatches send out the dread *lettres de cachet* to arrest a suspected traitor; Louis sent them in the name of the council. Since many of his officials held office by hereditary or traditional right, he was not in a position to get rid of them wholesale. Instead, he reduced the scope of their power and played one official against another, one administrative organ against another. He used special ad hoc commissions for particularly important and delicate matters that before would have been handled routinely by a council. The councils were relegated to the status of purely bureaucratic tools. Policy emanated from the king.

Intendancy was given its final form. Besides the duties that they had performed under Richelieu, intendants under Louis took over complete control of provincial and municipal government in time of war or crisis. In time of peace they performed a supervisory function in local government that greatly reduced the responsibility and power of the regular local officials. The provincial governors, who were drawn from the old nobility, became figureheads. The intendants were the eyes and ears of the central government, and upon their reports, surveys, and statistical tabulations the king based the decisions that moved the realm.

Louis completed the reduction of the parlements to impotency. In 1673 he decreed that the parlements were to record his laws at once and in their original form; objections to a law could be heard only once and only after it had been recorded. No longer could the parlements debate constitutional questions or take part in the formulation of general policy.

In all these changes Louis did no more than complete the bureaucratic developments that had been started in earnest under Henry IV and been advanced by Richelieu. Louis's main contribution was the orderly arrangement of governmental organs that previously had overlapped in jurisdiction and functions. The overlapping had been one means of control by which one group of officials watched another, but Louis meant to watch all by himself. The overlapping had created blind spots in which the administration could escape the surveillance of the king. Louis made the bureaucracy like the famous Hall of Mirrors at Versailles—a long chamber into every nook and cranny of which the king might see from a position of absolute centrality. As the mirrors reflected the sun throughout the hall, so the radiance of the Sun King was reflected everywhere in the administration.

Louis XIV came as close to erecting a police state as the limitations of communication and transportation in the period allowed. His political police were the intendants, spies, and other agents who sniffed out sedition and treason. The Bastille awaited the mighty or the humble. Men were seized by *lettres de cachet* and imprisoned indefinitely without recourse to trial or the possibility of acquittal. A standing army was ready at hand for the suppression of insurrection. Louis seldom sought to twist the processes of justice; he merely circumvented the whole system in cases of political crime, real or supposed.

The machinery of absolutism was a workable instrument to any ends that the absolutist monarch desired. Its effectiveness depended little on its popularity. Yet Louis intended good to come of it, and insofar as that good, personally conceived, corresponded to the good of France, the machinery was beneficial.

Absolutism in Economics and Religion

Louis's mediocre capacity would not have sufficed to undertake single-handedly the fiscal and economic reforms he envisaged. Although he trusted no man with the plenitude of his power, he permitted Jean Baptiste Colbert (1619–1683) a larger measure of responsible autonomy than any other minister. Colbert, who prided himself on never taking a vacation, was a brilliant administrator with an enormous capacity for hard work. Though not a personable man (he was nicknamed "The North" because, like the north wind, he was cold and surly), he was entirely devoted to the king and to making France great. Louis appreciated him and entrusted him with the direction of industry, commerce, agriculture, colonies, maritime affairs, art, and finances.

Louis's ambitious projects demanded vast amounts of money. The bulk of the state's revenues came from taxes levied on the king's poorest subjects. Nobles and clergymen, who owned most of the wealth, were exempted from virtually all government levies until years after Colbert's death. Colbert was unable to change this system, but he did introduce order into the financial administration, decrease the direct taxes paid by the common people, increase the indirect levies that everyone paid, and eliminate much graft. Under his able management revenues tripled, and for a few years receipts actually exceeded expenses. Louis's ever-increasing expenditures in peace and war made it impossible for prosperity to last. After the beginning of the Dutch War in 1672, outgo regularly exceeded income and was often twice as large. The government went deeper and deeper into debt. Colbert's exhortations to Louis to economize went unheeded.

ECONOMIC POLICY OF COLBERT

Colbert applied the policies of mercantilism (see pp. 355–360) to the French economy. "Colbertism," in fact, is sometimes used as a synonym for mercantilism. Colbert considered gold essential to the national well-being. Since France lacked ore deposits, it could increase its bullion stocks only by increasing the value of exports and decreasing the value of imports. Colbert believed that the total volume of trade and the total number of ships engaged in trade were all more or less fixed. The only way that one nation could increase its share was at the expense of another nation. He once called commerce "a perpetual and peaceable war of wit and energy among all nations."

Colbert devoted much effort to building up foreign trade, and he stressed the importance of colonies as sources of raw materials and potential markets for finished goods. His ambitions in this connection outran his capacities. Between 1664 and 1670 he granted chartered monopolies and other privileges to four companies to undertake French trade with the East Indies, West Indies, northern Europe, and the Levant. He hoped that the companies would revive France's moribund oceanic commerce, break the monopolies of the English and Dutch companies, exploit the colonies France already had, and help in adding new ones. The companies were supervised by the government, or more precisely by Colbert. Since neither he nor the other government officials had any practical experience in foreign trade, the companies soon foundered and in a few years were liquidated. Yet they were not complete failures, for they served to revive French overseas trade and to train French seamen and merchants in the ways of oceanic commerce.

Colbert undertook an expansion of domestic commerce through improved communications, including the betterment of road and river networks and the construction of canals, and through the reform of internal tariffs. The system of internal tariffs forced up the price of goods and impeded interregional trade. France had long been divided into two parts: the Five Great Farms (so called because the collection of tariffs had once been farmed out to private contractors under five separate contracts), which covered the northern half of France, and the rest of the country. Although there were no tariffs within the Five Great Farms, goods passing between the Farms and the other provinces paid heavy duties, varying according to the place where the goods crossed the line. In addition, shipments from certain provinces that had been recently acquired by France paid duties on entering any other part of the kingdom. Colbert could not abolish the division, principally because the tariffs were an important source of royal revenue, but in 1664 he issued a new schedule of tariffs between the Farms and the rest of France that simplified and somewhat reduced the rates.

Colbert expended much time and effort in trying to build up industry so that France would become as nearly self-sufficient as possible. Subsidies, monopolies, tax reductions, loans without interest, and a host of other aids were extended to manufacturers to stimulate productivity. He arranged for the immigration of hundreds of skilled foreign workers and forbade the emigration of French artisans. He established new industries with government aid, particularly in fields where there was little or no French production. In return for assistance the manufacturers had to submit to close governmental regulation. Though French industry had always been subjected to outside control by government, church, town, and gild officials, intervention reached a new peak under Colbert. His instruments of control were the once independent craft gilds. He drew up new gild regulations in consultation with gild officials. Manufacturers were compelled to join the gilds. In 1666 and 1670 he issued regulations standardizing the quality and size of all sorts of goods, especially cloth. A corps of state inspectors was established to see that the regulations were obeyed, and severe punishments were ordered for those who disregarded them.

Colbert's purpose was to raise French goods to such a high and uniform quality that Frenchmen and foreigners alike would prefer French merchandise. However, he was never able to enforce his system completely. He did not have enough inspectors and, more important, both manufacturers and consumers resisted his efforts at standardization. The manufacturers preferred their old ways, and the consumers often wanted goods of sizes and qualities different from the standards set by law. The regulations acted as an obstacle to experimentation and innovation on the part of producers and placed undue emphasis on the production of luxury goods, in which the gilds had traditionally dealt.

The great minister attempted to introduce improvements in agricultural production and promoted land reclamation and forestry. To build up a large and industrious population, he had the government forbid emigration, give tax exemptions to families with ten or more children, put difficulties in the way of people who wished to become nuns and priests, reduce the number of Church holidays from forty-one to twenty-four, and try to force vagabonds, beggars, and gypsies to find work by threatening them with the poorhouse or service in the Mediterranean galley fleet of the French navy.

Colbert accomplished much in his twenty-two years in power. On balance, however, the long-term results of his policies proved disappointing, for they failed to raise the level of the French economy. Although the wars and extravagances of Louis XIV were the chief causes for the failure to achieve economic growth, Colbert must share in the blame. The excessive paternalism of his system tended to stifle initiative without obtaining the advantages of planning. Planning was impossible because it assumed a greater capacity for control of the economy than either the physical power of the state or contemporary knowledge of economics allowed.

GALLICANISM

In his efforts to centralize and unify the realm the Sun King inevitably clashed with the papacy. From his forebears Louis had inherited the tradition of Gallicanism—control of the Church in France by the throne—and he stoutly defended it. He had the unwavering support of most of the French clergy. Very early in his reign quarrels broke out between Paris and Rome. The most serious occurred in 1673, when Louis demanded that he receive the *régale*, the income from vacant bishoprics until they were filled by a new bishop. In 1682 the dispute came before an assembly of bishops in Paris under the leadership of Bishop Bossuet, who was noted as a defender of Gallicanism as well as of the divine right of kings. The prelates drew up a statement known as the Declaration of Gallican Liberties. Its four articles reaffirmed the temporal supremacy of the king and restated the old claim that the doctrinal authority of the pope could be overruled by a Church council. The adamant posture of both sides raised the possibility that the French Church might break completely with Rome. The danger passed in 1693 when Louis, faced by a coalition of hostile Protestant powers and desirous of papal support, agreed to a compromise that was a victory for Rome. Louis greatly modified his claim to the *régale* and withdrew the edict by which he had made the four articles of the Declaration of Gallican Liberties part of French law. The French bishops retracted their support of the Declaration and humbly craved the pope's pardon.

Although Louis had no hesitation in disagreeing with the pope in matters pertaining to church-state relations, he felt himself at one with Rome in matters of faith. He was always a devout Catholic, and as he grew older, his piety increased and rigidified, accentuated by the influence of the deeply religious Madame de Maintenon. Any position that departed from a narrow Catholic orthodoxy was anathema to him. He believed, too, that in the interests of national unity and strength all his subjects should be of the same faith. His mixed religious-political motives explain his campaigns against the Jansenists within the Catholic Church and against the Huguenots outside it.

JANSENISM

The Jansenists owed their name and doctrines to Cornelius Jansen (1585–1638), a Flemish bishop. The kernel of their belief was that man attains eternal salvation only if God predestined him to it, and that God's gift of grace is irrespective of any good works that man may do. Predestinarianism and rejection of free will brought the Jansenists close to the doctrinal position of John Calvin; their enemies called them "warmed-over Calvinists." The Jansenists considered themselves loyal members of the Catholic Church who wanted to increase the personal holiness of priests and laymen and who opposed the Church's secular power. They complained that the pope misunderstood their position. They particularly condemned some of the Jesuits whom they called "Laxists" for too readily granting absolution of sins upon confession. The Jansenists held that such laxness made penance too easy and encouraged immorality. They themselves led puritanical lives and scorned the luxury and licentiousness that was then fashionable.

The movement had two centers, the monasteries of Port-Royal in Paris and Port-Royal des Champs near Versailles. A group of clerics and laymen attracted by the Jansenist doctrines settled near Port-Royal des Champs and dedicated themselves to a life of the mind and spirit. Among them was Blaise Pascal (1623–1662), scientist and philosopher. While living at Port-

Royal, he wrote *Provincial Letters* (1657), a scathing attack upon the Jesuits.

During the first decades of Louis's reign the Jansenist teachings attracted a number of important people. The king was alarmed by this development. He believed that the movement endangered both Church and state. He was also repelled by the Jansenist emphasis upon asceticism, which he took as a rebuke on his own style of life. His reactions were reinforced by the Jesuit priests who were his personal confessors. Louis urged that the movement be outlawed by the Church, but for a time the Jansenists enjoyed the protection of two successive popes who disliked the Jesuit order. The next pope, Clement XI, was more obliging; in bulls issued in 1706 and 1713 he condemned the Jansenist teachings. The leaders fled to Holland. Although the movement was heavily persecuted in France, it managed to live on there until the nineteenth century.

SUPPRESSION OF THE HUGUENOTS

The Huguenots had been destroyed as a separate political force in Richelieu's day. They were allowed, however, to keep the religious and civil freedoms that had been guaranteed them by the Edict of Nantes in 1598. There were about two million of these French Protestants, among whom were many men of unusual energy and ability. Usually excluded from important positions in public life, they became leaders in trade, industry, banking, and the professions. Their economic success was envied by the Catholic majority, who already despised them as heretics. The autonomy enjoyed by the Huguenot religious communities made them appear a dangerous republican influence. The Catholic majority looked upon the Edict of Nantes as a temporary political expedient and believed that one day all Frenchmen must be Catholics.

Louis shared these feelings. He was outraged that any of his subjects should be of a religion different from that of their sovereign and starting in 1679 he embarked upon a program of undermining the Edict of Nantes. He permitted the destruction of three-quarters of the Protestant churches (or "temples" as the Huguenots called them), placed restrictions on the subjects that could be taught in their schools, suppressed their special courts, billeted troops in their homes with orders to be as unpleasant as possible, and harassed them at every turn. Simultaneously he sponsored a vigorous campaign to convert Huguenots, offering them money, exemption from the dreaded billeting, and other privileges.

The Edict of Nantes was practically a dead letter by the time Louis officially revoked it in October, 1685. He claimed that so many Huguenots had become Catholics as a result of his conversion campaign that the edict was superfluous. The remaining Protestant churches were destroyed, Protestant religious services and schools were banned, torture and brutality were freely used to compel conversion, and refugees caught trying to leave the country were sentenced to the galleys. About 200,000 Huguenots, among whom were many of the wealthiest and most industrious, managed with the aid of friendly Catholics at home and fellow Protestants abroad to escape to England, Holland, Brandenburg-Prussia, and British America. A number of exiles made important contributions to the economic development of their havens and strengthened France's enemies. Their departure undoubtedly weakened certain sectors of the French economy, but recent study has shown that it was less disastrous than hitherto supposed. Many of those who remained in France practiced their religion in secret, and after Louis's death in 1715 persecution abated.

French Predominance

The principal aim of the foreign policy of Louis XIV was to make France the arbiter of Europe, exercising the primacy that had once belonged to the House of Hapsburg. Second, Louis sought to extend the boundaries of the realm to what would later be called the "natural frontiers" of France: the Rhine, the Alps, and the Pyrenees. His policy could only mean conflict with Spain—a conflict that put the seal to French predominance.

THE WAR MACHINE

Louis laid the foundations for his foreign policy by constructing with customary thoroughness the finest war machine in Europe. He was unalterably opposed to the traditional method of raising an army of semi-independent military chiefs and their private troops when the occasion demanded. Instead, he created the first great national army in Europe. It was directly under royal command. In 1667 the French army had 72,000 men; within ten years it had nearly quadrupled. Two men of extraordinary capacity—Louvois and Vauban—were the craftsmen of the new military force.

Michel Le Tellier, Marquis de Louvois and son of the minister of the same name who was one of the "Triad," was secretary of state for war from 1666 until his death in 1691. Louvois fashioned a close-knit fighting force of extraordinary discipline, high morale, and formidable power. A table of organization assigned the duties of every officer from ensign to marshal, with a rigid chain of command based on rank and, within each rank, on seniority. It remedied the worst aspects of the old system, by which officers had been recruited by purchase from a narrow social base. Pay scales for all ranks were fixed. Uniforms were widely adopted to improve morale and establish divisional distinctions within the army. Orders of merit and medals were instituted as rewards for valor and service. Military hospitals were built, and a pension plan was created for disabled veterans. Weapons were

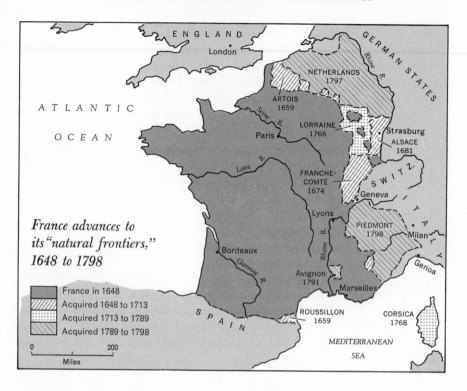

France advances to its "natural frontiers," 1648 to 1798

France in 1648
Acquired 1648 to 1713
Acquired 1713 to 1789
Acquired 1789 to 1798

0   200
Miles

standardized. In 1687 a way was devised of fixing a bayonet to a gun so that the weapon could be fired with the bayonet attached; this allowed infantrymen to fire and then charge and made pikemen unnecessary. An effective force of "dragoons" or mounted infantry gave increased mobility to the army. Much of the artillery corps was integrated with the regular army establishment. A complex logistical system was devised, with permanent arsenals and supply depots linked to permanent barracks located strategically throughout France. The militia was completely reorganized to provide a reserve of reinforcements for the line. In 1668 the inspector general's office was created to inspect troops and equipment, enforce discipline, ensure training, and report on the merits of line officers for command. The name of the first inspector general of infantry, Colonel Martinet, is still a synonym for a rigid disciplinarian.

Marshal Vauban (1633–1707), a man of low birth and high genius, was undoubtedly the greatest military engineer of the age. He was a master of fortification in an era when strategy entailed the taking of strong points rather than fighting pitched battles. He directed more than fifty sieges, devising parallel trenches, earthworks, and temporary fortifications to enable the army to besiege and reduce enemy forts with a minimal loss of troops. His own fortresses, ringing France and commanding the wilderness of Canada, were the epitome of scientific planning. Salients that projected out from the fortresses permitted a raking gunfire and made frontal attack suicidal.

Colbert was responsible for the birth of the French navy with Louis's grudging acquiescence. In 1661 the navy had 30 ships; in 1677 it had 199. Through technological advances and a system of shipyards and fleet staging ports, Colbert provided France with an effective sea force, which might have established the maritime supremacy of France in the 1690's if Louis had not cut its budget after Colbert's death. Instead, England gained command of the sea, a fatal blow to French ambitions for over a century to come.

THE WAR OF DEVOLUTION, 1667–1668

Louis's first bid for martial glory in the quest for international power came in May, 1667, when his armies invaded the Spanish territories of Franche-Comté and the Spanish Netherlands. This attempt to establish French hegemony on the corpse of Hapsburg power was based on the claim that the territories belonged to his wife, Maria Theresa, because of an inheritance custom in them called the law of devolution, by which children of the first marriage inherited private property in preference to children of the second marriage. Maria Theresa was the eldest daughter of the first marriage of Philip IV of Spain, who had recently died.

This labored justification for Louis's attack did not prevent his troops from winning immediate and sweeping victories. His triumphs alarmed the Dutch. Although they were long-time allies of France against the Spanish Hapsburgs, they did not relish Louis as a next-door neighbor. When Louis struck, they were at war with England. They speedily ended the conflict and in 1668 made an alliance with England and Sweden against France. The French realized that the balance of power was against them, and on May 2, 1668, they ended the war by the peace treaty of Aix-la-Chapelle. France returned Franche-Comté to Spain but retained some of the Flemish conquests. Louis's willingness to give up territories won by his troops stemmed from a secret treaty of a few months earlier with Emperor Leopold of Austria, in which they agreed to divide the Spanish Empire between them when Charles II of Spain died. Charles was then only seven years old and so sickly that he was expected neither to live long nor to have any children. Louis was willing to forego present annexations in the confident, expectation of getting much more in the future. Unfortunately for the schemers, Charles managed to live until 1700, although he remained childless.

THE DUTCH WAR, 1672–1679

Despite the gains that France had made in the short War of Devolution, Louis was furious with the Dutch for having dared to oppose him. He called them a "nation of fishwives and merchants." Moreover, Holland was France's chief commercial rival. Louis decided that the Dutch republic must be conquered. He made careful diplomatic preparations to isolate the enemy. By the judicious use of subsidies he obtained promises of neutrality from some of his fellow monarchs and promises of military aid from others. In 1672 a French army of 120,000 men marched into the United Provinces. The Dutch were greatly outnumbered, but led by the twenty-two-year-old Prince William of Orange, great-grandson of William the Silent, they managed to stall the French advances. Meanwhile they sued for peace, offering territorial concessions. Louis demanded more than they were willing to give. Other nations awoke to the danger of a French conquest in the Netherlands and combined against Louis to try to maintain the balance of power and prevent the French from establishing hegemony over Europe. A number of countries in the French camp switched over to the Dutch. Louis sought desperately for new allies but managed to hold only Sweden on his side.

Despite these odds, the French armies under the command of Marshal Turenne and Prince Condé, Louis's great generals, continued to win victories. In July, 1675, Turenne was killed in action, and soon thereafter Condé retired. The fortunes of war turned against the French and a stalemate developed. Peace negotiations began late in 1676. Louis decided to end the war when the Dutch leader, William of Orange, married Mary Stuart, niece of the king of England, and the English joined the Dutch against him. In the latter part of 1678 and early 1679 he signed a series of peace treaties with his opponents at Nijmegen in Holland. While giving up the Dutch conquests, he gained Franche-Comté from Spain and a line of fortified places in the Spanish Netherlands. The Peace of Nijmegen represented the peak of success for Louis's foreign ambitions. Although he had failed to destroy the Dutch, his armies had won general recognition as Europe's best, his new navy had given a good account of itself, he had strengthened his frontiers and added new territory, and he was acknowledged to be the most powerful monarch of Europe.

WAR OF THE LEAGUE OF AUGSBURG, 1688–1697

Louis was still not satisfied. Immediately after the end of the Dutch War he hit upon a new scheme to annex land on the northern and eastern borders. His plan was to take advantage of loose wording in the articles of the Treaty of Westphalia, which had given France certain lands "with their dependencies." It was unclear which territories were dependencies and which were not, and Louis arranged for the creation of special courts, called Chambers of Reunion, to settle the question. He took care to pack the courts with people who would decide in his favor. By this unscrupulous procedure he annexed all of Alsace and other territories, and he was able to occupy them quickly because he had kept a large number of men under arms after the close of the Dutch War.

Once again Louis overplayed his hand. The other powers feared that unless they checked Louis's ambitions, he would reduce them to satellites or, to use their phrase, he would establish a "universal monarchy." In 1686 Holland, Sweden, the German Protestant princes, Austria, and Spain formed an alliance against him called the League of Augsburg. England joined in 1689 after a revolution had placed Louis's implacable enemy, William of Orange, on the English throne as William III.

Knowing that war was certain to come, Louis decided to gain the advantage by taking the offensive. In 1688 he declared war on Austria and quickly gained several victories. When the other powers entered the conflict the French were put on the defensive. For a time they managed well enough, but by the end of 1693 Louis knew that he could not win and sued for peace. The allies spurned his offers and the war dragged on until 1696. By then the allies were becoming exhausted and peace was agreed upon at Ryswick in Holland. The terms of the treaty provided that Louis relinquish all territory he had acquired since the Peace of Nijmegen except Strasbourg. He made major commercial concessions to the Dutch, including the right to import salt herring and salt into France. He also had to recognize William of Orange as rightful king of England and promise not to aid the deposed Stuart line in any future effort to regain the English throne.

The Treaty of Ryswick was signed in 1698 by the major powers. Europe was once more officially at peace. The calm lasted three years, when a new and greater war broke out. This final and most costly of Louis's wars, the War of the Spanish Succession, lasted from 1701 to 1714. Because of its significance to the course of European history, it will be treated later in detail. It was a long and exceptionally bloody war, and although it was not a defeat for Louis XIV, it was also not a victory. The best that could be said of it from Louis's point of view was that he lost none of the border territories gained in earlier wars. He also managed to put a member of the Bourbon family on the Spanish throne, but he had to pledge that the French and Spanish crowns would never be united. This was a far cry from the ambitious plans of the Grand Monarch when he had first launched his troops against Spain in May, 1667. The half-century of war had indeed established France's "natural frontiers" and made Louis the most powerful monarch in Europe. However, the "natural frontiers" invited trouble, and for all of France's land might, Britain dominated the seas around Europe.

Cultural Glory of France

Louis's reign coincided with one of the greatest ages in the history of French literature and art. Although several of the outstanding figures in the outburst of genius had already produced their masterpieces before 1660, a good deal of credit for the flowering of culture belonged to the Sun King. Louis had a genuine taste for art and letters. He delighted in honoring creative artists, and he was a generous patron. He saw the artist and writer as instruments to glorify himself and to spread the fame of France.

ABSOLUTISM IN THE ARTS

As a result of his passion for control and regulation, Louis sought to impose central direction upon the creative arts. Colbert was entrusted with carrying out his aims. The conscientious minister applied as much energy and thought to the assignment as he did to fiscal and economic matters, and in the long run he was far more successful. The instruments he used to carry out his master's wishes were the academies. He took over direction of the Académie Française, founded by Richelieu, and the Academy of Painting and Sculpture, and he established five other academies—of the dance, letters, science, music, and architecture. The academies formulated standards for their respective branches of art and learning, trained students, and performed services for the state, such as preparing designs, decorations, and inscriptions for public buildings and monuments. In a sense their members were royal officials, receiving pensions and awards for their services. Art and architecture were in many ways as much a part of the whole structure of Louis XIV's absolutism as Colbert's mercantilism and Louvois' army.

Early in Louis's reign major French architecture was almost the personal domain of François Mansart (1598–1666), whose work was classical and restrained. His most serious challenger was Louis Le Vau (1612–1670), a master of the baroque splendor that Mansart found disagreeable. Both men were still free of the standards set by the academies. Jules Hardouin-Mansart (1646–1708) was not. As official architect to the king, he was the principal bureaucrat–architect responsible for the buildings at Versailles. The landscaping of the magnificent formal gardens was done by André Le Nôtre (1613–1700).

Until the end of the seventeenth century French painting was dominated by classicism. Classicism was embedded in the standards of the academy and given expression in the works of Charles Le Brun (1619–1690), decorator of Versailles, Louis's official art counselor, and director of the state-owned Gobelin tapestry works. During the last years of Louis's reign France produced a court painter of insight and subtlety in Antoine Watteau (1684–1721). He attained pictorial depth by masterful design and color, and artistic depth by an implicitly critical depiction of the elegant inanity of court life and the transitory glory of the Grand Monarch and his noble herd. Under Watteau's hand the polished veneer of Versailles appeared wafer-thin.

Literature, particularly drama, was the chief cultural glory of Louis's reign. The dramatists achieved a clarity and elegance of expression that have rarely been equaled. They drew much of their inspiration from classical antiquity, imitating the measure, discipline, and dignity of the Greek and Roman authors and choosing many of their subjects from classical history and mythology. The greatest of the French writers, like their classical models, presented what they thought to be universal principles of human behavior, applicable to all men in all times. This approach characterized French literature from the end of the sixteenth to the early eighteenth century. The period, known as the classical age of French letters, received its fullest expression during the years 1660–90.

Pierre Corneille (1606–1684) was the first of the great writers of tragic drama of the classical age. His masterpieces date from the time of Richelieu. Unlike the ancient Greek dramatists whom he admired so much, Corneille did not portray man as the victim of his destiny; he felt that human will could triumph over circumstances. *Le Cid* (1637), his most famous play, dealt with the youth of a partly mythical Spanish hero and marked the opening of a new era in French drama. The tragedies of Jean Racine (1639–1699), like those of Corneille, adhered to classical forms and concentrated on emotional conflicts. Unlike Corneille, Racine portrayed the human will as weak and vacillating. His most striking characters were women; his masterpieces—*Andromaque, Bérénice, Iphigénie,* and *Phèdre*—all bear the names of women.

In comedy Molière (1622–1673) was supreme. With sardonic humor he exposed the hypocrisy and affectation he saw about him. In *Tartuffe* he unmasked a pious fraud, in *Le Bourgeois Gentilhomme* he cruelly mocked the social climber, in *L'Avare* his pen speared the miser, in *Le Misanthrope* he lampooned the conformist—and so on through a whole gallery of social types. He also founded the Comédie Française, France's first state theater.

Among the prose writers La Fontaine (1621–1695) is best remembered for his *Fables.* They are vignettes drawn from his observations of society and nature and are universal and timeless in their quality. He portrayed people of all classes and held their failings up to gentle ridicule. The *Maximes* of the Duke de la Rochefoucauld (1613–1680) is another work of the period that has had undying fame. In the five hundred or so pithy sentences that make up the book la Rochefoucauld cynically analyzed the motives of human behavior to show that man rarely acts on the basis of unalloyed altruism.

HOW GRAND WAS THE GRAND MONARCH?

The impact of Louis XIV on contemporary Europe was nowhere more manifest than in culture. Imitations of Versailles sprang up all over Europe. French etiquette, cuisine, dress, and coiffure enjoyed an enormous vogue among Europe's elite. The styles of the French court painters and the literary techniques of the French dramatists and essayists were widely copied. Both mighty and puny princes made Europe a firmament of sun kings, each with its orbiting noble satellites. Taste meant French; French meant Louis XIV. The French language, fashioned by the authors of the classical age into an elegant and dramatic tongue capable of the most subtle gradations of meaning, became in the eighteenth century the language of polite society from the Atlantic to the Urals. In the more mundane areas of life, imitation was no less marked. Armies were reorganized on Louvois' model; Vauban's designs for fortifications were copied faithfully on every known continent. Monarchs aspired to, although they seldom attained, the administrative precision of the French bureaucracy. Imitation is one measure of grandeur, and since this imitation was explicitly of Louis XIV, it is a measure of the grandeur of the Grand Monarch.

What of contemporary French opinion? The paeans of praise from the court panegyrists, the harsh condemnation of La Mothe-Fénelon in 1694— "This is sufficient, Sire, to demonstrate that you have passed your entire life apart from the way of truth and justice"—and the vitriolic characterization of Louis in the Duc de Saint-Simon's *Memoirs* are a spectrum of opinion, every color determined as much by the personal prejudice of the writer as by the objective truth about the king. It was the price paid by an institution of state, which in its personification obliterated the person; there was no Louis as an objectively graspable personality. The answer to the question, how grand the Grand Monarch? lies neither in the degree of acceptance by the rest of Europe of the patterns he set nor in contemporary French reaction to him. It lies in the assessment of the success or failure of Louis XIV as the state.

Louis's reign divided naturally into two parts in the year 1685. Until that date he was continuously and increasingly successful; after that date he held his own at best in domestic political and foreign affairs, and economically he lost ground rapidly. Death claimed his ablest counselors and the men with whom he replaced them were not their equals in either ability or devotion. Married to Maintenon and infected with a new piety, Louis turned upon the Huguenots, forfeiting the contributions of many of his most competent subjects. The nations of Europe banded against him. Most significant, after 1688 the Dutch and the English under William of Orange, whose combined fleets were more than a match for Louis at sea, could count upon German states to make common cause against France on the Continent. Literally surrounded, Louis never again held the diplomatic or military advantage after 1685. The result was almost continuous war on four fronts— the Low Countries, Germany, the high seas, North America—from 1688 until the year before Louis's death in 1715. The drain on the economic strength of France was enormous. Despite Colbert's best efforts, the reign saw steady economic decline in agriculture. Colbert's efforts to stimulate manufacturing were not matched after his death in 1683, and the Huguenot persecution was economically a retrograde step. The downward trend in industry was accelerated after 1688 by the heavy fiscal demands of Louis's wars. Foreign trade was the sole exception to the general decline, although war took a heavy toll on seaborne commerce during the last quarter-century of the reign.

Louis's early victories entailed neither the financial expenditure nor the human misery with which he purchased the diplomatic and military stalemates of his last quarter-century. The end of his reign was destructive of all the promising vigor of his early personal rule. The Sun King was a pathetic figure in his last years. The Duke de Saint-Simon in his *Memoirs* summed up Louis's last years as "so little his, so continually and successively those of some others . . . pulled down under the weight of a fatal war, relieved by no one because of the incapacity of his ministers and his generals." Louis had outlived his children and his grandchildren when he died on September 1, 1715, after a long and painful illness. He had reigned for seventy-two years, ruled for fifty-four years, and they had all been *his* years. Yet for all the splendor and all the grandeur, the Grand Monarch tasted remorse before he died. His charge to his five-year-old great-grandson and heir, Louis XV, is the most authoritative word on his reign, "Do not imitate me in the liking I had for buildings, nor the taste I had for war. Try rather to preserve peace with your neighbors. . . . Always follow good advice. Try to help your people, which I unfortunately have been unable to do myself." In indicting so much of his life and ambitions, Louis made a striking confession: he had chosen the wrong paths to the glory and greatness of the state.

— CHAPTER TWELVE —

Absolutism in Austria, Spain, and Prussia

THREE absolutist dynasties played major roles in Western history during the last half of the seventeenth and first half of the eighteenth centuries: the Hapsburgs in Austria, the Hohenzollerns in Prussia, and the Bourbons in Spain. France under Louis XIV was the explicit model for absolutism in all three states. Each of the dynasties adapted the basic tools of absolutism to differing dynastic ends and circumstances. The Austrian Hapsburgs and Spanish Bourbons wished to revitalize their states; the Hohenzollerns intended to make Prussia a great power.

The Rise of the Austrian Hapsburgs

The Thirty Years' War left the Empire weaker than ever before. The Hapsburg ruler retained merely the shadow title of Holy Roman Emperor in Germany. Nevertheless, the Hapsburg dynasty continued to be a power in Germany. Until the unification of Germany under Prussia in the late nineteenth century, the dynasty remained a principal German ruling house and its fortunes were continuously linked with German power politics.

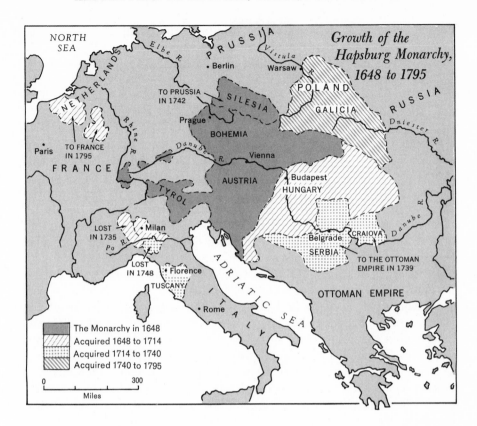

Growth of the Hapsburg Monarchy, 1648 to 1795

The Monarchy in 1648
Acquired 1648 to 1714
Acquired 1714 to 1740
Acquired 1740 to 1795

0 — 300 Miles

Disappointed in their long-cherished hope of building a strong empire in Germany, the Hapsburgs decided to base their power upon lands in Central and Southeastern Europe over which they held sovereignty. The new empire that they built was called Austria, or the Austrian Empire or the Hapsburg Monarchy; it never had an official name down to its disintegration during the First World War. It comprised the mainly German-speaking provinces of Austria, called the "hereditary provinces," as well as the Czech-speaking kingdom of Bohemia and the Magyar-speaking peoples of Hungary, both of which were acquired by the Hapsburgs in 1526. The three regions differed markedly from one another in language, culture, and traditions, and their distinctiveness was further complicated by the existence within each of minority ethnic cultures, mostly Slavic-speaking. Their one important geographic feature was contiguity; they formed a single, large mass in Central and southeastern Europe. No other bond united them except their recognition of a common sovereign who ruled from Vienna. The ability of the Hapsburgs to hold together this nameless agglomeration for over 250 years, and to impose a certain unity upon it and neighboring territories that were annexed in the course of time without destroying the unique integrity of its parts, was a tribute to their skill as rulers. If the greatest wonder was that the new Hapsburg empire lasted so long, an only slightly lesser marvel was how soon it made its weight felt in the power politics of the absolutist nation-states.

THE ABSOLUTISM OF LEOPOLD I, 1657–1705

The shift from German imperial ambitions to Austria-centered concerns had already been evidenced by the Hapsburgs during the Thirty Years' War. The new trend became the dominant theme of Hapsburg policy during the long reign of Leopold I (1657–1705). The second son of Ferdinand III, Leopold had been educated for the priesthood. He remained deeply religious throughout his life, the papal nuncio at Vienna once remarking that he was too pious for an emperor. He was a quiet, reserved man who loved books and music, whose private life was a model of propriety, and who hated to make decisions. He did not welcome his accession to the throne; it seemed to be an obligation imposed by God and wholly lacking in personal enjoyment. Scrawny and ugly, with the large pendulous lip of the Hapsburg men, he teetered on spindly legs. Unheroic and almost ridiculous, he appeared the antithesis of his glamorous cousin and lifelong opponent, Louis XIV. Yet he was no less conscious of his own dignity and had as great a sense of the mission of his dynasty. Throughout his reign three immense tasks preoccupied him: unification of the state; maintenance of the European balance of power against France; and defense of the realm against the Turks. He went far toward attaining his goals.

In 1657 the fortunes of his house were at a low ebb. War-torn Bohemia was exhausted and depopulated. The Turks held over two-thirds of Hungary. The principality of Transylvania, supposedly a dependency of the Hungarian crown, had become independent. In the western part of Hungary that was still under Hapsburg rule the Magyar magnates seriously restricted the sovereign's power. In all the Hapsburg possessions finances and administration were in confusion.

Each province of the monarchy had its own estates or representative assemblies, dominated by the provincial nobility and having extensive powers, including veto of imperial taxes. Leopold began to infiltrate the nobility and the high administration of the provinces with men of his own choice. The new nobility, who were usually not natives of their province and often of foreign origin, owed their property and their eminence to the emperor. They voted accordingly, so that in time Leopold transformed the estates from law-making bodies to law-accepting bodies—rubber stamps for his will.

Building on foundations laid by his predecessors, Leopold superimposed imperial administrative councils on the provincial political institutions. Although they did not displace local organs of government, the imperial agencies directed and controlled the provincial governments, administering the entire realm in the interests of the emperor. They were the principal instruments of monarchic centralization. The most important was the *Hofkanzlerei* or Court Chancellery. Leopold modeled his court at Vienna on Versailles, but unlike Louis XIV he used the court aristocracy in important posts, tying them yet closer to the throne. Men of non-noble and foreign origin were employed at all levels of the bureaucracy and, with the courtier-aristocrats, formed a supranational administration, loyal to the monarchy rather than to their provinces or native lands.

The Hapsburg standing army had come into being during the reign of Leopold's father, Ferdinand III. Leopold strengthened it so that it became one of Europe's largest. Until 1715 all the troops came only from the German-speaking provinces, whereas the officers, like the civil bureaucrats, were drawn from all parts of the monarchy and from abroad. Thus, the leadership of the army, like the bureaucracy, was supranational, owing its first allegiance to the emperor.

The imposition of religious uniformity was an essential part of Leopold's policies. By the end of the Thirty Years' War Protestantism had been rooted out from among the nobles and townspeople of the German provinces and Bohemia. It persisted among many of the peasantry who, ostensibly Catholic, practiced their religion in secret. Persecution by Church and state forced them to give up their faith or drove them out of their homelands. Despite his personal piety, however, Leopold did not tolerate interference by the Catholic Church in affairs of state and steadily increased his own power over the church.

As a result of his policies of unification and centralization, the Hapsburg Monarchy by the end of the seventeenth century had advanced far in the direction of monarchic absolutism. It lagged behind the France of Louis XIV in the degree of centralization and the extent to which it had subordinated particularism, but the task of unification that confronted Leopold was much more difficult than that which faced his Bourbon cousin.

HAPSBURG VERSUS BOURBON

The struggle against French domination of Europe was the second of Leopold's three chief preoccupations. Louis XIV's ambitions to expand his kingdom to the Rhine and the Alps would have been enough to raise the Hapsburgs against him, for they would have fought to keep him out of Germany, but the ancient Hapsburg-French rivalry was greatly heightened by Louis's claim to the Spanish throne. The Austrians were handicapped in their efforts to restrain Louis by having to fight the Turks and by the reluctance of the German princes, who were traditionally suspicious of Hapsburg ambitions in Germany, to offer assistance. After Louis's conquests in the second war against the Dutch, with whom Austria was allied, Leopold had to acquiesce to the French conquests at the Peace of Nijmegen, 1678–79. At the height of his power Louis was so contemptuous of his Hapsburg enemy that he boldly seized parts of the Holy Roman Empire through the Chambers of Reunion (see p. 272) and ringed the Austrian Monarchy by alliances with Brandenburg, Bavaria, Cologne, Sweden, Turkey, and Poland.

The Peace of Nijmegen was not without its advantages for Austria. It allowed Leopold to direct his full energies against the Turks. Victories over that old foe much enhanced Austria's power and prestige and enabled it to resume its anti-French activities. The Hapsburgs' leading part in the War of the Spanish Succession was rewarded at the Peace of Utrecht in 1713 with the cession to Austria of the Spanish possessions in Italy and the southern Netherlands.

EXPULSION OF THE TURKS

After the death of Suleiman the Magnificent in 1566 Turkish power steadily declined under a series of weak and degenerate sultans. In 1656 Mohamed Kiuprili became grand vizier and founded a vigorous dynasty of prime ministers who ran the state for the next forty years. In 1663 an army of 120,000 marched up the Danube to win new territories for the sultan. Under the auspices of Pope Alexander VII the Christian powers, including France, combined in the Holy League to stop the threat. In 1664 the League's army, composed chiefly of Hapsburg troops, vanquished the Turks at St. Gotthard in Hungary and compelled them to agree to a twenty-year truce with Austria.

The Vasvar truce, named for the Hungarian town where the agreement was made, divided Hungary between the Hapsburgs and the Turks. Many of the Hungarians who found themselves under Austrian rule preferred Turkish hegemony, under which they had enjoyed considerable autonomy and religious toleration. For forty years after the truce they were in almost uninterrupted revolt against Vienna, knowing that Hapsburg centralization would infringe upon their traditional liberties and that force would be used to coerce the many Protestants into becoming Catholics. Not unexpectedly, their rebellion received underground assistance from Louis XIV.

The Turks used the truce to consolidate gains they had made in the Mediterranean and to prepare for another invasion of the Hapsburg realm. Early in the 1680's they moved. The leaders of the Hungarian resistance offered themselves as allies and Louis XIV sent assurances that he would not come to Leopold's aid. By mid-July, 1683, the invading army of 250,000 Turks and Hungarians stood at the gates of Vienna. The city had but 14,000 soldiers to defend it. Pope Innocent XI's call for a crusade was ignored by Louis XIV, but Saxony, Bavaria, and Poland answered the summons. In a brilliant victory under John III Sobieski, king of Poland, the siege of Vienna was lifted in September. Europe hailed the Polish king with a line from the Gospel of St. John, "There was a man sent from God whose name was John."

Disagreements among the allies and Leopold's envy of the acclaim given Sobieski distracted the victors from immediate pursuit of the Turks. In 1684 a new Holy League mounted a vigorous campaign against the Turks by land and sea.[1] By 1697 the Hapsburgs had won nearly all of Hungary and Transylvania and part of Slavonia. By the Peace of Karlowitz, 1699, the Turks recognized these conquests and ceded Dalmatia, southern Greece, and the Aegean Islands to Venice, Podolia and the western Ukraine to Poland, and Azov in the Black Sea to Russia. The Peace of Karlowitz proved one of the great turning points in European history. It marked the end of the centuries-long Turkish menace to Europe, and it established Austria as the foremost power of Central and Southeastern Europe.

SUBJUGATION OF HUNGARY

Bureaucrats and priests followed the Austrian armies into Hungary. They used stern repression and terrorism to break the resistance of the Hungarians. Although the Magyar nobles were left in possession of their lands and peasants and were permitted to retain their provincial assemblies and national diet, they were forced in 1687 to renounce the traditional rights to elect their own king and to bear arms against him if they thought he had infringed their privileges. They agreed to make the Hungarian crown hereditary in the male Hapsburg line. Leopold further weakened Hungarian resistance by making grants of empty land in the newly won territories to non-Magyar nobles and by promoting the settlement there of German and Slavic peasants. Henceforth, imperial bureaucrats in Vienna administered Hungary. The Hungarians did not take easily to the new order. A rebellion, led by Francis Rakoczy, prince of Transylvania, and aided by France, broke out during the War of the Spanish Succession. After initial successes the rebellion was put down by Hapsburg troops in 1711.

The defeat of the Turks and the conquest of Hungary rounded out the work of Leopold. During his reign he had more than doubled the size of his dynastic patrimony, built up an administrative organization that held his polyglot Danubian realm together, and raised the monarchy to great-power status in Europe. Although he was not a Grand Monarch, he was an effective absolutist.

CHARLES VI, 1711–1740

Joseph, Leopold's son and heir, ruled only six years and died without children in 1711. The crown went to his brother Charles, who was the

---

[1] During this war the Athenian Parthenon, used by the Turks as a munitions magazine, was reduced to the present ruins when Venetian ships bombarded Athens in 1687.

Hapsburg claimant to the Spanish crown against Philip of Anjou, the Bourbon claimant. Charles had once dreamed of reuniting Spain and Austria, as in the great days of Charles V. More realistic matters claimed his attention when he became emperor, for pressing foreign problems beset him.

A brief war in 1716–18 against the Turks, who had made another bid for conquest, brought victories to Austrian armies led by Prince Eugene of Savoy and annexations of territory, most of which the Turks regained in another war twenty years later. More troublesome were the former Spanish territories in Italy, gained by Austria at the Treaty of Utrecht. The Spanish Bourbons were not reconciled to their loss and schemed to regain them. The balance of power was threatened by the Spanish ambitions, and a quadruple alliance of Austria, England, Holland, and France in 1718 prevented belligerent moves by Spain. The allied powers persuaded Philip V of Spain to renounce his claims, but his scheming on behalf of his sons, for whom he hoped to secure the Italian possessions as princedoms, continued to plague Austria.

Charles's principal foreign concern was dynastic. In 1713 he had made a secret agreement with the members of his family to guarantee the undivided inheritance of his dominions to his eldest son or, lacking a son, his eldest daughter. In 1719 he ordered the publication of this agreement, called the Pragmatic Sanction, in order to ensure the succession of Maria Theresa, his daughter and sole heir apparent, who had been born in 1717. He sought domestic and international consent for the sanction to forestall claimants after his death. The provincial estates of his own realm agreed readily enough, but foreign powers exacted diplomatic and commercial advantages in return for recognition of the sanction as inviolable fundamental law. By 1739 Charles had obtained the consent of all the powers except Bavaria and the Palatinate. In October, 1740, Charles VI died. Less than two months later Frederick II of Prussia invaded Austria, laying claim to part of Maria Theresa's inheritance despite Prussia's adherence to the sanction. In touching off the War of the Austrian Succession, he undid Charles's carefully spun diplomatic web.

FISCAL PROBLEMS AND THE PEASANTRY

Military expenditures, the drain of wars, court expenses, and fiscal mismanagement kept government finances in an unending state of crisis during the reigns of Leopold and his sons. Early in the eighteenth century the government made a determined effort to put its financial affairs in order, and for a few years conditions improved. Then Charles VI's heavy expenditures on his court and army once more brought a decline, so that when he died the state was near bankruptcy.

In its effort to increase revenues the government levied many new taxes, debased the currency, established monopolies, and took heavy mortgages on lands that belonged to the monarch. Fiscal problems impelled the state to interfere in the relationship between nobles and the peasants who lived on their lands. Nearly all the monarchy's peasants were serfs of the nobles or "hereditary subjects," as they were called in Austria, except in the Tyrol, where the peasantry was free. The serfs owed many obligations in cash, kind, and labor to their lords. They also paid taxes to the state for the land that they tilled for their own use. These taxes were the chief source of the government's income. The land that the peasants worked for their lords, the demesne land, was not taxed.

In Leopold's reign the government discovered that landowners were increasing their demesnes at the expense of serf land, thereby reducing the state's tax revenues. Moreover, the increase in demesnes forced the demesne peasants to spend more time in unpaid work for their lords, which reduced the amount of money they earned and consequently their taxes. Spurred on by peasant unrest as well as by loss of revenue, the government decided that in its own interests it should intervene to protect the peasants. Between 1680 and 1738 imperial decrees were issued to limit the lords' demands upon their serfs and to end the reduction in area of taxable land. Lacking adequate means of enforcement these laws were disregarded by the noble landowners, and the tax-paying capacity of the peasantry continued to decline.

The government sought to increase revenue by mercantilist devices. The Central European variety of mercantilism was called "cameralism," from *Kammeramt*, the German word for "treasury," because its primary purpose was to increase the sovereign's revenues. New industries were introduced and old ones expanded in hopes of stimulating economic growth, increasing tax income, and meeting domestic demands for goods that would otherwise have to be imported. The government attempted to promote commerce by road improvements and, during Charles VI's reign, by developing the Adriatic ports of Trieste and Fiume. Despite these efforts, economic development lagged. Many of the new enterprises failed, and most of the others barely managed to survive.

The Rise of the Spanish Bourbons

Charles II, king of Spain from 1665 to 1700 and a descendant of the first Hapsburg ruler of Spain, Charles V, presided over the decaying remains of Spanish power. His reign was a dreary tale. He was almost feeble-minded, and his weak constitution and failure to sire an heir made his thirty-five years on the throne a constant power struggle between Austrian and French partisans over the succession to the throne. Incompetence, laxity, and the rule of favorites continued to the end of Charles's reign. In 1680 he married Marie Louise of France, and on her death in 1689 he married Marie Anne of Bavaria. Each was a marriage of state, allying Spain first with France and then with Austria, and each spawned parasitic courtiers who used their influence in the interests of their patrons.

Both Austria and France sharpened their knives to carve up Spain as soon as the childless Charles should die. Tormented by courtiers and confessors, Charles first named as heir the Austrian emperor's grandson, Archduke Charles, and then a month before his death in November, 1700, named Philip of Anjou, grandson of Louis XIV. The imminent danger of a union of the French and Spanish thrones touched off the War of the Spanish Succession. France supported Philip; Austria, England, and Holland advanced the Archduke of Austria. After the long and brutal war Philip of Anjou was recognized in the Treaty of Utrecht (1713) as King Philip V of Spain but had to yield his rights to the French throne. Spain ceded its Italian possessions and the Spanish Netherlands to Austria, and Gibraltar and Minorca to Britain; Spain also gave slave-trading rights in Spanish America to the British. Spain was clearly the major loser in the war.

BOURBON ABSOLUTISM IN SPAIN

When Philip V took over the Spanish throne in 1700, his new kingdom was in a state of nearly total collapse. For almost a century Spain had been declining economically and its population had fallen from approximately seven million to less than five million. It suffered from chronic unemployment, and much land lay untilled. Taxes had increased without bringing government solvency. Steady devaluation of the copper currency resulted in an alarming inflation. The volume of shipping between Spain and its overseas empire had fallen to one-quarter of what it had been a century before. Industry stagnated and many trades disappeared. The power of the central government had declined, while the power of the nobility and the Church increased. During the seventeenth century the number of clergy and religious orders had approximately doubled, comprising an economically unproductive burden on the weakened country. Once noted for its prowess, the army had been reduced to a rabble of twenty thousand men; the fleet had dwindled to twenty rotten ships. Intellectual life had stagnated, and the clergy, who were formerly leaders of thought, had become notorious for ignorance and sloth. The future of Spain appeared bleak.

The new Bourbon regime embarked upon a program designed to reverse the country's decline. Under its guidance much progress was made during the eighteenth century: population increased and economic activity revived. Spain once again became an important power, although it never achieved the dominant position it had occupied in the sixteenth century. The instrument that the government used to achieve its goal was monarchic absolutism. The Spanish brand of absolutism was less dynamic and less creative than absolutism elsewhere. Its impact upon the traditional ways of life and administration was much less than that of other absolute monarchies. The personalities of Philip V (1700–46) and his son Ferdinand VI (1746–58), the first two Bourbon kings, had much to do with the relative timidity of Spanish absolutism, for absolutism reflected the strengths and weaknesses of the man at the head of state. In view of the personal qualities of Philip and Ferdinand, it was remarkable that so much was accomplished.

Philip resembled the half-witted Hapsburg Charles II more than his purposeful Bourbon grandfather Louis XIV. He was indolent, guilt-ridden, superstitious, hypochondriac, and dirty. His incompetency was relieved by the capacity of his second wife, Elizabeth Farnese, stepdaughter of the Duke of Parma, whom he married in 1714 and upon whom he depended for the rest of his life. Energetic and ambitious, Elizabeth acquired skill in the practice of ruling the state. Philip's successor, Ferdinand VI, seemed no stronger a man than his father. Yet he recognized his own lack of ability and was content to follow the domestic policies laid down in the preceding reign and to let more able men run the government for him.

Credit for the achievements of the reigns of the first two Spanish Bourbons belonged more to their ministers, supported by Elizabeth Farnese, than to the monarchs themselves. Philip arrived in Spain with a corps of French advisers who were trained in the methods of French absolutism. They immediately instituted a series of internal reforms designed to strengthen the state and increase the central power. Their work was continued in later years by a succession of competent ministers, among whom the most able was Cardinal Giulio Alberoni, who came to Spain from Italy with Elizabeth Farnese in 1714.

CENTRALIZATION

The Hapsburgs had not united Spain; they had merely imposed a central authority of king's councils upon the constitutions and laws of the feudal kingdoms comprising Spain. As long as the monarchs were capable, the council system worked effectively. From Philip III through Charles II— through the entire seventeenth century—the monarchs grew progressively weaker while the forces of particularism grew stronger. The Bourbon regime retained the councils but established an administrative organization to run them. Patterned after the French model, it had six ministries: foreign, navy, war, justice, finance, and the Indies. Each minister was to have full authority in his sphere and deal directly with the king, but the councils' wide jurisdiction over many routine matters and their collective authority weakened the independent power of the king's ministers.

In contrast to the compromise with the councils, the Bourbons established direct control over provincial and district administration. In imitation of the French system, intendants were made responsible for the main burden of government at the provincial level. The districts, which were subdivisions of the provinces, continued to be administered by *corregidors*, as they had been under the Hapsburgs. The corregidors exercised a wide variety of functions and for the mass of the Spaniards were the embodiment of centralized power.

When Philip came to the throne, two-thirds of the appointments to the multitudinous Church offices in Spain were made by the papacy, which gained a large income from vacant Church posts and from fees paid by Spaniards in Church courts. After the War of the Spanish Succession—during which the papacy had supported the Austrian claims—the Bourbon government entered into long diplomatic negotiations with Rome which finally produced the Concordat of 1753. The agreement gave the king the right of appointment held by the pope and the income from ecclesiastical vacancies, and it allowed him to tax Church land. A victory for royal absolutism, the Concordat did not end the resistance of important sections of the clergy, especially the Jesuits, to these extensions of royal power.

Philip's French administrators introduced changes in tax collection and made economies in administrative operations. Later ministers tried to encourage the growth of trade and industry by reducing or abolishing oppressive taxes that were inimical to development, introducing new industries, attracting skilled foreign workers, building roads, raising tariffs against imports, building up the merchant marine and navy, and enforcing regulations against smugglers who cut in on Spanish trade with her American possessions. As a result, the government achieved solvency and could carry out its domestic and foreign policies.

FOREIGN AFFAIRS

Under Bourbon rule Spain once again played an active role in European power politics. Philip's reign, born in war, saw Spain in almost constant conflict with other powers over Spanish claims to parts of Italy (he got Naples and Sicily for his younger son Charles in 1735), attempts to gain the crown of France, and diplomatic intrigues to recover Gibraltar from Britain. The last of Philip's struggles grew out of British smuggling activities in Spanish America. The clause in the Treaty of Utrecht allowing the British to import a limited number of slaves each year enabled the British to smuggle in more than the quota and to engage in commerce in other contraband. When they seized smugglers' vessels, Spanish coast guards manhandled British crews. In 1738 an unsavory British seaman, Captain Jenkins, presented before a bellicose Parliament his severed ear, claiming that it had been cut off by a Spanish coast guard, and Britain went to war against Spain. The War of Jenkins' Ear, undertaken for commercial ends rather than the vindication of Captain Jenkins, merged into the general European conflict of the War of the Austrian Succession in 1742. Spain stood with Prussia and France against Britain and Austria. Spain's contributions were appreciable and costly, but they were poorly rewarded. By the treaty ending the war in 1748 Spain regained for the younger brother of the king merely the Italian duchies of Parma and Piacenza. Ferdinand VI fought no more wars, even though Spain had made a remarkable comeback in the arena of dynastic power politics.

Compared to other absolutist monarchies, the achievements of the reigns of Philip V and Ferdinand VI were modest. Yet they placed Spain in the new current transforming the governmental structures of most European nations. They also prepared the way for more incisive changes under Ferdinand's successor, Charles III.

The Rise of Hohenzollern Prussia

At the end of the Thirty Years' War Germany was atomized into about 360 separate states. In addition, nearly 2,500 "imperial knights" held sovereign right as rulers of their own estates, although their properties averaged only about 100 acres each. None of the rulers conceived of a unified German state; atomization suited their individual purposes and ambitions. They followed independent courses to increase whatever power and wealth they possessed. Theoretically all were part of the Holy Roman Empire, and each sent representatives to the Imperial Diet, but the empire was no longer a viable political entity. Although the diet sat continuously at Ratisbon (Regensburg) from 1663 to the dissolution of the empire in 1806, its delegates spent their time in endless debate over singularly unimportant issues.

Among the many states, one was destined to unify Germany. The Electorate of Brandenburg had been ruled since 1417 by the Hohenzollern dynasty. During the first half of the seventeenth century the Hohenzollerns increased their holdings by inheritance and by the provisions of the Treaty of Westphalia to the extent that their realm became the largest of the German princedoms. Their possessions were scattered across northern Germany from the Polish to the Dutch frontiers. Each territory had its own government and laws, and like the Hapsburg domains the only common entity was the ruler, known by many titles, such as Elector of Brandenburg, Duke of Prussia, Duke of Cleves, and Count of Mark and Ravensburg. There was not a single name for the realm until 1807, when it officially became the Kingdom of Prussia. The estates (representative assemblies) of each territory passed on all legislation and taxation and, similar to the States of the Dutch provinces, they had independent fiscal, judicial, and administrative powers. The limitations on royal authority were particularly strong in the eastern provinces, where a numerous and assertive landed gentry, the Junkers, dominated the estates.

The Hohenzollern dominions were particularly hard hit by the Thirty Years' War. Brandenburg, the home territory, was occupied by foreign troops from 1627 to 1643, and other parts of the realm were held and fought

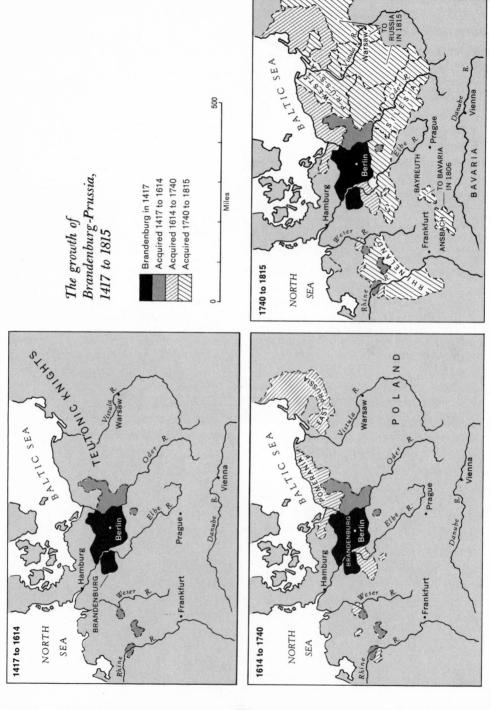

The growth of Brandenburg-Prussia, 1417 to 1815

Brandenburg in 1417
Acquired 1417 to 1614
Acquired 1614 to 1740
Acquired 1740 to 1815

Miles

0 — 500

1740 to 1815

1417 to 1614

1614 to 1740

over by rival armies. A number of cities and large stretches of the country-side lost many inhabitants. Organized economic life was almost completely disrupted. Even the most astute political observer of the mid-seventeenth century would have been reluctant to prophesy that within a century a unified, absolutist state would be formed out of this scattered and impover-ished agglomeration of territories.

Three circumstances worked to that end. The first and most important was that over four successive generations the Hohenzollern dynasty pro-duced one ruler of consummate genius, two others of extraordinary capacity, and one of better than average abilities. All four were infected with the ambition to be absolute within their territories and to be a power in Europe. The second circumstance was the accident that their territories were scat-tered from the Vistula to the Rhine rivers, providing bases for diplomatic and military operations throughout Germany. The third circumstance was one common to monarchies of the age: absolutism seemed the only guarantee of order and prosperity, both considerations made more pressing in Germany by the destruction and dislocation of the Thirty Years' War and the jungle-like power politics of dynastic statecraft.

THE GREAT ELECTOR, 1640–1688

Frederick William I of Brandenburg, known to history as the Great Elector, was the first of the creators of Prussian absolutism. Born in the early years of the Thirty Years' War, he grew up in troubled times. He received an excellent primary education and at fourteen went to Holland, where he studied for four years at the University of Leyden. He traveled much in the Netherlands, and from the practical Dutch he learned lessons about statecraft, economics, and religious toleration that proved useful in later years. He succeeded his father in 1640 at the age of twenty. Heavyset and above average in height, Frederick William had piercing blue eyes and a great beak of a nose that gave him an almost ferocious appearance. He was a man of seemingly inexhaustible energy. Strong-willed, imaginative, and daring, he feared nothing and refused to let failures discourage him.

He showed his mettle from the very start. Most of his possessions were held by foreign troops; he had no available revenues; and he could not depend upon his army. He immediately began to conciliate his domestic and foreign enemies, built up a small but efficient army, and managed to gain new territory in the Treaty of Westphalia. After the war he set out to weld his possessions into an absolute monarchy. Like his fellow absolutists in other lands, he accomplished this end by subjugation of the nobility, bureaucratic centralization, and establishment of a standing army under his control.

By gradual steps he deprived the provincial estates of most of their power. He persuaded the nobles to accept reductions in the power of the provincial estates by making them substantial concessions in other areas. For example, he ratified enactments that the Junkers had extorted from his predecessors, giving them greater power over their peasants. He legalized the conversion of the Junkers' landed estates from fiefs, held in return for service to the crown, into properties held in full ownership. He recognized the Junkers as the only class that was allowed to own rural property and confirmed their exemption from payment of taxes and import-export duties. Finally he reserved most of the highest ranks in the army and the civil bureaucracy for the nobility.

In the administration of local government Frederick William replaced the nobility with his own bureaucrats and thereby laid the foundation for the Prussian civil service. A governor and a staff of agents and commissioners of the central government ran each province. The towns were permitted to keep the appearance of self-government and to elect their own officials, but Frederick William's commissioners told them whom to choose. The entire civil service was directed from Berlin by the Privy Council of Brandenburg. The Privy Council had been established in 1604 when a previous Elector appointed a small group of men to serve as his private advisers. In 1651 Frederick William transformed the council into a ministry in which each privy councilor was responsible for the supervision of a province. The Elector dominated the council and established the administrative policy that it carried out. He chose the councilors from all parts of the realm and from abroad. Initially most of them were nobles, but after 1660 bureaucrats of middle-class origins became increasingly important in the council.

The army was the most important instrument that Frederick William used to achieve the goal of a powerful, unified state. The army, plagued by unruly and disloyal troops before 1640, was purged and brought directly under the monarch's control. The independent authority of regimental commanders was reduced, and their power to commission junior officers was removed. A rudimentary general staff was organized to exercise centralized control over the units. Frederick William undertook to train, equip, and discipline a relatively small army (during his reign it never numbered more than thirty thousand) that was recognized by both his allies and his enemies as one of the most effective in Europe. The army's major role in unification was simply its presence: it represented the monarch's power in every one of his far-flung territories. By the end of the reign it had also begun to serve as the tax-collecting agency of the state as well as its police force.

ECONOMIC POLICY

Frederick William's prime domestic concern was to maintain the army. Over half of the state's revenues went to this purpose. He enforced strict mercantilist policies—high tariffs, external trade restrictions, subsidies and monopolies to manufacturers to stimulate domestic industry—in order to enrich the realm and increase its population. Roads, canals, and harbor improvements were major state concerns, and an efficient postal system was established. Attempts were made to found overseas colonies and create overseas trading companies. Frederick William invited people from other parts of Germany and other countries to settle in Brandenburg and East Prussia; he offered them exemption from taxes for a period of years and gave them farm tools, seed, and cattle to get started. He welcomed religious minorities that were persecuted by other absolutist monarchs, particularly the Huguenots in France under Louis XIV. The exiles brought in new techniques and industries and assumed important roles in economic life. The nobles among them applied their talents to becoming officers in the army.

In common with all the mercantilist absolutist monarchs, Frederick William enjoyed only partial success in his economic ambitions. Population increased from about 600,000 in 1640 to about 1,000,000 in 1688, but the country remained so poor that there was little excess capital available for investment in new enterprise. The urban middle class, so vital to economic development in other lands, demonstrated little vitality and remained content with stagnant economic conditions and meager incomes. Economic growth lagged. Although he increased taxes, Frederick William was unable to raise enough money. He was forced to depend upon subsidies from abroad and upon income from the crown domain. The crown domain comprised the estates and other productive enterprises that were the personal property of the Hohenzollern rulers. It was scattered throughout the territories and constituted a sizable aggregate. By careful economizing he increased its yield until by his death it produced over half of the state's total revenue. Such a feat of economy was achieved nowhere else in seventeenth-century Europe.

FOREIGN POLICY

Frederick William's foreign policy was undertaken for prestige as much as for the defense of his scattered possessions. Few others matched his skill in forming alliances; at one time or another he was the ally of nearly every power. As a price for his support he exacted subsidies for the maintenance of the army. Most of the time he was in the anti-French camp, although for short periods he aligned himself with Louis XIV.

His principal achievement in foreign affairs was to win full control over East Prussia, long held by the Hohenzollerns as a fief from the king of Poland. In 1656 he allied Brandenburg-Prussia with Sweden against Poland, then adroitly changed sides when Russia, Denmark, and Austria came to Poland's aid. By the end of the war he had managed to gain the allies' recognition of his sovereignty over East Prussia. Since the new territory was not part of the empire, by this act he raised his dynasty above the other German princes. As sovereign duke of Prussia, he became one of the crowned heads of Europe.

Frederick William's long reign was a record of extraordinary success. He transformed a devastated and disjointed collection of territories into a centrally directed, albeit superficially united, state. He elevated his dynasty above the rest of the German ruling families. He created an army and a military tradition that remained the bulwark of Hohenzollern absolutism. Finally, he made his state a power to be reckoned with in Europe.

FREDERICK I, 1688–1713

The Great Elector's son and heir, Frederick I, was a timid and sensitive cripple, lacking his father's energy and drive. He sought to compensate for his defects by imitating the splendors of the court of Louis XIV. He surrounded himself with courtiers, musicians, artists, and servants. He built the luxurious palace and gardens of Charlottenburg on the model of Versailles. He founded the University of Halle in 1694, the Royal Academy of Arts in 1696, and the Berlin Academy of Sciences in 1700, all of which were destined to play an important part in Prussian intellectual life. Unlike his hero—and unlike his father—he did not exercise autocratic control over the government, and inefficiency and corruption appeared in the highest levels of the bureaucracy.

He shared his father's faith in military might as the source of power and built up the army to 40,000. His faith was vindicated in 1701 when the hard-pressed Emperor Leopold requested his assistance in the War of the Spanish Succession. In return for 8,000 men Leopold reluctantly agreed to recognize Frederick, his Brandenburg vassal, as king *in* Prussia, by virtue of his sovereignty over East Prussia. To placate the king of Poland, ruler of West Prussia, the "in" euphemism was used. Not until seventy years later, when Frederick's grandson annexed West Prussia, did the king *in* Prussia become king *of* Prussia.

FREDERICK WILLIAM I, DRILLMASTER

In 1713 Frederick was succeeded by his twenty-five-year-old son, Frederick William I. The new king was uncontrollably violent in temper, vulgar in speech and manner, scornful of education and culture, and so deeply pious that he considered theaters "temples of Satan" and closed them when he became king (later he allowed comedies to be presented in Berlin under strict censorship). He made a fetish of personal cleanliness, washing and grooming himself many times each day. He was so miserly that his own mother described him as avaricious. He had a mania about tall soldiers (he himself was only five feet five inches in height) and often judged the merits of his officers by their size, passing over able men for promotion because they were too short. He built up a 3,000-man personal guard, called the Potsdam Giant Regiment of grenadiers, recruited from all over Europe. Each guard was six to eight feet tall. The regiment was under his personal command and he delighted in drilling it for hours.

This uncouth neurotic was the most remarkable administrative reformer of his dynasty. He not only completed the work of centralization and despotic absolutism started by the Great Elector, but was the real father of Prussian militarism and Prussian bureaucratic efficiency. He called the army the "basis of his earthly bliss" and stated that upon it depended his "true interests, security, glory, and prestige." By spending four or five times as much annually on the army as on all other state activities, he increased its size from 40,000 to 83,000. It was the fourth largest army in Europe (after France, Russia, and Austria), although his state ranked only tenth in size and twelfth in population.

Previously the Prussian army had depended for manpower upon voluntary enlistment, impressment, recruitment in neighboring states, mercenaries and, in times of emergency, local militias. The king's harsh discipline encouraged desertion: between 1713 and 1740 over 30,000 soldiers fled the army. A new method of recruitment was obviously necessary, and in 1732 and 1733 decrees established the cantonal system of recruitment. Each regiment had a specific district or canton assigned to it. All young men in the district were enrolled upon the regimental recruiting list, and when the regiment could not fill its ranks from volunteers it drafted men from the list. All males were subject to call, but the bourgeoisie and upper stratum of the artisan class were generally exempted in the interests of promoting trade and industry. The conscripts came almost entirely from the least prosperous sections of the population, especially the poorest elements of the peasantry.

To promote efficiency and immediate obedience to orders the king introduced cruel discipline. Common soldiers were brutally whipped for the smallest offense. In 1714 Frederick William himself wrote the Infantry Regulations, governing every phase of the soldier's life in the garrison and in the field. The endless drilling and maneuvers that he prescribed made his troops the best trained in Europe.

THE OFFICER CORPS

An equally important innovation was to make the officer corps the monopoly of the landed nobility. Frederick William's grandfather had favored nobles for commissions, but he had allowed men of humble birth and foreigners to become officers and rise to high rank. At least three of the Great Elector's generals were sons of peasants, and in 1688 one-quarter of the officer corps were French Huguenots. Frederick William believed that Prussian nobles, accustomed to ordering about their serfs, would make the best commanders of the rustics who comprised the bulk of the army. He also had political reasons for drawing his officers exclusively from the landed nobility. Resistance to Hohenzollern absolutism persisted among the Junkers, and Frederick William was determined to stamp it out; his goal was to make the nobility "acknowledge no master but God and the King in Prussia." He made it illegal for nobles to enter the service of other monarchs. Lists were drawn up of all high-born youths between twelve and eighteen, and he personally selected boys from these lists for the cadet corps in Berlin, where they were trained for lifetime careers as army officers. By 1724 there were few noble families in all his possessions that did not have sons in the officer corps.

At the same time he provided solid advantages in the corps to hold the loyalty of the officers. To sons of families of small means he offered an education, a standard of living higher than any they could expect at home, and a social position second to none. The officer corps was the gateway to honor and prestige. The officer caste was a closed society and a superior one. At the same time there was complete social equality within it: everyone wore the same uniform (including the king, who always wore military dress), and only generals bore designations of rank. As a result the nobility came to regard military service as its natural profession, and the officer corps became the chief supporter of absolutism. Its members thought of themselves not as Brandenburgers or Pomeranians but as soldiers of the Hohenzollerns. The nobility, once so jealous of its independence, had become a service nobility identifying its interests with those of the monarch.

The army and military life loomed so large in Frederick William's state that his son and successor, Frederick II, called it the "Sparta of the North." Yet for all the importance attached to the army, Frederick William used it little. He blustered and threatened, but when armed conflict seemed imminent, he withdrew. Perhaps he loved his soldiers too much to see them killed, or perhaps he was at heart a coward and feared to risk his power on the field of battle. Only twice did his regiments march to war. In 1714 he helped the Danes against the Swedes, and in the War of Polish Succession (1733–35) he sent 10,000 men to aid the imperial forces, but peace was concluded before his troops saw action.

THE BUREAUCRACY COMPLETED

Frederick William carried his military scale of values over to the civil bureaucracy. It became as disciplined a machine as the army. He replaced the rule of councils that his grandfather had established with his own personal and direct rule. He set up a General Directory, headed by four ministers, as chief administrative agent of the central government and supervisor of the bureaucracy. Special bodies called Boards of War and Domain were established for each part of the realm. Their functions were similar in many ways to those of the French intendants. At the local level, tax commissioners were the agents of the central government in the towns, where all self-government had disappeared, while noble commissioners represented the state in the country districts.

The king managed his officials with an iron hand. Minutely detailed regulations and disciplinary rules were issued to guide the bureaucrats. Waste, slothfulness, corruption, deception, and disobedience were severely punished, sometimes even with death. Not only criticism of orders but initiative and self-reliance were considered acts of insubordination. Like the army, the civil bureaucracy became a special kind of organization with its own code, in which the supreme values were unswerving obedience, stern self-discipline, and hard work. Officials took a special pride in their jobs, saw service to the king as the highest duty and honor, and considered themselves superior to the people they governed.

"AN ARMY WITH A COUNTRY"

His army was so large and expensive that Frederick William had to mobilize the full resources of the country to support it. Years later a former Prussian general said of the Hohenzollern realm that it was "not a country with an army, but an army with a country that served as its headquarters and food supplier." Frederick William inherited a treasury that had been nearly emptied by his father's extravagances. By drastic reduction of non-military expenditures, efficient levying and collection of taxes, and skilful management of the crown domain, he doubled the state's revenues. He encouraged immigration to thinly populated territories (especially East Prussia), protected industry and agriculture with tariff barriers, and promoted industries that produced war materials, such as armaments or wool cloth for uniforms. Severe penalties were laid on people who did nothing gainful. When he met idlers on his walks through Berlin, he berated them and thrashed them with his cane. He even decreed that Berlin market women should spin, knit, or sew while waiting for customers or else lose their concessions.

Religion did not escape his surveillance. The pulpit became a loudspeaker to inculcate the duties of a citizen, particularly the prompt payment of taxes. Frederick William was an ardent Protestant and detested Catholicism, but he allowed his Catholic subjects religious freedom because he did not want them to emigrate and thereby decrease the population. He was less tolerant of Jews (there were about six thousand in his possessions), but he permitted them much economic freedom because he considered them useful in stimulating economic growth.

Frederick William's accomplishments were overshadowed by those of his more famous son, Frederick II, called the Great. Yet to the father belongs the dubious credit for founding Prussian militarism and despotism. It is little wonder that the Nazis considered him a great man and that a Nazi writer said, "Frederick William I speaks through Adolf Hitler."

Frederick the Great of Prussia

Frederick II won the appellation "the Great" by virtue of his military prowess, his success in establishing Prussia as a great power, and his intellectual capacity. His admirers hailed him as the colossus of the age. He spawned imitators in the age of "enlightened despotism" as Louis XIV had in the age of "divine right absolutism." Yet his detractors saw him as an evil genius—hypocritical, capable of any treachery, hungry for power and territory. He was, in truth, something less than a colossus and neither more nor less treacherous and power-hungry than most other monarchs of the age. He was simply more efficient and purposeful, while other absolutists succumbed to inertia. He was also calculating, bold, resilient, unceasingly industrious, cynical, and increasingly misanthropic as he aged. Above all, he commanded a state that was a military machine. It was not his creation, but he perfected it; its purpose was not his to choose, but he fulfilled it. The genius of Frederick II was to accept the Prussian military machine and the Hohenzollern goal of power and territorial aggrandizement and, with consummate skill and unswerving application, to use the one as the means to advance the other. His was a limited genius.

As a youth, Frederick was miserably unhappy in the barracks-room court of his father because he had a genuine love of music, art, and philosophy. He proved the most difficult cadet his father ever had, but the drillmaster king made a soldier of him. He burned the lad's books, broke his flutes, and thrashed him publicly. When the prince reached eighteen, he could take no more of the harsh discipline that caused peasants to desert the army in droves and was magnified many times over by his own sensitivity and his father's neurotic love-hate. He attempted to "desert" to France. Frederick was caught and forced to witness the beheading of his accomplice and best friend, a young officer named von Katte. He was even led to the scaffold himself in the belief that he, too, would die. After a spell in prison, Frederick bowed to discipline, took the wife his father chose, and accepted the life his father ordained. During his last illness in 1740 Frederick William said with a drill sergeant's pride, "I die contented since I leave such a worthy son and successor."

The reconciliation with his father was more than superficial. Although Frederick retained the serious intellectual and cultural interests of his youth —indeed, his reputation as an "enlightened despot" grew principally from such pursuits—culture was secondary to his furtherance of the traditional absolutist policies. They were his life's work. Though his commitment was as strong as his father's, his courage was greater. He was not simply a drillmaster. In 1740 within months of his accession at the age of twenty-eight he marched his army onto the field of battle. About one-quarter of his forty-six years on the throne were spent at war.

TUNING THE WAR MACHINE

Frederick changed no essential features of Prussian government, resting content to build on the foundations laid by the Great Elector and Frederick William I. At his accession he found the state administration and the army in excellent condition; he also found a huge cash reserve hoarded in casks in the cellar of the royal castle. He intervened far more frequently in the routine business of government than had his father, and he allowed his ministers less freedom of action. He made himself the single pivot for the whole government, the sole creator of policy. This herculean task was executed almost entirely by letter, since he rarely saw his ministers in person.

Frederick made personal tours of his territory to keep a close watch over the bureaucrats. In his snuff-stained, threadbare uniform "Old Fritz" (as he was called in his later years, not with much affection) was a familiar but awe-inspiring figure throughout his dominions to the end of his life. He used special agents, "Fiscals," and spies to sniff out corruption in the bureaucracy. On the whole, the civil servants performed their tasks efficiently, and they were well rewarded. Entrance into the service was gained by examination except for the top posts, for which nobles were favored. Promotion depended on merit.

Frederick's strong bias toward the nobility grew out of his belief that they alone possessed the superior natural qualities needed to lead and that they alone were moved by a sense of honor, enabling them to face danger and death unflinchingly and to serve without expectation of material reward. He scorned the bourgeoisie as money grubbers, incapable of self-sacrifice. If a bourgeois officer left the army in disgrace, he turned to another career; a noble in the same straits chose suicide as the only honorable course. Frederick used bourgeois officers only in the exigencies of war, dismissing them or demoting them when opportunity allowed. Since the Junkers had been transformed into a state nobility they no longer posed a threat to the absolutist state. They enjoyed the largesse due to the loyal, receiving advances of money as either gifts or low-interest loans. Frederick encouraged the establishment of mortgage loan banks, where estate owners could borrow at low interest against their property; the banks were the first formally organized agricultural credit institutions in Europe.

Frederick extended to the Junkers the strong assurance that the state would not interfere in the administration of their estates or the control of their serfs. However, a major grievance of the peasantry had been the extinction of their holdings by landlords who transferred the dispossessed peasants to their own demesne land as laborers. Frederick prohibited this practice in order to ensure that the peasants would have enough land to raise a family and provide him with more taxpayers and army recruits. It was his only major agrarian reform, and it was only partially successful: many nobles continued to dispossess their peasants. On the king's own domain, forming about one-third of the kingdom, Frederick limited the labor services of the crown serfs and in 1777 provided assurance of inheritance of peasant holdings.

Frederick, no less than his predecessors, subverted the country to the maintenance of the army. He retained the cantonal system of recruitment but increased the proportion of foreign mercenary soldiers from one-third to two-thirds of the total enlisted strength, because he judged that his subjects were more useful to the army as taxpayers and producers than as cannon fodder. He imposed rigorous and continual training on officers and discouraged their marriage as inimical to devotion to duty. The largely bachelor officer corps provided an added dividend in reducing expenditures on pensions to widows. Constant drill and inspection, an improved supply system, and regular maneuvers kept the army on a constant war footing. A master tactician, Frederick emphasized mobility, fast deployment of troops, flanking attack, and integrated artillery as an infantry-support weapon. Its discipline, training, and tactics made the Prussian army the terror of far larger enemies with greater resources.

STRATEGIST AND STATESMAN

Frederick II's wars belonged to the mainstream of eighteenth-century power politics and will be treated later. It is only necessary here to describe briefly the genius that won him so many victories. Frederick was first and foremost a strategist, and his statecraft turned on strategical considerations. His actions were always conditioned by one overwhelming defensive concern: some part or another of his extended realm was immediately vulnerable to every major power in Europe except Spain. Such vulnerability put a premium not only on military might but also on careful diplomatic arrangements to protect home base while the army was in the field. Frederick's plan of aggression was to engage in short, sharp, surprise actions against a power that was diplomatically off balance, if only momentarily so, and to seize and hold its territory with a minimum of troops. This pattern of aggression marked his first three campaigns and paid rich dividends on the first two occasions. Only on the third occasion did Frederick get in deeper than he had expected.

His first attack was on Austrian Silesia in the late autumn of 1740 (war was strictly a summer sport in eighteenth-century war manuals), and it touched off the War of the Austrian Succession. It was a surprise move, made in defiance of the Pragmatic Sanction but in the certainty that most of the major powers would come in against Austria. The mobility of the attack assured rapid victory and in 1742 Austrian peace overtures were accepted by Frederick, Silesia was ceded to him, and he left the war. The general war continued and when the tide turned in Austria's favor against the rest of the powers, Frederick renewed war on Austria to safeguard his gains. In 1744 he made a sudden attack into Bohemia. He quickly accepted Austrian peace proposals after inflicting a stunning defeat on Saxony, Austria's ally, in December, 1745 and again withdrew from the war. In his third campaign in 1756 Frederick undertook a "preventive war," because Austria, Russia, and France had concluded alliances that were clearly directed against him. Unfortunately the "preventive war" escalated into the Seven Years' War. (See pp. 375–376.) Frederick won spectacular victories, such as the one at Rossbach in 1757 in which he surprised a Franco-Austrian army three times as large as his on the march and routed it, inflicting 8,000 casualties (including 8 generals) for only 550 casualties on his side. Three times, however, Frederick was on the verge of utter defeat. He gained no territory at the peace in 1763 and was thankful to receive confirmation of his Silesian conquest of twenty years before.

The Seven Years' War had a chastening effect on Frederick. For the rest of his reign, he tried to avoid war. In the almost bloodless War of the Bavarian Succession, 1778–79, astute maneuvering of his army and a personal correspondence between Frederick and the empress kept Bavaria out of Austrian hands. In 1772 Frederick engineered the first partition of Poland in order to prevent a general war from growing out of the Austrian and Russian confrontation over Poland. His share was West Prussia. In the last year of his life he organized the League of the German Princes to prevent Austria from acquiring Bavaria.

ECONOMIC REVITALIZATION

The Seven Years' War, which ended midway in Frederick's reign, exhausted the Prussian economy. For the remaining twenty-three years of his reign Frederick tried to achieve the economic revitalization of Prussia. Silesia, his greatest conquest, proved invaluable. Rich in iron, coal, and lead and possessed of a highly developed textile industry, Silesia increased the Prussian population by half and provided a large area contiguous to the homeland of Brandenburg. After 1763 Silesia was exploited to the full.

Better farming techniques and the introduction of new crops (especially the potato), land reclamation by marsh drainage along the eastern rivers, and repopulation that drew in about 300,000 settlers, principally from other German states, resuscitated Prussian agriculture. Mercantile practices such as subsidies, monopolies, tariffs, export restrictions, and abolition of internal tolls stimulated industry and domestic trade, although they discouraged foreign commerce. The state assumed a number of sales monopolies, engaged in mining and lumbering, and by virtue of the royal domain became the largest grain producer. A state bank was established at Berlin in 1765 with branches elsewhere. It stimulated investment by extending credit, controlled the currency by issuing paper money, and made a profit for the state.

By the end of the reign Prussia had a fairly diversified economy and a high export rate, although overall external trade had declined. Heavy taxation, made heavier in the last decade, prevented the economic recovery from being reflected in the standard of living of the masses. The army of 200,000 rather than the masses lived off such fat as the land of Prussia produced.

REQUIEM

In 1786 the dying Frederick could look back upon a reign of extraordinary accomplishments. Following the course set by his predecessors, he had added imagination and daring to their ambitions. He audaciously gambled everything in two great wars, which he himself started and fought with incredible skill, and he won universal recognition of Prussia as a great power. He purchased victory by the purposeful and ruthless application of his will to every obstacle—foreign and domestic, friend and enemy. His achievements seized the imagination of all Germans and stimulated the awakening of German nationalism. According to the eighteenth-century poet Goethe, the giant of German literature, Frederick was "the polar star, who seemed to turn about himself Germany, Europe, nay the whole world." Friedrich Meinecke, a modern German historian, has written of Frederick that for the first time "cold and hard *raison d'état* took human form among us Germans." He excused Frederick's wars of aggression with the words, "He laid the foundations of Prussia's greatness and thus his action is justified by history." On March 21, 1933, Adolf Hitler chose Frederick's tomb as a suitable place to announce the official birth of the Nazi Third Reich.

CHAPTER THIRTEEN

Absolutism and Oligarchy in the East

ON THE EASTERN PERIPHERY of Europe absolutism gained a foothold, although the pattern of statecraft was not so monotonously absolutist as in the West. The Russian monarchy, initially far more despotic than Western monarchies, was made absolutist in the Western manner but with significant differences by Peter the Great (1682–1725). Denmark accepted absolutism without a murmur. Sweden's Charles XI (1660–97) initiated an absolutism that was the principal model for Russia and Prussia. Yet it was in the East that absolutism suffered some of its earliest reverses. Poland (like the Dutch Republic and England) never developed a successful absolute monarchy. The Swedish aristocracy took advantage of a defeat in war and a succession crisis to reverse absolutism in favor of a highly traditional variety of noble oligarchy. The Ottoman Empire, where a thoroughgoing Eastern despotism precluded Western absolutism, became increasingly atomistic in political and social structure at the expense of the sultanate. Even in Russia the era of weak tsars from 1725 to 1762 enabled the nobility to condition Russian absolutism in a way that was highly favorable to themselves. European absolutism was, in fact, far more uniformly potent in the Continental homeland than on the peripheries, east or west.

Russia Becomes a Great Power

The death in 1682 of the childless Tsar Fedor III precipitated a power struggle that threatened a new Time of Troubles. (See pp. 164–165.) After years of turmoil during which the throne was occupied jointly by Fedor's brother Ivan, a half-blind mental defective, and his half-brother Peter, Ivan died in 1696 and left Peter as the sole ruler. Peter's reign marked a major turning point in Russian history. Largely through his efforts Russia made its debut as a great power. At the same time, the blame for worsening many of the ills that plagued Russia must also be laid to him. More than most of his contemporary absolutist monarchs, Peter put the welfare of his subjects last.

PETER I, THE GREAT

Peter had the crudeness and ferocity of a savage. He was coarse in manner and speech and contemptuous of ordinary decency, took a special delight in torture, had a violent and uncontrollable temper, and reveled in obscene and blasphemous drunken orgies. He married a nobleman's daughter when he was sixteen, forced her into a nunnery when he tired of her, and after a series of casual liaisons with women of the lower class married a Livonian peasant girl who became Empress Catherine.

This uncouth giant—he was six feet nine inches tall—possessed great ability as a ruler. He dealt decisively with problems and had vast energy and drive. Despite the toll taken by dissipation, he had an almost incredible capacity for hard work. He personally drafted almost all of the many legislative acts of his reign and handled much of the diplomatic correspondence. Most important, he had a vision of what he wanted his empire to be— a great power with himself as its absolute master—and he never lost sight of that dream.

Peter sought to realize his dream by borrowing ideas and methods from the more advanced societies of the West. The first tsar to travel abroad, he made a number of trips to the West to observe and learn at first hand and induced hundreds of foreign technicians and artisans to come to Russia. His admiration for things Western was as excessive as all his other passions. With the exception of priests and peasants, his subjects were ordered to wear Western-style clothing and to shave their beards; those who would not shave were taxed in proportion to their wealth. He promoted the use of tobacco, hitherto condemned in Russia as sinful. He brought the Russian calendar into agreement with the European one; the Russians had formerly counted the years from what they believed was the date of the creation of the earth, September 1, 5508 B.C.

The most striking symbol of Peter's Western orientation was his new

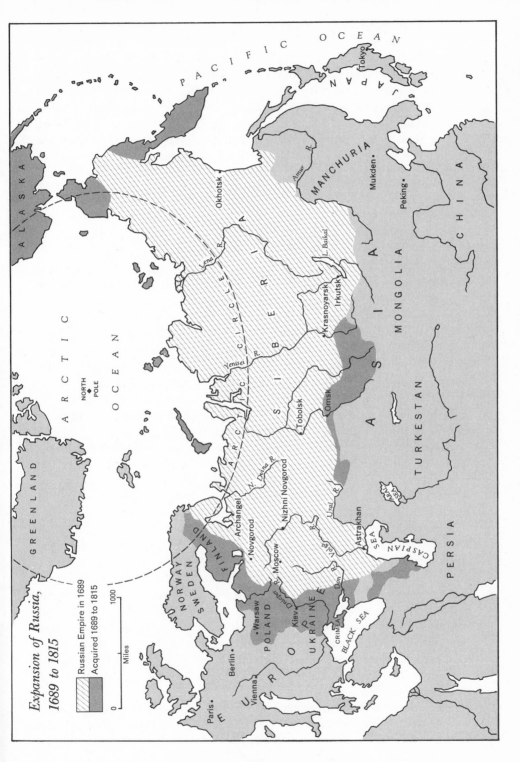

Expansion of Russia, 1689 to 1815

Russian Empire in 1689
Acquired 1689 to 1815

1000

Miles

0

capital of St. Petersburg. Moscow was too Russian and too set in its ways to suit him. In 1703 he chose a site in the far northwestern corner of the realm that had been recently won in battle from the Swedes. He could get no closer to the West and still be on Russian soil. There, in bleak malarial marshes, a new city rose at immense cost in lives and money. Unlike Versailles, St. Petersburg was not a monument to regal glory. It was a window on the West through which Peter wanted his people to look in order to be drawn from their traditional ways. St. Petersburg also testified to the tsar's ambition to make Russia a naval power, for it looked out over the Gulf of Finland to the Baltic Sea.

THE WARS OF PETER

From 1690 to 1724 Russia was at war continuously except for thirteen months. Nearly all the wars were of Peter's own making, undertaken to expand his territories and to gain ports on the Baltic and the Black seas that would be open all year (Archangel, Russia's only seaport, lay on the White Sea and its harbor was frozen for nine months of the year). Above all, the wars were meant to demonstrate Russia's might.

Although Peter warred against the Turks, his greatest enemies were the Swedes, who held Finland, Karelia, and Livonia and dominated the eastern Baltic. Peter allied Russia with Poland and Denmark to partition the Swedish possessions and in 1700 hostilities began. The Great Northern War, 1700–21, was contemporaneous with the War of the Spanish Succession; it was the northern theater of the general war that raged through Europe in the first decades of the eighteenth century.

The Allies' expectation of an easy victory reckoned without the military genius of the youthful Swedish king, Charles XII. A few months after the war began, Charles with just 8,000 troops smashed a Russian army of 40,000 at Narva, a Swedish fortress on the Gulf of Finland. Peter fled in terror from the battlefield and for a time was ready to sue for peace. Fortune reprieved him when Charles turned his attention to Poland for the next few years. Peter rebuilt and rearmed his shattered army and constructed a formidable fleet. In 1707 Charles invaded Russia in force. Peter's armies, reorganized and trained, fell back before the advancing Swedes, drawing them ever farther into the vast Russian plain. Like the later invaders Napoleon and Hitler, Charles encountered Russia's most potent ally, winter. The winter of 1708–09 turned out to be the worst in Europe for a hundred years. The Swedish troops suffered terrible losses. In June, 1709, weakened by their experiences, they met Peter's army in southern Russia at Poltava. The Swedes were routed and Charles fled; the victory resounded throughout Europe.

Peter's demand that Turkey give up Charles, who had taken refuge there, was refused. In the ensuing war Turkish victories forced Peter in 1711 to give up some of his recent territorial acquisitions. Humiliated, the Russians turned to the northwest, where they had better fortune, conquering most of the Swedish Empire by 1719 and invading Sweden itself. By the Treaty of Nystadt in 1721 Peter gained Livonia and Estonia on the Baltic and Ingria and Karelia on the Gulf of Finland. Russia emerged as a major power, to be increasingly involved in European affairs. To celebrate his victory, Peter gave himself the titles Father of the Country, Emperor, and the Great. As if to confirm his self-esteem, within a year of the Peace of Nystadt he led an army into the Caucasus and wrested territories on the shores of the Caspian Sea from the shah of Persia.

THE PETRINE REFORMS

Peter's wars were responsible for many of the innovations and reforms to which he owes his fame. His need for men, money, and matériel dictated the establishment of a more efficient government and one completely under his control. He introduced a series of administrative innovations aimed at ending the chaos into which the governmental structure had disintegrated. He divided Russia into provinces (eight in 1707, increased to twelve in 1720), each subdivided into counties and districts, and all staffed by bureaucrats of the central government, in imitation of Western organization. The reform of the central administration began in 1711 when Peter set up a body of nine members, called the Governing Senate, as the principal administrative and judicial authority of the empire. Although it sometimes had a limited legislative role, its primary function, as Peter described it, was "to collect money, as much as possible, for money is the artery of war." To this end the Senate exercised control over the fiscal system. When it became evident that the Senate alone could not perform all the functions of a central administration, Peter established nine bureaus to run each of the major branches of government, based on the Swedish system. Like their Swedish models, the bureaus were headed not by one man but by a board or "college" of eleven men who arrived at decisions by majority vote. Peter brought in a large number of foreign experts to act as advisers to these boards. Originally independent of the Senate, the colleges were put under the supervision of that body in 1721.

Peter drew his administrators and army officers from the nobility. Unlike Prussia, where the Hohenzollerns had to tame the nobility, the Russian nobles had a tradition of state service. Peter's mushrooming bureaucracy and his almost perpetual wars made him demand much more of them than had his predecessors. To reduce evasion of state service, a bureau registered all nobles and kept records of their service. The noble entered service at fifteen and remained till death or disability ended his usefulness. No more than a third of the males of a family could be in the civil bureaucracy; the rest had to be in military service. Young nobles began their army service as ordinary recruits in line regiments or, if they came from important families, in the three special guards regiments organized by Peter. After a suitable period of training they received commissions.

Convinced that the demands of the state outweighed all other considerations, including lineage, Peter established the principle that social distinction rose from state service and not from ancestry. In 1722 he introduced a Table of Ranks that created fourteen parallel grades in the military and civil services. Every bureaucrat and officer was supposed to begin his service at the lowest rank and work his way up. A commoner became a noble when he won a commission as second lieutenant or ensign, lowest of the fourteen military ranks, or was promoted to the eighth rank (collegiate assessor) in the civil service. This system made the nobility heavily dependent on the favor of the tsar. It remained in effect, with some modifications, until the 1917 revolution. Although persons with wealth or connections rose more rapidly than others and filled most of the higher posts, a career in government service proved to be the road to nobility and fame for many persons of humble origin, and in this way the reform served to democratize the nobility.

To systematize and simplify the fiscal and military obligations that he demanded of his subjects, Peter introduced two major reforms: the poll tax and conscription. His military expenses, which sometimes amounted to 80 per cent of the government's total expenditures, kept him in a perpetual financial crisis. His counselors had long advised the replacement of the tax on households (hearth tax), the chief source of revenue, by a poll tax on every male. In 1719 Peter ordered a census of every male, including infants but excluding the nobility and clergy. The estimated military expenditures were divided by the total number of males, and the quotient was the poll tax rate. The yield was not as high as expected because some peasants were unable to pay the tax or managed to evade it, but enough came in to allow Peter for the first time to solve his financial difficulties. An incidental effect of the poll tax was that it wiped out the last legal distinction between serfs and slaves. Slaves had not been subject to taxation because they were not considered legal persons. Now they were entered in the tax rolls as serfs.

The new system of conscription proved as effective in meeting the demand for soldiers as the poll tax was in satisfying the fiscal needs. Peter's predecessors had maintained a small standing army. After his defeat by the Swedes at Narva, Peter raised the army's size by drafting peasants and townsmen. The quota for each village or town was at first proportionate to the number of homesteads, but after the census of 1719 the quota was proportionate to the number of males in the community. The conscripts, who were between twenty and twenty-five when drafted, served for life. The system enabled Peter to increase his army from 35–40,000 in 1700 to over 200,000 at the end of his reign, reinforced by about 100,000 Cossacks and an undetermined number of troops from the non-Slavic peoples of the eastern frontiers. The system became a permanent part of Russian life, although the term of active service was reduced in later years.

In addition to the great increase of the army Peter created the Russian navy. He established shipyards, set aside forest tracts for ship timber, compelled state peasants to cut and prepare the timber, and set up factories for sails and naval stores. By the end of his reign he had 800 vessels and 28,000 sailors in the Baltic fleet—a force that played a large part in the victory over Sweden. After Peter's death the navy was neglected, and by the 1730's there were only about 15 seaworthy armed vessels under the Russian flag. The navy was later rebuilt, but Russia never became the sea power that Peter had hoped to make it.

Russian producers could not meet Peter's demands for military goods, and his depleted treasury made it impossible to buy the goods abroad. To build up the country's manufactures and increase the prosperity and therefore the taxpaying capacity of his subjects, Peter instituted a program similar to the mercantilist policies of his fellow monarchs in other lands. He established state-owned mines, foundries, arsenals, cloth factories, and other enterprises to make goods for the army and navy, imported foreign experts to run the plants and train native workmen, and sent young Russians abroad to learn new skills. Subsidies, monopolies, exemptions from taxes and military service, high tariff protection, and free importation of materials and equipment encouraged private entrepreneurs. Peter later turned over a number of state-owned enterprises to the new entrepreneurs. Thousands of state peasants were compelled to work at low wages in both state-owned and private enterprises. Despite extensive inefficiency and failure in the new industries, Peter's efforts established large-scale factory enterprise, which had before scarcely existed in Russia, as an integral part of the Russian economy. Especially successful was the development of iron and copper production in the Ural Mountains.

In order to promote internal commerce Peter embarked on an ambitious canal-building program designed to link the chief rivers of Russia. He made St. Petersburg the empire's center of foreign trade by decreeing that a number of rich merchants settle there, that certain products (hides, hemp, caviar, tar, and potash) that were important in Russian export trade be shipped only from there, and that dock charges be less there than in Archangel, which was previously the chief Russian port.

THE CHURCH, CULTURE AND EDUCATION

The Russian Orthodox Church's autonomy and great wealth posed a threat to Peter's ambitions for absolute power, and he resented the opposition of churchmen to his efforts to introduce Western ways into Russian life. When in 1700 the patriarch of the Church died, Peter left the office vacant and appointed a priest who was subservient to him as "keeper and adminis-trator of the patriarchal see." The keeper handed over the administration of Church property to a government bureau, which gave the clergy only a part of the income from their properties and put the rest in the tsar's coffers. In 1721 Peter abolished the office of patriarch and placed the direction of the Church under the Most Holy Synod, a committee of clergymen presided over by a layman, the Procurator, chosen by the tsar. The Church thereby became a part of the central administration, and whatever independent political influence it had once possessed disappeared. The Holy Synod survived until 1917.

Peter's reforming zeal extended to cultural matters. Through his efforts printing became much more common. Until the end of the eighteenth cen-tury all presses in Russia belonged to the state or the Church. Translations were made of European works, with the tsar himself supervising the choice of foreign books and personally editing the translations. Most of the books dealt with technical subjects, reflecting Peter's own interests, but historical and legal works were also published. In 1703 he established the first Russian newspaper. The Russian alphabet was simplified; thereafter the old alphabet was used only in Church texts. In 1702 he introduced the public theater into Russia when he imported a company of German actors. He established the first hospital and the first museum in his country. He was the founder of the Russian Academy of Sciences, which combined scientific research and teaching. In the beginning it was composed of seventeen scientists and eight students who were all of German origin, for Russia lacked both scientists and advanced students.

The low level of education in Russia disturbed Peter. At his accession the only schools were a few poorly attended theological seminaries. Since his military plans required trained officers he organized several military acad-emies whose students came almost exclusively from the nobility, although the schools were open to members of other classes. In 1714 he ordered the establishment of two technical schools in each province, but this effort to increase educational facilities proved a nearly total failure. Later a system of schools under Church supervision was established; by 1727 these schools had a total of about 3,000 students, most of whom were sons of priests training for the priesthood.

THE SUCCESSION

Peter despised his son Alexis, who was born of his first wife. Those who opposed Peter looked upon Alexis as the symbol of their discontent and as their potential leader. Although Alexis renounced his right of succession after Peter had a son by Catherine, his father still persecuted him and Alexis fled Russia. In 1718 he was lured back by promises of the tsar's for-giveness, only to be imprisoned and, with his father and other dignitaries watching, tortured to death. On the day before he was buried his father celebrated his demise with a particularly brilliant court ball.

The murder of Alexis availed Peter nothing, for his infant son by Catherine soon died. His sole direct heir was the son of Alexis. Determined that this boy should not succeed him, Peter decreed in 1722 that the tsar could name his own successor. Peter himself never got around to naming one, with the result that as he lay dying in 1725 at the age of fifty-two, his once-powerful constitution ravaged by dissipation, a new succession crisis threatened. At the last moment a palace coup by high officials and guards officers succeeded in having Catherine accepted as his successor. The peasant wench and one-time camp follower became Catherine I, Empress of All the Russias.

PETER IN RETROSPECT

Peter's fame survived the Communist Revolution. Indeed, he is as commanding a hero to the Soviets as he was to the Tsarists, who see many parallels between their efforts and his to equal and surpass the West. To the Soviets, his reforms were necessary to the creation of a powerful Russian state and he was the man who led the nation toward progress and enlightenment.

As Russia's might and involvement in European politics grew during his reign, Peter's accomplishments affected an ever-increasing number of other lands. Although all that Peter did was foreshadowed by his predecessors of the previous two centuries, the fact remains that he made Russia a European power, established her on the Baltic Sea, remedied the organizational shortcomings that had made previous regimes inefficient, and forced the people out of their intellectual isolation by his sponsorship of Western culture.

The Russians paid heavily for the achievements, more heavily perhaps than the subjects of any other absolutist monarchs of the age. The suffering, deprivation, and sacrifice caused by war was only a small part of the price. State service kept the nobility from the countryside, alienating them from the mass of the people and creating new and irreconcilable social antagonisms. The Westernized nobility with their new ways, new dress, and clean-shaven faces were set still further apart from the masses. New and onerous burdens were imposed on the peasantry by the state and by the lords, and millions who had been free were forced into serfdom or the less onerous but still unfree category of state peasant.

The oppressions of Peter were not accepted passively. Peasant revolts punctuated his reign, and thousands fled to the still unsettled frontiers. Feared and hated by his subjects, Peter seemed to them to fulfill the prophecy of the Scriptures as interpreted by the Old Believers, that he was the Anti-Christ incarnate. In retrospect, he was something less than that, though some of his influence was nearly as malignant.

THE RULERS, 1725–1762

From Peter's death in 1725 until the accession of Catherine II in 1762 the history of the tsars is a fantastic tale of depraved monarchs, corrupt favorites, and palace revolutions. Much of the blame was Peter's. In decreeing that the tsar could name his own successor, he had destroyed the principle of fixed succession, leaving the way open for intriguing adventurers to gain power by backing a successful candidate for the throne.

Catherine I was the first in a line of six bizarre creatures who held the throne until 1762. She was succeeded in 1727 by the son of the murdered Alexis, the eleven-year-old Peter II, who reigned just three years. Anna, daughter of Ivan V (Peter the Great's co-tsar) who reigned from 1730 to 1740, gave over the government to a group of German adventurers headed by her lover and whiled away her hours with extravagance and the collection of freaks, both animal and human. Her two-month-old grandnephew, Ivan VI, who was named her successor on her deathbed, reigned thirteen months until overthrown by a palace revolution that put Elizabeth, the thirty-two-year-old daughter of Peter the Great and Catherine, on the throne. Poor Ivan spent the rest of his life in confinement, reduced to idiocy by his long imprisonment and ill-treatment and finally murdered in 1764 at the command of the ruler when an attempt was made to free him.

Elizabeth (1741–62) possessed all the vices and none of the capacities of her parents. She took a succession of lovers, delighted in an immense wardrobe (including men's clothes), and left the government to favorites. Her successor was her nephew Peter, Duke of Holstein, whom she brought from Germany to Russia and married to a young German princess named Sophia, who was rechristened Catherine upon her conversion to Russian Orthodoxy for the marriage.

Peter III became tsar in early 1762 and reigned for a mere six months. Much of what is known of him comes from his wife—and usurper—and her adherents, and probably less than justice has been done him in most accounts. He was certainly peculiar, childish, and arrogant. In seeking reforms, he showed utter contempt for things Russian and idolized Frederick the Great of Prussia. A threat he made to secularize Church property cost him the support of the clergy; another threat to take away the special privileges of the guards regiments contributed to the loss of his throne. His wife Catherine and her lover Orlov won over the guards and seized the throne in June, 1762. Crowned Empress Catherine II, she assented to, if she did not order, the murder of Peter a few days after the coup.

PATTERNS OF CHANGE, 1725–1762

If attention is focused only on the tsars, Russian history from 1725 to 1762 seems a preposterous parade of lewd and deranged sovereigns, corrupt favorites, and rebellious guardsmen. When other facets of Russian life are examined, meaningful patterns appear. A new class cohesiveness developed among the nobles who won their freedom from the restrictions imposed upon them by Peter I; they became the real masters of Russia. The condition of the peasantry worsened, and Russia became increasingly involved in international affairs.

Peter I had welded the nobles into a single class held together by common interests and common class privileges. After his death the feeling of cohesiveness continued to grow until by the 1760's the nobles identified themselves as a corporate body all of whose members shared the same class interests. Despite strata within the nobility, ranging from fabulously wealthy aristocrats to petty landowners who were almost indistinguishable from peasants, noblemen stood together in their demands for greater privileges. The absence of a stable principle of succession to the throne and the character of the monarchs afforded the opportunity to attain their goals. The dependence of the sovereigns upon the nobility, particularly upon the predominantly noble guards regiments, to get and keep the throne enabled the nobles to exact increased privileges. Their most spectacular gain was the abolition of the hated requirement of service in the army or the bureaucracy. Gradual reduction of this obligation culminated in the abolition of all compulsory service for nobles in Peter III's reign.

The partial monopoly of the right to own land and serfs, won by the nobility in the seventeenth century, was made complete, although a few men of other classes continued to own serfs illegally. The police and judicial powers of the nobles over their serfs were so greatly expanded that the serfs were more than ever at the mercy of their lords. Many escaped to the eastern or southern frontiers of European Russia or fled across the western border into Poland. Peasant risings, sometimes of a handful of men and sometimes of thousands, were endemic. They were invariably crushed, sometimes with inhuman cruelty, but repression seemed only to encourage others to strike out against their oppressors.

In international affairs Russia played the great-power role that Peter had won for it, but government ineptitude limited Russian gains. In alliance with Austria Russia fought successfully to have the Russian candidate recognized as king of Poland in the War of the Polish Succession, 1733–35. War against Turkey in 1735–39 went badly, despite Austrian assistance after 1737, with no gains and heavy losses of men and money. War with Sweden in 1741–43 saw easy victories by Russian troops and occupation of most of Finland, but the concluding treaty brought only small territorial acquisitions. Russia stayed out of the War of the Austrian Succession until the last minute, entering only when a large annual cash subsidy from England persuaded her to send troops against France. Before the Russians saw action, the war was over, and Russia was not invited to the peace conference.

As the specter of Frederick II's expansionist ambitions grew in the 1750's,

Russian policy became markedly anti-Prussian. An Anglo-Russian agreement in 1756 aimed at Prussia was abruptly terminated in the same year when Britain allied herself with Prussia. Russia joined Austria and France in the Seven Years' War. Russian troops bore much of the brunt of the fighting against Prussia and with Austrian forces occupied Berlin in 1760. The death of Empress Elizabeth in 1762 saved Prussia, for her successor, Peter III, switched sides and ordered his troops to fight alongside those of his idol, Frederick II. The thousands of lives and millions of rubles that Russia had spent to defeat Frederick had gone for nothing because of the whim of the tsar. When Catherine became empress, she withdrew her troops from the war, so that Russia was not represented at the peace conference in 1763 and gained nothing.

CATHERINE II (1762–1796)

The accession of Catherine II restored the Russian throne to a centrality in Russian life that it had not had since the death of Peter I. Catherine, who was far superior to the grotesque creatures who preceded her, bears comparison with the outstanding rulers of the time. Nevertheless she was not without personal aberrations, her most renowned being the inconstancy of her affections. Most of her twenty-one known lovers held her devotion for only a brief time, but all of them were rewarded with rich gifts, and three of them had much influence in government. Gregory Orlov was all-powerful during the first decade of Catherine's reign; Gregory Potemkin exercised great influence from 1771 to 1791, long after Catherine had broken her romantic attachment with him; and Platon Zubov in his twenties was entrusted with great power by the infatuated sixty-year-old empress.

Catherine developed an interest in the writings of the Enlightenment in the early years of her marriage, and for the rest of her life she kept up with the latest intellectual and literary movements. She corresponded regularly with Voltaire, Diderot, d'Alembert, and other foreign intellectuals and expressed sympathy with many of the ideas that they supported. She also wrote plays and essays in French and Russian.

The empress's enthusiasm for the new ideas was only partly motivated by genuine intellectual interest. Realizing that the French philosophes were the opinion-makers of the day, she deliberately curried favor with them so that they would create an "image" of her as an enlightened ruler. It not only pleased her vanity but also served Russia's political interests. In her letters she discussed Russian developments, always in the best light. Her correspondents, flattered to receive imperial confidences, talked about them in influential circles (as Catherine knew they would) and created a favorable foreign opinion of her. Catherine's self-advertising campaign was strikingly successful. She owed her reputation for enlightenment—and her title of "Great"—to Western intellectuals, not to her record as a ruler.

Catherine's true importance for Russian history lay not in her philosophical views but in her pro-noble and anti-serf policies, her economic and fiscal measures, and her foreign policy.

CATHERINE AND THE NOBILITY

In striking contrast to the absolutists, including Peter the Great, who tried to restrict the privileges of the nobility, Catherine increased their privileges. Her reign turned out to be the Golden Age of the Russian nobility. She identified herself completely with the nobility and acquiesced in its demands even more than had her weak predecessors. She allowed the lords greater powers over their serfs and gave hundreds of thousands of state peasant families and their land to nobles, thereby converting the peasants into serfs. She established special banks to lend government funds to nobles and did not press them for repayment. Her pro-noble policy culminated in the Charter of the Nobility, which she issued in 1785. This long document confirmed the privileges that the nobles had already won, such as freedom from the service requirement. It exempted them from personal taxes, corporal punishment, and trial by judges other than those of birth equal to their own. The nobles of each province were organized into assemblies and given control over most of the governmental functions of the province, either directly or through officials they had chosen from among themselves. Thus Russian nobles were granted the right to form provincial estates entrusted with governmental functions at the very time when in other parts of Europe privileged noble assemblies were under heavy attack or no longer existent.

Catherine did not show the same regard for the Orthodox Church. Tsars had long struggled with the problem of controlling the great wealth of the Church. In 1764 Catherine ordered the secularization of Church property. All of its lands and serfs were turned over to a government bureau, many monasteries were closed, and henceforth the Church was supported by government funds.

The growth in the privileges of the nobility was accompanied by a steady deterioration in the condition of the peasantry. Serfdom reached its nadir during Catherine's reign. Both the lords and the state increased their demands, serfdom was introduced into the Ukraine (the southeastern region annexed by Russia in the seventeenth century), the sale of serfs without land was legalized, and hundreds of thousands of state peasants were compelled to work at low wages in privately owned factories and mines. During the first decades of Catherine's reign there was an ominous increase in peasant unrest and violence, culminating in a great uprising in 1773. A Don Cossack adventurer named Emilian Pugachev, who claimed to be Peter III and to have miraculously escaped assassination, vowed to right old wrongs of the people and promised land and freedom to his followers and death to their oppressors. Thousands of state peasants and serfs enlisted under his banner. Soon he was in control of much of the Volga valley. The government had to launch a full-scale campaign to crush the rebellion and capture and execute Pugachev. Terrible reprisals were visited on the rebellious districts. Official attempts to stamp out every memory of the rising, however, were less than successful. The peasants made a folk hero out of Pugachev as their defender against oppression. The rulers of Russia did not forget him either: from his time on they were haunted by the fear of a new Pugachev.

ECONOMIC REFORM

Catherine's economic policies proved to be the most progressive part of her program. In 1775 she abolished monopolistic privileges in trading and manufacturing and decreed that anyone could go into any kind of business, except distilling, which for some time had been an exclusive right of nobles. Nobles were the chief beneficiaries of the new policy: many of them established factories on their estates and used the serfs as unpaid laborers. Some peasants benefited, too, for many of them became active in cottage industry, and a few built up large enterprises.

This reform, combined with a general upswing in economic activity, was responsible for a remarkable growth of industry. The incomplete data available indicate that there were about 650 factories in Russia when Catherine began her reign and around 2,000 factories when she died. The most striking development was in iron production in the Urals. For a brief period in the last part of the century, that region was the world's chief producer of pig iron. The Russian plants, however, failed to adopt the new techniques developed in the West, and Russian production soon fell far behind that of Western iron-producing nations.

Catherine's government was active in bringing in colonists to settle uninhabited parts of the realm. The program, unsuccessfully attempted during Elizabeth's reign, was revived when Catherine ascended the throne. Most of the immigrants came from Germany. The government gave them land, loans, and subsidies to get started. Many of the colonists settled along the lower Volga, where their descendants retained the language, traditions, and culture of Germany until World War II, when their collaboration with the Nazi invaders persuaded the Soviet government to disperse them.

Much of the benefit of Catherine's economic policies was canceled out by her disastrous fiscal activities. When she came to the throne the gross mismanagement of government finances and the heavy cost of the war against Prussia had brought the state to the edge of bankruptcy. Catherine's fantastic extravagances, notably in gifts to her favorites, and the costs of her wars made matters worse. To cover the deficit the government in 1769 began to issue paper money, at first in limited quantities then in increasing amounts, producing serious inflation. The government borrowed abroad, contracting a huge foreign debt in addition to the many millions of rubles owed to Russian creditors, and increased the tax burden two and one-half times during Catherine's reign.

FOREIGN POLICY

In foreign policy Catherine's dream was to expand her realm at the expense of Poland and Turkey in order to make Russia the prime power of Europe. She remarked to a friend, "If I could live for two hundred years all of Europe would be brought under Russian rule." She did not achieve all her ambitions, but she added 213,000 square miles—an area as large as France—and 12 million people to the Russian Empire, and Russia's international prestige reached new heights.

The opening gambit in her drive for conquest came in 1764 when Catherine arranged to have a former lover, Stanislas Poniatowski, elected king of Poland after he promised not to oppose any of her policies in Poland. In 1768 this arrangement brought on war with the Turks who feared that Russian control of Poland would threaten the Ottoman Empire. The Austrians were also worried by Russian victories, not wanting Russian troops on their eastern flank, and they made an alliance with Turkey and prepared for intervention. The threat of Russo-Austrian war was averted through the diplomacy of Frederick II of Prussia. Although he had allied with Catherine in 1767 against Austria, Frederick had no wish to fight to guarantee Russian annexations in Turkey. In 1772 he suggested the partition of part of Poland among Austria, Russia, and Prussia, in return for Russia's giving up its Turkish conquests. Fearful of war with Austria, Catherine agreed.

The Turkish war was ended in 1774 by a treaty signed in the Bulgarian village of Kuchuk Kainarji. As the Treaty of Nystadt in 1721 had given Russia access to the Baltic Sea, the Treaty of Kuchuk Kainarji gave Russia access to the Black Sea. Turkey ceded the northern Black Sea coast from the Dnieper to the Bug estuaries, opened the sea to Russian shipping, allowed Russian merchants passage through the straits into the Mediterranean, and recognized the Crimea as an independent Tatar state (making it susceptible to Russian conquest). A vaguely worded concession by the Turks permitted Russia to represent Christian subjects of the Ottomans if they were not fairly treated; it was used in later years as the excuse for repeated Russian intervention in Turkish domestic affairs.

With Russian prestige at its height, Catherine could indulge in her dream of completely expelling the Turks from Europe and establishing a new Byzantine Empire in the Balkans. Her second grandson, born in 1779, was christened Constantine in anticipation of his becoming sovereign of the new empire centered in Constantinople. The Danubian areas were to be made into a separate kingdom under her favorite, Potemkin, as king. This ambitious "Greek Project," as it was called, received uneasy acceptance from Emperor Joseph II of Austria; a promise of territory in the Balkans to go to Austria helped persuade him to enter into a defensive alliance with Russia in 1781. Catherine annexed the Crimea and attempted to stir up rebellion against the Turks in the Balkans. In 1787 a showy river trip by Catherine, the Austrian emperor, and Western diplomats down the Dnieper into the Crimea, replete with signs along the river banks pointing "This way to Byzantium" and military and naval demonstrations, capped a series of provocations that moved the Turks to declare war on Russia. In 1788 Austria joined Russia, but withdrew three years later after heavy losses. In 1792 the Treaty of Jassy recognized a Russian victory, and the Turks ceded the rest of the north shore of the Black Sea to Russia. Austria's defection, however, caused Catherine to abandon the Greek Project.

Catherine's attention turned to Poland. Following an invasion by Russian troops in 1793, Russia and Prussia annexed more Polish territory in the second partition of that hapless country. Two years later Russia, Prussia, and Austria divided all that was left of Poland among themselves.

Intense russification and administrative unification of newly acquired territories were features of Catherine's expansion program. The new territories were divided into provinces and made subject to Russian law, institutions, and economic organization. Serfdom was introduced into regions taken from Turkey. In time many of the conquered peoples reconciled themselves to Russian domination. Others never ceased the struggle to regain independence.

THE BRIEF REIGN OF TSAR PAUL

Catherine was succeeded in 1796 by her son Paul, whom she despised and to whom she had never given any responsibility. Although Paul was clearly unbalanced mentally, he applied himself to needed reforms during his short reign. Among other things he established a fixed line of succession to the throne, thereby ending the uncertainties and schemings that had troubled the Russian succession since Peter's time. He began reforms in the central government in the interests of efficiency. He sought to help the serfs by recommending that they work no more than three days a week for their lords and ordering the construction of granaries in every village to store food for emergencies.

His mistake was to try to lessen the privileges of the nobility. He did not re-establish the service requirement but made it clear that he expected nobles to spend their lives in government service. He taxed noble land, abolished the provincial assemblies of the nobility, and imposed new disciplinary regulations on army officers. Discontent and disaffection spread among the nobility, and in March, 1801, a band of guards officers murdered him. His son and heir, Alexander I, knew about the plot to drive Paul from the throne, but it is not known whether he was aware that it involved his father's assassination. In any event, he did not punish the murderers. One of his first acts as sovereign was to restore to the nobility all the privileges that Paul had taken away.

The Decline and Disappearance of Poland

In 1772 Poland was the third largest state in Europe in area and stood fourth in population.[1] By 1795 Poland had disappeared as an independent state. Its tale of decay and disappearance is the strange story of a nation that committed suicide. Ultimate responsibility for Poland's obliteration lay with the Polish nobility, who ran the country and whose selfishness and perversity made Poland defenseless against aggression.

NOBLE OLIGARCHY

The nobility elected the king and in return for their votes exacted the assurance that the man elected would be nothing but a figurehead. The nobility, some 700,000 to 800,000 strong (approximately 8 per cent of the population), were predominantly petty country squires. Sixteen or seventeen families possessed enormous wealth, but the majority of the noblemen were miserably poor, half of them were all but landless, and many were barely distinguishable from the peasantry. Most of them were retainers of the wealthy lords and exercised their voice in politics according to the wishes of their patrons. The great lords struggled ceaselessly among themselves to attain political power, not hesitating to call in foreign troops or sell themselves for foreign subsidies.

Noble political power was concentrated in some fifty provincial assemblies, which were representative only of the nobility, unlike most other estates in Europe. The assemblies had ultimate power over national legislation, collected taxes, of which they turned over to the central government as much as they wished, and maintained their own armies. The assemblies elected the representatives to the diet, the only national authority other than the figurehead king. By the use of the *liberum veto*—merely rising and saying, "I object"—any noble deputy could force the dissolution of the diet, "explode" it, as it was called. The *liberum veto* not only dissolved the diet but nullified all measures previously adopted by that diet. Of the fifty-five diets convened between 1653 and 1764, forty-eight were exploded, their work undone. The one way to get around the *liberum veto* was the "confederation." Armed noblemen could with complete legality confederate and use force upon their opponents to push through legislation. The cure—"legally

---

[1] Russia and Sweden were larger; France, Russia, and Austria were more populous.

organized revolution" in theory, chaos in practice—was obviously as bad as the disease. Poland was, in effect, a loose federation of fifty or so little noble oligarchies without any effective central authority.

The nobility used its political power to free itself from compulsory military service and most taxes and to give itself a monopoly of land ownership, unlimited power over the peasantry (reduced to serfdom), and a monopoly of all higher offices in Church and state. Three-quarters of the population were serfs, unable to appeal to any higher authority for protection against their masters and reduced to misery. The townsmen were excluded from all political participation, and the towns, most of them little larger than villages, were firmly under noble control. Town life and the portion of the economy dependent upon it steadily declined. The Polish nobles boasted of their "golden liberty" and scorned the nobility of other lands as the "slaves of despots," but in reality they were ineffectual petty tyrants presiding over a nation in decay, bereft of the institutions or the economy requisite to defend itself against the effective despotisms of Russia, Austria, and Prussia.

Polish disunity went deeper than politics. Only about one-half of the population was Polish, one-third was Ukrainian and White Russian, and the rest was a mixed bag of Germans, Lithuanians, Armenians, and Tatars. The Poles and Lithuanians were universally Catholic, the Ukrainians and White Russians were Orthodox, the Germans were Protestant, and there were about one million Jews. During the Reformation, Poland had been among the most tolerant of nations, but in the later seventeenth and eighteenth centuries there was much oppression by the Roman Catholic Church, the official state religion. Many Orthodox peasants were forced to become Catholics, and other non-Catholics were deprived of their rights, restricted in the exercise of their religion, and on occasion victimized by mobs. Intolerance not only produced divisive discontent but also served Poland's neighbors, particularly Russia, as an excuse for intervention on behalf of coreligionists.

THE ROAD TO PARTITION

Poland's weakness became apparent during the reign of John Casimir (1648–68). Invaded by Ukrainian Cossacks, Russians, and Swedes, the country managed to survive their onslaughts but had to cede Livonia to Sweden in 1660 and the eastern Ukraine and part of White Russia to Russia in 1667. Poland's neighbors began to discuss the division of all of Poland among themselves. The succeeding years brought new wars and invasions, foreign intervention in Polish affairs, and heightened interest in the possible partition of Poland.

The question of what was going to happen to Poland and, if it broke up, who was going to get the pieces was a problem of major importance for the international balance of power. France saw Poland as a buffer state

The Cake of the Kings:
First Partition of Poland, 1773, engraving
by Le Mire after Moreau le jeune

*"The States bordering upon Poland have
so often been involved in the disorders
which have arisen during interregnums
in that kingdom, that the experience of
the past would in any case have led
the neighboring powers to occupy
themselves seriously with the affairs of
that State. . . . These powers have
agreed accordingly to attempt to reach
without loss of time a common
understanding, in order to restore
peace and good order in Poland, and
establish the ancient constitution of this
State and the liberties of the nation
upon a sound basis. Consequently . . .
[they] will put themselves in effective
possession of those portions of Poland
which are calculated to serve hereafter
as the most natural and secure boundary
between them."* Catherine II to the
Poles, reprinted in J. H. Robinson and
C. A. Beard, READINGS IN MODERN
EUROPEAN HISTORY (Boston, 1908).

against Russia. Austria saw Poland as a buffer against Russia and Prussia.
The Prussians wanted Polish territory so that they could unite East Prussia
with Pomerania and Silesia; since the mid-seventeenth century they had
been pushing the idea of partition at every opportunity. The Russians of
that day, like the Russians of today, felt that they had to dominate Poland
because if that country was truly independent or under the domination of
another power Russia's own security would be endangered. The Russians
and Poles were ancient enemies, but by the eighteenth century Poland
had become a Russian satellite. With Poland under their domination the
Russians had no special interest in splitting it up and therefore frustrated
proposals for partition.

PARTITION

Russian opposition to partition changed under Catherine II. Her support
of Stanislas Poniatowski for the throne of Poland precipitated the chain of
events that led in 1772 to the partition of part of Poland among Russia,
Prussia, and Austria. Poland lost almost one-third of its area and over a third
of its people. Russia took the largest but least prosperous share, Prussia took
the wealthiest, and Austria took the greatest in population.

Partition shocked many Poles into a new political awareness. They realized
that the only way they could save what was left of Poland was by a radical

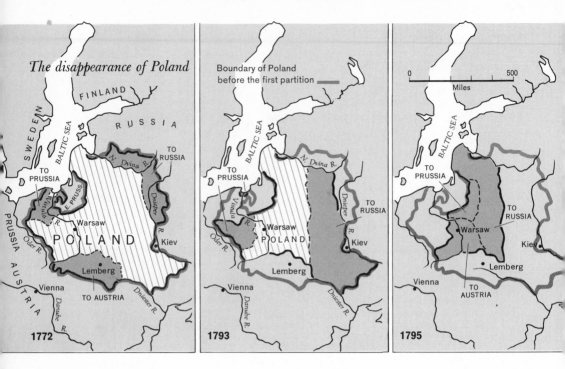

The disappearance of Poland

change in the form of government. This realization was stimulated by an intellectual revival, connected with the translation of writers of the Enlightenment like Montesquieu, Rousseau, and Adam Smith. Periodicals were founded and books and articles appeared that questioned such basic institutions of Polish life as serfdom, the election of kings, and the *liberum veto*. In 1788 the Poles summoned a diet whose members agreed to prohibit the *liberum veto* at its sessions. In 1792 after long deliberations the diet made the throne hereditary, gave the king substantial powers, provided for a council of ministers and an efficient organization of the central administration, established representation of the towns in the diet, and allowed townsmen to purchase rural property (previously a monopoly of the nobility) and hold high government offices.

The reforms, which won the acclaim of liberals in Western Europe, spurred a number of reactionary Polish lords to rebel against the new order. Catherine of Russia sent 100,000 soldiers to aid them on the pretext of "restoring Polish liberties," and soon Prussia sent troops to help the rebels. The Poles were compelled to abolish all the reforms and restore the anarchy that made them such easy prey. In 1793 Russia and Prussia agreed to a second partition of Poland. This time Poland lost about half of its remaining area and population. In 1794 a group of nobles again raised the banner of revolt, led by Thaddeus Kosciusko, who twenty years earlier had crossed the ocean to fight for American independence. Kosciusko assumed dictatorial powers and promised freedom to the serfs to win their support. Dissensions among the leaders, large Russian reinforcements, and the entrance of Prussian troops doomed the rebellion to failure. In 1795 Russia, Prussia, and Austria swallowed up the rest of Poland.

Poland had disappeared because its nobles, in pursuit of divergent and selfish interests, had awakened too late to the realization that responsibility is the price of privilege. Had they allowed Poland to develop a strong central government and thus be able to protect itself, the history of their country and of Europe would have been very different. The Polish problem did not disappear with the annihilation of the Polish state. The Polish people never gave up the resolution to regain their national identity, and control of Polish lands continued to be a source of contention among the great powers.

Scandinavia

ABSOLUTISM IN DENMARK

The defeat of Denmark in the First Northern War, 1655–60, afforded Frederick III (1648–70) the opportunity to break once and for all the nobles' domination of Denmark. The Danish nobility, comprising 500 to 600 families, controlled the central government through the king's Council of the Realm. They also controlled local government, monopolized the chief offices in state and church, owned half the country, paid no taxes, evaded military service, and had the greatest voice in the election of the king. Frederick, who was a national hero by virtue of his brilliant though hardly successful leadership against Sweden in the war, won the support of the clergy and townsmen of Copenhagen for a bold and bloodless coup d'état in October, 1660, by which he forced the nobility to concur in making him hereditary king of Denmark.

The coup established a limited hereditary monarchy. Frederick, however, took advantage of the confusion of his opponents to make himself an absolute ruler. In 1665 he promulgated a document called the *Kongelov*, the "King's Law," which accorded the monarch sweeping powers and declared him to be above the law as well as being the sole maker of laws. In only five years Denmark had been transformed from a state dominated by a noble oligarchy into the most perfect example of absolute monarchy in all of Europe.

Frederick was succeeded in 1670 by Christian V, but the real ruler of the country was a man named Peter Schumacher, son of a wine merchant. Schumacher, later ennobled as Count Griffenfeld, had been the chief author of the *Kongelov*. During his tenure of power he further developed the authority of the monarch. Griffenfeld was toppled from high office in 1676, but the policies he followed were pursued by his successors and accepted by the people. Not until 1848 was absolutism successfully challenged in Denmark.

In the seventeenth and eighteenth centuries Denmark was a much larger state than it is today. The royal possessions included Norway and the southern part of the Danish peninsula, now part of Germany. The realm included less than a million people, but its small population did not prevent Denmark from taking an active role in European affairs in the seventeenth century. In the eighteenth century it played only a small part in international politics, preferring to follow a policy of semi-isolation. In home affairs the old nobility declined in wealth and influence, while the royal bureaucracy gained in importance and status. Many of the bureaucrats were foreigners, chiefly from Germany. They owed their eminence to the king and were therefore loyal to him. The kings were an undistinguished, dreary lot, and under their uninspired leadership once-vigorous Denmark was turned into a backwater.

ABSOLUTISM IN SWEDEN

Once Charles XI of Sweden (1660–97) had attained his majority and retrieved Sweden's fortunes from its heavy defeats during the intervention in the Franco–Dutch War of 1672–79 (see p. 272), he, too, turned to the creation of an absolute monarchy. In 1680 he ordered an investigation of the abuses of the "regents" or great landed aristocrats who had ruled during his minority. With the acquiescence of the Riksdag (the estates) he punished the regents by excessively heavy fines. Another commission was appointed to reclaim crown lands and revenues given to the nobility by former monarchs. The "reduction," as the policy was called, was done with absolutist thoroughness. In 1652 almost three-quarters of the land in Sweden was in noble hands; in 1700 only a third remained with noblemen, a third with the king, and a third with the peasantry. The economic foundations of noble dominance were shattered, and the seizure of the lands enabled the monarch to attain fiscal solvency. Charles XI enjoyed the wholehearted cooperation of the clergy and the townsmen as well as the peasantry, who had been threatened with enserfment when the nobility dominated the state.

Bureaucratization was thoroughgoing. The new corps of civil servants was drawn from the minor nobility and professional classes and totally dependent on the king. The collegial system of administration that became the model for absolutist government in Russia and Prussia was Charles XI's creation. A large standing army was maintained by grants of crown land to officers and appropriation of part of the peasants' holdings in each district to support the volunteer enlisted men. The navy was built up to sufficient power to preserve communications in the far-flung reaches of the Baltic empire. The state Lutheran Church was brought firmly under monarchic control. Mercantilist policies were initiated to promote economic growth.

Charles XII of Sweden

"Charles XII, king of Sweden, dead at the age of thirty-six years and a half, after having experienced all the grandeur of prosperity, and all the hardships of adversity, without being either softened by the one, or the least disturbed by the other. . . . He carried all the virtues of the hero to such an excess as rendered them no less dangerous than the opposite vices. . . Severe to himself as well as to others, he too little regarded either his own life and labors, or those of his subjects; an extraordinary rather than a great man, and more worthy to be admired than imitated."

Voltaire, HISTORY OF CHARLES XII
(Boston, 1887).

Courtesy of Nationalmuseum, Stockholm

CHARLES XII OF SWEDEN

In 1697 Charles XII, aged fifteen, succeeded his father. Sweden's natural enemies Denmark, Russia, and Poland saw his youth as an opportunity to carve up the Swedish Empire. Their concerted attack touched off the Great Northern War of 1700–21. They underestimated their prey. Intelligent, courageous, and bellicose, Charles was a military genius. He fought a brilliant defense-offense against the forces allied against him in the first seven years of the war and brought Poland, Denmark, and Saxony to defeat. His disastrous invasion of Russia in 1707 ended in the Swedish rout at Poltava in 1709 and his exile in Turkey from 1709 to 1714, when he made a triumphant return to Sweden. Four more years of bitter warfare against the old enemies reinforced by Prussia and Hanover was a struggle against overwhelming odds. Killed in action in 1718, Charles was as worn out by the effort of war as was his land, which had lost almost a generation of its male youth and had consumed its prosperity in war. The peace treaties of 1720 and 1721 ended Sweden's hegemony in the north and her status as a major power; Livonia, Estonia, Ingria, and Karelia went to Russia, and all but a small part of her German territories went to Prussia and Hanover.

OLIGARCHY IN SWEDEN

Defeat and exhaustion in the Great Northern War and Charles's death without a direct heir (he never married) destroyed absolutism in Sweden. The nobility re-established its power by making the succession of Charles's sister Ulrica and her German husband conditional upon a new constitution that gave the Riksdag almost supreme political power, recreating noble

Sweden—The rise and decline of a Baltic empire, 1523 to 1815

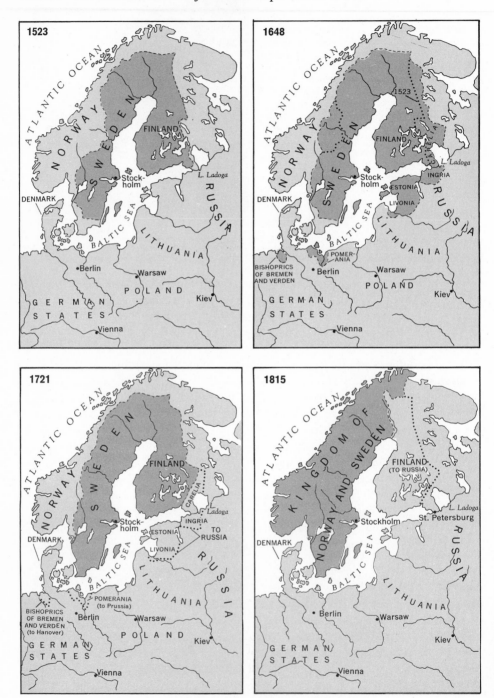

oligarchic rule in Sweden. The Age of Freedom, as its noble beneficiaries termed it, lasted from 1718 to 1772. Peace was the policy followed by Count Arvid Horn, the cautious and conservative noble oligarch whose twenty-year tenure in office enabled Sweden to regain much of her economic vitality. His fall in 1738, engineered by the war party intent on regaining Swedish glory, plunged Sweden into a war with Russia from 1741 to 1743, which cost it more territory in Finland. Until 1766 the war party retained power, disastrously allying Sweden with France and subverting Swedish interests to the French.

Corruption, misrule, and economic distress produced a reaction in favor of a strong monarchy. In 1772 Gustavus III (1771–92) forced the Riksdag to assent to a new constitution under which the king enjoyed command of the armed forces, the power to convene, terminate, and limit discussion in the Riksdag, and sole responsibility for foreign affairs. The constitution contained significant limitations on the king's power: the Riksdag had to consent to legislation, the declaration of war, and amendments to the constitution, and it levied taxes and controlled the state bank. The old absolutism was not re-established, but the Age of Freedom or noble oligarchy was ended.

The Ottoman Empire, 1656–1792

In the seventeenth and eighteenth centuries the Ottoman Empire plummeted from the pinnacle represented by the reign of Sultan Suleiman the Magnificent (1520–66). Degeneracy, corruption, internecine political strife, economic decline, and ethnic and religious antagonisms disrupted the internal life of the empire and cost it the external strength that had made it the most feared power in the sixteenth century.

The sultans were almost without exception weak and degenerate men, products of the incredible environment in which the royal princes were raised. The old practice of murdering the sons of the sultan was replaced in the late sixteenth century by locking them up with a harem and a few eunuchs in a separate part of the palace, called the Cage. One of them emerged to become sultan; the rest stayed until death, safely removed from power. Not unexpectedly, the chosen prince was often a puppet of oligarchic factions who were vying for power. The dominant figure was sometimes the grand vizier or a harem favorite such as the beautiful and ambitious Baffo, daughter of a Venetian nobleman, who was kidnapped and sold into Turkish slavery. She ruled for almost three decades during the reigns of her husband (Murad III) and her son (Mohamed III) in the late sixteenth century.

The lower levels of government reflected the decay at the top. Corruption and incompetence were endemic. The merit system was replaced by the purchase of offices and bribery to gain promotion. Tax collection was sold to the highest bidder and yielded a decreasing return as the taxes got heavier, since the profits went to the collector. The Janissaries, who were ostensibly the warrior backbone of Ottoman power and had been originally recruited from Christian boys to serve as the sultan's celibate slaves, were allowed to marry, to engage in trade and industry, and to enroll their sons in the Janissary corps. Increasingly recruited from the Moslem population, they became an unruly militia of merchants and artisans, only a fraction of whom were trained soldiers. By inciting mob violence they sometimes unseated the ruling faction and even overthrew sultans.

THE ADVENT OF NATIONALISM

The Ottoman Empire never became a nation-state. It remained an agglomeration of different ethnic groups and religions loyal to a community or a faith. Nationalist sentiment made its appearance in the Balkans, where the Christian peasantry in the heyday of the empire had been protected by strict sultanic regulations from arbitrary incursions by their lords, the Moslem cavalrymen ("spahis"), who held the land from the sultan by military-service tenure. In the era of decline the spahis took advantage of the government's weakness to disregard the regulations, convert the fiefs into hereditary possessions, and exploit the Christian peasants. The peasants lost their hereditary right to their holdings, and extortionate rents and taxes placed them in perpetual indebtedness to the spahis, ending their freedom of movement and reducing them to near-serfdom. The peasants erupted periodically into insurrection or fled to the mountains and forests to form outlaw bands that robbed Turks and raided rich Christian monasteries. The bandits (called haiduks in Serbia and klephts in Greece) had no ideological commitment, but they created a Robin Hood-like romantic tradition of defiance to Ottoman authority which nurtured nationalistic consciousness.

In the late eighteenth century nationalist movements developed in the Balkans under the leadership of the Christian middle class, whose trade contacts with the West enabled them to judge the backwardness of the Ottoman Empire. They imported Western books, sent their sons to study abroad, and established schools free from control of the Orthodox Church, which was tainted by its collaboration with the Turks. The French Revolution awakened in the Balkan minorities, who were already deeply influenced by the Enlightenment, the same passions that moved Western men: national determination and liberty.

EXTERNAL IMPOTENCE AND TERRITORIAL DECLINE

The Thirty Years' War gave the Ottomans a breathing spell from foreign embroilments, since their European enemies were at one another's throats. In the second half of the seventeenth century the Turks engaged in a series of wars with Christian powers and in 1683 pushed westward as far as

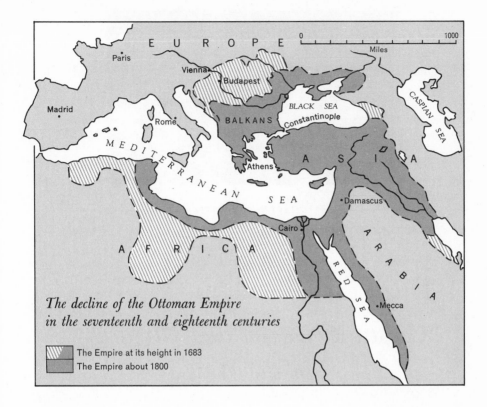

*The decline of the Ottoman Empire
in the seventeenth and eighteenth centuries*

The Empire at its height in 1683
The Empire about 1800

Vienna. (See p. 282.) The Treaty of Karlowitz in 1699, ending the war between Turkey and the Holy Alliance, cost the Ottomans much of their territory and freed Christian Europe from the old threat of Turkish aggression, but it also presented a new problem. Was the Ottoman Empire to be carved up, and if it was, which powers were to get what pieces? Labeled the Eastern Question by nineteenth-century statesmen, this issue was to haunt European international affairs until the dissolution of the Ottoman Empire in 1918.

Despite several wars, for sixty years after Karlowitz the Turks managed to avoid serious territorial losses. Then the accession of Catherine II in Russia threatened to be as disastrous for Turkey as it was for Poland, since Russian aggression engendered a new string of wars. The first partition of Poland saved Turkey from partition, but the Ottomans had to cede a great segment of territory to the Russians in the Treaties of Kuchuk Kainarji (1774) and Jassy (1792). Had Catherine been able to carry out her Greek Project the Balkan peninsula would have been divided between Russia and Austria. Instead, it remained under Ottoman rule until the nineteenth century, when one after another the Balkan peoples won precarious national independence with the assistance of the Christian powers, whose interests were anything but altruistic.

CHAPTER FOURTEEN

Constitutionalism and Oligarchy
in the West

Two NATIONS in Western Europe swam against the tide of absolutism in
the seventeenth century: the Dutch Republic and England. By the end of
the century, when Louis XIV's France had become the model for absolutism,
as his Versailles was for the absolute monarch's palace, these two nations
stood alone as oligarchies of wealth in which the oligarchies wielded ultimate power from bastions constitutionally bulwarked against a strong executive. Both oligarchies had been tried in contest, and both had triumphed.
It is difficult to assign common causes for their victories. Both states
were Protestant, and both were colonial and commercial sea powers,
having vital economies in the hands of strong and cohesive urban middle
classes—although there were wide differences between their policies, economies, and social structures. Perhaps most significant was the survival and
continued vitality of their representative institutions: the provincial States
in the Dutch Republic and Parliament in England. Their survival depended
in turn upon revolutions in both countries at a time when monarchy
was not able to repress the representative institutions, in the Dutch struggle
for independence from Spain in the late sixteenth century and the English

civil wars of the mid-seventeenth century. These revolutions, spawned by specific grievances originating in monarchic policies, strengthened the representative institutions at the expense of the executive.

The Dutch Oligarchy, 1660–1766

1660 represented the high point of the Dutch oligarchy. For ten years after the death of Stadholder William II in 1650 no member of the House of Orange had held the highest national and provincial offices in the republic, and since 1653 Jan De Witt, the oligarchy's chosen leader as grand pensionary of Holland, had directed the affairs of state with singular ability and great restraint. It was the golden age of Dutch republicanism. True, a war with England in 1652–54 had given the more cautious merchant-oligarchs pause, for English sea power coupled with England's ambition to cut into the Dutch carrying trade in ocean commerce raised a disturbing prospect. But Spain, the traditional enemy, had recognized Dutch independence in 1648 and was obviously a declining power. Portugal appeared a greater threat to Dutch interests after it regained control over the territories in Brazil into which the Dutch had made deep inroads. Successful intervention by the Dutch in a Swedish-Danish war in 1657–60 prevented Sweden from controlling the Baltic trade, a mainstay of Dutch commercial strength. Amsterdam was at the height of its vitality as the financial heart of the world; it and the other great Dutch commercial cities had triumphed at the expense of Antwerp in the Spanish Netherlands. Everywhere—Brazil alone excepted—Dutch colonies flourished, and the Dutch primacy in the carrying trade was not yet in question. Never had the nation been more prosperous, and the then current comparisons of the republic with Venice in its heyday and even with republican Rome were not so fanciful.

REGENTAL OLIGARCHY

From the beginning the republic was a loose confederation of seven provinces, each governed by its own representative assembly or States, and each States sending a delegation to the States-General, which was responsible for the conduct of foreign affairs and defense but little else. The province of Holland was pre-eminent in the republic, its States comprising the representatives of the eighteen towns of the province, each with one vote, and the representative of the old nobility with one vote. Sober, dignified, responsible, moderate, and God-fearing (though seldom preacher-fearing), the urban oligarchs of Holland or "regents," as they were known, ruled for the general welfare but without respect for the general will. There was no democracy in the republic. The regents, in whose persons were joined political power and wealth, held all the major offices, executive and judicial. They controlled the town governments, the States, and the States-General.

The regental oligarchy was a closed society. Closely connected by marriage and common economic interests as well as by shared responsibilities of government, the regent group was virtually hereditary and self-perpetuating. This urban upper middle class had wholly eclipsed the old nobility in the provinces of Holland and Zeeland, and in the other five provinces dominated the nobility. Although the lower middle class was politically conscious, it was excluded for the most part from political life, and its only organized political bodies, the craft guilds and civic guard (local militia), were closely controlled by the regents. The regents were not immune to popular pressure, but they were adroit in channeling and generally withstanding it. Because of their unchallenged pre-eminence, they could afford to allow a remarkable freedom of expression and criticism and extensive religious toleration. The most serious threat of disruption came not from the old nobility nor the lower middle class but from the firebrand ministers of the staunchly Calvinist Reformed Church, the established church of the republic, though only a minority of the population belonged to it. Popular pressure became dangerous only when the more fanatical ministers could fix upon an issue and use it to challenge the religious orthodoxy of the regents. In such circumstances the regents had to give up momentarily their accustomed tolerance and moderation if they were to turn off the clerical attack.

Two basic divisions within the republic threatened the primacy of the oligarchy and even the life of the republic. The first was the geographical distinction between the two "seaward" provinces (Holland and Zeeland) and the five "landward" ones (Friesland, Groningen, Overijssel, Gelderland, and Utrecht). The dominant maritime and commercial interests of the former sometimes conflicted with the agrarian concerns of the latter. Though all the provinces were supposed to contribute to the maintenance of the navy and the protection of the merchant marine, Holland and Zeeland shouldered the principal expense and the landward provinces were constantly in arrears for their agreed proportion of the navy's cost.

The second division was political: the fundamental division between the "Orangists" and the "Statists." The former sought greater unity under the leadership of the stadholder-captain-general of the House of Orange, while the latter were determined to preserve provincial autonomy, the sovereignty of the provincial States, and thus the oligarchic pre-eminence. The Orange dynasty had provided the young republic with a symbolic personification of its independence and integrity. The heroism of William the Silent, stadholder from 1579 to 1584, had been the birth glory of the nation, and his successors, Maurice of Nassau (1585–1625) and Frederick Henry (1625–47), had been indomitable, brilliant warriors. As servants of the provincial sovereignty that effectively limited their urge for power, they won the admiration of all Dutchmen, even those who adamantly opposed any accretion of authority by the dynasty at the expense of provincial sovereignty. The Statists did not reject the leadership of the Orange stadholder, but only his predilection for centralization and his dynastic ambitions. In turn, the Orangists respected the Statists' rejection of anything approaching a centralized monarchy, and at its most extreme their demand was merely for a stronger federal system under Orange auspices. The independence of the Holland oligarchy and the fact that Holland and Zeeland provided most of the wealth, almost all of the sea power, and the largest number of men for the defense of the republic, discouraged any other Orangist ambitions. The political realism of both Orangists and Statists, their mutual respect, and common necessity resulted in a marked lack of destructive political antagonism between them. Nevertheless, Dutch politics could be brutal and occasionally disruptive of unity, even in the face of an external enemy. This was never more evident than in the golden age of republicanism when there was no stadholder.

JAN DE WITT

Jan De Witt (1625–1672), was the epitome of the Holland oligarch. In a period of fast-shifting foreign relations when new alignments of the European powers were under way, De Witt, leader of the republic from 1653 to 1672, faced challenges comparable to any faced by stadholders since William the Silent. His leadership in war—with England in 1652–54, with Portugal over Brazil in 1657–61, with Sweden over the Baltic in 1657–60, with England again in 1665–72, and finally with France in 1672—was never less than competent, often brilliant, and always courageous. His statesmanship was of a high order. He recognized that the interests of the republic could only be served by a tenacious defense of Dutch commercial and colonial activity. He built up Dutch finances after every war, rearmed the reluctant nation, and often provided direct military leadership. Though forced out abruptly in 1672 when French armies cut deep into Dutch territory, De Witt was far less responsible for that disaster than the oligarchs, who had countered his attempts to build Dutch power as vigorously as they had countered those of the Orange dynasty. Like Oldenbarneveldt before him (see p. 246), he was requited for his decades of service to the republic and to Dutch independence and prosperity by death—torn to pieces by a howling mob.

The French invasion was the immediate cause of De Witt's fall and also of the decline in dominance of the regental oligarchy. William III of Orange was called to the stadholdership of Holland on July 4, 1672, and four days later he was made captain and admiral-general of the States-General. It was not simply the Orangists who called upon him; it was also a beleaguered nation, which traditionally turned to Orange for leadership in times of trouble. The more profound causes of the decline of the oligarchs stemmed from the inherent divisions within Dutch politics. The Holland and Zeeland oligarchs had neglected the army. Maritime-oriented, they were reluctant to admit the threat of French invasion overland, and they had a traditional class distaste for the noble-officered army In a period of supposed security on land and war at sea vitally affecting their commercial and colonial interests they had maintained only the navy. Religious antagonism had also broken out with increased virulence because of a new demand by militant Calvinist Reformed ministers in the 1660's for a greater voice in affairs of state in order to repress Catholicism and the non-Reformed Protestant sects. Characteristically, De Witt had withstood the demand. The militant Reformed, with an increasingly large following among the urban lower middle class, saw Orange as the natural counterpoise to the regents. Finally, the basic cause of the oligarchs' decline was the very weakness of the union and the autonomy of the provinces, which permitted the decline of the army for want of support and bred factionalism among the regents. Regental oligarchy was workable only so long as confidence in the regents was widespread. When that confidence cracked, there was no practical alternative to a prince of Orange as the champion of the nation and the bridge over divisions and factionalism.

WILLIAM III

William III directed the fortunes of the republic for thirty hazardous years. For the last thirteen of those years he was also king of England. His accession to the stadholdership in 1672 at the age of twenty-one came at the republic's darkest hour in a century. He was the architect of its brilliant resistance to Louis XIV's aggression, and after six years of hard fighting he brought peace in 1678 without loss of territory. For the rest of his life William had one consuming passion: containment and destruction of the aggressive ambitions of Louis XIV of France. After he became England's king in 1689, he used English wealth and power in this struggle.

William's singleness of purpose accounted in part for his unwillingness in 1672 to grasp the opportunity to rout the Statists, reduce regental power, and establish a more cohesive union under an Orange executive who would have been constitutionally more powerful than the stadholder and captain-general. In 1672 emissaries of his uncle, Charles II of England, in league with Louis XIV, offered the young captain-general the assistance of the two monarchs in making him king of the Dutch nation in return for small cessions of territory and his receiving the crown from them. William's answer was a more vigorous prosecution of the war against France and England. He rested satisfied with turning out De Witt's supporters in the town governments, the provincial States, and the States-General and replacing them with more pliant Orangist adherents. He did not attempt an organic reorganization of the cumbrous machinery of the republic, for he did not want to jeopardize the unity of the nation when it was beset by Louis XIV. When William died in 1702 without a direct heir, the regental oligarchy took control once again in the longest, the last, and the least successful of the periods without a stadholder, from 1702 to 1747.

THE REPUBLIC, 1702–1766

For the Dutch the eighteenth century marked a period of economic decline, costly and relatively unsuccessful involvement in far-flung wars, and an end to the vitality of the regental regime. The barrier towns ceded to the Dutch by the Peace of Utrecht in 1713 as protection along the republic's southern border perpetuated the landward orientation of Dutch policy at the expense of the traditional maritime defense. The decline of the Dutch navy led to neglect of the republic's overseas interests. Moreover, war on the scale it was fought in the eighteenth century was such a heavy drain on the resources of the small nation that it could not afford to remain a competitor of Britain and France. It became dependent upon its British ally for protection landward and, increasingly, seaward. The price exacted by the ally was the encroachment of British merchants upon the Latin American trade, once the preserve of the Dutch.

During this period the regental oligarchy seemed to lose its sense of responsibility and cohesiveness. It became increasingly smaller in relation to the total population: since 1600 the population of the republic had almost doubled, but the oligarchy had remained the same closed group of families, jealously guarding its political and economic dominance. Luxury became the way of life of the oligarchs, whose sobriety and sensibleness had once been their hallmark. Interest in country estates replaced their former urban preoccupation and many among them aped the ways of the nobility. Factionalism, corruption, and self-satisfaction enervated the oligarchy, which had no other claim to leadership and power than its energy and success. Half-hearted attempts to strengthen the union foundered on oligarchic exclusiveness and town rivalries, and only served to make more rigid the jealous guarding of provincial sovereignty. In 1747 an invasion by France during the War of the Austrian Succession produced the familiar historical phenomenon—a call to William IV of Orange-Nassau (1711–51). He was invested with a hereditary stadholdership of all seven provinces and the captain-generalship. He died after only four years of rule. Since his son, William V (1748–1806), was only three a regency was established which lasted until 1766.

Triumph of the English Oligarchy, 1660–1689

In 1660, after eleven years of exile on the Continent and one unsuccessful attempt to gain his throne, Charles II returned to England and the crown at the invitation of the reconstituted Parliament. Almost twenty years before that same Parliament had taken up arms against his father, Charles I, and set in train two civil wars, ending with Charles I's execution in 1649. After that England had passed through a republican experience based on the notion "that the people are, under God, the original of all just power." The experiment in republicanism had two casualties: republicanism itself, bankrupted by its failure to find a legitimate foundation for power; and absolutism. If monarchy was vindicated in 1660, absolutist monarchy was not, and it was clear that Charles I's rule without Parliament could never be repeated. Absolutism was not a viable goal of monarchy in a nation in which men of property had made war upon and destroyed a king. The cynical, thirty-year-old Charles II recognized this prime fact of monarchic life in England and, as he flippantly remarked, had no intention of going upon his travels again.

THE POLITICAL SETTLEMENT OF 1660

In the settlement of 1660 there was no attempt to deal with the broad issues that had precipitated revolution, destroyed a monarch, and established a republic. No attempt was made at a fundamental restatement of the relations between king and Parliament. The settlement was political rather than constitutional. All acts that had passed the Long Parliament in 1640–42 and received Charles I's assent were held to be legally valid; all other enactments were ignored. Consequently the settlement confirmed the abolition of ship money and other nonparliamentary revenues levied by the king's prerogative during Charles I's "personal rule" in the 1630's; abolition of the Privy Council's domestic criminal jurisdiction in the Star Chamber and of the High Commission court, which had enforced conformity to the state Church of England; and reduction of the king's power to imprison without trial—all enacted in 1641 and assented to by Charles I. It also confirmed the statute of 1641 requiring that Parliament be summoned at least every three years. Although the monarchy was re-established without a definition of the limits of its authority, it could not be absolutist.

The restoration of Charles II had been possible only because the landed aristocracy—nobility and gentry—had made common cause with the upper middle class urban merchants to protect their property and preserve order— an order that in the confused months following Oliver Cromwell's death in 1658 had been rapidly dissolving. These were the oligarchs, and although they differed over specific political issues in the next three decades, they were always prepared to coalesce in defense of property and Protestantism.

The land settlement of the Restoration returned to the king, the Church, and the royalists all lands confiscated from them. Nevertheless, a great many who had acquired such lands during the revolutionary decades retained possession. Lands sold by royalists to pay the heavy fines levied on them by the victorious Parliamentarians in the 1640's and 1650's remained with the purchasers. Those who had bought Crown lands generally managed to keep them on long-term leases at low rents. Thus men of property had a special stake in avoiding a revival of monarchic pretensions.

THE RELIGIOUS SETTLEMENT OF 1660

By avoiding basic issues, the political settlement of 1660 held out promise of a successful new beginning for English political life. The settlement in religion was less auspicious. In the Declaration of Breda in 1659, presenting the terms on which he would return to the throne, Charles had made a faint promise of religious toleration to Protestants who could not accept the tenets of the Church of England, such as the Presbyterians, Congregationalists, Baptists, and Quakers. These were the heirs of Puritanism, who would henceforth be called Dissenters. After the Restoration an attempt at reunification under the Anglican Church failed. As a result of the election of a new Parliament in 1661 with a staunchly Anglican and royalist majority, called the Cavalier Parliament, a series of repressive measures against the Dissenters were enacted between 1661 and 1665. Inappropriately called the Clarendon Code after Charles's chief minister, the Earl of Clarendon, who in fact opposed several of the measures, the new legislation excluded all but Anglicans from national or local government, prohibited Dissenting religious services with more than five people present except in a private household, and forbade Dissenting clergymen to come within five miles of the place where they had been ministers.

Charles was interested less in toleration for Protestant Dissenters than in toleration for Roman Catholics. His own brother and heir presumptive James, Duke of York, was a Roman Catholic, and Charles himself, in secret provisions in the Treaty of Dover with Louis XIV in 1670, promised to declare himself a Catholic at an opportune moment in return for a large subsidy from France. In 1673, just as Charles was taking England to war in alliance with France against the Dutch, he issued a Declaration of Indulgence suspending the laws against both Roman Catholics and Dissenters. Parliament, attacking this use of the royal prerogative to block legal proceedings, passed the Test Act, banning Catholics and Dissenters from civil or military office. Charles, at war and in need of parliamentary revenue, could not afford to veto the Test Act. Its first victim was his brother James, who had to resign his admiralship of the navy.

THE CATHOLIC SPECTER

The 1670's were dominated by Charles's pro-French policy and by the growing fear of a revival of Catholicism. The two were intimately connected, for when the secret terms of the treaty of 1670 leaked out, the pro-French policy was seen as a league with the "Romish anti-Christ." The presence of the Catholic James a heartbeat away from the throne heightened the fear. French subsidies enabled Charles to survive without long parliamentary sessions, and the old suspicions of personal rule began to revive. The marriage of James's eldest daughter Mary to the Dutch stadholder William III in 1677 as a sop to Protestant sensibilities did little to allay fears. In 1678 a wave of anti-Catholicism broke out in the wake of a far-fetched report of a "Popish Plot," fabricated by a charlatan named Titus Oates, claiming that the Catholics planned to murder the king, massacre Protestants, and bring about a French invasion of Ireland. Anti-Catholicism gained new strength in Parliament, and only by the dissolution in January, 1679, of the Parliament which had sat since 1661 did Charles prevent a move to exclude James from the succession.

The unresolved conflict over religion had precipitated a falling-out between king and Parliament that now took on constitutional proportions. During its long life the Parliament of 1661–79 had become less vociferously Anglican and Royalist as by-elections to fill vacancies brought in younger men with less vivid recollections of the horrors of the civil wars and the republican experiment. An opposition had grown up in Parliament that lacked the ideological frame of the opposition of 1640–42 but had a similar suspicion of the king's sincerity and a wholehearted detestation of the likelihood of a Catholic ruler. Effectively led by a former minister of Charles II, the Earl of Shaftesbury, the new opposition rallied all who feared a Catholic conspiracy, including some staunch Anglicans. Merchants, artisans, Dissenters, and a great many substantial farmers supported the opposition, as well as men of landed property whose fortunes had been made in the 1650's. The few remaining republicans and ex-Levellers (see p. 240) also made common cause with the opposition.

Between March, 1679, and March, 1681, three Parliaments of short duration wrestled with the exclusion of James from the succession, and except for the reluctance of the House of Lords, Parliament would have passed such a bill. The elections to each Parliament returned a larger proportion of the opposition. Yet after Charles had dissolved the last of these three "Exclusion" Parliaments, he was able to rule for the remaining four years of his life without another Parliament. This strictly illegal action was possible only because increased prosperity had brought a greater yield from taxes already granted him and because French subsidies had made him independent of new parliamentary appropriations. Charles recognized that the opposition was creating its own reaction, especially among Anglican landowners who were fearful of its Dissenter tone and its republican element. To these men exclusion of a lawful successor, even if Catholic, carried reminders of the revolution of the 1640's. They believed in passive obedience to the will of the monarch, as the Church and tradition instructed them.

REACTION

In 1682 Charles felt strong enough to move legally against the opposition. Shaftesbury was accused of treason, and though he was acquitted by a highly favorable London jury he was forced to flee to Holland, where he died shortly afterward. In the next year the uncovering of a plot by republican extremists to kidnap the king (the Rye House Plot) and the execution for treason of two leaders of the opposition for alleged complicity in plans for a revolt, discredited the opposition and enabled Charles to establish his ascendancy.

Charles's victory was not a triumph of personal rule so much as a triumph for the coalition of king and Anglican landowners. The opposition, derisively nicknamed Whigs after Presbyterian guerrilla fighters in the west of Scotland, still possessed an organization. The Anglican landowners, called by their opponents Tories after Irish Catholic bandits who preyed on Protestants, were less well organized, and their continued adherence depended on the king protecting the Church of England.

Charles II died in February, 1685. His Catholic brother succeeded as James II. A staunchly Tory Parliament voted James an ample life income. In June both a Protestant rebellion in Scotland led by the Duke of Argyll and an invasion of the southwest of England by Charles II's illegitimate son, the Duke of Monmouth (whom Charles had exiled to Holland in 1683) and a handful of exiled radical Whigs were put down with severity, and Argyll and Monmouth were executed. James, encouraged by the loyal enthusiasm with which his success was greeted, demanded the repeal of the Test Act and the acts of the Clarendon Code that barred Catholics from office. The rebellions had also given James an excuse to keep an army encamped on the outskirts of London. Parliament, even with its Tory majority, protested the presence of the troops and refused to repeal the Test Act, which moved James to adjourn it in November, 1685. It was never reconvened. James then embarked upon a policy of naming Catholics to posts in the government, local governments, army, navy, universities, and even the Church of England. Early in 1687 a Declaration of Indulgence suspending all laws that excluded Catholics and Protestant Dissenters from office thoroughly alienated the Tories while it won few Dissenters (most of whom were Whigs). James's actions seemed to forebode Catholic absolutism, for which the only model was the France of Louis XIV. When in 1688 the

Archbishop of Canterbury and six other bishops, after refusing to read a second Declaration of Indulgence from their pulpits, were tried for sedition and acquitted by juries, it was evident that the Tory adherence to James was at an end.

"THE GLORIOUS REVOLUTION"

The birth of a son to James and his Catholic queen in June, 1688, coalesced Whig and Tory into revolutionary action. They invited Dutch stadholder William III and his wife Mary, Protestant daughter of James II by his first wife, to assist them in protecting the Protestant religion in England. In November, 1688, William and a small expeditionary force landed in England and moved slowly toward London, gathering support from landowners and towns on the way. In panic, James and the royal family fled for France, only to be captured and returned to London. This embarrassment was rectified by allowing them to escape again. Literally without a shot fired a dynasty had fallen and a revolution had taken place, a revolution more superficial in the event but more profound in result than that of forty years before. This time the oligarchy—Whig and Tory, landed and mercantile—was firmly in control, and republicanism and Leveller radicalism were nowhere evident. Not the continuance of monarchy but only the person of the monarch was at issue.

A "Convention" (it could not legally be called a Parliament since no king had summoned it) was convened in January, 1689, to settle the question of the crown. It agonized over the precise legal formula to justify an act of usurpation by invitation. It found the justification in James's flight, which was tantamount to "abdication." The Convention offered the crown to William and Mary as joint sovereigns, "whom it hath pleased Almighty God to make the glorious instrument of delivering this kingdom from popery and arbitrary power." Accompanying the offer, though not a condition of it, was a Bill of Rights. Accepted by the new sovereigns and enacted into law, it guaranteed the right of petitioning the king, of bearing arms (Protestants only), of freedom of election to and debate in Parliament, of frequent meetings of Parliament, and of reasonable bail and jury trial. It also declared illegal the suspending of laws by the king and the levying of revenue and the keeping of a standing army in peacetime without Parliament's consent. Rather less than its illustrious American derivative of a century later, the Bill of Rights was a guarantee of the individual rights of Englishmen. More definitely it was a charter of independence for Parliament. A limited liberty of conscience was granted to Protestant Dissenters by the Toleration Act, in recognition of the Dissenters' opposition to James. The Toleration Act, though it preserved the exclusion of Dissenters from office, permitted them considerable freedom of worship.

JOHN LOCKE AND OLIGARCHY

The "Glorious Revolution of 1688"—as Whigs would honor it for centuries to come—found its prophet, its apologist, and its theoretician in John Locke (1632–1704). Confidant and assistant for fifteen years to the Earl of Shaftesbury, the opposition leader, Locke lived in exile in Holland from 1684 until the advent of William III early in 1689. His political philosophy undergirded the political theories of the French philosophes of the Enlightenment, furnished the framework for the American Declaration of Independence in 1776, and dominated English political theory to this day. In 1690 Locke published his *Two Treatises of Government*, written between 1679 and 1683 as an unpublished contribution to the exclusion controversy. Upon its publication, the *Two Treatises* provided a persuasive rationale for the events of 1688–89.

Locke rejected the accepted way of justifying a political position by appealing to history in general and to legal precedent in particular. Instead, he sought justification in an older tradition, appealing to fundamental natural law revealed not by history but by the use of reason. Like Thomas Hobbes and other predecessors, Locke used a "state of nature"—the absence of government—as a starting point for theory and as a device to invoke natural law to buttress immediate political arguments. Locke argued that men are created with equal rights to life, liberty, and estate. No man can exercise authority over another. All men are governed by natural law, and since all are essentially rational, they can discover and apply natural law. Political institutions did not exist in the state of nature. In this way Locke laid the natural law foundations for equality as existing before the advent of government. When government came into being it was by agreement, a contract among men in the state of nature, by which they gave the political authority the responsibility to preserve and protect their property.

Such a contract could have engendered a thoroughly egalitarian democracy (and this construction has been put by later political philosophers upon Locke's intentions). Democracy did not result, however, because two other developments occurred in the state of nature before the contract bringing government into existence. First, inequality of property grew out of an agreement among men in the state of nature to translate not only their labor and the fruits of the earth but the land itself into money with which men might further increase their property by purchase. Second, natural law gave man the right to dispose freely of his own property, including the "property" of his own labor. Men sold their labor to other men and became employees, their labor becoming part of the employer's property. In his later studies, *Some Considerations of the Consequences of Lowering of Interest and Raising the Value of Money* (1691) and *The Reasonableness of Christianity* (1695), Locke observed that from these two developments came both the differences in property and, significantly, the differences in the rational capacity of men in contemporary society. When in the process of a money economy a few men had appropriated the greatest part of the property (including the labor of other men), those without property, who had to spend their lives in merely sustaining themselves, could not raise their thoughts to higher things, could not have the leisure to reflect upon nature and its laws, could not use their rationality to the full. Even before government was formed by agreement among men in the state of nature, the majority of men had been relegated to a status that would not enable them to participate in political life.

After the advent of government all citizens were protected in their right to life, liberty, and estate, but those few who had gained the greatest part of the property alone controlled government. All men *tacitly* agreed to obey the laws of the government, but only the latter class contracted *explicitly* to form a government. If the government broke the contract that class could change the government. The government broke the contract if it failed to protect property or if it attacked property itself. By majority decision the propertied class determined when the contract had been broken. Thus in 1688 men of property changed the government from James II to William III and Mary because James threatened property. This was the triumphant justification accorded the Revolution of 1688 by Locke's theory.

Locke did not set out to protect individual rights. Such a reading of Locke was peculiarly American and intimately connected with the development of the American Constitution. Locke sought to protect the rights of property owners, not only against government tyranny but also against the propertyless. His theory did battle for the oligarchy against both these foes during the century and a half of the oligarchy's dominance.

The Augustan Age of English Oligarchy, 1689–1760

> A pleasing Form; a firm, yet cautious Mind;
> Sincere, though prudent; constant, yet resign'd:
> Honour unchang'd, a Principle profest,
> Fix'd to one side, but mod'rate to the rest:
> An honest Courtier, yet a Patriot too;
> Just to his Prince, and to his Country true:
> Fill'd with the Sense of Age, the Fire of Youth,
> A Scorn of Wrangling, yet a Zeal for Truth;
> A gen'rous Faith, from Superstition free;
> A Love to Peace, and Hate of Tyranny;
> Such this Man was; who now, from earth remov'd,
> At length enjoys that Liberty he lov'd.

Thus the poet Alexander Pope eulogized his friend Sir William Trumbull, attributing to him all the virtues of the eighteenth-century oligarch. Trumbull, a good Whig in the third generation of a family of officials, had faithfully served Charles II, James II, and William III in embassies and high office. Pope's elegant excessiveness was like that of the age, which in its manners and mores sought the simplicity of republican Rome, but in its thrust and ambition reflected the imperial glory of the Rome of Emperor Augustus.

THE OLIGARCHY

In 1696 Gregory King, a statistician, calculated that eight years earlier there had been 1,360,586 families in England. Of these, (1) 160 were headed by noblemen, (2) 26 by bishops, (3) 16,400 by landed gentlemen, (4) 10,000 by officeholders, (5) 10,000 by merchants, (6) 10,000 by lawyers, (7) 10,000 by clergymen, (8) 16,000 by persons in sciences and the liberal arts, and (9) 9,000 by army and navy officers. By the broadest interpretation the oligarchy of England comprised these 81,586 families or 6 per cent of the families in the nation. By the narrowest interpretation the oligarchy consisted of the first six categories, totaling 46,586 families or about 3 per cent of the families in the nation. In the broadest interpretation, status is the determinant; in the narrowest, wealth and political power are the determinants. Either way, the oligarchy formed only a fraction of the nation.

From it were drawn those who sat in Parliament and those who controlled election to the House of Commons. They comprised the bureaucrats who ran the state, the officers who directed its military might, and the lawyers who staffed the law courts and determined precisely the "undoubted rights and liberties" of Englishmen. The landed gentry filled the important local offices in the counties, such as justice of the peace and deputy-lieutenant in control of the militia. The merchants governed the towns, in which increasing numbers of Englishmen were coming to live. The clergy held the pulpits and monopolized education from the village school to the two universities, Oxford and Cambridge. In the hands of these oligarchs rested by far the largest part of the nation's acreage and its commerce and burgeoning industry.

Not unnaturally, in an age in which oligarchy had triumphed and stood unchallenged, these fortunate few had a livelier sense of what divided them among themselves than of what united them against the monarch above and the masses below. Social status was a horizontal divider; the Duke of Devonshire would have been extremely annoyed had he been mentioned in the same paragraph with a Bristol tobacco importer. The nobility comprised a traditional and legally defined elite, little debased by their steady increase in number throughout the eighteenth century. They, together with the twenty-six bishops and, after 1707, sixteen Scottish peers, sat in the House of Lords, the upper house of Parliament. The landed gentry covered four degrees of rank (gentleman, esquire, knight, and baronet) and a wide range of wealth. They were the supreme local powers in the counties and the largest element elected to the House of Commons. The officeholders were socially indistinguishable from the gentry, being of the same ranks, but were functionally distinct and congregated principally in London. The army and navy officers were drawn almost exclusively from the gentry, and those who survived the service generally died on modest landed estates.

Physicians, academics, and artists were gentlemen by courtesy and never enjoyed higher status or prosperity than in the eighteenth century. The clergy (except Dissenter parsons) were generally university graduates, many of them younger sons of gentlemen and noblemen, and were dependent upon the landed aristocracy for their livings. The alliance between the gentleman's manor house and the parson's vicarage was never stronger than in the eighteenth century, and the upper ranks of the clergy were highly acceptable socially. Poverty among the clergy, of which there was a good deal, at least was genteel. The merchants varied widely in wealth and political power. The greatest were almost merchant princes, allied with the landed aristocracy by marriage and economic interdependence. The great merchants of London were financiers, the creditors of kings, nobility, and gentry, who could expect office, honors, and even nobility. The successful merchant, whether in London or in the provincial towns, could establish himself on the land and his progeny in the gentry. Merchant control of town government meant control over most of the seats in the House of Commons. The generally rising economic prosperity of the eighteenth century, intimately connected with colonial trade and Britain's growing sea power, tied the merchants closely to politics.

The oligarchy was also divided vertically, between those whose lives were passed in the counties and those who congregated in London. This division was more meaningful than any other in the first half of the eighteenth century, and it reflected a political change completed by 1688–89. Before the labels "Whig" and "Tory" came into being, those opposed to monarchic policies were called the "Country party" and those supporting the king were called the "Court party." Thus, before 1688 Whig-Country and Tory-Court were the identifications. Although both invited William III to assume the throne, it was the Whigs rather than the Tories who enjoyed William's confidence. The Tories had been too closely allied with Charles II and too supine toward James II to reap the benefits of their defection from the doctrine of passive obedience to the monarch. The defection caused a crisis of conscience among the Tories, some of them becoming politically neutral, others becoming "Jacobites," favoring the return of James II (Jacobus is the Latin name for James). The commercial connections of the Whigs made them readier supporters than the Tories of William's wars against France. Neither were the Tories in favor of the limited toleration accorded Dissenters.

Under Anne, William's successor, the Tories had a brief period in office from 1711 to 1714; but after Anne's death an abortive Jacobite rising in 1715 against the succession of the Elector of Hanover as George I discredited Toryism, even those Tories who were not Jacobites. The Tories then became the "Country party" and the Whigs the "Court party"—the former in opposition, the latter in office. The "Court party" comprised the great landowners, including a growing number of peers and many of the upper gentry, officeholders, lawyers, bishops and higher clergy, and the merchants. The "Country party" comprised the "country gentry," those with no more ambition than to dominate their county society and with a new-found distaste for London, and the country parsons. These designations were more realistic than the labels "Whigs" and "Tories," which continued in political currency though with decreasing relevance to political positions in 1688 as the memories of that year grew fainter.

London was the heart of the "Court" oligarchy. It was the site of the king, Parliament, the hierarchy of the Church, the bureaucracy, and the courts of law, as well as the commercial center of Britain. London's four points of power and wealth were its business houses, its coffeehouses (one, Mr. Lloyd's, became the insurance exchange of London and is still a household word: "Lloyd's of London"), its fashionable mansions, and above all its most exclusive club, Parliament. A remarkably free press supplemented gossip and debate in keeping the oligarchy alive to events. Coarse, slummy, filthy, foul from coal smoke, disease-ridden, a horror to 95 per cent of its half-million inhabitants, to the 5 per cent in positions of power in eighteenth-century Britain London was the universe.

PARLIAMENT AND KING

Glorious '88 was above all the victory of Parliament. Little in the settlement trenched specifically on royal power, but no monarch ever after could forget that William III and Mary had received their crowns from Parliament, or that George I (1714–27) had been placed on the throne by an act of Parliament in 1701 that passed over fifty-seven Roman Catholics with a better hereditary claim in order to ensure a Protestant succession. Parliament, holding the purse strings and the last word in keeping a standing army in being, continuously and routinely participated in affairs of state.

The House of Lords, which had about two hundred members, could in fact seldom turn out more than fifty for its meetings. Its prestige was not lessened, but its power had been eroded in the period 1660–88 by the assumption of control by the House of Commons over granting parliamentary revenue. In the Augustan age of oligarchy the Lords did indeed manage the Commons, but did so through the great peers of the "Court party" who exercised control over elections to the lower house. There were 513 members in the Commons for England and Wales; after the union of Scotland with

England to form Great Britain in 1707, there were 45 members for Scotland. Members from England's 40 counties, returning 82 MP's, were elected by all owners of land that produced an income of at least 40 shillings a year. The bulk of the members were elected by towns, however, the narrowest franchise being that of the "rotten borough" of Old Sarum, whose two MP's were returned by no more than three electors, and the broadest being Westminster, adjacent to London, with almost universal male suffrage. Out of a population of between six and seven million only 250,000 had the suffrage.

The extent of the franchise was important only as it affected the price paid by an aristocratic patron to buy the election of an adherent. The most venal constituencies were the "pocket boroughs," whose right of representation was controlled or virtually owned by an individual. Other boroughs held out for high prices, and a few followed a fairly independent line. The county constituencies were thoroughly controlled by the country gentry and comprised the bulwark of the "Country party." Every attempt was made to avoid an election contest, for it was likely to cost both sides heavily in beer and tobacco, pensions and jobs. It was the expense of an election, whether contested or determined by agreement (usually by giving one seat of the constituency to the man promoted by one faction and the other to his opponent) that put the Commons in the hands of the wealthy noble patrons, the Whig oligarchs.

Party as such in Parliament did not exist. The Whig and Tory labels are of no use in analysis. Three broad divisions were discernible: (1) the members of Parliament who were officeholders and pensioners and who always supported the government, no matter who controlled it; (2) the independent country gentlemen at the other extreme; (3) in the center, the political factions, contending for power, but in fact composed of groupings held together by common interests following one or another of the political leaders who contested for power.

From the accession of George I in 1714 to the accession of George III in 1760 three major administrations held office by skilfully manipulating and balancing the competing interests of the members of Parliament. From 1721 to 1742 Sir Robert Walpole as chief minister led Britain in a period of peace and commercial expansion. From 1743 to 1754 Henry Pelham, supported by the patronage manipulations of his brother the Duke of Newcastle, fought the War of the Austrian Succession and weathered a final Jacobite rising in 1745 in Scotland in favor of Prince Charles, grandson of James II. From 1757 to 1761 William Pitt, sustained by Newcastle's patronage though heartily disliked by both that politician and King George II, fought a victorious war for colonies and commerce with France, which ended in 1763 with the loss of France's empire in North America and the triumph of English hegemony in India. (See p. 376.) Although these three administrations were based on venality, each in its time represented

King George I of England,
by Sir Godfrey Kneller
". . . *The King's character may be comprised in very few words. In private life he would have been called an honest blockhead. . . . No man was ever more free from ambition; he loved money, but loved to keep his own, without being rapacious of other men's. . . . [H]e was more properly dull than lazy, and would have been so well contented to have remained in his little town of Hanover, that if the ambition of those about him had not been greater than his own, we should never have seen him in England. . . . Our customs and laws were all mysteries to him, which he neither tried to understand, nor was capable of understanding if he had endeavoured it.*" Lady Mary Wortley Montagu (1689–1762), in ENGLISH HISTORICAL DOCUMENTS (London, 1957), Vol. X. Courtesy of the National Portrait Gallery, London

the best interests of the oligarchy of great noble landowners and London merchant princes.

While Parliament was guarding the oligarchy's interests, the king did not remain neutral. William III, an executive by training and by the necessities of war, intimately and continuously directed his own administration. His successors were Anne (1702–14), a woman of modest attainments; George I (1714–27), a German prince who knew no English and preferred his native Hanover; and George II (1727–60), who though Hanoverian understood the English situation and relied heavily on Walpole, Pelham, and Pitt. These three monarchs were circumspect and realistic. Entrusting their affairs to ministers who were competent politicians, they used royal patronage increasingly to build up a "king's interest" in Parliament. No ministry could survive without the votes of the "king's interest," that is, without the king's confidence. This situation produced a stability in relations between the throne and Parliament that had been absent before 1688. Anne was the last monarch to veto a bill passed by Parliament (in 1707). This indicated not so much the erosion of royal power as the weightiness of the royal influence in Parliament and the identification of successive monarchs with the oligarchy's aspirations. What would happen if either king or Parliament upset the balance remained to be seen.

THE AGRICULTURAL REVOLUTION

The triumph of oligarchy produced economic advances on all fronts because it was above all an oligarchy of wealth. The interest in amassing profit was not hard to understand in the case of merchants. It can be easily overlooked in the case of the landed aristocrats if one fails to realize how recently arrived many of them were, how committed to modern economic methods, and how closely land and trade were linked, despite high-sounding titles and aristocratic pomp and circumstance. Capitalism was not confined to the countinghouses of London. The "improving" landlord who farmed for profit became common. The growing concentration of large estates in fewer hands (a development that originated in the redistribution of land during the 1650's) stimulated the drive for "profit by improvement."

"Improvement" meant first of all demanding higher rents from tenant farmers, a practice which had been constant since Tudor times and which the tenants were powerless to halt. The customary laws of the manor that might have protected the tenant became increasingly feeble as manorialism declined. Rent gouging worked terrible hardships, but it produced a more energetic, productive, and resourceful tenant farmer.

Improvement also meant enclosing the ancient open fields of the medieval manor, consolidating into a single holding the strips held by the individual farmer in the open fields, and eliminating the tenants' rights to graze their cattle and gather firewood on the common and wastelands of the village by enclosing and apportioning them among those with property rights to them. This process had been going on since the fifteenth century, and by 1700 nearly half of the land in cultivation was enclosed. Enclosure created more economical farming units and made possible new practices promoting productivity. This consideration prompted a steady increase in enclosure in the eighteenth century by acts of Parliament. Unlike enclosures by consent, which in the sixteenth and seventeenth centuries had usually been extorted by the landlords and larger farmers, parliamentary enclosure provided some safeguards for small owners. Eighteenth-century enclosure did not wipe out small owners. It did freeze the size of their holdings while increasing the holdings of the larger owners.

There is much evidence that new methods of increasing production, the third facet of improvement, provided agricultural employment for those whom enclosure had dispossessed. The new methods increased profits and wages and provided sustained, year-round employment. Three great improving landlords showed the way: Jethro Tull, Charles Townshend, and Robert Bakewell. Tull (1647–1741) introduced deep plowing, deep sowing, and cultivation to root out weeds. Townshend (1674–1738) after a career in politics retired to farming and on his Norfolk estates perfected crop rotation by the use of turnips and other root crops to restore fertility to the soil. "Turnip" Townshend's methods increased productivity to an important extent, since he planted all his fields every year, whereas under the old system one-third of the fields lay fallow each year. Turnips and clover provided fodder, making it possible to sustain cattle over the winter for slaughter at the most advantageous time. Bakewell (1725–1785) revolutionized stock raising by instituting selective breeding, which improved the strains of sheep, cattle, and horses and produced heavier, less disease-prone beasts than had indiscriminate breeding on common lands.

Dutch and British Oligarchy Beset, 1760–1790

By 1760 the constitutionalist oligarchies of the Dutch Republic and Great Britain for over half a century had things pretty much their own way. For both oligarchies the mid-eighteenth century represented a turning point in their fortunes: in the Netherlands the regental oligarchy was attacked from below, and in Britain the landed and commercial oligarchy was pressed from above and threatened from below.

WILLIAM V OF THE NETHERLANDS AND THE PATRIOTS

William V, hereditary stadholder who had been subject to a regency since his father's death in 1751, came of age in 1766. An ineffectual ruler, he was backward-looking and unimaginative. His viewpoint, traditionally Orangist and pro-English, was reinforced because his mother was the daughter of George II of England; he confessed himself to be "no friend to novelties." He was to see many of them.

Much against William's will, the Statist regents of Holland seized on the American Revolution as a chance to engage in trade and investment at British expense. British attempts to cut off that trade forced them into war with Britain in 1780. The war revived the old Statist-Orangist rivalry and added a new third force in Dutch politics, the Patriots, who were encouraged by the example of the American Revolution. The Patriots were a strange amalgam of landward nobles, Roman Catholics and non-Reformed Protestant sectaries, middle class burghers not of the regental oligarchy, and lower middle class craftsmen. Anti-Orangist because of a strong republican bent and anti-Statist because they meant to dismantle the regental monopoly of Dutch political life, the Patriots at first made common cause with the regents against the Orangists. In the province of Holland in 1782–83 they agitated successfully for a reduction of the stadholder's influence in appointments to town governments. In Utrecht the movement took on a more radical complexion: lower middle class burghers, led by Peter Ondaatje, a redoubtable student orator, forced the town council to accept overseers from the lower middle class to sit with the regents' council. The humiliating peace concluded with Britain in 1784 swelled the ranks of the Patriots, and by

1786 they had gained control of Holland, Groningen, and Overijssel. The movement became increasingly insistent upon the introduction of full democracy in the republic. Its influence crested in 1786 when the States of Holland deposed William V as stadholder of that province and the Utrecht town council was reconstituted by popular election.

The Patriots' radical wing was a paramilitary force called the Free Corps, which in 1787 clashed with William V's troops and threatened civil war. Yet within a matter of months the movement had collapsed, and some thousand Patriots fled in exile abroad, mostly to France. The Patriots fell not before internal reaction but before external force. The French had armed and actively supported the movement because of its anti-British sentiments. The British grasped the opportunity afforded by imminent civil war to promote an expeditionary force of Prussian troops—William V's wife was the sister of Frederick William II of Prussia—and the show of force scattered the Patriots. A mild repression followed, in which the regental oligarchy excluded from power all those suspected of Patriot sympathies and heavily censored the press. The Orangists' and regents' relief at being spared was relatively short-lived. The Patriot movement continued underground, and when French Republican armies invaded the Netherlands during the French Revolution, the Patriots in hiding and those returning with the French army deposed William V in 1795 and established a more representative government than any proposed by the Patriots a decade earlier.

BRITAIN'S "PATRIOT KING": GEORGE III

"Born and educated in England, I glory in the name of Britain, and the peculiar happiness of my life will ever consist in promoting the welfare of a people, whose loyalty and warm affection to me, I consider the greatest and most permanent security of my throne." Thus George III (1760–1820), aged twenty-two, pronounced his patriotism in his first speech to Parliament. These words were the death knell of the administration of the great William Pitt, for George meant to be his own chief minister, to regain the reins of administration, to arrest the tendency of ministers to stand humbler before the Commons than before the king, and to be the "Patriot King" and leader of his people. He had no intention of being an absolute monarch, for he took pride in what he once called "the beauty, excellence, and perfection of the British Constitution"; but his assertion of royal power would end the free-wheeling oligarchism that had been the habit of English politics for over half a century. Moral, courageous, and industrious, George III had a high sense of duty but too little flexibility. His collision with the oligarchy did not bring the settlement of 1688 into question, but it weakened king and oligarchy in the face of new pressures from below.

Pitt was dismissed in 1761, and the Earl of Bute, pompous tutor of George, replaced him. By a more venal use of patronage than any the age had seen, Bute built up an expanded "king's interest" in Parliament. A dreary succession of ministers, alter egos of George-who-would-be-king, dominated the 1760's. The new Tory ministers were a sad lot—incompetent, inexperienced, and unimaginative. They must take the responsibility for failing to cope with the sentiment for independence manifested in the American colonies. However, neither they nor the king can be blamed entirely for the end of the Augustan age of oligarchy. By 1760 there was already a ground swell of resentment that would have major future political implications. The attack was mounted from two divergent quarters, both rooted in the urban middle class, which had become disenchanted with the elegance and dominance of the oligarchy.

JOHN WESLEY AND JOHN WILKES

In the religious reform movement called Methodism, John Wesley (1703–1791) created the tightest-knit organization and most formidable body of opinion in Britain in the last half of the eighteenth century. Methodism was overtly a two-pronged attack on oligarchy: against the luxurious indifference to the work of God on earth exhibited by the Anglican Church, of which Wesley lived and died an ordained minister, and against the luxurious elegance and moral depravity of those of wealth and position who dominated society. Yet Methodism never questioned the validity of the Anglican Church, and it never mounted a political attack on oligarchy or the established institutions of government. Its message to the poor of Britain was to offer them hope for a better life in the next world, not hope for much improvement in this. In this respect Methodism proved a bulwark of the old order. The greater impact of Methodism, however, was destructive of oligarchic monopoly. Wesley's major appeal was directed to the thrifty, hard-working lower middle class, who by force of will and drudgery were fashioning new lives for themselves in the burgeoning industrial economy of Britain. Methodism's anti-intellectualism, mystical message, Biblical fundamentalism, and stress on the sinfulness of the flesh afforded its hundreds of thousands of converts a pride and integrity which, while immunizing them to the blandishments of radical politics, gave them a new cohesiveness and identification.

John Wilkes (1727–1797), rake and rogue, was the antithesis of John Wesley. Many in the lower middle class whom Wesley did not move, Wilkes did. Following an attack on the king in 1763 in his scurrilous weekly *The North Briton,* Wilkes was forced to flee from criminal prosecution because George had him expelled from the House of Commons and thus deprived him of his legal immunity as a member of Parliament. In 1768 he returned, ran for Parliament from Westminster, and was elected, only to be expelled again. Elected twice more by the craftsmen and little shopkeepers in that constituency, the only one in Britain with nearly universal male suffrage, Wilkes became the champion of the lower middle class, challenging king and Parliament. Finally, with the never-quiescent London mob marching through the streets shouting "Wilkes and Liberty" and the metropolis on the verge of revolt, he was seated in 1774. Though no paragon of virtue, in his long battle to uphold liberty he had exposed parliamentary venality and monarchic influence in the Commons, forced Parliament to allow reporting of its debates, secured legal recognition of the right of the individual not to be arrested on unspecified charges, and awakened a popular concern with the "undoubted rights and liberties of Englishmen" which proved a powerful solvent of oligarchism.

WAVE OF REFORM

Wesley had demonstrated the moral shortcomings of Augustan elegance, and Wilkes had shown its political depravity. Wesley inspired a reform movement within the Anglican Church, Evangelicalism, which through its spokesman in Parliament, William Wilberforce (1759–1833), pressed for legislation abolishing the slave trade and for more humane treatment of natives in Britain's empire. Wilkes inspired a radical political movement of Dissenters who, excluded from office by the Test Act, agitated for universal manhood suffrage and wholesale reform of Parliament. Richard Price, Joseph Priestley (who won fame as a chemist), and John Cartwright were the fathers of British lower middle class radicalism, which in the 1780's moved the more perceptive of the oligarchs to attempt modest reforms in order to stave off unrest and possible rebellion.

The American Revolution was a powerful persuader in the direction of reform. Edmund Burke (1729–1797), a political theorist and practical politician who had sought a settlement of American grievances, later argued for reform of the most glaring inequalities and abuses in the election of members of Parliament. It was an uphill fight, made more difficult by the occupation of London by a mob during a week of anti-Catholic rioting in 1780 (the Gordon riots), an episode hardly likely to inspire confidence in the political stability of the masses. The unrest in Ireland that followed the American Revolution brought home to the oligarchy as nothing else could have the necessity for change. Burke, who was himself an Irishman, urged concessions to Irish demands and the most sweeping reforms, including allowing Irish Catholics to vote and hold office. In 1782 Burke and the parliamentary faction of Lord Rockingham, of which he was a leading member, had their opportunity when George III reluctantly called Rockingham to form a ministry to end the war with America.

In three short months in office, ending with Rockingham's death, this reform administration made a just and honorable peace with the American colonies and introduced and drove through Parliament legislation barring government contractors from Parliament and reforming the worst abuses of the patronage system. Concessions to Ireland were made, culminating in an act making the Irish Parliament autonomous and independent from the direct royal control that had subverted its authority for three centuries.

WILLIAM PITT THE YOUNGER

With Rockingham's death in July, 1782, George III managed to pull down his ministry. He could not, however, replace it with another inept, rubber-stamp ministry to enable himself to play prime minister. In December, 1783, after a series of coalition ministries he called William Pitt, twenty-four-year-old son of the great William Pitt, to form a ministry. Ambitious but honest, adroit, and courageous, young Pitt enjoyed the king's support and the good will of the trading interests of London. He slowly but surely fashioned a following in the Commons by prodigal use of patronage and swamped the old landed aristocracy in the Lords by persuading the king to create almost a hundred new peers, many of them London businessmen. Determined upon economic and fiscal reform, Pitt reduced tariffs, introduced modern budgetary practices into government finance, and began a reduction of the public debt. He encouraged trade with the United States and reorganized the East India Company's government of India, preserving the company's power but purging its administration of the abundant invitations to corruption that marred its governance in the previous decades. Pitt made a half-hearted stab at parliamentary reform and the abolition of the slave trade, in which he assumed the mantle of Burke and Wilberforce while lacking their commitment and zeal. William Pitt was not a reformer; he was an astute politician who intended to remain in power while introducing sound administrative practices, encouraging commercial prosperity, and making government fiscally solvent.

Pitt's first ministry lasted from 1783 to 1801—the longest since Walpole's. His major domestic accomplishments were almost wholly confined to the first decade of the ministry; the second decade was dominated by the French Revolution and the war against France, in which Pitt and Britain played a major role in the coalition of European powers to check the spreading "contagion" of republicanism. The French Revolution's repercussions in Britain were immediate and disquieting. Tom Paine's *Rights of Man*, published in 1791 and 1792, appealed to the British to overthrow monarchy and organize a republic, striking a responsive note in the radical underground. Pitt took strong repressive measures against radical agitation. There were, in fact, few radicals; Wesley's political conservatism proved more influential among the loom operators, weavers, miners, and cobblers. Burke's attack in 1790 on the Revolution, with its grim prophecy of violence, helped to disabuse intellectuals who had been inclined to greet the Revolution as the dawn of a new day for representative government and political liberty.

The French Revolution's excesses, manifest by 1792, discredited reform in Britain. The oligarchy was given a respite. Pitt's two decades in office at a critical juncture in the challenge to the old order by the still inchoate new order can be superficially seen as a reactionary resistance to change. In fact, however, Pitt made a notable contribution to the transformation. He re-established the good name of Parliament which had fallen into odium during George III's essay into parliamentary leadership. He trained an extraordinarily able group of young ministers who in the next generation would effect reforms that he himself could not accept. He forged groups of disparate "interests" in Parliament into something like a party and thereby pointed the way to the parliamentary practice of the nineteenth century. His commitment to good government, sound financing, and a burgeoning economy brought a new spirit to government that helped to make nineteenth-century administration more honest and more effective than any the nation had known before. Above all, by conditioning the oligarchy to face change and by diluting the oligarchy with new money and new men, William Pitt contributed to the stability with which English constitutionalism would accommodate the press for democracy in the nineteenth century.

CHAPTER FIFTEEN

Wealth, War, and Empire

In *Leviathan* Thomas Hobbes described the conduct of nations toward each other in these words: "Kings, and persons of sovereign authority, because of their independency, are in continual jealousies, and in the state and posture of gladiators; having their weapons pointing, and their eyes fixed on one another; that is, their forts, garrisons, and guns upon the frontiers of their kingdoms; and continual spies upon their neighbours; which is the posture of war." Each state utilized all the means at its disposal—diplomatic, military, and economic—in pursuit of survival and aggrandizement. Economic rivalry increasingly became a cause of international tension, much as religious disputes had earlier done in Europe. During times of peace nations thought of trade as unarmed warfare between rivals, and they did not hesitate to resort to armed conflict in order to strengthen their own trading position or to cripple and destroy that of their competitors.

Power and Plenty: The Policies of Economic Nationalism

The economic policies of nation-states in the early modern period had a dual purpose: to build up economic power to strengthen the state, and to use the power of the state to promote economic growth and enrich the nation. In the words of Sir Josiah Child, British merchant and politician of the late seventeenth century, "power and plenty ought jointly to be considered." These aims and the measures the states took to achieve them are customarily lumped under the label "mercantilism," a word coined in the latter part of the eighteenth century by Adam Smith, Scottish economist and critic of economic nationalism.

In pursuit of their dual objectives policy makers had to deal with the conflicting desires of both their own subjects and rival nation-states. In medieval times municipalities and other local government units had possessed extensive powers of economic control and regulation. They levied tolls or tariffs on goods entering and leaving their jurisdictions. Local gilds of merchants or artisans fixed wages and prices and otherwise regulated the conditions of life and work. The policies of economic nationalism represented a transfer of these functions from the local to the national level, where the central government attempted to create a state that was unified economically as well as politically.

At the same time that they were seeking to impose economic and political unity on their subjects, the rulers of nation-states were engaged in aggressive competition with one another for extension of territory and control of overseas possessions and trade. They did so partly to make their countries self-sufficient in war, and the very attempt to gain more territory or trade at the expense of others often led to war. Thus economic nationalism aggravated the antagonisms engendered by political rivalry among the rulers of Europe.

CHARACTERISTIC POLICIES

Nations sought to accumulate stores of gold and silver in the belief that a plentiful supply of money would alone stimulate trade and finance war. Since few European countries had mines producing gold and silver, the acquisition of colonies that possessed them was a major goal of exploration and colonization. The colonies of France, England, and Holland produced very little gold or silver, so that the only way for these countries to obtain supplies of the precious metals (apart from conquest and piracy, to which they also resorted) was through trade.

If a country sold more than it purchased abroad, it was thought to have a "favorable balance of trade" because it could take the difference in bullion. Ideally, according to this theory, a country should only sell and should purchase nothing abroad. Practically, however, no state could do so, and the questions arose: what to export and what to import? Because of the high incidence of poor harvests and periodic famines, countries sought plentiful domestic supplies of grain and other foodstuffs and usually prohibited export of all but the surplus. At the same time they encouraged

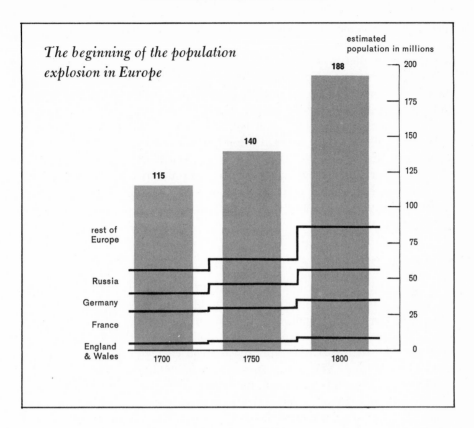

The beginning of the population explosion in Europe

estimated population in millions

manufactures, not only to have something to sell abroad but also to further self-sufficiency by broadening the range of their own production.

In order to encourage domestic manufactures, foreign manufactures were excluded or forced to pay high protective tariffs. Export of domestic manufactures was subsidized. Colbert issued elaborate regulations governing the quality of French manufactures to enhance their reputation. Sumptuary laws (laws governing consumption) attempted to restrict the consumption of foreign merchandise and to promote that of domestic manufactures.

Large merchant navies were valued highly because they earned money from foreigners by providing them with shipping services and because they encouraged domestic exports by providing cheap transport. Moreover, the chief difference between a merchant ship and a warship was the number of guns it carried, so that a large merchant fleet could be quickly converted to a navy in case of war. Most nations had "navigation laws," which restricted the carriage of imports and exports to native ships and in other ways promoted the merchant marine. Governments also encouraged fisheries as a means of training seamen and stimulating the shipbuilding industry, as well as of making the nation more self-sufficient in food supply and furnishing a commodity for export. The extensive herring fisheries of the Dutch were a prime example. Underlying the emphasis on merchant marines was the notion that there existed a fixed and definite volume of international trade. According to Colbert, all the trade of Europe was carried by twenty thousand ships, of which more than three-fourths belonged to the Dutch. Colbert reasoned that France could increase its share only by decreasing that of the Dutch, an objective for which he was prepared to make war.

Theorists of all nations stressed the importance of colonial possessions as an element of national wealth and power. Even if colonies did not have gold and silver mines, they might produce goods not available in the mother country, which could be used at home or sold abroad. The spices of the Orient, the sugar and rum of the West Indies, and the tobacco of Virginia served such purposes.

NATIONAL DIFFERENCES IN ECONOMIC POLICY

Despite similarities, each nation had distinctive economic policies derived from peculiarities of local and national tradition, geographic circumstance, and possibly most important, the character of the state itself. Advocates of economic nationalism claimed that their policies were designed to benefit the state. But what was the state? It varied in character from the absolute monarchies of Louis XIV and most other Continental powers to the burgher republics of the Dutch, the Swiss, and the Hanseatic cities. In no case did all or even a majority of the inhabitants participate in the process of government. Since the nationalism of the early nation-states rested on a class, not a mass, basis, the key to national differences in economic policy should be sought in the differing composition of the ruling classes.

In France and other absolute monarchies the wishes of the sovereign were paramount. Although few absolute monarchs had much understanding or appreciation of economic matters they were accustomed to having their orders obeyed. The day-to-day administration of affairs was carried out by ministers and lesser officials, who were hardly more familiar with the problems of industrial technology and commercial enterprise and reflected the values and attitudes of their master. Elaborate regulations for the conduct of industry and trade added to the cost and frustration of doing business and encouraged evasion. According to legend, after one of Colbert's successors had outlined a program of new and expanded trade regulations to a delegation of influential French merchants, he asked what more he might do for them. They replied, *"Laissez nous faire"* (let us alone). On large issues absolute monarchs often sacrificed both the economic welfare of their subjects and the economic foundations of their own power as a result of their ignorance and lack of concern. Thus, in spite of its great empire the government of Spain continually overspent its income, hamstrung its merchants, and steadily declined in power. Even France under

The Royal Exchange, London, by J. Chapman

"Nor is trade itself in England, as it generally is in other countries, the meanest thing men can turn their hand to; but, on the contrary, trade is the readiest way for men to raise their fortunes and families. . . . [A]n estate's a pond, but trade's a spring: the first, if it keeps full . . . it is well, and it is all that is expected; but the other is an inexhausted current, which not only fills the pond and keeps it full, but is continually running over, and fills all the lower ponds and places about it." Daniel Defoe, THE COMPLETE ENGLISH TRADESMAN (1745), reprinted in THE NOVELS AND MISCELLANEOUS WORKS OF DEFOE (Oxford, 1841), Vol. XVII.

From an original print in Guildhall Library, London

Louis XIV, the most populous and powerful nation in Europe, could not easily support the continued drain of its wealth for the prosecution of Louis's territorial ambitions and the maintenance of his court. When he died, France hovered on the verge of national bankruptcy.

The United Netherlands, governed by and for the wealthy merchants who controlled the principal cities, followed a more informed economic policy. Living principally by trade, it could not afford the restrictive, protectionist policies of its larger neighbors. It established free trade at home, welcoming to its ports and markets the merchants of all nations. On the other hand, in the Dutch empire the monopoly of the Dutch traders was absolute.

England lay somewhere near the center of the spectrum. The landed aristocracy had been recruited primarily from recently risen merchants and mercantile-connected lawyers and officials, and great merchants had long taken a prominent part in government and politics. After the revolution of 1688–89 their representatives in Parliament held ultimate power in the state. The laws and regulations that they made concerning the economy reflected a balance of interests, benefiting the landed and agricultural resources of the landowners while they encouraged domestic manufactures and assisted shipping and trading interests. The most distinctive feature of England's economic policy was the relative freedom from restrictive legislation enjoyed by its merchants and manufacturers. This freedom, together with favorable commercial legislation (such as giving the business customs of merchants the force of law) and stimulation of foreign and colonial commerce, enabled them to lay the basis for subsequent rapid economic progress.

Europe Overseas: Colonies and Commerce

During their overseas expansion Europeans possessed two advantages that facilitated their conquest and subjugation of alien peoples. They had a superior technology—ships and navigational techniques, gunpowder and firearms, tools and techniques of production which enabled them to reproduce in strange and sometimes hostile environments the material features of European life. Psychologically they had the advantage of believing firmly in their own moral superiority because of their Christian faith. Whether Protestant or Catholic, they felt that God had given them license to conquer, to massacre if necessary, to destroy civilizations, and to subject whole races to slavery.

The Europeans also knew what they wanted. They were purposeful and prepared in the fashion of a businessman or an engineer, whereas the peoples with whom they came into contact were for the most part psychologically unprepared, organizationally weak, and subject to divided counsels. Among the world's great cultures only the Chinese and Japanese, who themselves had strong feelings of moral superiority, were able to withstand the European onslaught. In short, Europeans brought to the task of conquering and exploiting the world the zeal of the crusader, the rapacity of the warrior, and the shrewdness of the merchant.

THE SPANISH AND PORTUGUESE EMPIRES

The way in which colonies were governed differed from country to country. The Spanish regarded their empire essentially as a source of precious metals and as an extension of Spain. Spanish institutions, such as the "latifundia" or great estates that had existed in Spain from Roman times, were transplanted to the New World. The Inquisition was carried overseas. The Spanish followed a very restrictive colonial policy, controlling immigration (for example, no "heretics" or non-Catholics were allowed to immigrate) and regulating trade minutely. Little intracolonial trade was allowed, and practically no trade was permitted between the colonies and foreign powers. Trade between Spain and its empire became the monopoly of a privileged group of merchants enjoying royal favor. Spain and its colonies did not progress economically in the seventeenth and eighteenth centuries, as did its rivals.

The Portuguese Empire in the East was at first exploited as a royal monopoly for the benefit of the king and his favorites. In the years from 1580 to 1640, when Portugal was under Spanish rule, the Portuguese lost the greater part of their overseas possessions to the Dutch. After winning back their independence, the Portuguese regained their Brazilian empire and re-established control over colonial trade in a manner similar to Spain's; and like Spain, Portugal and its empire failed to progress economically.

THE DUTCH

Spain and Portugal had seized the most lucrative and attractive overseas dominions early in the sixteenth century and excluded other Europeans by force of arms. Adventurers from other lands sought new routes to the Orient through Arctic seas, hoping to discover a northeast or northwest passage to China and Japan, but their efforts proved fruitless. The Dutch, however, had little reason to complain, for the Netherlands held a privileged position in the Spanish Empire. The Dutch and the neighboring Flemings reaped a large share of the profits of colonial trade by supplying Spanish and Portuguese colonial merchants with manufactured goods and distributing colonial produce in Northern Europe.

The Dutch war for independence in the late sixteenth century interrupted commercial relations between the northern Netherlands and Spain. The Dutch continued to trade with the Portuguese Empire via Lisbon, but in 1592 after an abortive Portuguese revolt against Spain the Spanish authorities closed the port of Lisbon to Dutch ships. Heavily dependent upon maritime commerce, the Dutch immediately began building ocean-going ships capable of the months-long voyage around South Africa to the Indian Ocean. So successful were these early voyages that in 1602 the government of the United Provinces, the city of Amsterdam, and several private trading companies formed the Dutch East India Company with a legal monopoly of trade between the Indies and the Netherlands.

Taking advantage of the weakness of Portugal under Spanish rule, the Dutch East India Company expelled both the Portuguese and English interlopers from the fabulous Spice Islands and Ceylon. The Dutch had too few people to undertake large-scale colonization, so they set up strongly fortified trading posts, made treaties with the native rulers, and strictly controlled the export of spices to Europe. From their bases in the East Indies and Ceylon they carried on trade with Japan, Formosa, the China

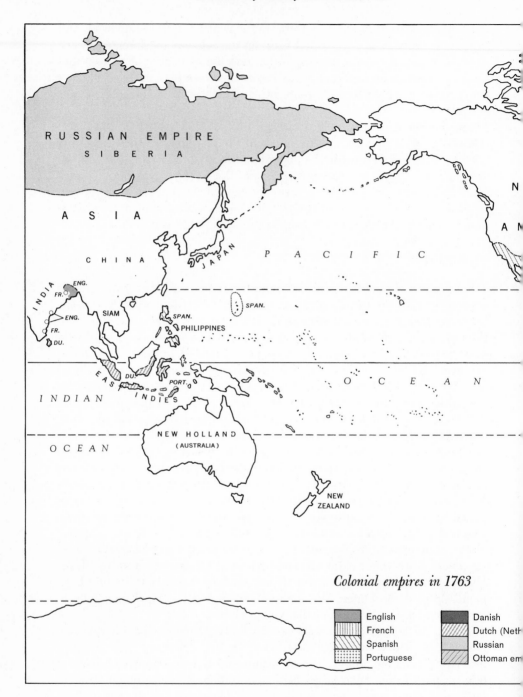

Colonial empires in 1763

English		Danish
French		Dutch (Neth
Spanish		Russian
Portuguese		Ottoman em

coast, and India and settled a few colonists at the Cape of Good Hope to maintain a victualing station. The Dutch in the Indies followed a policy of monopoly and strict exclusion of both foreigners and Dutch traders who were not members of the East India Company. The Company was a government within a government with nearly unlimited sovereignty in the Indies.

In the Western Hemisphere Brazil, a possession of the Portuguese crown, tempted Dutch adventurers. Again taking advantage of the weakness of Portugal, the Dutch established colonies on the Brazilian coast in 1624 and attempted to take control of the entire area. They failed to reckon with the Portuguese colonists in Brazil itself, who were resentful of Dutch intrusion and expelled the new settlers from all but one province in the north (Surinam or Dutch Guiana) and a few islands in the Caribbean.

In the same year in which the Dutch inaugurated their attempt to colonize Brazil another group of Dutch settlers founded the city of New Amsterdam on the southern tip of Manhattan Island. Dutch claims in the area dated from the voyages of Henry Hudson, an Englishman sailing under Dutch auspices at the beginning of the seventeenth century. The Dutch laid claim to the entire Hudson Valley and surrounding areas, founded Fort Orange (Albany), and under the patroon system of land ownership established families such as the Rensselaers and Roosevelts who were destined to play a great role in the history of the United States.

ORIGINS OF THE FRENCH EMPIRE

At the beginning of the sixteenth century the French took an active interest in the exploration of North America, especially in the vicinity of the St. Lawrence River, which they hoped would prove to be the long-sought northwest passage to the Orient. Early attempts at settlement in the area failed, and in the second half of the century religious warfare and dynastic strife inhibited further efforts. After the re-establishment of strong government under Henry IV and Richelieu the French embarked on an ambitious program of conquest and colonization. Almost simultaneously they undertook trading expeditions to India, participated in the Dutch attempt to take over Brazil, seized West Indian islands from Spain, and made extensive explorations and some settlements in North America. In 1608 they established their first permanent base in North America at Quebec and named the surrounding area New France. They explored the entire basin of the Great Lakes and in the second half of the century extended their explorations to the Mississippi Valley.

In spite of their great effort and many substantial achievements, French colonial enterprise made little progress in the seventeenth century. The French colonies suffered simultaneously from excessive paternalism and inadequate support, the latter due in part to the magnitude of the French effort, but even more to the government's preoccupation with Continental affairs. As late as 1660, half a century after the first settlement, all Canada contained only 2,500 colonists, a fraction of the number of Frenchmen in the few sugar islands of the West Indies.

BEGINNINGS OF THE ENGLISH COLONIAL EMPIRE

The English made an early attempt at exploration and discovery under the Cabots at the turn of the fifteenth century, but the results of the mission were not promising for its mercantile supporters. What little overseas expansion the English undertook was for trade rather than for empire, and in the first half of the sixteenth century they were preoccupied with dynastic, diplomatic, and domestic problems. In the second half of the century interest in overseas trade and settlement revived, heightened in the last decade of the century by the publicist Richard Hakluyt's stirring accounts of voyages of exploration. The voyage of Richard Chancellor and Hugh Willoughby in 1553 through arctic waters into the White Sea was a failure as far as discovering a northeast passage to the Orient was concerned (as were subsequent attempts to find a northwest passage), but it resulted in the establishment of trade relations with the growing Russian Empire and, through it, with the Middle East. The experience led to the formation of large chartered companies, each endowed with a legal monopoly of trade with a particular area, such as the Muscovy Company, the Levant Company, and the East India Company. Under Elizabeth I daring sea captains made privateering raids on Spanish ships and colonies in the New World. One of these captains, Sir Francis Drake, after raiding Spanish colonies on the west coast of South America sailed up the coast of California, crossed the Pacific, and returned to England in 1580 by way of the Indian and Atlantic Oceans, the second circumnavigation of the globe.

Two brief attempts by Englishmen to found settlement colonies in North America during the reign of Elizabeth ended in failure, but in the first half of the seventeenth century England established successful colonies in Virginia (1607), New England (1620), and Maryland (1632), as well as on islands in the West Indies. The English colonies differed from those of other countries in that they were founded primarily under private rather than governmental auspices, although in most cases the founders obtained governmental authorization. They also originated from a variety of motives. The Virginia settlement, for example, was promoted by a company of London merchants and financiers as a commercial enterprise. After the settlers failed to discover gold or other readily exportable commodities, the settlement's future looked bleak until the introduction of tobacco cultivation in 1612. The Pilgrims were separatist puritans who after a brief sojourn in Holland, where they sought religious freedom, emigrated to America in 1620 in order to preserve both their English nationality and their religious independence. Boston was settled by puritans in 1630 and grew rapidly as a result

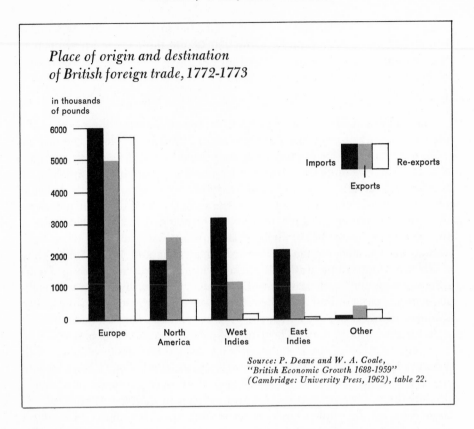

Place of origin and destination of British foreign trade, 1772-1773

in thousands
of pounds

Imports   Exports   Re-exports

Europe   North America   West Indies   East Indies   Other

Source: P. Deane and W. A. Coale,
"British Economic Growth 1688-1959"
(Cambridge: University Press, 1962), table 22.

of Archbishop Laud's persecution of puritans in England during the 1630's. Maryland represented a blend of religious and economic motives: the Calvert family obtained a royal grant for pecuniary gain but also used the colony as a haven for their Catholic coreligionists.

Although the English-speaking population of North America was no greater than 100,000 in 1660, important traditions had already been established which have exerted a profound influence on the subsequent history of the continent. One of the most important was the pluralism (including religious pluralism) inherent in the mode and places of settlement—a variety induced by the exigencies of a difficult new environment. Other traditions were a strong desire for individual liberty and the wide latitude permitted individual initiative and enterprise, tempered by the necessity for collective agreement and action exemplified by the Mayflower Compact. In 1619 the first representative assembly in the Western Hemisphere met in Jamestown, Virginia, establishing a precedent that has contributed vitally to both the moral and material strength of America. In the same year another, less happy precedent was established in the same colony: the introduction of the first Negro slaves.

Dynastic and Imperial Statecraft, 1700–1763

Dynasticism was the escalation into national policy of the tendency of an absolute monarch to consider his realm as the patrimony or hereditary endowment of his dynasty, and to view his dynasty's interests as distinct from and paramount to the interests of his subjects. According to this view, the monarch's kingdom and his subjects served merely to increase the power and glory of his family. Narrow considerations of dynastic interest often gave form and content to relations among the states of Europe. Marriage alliances between the royal houses and treaties and agreements establishing rights of succession were the staple of diplomatic activity and the fountain of war. War was primarily a means to assert a claim to territory based upon rights of marriage or succession. A marriage between two houses would in an instant ally two powers; the birth of an heir to such a marriage might result in the eventual union of the two powers. Either situation could provide a sudden, enormous accretion of wealth, territory, and population to an aggressive monarch. Almost in a matter of days the whole power structure of Europe might be drastically changed.

The fluidity created in international relations by dynasticism provoked a form of reaction: the balance of power. European monarchs could hardly question the universally recognized legal rights and benefits of marriage and succession. They could and did demand that the exercise of those rights and the settling of those benefits not result in so large and sudden an accretion of power to any one monarch that the power structure of Europe was unrecognizably changed and the balance of the powers upset. They formed coalitions strong enough militarily to outweigh the monarch who threatened to become too powerful. Two avenues for redressing the balance were open to the coalition: it might compel assurances that a marriage and potential succession would never result in the union of two crowns, or it might exact a cession of territory to another less formidable power in return for international recognition of the territory acquired by dynastic policy. The inherent difficulties of getting together a coalition in the face of a threat meant that the balance of power seldom worked effectively until the aggressor had made considerable headway. It always depended upon the intervention of one or two major powers whose concern stemmed less from a commitment to the balance of power than from their own dynastic ambitions.

PATTERNS OF WAR, 1651–1697

War was the logical extension of diplomacy. It served as the instrument both of dynastic aggression and of the balance of power summoned to contain it. The balance of power was not intended to preserve peace so much as to make war only moderately profitable to the victor and not crushing to the vanquished. In the late seventeenth and first half of the eighteenth centuries war involved almost all European powers; it was fought on many fronts (including the colonies); it demanded heavier expenditures on more ornate fortifications, increased fire power, improved supplies, larger armies of better-paid troops, bigger fleets of grander ships, and more guns; and destruction of enemy commerce was accepted as a prime strategy of maritime belligerents.

The wars of Western European powers in the second half of the seventeenth century were usually three-cornered affairs, involving the Dutch, French, and English, with incidental participation by other powers. The conflict between the English and Dutch in the mid-seventeenth century was the first almost wholly commercial war. In 1651 the English Parliament passed a navigation act forbidding the importation into England of any goods except those transported in English ships or ships of the nation producing the goods. Aimed directly at the Dutch carrying trade, the law provoked a maritime war that lasted two years. The war gave such an impulse to English commercial expansion that in the next few years England took the first steps toward becoming a Mediterranean naval power, became a commercial rival to the Dutch in the Baltic, and emerged as a commercial carrier of the first rank. The challenge of England's expansion coupled with the failure of the Dutch to regain a foothold in Brazil in the war with Portugal in 1657–61 signaled the approaching end of Dutch commercial primacy and assured the loss of the most important of their colonies in the Western Hemisphere.

In 1664 the English seized New Amsterdam from the Dutch, named it New York, and inaugurated the second Anglo-Dutch War (1665–67), in which France and Denmark joined the Dutch. In 1667 Louis XIV invaded the Spanish Netherlands to begin the short War of Devolution. To meet this greater threat, the English and the Dutch made peace—the Dutch recognizing the English conquest of New York—and in 1668 they formed with Sweden a triple alliance directed against Louis. The French quickly agreed to peace. Louis then bought off Charles II of England and in 1672 opened an aggressive war upon Holland, which lasted until 1679 and brought most of France's traditional dynastic enemies together on the Dutch side. (See pp. 271–272.)

The War of the League of Augsburg (1688–97) was transitional from the seventeenth-century pattern of war to that of the eighteenth century. It began when Louis XIV laid claim to the Rhineland Palatinate on dynastic grounds. This evoked a counter-response from the Protestant powers, the Holy Roman Emperor, and Spain, the latter fearful of Louis's intentions toward the Spanish Netherlands. The war had a new dimension in that it combined operations—maritime and military, continental and colonial—which foreshadowed all eighteenth-century dynastic and imperial warfare. French sea power enabled the deposed James II of England and a French army to open a front in Ireland against William III, newly crowned king of England. English naval power prevented further French troops from reaching Ireland, however, and at the Battle of the Boyne in 1690 William led his troops to victory over James's army. An Anglo-Dutch naval victory off La Hogue, France, in 1692 ended a projected invasion of England and swept the French fleet from the sea. In North America French Canadian colonists and New Englanders fought one another in what they called King William's War, marked by attacks on frontier strong points and raids by Indian allies of the French on isolated towns and farms in Maine and Massachusetts. The cockpit of the war was the Spanish Netherlands and the Rhineland; the battles at sea and the skirmishes in the colonies were peripheral. Yet the periphery was already assuming an importance that would increase, not diminish.

The wars of the last half of the seventeenth century left the Dutch Republic a second-class power with a shrinking empire and a shrinking economy. England, in contrast, experienced a burst of economic enterprise, enlarged its navy and merchant marine, created an effective standing army, added to its colonial possessions, created the Bank of England in 1694 as the financial resource for further colonial and commercial expansion and the reservoir to finance war, and entered the eighteenth century as Europe's foremost maritime power and leading contender for empire. France's dominance on the Continent was shaken but not cracked, and France remained a power of the first rank. In the rivalry between the two great Western powers England held an advantage. England's navy had grown as France's had diminished; and unlike France, which had been drained by three decades of costly land wars, England had the economic wherewithal to meet the price of war on three fronts—the Continent, the colonies, and the sea.

THE WAR OF THE SPANISH SUCCESSION, 1701–1714

The Treaty of Ryswick in 1697, ending the War of the League of Augsburg, marked a setback for the ambitions of Louis XIV. His expansionism had been effectively checked by the operation of the balance of power both on the battlefield and at the peace table. The Sun King's last war, only four years after Ryswick, resulted from Louis's taking advantage of the last opportunity left him for extension of his power in Europe: to place his grandson on the Spanish throne.

The succession to the Spanish throne was the type of dynastic issue certain to provoke an international crisis. Charles II of Spain was a childless invalid, so that the Spanish Hapsburg line faced certain extinction. In anticipation of this event Louis XIV had long plotted to make the throne of Spain part of the Bourbon patrimony, claiming it for his family through his mother and his wife, both of whom were daughters of Spanish kings. He was not the only claimant. Both the mother and the first wife of Emperor Leopold of Austria were daughters of Spanish kings, and Leopold demanded that Spain become part of the patrimony of his house, the Austrian Hapsburgs.

The other European powers were understandably disturbed at the prospect of the union of the Spanish Empire—including Spain, the Spanish Netherlands, Spain's Italian possessions, and her overseas empire—with either Austria or France. The Spanish succession became the subject of diplomatic negotiations and treaties proposing the partition of the empire among the Bourbon and Hapsburg claimants. Charles refused to consider splitting up his realm, and in 1698 he named Emperor Leopold's grandson, the seven-year-old Electoral Prince Joseph Ferdinand of Bavaria, as his sole heir. A few months later the boy died, and new intrigues and new plans for partition got under way. Driven to distraction, Charles in October, 1700, signed a new will naming Philip of Anjou, second grandson of Louis XIV, to succeed him. Soon thereafter Charles died.

The news of the choice of a Bourbon heir aroused much excitement and war talk in the courts of Europe. Louis hastened to give assurance that the thrones of Spain and France would never be held by the same person, and it seemed as if war could be averted. Then by a series of diplomatic blunders Louis destroyed the hopes for peace. He declared that Philip of Anjou, now Philip V of Spain, and his descendants still had rights to the succession to the French crown, sent French troops into the Spanish possessions in the Netherlands and Italy, and broke a promise he had given in the Treaty of Ryswick by recognizing the son of the deposed James II of England as rightful king of England. These acts were too much for the other powers. On May 15, 1702, England, Holland, and Austria declared war on France and Spain; the allies were eventually joined by Prussia and other German states, Portugal, Denmark, and Savoy.

The troops and ships of the allies far outnumbered those of Louis, and in Prince Eugene of Savoy, French-born commander of the Austrian forces, and John Churchill, first Duke of Marlborough (and ancestor of Winston Churchill), they had two of the greatest generals of modern times. After a bad start the allies rolled up a series of major victories—Blenheim (1704), Ramillies and Turin (1706), Oudenarde (1708), and Malplaquet (1709). They pushed into Spain, drove out Philip, and put Charles, second son of Emperor Leopold, on the throne.

The principal front of the war was the Spanish Netherlands and Germany. There was only one major sea fight. The English and Dutch fleets kept French and Spanish shipping off the seas while they freely transported their own troops and supplies. After the French fleet at Toulon had scuttled itself for fear of capture, the Mediterranean became an English ocean; from Gibraltar (taken in 1704) and Minorca (taken in 1708) the English fleet commanded the whole of that ancient sea. The war in North America, called Queen Anne's War after William III's successor, was an adjunct to the

European struggle. It was both more intense and more extensive than King William's War. After two unsuccessful attempts British colonial forces finally captured the French base at Port Royal, Nova Scotia, as a result of their superior sea power; but two English attempts to loosen French control of the St. Lawrence River failed, and French raids on Newfoundland stung English pride. The war in North America was not decisive for either side.

The allies' invasion of France in 1708 moved Louis to sue for peace. His overtures were spurned by the allies, who were intent upon humbling the Grand Monarch. Louis seemed ready to yield, when in an incredible outburst of national pride and cohesiveness his subjects rallied around him and reinvigorated the French war effort. In 1712 the army of this seemingly defeated nation won its one great victory of the war at Denain in northern France. In Spain, too, the people had taken up the cause of the French, and aided by French troops, they restored the Spanish throne to the Bourbons.

These amazing reversals made the allies view the peace proposals with more interest. Meanwhile, a political change in England in 1710, when a Tory government pledged to end the war came into power, foreshadowed the withdrawal of England. Negotiations were resumed, and after long parleys France signed separate peace treaties with all her enemies except Austria on March 31, 1713, at Utrecht, and with Austria on March 6, 1714, at Rastadt. The chief provisions of the agreements were: (1) Philip of Anjou was recognized as king of Spain, but the separation of the thrones of France and Spain was declared to be inviolable law; (2) Spain ceded Naples, Milan, Sardinia, and the Spanish Netherlands (henceforth the Austrian Netherlands) to Austria, and Gibraltar and Minorca to England; (3) France ceded the Hudson's Bay territory, mainland Nova Scotia, Newfoundland, and St. Kitt's in the West Indies to England; (4) Spain gave the English the exclusive right for the next thirty years to import up to 4,800 slaves a year into Spanish America and to send one trading ship a year with 500 tons of merchandise (later increased to 650 tons). The English agreed to give the Spanish king one-fourth of their profits on the slave trade. This slaving privilege, called the *Asiento* (contract), had been held by the Genoese until 1702 and then by the French.

France came out of the great war much better than it had reason to hope. Louis had succeeded in establishing the Bourbon family on the throne of Spain and managed to retain territories in Europe that he had annexed in earlier wars. Spain had provided the victorious allies with most of their spoils of victory.

THE LONG PEACE, 1714–1740

The peace treaties brought a welcome end to nearly three decades of general war. Coincidentally death made a clean sweep of the generation of kings and statesmen who had been the architects of the wars. New men and a new interest in peace held sway. In France Louis XIV's death in 1715 brought his five-year-old great-grandson Louis XV to the throne under a regency. The succession in 1714 of George I of the German House of Hanover brought a change of dynasty to England. Frederick I of Prussia was succeeded in 1713 by Frederick William I, who, though a renowned militarist, displayed a life-long reluctance to use his troops for more than playing soldiers. In Austria Charles VI became emperor in 1711 and found his new eminence more than adequate consolation for the loss of the Spanish throne that he had held so briefly. In Holland the death in 1720 of the grand pensionary Anthony Heinsius, who had controlled Dutch policy since 1702, made an effective break with the wartime past. Only Philip V, the new Bourbon king of Spain, smarting from the loss of Spanish possessions and spurred on by his second wife Elizabeth Farnese to find an Italian crown for their son Don Carlos, wanted war. In 1717 and 1718 Philip seized Sardinia and then Sicily, only to be forced in 1720 by British naval and French army action to give up his conquests and promise to abandon his Italian claims. The powers did not want a general war.

Peace was assured for a time by a remarkable alliance between Great Britain and France to preserve the balance of power. The alliance was joined by the Dutch in 1717 and by Austria in 1718, after which it was called the Quadruple Alliance. Until 1733 the alliance worked effectively, owing in part to the willingness of the powers to cooperate in settling crises raised by Elizabeth Farnese's continual machinations on behalf of Don Carlos, and in part to the interest of the British chief minister Robert Walpole (1721–42) and his French counterpart Cardinal Fleury (1726–43) in keeping the peace.

A war in 1733–35 between France, Spain, and Savoy on the one hand and Austria on the other over the Polish succession did not become general, primarily because Britain remained neutral. The outbreak of war between Britain and Spain in 1739 was more ominous. In a burst of bellicosity Whig commercial interests in Parliament demanded war with Spain after Robert Jenkins, an obscure English sea captain, displayed before the House of Commons what purported to be his ear, cut off in 1731 by Spanish coast-guards off Havana. Tightened up by Bourbon efficiency, the Spanish colonial administration had been enforcing the *Asiento* clause to the letter, with palpable injury to English smugglers. Over Walpole's vehement objections George II and the Whigs took England into the War of Jenkins's Ear, which merged into the general struggle precipitated in 1740 by the attack of Frederick II of Prussia on the Silesian territory of Austria in defiance of the Pragmatic Sanction that guaranteed the claims of Empress Maria Theresa to all the Austrian possessions. (See p. 284.)

THE WAR OF THE AUSTRIAN SUCCESSION, 1740–1748

Had Frederick not invaded Austria, war would doubtless have broken out anyway. There were three claimants to the Austrian inheritance: Philip V of Spain, Charles Albert of Bavaria, and Augustus III of Saxony. A disputed succession in a major state could result only in a general war. The French—who even before Frederick's attack had decided to intervene on Spain's side in the War of Jenkins's Ear—formed a coalition with Prussia, Spain, Bavaria, and Saxony against Austria, while Britain and Holland allied themselves with beleaguered Austria. The coalition fell apart when in 1742 Frederick concluded a separate peace with Austria in return for Maria Theresa's recognizing his possession of Silesia. When Austria then began to win battles, Frederick, fearing that Maria Theresa would regain Silesia, re-entered the war, forced Austria to reconfirm his right to Silesia, then in 1745 again withdrew.

Britain gave financial aid to Austria but, lacking adequate land forces, was not of much help in the fighting in Europe. However, British military and naval action in the New World and on the high seas offset the reverses in Europe and balanced the scales of war. The fighting in "King George's War," the name given the North American phase of the conflict, was significantly fiercer than earlier colonial struggles. French attacks on Nova Scotia and Massachusetts from the citadel of Louisburg on Cape Breton Island provoked a counterattack by English troops and Massachusetts militia in 1745 in which they captured that great fortress commanding the mouth of the St. Lawrence River. The British fleet was thus afforded unhampered access to the seaway and threatened the very existence of French Canada.

For the first time India became a theater of a European war, albeit a secondary one. The French and English East India companies, which had full political powers within their "factories" or trading stations and were in effect states, did battle with one another. It was a purely commercial warfare, for which each side received only limited governmental assistance. The success of a small British fleet in disrupting French trade in the Indian Ocean moved the French company's governor, Dupleix, to take the English factory at Madras in 1746.

As a result of naval victories by the British admirals Anson and Hawke in the West Indies in 1745, the lucrative French trade with her sugar islands was almost strangled. French privateering (quasi-official commerce raiding) in the Atlantic and Indian Oceans could not balance the heavy commercial losses suffered by France from the British naval blockade and destruction of French shipping. Because these losses raised the specter of the loss of her colonies, they moved France to agree to peace in 1748. Considerations of colonies and commerce had come to dominate the Anglo-French rivalry and even to dictate the Continental policy of France.

The Peace of Aix-la-Chapelle in 1748 was first agreed upon secretly by France, Britain, Spain, and Holland and then reluctantly accepted by Austria. The peacemakers made an effort to return Europe to the balance of power that had been established at the end of the War of the Spanish Succession. They decided on the restitution of all conquests in Europe and overseas, except for Prussia's annexation of Silesia. Maria Theresa and her advisers would have been far happier if the treaty had allowed her to regain Silesia and to give up the Austrian Netherlands, which had been occupied by the French during the war, but her English and Dutch allies demanded that she keep the Austrian Netherlands in the interests of a balance of power. Her right to the Hapsburg patrimony was recognized, although she had to cede three Italian duchies to a Spanish Bourbon prince. The right of the House of Hanover to retain the succession in both its German lands and Great Britain was confirmed.

Aix-la-Chapelle witnessed the emergence of a new great power—Prussia. Frederick's annexation of Silesia doubled Prussia's population and added greatly to its economic resources, while his skill on the battlefield won him the respect of the other powers. The Hapsburgs once again had survived an effort to drive them from their high position and to partition their empire. Now, however, they were faced with a new rival for the domination of Germany. Maria Theresa knew that in order to crush Prussia, she had to win back Silesia; and Frederick was resolved to hold it. Because of the Peace of Aix-la-Chapelle, war in Central Europe was unavoidable. Nor did the peace settle anything for France or Britain except to establish a resolve on either side that the struggle for colonies and commerce must have another, and perhaps final, round.

THE "COLD WAR" OF 1748–1754

Neither the French nor the British governments yet recognized the full implications of their imperial rivalry. But at least one Frenchman and one Englishman did. Joseph François Dupleix, governor of the French East India Company, was in conflict with the company's purely commercial policies and sought to make the French trading stations militarily self-sufficient by raising revenues within the native states and leaguing with the native rulers. From the principal French base at Pondicherry he extended French influence over Indian rulers along much of the southeastern coast of India by supplying his clients with arms and modern military training and unleashing them on neighboring princes who were friendly to the British East India Company. From 1750 until Dupleix's recall to France in 1754 for defiance of company policy, the French and English companies fought each other behind the façade of native rivalries. Dupleix's nemesis, a young official of the English company named Robert Clive, wisely copied

Dupleix's strategy and built up a system of clientage among the native princes while Dupleix's successor dismantled the French system.

Along the West African coast cold war "incidents" between French and English slavers were commonplace. In the West Indies French occupation of neutral islands used as bases by English smugglers resulted in a tense naval confrontation. Far more serious was the French decision to contain the British in Nova Scotia and to close the Ohio country to English settlers pushing westward from Pennsylvania and Virginia. French troops were poured into the Ohio Territory and an arch of forts was constructed from the St. Lawrence to central Illinois. The keystone of the arch was completed in 1754 with the construction of Fort Duquesne at the head of the Ohio River, where Pittsburgh now stands.

The governor of Virginia, the colony that claimed what is now western Pennsylvania and Ohio, dispatched a young Virginia militia colonel to warn off the French at Duquesne. He was rebuffed. On the trek homeward, Colonel George Washington's party met a French patrol, a volley of shots was exchanged, and the French officer in charge was killed. Washington constructed a rude wooden palisade—aptly dubbed Fort Necessity—and stood off a larger French force for some days before surrendering on July 4, 1754. This border incident started the colonial conflict called the French and Indian War, from which in two years would stem the greater European conflict that raged for nearly seven years.

THE SEVEN YEARS' WAR, 1757–1763

The Anglo-French war was fought in a desultory fashion from 1754 to 1757. Formal British infantry tactics in North America were suicidal in the face of French and Indian ambushes, such as that which killed General Braddock in 1755 and routed his forces on their way to attack Fort Duquesne. The British managed only to break the French grip on the perimeter of Nova Scotia. British naval action proved abortive. Yet the French, fighting defensively, scored only one victory—the capture of the prime Mediterranean base of Minorca.

Although a profound change in the alliance system of Europe did not by itself provoke the general war, it determined the sides that would fight it. The Diplomatic Revolution of 1755–56 was a dramatic break with the dynastic past when France and Prussia had been allied against their hated rivals Britain and Austria. In 1755 Britain made an alliance with Russia, sworn enemy of Frederick, to protect George II's Hanover against a possible Prussian attack. Then in 1756 Britain, troubled by reports of overtures for an alliance between its ally Austria and the Hapsburgs' ancient foe France, concluded an agreement with Frederick to oppose the entry of any foreign troops into Germany (the Convention of Westminster). The French and

Austrians were outraged by this betrayal by their respective allies and moved closer to an alliance. The Russians, too, were indignant at Britain's action; they allied with Austria to partition Prussia and reduce it to an insignificant German princedom.

Frederick, well informed of all these supposedly secret negotiations, decided in August, 1756, to take his enemies by surprise and attack Austria's ally Saxony. His aggression plunged Europe in 1757 into seven years of general war, in which France, Austria, Saxony, and Russia were ranged against Prussia and Britain.

Frederick fought an amazing war—eight battles lost, eight won—and his state was dangerously close to annihilation in 1761. To Frederick Britain owed the major debt for a deflection of French arms and effort that enabled the British to wrest an empire from the French. After the accession to power of William Pitt in 1757 Britain supported Prussia on the Continent with huge subsidies while applying the British navy and British troops to stripping France overseas. With Frederick's first major victories on the Continent the stripping began. In 1758 Louisburg, Fort Duquesne (renamed Fort Pitt), and the French slaving stations in West Africa were taken. In 1759—called by the English the year of miracles—the French fleet was destroyed at Quiberon Bay, Wolfe prevailed over Montcalm and Quebec fell, the principal French Caribbean islands were taken, and the French were defeated in India. By the time George III, the new king, sacked Pitt in favor of his Tory favorite in 1761, the imperial victory over France had been assured. France sued for peace.

That France did better in the peace than her performance in the war warranted owed much to the genius of her chief minister, Choiseul, and much to the absence of Pitt, who had fallen from office in 1761. Nonetheless, the Treaty of Paris in 1763 was crushing for France. She lost all her North American possessions except two islands off Newfoundland. Spain ceded Florida to Britain. Britain returned to France all but one of her Caribbean islands. Despite the return of her stations in India, France's power there was destroyed; and in Africa she lost her major slaving stations to the British. Britain had decisively won the struggle for colonies and commerce. Yet in the triumph were sown many of the bitter seeds that would in twenty years cost Britain a large part of its empire, lost not to a foreign power but to British colonists.

The American Revolution, 1763–1783

The revolt of Britain's American colonies was intimately connected with Britain's victory over the French. The colonists had contributed little either in money or in men to the victory. The war had been won by British troops and paid for by British taxes. When it was over the government in London decided that the colonies should bear a larger share of the costs of their government and defense. The efforts of the British to impose taxes on the colonists and systematically collect them met with stubborn resistance and led finally to the widespread belief that the colonies had come of age and should free themselves of their motherland.

THE AMERICAN COLONIES

By 1763 the white population of the colonies was over 1.5 million and was growing rapidly from continuous immigration and a high birth rate. It was still principally of English extraction, but more recent waves of immigration had brought large numbers of German Protestants and Scotch-Irish (Scottish settlers in northern Ireland). Protestantism—Congregational, Presbyterian, Anglican, Quaker, Reformed, and Lutheran—was the majority faith. Literacy was high, newspapers were numerous and avidly read, and the colonies boasted nine colleges of higher learning, producing clergymen, lawyers, physicians, and teachers. The colonial assemblies had grown in importance and power since their beginnings in Virginia in 1619. Compared with other eighteenth-century legislatures, they were broad-based. Although the franchise was limited to property holders, property holding was widespread, especially in the small-farm regions of New England, Pennsylvania, and North Carolina. All but one of the colonies had fairly well-established aristocracies, but they were founded on wealth, not birth or title. The aristocracy of merchant wealth dominated the major urban centers of the colonies: Boston, New York, Philadelphia, Charleston. The landed aristocracy had grown wealthy at the expense of small farmers, but the latter had merely pushed westward to new soil. There was no tenant peasantry except in New York, although in the southern colonies there were 175,000 Negro slaves.

No other bond among the colonies was so impressive as that of their economy. In the first half of the eighteenth century the colonial economy had burgeoned. The iron industry throughout the northern two-thirds of the colonies; shipbuilding in New England; naval stores (spars and masts in New England, pitch, tar, and turpentine in the Carolinas); tobacco, rice, and indigo in the South; and livestock and market produce in the Middle Atlantic colonies and southern New England could compete with the same industries elsewhere in the world in both quality and quantity. A sizable portion of the empire's carrying trade was in the hands of colonial shippers. There was little to hamper trade among the colonies, and the specialization among regions in production and commerce was so complementary as to create an integral colonial economy. For example, the southern plantation colonies depended on the ships of New England to transport their cash crops and to bring in the slaves to produce them, and also on the rum of New England (distilled from West Indian molasses) to purchase slaves in Africa. The colonies were separate political entities, but economically they were closely united.

The colonies also had a common language, a common legal tradition, and common political institutions. The common law of England was the heritage of all the colonies. The abundant litigation of the colonists in scores of courts great and small pressed the law into every man's consciousness, and service on the magisterial bench and jury duty were schools for statecraft and government. The common law provided the framework of the colonial assembly, the political institution common to all the colonies. By virtue of the assembly's power of the purse, it was independent of the governor, who represented the imperial government's interests. The colonists spoke the same language, and they also spoke the same jargon, the language of law, with its notions of "right," "property," and "liberty" and their embodiments in an independent judiciary, trial by jury, and a representative legislature.

Yet on the surface these bonds seemed to count for little. Jealousies among the colonies were many, not the least of which was antagonism over boundaries, especially in the West. Indifference to the problems of neighboring colonies was widespread. The colonies had sprung from different origins, and poor land communications created intense localism. Each colony conceived of its tie with the mother country, three thousand miles away, as more potent and meaningful than its tie with a neighboring colony across a river or a parallel of latitude. To the colonists the mother country was a tolerant or indifferent, basically beneficent, seat of power, imposing commercial laws ostensibly for the benefit of all (readily broken by individuals when it was to their profit), providing protected markets and subsidies for colonial products (though the colonial merchants had no qualms about selling to the highest bidder, even to the enemy in wartime), and affording naval protection (at no cost to the colonies and a good profit to the producers of ships and naval stores). Colonists took pride in the vast British Empire and in the representative Parliament in England that ruled lightly in the interests of an oligarchy with whom the colonial oligarchs had close business ties. There was pride among the colonists because of their identification with Englishmen in the overthrow of despotism in 1688. In 1763, therefore, beyond the routine friction engendered by commercial laws and their haphazard enforcement, the occasional veto of colonial legislation by the Privy Council in England, and the carping of colonial governors about the colonies' unconcern with the pressing problems of empire, there was nothing to hint at the division that would soon overtake the colonies and the mother country. The most apparent safeguard to the imperial tie of each colony was the absence of any sense of common cause with other colonies.

THE PROVOCATIONS

The years 1759–66 changed all this. A series of provocative actions by the home government seemed to threaten the practical autonomy of the colonies. The actions stemmed from a desire by the government both to discourage the widespread illicit trade of the Americans with France, which had gone on in war and peace, and to shift the burden of defense of the colonies to the colonies themselves. In 1759 the Privy Council's power to veto Virginian colonial legislation was made more effective by suspending such legislation until the Council had passed upon it. The independence of the judiciary in New York and New Jersey was restricted in 1761, apparently in the hope that more pliant judges would deal more effectively with smugglers. In the same year broad powers of search were given to customs officers in Massachusetts. In 1763 the home government under George Grenville moved to enforce all the commerce laws by sending warships into American waters to assist the customs service. In the next year the American Act imposed new restrictions on colonial trade and levied taxes in the colonies to support a standing army in America. A newly established admiralty court in Nova Scotia with jurisdiction in sea commerce cases seemed to threaten a basic liberty, since trials for smuggling in that court were to be without jury. Feelings were further aroused by the schemes of the established Church of England to proselytize in New England, the jealously guarded preserve of the puritans' descendants. Boston Congregationalist minister Jonathan Mayhew spoke for many: "Is it not enough, that they persecuted us out of the old world? Will they pursue us into the new to convert us here?"

The Stamp Act of 1765 provoked almost open rebellion in the colonies. The tax, a levy on every printed paper and legal document, raised the thorny question of the authority of the British Parliament to tax colonies. The colonists argued that since they were not represented by members in Parliament, that body could not take away their property by taxation. The London government replied that the colonies were "virtually represented" in Parliament because every member represented the whole empire, not just the constituents who elected him. Collectors of the tax in the colonies were attacked by angry mobs, English goods were boycotted, and unstamped newspapers and legal documents were used without respect for the law. Most significant, nine of the colonies sent delegates to a "congress" in New York to draw up resolutions denying Parliament's power to tax them. What the threat of the French and Indians had never been able to do, the provocation of Parliament had done, at least temporarily—unite the colonies in common cause.

Although the Stamp Act was repealed in 1766, within a year another affront occurred when the home government ordered colonial legislatures to maintain British troops billeted in the colonies. The colonies' recalcitrance resulted in the imposition of duties on tea, glass, paper, and other items by the chancellor of the exchequer, Charles Townshend, and a tightening of the customs service. This led to another convention of colonial representatives in 1768 and the brawl in Boston known as the Boston Massacre in 1770, in which British troops shot down five rioters. After 1770, when the Townshend duties were repealed on all items but tea, an uneasy truce prevailed until a rash of incidents in 1772 resulted in the creation in Boston of the Committee of Correspondence, a resistance organization headed by the volatile Sam Adams. It found its first issue in the granting of a government monopoly to the East India Company to import tea into the colonies. The colonial reaction was the Boston Tea Party in December, 1763, which moved the imperial government to close the Port of Boston, to alter the constitution of Massachusetts and strictly limit the town meetings (the heart of Massachusetts government), and to billet troops in Boston to enforce order. Boston, unrepentant, through its Committee of Correspondence encouraged the creation of similar bodies in other colonies.

The Quebec Act of 1774, which established representative government in that former French colony, gave broad privileges to the Roman Catholic Church, and closed off immigration from New York, Pennsylvania, and Virginia into the Ohio country, made those colonies receptive to the complaints of Massachusetts. In September, 1774, the first Continental Congress met in Philadelphia to resolve that the "English colonists . . . are entitled to a free and exclusive power of legislation in their several provincial legislatures"—a challenge to Parliament's supremacy. Shortly before the scheduled convention of the second Continental Congress, a clash of arms between the Massachusetts militia and British regulars at Lexington Green and Concord Bridge on April 19, 1775, began the War of Independence.

THE WAR

Contrary to almost universal expectations, the revolutionary movement did not collapse. In their challenge to Parliament the colonists had taken the first step toward both the equality of man and republicanism. These notions were merged with the Lockean defense of property and the right to preserve it by rebellion against tyranny in that charter of freedom, the Declaration of Independence, the promise and inspiration of Americans in search of independence.

The war was long and hard. Colonial particularism hampered the war effort. Washington's Continental Army relied upon the unreliable colonial militias. The bold attacks of John Paul Jones's frigates in British waters did not constitute a navy in action. Hit-and-run warfare on land and sea was the only possible strategy for the Americans; formal battles almost always went to the British, and only the mediocrity of British field commanders

The Declaration of Independence, by John Trumbull

"What then is the American, this new man? . . . He is an American, who, leaving behind him all his ancient prejudices and manners, receives new ones from the new mode of life he has embraced, the new government he obeys, and the new rank he holds. . . . Here individuals of all nations are melted into a new race of men, whose labors and posterity will one day cause great changes in the world. . . . The American is a new man, who acts upon new principles; he must therefore entertain new ideas, and form new opinions. From involuntary idleness, servile dependence, penury, and useless labor, he has passed to toils of a very different nature, rewarded by ample subsistence. This is an American." J. H. St. John de Crèvecoeur, LETTERS FROM AN AMERICAN FARMER (1782).

Courtesy of Yale University Art Gallery

prevented disaster for the American cause. The turning point came with the surrender of the British General Burgoyne and his guerrilla-ridden army at Saratoga in 1777. Britain lost her sole chance to cut the colonies in two, and the victory convinced the French to come in on the American side the next year. From that point the old Anglo-French struggle resumed. The French, joined by Spain in 1779, supplied a fleet sufficient to prevent regular supplies from flowing to the British armies; and a sizable force of French regulars and some able field officers gave real substance to the Continental Army. At Yorktown, Virginia, on October 17, 1781, the surrender of Britain's largest American army all but ended the war. For the remaining two years of war Britain effectively defended the rest of her empire against France and Spain.

THE "GREAT EXPERIMENT"

By the Treaty of Paris in 1783 Britain recognized American independence. The new nation's boundaries were drawn at the Canadian border, the Mississippi, and the Florida border, a settlement productive of disputes with both Britain and Spain in years to come. A new nation began its "great experiment," not yet prepared for the union that alone could preserve it, watched wonderingly by the European world, not quite sure of what it had spawned in this first rebellion of European colonists against a mother country. One realization stuck: liberty and the equality of man were no longer mere philosophic abstractions. Frenchmen—both those who like the Marquis de Lafayette and the Comte de Rochambeau had fought in America and the French *philosophes* who were spellbound by Benjamin Franklin in the salons of Paris—saw the great experiment as having direct applicability to France's own political malaise. In January, 1789, a bare six months before the outbreak of the French Revolution, Thomas Jefferson wrote from Paris to an English friend: "Though celebrated writers of this [France] and other countries had already sketched good principles on the subject of government, yet the American War seems first to have awakened the thinking part of this nation in general from the sleep of despotism in which they were sunk." The new world had stepped in, not to "redress the balance of the old" but to help upset it.

CHAPTER SIXTEEN

The Age of Science

THE SEVENTEENTH CENTURY was born in dissonance and disorder, in the clamor of competing faiths, in the continuing confrontation of the most divisive forces the European world had yet unleashed. The Reformation, wars of religion, and the Dutch revolt dominated the late sixteenth century and spilled over into the next. The first half of the seventeenth century sustained its birthright. The Thirty Years' War was a complex of dynastic rivalries, religious hatreds, and power collisions, accompanied or followed by revolutions in Spain, Portugal, England, France, Poland, Naples, and Savoy as well as coups d'état in Holland and Sweden. By mid-century there was a discernible sentiment to achieve harmony and end disorder. It found many outlets during the succeeding decades. The ready acceptance of absolutism in France, Spain, the Hapsburg Empire, many of the German states, Scandinavia, and Italy was an acceptance of order. Although the restoration of Charles II in England was not a triumph of absolutism, it was a victory of the landed and commercial oligarchs whose aim was order. The balance of power was a device of order in the international relations of states. Even in the clashes of arms—and there were many in the latter half of the seventeenth century—order manifested itself in the new naval tactics of the line formation, in the disciplined troops massed in serried ranks, in the splendidly symmetrical designs of Vauban's forts, and in the measured pace of siege warfare.

Nowhere was the search for order more apparent, and nowhere did it leave a richer heritage, than in the realm of the intellect, above all in the labor of scientists during the decades between 1650 and 1720. The word "scientist" should not be taken in the narrow modern sense of a physical scientist, for the scholars of that day comprised a readily identifiable community of intellectuals with interests ranging over the three areas known today as the natural sciences, social sciences, and humanities. They had a profound impact on their own age and an even more profound impact on the next, the Age of the Enlightenment.

The Scientific Community of Intellect

The great breakthrough in science had taken place in the century between the publication in 1543 of Nicholas Copernicus's *Six Books Concerning the Revolution of the Heavenly Spheres* and in 1632 of Galileo Galilei's *Dialogue on the Two Chief Systems of the World*. The next stage in the evolution of modern science produced some men of equal genius and many more of lesser talent. It also provided improved technical apparatus for the experimentation that Sir Francis Bacon had so strongly urged. It saw the growth of official interest in science because of the technological benefits that might be derived from it. For example, much of the stimulus for astronomical and optical investigation stemmed from a desire to make a science of the art of navigation in an age committed to sea power. In the late seventeenth century science captured the interest and imagination of all who would consider themselves learned, becoming an integral part of erudition even though it was not yet accepted in the universities. Those traditional centers of learning were still dominated by the formal, Aristotelian curricula of medieval scholasticism larded over with Renaissance classicism. Men of learning formed an international community of the intellect, which became a distinctive feature of scientific endeavor of the period.

Each of the European world's earlier communities of intellect—the monasteries of the early Middle Ages, the universities of the late Middle Ages, and the academies of the Renaissance—had its own fundamental concepts, methodology, philosophical system, and sense of corporate identification. The new scientific community was no exception. Its fundamental concepts were the reasonableness of nature and the capacity of man to comprehend the rational order of nature by observation and the use of reason. These fundamentals, the methodology to use them, and the resulting philosophical system were in great part fashioned by two illustrious men of the previous generation: the Italian Galileo Galilei and the Frenchman René Descartes.

Galileo had shown that to understand the physical world man would have to use empirical analysis and would have to express that analysis mathematically. Implicit in his discoveries and method was the jettisoning of the speculative Aristotelian metaphysics that had hitherto dominated explanations of the physical world. Descartes had postulated a universe whose mechanism could be discovered and expressed mathematically, and he had provided a method for the scientist to follow. The natural assumption of his mechanical universe was that the universe was one of order not chaos, rational not accidental, and consequently a universe operating by universally applicable physical laws. It was the clarity of this vision that made all of the scientists after Descartes "Cartesians" in some measure.

THE VIRTUOSI

The scientists of the generation after Descartes, who died in 1650, did not confine their search for universal laws of nature to the heavens or physical bodies on earth; they took a general interest in the arts and sciences. The breadth of their interests was a measure of their fervency and their confidence in the new scientific method. The age had a name for them: *virtuosi*. It was an apt name, smacking of the manliness of the Renaissance's *virtù*, of the masterfulness of an accomplished mind, a sure hand, and a restless spirit. These men spread themselves broadly over the realm of knowledge, but they were not dilettantes. Their achievements in the brief compass of three-quarters of a century represented a brilliant outburst of intellectual vigor rarely matched in any other epoch of so short a duration in the history of the Western world.

Cooperation and communication were the keynotes of the intellectual community of the virtuosi. They formed academies or societies in which they congregated regularly, read papers, conducted demonstrations, disputed, and conversed. The earliest societies, in Rome and Florence, were short-lived, as were a number of local societies in France, Germany, and England; but the Royal Society of London for Improving Natural Knowledge, chartered in 1662, and the Academy of Sciences in Paris, founded in 1666, still exist. The academies often began more scientific projects than they could complete; the scientists soon learned that science's technical capabilities fell far short of its speculative ambitions. Ample royal and noble patronage provided support for experiments beyond the means of individual scientists. The secretaries of the academies were voluminous correspondents and able propagandists of the new science, though with few exceptions—such as Robert Hooke of the Royal Society—they themselves were not creative scientists. They furnished the web of cooperation and communication that made the new science truly international, and they carried its gospel to the educated of Europe, giving science a great vogue among Europe's elite.

The communities of virtuosi were remarkably open for an age still hierarchically stratified. Bishop Thomas Sprat (1635–1713), a founder-member and historian of the Royal Society, boasted of the Society: "It is to be noted that they have freely admitted Men of different Religions, Countries, and Professions of Life. . . . For they openly profess, not to lay the Foundation of an English, Scotch, Irish, Popish, or Protestant Philosophy; but a Philosophy of Mankind." The Royal Society was almost as open as Sprat claimed, and probably the only test was the implicit one that its members not be atheists. A number of clergymen were among its luminaries, and all its members were vociferous in their commitment to the proposition that there was no conflict between science and religion. Despite the sometimes profound differences of background, accomplishments, interests, and scientific opinions, despite some very virulent personal antagonisms, virtuosi sought each other's company for the mutual intellectual stimulation the community provided. Physicists, astronomers, philosophers, naturalists, architects, physicians, political economists, and political theorists met on the common ground of curiosity about the universe, man, and his society.

The Physical World

The commanding genius of the scientific community was Sir Isaac Newton (1642–1727). In his early twenties, while staying at his mother's farm at Woolsthorpe for eighteen months (from 1665 to 1667) to escape an epidemic that had forced a mass exodus from Cambridge University, he formulated in his mind three supremely important scientific discoveries. He arrived at the fundamental notion that particles of matter attract each other or "gravitate" toward each other; he perfected a new mathematical method, the calculus; and he reached tentative conclusions about the composition of light. There is no parallel in all recorded history to such intellectual creativity in so short a span of time.

THE NEWTONIAN SYNTHESIS

Newton's prodigious achievement was to bring together Kepler's explanation of planetary motion and Galileo's of terrestrial motion into a unified theory. Kepler had shown that the heavenly mechanism runs according to three rules: the law of elliptical motion, the law of equal areas, and the harmonic law of planetary motion. (See pp. 192–193.) Galileo's experiments with earthly objects had shown that there are two "forces" working on a body in motion, one horizontal and the other vertical. Consequently, the body's trajectory or path is a parabola, in which the body describes equal distances horizontally in equal times but accelerates vertically downward, so that in each successive time interval it travels a greater distance than before. Galileo had also demonstrated that the downward acceleration of a body in motion is independent of the weight of the body. Clearly, something else besides weight had to explain the uniform acceleration of a falling body. It was for Newton to calculate gravity and to demonstrate that it is a single universal force acting on both Kepler's heavenly bodies and Galileo's earthly bodies, accounting for the elliptical orbits of the former and the parabolic trajectories of the latter.

Newton postulated that the attraction of gravity varies directly as the product of the masses of the two bodies and inversely as the square of the distance between them. Newton's proof of the theory turned on his demonstration that the rate at which the moon is "falling" toward the earth is the same as that of a falling terrestrial body: sixteen feet per second. To determine the distance between the centers of the moon and the earth, it was necessary to calculate the exact radius of the earth. In the 1660's Newton used the accepted calculation of the earth's radius, which had come from ancient times, and found his calculations to be in error by about 15 per cent. He abandoned his theory as untenable. The fault, however, lay not in the theory but in the mistaken calculation of the earth's radius. In 1670 the French scientist Jean Picard (1620–1682) provided the figures for an accurate measurement of the earth's radius. In 1684 at the urging of Edmond Halley, a fellow member of the Royal Society who had been discussing the possibility of a force such as gravity with two other members, Christopher Wren and Robert Hooke, Newton recomputed his proof, this time using the correct radius of the earth. The new calculations banished the 15 per cent error of his earlier calculations, and the ideas which he had turned over in his mind since the days at Woolsthorpe fell into place. In 1687 he published in Latin the massive treatise *Philosophiae Naturalis Principia Mathematicae* (Mathematical Principles of Natural Philosophy).

The *Principia* incorporated Newton's demonstration of the law of gravity explaining the motion of the planets and their satellites. It also cast a wider net. On Galileo's foundations Newton constructed the science of mechanics, defining force, momentum, and inertia with the precision of mathematics. He disposed of Descartes' theory that the planets were held in an invisible fluid that filled all space and whirled around the sun, by showing with precise calculations that the motions of a body carried in a vortex would not follow Kepler's laws. From gravity he demonstrated that the pull of the sun and the moon cause the tides, that comets are under the influence of the sun's attraction and their orbits can therefore be calculated, and that the earth and the other planets are flattened at their poles. He showed that the sun's gravitational pull on the earth's slight bulge at the equator produces a slight twisting force that explains the phenomenon known as the "precession of the equinoxes"—the very slow change over the years in the position of the sun with respect to the fixed stars at the spring and autumn equinoxes. Newton had indeed ordered the universe.

The *Principia* was a difficult book even for skilled mathematicians, in part because Newton chose to use the theorems of classical geometry for his demonstrations instead of the calculus, although he must have used the calculus to work out and test the theorems. He did so presumably because he admired the mathematical methods of the ancients and because he wanted to make his book as abstruse as possible so as to avoid the criticisms of those whom he called "little smatterers in mathematics."

It took the scientific community nearly half a century to grasp all the implications of Newton's achievements. Once understood, the *Principia* became the classical textbook of physics until the first part of the present century. Only with twentieth-century physics and its improved apparatus has the dominance of Newtonian mechanics been reduced in the light of its inapplicability to much of the phenomena of the atom and the farthest reaches of space.

THE CALCULUS AND THE COMPOSITION OF LIGHT

The calculation of Newton's mechanics had depended upon Newton's discovery of the calculus, the mathematics of infinity, of variables and probables. The early seventeenth century had been remarkably productive of mathematical innovation. The Scot, John Napier, had invented logarithms and pioneered the use of decimals. Descartes' analytical geometry was the most commanding step forward before the calculus. Men of such opposed ideological views as the French Jansenist, Blaise Pascal, the Italian Jesuit, Bonaventura Cavalieri, and Newton's countrymen, the Puritan Parliamentarian, John Wallis, and the High Anglican Royalist, Isaac Barrow, all contributed elements to the mathematical study of infinity which Newton incorporated in his calculus. Newton did not so much invent as perfect differential calculus when, during those eighteen months at Woolsthorpe, he used it for the initial calculations of the theory of gravity. He did not tell any of his fellow mathematicians about his findings for several years and would not allow them to be published for thirty years. Meanwhile the German mathematician and philosopher Gottfried Wilhelm von Leibniz (1646–1716), ignorant of Newton's work, independently developed the method of the calculus and published his results in 1675. A rancorous controversy that arose over who was to be honored as the first discoverer for decades robbed English mathematicians of the benefits of the Continental improvements in the calculus, based on the more general and simply notated calculus of Leibniz.

The science of optics developed rapidly in the century following Galileo's improvement of Dutch telescopes in 1609. True to its origins in the technical side of instrument-making, optics provided the starting point for the study of the composition of light. The best lens of the day tended to color the image seen in it, a phenomenon apparent in the prism, which in refracting light breaks it up into the color spectrum. When Newton began to experiment with prisms it had already been established that white light was an amalgam of all the colors of the spectrum. Newton resynthesized white light from colored light by means of a lens to give final proof of the composite quality of white light. From these experiments Newton developed the reflecting telescope, which is still used for the largest optical telescopes. He also developed a theory of light that is still applicable. With Robert Hooke and Christian Huygens (1629–1695), the great Dutch optical technician, astronomer, and physicist, Newton agreed that light moves in waves. He proved the periodicity, or wave lengths, of light waves, and he went further than either of them in advancing the theory that light consisted of streams of particles emitted sporadically from the light source.

BOYLE AND THE FOUNDATIONS OF CHEMISTRY

The inquiring mind of Galileo had encompassed the study of gases as well as mechanics, optics, and astronomy. He invented the parent instrument of the thermometer and the barometer and first weighed air. In 1643 his secretary Evangelista Torricelli (1608–1647) invented the mercury barometer, which clearly proved that a vacuum could exist (contrary to Aristotle's dictum that "nature abhors a vacuum"), and suggested that variation in the weight of the outside air caused the mercury to rise or fall in the barometer. Three years later Blaise Pascal tested the principle and demonstrated that on top of a mountain the mercury would fall, from which he surmised that the weight of the outside air was less than at a lower altitude. By 1650 Otto von Guericke (1602–1686) made the first air pumps. With his "Magdeburg hemispheres," from which he pumped as much air as he could, he showed that teams of mules could not pull the hemispheres apart because of atmospheric pressure, that in a vacuum life and combustion are extinguished and the passage of sound is halted, but that light is not stopped in its passage.

Robert Boyle (1627–1691), youngest son of the Earl of Cork, had been drawn to science while he was a student at Oxford. He became an inveterate experimenter, recording his findings in minute detail. Although he lacked mathematics, his industry, ingenuity, and patience gave a new respectability to experimentation, which previously had been considered chiefly as a method of demonstration rather than inquiry. In experiments in 1659 Boyle dealt with the physical problems of air but his conclusions were those of a chemist. Torricelli and Pascal had held that the *weight* of air causes the movement of mercury in the barometer's column. Boyle theorized that it is in fact the *pressure* of air that accounts for the phenomenon. He established that air is a gas, with a definite pressure, and he postulated the law, named for him, that the pressure of a gas varies inversely with its volume. His other physical experiments as to the function of air in propagating sound, the expansion of water in freezing, and specific gravities and hydrostatics were valuable. But his greatest contribution rested in framing the science of chemistry.

Boyle conceived of chemistry as the study of the composition of substances, and he had the notion that elements are the irreducible constituents of material bodies. He analyzed the ingredients of chemical mixtures and compounds and furthered knowledge of specific substances. In common with most scientists of his day he held that matter is composed of atoms. Unlike them, he ascribed to atoms most of the chemical and physical phenomena he studied: "I look upon the phenomena of nature to be caused by the local motion of one part of matter hitting against another." This notion had important consequences, although an atomic theory as a usable facet of physics and chemistry was still far distant. The immediate result of Boyle's chemical investigations was to take the study of chemistry away from the alchemists and to exalt it above the pharmacological concerns of medicine. In Boyle's work originated the branch of science that a century later would flourish in the genius of Lavoisier.

PHYSIOLOGY

With William Harvey's (1578–1657) discovery of the circulation of blood the study of the human body passed from the realm of mere anatomy (the structure of the body) to physiology (the functioning of the body). The change here, as elsewhere, owed something to Descartes: his conception of the human body as a machine put a premium on physiology rather than anatomy as its proper study. The increasing technical refinement of optical instruments made possible tremendous advances in physiology in the late seventeenth century. The construction of magnifying lenses by Dutch craftsmen launched microscopy. Jan Swammerdam (1637–1680) discovered red corpuscles in the blood and the valves of the lymph glands, and he made a major contribution to biology by dissecting insects and classifying them according to their development. When in 1660 the Italian Marcello Malpighi (1628–1694) dissected and microscopically studied the frog, he supplied the missing link in Harvey's circulatory system: the capillaries connecting arteries and veins. He described the structure of the human lung, the brain, the spinal cord, and cell tissue, and he founded embryology with his investigations into the development of the fetal chick. The Dutchman Anton van Leeuwenhoek (1632–1723) discovered bacteria and spermatozoa, described the lens of the eye, and distinguished between voluntary and involuntary muscles. These men were observers and collectors of data, not theoreticians fashioning new explanations of the microscopic universe opened to them. It would be a century and a half before such rich discoveries spawned a sufficient conceptual structure in biology to begin to explain adequately the generation of life, the working of the nervous system, the particular functions of principal bodily organs, and the nature of cell tissue in plants and animals.

For the moment the prime effect of these investigations was to add greatly to the pitifully small corpus of knowledge about the workings of the living organism.

THE NATURALISTS

Significantly, neither biology nor geology produced a Newton or a Boyle in the period 1650–1725. The virtuosi who engaged in biological and geological investigations are best called naturalists: those who observe and describe but do not attempt to make the scientific inferences that lead to general scientific truths. Few of them suspected how ancient the earth is— how old life upon it is. In the seventeenth century, though fossils and earth stratification had long been noticed by miners, the world was still supposed to have been created about 4000 B.C. Ingenious explanations were advanced to dismiss fossils: they were seeds that had grown into the rocks rather than out of the ground, or they were put by God into rocks to test man's faith in the Biblical account of the Creation. By the end of the seventeenth century naturalists admitted that fossils had indeed once been organic but claimed that they had been killed by the Flood in Noah's time, which by their reckoning came well after 4000 B.C. There was nothing in the scientific revolution in mechanics and astronomy, or in its postulate of a mechanical universe that apparently had always existed, to point to a historical process— an evolution—involving the earth and life upon it.

The most important naturalist (and perhaps the most attractive of the virtuosi) was the Englishman John Ray (1627–1705). Modest, open to new ideas, and utterly honest, Ray argued persuasively for the organic origin of fossils and perceived that the earth is much older than men thought. His extraordinary methodicalness and acute powers of observation, married to abundant zeal, allowed him to produce between 1686 and 1710 an impressive series of volumes describing and classifying plants, animals, birds, fishes, and insects.

From a genius who posited the laws of a mechanical universe to a man of more modest talents laboriously classifying thousands of creatures may seem a comedown. But postulating laws of a mechanical universe required a slighter break with the metaphysical past and a lesser challenge to accepted religious authority than postulating laws of biological origin. A Newton was possible in the seventeenth century; a Darwin was not.

The Psychic World

The very discrepancy of achievement between the physical sciences and the life sciences in the seventeenth century had one important result. The virtuosi who turned to the world of man's mind, the psychic world, brought to it mechanistic preconceptions derived from the brilliant achievements in physics. To the planets in the heavens and the moving bodies on earth they added man as an intricate particle of matter obeying mechanical laws. They nevertheless knew less about him—less of how he functions and how he came to be as a species or an individual—than they knew about the universe. Physics proved to be a poor foundation for the study of man's psyche, and the embryonic stage of the life sciences could not provide an alternative to the mechanical analogy in an age when the aspiration of man to know everything, and his unbounded confidence that he could, far outran his knowledge of himself.

Descartes' conception of man as a machine was fundamental to the investigation of the psychic world in the Age of Science. The physical actions of the human body, he wrote, are mechanically explicable: "I say, that you consider all that these functions follow naturally in this machine simply from the arrangement of its parts, no more and no less than do the movements of a clock." He argued that the human body is occupied by a rational, immaterial "soul" or mind, however, and that this soul is married to the material body by the pineal gland in the brain. He attempted to give a crude physiological explanation of the way in which the pineal gland transmits the soul's perceptions to the body's actions. Since what the soul perceives is transmitted to it by the senses and since the soul is given only a replica of the external object, it follows that the transmission mechanism might distort reality. Hence "I think, therefore I am"—Descartes' great single certainty—is the one clear truth that man can rely upon, for the tree in front of him, apprehended in his mind, exists for him only in its replica state.

LOCKEAN ENVIRONMENTALISM

In *An Essay Concerning Human Understanding* (1690), John Locke sought to determine what knowledge is, how it is acquired, and how far it extends. He started with a simple premise that man's mind at birth is a blank page. "Let us then suppose the mind to be, as we say white paper, void of all characters, without any ideas—how comes it to be furnished?" His answer was that ideas are furnished by the perception of our senses, and reflection on these perceptions. Thus, all man's ideas depend upon both experience and reason.

Locke took pains to point out that the certainty of knowledge is extremely limited, though the precise limits of certainty are more or less dependent upon the kind of knowledge. He described four kinds of knowledge: (1) analytical knowledge—ideas springing from the comparison of ideas, (2) mathematical and ethical knowledge, (3) scientific knowledge of the physical world, and (4) knowledge of the existence of one's self, the world, and God. Knowledge of the physical world is the most limited, for when the external object is no longer within range of the senses its continued existence can only be presumed—a sad thought for the virtuosi, but Locke reassured them that despite its limits, knowledge of the physical world derived from experience and fashioned by reason is enough to enable man to carry on bravely in this life, to be more than merely a chip on an ocean of infinite unknowingness.

Locke's emphasis on "experience" and "reason" made a tremendous impression on thinkers for three-quarters of a century. By the use of reason man might condition his environment, which is the source of human experience. A changed environment would in turn result in changed experience. Locke had denied the existence of innate ideas in the mind of man, but implicit in his philosophy of knowledge was an invitation to man to change his environment so as to make innate in it experiences which would scribble on the "white paper" of minds yet unborn.

LEIBNIZ'S INNATISM

Locke had conceived of a thing as having two qualities: a "primary" quality (its physically expressible attributes such as size, shape, motion, or number), and a "secondary" quality (its derived properties such as beauty, luster, taste, or color). He argued that although secondary qualities depend on somebody to perceive them, primary qualities exist whether there is someone to perceive them or not. The German virtuoso Leibniz undertook a critique of Locke's *Essay* that turned on this question of primary and secondary qualities. Leibniz made no distinction between the two. Both primary and secondary qualities are equally certain, for what the mind perceives is a perfect reflection of reality. Leibniz argued that knowledge is perceived not at all by the senses but is a creation of the mind. All ideas are innate, to be worked up into knowledge by the rational operation of the mind. Leibniz had no need to slide over the relationship between body and mind, as Locke had done, since there is no connection between body and mind; both work separately from each other but in perfect harmony because they obey the same laws of nature. Neither was he compelled, as Locke was, to argue that God is a demonstrable truth, for faith and reason, like body and mind, are harmonious though separate, and God must be the origin of such harmony.

The Social World

The virtuosi found it easier to postulate mechanistic "laws" for the functioning of men's minds than for their collective behavior in society. Too little was known about the mind, and far too much about society, even if knowledge of society was not very systematic. Social theory bore somewhat the same relationship to psychology that biology bore to physics: abundant data, readily observed, tended to defy arrangement, not least because the conceptual framework by which something might be made of the data was extremely rudimentary.

For two centuries theorists had been dismantling the medieval view of social structure, even though in practice much of that structure still remained as the bulwark of monarchic absolutism. Men had become aware of other ways of conceiving of society than the traditional hierarchic one. The intellectual ferment of the seventeenth century provided new strength to their reassessments. If the virtuosi who turned their attention to society were not Newtons or Lockes, their efforts were nonetheless productive of basic and bold new departures in man's view of his social world.

THE POLITICAL ECONOMISTS

The best economic minds of the Age of Science often receive too little credit for providing the foundation of modern economics; that credit is usually given to the eighteenth-century French physiocrats and Adam Smith. Although the earlier economists remained within the context of the mercantilist theory they nevertheless asked more penetrating questions than their predecessors had about such basic matters as price and value, and they formulated more sophisticated answers. The most important of these economists was the English virtuoso Sir William Petty (1623–1687), physician, wealthy landowner, and one of the first fellows of the Royal Society. Possessed of a breadth of vision that freed him from the shackles of orthodox mercantilist thought, he achieved a level of analysis not surpassed for a hundred years. No less an authority than Karl Marx labeled him the founder of political economy.

Petty made notable contributions to both the theory of economics and its methodology. He postulated the labor theory of value, in which labor was the source of wealth and the measure of value—a doctrine that the classical economists of the early nineteenth century and Karl Marx would raise to a Newtonian-like axiom of economics. He understood the advantages of the division of labor in reducing the price and raising the quality of a product. Atlhough his views on foreign trade were colored by mercantilist notions, he recognized that restrictions on the export of gold and silver hampered economic growth, and he realized, too, that not only a deficiency of money but also an excess of it could damage a nation's economy.

Petty can rightly claim to be the founder of comparative social statistics as a science. While serving as a physician to Cromwell's troops in Ireland in the 1650's he saw how inefficiently the lands granted to soldiers there were surveyed. He produced a far more accurate survey, which took account not only of acreage and declared value, but of the quality of the land, population, and crafts as well. His motives were not wholly altruistic: he carved out a huge estate for himself in Ireland, upon which he set up model iron works, quarries, lead mines, and fisheries.

The statistical methods introduced by Petty were utilized by two of his countrymen, Charles Davenant (1656–1714) and Gregory King (1648–1712). In 1696 King made such an accurate estimate of English population on the basis of tax returns that the results have not been seriously questioned since. Both Davenant and King divided the population into those who increase the nation's wealth and those who diminish it, based on whether they were a contribution to or a drain on capital investment. They both mirrored a concern about overpopulation and poverty that was characteristic of Western Europe during the seventeenth century. Since the mid-sixteenth century England, the Low Countries, and France had undertaken exceptional efforts to cope with pauperism by government action. It fell to an English virtuoso of the Royal Society and a chief justice of England, Sir Matthew Hale (1609–1676), to fix poverty clearly as a social evil resulting from economic causes, not from the moral depravity of the poor. In *Discourse Touching Provision for the Poor,* published in 1683, he argued that crime could be reduced by solving the problem of poverty through economic improvement.

Petty's Dutch counterpart was Pieter de la Court (1618–1685), a Leyden clothier, whose *True Interest and Political Maxims of Holland,* written in the 1660's, made a comprehensive and searching sweep of the political, social, and economic aspects of the Dutch Republic and attempted to establish guidelines for sound policy by subjecting old assumptions of government to the light of reason. Like Petty, he regarded the restriction on the export of bullion as inimical to Dutch commerce.

Jean-Baptiste Colbert, Louis XIV's minister, ranks with the other leading political economists of the age. Founder of the French Academy of Sciences and a patron of the new science, he sought to implement a coherent, organized economic policy. He left behind no corpus of written work, and his strong protectionist mercantilism obscured the novelty of many of his theories of domestic economy, but his papers indicate a Cartesian-like, mechanistic approach to economics. In Marshal Vauban (1633–1707) France produced not only a new-model soldier but also a new-model economist. In *Project for a Royal Tithe* (1707), suppressed by royal mandate as subversive, he urged the uniform application of a 10 per cent tax on all Frenchmen, ending the privileged exemption of the nobility. To Vauban, tax privilege was economic suicide for France, for it placed an intolerable tax burden upon the peasantry, whose labor he considered to be the mainstay of France's wealth.

THE HISTORIANS

The treatment of the past in the Middle Ages had been an adjunct to philosophy, with Divine Providence as the determining force in human affairs. The Renaissance humanists, inspired by both their reverence for antiquity and their contempt for medieval culture, began to conceive of the story of the past as a distinct branch of knowledge that would provide the model of classical society for European man's imitation. They put their historical accounts into a secular framework, sought causation in human motives and decisions rather than in the workings of Providence, and concerned themselves with the basic problems of history—relevance of the past to the present and how the present grew out of the past. The religious controversies of the Reformation stimulated the study and writing of history, since Catholics and Protestants alike turned to the record of the past to establish the rightness of their own positions and to attack the claims of their opponents.

In the sixteenth and seventeenth centuries the conscious mining of the past for the purpose of polemics developed into a fine art. Increasingly the focus shifted from religious to political questions. The origins of this shift lay in the work of legal scholars attempting to use history to justify the growing monarchic power. The polemics were supplied both by those who exalted this power and by those who attempted to restrict it.

The historical endeavors of the century laid the foundation for historical method and provided much factual material. In England historian-polemicists began the serious study of the English medieval past that was to bloom in the nineteenth century. Anglo-Saxon language and literature, feudalism, medieval institutions, monastic history, and the origins of English common law received attention. In the Dutch Republic and Germany historians created national histories in defense of Dutch merchant oligarchs and German princes against monarchic pretensions. Leibniz undertook a monumental history of the dynasty of his patron the House of Brunswick, beginning in 768; when he died, he had only reached 1005. In France a group of Jesuits who were called Bollandists in honor of one of their more eminent members, Jean Bolland, sought to establish the lives of the saints on historically sound grounds by collecting and editing masses of texts. The Maurists, monks in the Benedictine Congregation of St. Maur in Paris, led by Jean Mabillon, created methods of textual criticism and the study of the internal structure of historical documents that remain to this day the basic tool of ancient and medieval historians. Charles Du Cange, a French government official, compiled the first and still the greatest dictionary of early medieval Latin. Scholars authenticated old manuscripts and weeded out forgeries, studied ancient coins and established the science of numismatics, and made critical analyses of old inscriptions. The chronology of human history came under intensive examination, primarily because new knowledge about the ancient empires of China and Egypt had thrown doubt on the traditional chronology based on the Bible. By the end of the century the assurance with which historians had once accepted that chronology had vanished.

REASON VERSUS HISTORY

To a virtuoso committed to the pure light of reason, history was merely another form of challengeable authority, no better than metaphysics and perhaps more insidious. More specifically, Locke, in the *Essay on Human Understanding*, pointed the way explicitly to understanding man, implicitly to improving his condition. Reason founded on experience was the only path; authority, historical or otherwise, was irrelevant. Above all, in the Lockean scheme of knowledge experience could only be personal, never collective, and hence history (collective experience) was an impossibility.

The 1690's witnessed more than just Locke's blow at the usefulness of history. In 1697, Pierre Bayle's *Historical and Critical Dictionary* dealt an almost mortal blow to history. Bayle (1647–1706), a Huguenot converted to Roman Catholicism by the Jesuits, reconverted to Calvinism, an exile in Holland from persecution in France for his Calvinism, removed from his chair in the Calvinist university of Rotterdam for his skepticism, was a walking pincushion of persecution. By patent ridicule, subtle irony, and murderous criticism in the light of reason, the *Dictionary* stripped all the history, secular and especially ecclesiastical, upon which Bayle could lay his hands, of its factualness and its authority. In a different atmosphere and within a different framework of knowledge than that afforded by Locke, Bayle's brilliant work might only have served to exorcise error from history. In his generation, Bayle's criticism consumed history. If history was to be reborn from the destructive onslaught of Bayle's criticism and its obsolescence through Locke's psychology, it would have to be structured on rational laws, and experience would have to be conceived of as collective (societal), not merely individual (psychic).

VICO AND THE SCIENCE OF HISTORY

A Roman lawyer holding a professorship of rhetoric in Naples, the intellectual backwater of the age, undertook to be the Newton of history, the discoverer of the laws of man's collective behavior in the operation of man's past. Giambattista Vico (1668–1744) is today claimed as a founding father by both sociologists and historians. Three strains merged in him: the vital historical activity of Roman lawyers in political polemics during the previous two centuries, the philological studies which were a feature of seventeenth-century letters, and the new science of mechanical laws and reason fashioned from experience. The richness of this patrimony, unique among the virtuosi, enables him to escape categorization as a Cartesian or a Lockean. His was a highly original mind, and more in intention than in the specifics of his endeavor he stood with the other virtuosi.

The title of Vico's masterpiece is almost a statement of his thesis: *Principles of the New Science of Giambattista Vico Concerning the Common Nature of the Nations* (1725, much revised 1730). Vico posited a "natural law" of peoples, common to all peoples, that explained the growth of human societies ("nations") and their institutions from the moment when brutish creatures became men. The first stage of civilization was born in the foundation of the institutions of religion and marriage when a fearsome thunderclap drove male and female, hitherto breeding promiscuously, into caves to become lifelong mates. This first stage was the age of gods, in which men communicated by signs and simple words related to physical objects, for observance of religious rituals was more important than discussion. The second stage was the age of heroes, in which men spoke in images and metaphors, wisdom being poetic. The third stage was the age of men, in which men communicated in words of commonly agreed and specific meaning, wisdom being conscious and rational. A distinct form of government and jurisprudence corresponded to each stage of civilization. History moved in cycles, the change from one stage to the next being accomplished by a process both of growth and decay.

Vico's contemporaries found his work strange, indeed ominous. His theory of historical cycles seemed to deny the never-ending progress of man which, by 1725, was already an article of faith of intellectuals. He appeared to make a historical reality of a state of nature, which in Hobbes had been a philosophical presupposition and in Locke a symbolic convenience. Vico demanded a sophistication in dealing with past reality which was foreign to a generation that had consigned history to the rubbish heap along with irrational metaphysics. Yet Vico had demonstrated even to the satisfaction of the most skeptical of his contemporaries that experience could be collective. His rigid intellectual honesty by introducing complications in the clean, neat world of unending progress through reason, cost him his audience in the Age of Enlightenment which succeeded the Age of Science. Vico's day came when the Enlightenment had run its course and German historians in the early nineteenth century took up the serious task of writing scientific universal history.

RETROSPECT

The achievements of the Age of Science are not easily explained. They depended in part on the accident of genius. They were founded on the decisive breakthrough in understanding the physical world during the previous century and on the development of procedures of empiricism and mathematics. They owed a great deal to the more material attributes of the seventeenth century, that is, the fact that patronage was attracted by the prospects of technical advance through science. In no small part they can be traced to the extraordinary community of intellect that provided companionship of the mind, a sounding board for ideas, and an exhilarating sense of common destiny on new frontiers of knowledge.

These achievements accomplished the end of the Age of Science. Science, represented in the accomplishments of the virtuosi, had by the second decade of the eighteenth century become the new order of the European intellect, and in so becoming had effectively established itself in place of the old order it had destroyed.

By 1720 the virtuosi had furnished their successors (and imitators), the *philosophes* of the Enlightenment, with a matchless patrimony: their methodology, their intellectual substance, their means, and indeed many of their ends.

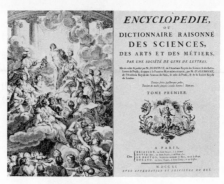

CHAPTER SEVENTEEN

The Enlightenment

THE NEW INTELLECTUAL ORDER that grew out of the achievements of the Age of Science was above all one of certainty—certainty in the value of experience, certainty in the ability of reason to solve all problems, certainty that the real world is indeed as man perceives it. Impressed by the success of the natural scientists of the seventeenth century in discovering the laws of the physical universe, the men of the eighteenth-century Enlightenment believed that they could uncover the laws governing human institutions and human behavior. They faced the future with optimism, thinking that the laws of human society, once determined, could be used to increase man's welfare and happiness and to guarantee unending progress in the human condition. Not everyone shared their new faith, and even among those who did there was no rigorous uniformity of outlook. Nevertheless, certainty, optimism, and a belief in progress were the trinity that furnished most intellectuals with their creed. The Enlightenment was an era when men tended to see everything in the pure light of reason. For over three-quarters of a century faith in reason dominated the intellectual life of Europe.

INTELLECTUAL ROOTS OF THE ENLIGHTENMENT

The men of the Age of Reason modified, sometimes clarified, and popularized the ideas they inherited from the seventeenth century. A process of selection was involved. The rules laid down by Descartes in the *Discourse on Method* (see pp. 199–200) were generally acceptable. On the other hand, Descartes' conception of the operation of the universe gave way around the 1730's to Newton's mechanics, though in France national pride delayed the final abandonment of Cartesian cosmology until after the middle of the century. The men of the Enlightenment also rejected Descartes' theory of knowledge, that the mind at birth possesses certain innate ideas from which by deduction we arrive at true knowledge about the world, in favor of the environmentalism of John Locke. Locke's doctrine, with its implicit premise that man could improve himself by a better environment and education, offered a theoretical justification for the Enlightenment's belief that man and society could be reshaped in accordance with natural law.

The ethical concerns that motivated the rational endeavors of the Enlightenment were derived from the best aspirations in the Christian tradition. However, the dogmatic, metaphysical, and mystical qualities of orthodox Christianity had been culled out during the seventeenth century, leaving only the ethics. Deism, the religion of reason that had been developed during the seventeenth century, became the new orthodoxy of the Enlightenment.

THE ADVENT OF DEISM

Traditional religion was shaken by the new awareness of reason and fact of the Age of Science. The contrast between the mechanical, predictable workings of nature and the miracles related in the Bible was disturbing, and belief in the historical accuracy of the Bible was shaken by the textual criticisms of such scholars as Thomas Hobbes, the English philosopher; Baruch Spinoza, a Dutch Jew; and Richard Simon, a French priest. Their studies showed that many parts of the Bible were actually written much later than Biblical times, that the text had undergone numerous alterations and additions and contained obvious contradictions, and that Biblical chronology did not agree with the chronology derived from ancient secular sources.

The increasing knowledge of non-European cultures intensified the questioning of orthodox Christianity. Travelers told of peoples who had never heard of Christianity and who had their own systems of religious and moral values that they believed were the only true ones sanctioned by God. The religions of the Far East especially, and the cultures built upon them, seemed hardly inferior. Some intellectuals began to adopt a relativistic attitued toward religion, maintaining that the doctrines of Christianity were not necessarily superior to those of any other creed.

This skeptical attitude toward Christianity was not a new phenomenon. Renaissance humanists, inspired by their study of classical writings, had counseled men to abandon rigid doctrines and opinions. The religious wars and persecutions of the sixteenth and seventeenth centuries had moved some thoughtful men to doubt the certainties claimed by the opposing creeds. Appalled at the horrors perpetrated in the name of religion, they urged toleration and recognition of the impossibility of proving the superiority of any one creed. Michel de Montaigne (1533–1592) was one of the first to react in this way. Custom, he said, dictates our religion just as it dictates the style of our clothes. Each religion uses the same arguments to prove that it alone is the only true faith. There is no way for man to know which one is right.

PASCAL AND SPINOZA

Most intellectuals of the seventeenth century viewed the conflict between the new knowledge and traditional religion with equanimity; to others it brought anguish of heart and mind. Blaise Pascal (1623–1662), the seventeenth-century French mathematician and philosopher, voiced the dilemma most clearly. He wrote that he felt himself "engulfed in the infinite immensity of space whereof I know nothing, and which knows nothing of me. The eternal silence of those infinite spaces terrifies me." Using the method of Cartesian doubt, he tried to convince himself that God exists by doubting all traditional doctrine and evidence. He concluded that reason could not persuade man to believe in God; he must accept that belief on faith alone. "The heart has its reason," he wrote, "which the mind does not know . . . and this is the essence of faith, that God is known to the heart and not to the reason." In a famous passage known as "Pascal's wager" he said, "We can say 'Either God is, or is not.' . . . What will you wager? You can argue reasonably in favor of either." He felt that the odds stood heavily against God's existence, yet he urged men to bet that God does exist. For if there is a God, the believer gains eternal life; if God does not exist, man loses nothing.

Pascal's despair was not shared by his contemporary Baruch Spinoza (1632–1677). Born in Amsterdam of a Portuguese Jewish family and educated in both religious and secular lore, Spinoza earned his living as a lens grinder. He adopted the mathematical method of Descartes for his own thinking because it allowed him to describe phenomena objectively, without ascribing cause or purpose; but he rejected the chasm between the material world and the immaterial mind postulated in Cartesian dualism. (See p. 199.) He argued that matter and mind are both aspects of God and have no existence apart from him. God is the only reality in the universe and is immanent in all matter and thought. Spinoza rejected the validity of orthodox religious concepts of God and denied the divine inspiration of the Bible. God is not the personal, loving Deity who heeds men's prayers and who causes everything. God *is* everything. Spinoza's philosophy, called pantheism, was branded atheism by Christian and Jew alike, and his teachings were denounced. Some who read Spinoza, however, found solace in his words, for he seemed to have closed the gap between the mechanism of the new science and belief in God.

NATURAL RELIGION

Spinoza's pantheism did not satisfy most of those who felt that orthodox religious dogma could not be reconciled with reason and fact. For these men satisfaction was found in a new kind of religion called natural religion or deism. By the late seventeenth century natural religion had become the vogue among the virtuosi. Newton, Boyle, Locke, and many lesser minds wrestled with the definition of the exact nature of God, producing theological works as voluminous as their scientific treatises. They believed that both reason and nature reveal the existence of God, of a natural order of morality that shows man the difference between good and evil, and of a life after death with reward or punishment for man's deeds. Vehement in their denunciation of atheism, they conveniently accepted the doctrines of Christianity that coincided with what they believed were natural principles and rejected the rest as being the products of superstition. They compared the universe to a precisely made machine, such as a watch, and placed God in the role of the Watchmaker. He had made the universe and set the laws by which it operated. Once it was started He had no need to concern Himself with its workings, for as His creation it ran perfectly.

The Circles of Enlightenment

Although the Enlightenment was an international movement, its center was in France, and since the center of France was Paris, so the center of the Enlightenment was Paris. France had already established its cultural supremacy along with its military might under Louis XIV; and though its military might diminished, its cultural supremacy increased. Courtiers and scholars in Berlin, Warsaw, and St. Petersburg spoke and wrote in the elegant French of Molière, scorning their native tongues as uncultured. Paris became the Mecca of the philosophers, writers, and artists of all Europe, who visited and studied there and returned home to spread French influences. French intellectuals and artists were much in demand at the royal courts and cultural centers of other lands.

Great Britain also played a leading part in the movement. In addition to the fundamental contributions of Newton and Locke to the thought of the Enlightenment, the English political structure, with its limitations on royal power and its system of representation, fascinated Frenchmen. Many studied it at first hand, returning home filled with enthusiasm for the system and usually with a good deal of misunderstanding about how it actually operated.

THE NEW READING PUBLIC

A remarkable expansion in the reading public during the eighteenth century helped to bring about a wide diffusion of the ideas of the Enlightenment. For the first time in history a mass reading public appeared, made up chiefly of members of the growing educated middle class, but also including many nobles, some city artisans, and a small number of country people. Private libraries in the homes of the well-to-do became more common. Books, pamphlets, and magazines poured from the presses. The number of newspapers multiplied, most of them journals of opinion more than of news. The coffee houses, cafés, clubs, and reading rooms that became so popular in Western Europe subscribed to newspapers and magazines for their patrons to read. In 1720 Paris had over three hundred cafés, each with its own clientele, drawn mainly from the middle class, who came regularly to read the journals and talk about the ideas discussed in them. A coffee house in the provincial city of Strasbourg in Alsace in the 1780's received eighty-six periodicals in four languages.

In England, the Dutch Republic, and British North America the press was either free or subject only to a mild censorship. Censorship in other lands varied in severity, and enforcement was generally sporadic. To escape the censor's ban books and newspapers were often published clandestinely, smuggled in from abroad, or laboriously copied by hand and passed from reader to reader. Their illegality increased their attractiveness, so that censorship actually helped propagate the new ideas.

SOCIETIES AND SALONS

Learned societies patterned on the societies of the virtuosi were founded across the Western world from St. Petersburg, where Peter I established the Russian Imperial Academy of Sciences in 1724, to Philadelphia, where under Benjamin Franklin's leadership the American Philosophical Society came into existence in 1743. Such societies sponsored experiments, lectures, publications, libraries, and museums. They enjoyed such high prestige that their sponsorship of a new social or scientific theory did much to make it popular among the educated classes.

In Paris, and to a lesser extent in other cities, salons became fashionable. They were usually conducted in the homes of gifted women of wealth, where writers, clergymen, bankers, businessmen, and aristocrats met regularly for conversation, intellectual stimulation, or just to be seen. Much of the talk was little more than idle chatter; elegance of expression, malicious wit, and clever epigrams were more valued than profundity. Nonetheless the salons brought together as equals men of different ideas and social origins, and inevitably they influenced one another. Aristocrats were persuaded to adopt liberal social and political views that ran counter to their own class interests. Writers, many from relatively humble backgrounds, gained a polish, self-confidence, and sophistication that made them more effective propagandists.

The international secret order of Freemasons provided an especially effective medium for transmission of the ideas of the Enlightenment. It had originated in the Middle Ages, when stone masons joined together into lodges to preserve their professional secrets. The order persisted in England into the eighteenth century, by which time it was composed entirely of professional architects, nobles, and intellectuals. After the union of four lodges into a Grand Lodge in London in 1717 all pretense of craftsmanship was abandoned, although the old symbols and rites that supposedly originated with King Solomon, the mythical founder of the order, were preserved. The English Freemasons dedicated themselves to the religion of reason, the creation of a moral and social order based upon the principles of reason, and the establishment of liberty and equality.

Through the initiative of merchants, diplomats, soldiers, and even prisoners of war, Freemasonry spread with remarkable speed to nearly every European land, to British North America, and even to India. It linked men of like views throughout Western society and acquainted them with the principles of the Enlightenment. Washington, Franklin, Jefferson, and many other leading Americans were Masons. In Europe even royalty belonged: Emperor Francis I of Austria was a member, and Frederick II of Prussia became master of a lodge in Berlin.

The Philosophes

In the seventeenth century many of Europe's intellectual leaders had been mathematicians and scientists. In the eighteenth century the leaders of intellectual life were those who called themselves *philosophes*, "philosophers." It was a misnomer. They did not concern themselves primarily with technical philosophical speculations, and with a few notable exceptions they were not creative thinkers. They were popularizers and propagandists of the ideas developed by the virtuosi. They were less enamored with advancing knowledge for its own sake than with using knowledge to refashion ethics and to reconstruct society according to reason and natural law. In pursuit of that goal they turned out histories, plays, novels, scientific treatises, political pamphlets, and literary and art criticism, as well as philosophical tracts. Seeking to reach as wide an audience as possible, they wrote in the vernacular rather than in Latin. They deliberately culti-

Philosophes Dining, engraving after Hubert. Voltaire (1) presiding, Le Pere Adam (2), L'Abbe Mauri (3), d'Alembert (4), Condorcet (5), Diderot (6), Laharpe (7).
". . . *Reason is to the* philosophe *what grace is to the Christian. Grace causes the Christian to act; reason causes the* philosophe *to act. . . . Truth is not for the* philosophe *a mistress who corrupts his imagination. . . . He does not confuse it with the probable . . . Civil society is, so to speak, an earthly deity to him; he burns incense to it, he honors it by his integrity, by his rigorous attention to his duties, and by a sincere desire not to be a useless or embarrassing member of it. . . . The* philosophe, *then, is an honest man who is guided in everything by reason. . . ."* ENCYCLOPÉDIE (Neufchâtel, 1775), Vol. XII.

The Mansell Collection

vated a limpid, easy style to attract the average educated reader. Many of them earned their living with their pens, unlike intellectuals of preceding eras, who had been men of wealth and leisure, clergymen, or professors, or had been supported by wealthy patrons.

Beyond a faith in reason the philosophes did not share a common program of action; indeed, they often plunged into rancorous disputes with each other. Their doctrines ranged through many shadings of liberal and radical thought. Yet almost without exception their views suited the needs and demands of the growing middle classes from which most of them came. They were not conscious supporters of middle-class supremacy; they considered themselves defenders of the rights and liberties of all men, not those of one particular group, and their ideas attracted aristocrats and even kings. Nevertheless, they found their most numerous and ardent supporters among the bourgeoisie, who had long suffered under arbitrary rule and aristocratic domination. When in the nineteenth century the middle classes finally gained social and political equality, they appropriated wholesale the principles advocated by the philosophes for the foundation of their new order.

DOCTRINES OF THE PHILOSOPHES

In assuming that they could provide the same sort of orderly, mechanical explanation for the workings of society that the natural scientists had provided for the planetary system, the philosophes failed to recognize the all-important qualitative differences between the methods of Newton and their own. Newton contented himself with explaining how nature operates and did not inquire into the intent of nature or concern himself with ethical considerations. Neither was Newton particularly interested in the utility or the practical application of his findings. In contrast, the philosophes began with certain ethical premises and with the utilitarian conviction that knowledge must serve to improve material welfare. They assumed that existing social and political institutions were contrary to man's best interests and were therefore contrary to nature. Because their own tenets were based entirely upon reason, they assumed that these tenets were in accord with natural law and so were ethical and useful to mankind.

Most philosophes had a firm faith in the inevitability and uninterrupted continuity of human progress. Each generation benefits from the advances made by its predecessors. The idea of inevitable progress, like so much else in the Enlightenment, had been implicit in seventeenth-century thought. There had even been a literary feud in France and England in the seventeenth century known as the quarrel of the Ancients and the Moderns which had centered around the comparative merits of the classical age and their own time, with the Moderns asserting that the present was better because it could build on all the achievements of the past.

The optimism of the philosophes reached its climax in the work of the Marquis de Condorcet (1743–1794). In *The Progress of the Human Mind,* published in 1793 during the French Revolution, Condorcet prophesied that man was destined for unceasing improvement in all his faculties since he had found the sure method of reaching truth through reason and had adopted enlightened policies in government. "No bounds have been set to limit the improvement of the human race; the perfectibility of man is in reality indefinite," said Condorcet. Ironically, he was hiding from political enemies during the Reign of Terror when he wrote these words. Soon after his capture he died in prison—perhaps by his own hand.

The philosophes' critical attitude toward the European society of their own time led them to idealize societies in remote, non-Christian parts of the globe, though they often knew little about these regions. They assumed that distant peoples had far more natural morality and virtue than Europeans did. The Chinese sage became an especially favored stereotype of wisdom and cultivation. Later in the century some philosophes portrayed the American Indian as a "noble savage," the unspoiled child of nature whose simplicity and natural morality put the corrupt civilization of Europe to shame.

THE GREATEST OF THE PHILOSOPHES

Voltaire (1694–1778) has been well described as "the spirit incarnate of the Enlightenment, with all its virtues and all its faults." Born in Paris into a prosperous bourgeois family called Arouet, he early assumed the pseudonym Voltaire. At seventeen he wrote his first work; by the time of his death at eighty-four his published writings filled more than seventy volumes. Plays, novels, histories, poems, political pamphlets, treatises, and thousands of letters poured with equal ease from his pen, all stamped with a lucid style, incisive logic, irony, and never-failing wit. "In Voltaire's fingers," said Anatole France, "the pen runs and laughs." His literary skill, his learning, his wit, and his thirst for controversy made him Europe's best-known man of letters and the idol of intellectuals everywhere.

During his twenties Voltaire was twice imprisoned in the Bastille for disrespect to high aristocrats. Outraged by this injustice, he went into self-imposed exile in England for three years, immersing himself in English culture and becoming its great admirer. In 1733 after his return to Paris he published *Philosophical Letters on the English,* in which he compared the freedom of the press, speech, and religion, equality before the law, and equal taxation he felt existed in England with the injustices and inequities of caste-ridden France. The French government condemned the book, and Voltaire escaped another imprisonment only by again leaving Paris to live on France's eastern frontier. While in England Voltaire had acquired an enthusiasm for the works of Newton and Locke, and he became the leading popularizer of their ideas in France and Europe. His passion for physics even moved him to dabble in experiments in a laboratory set up in his home.

In 1749 Voltaire accepted the repeated invitations of Frederick II of Prussia, who fancied himself a philosopher-king, to live at his court. Voltaire sojourned at Potsdam for two years, but the clash of these two strong personalities produced an impossible situation and the Frenchman left. Since his writings, pensions from wealthy patrons, and shrewd investments had brought him a fortune, he decided to buy an estate at Ferney, then in Switzerland near the French border, where he lived for the rest of his life.

At Ferney, safe from molestation by the French government, Voltaire turned his attention increasingly to philosophical and political matters. He produced a stream of pamphlets, many aimed against the irrationality of Christian dogma and the bigotry of the clergy. An avid disciple of Pierre Bayle (see p. 397), Voltaire used material from the *Historical and Critical*

Dictionary in his own campaign against religious intolerance and persecution—a campaign that has been described as probably the greatest contribution ever made by one man to the freedom of conscience. He took as his war cry the phrase *Écrasez l'infâme*, "Crush the infamous thing," meaning the Roman Catholic Church.

The most famous of his battles for human freedom concerned a Protestant family in Toulouse named Calas. The father had been tortured and executed on the false charge of murdering one of his sons to prevent his conversion to Catholicism, and his two daughters had been immured in convents. The youngest son managed to escape and went to Ferney to seek Voltaire's help. The philosophe's outrage at Calas's condemnation for what he believed and not for any crime he had committed set him on a campaign to right the injustice. It lasted three years, during which time he said he never permitted himself to smile. He wrote pamphlets, sent letters to important people, and collected a defense fund, to which Empress Catherine II of Russia, George III of England, and the king of Poland contributed. His unrelenting pressure finally compelled the courts to declare Calas innocent. The chief judge responsible for the miscarriage of justice was dismissed, and Calas' daughters were released. In another case he spent nine years clearing the family of a Protestant named Servas, who had also been unjustly accused of murdering his daughter because she was about to become a Catholic.

THE RELIGION OF REASON

Voltaire, like most of his fellow philosophes, was a deist. Reason told man that God exists, for there had to be a First Cause. "If God did not exist, it would be necessary to invent him," said Voltaire. The Supreme Being, as the deists preferred to call God, had created a harmonious, ordered universe that ran according to eternal physical and moral laws. A school of thought called Optimism maintained that the world was not perfect, for only God could be perfect, but that it was the best of all possible worlds as far as humans could hope to understand it. Voltaire was an Optimist until the great Lisbon earthquake of 1755 and the outbreak of the Seven Years' War in 1756 compelled him to abandon Optimism because he could not reconcile the senseless suffering in those two disasters— one natural and one man-made—with the belief that this was the best of all possible worlds. He summed up his changed viewpoint in *Candide*, the immortal novel written in just three days in 1759. Candide, educated in his sheltered youth in the philosophy of Optimism, after exposure to the ways of the world defined Optimism as "the mania for pretending that all is well when all is ill."

Although relatively few people subscribed to the religion of reason, their influence far exceeded their number. The devotees of deism included some of the most important people of the time, including rulers and ministers of state. In America such leaders as Thomas Jefferson, Benjamin Franklin, and John Adams adopted reason as their guide to religious faith. Yet deism did not survive the era of the Enlightenment. Too cold and abstract for the masses, who much preferred the color, symbolism, and personal God of orthodox Christianity, it also lost its hold on the intellectuals. They came to realize that the arguments used by deists against Christianity could be turned with equal deadliness against the religion of reason itself. This realization persuaded some to retreat to skepticism or agnosticism. The more advanced skeptics went beyond agnosticism to complete materialism and atheism, holding God to be an unnecessary hypothesis. They maintained that the universe has always existed and that matter, by its nature, has the capacity for motion, sensation, and even thought. Baron d'Holbach (1723–1789), a German nobleman who became a French philosophe, was the best-known defender of this doctrine.

Although deism did not survive the Enlightenment, its attacks on traditional religion helped weaken the established churches during the eighteenth century. Some churchmen, including persons of high ecclesiastical rank, became supporters of the religious views of the Enlightenment, and in many areas their attitude adversely affected the morale of the lower clergy. The Church lost intellectual prestige, for now intellectuals held traditional religious philosophies in low esteem. Corresponding with the decline of religion's influence was a decline in the Church's political influence.

TOLERATION AND HUMANITARIANISM

The philosophes linked their attack on religion with a demand for toleration. They pointed out that it is irrational and immoral to force a man to believe that which his conscience will not let him believe. Intolerance is not only incompatible with religious precepts of charity and love; it is also uncivilized. Religion, they held, is a matter of individual conscience, over which the state should have no control. Many who advocated toleration, however, sometimes proved unwilling to extend it to everyone—atheists and Moslems were still anathema, and the traditional Catholic-Protestant rivalry still made zealots of men who had no use for the theology of either.

Faith in reason led also to a demand for humanitarian reforms. It seemed barbaric to rationalists that in the enlightened eighteenth century the law still permitted cruelty and inhumanity. Slavery and the horrors of the slave trade aroused indignation and pressure for reform. Inhumane treatment of the insane and criminals came under attack, and the first steps were taken to improve conditions in asylums and jails. In an *Essay on Crimes and Punishments* (1764) the Italian philosophe Cesare Beccaria argued for the application of reason to the administration of justice. Laws, he said, should be invariable, fair, and clearly stated. The aim of punishment should be not vengeance but the deterrence of further crime. The penalty should fit the crime; justice should be swift; torture and capital punishment should be abolished as useless and contrary to natural right. The state should by education and rewards for good deeds try to prevent crime. Beccaria's book won great acclaim, was quickly translated into other languages, and stimulated penal reform movements in France, England, and Russia.

THE PHILOSOPHE-POLITICAL THEORISTS

The majority of political theorists among the philosophes spun their webs of theory from unproven assumptions. They generally believed that human nature is everywhere the same so that differences among nations and societies arise not from differences in human nature but from irrational customs and traditions. The principles or natural laws underlying human behavior and institutions can be determined by the use of man's reason. It was assumed that man is by nature rational, basically good, and educable, and that he will accept the natural laws once they are discovered, and follow them to construct societies that will maximize human welfare. Oppressive social, economic, and political institutions were merely the creation of rulers and the Church. Such views explain why most of the philosophes paid slight attention to the historical development of social and political institutions and grossly underestimated the extent to which history determines the structure of social relations.

The philosophes shared a basic conviction that society should be organized for the good of all its members, not just for the benefit of a ruling elite, and that natural laws provide the guidelines to reach this goal. Although they thought in terms of national states, their belief in natural law and man's rationality produced a cosmopolitan outlook. With the triumph of the principles of reason would emerge first a united and uniform European civilization, ultimately a world civilization in which all nations would participate equally and wars would disappear.

Following the pattern set by earlier political theorists, especially John Locke, the political theorists assumed that governments and organized societies started when men formed contracts with one another to protect their rights. They argued that one of man's rights is to revolt against the government if it fails to protect his other rights. Few of the political theorists, however, supported democratic or representative forms of government. They favored absolute rule by an enlightened despot, assisted by an elite of educated men, who would follow the dictates of reason and introduce necessary administrative reforms, establish freedom of thought and religion, and promote material, technical, and educational progress.

Voltaire, who abhorred the idea of government by the people, wrote, "No government can be in any manner effective unless it possess absolute power."

MONTESQUIEU AND CONSTITUTIONAL GOVERNMENT

Charles de Secondat, Baron de Montesquieu (1689–1755), was the most sophisticated of the Enlightenment's political theorists. Unlike the majority of his brethren, he was no fancier of enlightened despotism, and he was unwilling to make the assumption that human nature was everywhere basically the same. As a wealthy member of the French *noblesse de la robe*, Montesquieu opposed the absolutism of the French throne, as much for its ineffectiveness as for its repressiveness. He was, however, far more than a spokesman for special class interests, and he deservedly occupies a high place among the architects of modern constitutional government.

Montesquieu's first work, *Persian Letters* (1721), used the device of an imaginary correspondence between two Persian travelers in Europe to satirize the institutions and customs of his own society. Encouraged by the book's success to devote himself to scholarship and writing, Montesquieu in 1726 sold his seat in the *parlement* (law court) of Bordeaux and set out on a long European tour to find out firsthand about conditions in other lands. The trip included a stay of eighteen months in England, where he acquired a lifelong admiration for the English political system that deeply influenced his thought. After his return home he spent nearly two decades studying and writing, and in 1748 he published his masterpiece, *The Spirit of Laws*.

Montesquieu employed a comparative method to examine a number of political systems, ancient and modern, and to discover the fundamental principles upon which they rested. Dividing governments into republics, monarchies, and despotisms, he concluded that the form of government differed among nations according to their natural environment, their history, and their social and economic conditions. Republics depended upon the public spirit or civic virtue of the people; monarchies depended upon honor in the sense of distinctions awarded outstanding subjects by the monarchs, and despotism depended upon the fear in which the people held the despot. His researches convinced him that republics flourished only in small countries or city-states, monarchies worked best in nations of moderate size in temperate zones, and despotism was most suited for large empires in hot climates.

He urged France to follow the English pattern of the separation of powers as the best guarantee for the preservation of individual rights. In England, he said, the executive, legislative, and judicial authorities were independent of each other and balanced and checked one another, thereby preserving individual liberty. He did not recommend that France duplicate the English system in every detail, proposing instead that governmental power be divided among the king and such traditional "intermediate bodies" as the organized nobility, the *parlements,* the provincial estates, and the chartered towns. Actually, Montesquieu erred in his analysis of the course of English constitutional development, for the revolutionary settlement of 1689 had established the supremacy of Parliament, so that even when Montesquieu wrote, the English system of government was moving toward the concentration in the hands of Parliament of the executive and legislative powers, rather than their separation. Nonetheless, Montesquieu's exposition did much to make the tripartite division of ruling power the model for liberals who wanted to protect the freedom of the individual citizen. It had a potent influence on the drafters of the American Constitution in 1789 and the drafters of many other constitutions during the nineteenth century.

The Encyclopedists and the Progress of Science

In no other facet of the Enlightenment were the philosophes' ideas, outlook, and interests better epitomized than in the great cooperative work of the *Encyclopédie.* Its publisher originally intended it to be a simple translation of a two-volume English encyclopedia, but the plans changed when a hitherto obscure philosophe named Denis Diderot (1713–1784) took over the editorship. Diderot saw in the project the opportunity to create a reference work that would instruct its readers in the rational, scientific, and utilitarian spirit of the Age of Reason. Although most of the articles were handled by second-raters, some of the most important philosophes, including Voltaire, were among the contributors, and the eminent mathematician Jean d'Alembert agreed to serve as Diderot's associate in editing the volumes. The word "encyclopedist," used to describe the contributors, became synonymous with "philosophe."

The *Encyclopédie* comprised seventeen volumes of text and eleven volumes of plates. The first volume appeared in 1751, and the last in 1772. Later five supplementary volumes appeared, but they were not edited by Diderot. Although the set was expensive, the *Encyclopédie* was a great success. Over 4,300 people subscribed to the first edition, and it rapidly went through six more editions. Its articles reflected the philosophes' faith in reason and science and their deep interest in technology and material progress. The *Encyclopédie's* subtitle was *An Analytical Dictionary of the Sciences, Arts, and Trades,* and long articles and carefully engraved illustrations provided detailed information about many manufacturing processes.

The Catholic Church denounced the *Encyclopédie* as the "gospel of Satan," and the French government twice revoked the license to publish the work. D'Alembert, alarmed by the second revocation, withdrew from

Agriculture in Eighteenth-Century France

This engraving from the Encyclopédie *typifies the didactic purpose of Diderot and his collaborators. It shows how tillage should be done, rather than how it was actually done. The plow (fig. 1), modeled after the type designed by Jethro Tull, the English agriculturist, the seeder (fig. 4), the spike harrow (fig. 6), and the roller (fig. 7) were all improved or new farm implements that were still almost unknown in French agricultural practices. Notice, too, the use of horses as draught animals, rather than the slower and less efficient oxen.* C. C. Gillispie, ed., A DIDEROT PICTORIAL ENCYCLOPEDIA OF TRADES AND INDUSTRY (New York, 1959).

collaboration, but the undaunted Diderot managed to overcome these difficulties and carried the work through to completion. The dangers of censorship and suppression, however, forced the encyclopedists to use innuendo and indirectness in the articles. They inserted political and religious criticism in unlikely places. The article on the goddess Juno cast doubts on the Biblical account of the Virgin Mary; the article on salt recounted the injustice to the poor of taxes levied on necessities, including the hated salt tax; and the article on Geneva contained indirect criticism of the French government.

NATURAL SCIENCES

The men of the Enlightenment took special pride in the accomplishments of the natural scientists. Academies, public lectures, journals, and popular books spread a knowledge of science among educated laymen. Science became fashionable, experiments were performed in salons, and prominent people dabbled in it, including monarchs. Benjamin Franklin's electrical experiments thrilled the powdered beauties of the Parisian salons. The overall accomplishments of eighteenth-century science, however, lagged behind the work of the giants of the seventeenth century. In the main the physicists, astronomers, and mathematicians of the Enlightenment devoted themselves to consolidating the discoveries of the preceding century. Their work was derivative rather than fundamental. The French mathematicians d'Alembert, Laplace, and Lagrange gave Newtonian mathematics a more precise expression. Better methods for teaching were introduced. Marked improvements in scientific instruments such as the thermometer, barometer, balance, and lenses facilitated experimentation.

Important advances were made in understanding the forms of energy. Research on the properties of heat, chiefly by the Scottish professor Joseph Black (1729–1799), provided a precise quantitative and conceptual foundation for its study. Serious investigation of electricity began, and became the most progressive branch of eighteenth-century physics. Outstanding work in this field was done by the Italians Luigi Galvani (1737–1798) and Alessandro Volta (1745–1827), the second of whom invented the battery, the first usable source of electricity; Benjamin Franklin (1706–1790), who contributed the concept of positive and negative charges and studies of conduction; and the Frenchman Charles Coulomb (1736–1806), who began the quantitative study of electricity. The leading contribution to biology was the system of classification perfected by the Swedish botanist Carolus Linnaeus (1707–1778). The next step was suggested by Jean Baptiste Lamarck (1744–1829), curator of the Jardin des Plantes in Paris, who advanced a theory of evolution that explained changes in species as a result of adaptation to changing environment. Near the end of the Enlightenment several chemists—notably the Frenchman Antoine Lavoisier (1743–1794), whose experiments showed the importance of precise quantitative techniques—began a revolution in the concepts and methods of chemistry that was to bear brilliant fruit in the nineteenth century.

THE STUDY OF HISTORY

Montesquieu alone among the principal philosophes took into account historical factors in explaining the nature of contemporary society. Other philosophes, however, were not loath to use history to persuade people of the truth of the doctrines of reason. History was "philosophy teaching by example." A number of philosophes turned their talents to the writing of historical syntheses to illustrate the workings of reason in mankind. Voltaire wrote histories of European civilization from the time of Charlemagne to the eighteenth century in which he tried to demonstrate how reason had evidenced itself in historical evolution. Turgot in *Discourses on Universal History* took as his purpose the discovery of the laws of social development. Condorcet's *Outline for a Historical Presentation of the Progress of the Human Mind* portrayed the steady progress of mankind through the ages. The pre-eminent historian of the eighteenth century, the Englishman Edward Gibbon, in *The History of the Decline and Fall of the Roman Empire* blamed the collapse of Imperial Rome on the rise of the anti-rational Christian faith.

Counter-Enlightenment

Reaction against the ideas of the Enlightenment came from men who were within the main stream of eighteenth-century intellectual endeavor and from men who stood apart from it. Both groups, for different reasons, rejected the conviction that the unaided human reason could propound the explanation of the universe and man.

RELIGIOUS REVIVAL

Enthusiasm for the religion of reason, as indeed for all the ideas of the Enlightenment, was confined mainly to the minority of the cultured in the upper strata of society. It held little appeal for ordinary people, nor did it satisfy some religiously inclined members of the educated upper classes. In addition, the inroads made by rationalism and religious liberalism among the clergy of the traditional churches disturbed people of deep religious feeling. They wanted a "religion of the heart" rather than a religion of reason. In their search for a more emotionally satisfying religious experience many of them joined mystical or semimystical sects that arose in the eighteenth century.

In Germany a rebirth of pietism emphasized the importance of inner religious experience, a spiritual awakening, and a "second birth" in conversion. Count von Zinzendorf (1700–1760), leader of the movement, drew on the mystical doctrines of seventeenth-century Pietists to preach a personal and emotional faith to his followers. Zinzendorf's sect, called the Moravian Brethren, was founded early in the 1730's and established settlements in North America centering around Bethlehem, Pennsylvania. A similar movement, Methodism, grew up within the Church of England, led by the Anglican minister John Wesley (1703–1791), and finally in the 1790's it broke away to form an independent church. (See p. 351.) In North America a revivalist movement known as the Great Awakening swept through the British colonies in the 1730's and 1740's, led initially by the redoubtable New England Congregationalist Jonathan Edwards (1703–1758). All three of these Protestant pietist movements were closely connected: Wesley's relations with Zinzendorf and his followers led to Wesley's mystical conversion in 1738, and Edwards' rustic revival in the 1730's prepared the way for the first successful Methodist mission to the colonies in 1740.

Within the Roman Catholic Church Jansenism gained new adherents in France and a few in other lands. From the Jansenist revival in France emerged a radical group, the Convulsionists, who heard apocalyptic prophecies and saw miracles in a Parisian graveyard in which a martyr to the cause was buried, until the government closed the graveyard in 1732.

In the intellectually isolated Jewish communities of Eastern Europe a revivalist movement called Hasidism, from the Hebrew word for pious, won thousands of adherents. Founded in Poland in the late 1730's by Israel ben Eliezer (1700–1760), a simple laborer whose followers called him Master of the Good Name, Hasidism taught that joyous religious fervor brought man into direct communion with God and was superior to the theology expounded by the rabbis. Mysticism even made inroads into Freemasonry, the bastion of rationalism. Mystical ideas and ceremonies, inspired by the desire for spiritual regeneration through direct supernatural contact with God, appeared among Masons in Germany, Russia, and France.

PHILOSOPHIC REACTION

Since the religious revival deliberately rejected science and formal philosophy, it hardly touched the intellectuals. They were reached by men of their own kind, who questioned the fundamental assumptions of rationalist philosophy in philosophic circles.

The skepticism of the Scottish philosopher David Hume (1711–1776) struck a hard blow at faith in natural law as well as religion. Hume insisted that man can accept as true only those things for which he has the evidence of factual observation. The philosophes lacked such indisputable evidence for their belief in a perfect Creator or in the existence of natural law and natural morality. Such assumptions may be true, said Hume, but we have no way of finding out and never will have, nor are we able to disprove completely the opposite assumptions. "A total suspense of judgment," he concluded, "is our only reasonable resource." Faith in reason cannot be maintained either. According to Hume, man's nature is the product of habit and custom, and most of his opinions are the result of his early education and environment. Human nature, therefore, can never be explained by reason or reduced to universal natural laws.

Hume belonged to the Enlightenment, although he questioned its fundamental assumptions. A more damaging assault was made by Immanuel Kant (1724–1804), particularly in *Critique of Pure Reason* (1781). Kant was a professor of philosophy at the Prussian University of Königsberg. Educated as a Pietist, he was relatively immune to the blandishments of the philosophes. Kant agreed with Hume that science and reason do not provide man with indisputable explanations of such problems as the existence of God, moral law, and immortality. Science, according to Kant, can describe the phenomena of the material world but cannot provide a guide for morality. There are, however, certain human experiences or feelings, such as conscience, religious emotion, and awareness of beauty, whose reality cannot be doubted even though science cannot explain them. These intuitive instincts, implanted by God, make man aware of the difference between good and evil. Kant called this awareness the "categorical imperative." It cannot be denied; it compels man to make a choice between right and wrong. By his insistence that science is limited in scope and that science and morality are separate branches of knowledge, Kant opened the way to new views of man's role and destiny that refuted the rationalism of the Enlightenment. His philosophy became the point of departure for nearly all nineteenth-century philosophical speculation.

JEAN JACQUES ROUSSEAU (1712–1778)

Even though he is counted among the greatest of the philosophes, Jean Jacques Rousseau was the seminal figure in the reaction against rationalism. The new movement called romanticism that was destined to supplant rationalism as Europe's dominant philosophy sprang principally from his writings.

Born in Geneva into a lower-middle-class Protestant family, Rousseau had a neglected and unhappy childhood, ran away at sixteen, and never afterward found a place in which he felt completely at home or friends in whom he had full confidence. For years he earned a precarious living. After he became famous, he lived mainly on the generosity of friends or the patronage of important people, and he usually repaid his benefactors with ingratitude and incivility. In spite of universal recognition, throughout his life he felt insecure and alienated from society.

His unhappy life had much to do with shaping his thought. He believed that man in the state of nature, without civilization, is fundamentally good. Nature has given man warmth of feeling, sincerity and simplicity of heart, and love and sympathy for his fellow man. Civilization has corrupted him; the progress in the arts and sciences in which the men of the Enlightenment took such pride actually debased man. Rousseau found the origin of society's ills in the introduction long ago of private property. This had given rise to inequality, avarice, envy, wickedness, class struggle, war, and not the least in the catalogue of woes, government itself, established by man to protect his property.

Rousseau maintained that the natural, good qualities in man stem from his emotions, while the evil qualities come from his reason. Man should therefore rely on his heart and not his head. In contrast to his fellow philosophes, Rousseau believed that intuition and emotion provide far better guides to action than reason and philosophy. Such simple natural joys as family life, humble toil, and above all a feeling of community with our fellow men give meaning and value to life. Religious reverence and belief in God belong among the natural emotions, too, though Rousseau himself did not subscribe to any formal religion.

Rousseau admitted that his description of the state of nature and the origin of civilization were not historically true. He explained that he employed these concepts as hypothetical arguments "to throw light on the nature of things, rather than to show their true origins." He recognized that man could not slough off civilization and return to his primitive state. Nevertheless, in his extremely influential novels, *La Nouvelle Héloïse* (1761) and *Émile* (1762), he tried to fashion a program of reform in education and environment (he was a good son of the Enlightenment in his environmentalism) that would enable man to preserve uncorrupted his innate feelings for justice and virtue. Rousseau urged a return to nature as far as possible. He was no fraudulent nature-lover; in the Jardin des Plantes in Paris his large collection of pressed flowers, neatly classified, can still be seen.

In *The Social Contract* (1762) Rousseau addressed himself to the more serious problem of devising a government that would preserve, as much as possible in modern society, the natural equality of man. In so doing, he contradicted his earlier arguments favoring unlimited individual freedom. *The Social Contract* proposed a system of government in which each individual would surrender all his natural freedoms to everyone else in his society. Rousseau argued that when men left the state of nature they made a contract with each other to subject themselves to what he called the "general will." This general will is more than a decision of the majority, which he called the "will of all." The general will represents the real will of each individual in the society, even though the individual himself might not realize it. The general will is always in the best interests of everyone. It aims at both the well-being of the entire society and that of each person within the society. True freedom consists in giving complete obedience to the general will, since each person's best interests are contained in it. If individuals place what they mistakenly consider to be their own best interest above the general will, inequalities, injustices, and impairment of freedom will result. Anyone who tries to do this must be compelled to follow the general will. As Rousseau put it, "he must be forced to be free." Rousseau provided no machinery for the discovery of the general will, though he thought that the will of all would sometimes coincide with the general will. Nor did he realize that to coerce a person to accept a pattern of behavior that somehow had been defined as the general will could lead to the negation of individual freedom and the tyranny of the strongest.

During Rousseau's lifetime *The Social Contract* was little read and poorly understood. Two decades after his death, much better understood, it became the ostensible model for Robespierre's Republic of Virtue in revolutionary France. It has since enjoyed a long vogue, drawn upon by theorists of both democracy and authoritarianism. All who have sought to use it either for theory or in practice have had to make their peace with its essential, inescapable conclusion—that society's corporate will dominating the will of its members makes all men equal but equally unfree.

RETROSPECT

In retrospect, the Age of Reason takes on a peculiarly unreal tinge. The eighteenth century ended in the convulsions of riots and revolution, massacres and mass executions, the establishment of the first genuine hegemony over the breadth of Europe since the Roman Empire, and a world war of gigantic proportions lasting over two decades. Much of the slaughter, rapine, and conquest were done in the name of the principles that had been the articles of faith of the philosophes.

In his near classic *The Heavenly City of the Eighteenth Century Philosophers* (1932) the American historian Carl Becker argued that the Age of Reason was in reality an age of faith. The philosophes replaced traditional religion with a new faith in science and reason, and they looked forward to a better world with as much confidence as the theologians of the thirteenth century had looked forward to perfect happiness in life after death. In fact there was a wide variety of views among the philosophes and there were many who did not share a wholly optimistic faith in progress, in the natural goodness of man, or even in reason.

For all of the philosophes' naiveté and ultimate ineffectualness, the Western world owes much to them. Tolerance, a decline in superstition, belief in the dignity and inherent rights of the individual, freedom of thought and expression, liberal political ideas, a conviction that governments should rule for the benefit of the governed, humanitarianism, and enthusiasm for education—in one guise or another all are our heritage from the Enlightenment.

CHAPTER EIGHTEEN

The Crisis of Absolutism

ABSOLUTISM in the mid-eighteenth century looked different from that epitomized in Louis XIV; indeed, contemporaries viewed it as a new variety of absolutism, which came to be called "enlightened despotism." With hardly an exception men of the eighteenth century compared the old absolutism unfavorably with the new. Monarchs who were not considered enlightened were disapproved; those who were enlightened were applauded. What contemporaries failed to see was how fragile absolutism—enlightened or otherwise—was by the mid-eighteenth century, and how little time it had left.

Enlightened Despotism

Enlightened despotism was the attempt of rulers or their ministers to apply the political tenets of the philosophes to the practice of absolutism. To justify their claims to absolute power, enlightened despots appealed to reason and to a secular and utilitarian concept of monarchy rather than to divine right or dynastic prerogatives. Thomas Hobbes in *Leviathan* had provided their fundamental argument: reason demonstrates that government functions best when it is headed by an autocratic ruler, and that the alternative to absolutism is anarchy. Reason also demands that the monarch accept as his objectives the increased prosperity of his subjects and their uninterrupted progress, and that he incorporate the principles of the Enlightenment into his government to reach these objectives.

It should not be assumed, however, that the enlightened despots were altruistic philosopher-kings. They believed that their own interests could best be served by reforms inspired by the philosophy of reason. Greater prosperity that increased the wealth and number of their subjects also provided the royal treasury with more tax revenues and the royal army with more soldiers. Rational reforms of administration strengthened the central government and increased its efficiency. The political and dynastic considerations that had moved the absolute monarchs of preceding generations had not vanished. They were only muted, and they always prevailed when they came into conflict with the doctrines of the philosophes.

Enlightened despots sat on the thrones of Prussia, Austria, Spain, Portugal, Sweden, Denmark, and a number of small German and Italian states. There was one notable impostor, Catherine II of Russia, whose enlightenment was a pose, not a practice; few governments have been less enlightened than her regime. Significantly, no French monarch's name can be added to the list, though not for want of trying by a few of their abler ministers.

The enlightened despots followed similar patterns of reform and innovation. They all sought to increase the level of agricultural productivity by sponsoring improved techniques, and often they tried to improve the economic and legal status of the peasants, who were by far the most numerous of their subjects. They reformed judicial procedures, codified and simplified laws, abolished or limited torture and inhumane sentences, and promoted better public health, hospitals, and asylums. They supported scientific, technical, and literary activities and attempted to raise the level of popular education. In religious matters they were strongly secular and, almost without exception, more tolerant than their predecessors. In Catholic states this secularism manifested itself in restrictions on papal influence over the Church. In several countries the Jesuits were expelled, and finally in 1773 the pope was persuaded to suppress the order. It was not re-established until 1814, by which time the doctrines of the Enlightenment had fallen into disrepute among monarchs.

PRUSSIA

Frederick II of Prussia (1740–1786), the first monarch to proclaim himself a disciple of the Enlightenment, once told a philosophe, "Philosophes such as you teach what ought to be, and kings are there to carry out that which you have conceived." Actually, Frederick's enlightened despotism was raised on the solid and wholly unphilosophical foundations laid by his drillmaster father, Frederick William I. Little in the practice of his regime can be ascribed specifically to the Age of Reason. It was his style of rule and his intellectual predilections more than the introduction of enlightened reforms in government that admitted Frederick to the ranks of the enlightened despots.

He read widely and wrote long treatises on history and government, besides many poems and essays, which gained him the reputation of being a minor philosophe. His contemporaries always remembered him as the young Prometheus bound, desirous of giving himself to philosophy but frustrated by his father's boorishness and brutality. His first published treatise on politics, appearing in 1740 and called *Anti-Machiavel*, assailed the principles of Machiavelli as immoral. A few months later, however, Frederick launched an unprovoked attack on Austrian Silesia; from the very start of his reign he was not one to permit the humanitarian and pacific ideals of the philosophes to stand in the way of his political ambitions. He wrote and spoke only in French, for he said that German was "unmanageable and lacking in grace." He looked to French thinkers for intellectual inspiration and took much pleasure in the friendship and correspondence of French philosophes.

Convinced that government could be reduced to a science, Frederick held that the state was the supreme authority, with all persons, including the king, subordinate to its interests. The king was simply the chief official or, as Frederick put it, "the first servant" of the state, whose function was to promote the welfare of his people. To do so he must have absolute power, for "The prince is to the society what the head is to the body." (Frederick's analogy was not particularly original; William Harvey, discoverer of the circulation of the blood, had made the same point a century earlier in a political essay addressed to Charles I.)

Frederick's reform of the judicial system made Prussian justice the most incorruptible and efficient in all Europe. He laid the foundation for reform and codification of Prussian law and abolished the use of torture except on charges of treason and murder. He won special acclaim for introducing limited freedom of speech and the press. He was himself indifferent to religious faith and urged tolerance on his subjects. His own tolerance, however, did not extend to Jews, whom he excluded from the civil service, the professions, agriculture, and most trades, and from whom he extorted large sums of money through special taxes.

AUSTRIA: MARIA THERESA

The first victim of Frederick's aggression was Maria Theresa of Austria (1740–80), who was not counted among the enlightened. She was less fortunate in her inheritance than was her Prussian archrival, for a defeated army, an empty treasury, and a state on the brink of dissolution constituted her patrimony in 1740. The first eight years of her reign were given over to the desperate defense of her realm following Frederick's invasion of Silesia. As soon as hostilities were ended, Maria Theresa dedicated herself to remedying the frailties that had brought her monarchy so close to dissolution. Her motives were simple: to assure that she would not lose another war with Frederick, and to regain Silesia. The latter was not accomplished, but under her leadership Austria did become far stronger and more unified. Maria Theresa's rivalry with Frederick, rather than the tenets of the Enlightenment, moved her to transform Austria.

Beautiful, gay, devoutly Catholic, and wholly without pretence of intellectuality, Maria Theresa bore no visible signs of greatness. Yet she had a strong sense of duty, was resourceful and courageous, sensible and intelligent, and was masterful in turning her feminine charm to get her way. Never loosening the reins of personal control, she readily accepted the services of ministers who were more creative and intellectual than she was. Prince Wenzel von Kaunitz, in effect a coruler; Count Ludwig Haugwitz, an administrator of extraordinary talent; Count Rudolph Chotek, an able financier; and many lesser servants were sympathetic to the Enlightenment. The interplay between their more advanced views and her innate conservatism and pragmatic good sense produced a workable amalgam of reform for Austria.

The state's most pressing need was a reorganization of the central administration, for all other reforms depended upon its efficiency. Through Haugwitz's efforts the administrative system was rebuilt along the Prussian pattern. A central bureau, the Directorium, modeled after the Prussian General Directory, was established to exercise overall supervision. A Council of State, created to serve as the empress's advisory board, examined all projects of reform and made appropriate recommendations to the sovereign. To carry through this program of centralization it was necessary to reduce drastically the traditional privileges of the provincial estates. These bodies persisted, but their legislative and administrative functions were taken over almost entirely by agencies of the central government, staffed by German Austrians, under the control of the Directorium. A High Court of Justice was set up for the entire state, provincial law codes were recast, and a new criminal code was promulgated. Reform was instituted in the army, too, including establishment of a system of conscription, adoption of the Prussian tactics of swift deployment and rapid fire, creation of a military academy to train officers (all of whom were nobles), and standardization of uniforms.

Recognizing the need for improvements in the condition of the peasantry, the chief source of revenue and recruits, the government set out on a program of agrarian reform. Most of the empire's peasants were serfs, and the government's aim was to improve the condition of their servitude, not free them from it. Beginning in the 1760's codes were issued for each province regulating the relationship between lord and peasant, fixing the amount of dues and services the peasant had to pay his lord, protecting the peasant's rights in the land he tilled, allowing him more personal freedom of movement, and reducing the lord's police and judicial authority over the peasant. Special governmental agencies were established in each province to enforce the provisions of the codes. In the last years of Maria Theresa's reign a step was taken in the direction of abolishing serfdom. Peasants who lived on estates owned by the crown were freed of their servile obligations and became renters of the land they worked. The government's hope that private landowners would follow its example was in vain, for only a handful of proprietors adopted the system.

In addition to limiting the power of the lords over their peasants, the government subjected them to a property tax on their demesne land—land that was tilled for them by their peasants. Although the tax rate was not as high as that paid by the peasants on the land they tilled for themselves, it established the principle of the tax liability of all subjects, regardless of class.

The empress and her advisers realized the value of education in making good citizens. Influenced by Gerhard van Swieten, a Dutch doctor who served as both Maria Theresa's physician and her adviser on educational matters, the empress promulgated a decree in 1774 establishing elementary schools supported by local and national funds, to be attended by all children between six and thirteen. Technical and classical high schools and teacher training schools were founded, and major reforms toward modernization were made in the curriculum of the University of Vienna.

Maria Theresa's reforms applied almost without exception only to the German and Bohemian parts of her realm. Hungary, Belgium, and Lombardy, all parts of the Hapsburg patrimony, were maintained as separate states with their own institutions. The empress and her advisers realized that attempts to extend the reforms to these regions could well lead to serious political difficulties and even revolt. The Hungarians especially resented Austrian rule and had bitter memories of the Hapsburg conquest. Maria Theresa changed all this when in 1741 she appeared personally before the Hungarian estates, with her infant son in her arms, to implore aid against Prussia. Her beauty, courage, and glowing words captured the minds and hearts of the Magyar aristocrats, who with shouts of enthusiasm promised her 100,000 men. It was the turning point in the history of Austro-Hungarian relations; from then onward the Hungarian nobility counted itself among the strongest supporters of the House of Hapsburg. Maria Theresa wisely rewarded them with high offices, titles, and land, lured them to Vienna, and educated their sons with her own in a private academy, suitably named the Theresianum. While Hungarian affairs were increasingly handled in Vienna and the chief officials of Hungary became functionaries of the crown rather than of the Diet, the empress was careful to retain Hungary's status as a separate part of her realm, to exempt it from nearly all her reforms, and to treat the Magyar nobles with special consideration.

In 1765 when Maria Theresa's husband died, their eldest son, Joseph, succeeded his father as Holy Roman Emperor and became coruler with his mother. Headstrong and infatuated with the ideas of the Enlightenment, Joseph had no patience with his mother's pragmatic and cautious method of government. There were many harsh words between them, but as the junior partner, Joseph had to yield. His chance finally came when the empress died in 1780.

JOSEPH II

Events were to prove that the son was not as capable a ruler as the mother had been. His doctrinaire implementation of the tenets of the philosophes was so extreme that his reign turned out to be one of revolution from above and failure. Like Frederick, he described himself as "the first servant of his people." All that the state did was to be done for the people, but nothing was to be done by the people. He, the enlightened despot, knew what was best for them. Concentrating administration in his own hands, he attempted to reorganize the entire empire into a uniformly rational pattern. Indifferent to the marked regionalism of the realm, he divided it into thirteen large districts, subdivided each into smaller units, staffed the new administrations with his own bureaucrats, and made German the only official language except in the Austrian Netherlands and Lombardy. He created a secret police whose task was to maintain rigid surveillance of the bureaucrats and of the political opinions of his subjects. He simplified the court system, establishing equal punishment for the same offenses regardless of the culprit's social standing, and he drew up law codes in which, among other things, the death penalty was abolished for many offenses for which it had hitherto been imposed.

Joseph's enlightened views made him a defender of religious toleration. One of his first acts was to make Protestants, Eastern Orthodox, and Jews equal with Roman Catholics before the law and allow them to hold public office and have their own schools, churches, and seminaries. He sought to increase state control over the Church at the expense of Rome, dissolving over seven hundred of more than two thousand monasteries on the grounds that the monks and nuns were unproductive. The income from these confiscated properties went to support schools, charitable institutions, hospitals, parish priests, and the ex-monks themselves. Education was freed of Church control, and marriage was made a civil contract. Bishops were made to swear allegiance to the state, and new bishoprics were created in which Joseph installed men of his own choosing. Rome's protests, even the pope's personal visit to Vienna, were of no avail. In modifying but not abolishing

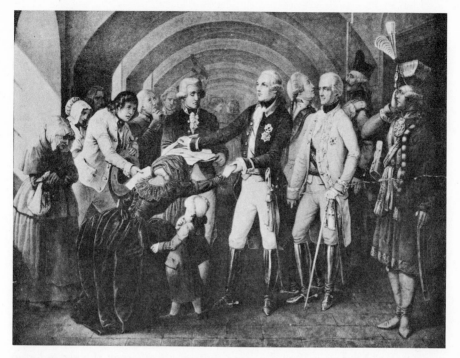

Joseph II Grants an Audience to a Subject, drawing by Ritter von Perger, lithograph by S. Bauer

"Since the good can only be of one kind, namely that which serves all, or at least the greatest number . . . and since equally all provinces in the monarchy must constitute only one whole, all jealousy, all prejudice, which until now has existed frequently among nationalities must cease. . . .

"He who wishes to serve the state must think of himself last. . . . Only one intention can guide his action, the greatest good and usefulness for the greatest number." From Joseph II's Instructions to His Bureaucracy (1783), reprinted in E. M. Link, THE EMANCIPATION OF THE AUSTRIAN PEASANT 1740–1798 (New York, 1949).

Courtesy of Heeresgeschichtliches Museum, Austria

state censorship, Joseph let loose a stream of books and pamphlets, many of them attacking the Catholic Church and supporting the doctrines of the Enlightenment.

Although Joseph never completely abandoned the prevailing mercantilist views and, in fact, raised the already high tariffs, he was strongly influenced by the physiocratic theories of economic freedom so popular among men of the Enlightenment. The government began to relax its regulation of trade and manufacturing, and to reduce its subsidies to private enterprises. The contrast between the conservatism of Maria Theresa and the revolutionary fervor of her son was nowhere more clear than in their respective handling of the agrarian question. In 1781 he issued a decree giving peasants their personal liberty. Serfdom was abolished, although if the

427

peasant remained on the lord's estate, he still had to pay him certain obligations in labor, kind, and cash. Other decrees in succeeding years protected the peasant from eviction from his holding and gave him the right to pass it on to his children. Finally in 1789 Joseph ordered that all the dues and services paid by more prosperous peasants to their landlords be converted into money rent. By the same law he equalized the land tax rates of the peasantry and the nobility.

A few months after the promulgation of this decree Joseph died, a broken man of forty-nine. Almost without exception his reforms had failed. Hungary and Belgium were in revolt against centralization. The nobility were outraged and on the verge of rebellion against the agrarian reforms and the loss of class advantages. Even the peasants were in revolt because the opposition of the nobles had compelled Joseph to suspend implementation of the agrarian reforms of 1789 and because these reforms extended only to the wealthier peasants. The war with Turkey into which Austria had been drawn in 1788 was going badly, and economic depression heightened Joseph's sense of failure. Bitter and disillusioned, he repealed some of the reforms shortly before his death in 1790 and was said to have been on the point of repealing them all. He summed up his career in the epitaph he wrote for himself: "Here lies a prince whose intentions were pure, but who had the misfortune to see all his plans miscarry." Joseph tried to go too fast and too far—Frederick II said of him that he always took the second step before he took the first. He was a revolutionary without a party to support him and without public opinion behind him.

He was succeeded by his brother Leopold II, who as Grand Duke of Tuscany had been one of Europe's most enlightened and most successful rulers. Leopold saw his mission as the restoration of internal unity to the empire. In his brief two-year reign he repealed most of Joseph's revolutionary legislation, although he refused to be cowed into utter reaction. Above all, he refused to give in to demands of nobles that he abolish the agrarian reforms of Joseph and those of Maria Theresa as well. He repealed Joseph's never-enforced agrarian law of 1789, but the peasants retained their freedom to choose their own occupations, to move about as they wished, to marry whom they pleased, and to occupy permanently their holdings.

SPAIN

In contrast to its fiasco in Austria, enlightened despotism in Spain under Charles III (1759–88) piled up a record of achievements. King of Naples before succeeding to the Spanish throne, Charles was a man of average intelligence but of much experience in ruling, who was possessed of a desire to better the well-being of his subjects. Aware of his own intellectual limitations, he leaned heavily on able ministers who were deeply affected by the ideas of the Enlightenment.

Charles continued the policy of administrative centralization initiated by his Bourbon predecessors, revised the tax structure, ended many oppressive levies, and arranged for a more equitable distribution of the tax burden by a kind of graduated income tax. Though a devout Catholic, he completed the subordination of the Church to the state. In 1767 he expelled the Jesuits, the chief opponents of state domination of the Church, and curtailed the powers of the Inquisition, which the Jesuits had controlled. Concerned by the ignorance and superstition of many priests, he attempted reforms in clerical education, issued regulations tightening monastic discipline, and appointed able men to bishoprics. He freed those of Jewish descent from the legal handicaps that barred them from military service and from many trades, although practicing Jews were still excluded from the country. He tried without success to end begging, a perennial problem in Spain, by establishing workhouses and asylums and by sending mendicants into the army; the practice was too widespread and the state's resources too limited. Humanitarian legislation was issued to protect Negro slaves in Spanish America. His educational reforms were especially ambitious. He promoted primary and vocational schools, strengthened university faculties, and introduced new curricula, including courses in science, despite protests from conservative academics that Newtonian physics did not help a student become a good metaphysician.

Charles was particularly concerned with economic problems. His government introduced measures to increase farm output by reclaiming land, bringing in foreign colonists, flood control, irrigation, and reforestation. It also adopted measures designed to increase peasant proprietorship and to decrease large-scale land ownership by absentee landlords. The privileges of the Mesta (see p. 186), the association of sheep raisers, were greatly reduced, notably the right to graze its flocks on common land and to prevent enclosures. Measures directed at stimulating industry included the importation of foreign artisans, the opening of government-owned factories in new industries, construction of roads and canals, standardization of weights, measures, and coinage, a postal system, and drastic revision of internal tariffs. Royal support given to some seventy private societies throughout Spain called *Amigos de País* (Friends of the Country), composed of leaders in economic and intellectual life, promoted technical schools, new industries, and model farms. These public and private activities stimulated a marked increase in Spanish industrial and agricultural production.

The promise of continued development held out to Spain by Charles's reign was not fulfilled. He was succeeded in 1788 by his dull-witted and pleasure-loving son Charles IV. The new king had no interest in following his father's policies; the old groups regained power, misrule and immorality became the order of the day, and the fortunes of Spain descended to a new low.

PORTUGAL

The decay of Portugal was momentarily halted during the reign of Joseph I (1750–77). The Marquis de Pombal, one of Joseph's ministers, so distinguished himself in directing the reconstruction of Lisbon after an earthquake and tidal wave in 1755 leveled the city and killed nearly thirty thousand people that the king gave him his unlimited trust. Pombal, infected with the ideas of the Enlightenment, believed that only absolute monarchy could save Portugal. He set out to crush the coalition of wealthy nobles and Churchmen, particularly the Jesuits, who shared power with the throne. In 1758 the uncovering of a plot against the crown gave him his opportunity. He ordered the execution or imprisonment of leaders of the aristocracy and in 1759 succeeded in having the Jesuits expelled from the country.

Now able to carry out a reform program without interference, Pombal overhauled the administrative machinery of the state, sacked a host of useless officials, ended the nobility's monopoly of government posts, introduced the merit system into the civil service, reformed tax collection, and reduced corruption so that the government's revenues rose sharply. Tackling the problems of economic growth, he established trading companies, stimulated new lines of production, abolished internal tolls, and ended tariffs between Portugal and her colonies. Full civil liberties were extended to persons of Jewish ancestry, slavery was abolished, and a national educational system was created. Legal codification was projected. At the same time Pombal was a ruthless man, whose spies were everywhere and who filled the prisons with those who disagreed with him. When Joseph died in 1777, Pombal's foes at court had him dismissed, his reforms languished, and Portugal soon fell back into its old torpor.

SCANDINAVIA

In Sweden and Denmark enlightened despotism was short-lived and demoniacally violent in its end. In Sweden Gustavus III (1771–92) ended noble domination by a coup in 1772. Initially popular, nearly absolute in authority, and a devotee of the Enlightenment, Gustavus instituted a series of reforms that included tax revision, judicial reform and the abolition of torture, the lifting of internal tariffs, religious toleration, a free press, and educational reform. In the second decade of his reign the old conflict with the nobility broke out again, fired by the king's heavy military expenditures and reverses in war. Supported by the middle and lower classes, Gustavus triumphed briefly in a second coup d'état in 1789 and won still greater powers for himself, only to be shot in the back at a masquerade ball by a group of nobles in black masks.

In Denmark King Christian VII (1766–1808) suffered from insanity. In 1768 he engaged a new German physician, the young and handsome Johann

Friedrich Struensee, ardent disciple of the Enlightenment. The new doctor quickly managed to make himself chief adviser of the king and lover of the queen. By 1770 he ruled Denmark in all but name, and in two whirlwind years he introduced almost all the reforms associated with enlightened despotism. In 1772 a palace revolution, supported by the king's mother and brother, overthrew him, and he was executed. Many of his reforms were undone, yet his innovations paved the way for progressive measures in later years.

THE CRISIS OF ABSOLUTISM

Enlightened despotism hardly worked wonders anywhere. If undertaken in the pure light of reason without the political wisdom and energy of a Frederick II, Maria Theresa, or Charles III of Spain, it worked not at all. Everywhere in Europe in the middle years of the eighteenth century despots —both enlightened and unenlightened—confronted a dangerous new phenomenon. The nobilities of Europe, no longer content to remain satellites in the galaxies of sun kings, began to reassert themselves from the islands of privilege left to them by the absolutist state. Enlightened despotism tended more to aggravate the monarch's position than to improve it, for the reform programs impinged on the vested interests of the nobility and provided it with a tangible target for attack. Some absolutist monarchs effectively met the challenge, principally in Eastern Europe; those in Western Europe were seldom able to contain noble assertiveness so easily. Nowhere was this plainer than in the state that had set the pace for absolutism in all of Europe, that had provided the first and greatest sun king— France.

The Failure to Renovate France

LOUIS XV

Over a century ago the French historian Alexis de Tocqueville wrote of Louis XV, king of France from 1715 to 1774, great-grandson and successor of Louis XIV: "Had there been on the throne a ruler of the calibre and temperament of Frederick the Great, he certainly would have carried out many of the great changes in social conditions and in the government that were made by the Revolution, and not only would have kept his crown but would have greatly increased his power."

The invidious comparison of Louis XV with Frederick II of Prussia was apt. The comparison had to do not with enlightened despotism, but with the characters of men. Louis had few of the qualities of leadership that characterized the great Prussian. He was intelligent, able, and quick, but he lacked strength of character, application, and all those other capacities which absolutism demanded of kingship and which Frederick possessed. Louis XV preferred the continual diversions provided by hunting and by such famous charmers as the Marquise de Pompadour and the Countess du Barry. Although not unique failings for the age, the sovereign of a great state could ill afford to spend so much time in these pursuits. Louis XV was a perpetual adolescent called to do a man's job.

Louis was five at his accession, and the first eleven years of his reign were passed under a regency filled with strife, intrigue, and indecision, presided over by two successive regents, the Duke of Orleans (1715–23) and the Duke of Bourbon (1723–26). Neither was particularly competent, and both were intent upon keeping their young charge as irresponsible as possible. By the time he had tired of Bourbon's intrigue and banished him in 1726, Louis had developed a fine taste for indolence and a suitably bored expression to go with it. For almost two decades he had the good sense to leave government to his capable, cautious, and honest old tutor Cardinal Fleury while he prolonged his youthful insouciance.

FLEURY'S ADMINISTRATION

Fleury's regime, lasting from 1726 until his death in 1743, was the sole extended period of political stability and peace that France knew in the eighteenth century, and Fleury was primarily responsible for it. He was the only chief minister of Louis XV who was not dismissed from office. He was a shrewd diplomatist, bent on peace and the containment of peripheral brushfire wars that might have set off a general war. With hardly a shot fired, he raised France's international prestige to a level it had not held since 1690, when the system of coalitions against Louis XIV had been perfected. He was a capable and steady administrator, summoning the best talent available. A number of the major ministers under Fleury were former intendants, men who had learned administration from the bottom up and retained a sharp sense of how policy made at Versailles might look different at Marseilles, Toulouse, Bordeaux, Tours, Rouen, or Strasbourg. There was nothing particularly brilliant about their administration; they were orthodox, methodical, honest, and effective. These qualities alone made them unique in eighteenth-century France. Some modest steps forward were taken. The codification of France's chaotic complex of laws and jurisdictions begun under Colbert was continued, Jansenism was quieted, and the mounting assertiveness of the nobility in the parlements was contained, for the last time.

With peace and an honest administration France began to recuperate from the loss of men, money, and matériel suffered in Louis XIV's wars. French commerce revived, to the alarm of the English, and France's increasing fleet of merchant ships began to mount a challenge in the carrying trade of both slaves and general cargo. Fleury's diplomatic success with the Turks once more opened up the Levant trade for France. The growth of French ports, on both the Atlantic and the Mediterranean, reflected commercial advance. Industries connected with colonial trade flourished, particularly distilling, sugar refining, cotton manufacturing, and shipbuilding. The systematic improvement of roads undertaken by Fleury with the forced labor of the peasantry (corvée) gave France a justifiably famous system of straight, ample, paved roads.

Events proved that the half-century from about 1725 to 1775 constituted the French monarchy's last opportunity to stave off disaster. It was a period in which the alternatives were a thoroughgoing renovation of France's governmental financial structure or continued decay, encouraging an assertion of the nobility's privilege and ultimately rebellion against absolutist monarchy.

THE DEAD HAND OF COLBERT

Fleury had been content to allow the French economy to proceed on its own within the traditional system of governmental surveillance and interference. It was the last time that the system of Louis XIV's Colbert, built on foundations dating back to Henry IV's Sully, worked moderately well. Colbert had fastened on France an elaborate system of *inspecteurs, controlleurs,* corporations of craftsmen, high-tariff mercantilism, and subsidization of luxury industries that was intended to prevent the ravages of unbridled domestic competition and to protect French industry from foreign competition. These controls turned out to be principally a means to raise revenue and to remunerate officeholders. They were an impediment to the growth of large industry, the introduction of technical improvements, and the development of a progressive market economy.

Colbert's reforms in government finance had been bold for the 1670's, but within half a century they had become insufficient to ensure the government's solvency even in peacetime, and they had fixed a rigidity on the fiscal structure that discouraged improvement. Colbert had been unwilling to tamper with the direct taxes from which most of the nobility and all of the clergy were exempt (the clergy paid the state a ridiculously small sum called a "free gift"). He had preferred to tighten up the collection of taxes and to increase indirect taxes, such as tolls, customs, and the hated salt tax. All efforts at increasing direct taxation were either defeated or watered down and the burden was shifted to the peasantry, non-noble landowners, and townspeople. At the same time the exempted class of nobility was growing as successful merchants, lawyers, and bureaucrats bought themselves or their sons into the nobility. While the nobility was prepared to shift any new tax likely to fall upon them onto the peasantry, they also jealously resisted any attempt to increase taxes on the peasantry because that reduced the nobility's chief source of income, rents from their peasants. To make up the difference between tax revenues and expenditures the government was thrown back on the sale of offices and honors, payments from private industry to escape inspection and control, and the floating of loans. These expedients were the equivalent of foregoing future profits for immediate gains, since the sale of offices and honors exempted that many more people from taxes, and the loans necessitated the payment of interest at increasingly stiff rates as the government's credit declined, especially in wartime.

LAW'S PANACEA

One notable attempt to stir up the stagnant waters and provide greater revenue for the state was the scheme of the mercurial Scottish financier, John Law (1671–1729). Son of an Edinburgh goldsmith, he was a student of mathematics and political economy and a prodigious gambler. While living in exile in France during the last years of Louis XIV, he became an intimate of the Duke of Orleans over the gambling tables. When Orleans became regent in 1715, Law settled in Paris.

Law's scheme was not unsound. The crux of it was to spur economic expansion by increasing the amount of money in circulation in France. The regent was impressed. In 1716 Law received a charter for a joint-stock bank in Paris with the right to issue notes acceptable as money. Two years later the government bought out the stockholders and Law's bank became the royal bank under Law's direction. By 1720 it had issued twice as much in paper notes as there had been currency in circulation when it was established. In 1717 Law expanded his operations by founding the Company of the West, a trading company known popularly as the Mississippi Company, to which the government awarded the monopoly of trade with France's Louisiana territory. Two years later the company absorbed other French overseas trade monopolies, and the name was changed to the Company of the Indies. Law's enterprise now held the monopoly of all French colonial trade. In addition, it purchased the right to collect indirect taxes in France, to mint money, and to service the government debt. In 1720 it merged with the royal bank. In that same year the Scottish adventurer, who had recently adopted French citizenship and the Catholic faith, was appointed controller general of finance, the principal fiscal post in the government. France's economy was in Law's hands.

Law's plans for economic and fiscal reform were all-encompassing. A revival of Vauban's 10 per cent tax applied to everyone, uniform tax collection, dissolution of unnecessary offices, capital loans to manufacturers at reasonable rates to encourage industry, and a government program of public works were blueprinted. That was where they remained. Law had financed the Company of the Indies by selling its stock on easy terms and paying high dividends, while his bank flooded the country with new paper currency so that people had much more money to spend and to invest. By overselling the potential of the commercial enterprise and by inflating the currency, he produced a fever of speculation that he could not control. In the spring of 1720 investors realized that the stock of the company was fantastically overpriced and began to sell. The price slipped, panic swept the market, and the price plummeted. Law tried desperately to stave off collapse, but by October, 1720, he and his scheme were bankrupt. The royal bank closed, and Law fled France. The company lost most of its privileges but managed to survive as a modestly successful enterprise for several more decades.

This strange episode, called the Mississippi Bubble, had lasting effects on the French economy. A few, including some wealthy financiers, made great fortunes by selling out early. Thousands of others were ruined. The disaster marked the end to Law's proposed reforms of government finance as well as to the already fragile public confidence in the government's credit and solvency. Frenchmen acquired a distrust of central banks, paper money, and stock companies that was not dispelled for many years.

THE REGAL INTERREGNUM

Fleury died in 1743 in the midst of the War of the Austrian Succession. Instead of appointing another first minister, the thirty-three-year-old Louis in an unsustained burst of application to affairs of state, set out to rule. For two decades France's government was that of a caretaker, with the owner of the house playing caretaker. It was a government of secret diplomacy known only to the king (who hardly kept the threads of it straight in his own mind), of palace intrigue and government by playing one faction off against another, of inaction, drift, and contradiction. Madame de Pompadour, the king's mistress, was not, as legend has maintained, the real ruler of France, but she might as well have been. Ministers came and went—only the king remained. Every minister was under constant barrage from his enemies and ultimately fell afoul of Louis.

The ablest was Machault d'Arnouville, a former intendant, who as controller general from 1745 to 1754 managed to finance the War of the Austrian Succession in spite of the archaic fiscal system. He had the temerity to attempt the imposition of a uniform 5 per cent income tax on everybody, including nobility and clergy. The bold attempt failed in a howl of opposition from the parlements and the Church, and his fall from power was compassed by the customary intrigue.

Defeat in the Seven Years' War compelled Louis to choose a chief minister who was a not unworthy successor to Fleury. The Duc de Choiseul salvaged some of France's fortunes at the Peace of 1763. He also retired Louis to his pleasures and provided something like consistency in administration from 1758 to 1770. The one task he did not tackle was financial reform. Quietism was his policy, and his tacit alliance with the nobility in their reassertion of power in the parlements assured the preservation of the existing feeble fiscal structure.

THE PHYSIOCRATS

By the time of Choiseul's administration a theoretical basis for the renovation of the economy was not wanting in France. A distinctive group of philosophes had emerged, enthusiastic for economic engineering on the premises of the Enlightenment: rationality, mechanical laws, and progress. Called physiocrats, these men suggested practical solutions for all of France's economic problems, not least for the state's.

The originator of the physiocratic school was François Quesnay (1694–1774), Louis XV's physician. A contributor to Diderot's *Encyclopédia*, Quesnay based his economic theories upon the concept of a natural order that was universal and without flaw. He and his followers maintained that the basis of the natural order in economic life was the right of private property, and that it was the state's obligation to protect that right but not to interfere with it through regulations and restrictions. They condemned the regulatory policies of Colbert as harmful to economic progress and coined the antimercantilist battle cry, "laissez faire, laissez passer." With a few earlier English economists, notably Sir William Petty, they shared the merit of discarding the mercantilist belief that trade and commerce were the only means of enriching a nation. Instead, they transferred the power of creating wealth to the realm of production—above all, to agricultural production.

They argued that only land (including natural resources) produced a surplus or "net product," as they called it, over the amount expended in working it. In contrast, the manufacturer and trader were "sterile" as far as producing wealth was concerned: the manufacturer only gave new form to the materials produced by the earth, and the trader only transferred these materials from one person to another. Neither produced a "net product" or added to the wealth of the country. It followed that everything possible should be done to encourage the development and prosperity of agriculture, including an improvement of the means of transportation and the removal of tariffs and tolls that impeded the free circulation of agricultural products both within France and to other lands.

The physiocrats' analysis of the central role of the land in economic life provided them with a solution to the perpetual crisis in French government finances. They proposed that the existing complicated, inequitable, and inadequate tax structure be replaced by a single tax, the *impôt unique*, to be levied on the net product produced by the land. This tax, which should not exceed one-third of the surplus gained from the land, would be easy to levy once the productive capacity of all the land in the kingdom had been determined by government survey, would be simple to collect, and would be levied on those best able to bear taxation. Most important, the taxpayer would pay the *impôt unique* out of clear, net gain, so that the government would not be siphoning off money that should be reinvested to create new wealth. The economy would then prosper, the net product would increase, and the resulting income from the single tax would provide the state with all the revenue it needed.

In a work entitled the *Tableau économique,* printed at the palace at Versailles in 1758, Quesnay analyzed the movement of the net product among the different economic groups in society. Inspired by the analogy of the circulation of blood through the body, Quesnay tried to show that wealth will freely circulate if an economy is unobstructed by barriers raised by government regulation. The *Tableau* rested upon arbitrary and unreal assumptions, such as that of constant prices, an unchanging net product, arbitrary assignments of the amount of goods that each class was expected to purchase from the others, and of course the fundamental fallacy that only land produces wealth. It nevertheless represented the first comprehensive attempt to trace the relationships of economic groups. Contemporaries hailed it as a triumph of science and reason. One true believer compared it with the invention of money and writing as one of the most important discoveries of the human mind.

Agricultural progress and fiscal reform were not the only parts of the physiocrats' program. For the economy to grow, the natural order required that the individual have freedom to buy and sell as he pleased, that guilds be abolished, that restraints on freedom of competition be barred, and that men and goods be able to move freely within France with a minimum of restriction. These material rights would be of no avail unless they were reinforced with freedom of speech, press, and conscience. Despite their defense of individual freedom, most of the physiocrats strongly supported enlightened despotism, which they called "legal despotism," as the best form of government. Only under a single, absolute authority, guided by the counsel of men infused with the doctrines of the Age of Reason, could the natural order triumph. They failed to realize that such a despot would have to be singularly enlightened and singularly self-restrained, for the role assigned to him by the physiocrats was little more than that of a policeman enforcing the "natural and essential laws" of society.

The physiocrats did not all share Quesnay's doctrinaire repudiation of the productive importance of commerce and industry. Gournay (1712–1759), one of the earliest and most important members of the school, accorded larger significance to those sectors of the society. Another was Anne Robert Jacques Turgot (1727–1781), who could never quite accept the idea that only land produced a net product or that all classes except that which worked the land were "sterile producers." Turgot eventually was given the opportunity to try to renovate France's economy and government finances through physiocracy—and failed, though neither through much fault in himself nor in physiocracy.

THE PARLEMENTS AND THE NOBLE ASSERTION

To understand what did destroy the opportunity for reform presented by Turgot's tenure as controller-general (1774–76), the history of the parlements after the death of Louis XIV must be outlined. The Sun King, following a policy inherited from Richelieu, had whittled away at these traditional courts in Paris and the provinces because they were instruments of noble political ambitions and preserves of noble privilege. He had abolished their veto of legislation by royal decree. The parlements were awed by Louis XIV and remained acquiescent. The weakness of the central government under Louis XV, however, encouraged the parlements to reassert themselves against royal authority. The king had almost no control over their composition, and although they had no ultimate power over legislation, they could still force the king to override their stand against unpopular legislation and they could still act as sounding boards for dissidence and opposition.

The first serious clash with the parlements came over Machault's attempt to impose a uniform 5 per cent income tax. The parlements objected vociferously, the Paris parlement declaring the tax illegal. Since the levy would touch the clergy, the parlements rallied the Church, and together they forced Machault to abandon the tax. For the next two decades king and ministers alike moved warily in dealing with the parlements.

In 1766 the parlements threw down a challenge to royal authority that Louis could not ignore. The crisis began in Brittany, where the provincial parlement, in company with the Breton estates, fell into a bitter quarrel with the central government over charges that the royal power had disregarded provincial rights in the construction of roads in Brittany for military defense during the Seven Years' War. The dispute reached a climax when the leader of the parlement was arrested for his violent speeches against the military commander of the region. Other parlements joined the Bretons in denouncing the central government. They made such extreme assertions of their own power that they threatened the sovereignty of the throne and Louis could no longer tolerate the subservience of his chief minister, Choiseul, to the parlements.

Effective power in internal affairs passed to René Maupeou, a lawyer and a bitter opponent of the parlements. Maupeou skilfully provoked the Paris parlement into overt opposition to the king's authority, and early in 1771 he had the leading magistrates arrested, abolished the Paris parlement and set up six new courts for Paris (derisively called "Maupeou parlements"), with judges named by the king. In the wake of this shattering victory Maupeou set on foot wholesale changes in the law in order to curb noble privilege. His colleague Abbé Terray, controller-general of finance, began a fiscal reform aimed, like Machault's income tax, at a more equitable distribution of taxes, attempted to have more accurate assessments made of taxable income from land, and introduced other measures to increase state revenues. Maupeou's and Terray's work had only begun when Louis XV died of smallpox in 1774. Louis XVI, his grandson and successor, wanted above all to be mindful of the needs and wishes of his subjects and to dis-associate his reign from that of his arbitrary and now discredited grandfather. Heeding the protests of the members of the parlements who had organized demonstrations to try to show wide public support for their demands, Louis dismissed Maupeou and restored the old parlements.

France on the Eve of Revolution

The new king, twenty years old, was devout, shy, kind, and moral, a skilful locksmith and an adoring husband. He was also dull, poorly read, and no more capable of application to the labor of an absolutist monarch than was his recently deceased grandfather. He was destined to die not for his vices (the worst of which was his irresolution which could only appear to his enemies as duplicity) but for his absence of kingly virtues. His wife Marie Antoinette, daughter of Empress Maria Theresa, cut a sharp contrast. Quick, charming, frivolous, extravagant, and haughty, she enjoyed an ascendency over her slow husband that no mistress had ever exercised over Louis XV. Although her extravagance was not, as once believed, responsible for the monarchy's bankruptcy, it epitomized to an increasingly hostile nation all that was decadent in absolutism.

TURGOT, NECKER, AND CALONNE

Shortly after Louis's accession his chief adviser, Jean Maurepas, decided that for "public relations" the government needed a known reformer in high office. The physiocrat Turgot was summoned to the controllership of finance. Turgot had served for twelve years as intendant of the city of Limoges in central France, where he had distinguished himself by his energetic and imaginative leadership. Among his achievements were founding the Limoges pottery works, using paid labor to build roads and bridges instead of the compulsory corvée of peasants who received no wages for their work, equalizing the collection of taxes as far as he was able, and financing public works at low rates of interest. Turgot's experience in administration and reputation as a physiocrat awakened hopes that he would be the great innovator and reformer that the government needed so badly.

His first fiscal reforms were cautious, though promising, including reduction in court expenses and in pensions paid by the government to favored persons, simplification of the system of tax collection, and moves to bring the finances of other ministries (notably the ministry of war) under the surveillance of the controller-general. Turgot mounted his greatest offensive in the sphere of government control of the economy. His spearhead was the physiocratic doctrine of freer internal trade. He loosened the restrictions on grain movement after the bad harvest of 1774 in an attempt to cope with the grain scarcity and supply Paris with bread. Despite his caution, there was much opposition. Undeterred, early in 1776 he submitted to the king six edicts for reform, extending earlier edicts for freer trade in grain, abolishing offices for enforcing restrictions on trade in agricultural produce, abolishing the corvée, establishing a general tax on all proprietors of land for the maintenance of roads, and abolishing the corporations of craftsmen established by Colbert. The outcry was enormous. Clergy, nobility, financiers, colleagues in the ministry, and the craft corporations united in common cause. The opposition coalesced in the reinstituted parlement of Paris. Turgot persuaded Louis XVI to ram the six edicts through over the parlement's objections, but he was dismissed shortly afterward, and his reforms were quietly dismantled. With them ended the last great hope for the renovation of France. As ominous as his defeat was, more ominous was the means: the revolt of the nobility in the parlement reinforced by a broad and powerful segment of French opinion.

Jacques Necker, a Swiss banker and Turgot's successor in charge of finance from 1776 to 1781, played at reform. With an uncanny gift for self-advertisement he mounted a massive campaign to prove that the state's finances were never better. In fact, they were never worse. The government was in debt beyond repayment. Yet Necker's fall in 1781 was not owing to this deception but the result of his ambitious demands for more power.

In 1783 Charles Calonne, another former intendant, was made controller-general. Masterful and energetic, Calonne determined upon a plan of reorganization of the state's finances that owed much to the ideas of Turgot. He urged a new tax on landed income to be paid by all landowners, whether clergy, noble, or commoner; pressed for the abolition of restrictions on economic initiative; and proposed to gain the cooperation and understanding of the nation by presenting his program to provincial assemblies elected by all taxpayers, in which no distinction would be made among social classes. The king gave his support to these proposals. In February, 1787, at Calonne's behest he summoned an Assembly of Notables—a selected group of prelates and great noblemen—on the assumption that the parlements could not be persuaded to accept Calonne's tax but that the Notables could. Calonne's failure to persuade them sealed his dismissal.

His successor, Loménie de Brienne, the "enlightened" archbishop of Toulouse, faced the parlements with Calonne's proposals. The parlement of Paris, warmly supported by the provincial parlements, rejected the proposals and called for the summoning of the Estates-General of France, which had last met in 1614–15. The convening of the Estates-General, with its preponderance of the clergy and the nobility, could only have spelled disaster to Louis XVI. He had reached the same point that Louis XV had reached in 1771 when his authority was challenged by the parlements, and he chose the same course of action. He first banished the parlement of Paris in 1787, recalled it shortly afterward, was harassed by it for the next six months, and finally adopted the "Maupeou solution." In May, 1788, all the parlements of France were suspended, and new courts were established to take their places.

It was too late. The parlements resisted, supported by the nobility, the clergy, and the bourgeoisie. Riots in a half-dozen provinces and resistance everywhere forced Louis's capitulation. In August, 1788, the suspension of the parlements was rescinded, Brienne was dismissed, and Necker was returned to power. On September 23 the parlement of Paris returned to the metropolis amidst tumultuous celebrations to register a decree summoning the Estates-General to meet on May 1, 1789. The rebellion of the aristocracy had triumphed; the king had been defeated; and privilege, it seemed, had been confirmed.

THE ARISTOCRATIC REBELLION

The aims of the nobility as voiced in the parlements—such as the aggrandizement of their political power and the preservation of their privileges, especially exemption from taxation—were no more striking than the words in which they were expressed. In the years after Louis XIV's death when they were trying to revive their old privileges, the parlements had used the traditional historical arguments that they were the "sovereign courts" descended from the medieval king's council. Then around 1750 the notions of the Enlightenment began to creep into their arguments. The constitutionalism of Montesquieu enjoyed an extended vogue. Locke's idea of a contract between king and people was developed into a full-blown theory, replete with allusions to the "nation," "free consent," "liberties," and "the general will." All this smacked of self-delusion and even fraud, for the parlements, claiming that they were defending the "liberties of Frenchmen," conceived of those "liberties" as no broader than their own vested privileges. Nevertheless, the claim elicited the support of all those hostile to absolutism.

The parlements similarly interpreted the ideals of the American Revolution to reinforce the nobility's rebellion. They identified the American struggle against the tyranny of George III with their own struggle against the tyranny of Louis XVI. The patently conservative features of the American rebellion reassured them that there had not been a social revolution in North America. George Washington was easily classed as a noble, and

The Peasantry Bearing the Priesthood and the Nobility on Its Back, eighteenth-century cartoon

Oct. 17th, 1787. . . . Dined today with a party, whose conversation was entirely political. . . . One opinion pervaded the whole company, that they are on the eve of some great revolution in the government; . . . no minister existing . . . to promise any other remedy than palliative ones; a prince on the throne, with excellent dispositions, but without the resources of a mind that could govern in such a moment without ministers; a court buried in pleasure and dissipation . . . a great ferment amongst all ranks of men, who are eager for some change, without knowing what to look for, or to hope for; and a strong leaven of liberty, increasing every hour since the American Revolution." Arthur Young, TRAVELS IN FRANCE DURING THE YEARS 1787, 1788, & 1789 (Cambridge, 1929).

The Bettmann Archive

it was a small step to identifying the resistance of the colonial legislatures with the resistance of the parlements. There were, as the enemies of privilege would shortly prove, other ways to interpret the Enlightenment and the American Revolution. But their first effect was to strengthen the noble reaction by supplying the rhetoric of a French opinion beginning "to talk republican language even before it had thought republican thoughts." [1]

---

[1] Alfred Cobban, *A History of Modern France,* I (1957), p. 117.

442

CHAPTER NINETEEN

The French Revolution

THE FRENCH REVOLUTION ranks with the Reformation as one of two great watersheds in the history of the European world. Into it virtually all of the past flowed; from it virtually all of the present has come. Every revolution since has been a variation on the theme of the French Revolution. In the streets of Budapest in 1848, 1918, and 1956, Hungarians sang the "Marseillaise." The Russian revolutions of 1917—both Kerensky's and Lenin's—paid homage to the epoch of revolutions inaugurated at the Place de la Bastille on July 14, 1789. Much of the French Revolution survives only in form—Lenin was neither a Robespierre nor a Babeuf. Yet the change of substance into form is the way the past is preserved to influence the future. It is the translation of the "what was" into the "what will always be" in history, which in the case of the French Revolution has made of us all its children.

The Coming of the Revolution, 1788–1791

Between the end of September, 1788, and the convocation of the Estates-General in early May, 1789, the great topic of dispute was the composition of the Estates-General. Historically it consisted of three houses representing the three estates: the First Estate or the clergy, the Second Estate or the nobility, and the Third Estate or the commonalty. Each met and voted separately. The will of the Estates-General was expressed by either the unanimity of all three houses or a majority of two. The dispute in 1788–89 stemmed from a realization that the interests of the clergy and the nobility in preserving their privileges were likely to coincide to the detriment of the commonalty, so that the First and Second Estates might consistently thwart the desires of the Third. Such a possibility had not been questioned before; now it was a stormy issue.

In the seven months before the convocation of the Estates-General hundreds of pamphlets poured out on both sides of the question. The two consistent positions of those advocating change were that the representation of the Third Estate should be doubled and that voting should be by head, each deputy of all three houses having one vote and the will of the whole Estates-General being a simple majority of the voting deputies. Convinced that the great threat to the monarchy was still the nobility, Necker in December, 1788, persuaded the king to double the representation of that house.

THE THIRD ESTATE

"What is the Third Estate?" asked the Abbé Sieyès rhetorically in a pamphlet of that title published in February, 1789. "The Third Estate is a complete nation," he answered. Sieyès was one of a group of clergy and nobility who felt that the salvation of France from both absolutist monarchy and noble and clerical privileges lay in the Third Estate. Although the Third Estate was something less than a nation, it was the greatest segment of the society. It was also the most complex of the three social orders, comprising the peasantry, the bourgeoisie, the professionals, and the urban workers.

The peasantry constituted over four-fifths of France's twenty-five or twenty-six million people. Many peasants owned all or part of their holdings, and over one-third of France's soil was their property. Most of their holdings were too small to support them, however, and only by renting additional land or working part-time for a larger landowner or in trade could they survive. They also had to pay obligations to the nobles to whom their land had once belonged, which varied from place to place but usually included fees for using the village mill, bakery, or wine press and an annual small payment in cash or produce. These obligations were remnants of the feudal past, when the lords had exercised the powers of government over the peasants on their property. In addition, the peasants paid both a tithe to the church and the direct taxes. Peasants who owned no land either rented a holding from a landowner for a money rent or a share of the crop or hired themselves out as farm laborers. Serfdom had nearly disappeared. Estimates of the number of peasants who were serfs—that is, who actually belonged to

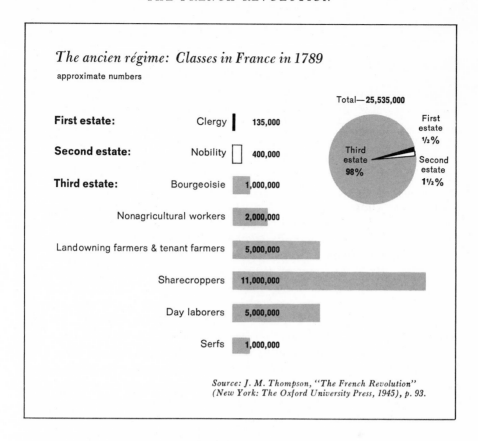

The ancien régime: Classes in France in 1789

approximate numbers

Total—25,535,000

First estate:	Clergy	135,000
Second estate:	Nobility	400,000
Third estate:	Bourgeoisie	1,000,000
	Nonagricultural workers	2,000,000
	Landowning farmers & tenant farmers	5,000,000
	Sharecroppers	11,000,000
	Day laborers	5,000,000
	Serfs	1,000,000

First estate ½%
Second estate 1½%
Third estate 98%

Source: J. M. Thompson, "The French Revolution" (New York: The Oxford University Press, 1945), p. 93.

lords—run from 140,000 to 1,000,000, most of whom were in the eastern provinces of Franche-Comté and Lorraine, only recently annexed to France.

Even well-to-do peasants lived humbly in order to avoid increased taxes. The available evidence indicates that after a gradual improvement over half a century the economic position of the peasantry worsened in the decade immediately preceding the Revolution. Poor harvests, a general rise in prices, and the nobility's reassertion of its privileges brought about the decline. The nobility, pressed by the price rise and determined to maintain the higher standard of living afforded by the general economic advance of the era, collected feudal dues more rigorously, revived forgotten obligations, and increased the rents of their peasant leaseholders and sharecroppers. The peasantry had long grumbled at the obligations due their lords, for which they received no services in return. With increased dues the customary discontent took on dangerous proportions.

Nearly two million members of the Third Estate lived in the cities and towns. Most of them were craftsmen and hired workers. The workers were concentrated in a few centers, notably Paris, Marseilles, Rouen, and Bordeaux, and some were organized into embryonic unions to better wages and working conditions. Like the workers, the craftsmen or lower segment of the bourgeoisie were particularly hurt by the increase in food prices brought on by the succession of poor harvests. The upper segments of urban society, the middle and higher bourgeoisie, were jealous of preserving the social distinctions between themselves and the smaller bourgeoisie and workers. Always conscious of their social inferiority to the nobility, they began openly to resent the privileges of the nobility. The nobility's increasing monopoly of office and reassertion of noble privilege in the parlements intensified the hostility. The nobility's arrogance was made even less bearable by their obvious new power.

It was the Third Estate, more particularly the bourgeoisie, for whom the Enlightenment had the greatest meaning. By virtue of its utilitarian motivation, its appeal to rationality, its emphasis on material well-being, and its defense of individual rights, the Enlightenment was absorbed by the middle-class merchants, manufacturers, lawyers, physicians, teachers, and journalists, whereas it only softened the veneer of some of the nobility. The burden of the philosophes' message was an attack on privilege—noble and ecclesiastical explicitly, monarchic implicitly. Religious toleration, humanitarianism, freedom of the individual, and reforms to free economic endeavor from injurious restrictions were all facets of a way of life that the old order—the *ancien régime*—in state and Church could not accept, though the philosophes had never given up hope that the absolutist monarch might be converted to their faith and work the reforms they sought. Above all, the philosophes called men to scrutinize existing social and political institutions in the pure light of reason. Many among the bourgeoisie had done so, and the France they saw in 1789 was a ramshackle edifice compared to the philosophes' blueprints. Few of the philosophes had urged revolution; few of the Third Estate had planned revolution in 1789. The Revolution issued from the spontaneous reactions to events of men interested in change rather than from a massive conspiracy to effect a new order. But the goals of change would have to bear some resemblance to the programs of the philosophes, the justification of events after the act would have to be couched in language furnished by the Enlightenment. In eighteenth-century France there were no ideological alternatives to the Enlightenment to mold the new order.

THE FIRST AND SECOND ESTATES

The 400,000 nobles in the Second Estate were divided into nine principal ranks, ranging downward from the great aristocracy through the nobility of the parlements to the tattered *hobereaux* (literally "hawks") in the provinces, eking out a meager living on a few ancestral acres. They were united only in their determination to preserve their privileges and expand their power, at the expense of both the monarchy and the bourgeoisie and to the deprivation of the peasantry. The successors of Louis XIV had assisted the nobles by failing to choke off the demands of the parlements. The bureaucracy, which under Louis XIV and his immediate predecessors had been drawn primarily from the bourgeoisie, was increasingly recruited from the nobility.

The divisions and contrasts within the First Estate or the clergy were almost as marked as those within the Third. The clergy numbered about 130,000. At the top was the hierarchy of archbishops, bishops, and heads of monastic houses, almost all of whom had noble origins. Intermediate were the cathedral clergy and priests charged with administrative responsibilities. The rest of the clergy were about equally divided between monks and friars of religious orders and parish priests. The Church was wealthy. It was the largest landed proprietor in France and derived large revenues from tithes, endowments, and gifts. The hierarchy and administrative clergy lived in opulence, and most monasteries were not characterized by sackcloth and ashes. Yet most of the parish clergy lived in extreme and parasitical poverty. The tithes intended for their support were siphoned off to the greater clergy, so that they were forced to wring from the peasantry every fee they could. The parish priest's discontent found an outlet in demands for a more democratic structure of Church government. If voting in the Estates-General were by head, a fair proportion of the representatives of the clergy could be expected to align themselves with the Third Estate against the nobility and their own ecclesiastical overlords.

THE ESTATES-GENERAL

Besides doubling the representation of the Third Estate, Necker introduced other far-reaching innovations in the instructions attached to the summons to the Estates. Each estate was to elect its deputies. In the past those sitting in the Estates-General held their seats by personal right, appointment, or right of office. Although Necker's order was hedged with procedures for the indirect election of deputies from the Third Estate by electors chosen by the voters, it was tantamount to universal manhood suffrage. Each of the forty thousand local meetings convened to choose electors was also instructed to draw up a *cahier* or list of grievances, to be incorporated into a general cahier for the district, which would serve as instructions for the district's delegates to the Estates-General. The cahiers touched on all matters of concern, local and national, and though respectful in tone, were a terrible indictment of the France of that day.

In the elections in the early spring of 1789, 300 clerical deputies, mostly from the lower clergy, were returned to the First Estate; 300 noble deputies, primarily country rather than court nobles, were returned to the Second

Oath of the Tennis Court (June 20, 1789), by Jacques Louis David
*"The National Assembly, considering that it has been summoned to establish the consti-
tution of the kingdom, to effect the regeneration of public order, and to maintain the true
principles of monarchy; . . . decrees that all members of this Assembly shall immediately
take a solemn oath not to separate, and to reassemble wherever circumstances require,
until the constitution of the kingdom is established and consolidated upon firm
foundations; and that, the said oath taken, all members and each one of them
individually shall ratify this steadfast resolution by signature."* Reprinted in J. H.
Stewart, A DOCUMENTARY SURVEY OF THE FRENCH REVOLUTION (New York, 1951).

Courtesy of The Louvre

Estate; and 648 commoner deputies, most of whom were bourgeois and over
half of whom were lawyers, with only a handful of peasants and workers,
were returned to the Third Estate.

The Estates-General convened at Versailles on May 4, 1789. The representatives of the Third Estate insisted that the three estates meet as a single
body and that the representatives vote as individuals, a procedure that
would assure the Third Estate's dominance, since with its doubled membership and the support of some clergy in the Second Estate it could outvote
the rest of the Second and the First Estates. When the government refused to accede to this demand a deadlock ensued that lasted for six
weeks. Finally, on June 17 the Third Estate, joined by a few supporters
from the clergy, declared itself a National Assembly and the only true representative of the nation. This was revolution. Three days later a gathering
of the self-styled National Assembly found the doors of their chamber
locked. Unaware that this was merely to allow for the preparations for a
joint session at which the king was to speak, and angry at what appeared
to be a lock-out, the deputies withdrew to a large tennis court nearby and
solemnly swore not to disband until they had drawn up a constitution limiting the powers of monarchy.

The Tennis Court Oath cemented an alliance between the king and the nobility that had begun to form earlier in the face of the demands of the Third Estate. At the royal session on June 23 the king's long-awaited plan for reform proved to be a capitulation to the demands of the nobility. Louis directed the estates to meet separately. Two days later 170 of the clerical deputies and 50 of the nobles joined the meeting of the Third Estate to show their opposition to the king's order, and on June 27 Louis revoked his order and directed the estates to meet together and vote by head. At the same time, influenced by the most reactionary of the court nobility, Louis called 18,000 troops to Versailles to "maintain order." On July 11 he dismissed Necker, who had been hailed by the Third Estate and its allies when the three estates had met together for the first time on June 30.

EMERGENCE OF THE PARIS MOB

The monarch's and nobility's fear of popular support for the Third Estate was manifest in the dispatch of troops to Versailles. They would have proved more useful in Paris. A worsening economic situation had coincided with the political upheavals of the past two years. The decline of the French economy since 1778 was quickened by a commercial treaty with Britain in 1786 that flooded the French market with cheaper British wares and caused a business recession and unemployment. A bad harvest in 1788 brought a sharp increase in the price of food in the early spring of 1789. The sufferings of the urban workers, the smaller craftsmen, and the small peasants who could not profit by the scarcity, burst out in bread and grain riots in the spring and early summer. In July, 1789, the price of bread was higher than at any time in the previous three-quarters of a century. Hunger and unemployment stood behind the emergence of the Paris mob.

The emergence of the Paris mob was the first manifestation of political violence in the Revolution and an event of enormous consequences. Workers and craftsmen, aroused by agitators and alarmed by the concentration of troops at Versailles, ransacked public buildings and arsenals in search of weapons to arm themselves. On July 14 they attempted to storm the Bastille, an old fortress used as a prison and supposed to be filled with political prisoners. The small contingent of guards fired into the mob, killing nearly a hundred. After a promise of safe-conduct had brought out the guards, they were slaughtered by the frenzied crowd and the cells were thrown open to disgorge a total of seven prisoners—four counterfeiters, two lunatics, and a dissipated young noble. The mob began to tear down the Bastille but, finding the task wearisome, moved toward the city hall with the head of the Bastille's governor on a pike. Another mob at the city hall was already in action, and the head of the chief of city administration was soon hoisted aloft on another pike. In the next few days slaughter was random, and the bourgeois leaders of Paris, thoroughly frightened, appointed as mayor Jean

Sylvain Bailly, astronomer and prominent deputy to the Third Estate, and established a National Guard to protect life and property under the command of the Marquis de Lafayette.

With Paris lost and a mob on the rampage, Louis tried to placate the people by sending the troops away from Versailles, recalling Necker, and accepting the new city government of Paris. On July 17 Louis XVI, king of France, went to the city hall of Paris to receive from Bailly a blue, white, and red cockade, the revolutionary emblem: blue and red for the city of Paris, significantly surrounding white, the color of the house of Bourbon.

THE *GRAND PEUR*

In the countryside wild rumors of brigands in the pay of nobles who looted and burned the homes and fields of honest folk roused the peasantry into an outburst of collective mania known as the *Grand Peur,* the Great Fear. The rumors were groundless, and peasants found no brigands, yet in their inflamed mood they decided to move against their old oppressors, the lords. The *Grand Peur* became a general, nationwide, agrarian insurrection, the peasants swarming into manor houses and demanding the destruction of records listing the obligations they owed the lords. The noblemen and their agents who resisted were murdered and their houses fired.

The deputies to the National Assembly were now as fearful of insurrection as the king himself and realized that only swift capitulation could pacify the peasantry. At a dramatic night session on August 4, 1789, the Assembly ordered the abolition of all feudal dues and privileges, ended tithes, and emancipated France's serfs. That same night the Assembly approved the principle of equal taxation for all classes, ordered the end of the sale of public offices, and decreed that every citizen was eligible for any civil, military, or Church office.

THE RIGHTS OF MAN AND THE RELUCTANT KING

The Assembly then turned its attention to drafting a constitution. As a prelude, the Assembly on August 26, 1789, issued a Declaration of the Rights of Man and Citizen. This great document owed its tone and content to the ideas of the Enlightenment and to the American Declaration of Independence and the Virginia Bill of Rights of 1776. It asserted as its first principle that all men were born and should remain free and equal in rights. Guaranteeing freedom of speech, press, and worship and freedom from arbitrary arrest and punishment, it declared that the only sovereign was the nation itself. Posted all over France, it was quickly translated and broadcast throughout Europe to spark the aspiration for liberty and equality everywhere.

The king withheld approval of the decrees of August 4 and the Declara-

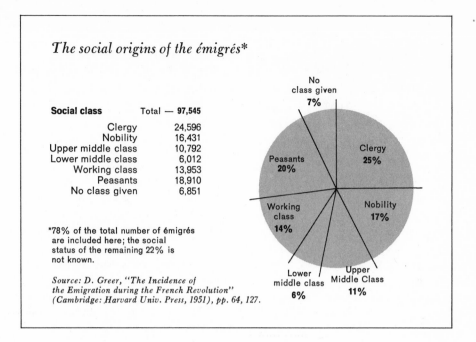

The social origins of the émigrés*

Social class	Total — 97,545
Clergy	24,596
Nobility	16,431
Upper middle class	10,792
Lower middle class	6,012
Working class	13,953
Peasants	18,910
No class given	6,851

*78% of the total number of émigrés are included here; the social status of the remaining 22% is not known.

Source: D. Greer, "The Incidence of the Emigration during the French Revolution" (Cambridge: Harvard Univ. Press, 1951), pp. 64, 127.

No class given 7%
Clergy 25%
Peasants 20%
Nobility 17%
Working class 14%
Lower middle class 6%
Upper Middle Class 11%

tion of the Rights of Man. He also refused to accept the proposed articles for the new constitution that provided for a unicameral legislature and limitation of his power to veto Assembly legislation. His recalcitrance fed the suspicion that he planned to use force to overthrow the revolution, and suspicion turned to certainty when his brother, the Count of Artois, and other court aristocrats left France. These émigrés, the first of thousands to flee France, sought to stir up the other governments of Europe against the Revolution.

Despite Bailly's and Lafayette's efforts to control the Paris mob, it was being skilfully incited by golden-voiced agitators. Stirred by the threat of counterrevolution and driven by hunger, the Paris populace's radical elements were easy prey to the call for direct action. It came on October 5, 1789, when a mob of market women, housewives, and the ever-present agitators walked to Versailles—the "March of the Women"—followed by a contingent of the bourgeois National Guard. The women went first to the National Assembly, where they demanded that the price of bread be lowered, then forced their way into the king's residence and surrounded Louis. To restore order, Louis agreed to go to Paris with his family to live. The victorious women marched back to the city with the royal carriage in their midst, bearing Louis, Marie Antoinette, and their son, or as the women called them, "the baker, the baker's wife, and the baker's little boy." The royal family never saw Versailles again. They were prisoners of the people of Paris and pawns to the fortunes of the Revolution. A few weeks later the

Assembly moved to Paris, exposing itself to popular and radical pressures, for its galleries were filled daily with raucous crowds whose applause or hisses influenced the deputies. Conservative deputies, fearing that the Assembly would give in completely to the pressures, began to drop out; some emigrated.

THE CONSTITUENT ASSEMBLY

The National Assembly, now called the Constituent Assembly because it was preparing a constitution, promulgated a series of sweeping reforms that revealed the bourgeois concerns of the deputies. It preserved the hereditary monarchy but sharply curtailed the powers of the king. In the interest of more efficient administration it scrapped the old administrative divisions and divided the country into eighty-three departments, each sub-divided into districts, cantons, and communes, with all local offices elective. The right to pass laws, levy taxes, override the king's veto, and control government expenditures was to be exercised by a unicameral legislature called the Legislative Assembly, comprised of elected deputies. Despite the guarantees of the Declaration of the Rights of Man and Citizen, suffrage was limited to so-called "active citizens"—men who paid a certain minimum in taxes. Moreover, the "active citizens" voted only for electors, who then chose the deputies to the Legislative Assembly as well as local officials. The tax qualification for an elector was so high that in all France only fifty thousand men could qualify. Some nobles and a few wealthy peasants were in the high tax bracket, but most of the fifty thousand were members of the bourgeoisie. In the *ancien régime* political power had followed ancestry; now it followed wealth.

The Constituent Assembly's solution for the state's financial problem was a simple and thoroughgoing attack on the old order. In November, 1789, the Constituent Assembly confiscated all Church property and the estates of the nobles who had fled France. It then paid off the government's creditors, most of whom were bourgeois financiers, with special financial notes called *assignats*. These notes could be used to buy the confiscated lands, which were sold to the highest bidder. In this way most of this property went into the hands of the bourgeoisie, who either kept it or sold it at a profit to speculators or to peasants.

The bourgeoisie adhered to the physiocratic tradition of opposing restrictions on trade and industry and favoring free enterprise. The Constituent Assembly abolished the craft corporations on the ground that they were monopolies, and it threw open all trades and businesses to everyone. Characteristically the Constituent Assembly also outlawed *compagnonnages*, the clandestine trade unions organized by workers long before the Revolution, and decreed that wages should be determined individually between each worker and his employer.

THE CIVIL CONSTITUTION OF THE CLERGY

The confiscation of Church property and the abolition of tithes deprived the clergy of its means of support. To maintain the clergy and ensure the Church's complete subordination to the state, the Constituent Assembly promulgated the Civil Constitution of the Clergy in July, 1790. Bishops and priests were to be chosen by the same electors who chose the delegates to the Legislative Assembly and the local officials, and they were to be paid by the state. Archbishoprics were abolished, and the number of bishoprics was reduced from 130 to 83—one for each department. When the constitution was submitted to Pope Pius VI for his approval, he not only rejected it but denounced all the works of the Assembly, including the Declaration of the Rights of Man and Citizen. The Assembly countered by ordering all French clergymen to swear allegiance to the Civil Constitution of the Clergy. Half refused. Called "nonjuring" or "refractory" priests, they condemned the "constitutional" clergy (those who swore allegiance) for being disloyal to the Roman Catholic Church, and they became bitter foes of the Revolution. Since they were numerous and popular, especially with the peasants, the government had no choice but to tolerate them. They remained islands of reaction and potential leaders of counterrevolution.

The Constitutional Monarchy, 1791–1792

The Constituent Assembly incorporated the reforms in a national constitution proclaimed in September, 1791. It then disbanded, having in little more than two years transformed France into a limited monarchy, swept away the remnants of feudalism, instituted equality before the law, reorganized the national and local administrations, established free enterprise, and made the clergy officials of the state. Satisfied that the Revolution was over, the deputies did not suspect that the regime they had fashioned would last barely ten months—or that the Revolution had only begun.

The first blow to the durability of the new regime came even before the promulgation of the constitution. Louis XVI, dismayed at the course of events and strongly influenced by Marie Antoinette, decided to flee France and appeal to his fellow monarchs for help. On the night of June 20, 1791, the disguised royal family bundled into a coach with a few servants and headed for the eastern frontier. Recognized when the coach stopped next morning to change horses, Louis was arrested at the village of Varennes and taken back with his family to Paris. The "Flight to Varennes" and a note denouncing the Revolution, which Louis had left behind when he fled, made it clear that he had joined the counterrevolutionaries. Obviously a constitutional monarchy headed by a king opposed to its principles had slight chance of success, and radicals demanded the establishment of a republic. The majority, however, still wanted a king, and after making a show of penitence, Louis was reinstated. The institution of monarchy had been badly shaken.

EXTERNAL REACTION

Another blow came from outside France. Absolutist monarchs elsewhere recognized that the doctrines of the French Revolution endangered their own regimes. The Declaration of the Rights of Man and Citizen had spread its message. Unrest and demands for reform by bourgeoisie and peasants appeared in Germany, Italy, the United Netherlands, and Britain. French aristocratic émigrés pressed unceasingly for war against the Revolution. Reluctant to start such a conflict, the monarchs nevertheless felt that something had to be done. In August, 1791, Leopold II of Austria, uncle of Marie Antoinette, and Frederick William II of Prussia met at Pillnitz in Saxony and issued a joint declaration pledging the use of force to help Louis restore absolutism and order in France if the other major powers would join them. Leopold knew that Pitt, the British prime minister, opposed intervention because war would make it impossible to carry through his domestic program. The Declaration of Pillnitz, therefore, was an empty gesture. It had an enormous impact in France, however, for it seemed to prove that Louis was in league with foreign monarchs and émigrés to overthrow the Revolution.

Pillnitz widened the gap between those who favored the constitutional monarchy and the more extreme revolutionaries. The division was apparent in the personnel of the new Legislative Assembly that met in October, 1791 —the Constituent Assembly had by its own decree excluded its members from standing for election to the Legislative Assembly. Of the new assembly's 745 members, 264 supported the constitutional monarchy and 136 opposed it; the remainder were uncommitted. In the Legislative Assembly's sessions the supporters of the monarchy chose to sit on the speaker's right, the radicals on his left, and the uncommitted between the two extremes, this was the origin of the expressions "Right," "Left," and "Center" that are part of our modern vocabulary of political reference.

THE CLUBS

Outside the Legislative Assembly the delegates grouped themselves into political clubs. The club called Friends of the Constitution (later changed to Friends of Equality and Liberty), and popularly known as the Jacobin Club because it met in a former Jacobin (Dominican) monastery, emerged as the most important of these organizations. Originally including many moderates, the Jacobin Club soon fell under the control of the radicals and with the resignation of the moderates it became the chief leftist organization. Despite its radicalism, the club's members were from the middle class, and some were from the upper bourgeoisie. Affiliated Jacobin clubs formed all over France, with the Paris club as their central chapter. In the Assembly itself the Left was dominated by a faction of the Jacobin Club called the Girondists, so called because its leaders represented the department of the Gironde around Bordeaux.

Continuing economic difficulties and ceaseless agitation against the Revolution by both nonjuring priests inside France and émigrés outside France played into the hands of the extremists. Convinced that the Revolution would not be safe until its ideas had triumphed in other lands, they urged an international revolution led by the French that would overthrow kings and set up republics. Their desire for war was supported by conservatives who hoped that a military effort would unite the country behind the king and the constitutional monarchy. The war party's arguments were given point by the formation of an alliance between Austria and Prussia, which included proposed annexations of French territory. The accession of Francis II to the Austrian throne in 1792 helped to strengthen the fear of enemy invasion, for Francis was known to be much more conservative than his father Leopold II. On April 20, 1792, the Legislative Assembly declared war on Austria. Prussia and Sardinia soon allied themselves with Austria.

WAR AND THE END OF THE MONARCHY

The French army was poorly trained and equipped and lacked experienced leaders because so many of its officers had become émigrés. It suffered a string of reverses, and within weeks enemy troops led by the Duke of Brunswick were on French soil. There was turmoil in Paris. On June 20 a mob poured into the palace of the Tuileries, where the king now lived, mocked him, and made him put on the red liberty cap that had become the symbol of the Revolution. When the Duke of Brunswick learned of the insult he issued a manifesto on July 25 threatening to level Paris if the royal family was molested and inviting all Frenchmen to unite with him against the Revolution. The manifesto served only to raise patriotic fervor to fever pitch. Bands of volunteers streamed into Paris on their way to the front, and among them was a contingent from Marseilles singing a stirring march, since become the national anthem of republican France, the "Marseillaise." Its words caught the spirit of the moment:

> Arise ye children of the Fatherland,
> The day of glory has arrived . . .

The Brunswick Manifesto went far toward sealing the fate of the constitution and its monarch. It gave the radicals a lever of public opinion to topple the constitution. The Paris mob had been relatively restrained since July of the previous year, when Bailly, Lafayette, and the National Guard had repressed with gunfire a mass demonstration against the monarchy at the Champs de Mars. Now the mob was brought into action again by the extremists. The enemy's close approach to Paris provided an opportunity for Georges Jacques Danton and other Jacobin extremists to rise in revolt against the government. Provincial troops on their way to the front and Parisians stormed the Tuileries and butchered the king's guard. Louis and the royal family had already fled to the Legislative Assembly for protection. They found none. The Assembly, cowed by the rising of which they were as much the intended victims as the king, deposed Louis XVI, imprisoned him and his family, and ordered the election of a National Convention by universal male suffrage to draw up a new constitution. The events of August 10 and the continued advance of the enemy gave an excuse for the mob to vent its hatred in an orgy of bloodshed. Declaring that the enemy within must be destroyed before the invader could be repulsed, mobs stormed the jails in early September and murdered over a thousand prisoners, both men and women, whom they claimed were counterrevolutionaries. With these "September Massacres" as a backdrop, the hastily elected National Convention held its first session on September 20, 1792 On that same day French troops at Valmy halted the enemy advance. On September 21 the Convention abolished monarchy, and the next day it proclaimed the Republic.

The Republic of Virtue, 1792–1794

Republics were a rarity in absolutist Europe. There were only Genoa, Venice, the Dutch Republic, and the Swiss Confederation. Of these four, Genoa and Venice had long since decayed, the Dutch Republic was in decline with its Orange stadholder well on the way to monarchy, and the Swiss Confederation was stagnant, with its young men still entering foreign service as mercenary soldiers (the guards butchered by the mob at the Tuileries on August 20 were Swiss). One republic of ex-Europeans in North America was just beginning to perfect a "more perfect union." The very word "republican" reeked of radicalism. With the greatest state of Europe now a republic and breathing a revolution of "liberty" and "equality," Europe seemed to be standing on a precipice. France, in fact, was, for the most terrible days of revolution stretched just ahead.

Although the majority of the delegates to the Convention were moderates, its leadership was all Jacobin, among whom Danton was the most prominent. The Jacobins were now badly divided. The violence of the events of August and September had repelled the Girondists, who stood for a moderate bourgeois republic and opposed domination by Paris and the mob. They comprised the Right in the Convention. The radical Jacobins were the

Left. They sat in the highest seats in the amphitheater in which the Convention met and were aptly named the Mountain.

"CITIZEN CAPET"

The Girondists and the Mountain split irrevocably on the king's fate. Both agreed as to his treason, but the Girondists desired to delay his trial by the Convention. Outvoted, they sought clemency for him, recognizing that his execution would have unfavorable repercussions abroad. The Mountain demanded his death. After long debate the Mountain won by a small majority, and on January 21, 1793, "Citizen Louis Capet," as Louis XVI was now called, went to his death under the guillotine.

Prior to Louis's execution French armies had occupied Belgium, the Rhineland, and Savoy. Flushed with triumph, the Convention announced to the world in November, 1792, that the French Republic would come to the aid of people everywhere who wished "to recover their liberty." European powers that had until then remained neutral laid plans for action. The Convention anticipated them by declaring war on England and Holland in February, 1793. A month later Spain joined the anti-French alliance. This was the first of many coalitions against France. It put almost all of Europe at war with her. The military pressure was enormous, but luckily for France the allies were suspicious of one another, and the attention of the Austrian and Prussian governments was diverted by their anxiety over getting as much as possible in the last partition of Poland.

Internal troubles added to the problems France faced. The execution of the king and military recruiting stirred up rebellion among the devoutly Catholic and royalist peasants of the Vendée in western France. Prices continued to rise as a result of serious food shortages. A group of extreme radicals, called the *Enragés,* agitated for price controls and rationing. In the Convention the chasm widened between the Girondists and the Mountain. In May, 1793, the Paris mob once again seized the initiative on behalf of the most radical faction. It invaded the Convention and demanded the expulsion of the leading Girondists. Those not arrested fled into hiding.

ROBESPIERRE AND THE TERROR

The Mountain was supreme. As its first move it drafted a new constitution which among other democratic features included an end to property qualifications for the suffrage. The constitution never went into effect. The military and domestic troubles that had brought the country to the edge of collapse gave the Mountain an excuse for dictatorship. The Convention declared that the government would be "revolutionary until the peace." It established an emergency government with almost unlimited powers to

Prisoners Arriving at Jail during the Reign of Terror, by Polignac
*"It has been said that terror is the means by which a despotic government rules . . .
When despots rule because their subjects are terrified, the despots are justified—
as despots. You put down all the enemies of freedom by means of terror, and you are
justified—as founders of the Republic. The government of the Revolution is the
despotism of liberty against tyranny. Must might be used only in order to protect crime?"*
Robespierre justifies the Terror in a speech of February 5, 1794, reprinted in SPEECHES
OF MAXIMILIEN ROBESPIERRE (New York, 1927).
Courtesy of Musée de Carnavalet; photograph from Bulloz

direct the nation until the dangers were overcome; only then would the new
constitution be implemented. A Committee of Public Safety, composed of
nine (later twelve) deputies chosen by the Convention, became the supreme
administrative and policy-making authority. The Convention itself became
a rubber stamp. Maximilien Robespierre (1758–1794), provincial lawyer
from Arras, disciple of Rousseau, incorruptible champion of democracy,
idealist, and fanatic, emerged as the dominant member of the Committee.
A Committee of General Security, named by the Committee of Public
Safety, held supreme police power, and a Revolutionary Tribunal tried
counterrevolutionaries with utter disdain for legal niceties.

This was the machinery of government that in September, 1793, instituted
the Terror. In the name of saving the Revolution from its internal enemies
hundreds of thousands were at one time or another imprisoned, and some
twenty to forty thousand heads rolled. More than two-thirds of those
executed were peasants, workers, and small craftsmen. Although legend
has it that those who suffered most were from the first and second estates,
only 8 per cent of the victims were noblemen and only 6 per cent were
clergy. The dead included all sorts and conditions of men, from dissipated
young noblemen and obscure peasants and artisans to the brilliant chemist
Lavoisier, whose epitaph, spoken by his friend and fellow scientist Joseph

Lagrange, can stand for all those of talent who died in the Terror: "It required but a moment for this head to fall and a hundred years perhaps will not suffice to produce the like." The dead ranged over the entire political spectrum, from Marie Antoinette through the Girondists to the *Enragés* on the left. The vivacious Madame Roland, in whose *salon* the Girondists had congregated, spoke history's judgment of the Terror a moment before she died: "O Liberty, what crimes are committed in your name!"

The Committee of Public Safety well recognized that the real threat to the Revolution came less from the poor wretches on their last ride to the guillotine than from the armies massing on France's borders. Under universal conscription, the *levée en masse*, almost all able-bodied, unmarried men between eighteen and twenty-five were mobilized, and by the spring of 1794 France's army stood at eight hundred thousand, the greatest in Europe's history. Mobilization of the entire French economy for war was another innovation. Some economic controls, such as ceilings on prices and wages, rationing, and prohibitions against hoarding, proved difficult to enforce. The overall effort, however, was highly successful. By October, 1793, the armies of the First Coalition had been repulsed, and French troops reached what Danton referred to as the "natural frontiers" of France—the Rhine, the Alps, the Pyrenees, and the Atlantic. The army of the Revolution had accomplished what Louis XIV could not accomplish. The newly won territories were either incorporated into France or turned into satellite states.

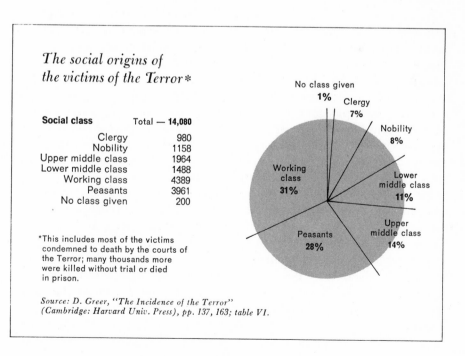

The social origins of the victims of the Terror*

Social class	Total — 14,080
Clergy	980
Nobility	1158
Upper middle class	1964
Lower middle class	1488
Working class	4389
Peasants	3961
No class given	200

No class given 1%
Clergy 7%
Nobility 8%
Lower middle class 11%
Upper middle class 14%
Peasants 28%
Working class 31%

*This includes most of the victims condemned to death by the courts of the Terror; many thousands more were killed without trial or died in prison.

Source: D. Greer, "The Incidence of the Terror" (Cambridge: Harvard Univ. Press), pp. 137, 163; table VI.

VIRTUE TRIUMPHANT

With its domestic enemies disappearing under the scourge of the Terror and its foreign enemies in retreat, the revolutionary government sought to reshape France's institutions and the tenor of French life. With the zest of the pure and righteous who have struck down privilege the radicals established a "Republic of Virtue." Christianity was equated with counter-revolution, and a program of de-Christianization raised the "Cult of Reason" in its place. Several thousand churches became "Temples of Reason"; the Virgin and other saints gave way before such "Revolutionary saints" as Rousseau and Voltaire. As a shrewd politician, Robespierre recognized that the Cult of Reason would alienate many from the Republic, but as a deist he believed that the "Supreme Being" had led France into becoming the Republic of Virtue and that credit should be given where it was due. Therefore in June, 1794, he introduced the "Worship of the Supreme Being" at a formal pageant, a parody of the Catholic liturgy done in utter seriousness.

A new calendar was introduced that did away with Sunday and all Church holidays, destroying the old Christian associations for calculation of time, and reduced the number of holidays—hard work became an attribute of patriotic virtue. September 22, 1792, the day on which the Republic had been proclaimed, was designated as the beginning of Year I. The year was divided into twelve months of thirty days each, and the months were named after the appropriate seasonal characteristics: for example, the autumn months were *Vendémiaire,* "grape harvest"; *Brumaire,* "misty"; and *Frimaire,* "frosty." Each month comprised three periods of ten days, the tenth day being given to rest. The five or six days remaining at the end of the year to adjust the new calendar to the solar year were made national holidays to celebrate the Revolution. The new calendar lasted until 1806, when Napoleon abandoned it, to no one's regret.

Virtue had no place for inequality or any remnant of the ancien régime. *Monsieur* and *Madame,* the old forms of address, were replaced by *Citoyen* and *Citoyenne* (citizen). The knee breeches (*culottes*) of pre-Revolutionary fashion disappeared, and good Republicans wore the trousers of the Parisian working class, the *sansculottes* (without breeches). Republican Rome was taken as a model. Women wore loose robes, sandals, and flowing natural hair, rather than the wigs of the court ladies. Simple classical furniture replaced the studied ornateness of the style of Louis XVI. The theater and the press became instruments of republican propaganda. Even playing cards were purified of the base remnants of monarchy: the King, the Queen, and the Jack of Spades went the way of Louis XVI, Marie Antoinette, and the counts of France. The new cards depicted soldiers, workers, La Belle Liberté, Rousseau, and figures of classical republican antiquity such as Brutus and Cato.

For all this excess, one lasting, substantial reform was undertaken. A commission under the scientist Joseph Lagrange fashioned the metric system of weights and measures, a rational and standardized decimal system. This improvement over chaotic local variations was adopted all over Europe and has survived to this day, with only the English-speaking peoples resisting its virtues.

VIRTUE DETHRONED

In his ruthless drive to save the Revolution as he conceived it, Robespierre antagonized and alienated the extreme radicals of Paris, called Hébertists. He ended their control of the Paris city government and then guillotined Jacques Hébert, their leader, and others. A few days later he turned on Danton and his followers, accused them of treason because they favored relaxing the Terror, and had them guillotined. Robespierre's own colleagues on the Committee of Public Safety suspected that they might be next. Continued French military success undermined whatever necessity might have justified the Terror. The fears of those who suspected that they would soon become Robespierre's victims seemed confirmed by a speech he made to the Convention denouncing the delegates who opposed him. The next day, 9 Thermidor in the Republican calendar (July 27, 1794), these delegates rose to denounce Robespierre and stampeded their fellow members into ordering his arrest. The Paris city government, staffed by Robespierre's supporters, tried unsuccessfully to rouse the people of Paris on his behalf; it was the first time the Paris mob had failed to respond to a radical call to arms. On July 28 the dictator, half-dead from a pistol wound in his jaw that may have been self-inflicted, was guillotined along with several scores of his followers. The Republic of Virtue died with them.

Reaction and Irresolution, 1794–1799

THERMIDOREAN REACTION

The happenings of 9 Thermidor provoked an unexpected change in the attitude of the public—a change so pronounced that the period has become known as the Thermidorean Reaction. Public opinion, hitherto repressed by fear of the Revolutionary Tribunal, clearly favored a relaxation of tension. The end of the Republic of Virtue was greeted with enthusiasm. Amusements and luxuries that had been frowned upon as unrepublican and decadent reappeared overnight. Knee breeches came back into style, and women turned away from severe, classical fashions to revealing and luxurious dresses. Vulgar ostentation became the vogue. Gangs of young fops, *jeunesse dorée* (gilded youth), wandered the streets of Paris beating up *sansculottes*. In the provinces gangs of royalists calling themselves Com-

began their own "white terror" against the former Jacobin
ιy Catholic churches reopened, and numerous nonjuring
,ed to Paris.

firebrands in the Convention hastened to abandon their revo-
.rdor. The powers of the Committee of Public Safety were cur-
ιe Revolutionary Tribunal was restricted in its activities and, in
olished. The Jacobins were completely discredited, their provincial
.es died out, and in November, 1794, the headquarters in Paris was
closeu. Jacobins who had played leading roles in the Terror were punished,
and many of those whom they had imprisoned were released. Thousands of
émigrés returned home. The repeal of price controls and other economic
regulations encouraged speculators and profiteers. The resulting inflation
hit the poor hard, and there were food riots and small insurrections. The
lowly and the exploited, now lacking leadership, were easily repressed.

The demand for a return to normal conditions included a desire to end
the war. Peace was made with Holland, where a satellite republic had been
established after the French invasion. Peace was also made with Prussia,
three small German states, and Spain. France won recognition of her conquest of the left bank of the Rhine and the Spanish part of the island of
San Domingo in the West Indies. Austria, England, and Sardinia remained
at war with the Republic.

THE CONSTITUTION OF THE YEAR III

Despite talk about a restoration of the monarchy, the bourgeoisie were
determined to keep France under the rule of the middle class. Since they
were in control of the Convention their wishes prevailed in the new constitution, the Constitution of the Year III that went into effect late in 1795.
It was the third since 1791, supplanting the never-implemented constitution
of 1793. Suffrage depended upon a property qualification, literacy, and
having a trade or profession. The voters chose electors, who selected officials
and members of the legislature. The property qualification for electors was
so high that only about twenty thousand men were eligible in all France—
less than the fifty thousand potential electors under the 1791 constitution
establishing constitutional monarchy. The legislature consisted of a Council
of Five Hundred that initiated legislation and a Council of Elders, with
250 members, that approved or disapproved the legislation proposed by the
Council of Five Hundred. The Elders appointed an Executive Directory
of five men from nominees submitted by the Five Hundred, to serve for
five years.

Conservative as these new arrangements were, they still offended rightists
and royalists. To prevent the Right from gaining control of the new government—which would have brought revenge down upon the heads of all who
had voted for the death of Louis XVI—the bourgeois Convention decreed that

two-thirds of the members of the two new Councils must be members of the outgoing Convention. This brazen self-interest outraged the rightists of Paris, and on 13 Vendémiaire (October 5, 1795) thousands of them rose in insurrection. The government turned its defense over to Napoleon Bonaparte, a twenty-six-year-old brigadier general of artillery who chanced to be in Paris without a command. He ordered his cannon outside the Tuileries to fire point-blank into the advancing mob. The legendary "whiff of grapeshot" broke the insurgents' ranks, and they fled, leaving their dead and wounded in the streets.

THE DIRECTORY

The new regime, called the Directory, inherited massive problems. The Directors were not equal to the task. Beset by internal disorder, enemies on both the right and the left, economic troubles, and the need to continue the war, the Directors failed to respond quickly and effectively to crisis. The Vendée revolt broke out again, and elsewhere bandits terrorized the countryside. The royalists were in touch with Louis XVI's brother, the Count of Provence, whom they called Louis XVIII (Louis XVI's young son, the Dauphin, had died in prison). In 1795 he issued a declaration from his exile in Italy, announcing that when he regained the throne he would restore the ancien régime and punish those prominent in the Revolution. This threat shored up popular opinion behind the Directory and confirmed its resolve to prevent the re-establishment of the monarchy.

On the left, radical working-class leaders hatched secret plots to overthrow the regime. François Émile Babeuf, self-styled "Gracchus" in commemoration of the ancient Roman popular leaders of that name, formed the Society of Equals. Advocating the abolition of private property and parliamentary government and the introduction of a planned socialist economy, the society recruited about two thousand active members and nearly twenty thousand supporters. Babeuf, a journalist, and the other leaders were middle-class intellectuals, but their followers came mainly from the working class, especially poor craftsmen in Paris. In the spring of 1796 the Babeuvists plotted rebellion. Betrayed and captured, Babeuf was guillotined, the other leaders were executed or deported, and the movement collapsed. This minor, tragic episode has gained historical fame because Babeuf's doctrines foreshadowed some of the socialist programs of the nineteenth and twentieth centuries.

EMERGENCE OF BONAPARTE

In March, 1796, General Napoleon Bonaparte, savior of the Directory, was given command of the French army in Italy. He defeated the armies of Austria and Sardinia, set up the Cisalpine Republic in the valley of the Po and the Ligurian Republic in the old Republic of Genoa, making them French satellites, and pushed to within seventy-five miles of Vienna. The Austrians sued for peace, and in the Treaty of Campo Formio in October, 1797, they recognized the French annexation of Belgium, the left bank of the Rhine, and the Ionian Islands. As compensation, Austria was allowed to annex the Republic of Venice, thereby ending the thousand-year independence of that ancient state. Bonaparte was the talk of France.

Elections had been held in March, 1797, for the two councils, and the royalists had gained majorities. The dismayed republicans asked Bonaparte for help. On 18 Fructidor (September 4, 1797) the Councils, protected by a military force commanded by an aide of Bonaparte, annulled most of the elections of the royalists. Having by this coup d'état forfeited its claim to be a constitutional government, the Directory henceforth clung to power only by such illegal acts as purges and quashed elections.

The conclusion of peace with Austria left Britain alone at war with France. General Bonaparte took command of an army supposed to invade England. He decided, instead, to strike at British economic supremacy by invading Egypt and thereby cutting off Britain's eastern and Mediterranean trade. He enjoyed some initial successes against the Turks who controlled Egypt, until a British fleet under Admiral Horatio Nelson defeated French naval forces in Abukir Bay at the mouth of the Nile in August, 1798, and isolated Bonaparte and his army in Egypt. It was Napoleon Bonaparte's first major defeat.

The fear of French expansion in the Mediterranean, awakened by Bonaparte's invasion of Egypt, persuaded England, Austria, Russia, Turkey, Naples, Portugal, and the Papacy to form the Second Coalition against France early in 1799. Russian and Austrian troops commanded by Marshal Alexander Suvorov drove the French out of Italy. Other allied forces invaded Switzerland and the Netherlands. These military reverses bred still more discontent with the Directory. In 1799 the opposition made such great electoral gains that the Directory was afraid to invalidate them. Bonaparte, who was still in Egypt, saw these developments as an opportunity to win greater prominence for himself. Leaving his army to its fate, he managed to slip through the British fleet with a handful of men and returned to France, where he was greeted with great enthusiasm. He offered himself to those seeking to overthrow the Directory. On 18 Brumaire (November 9, 1799) the plotters moved. The next day troops invaded the meeting of the Council of Five Hundred and overthrew the Directory. A provisional government headed by three consuls took control, with Bonaparte as First Consul. The rebels carefully retained the republican form of government— but only the form. The coup d'état of 18 Brumaire in fact marked the end of the First French Republic.

Impact of the French Revolution

In the context of Western history, the French Revolution emerges as part of a democratic surge felt throughout much of the Western world in the last four decades of the eighteenth century. Although the French Revolution was the most spectacular manifestation of the surge, demands for the abolition of special privilege and for political equality were not unique to France. They had been voiced by people of other nations well before 1789, not least in the American colonies of Britain.

Nonetheless, the French Revolution accomplished the rapid spread of democratic ideas. Its doctrines were highly exportable, for they spelled out the rights of man everywhere. The news of the great happenings in Paris inspired democratic-minded men in other lands and converted the timid. The news of absolutism and privilege overthrown struck terror into the hearts of rulers and statesmen and moved them to adopt repressive measures against the threat of popular government.

THE BRITISH ISLES

In Britain the events of the French Revolution encouraged men of the lower-middle and working classes to form clubs and societies demanding the principles the French were preaching. Many of these organizations entered into correspondence with members of the National Assembly in France and with various Jacobin clubs. The Revolution was hailed in artistic and literary circles, where the French were thought to have inaugurated a new age in which man was freed from the shackles of the past. Their reaction was summed up by the poet William Wordsworth, who many years later wrote:

> Bliss was it in that dawn to be alive,
> But to be young was very heaven!

Others, however, spoke out strongly against the Revolution. The greatest was Edmund Burke. His *Reflections on the Revolution in France* (1790) attacked the principles of the Revolution as abstract and dangerous, argued that a nation cannot break with its own traditions and character, and prophesied that the Revolution would lead not to the ideal society promised by its partisans but to violence and dictatorship. Many pamphlets appeared to rebut his arguments, the most successful being *The Rights of Man* by Thomas Paine, but events proved Burke's prediction correct.

The popularity of the Revolution—Paine's pamphlet sold tens of thousands of copies—alarmed many of the ruling class. Alarm turned into active repression when the French abolished the monarchy and offered aid to all people in the struggle against their rulers. Despite a trial of British radical leaders for treason and severe penalties handed out to them, the agitation and meetings continued. In 1795 and 1799 Prime Minister William Pitt put through Parliament stringent legislation, making it treason to speak or write against the government and prohibiting large public meetings. In 1799 the Combination Acts forbade workmen to unite in clubs and societies for the purpose of improving their wages or working conditions; in short, labor unions were declared illegal. This wiped out centers of revolutionary propaganda and also provided employers with a powerful weapon against labor. Thus in Great Britain conservatism and reaction were strengthened for a time as a result of the French Revolution.

In Ireland young patriots, detesting Britain's rule, hailed the Revolution. In 1791 Wolfe Tone (1763–1798) organized the Society of the United Irishmen. It soon abandoned its original purpose, parliamentary reform, in favor of establishing an Irish republic. After the Franco-British war had begun in 1793, Napper Tandy (1740–1803) and other United Irish leaders conspired with the French to send troops to free Ireland from English rule. The French invasion attempts were repelled, and a number of the Irish leaders were taken by the British. Tone committed suicide before execution, and his brethren were hanged, but with them had been born nineteenth-century Irish nationalism.

CONTINENTAL EUROPE

In Germany the events of 1789 elated many intellectuals, but they lost their enthusiasm after the September massacres and the execution of the king. German rulers met the threat of the Revolution by making their regimes more repressive in order to throttle at the outset any radical tendency. In Italy, intellectuals greeted the Revolution joyously, and revolutionary clubs were organized. Bonaparte's conquests in northern Italy and the establishment of the Cisalpine and Ligurian Republics caught the imagination of the people, and Italians began to dream of a free, united Italy.

In the Austrian Netherlands (Belgium) a group of liberal bourgeois intellectuals called Vonckists (after their leader J. F. Vonck) had cooperated with conservative groups in the rising against the reforms of Emperor Joseph II, only to be turned on by their conservative allies when they proposed moderate liberal reforms to broaden representation in the estates. Priests assailed the Vonckists as disciples of Voltaire, and there was a mass rising against them. Hundreds fled for their lives to France. Later, when they were able to return home, they agitated for a republic on the French model. The Belgian masses under reactionary clerical leadership opposed these revolutionary ideas, and in 1795 after the French had annexed Belgium and introduced republican reforms, there were popular risings and unrest, which were as much nationalist as antirepublican.

Following the abortive revolution of the middle-class liberal Patriots in the United Netherlands, suppressed in 1787, the leaders took refuge in France. They were enthusiastic supporters of the Revolution, and when France declared war on the United Netherlands in 1793, two thousand Patriots entered the French forces to serve in the Netherlands. With the French conquest northward these refugees came into their own. Under the French aegis and with the support of resident Dutchmen who had already embraced the Revolution's tenets in their societies and literary clubs, they established the Batavian Republic (Batavia was the Roman name for the Netherlands). Its constitution and laws were modeled on the French, and the Batavian Republic was a satellite of France. In 1798 a radical minority staged a coup d'état with the help of the French troops stationed there and established a unitary state by abolishing the old provincial sovereignty. Within five months the regime met its "Thermidorean Reaction" and was replaced by a more moderate government.

The return home of the exiled Dutch Patriots in French uniforms to fashion a satellite state for France bore witness to how deeply the ideas of the French Revolution had affected some men. Imbued with fervor for the rights of man, they were prepared to serve a traditional enemy and subject themselves and their nation to foreign domination. When Napoleon Bonaparte in his limitless ambition embarked on a Europe-wide conquest, one of his most potent allies was this fervor. Coming as a liberator and the instrument of the rights of man, Bonaparte had already half-defeated his opponents. The irony was that the very nationalism that had summoned Frenchmen to save the fatherland when "the day of glory had arrived" would manifest itself among France's satellites to help ensure Bonaparte's ultimate defeat.

--- CHAPTER TWENTY ---

The Napoleonic Era

Napoleon Bonaparte

First Consul Napoleon Bonaparte, despite his short stature, was striking in physical appearance, with a large head, swarthy complexion, sharply cut features, and brilliant steel-blue eyes. Born in 1769 on the island of Corsica (annexed to France from Genoa the year before his birth), he was the second of five surviving sons of a noble but impoverished family of Italian origin. At the age of ten Buonaparte—as he spelled his surname before frenchifying it in 1796—entered a French provincial military school as a scholarship student. Discipline was lax, the studies were general and pointless, and the lad applied himself with zeal only to mathematics and Roman history. In 1784 he was accepted at the military academy in Paris, where he began a year of hard, creditable study in artillery, which won him a cadetship in the army in 1785 and a commission the next year. Both at the military schools and in his first post aristocratic colleagues taunted him for his Corsican origin and poverty.

On frequent furloughs home between 1786 and 1793 Napoleon engaged in the Corsican independence movement, in which his older brother Joseph was prominent. An ardent Corsican patriot and avid reader of Rousseau, young Napoleon resolved to free Corsica from "French tyranny." The

National Assembly's declaration of November 30, 1789, extending to Corsica the rights and liberties of all Frenchmen and the reforms of the Revolution, dampened his insular patriotism and caused him to embrace the Revolution. He became increasingly republican, and when in 1793 the ruling faction in Corsica repudiated the Revolution, he and his family were forced to flee. Henceforth Napoleon Bonaparte's fortunes were irrevocably linked to France —and shortly France's would be linked to him.

THE MAN

The tendency in dealing with Napoleon is to paint him either in the gigantic proportions of a superman or in the smudged lines of an enigma. He was neither. Although he spent the last years of his life fashioning his own legend, he could not cover the tracks he had left in his passage. Courage, resourcefulness, keenness, and decision—these soldierly qualities distinguished this superb leader of men who was an inspiring field commander, master tactician, and bold strategist. In later years, even in defeat, he never forfeited the admiration of his generals, the devotion of his staff, and the love of his soldiers. Personal magnetism marked his relations with almost all who came into contact with him. Whether charming and gay, angry, maniacal, or morose, he dominated everyone in his presence. An overbearing egotism was both a pose and the very substance of his being. He was capable of continuous, slavish toil on any task he set himself. Precision and orderliness, a passion for arrangement and symmetry, were dominant motifs in his chamber, his chancellery, and his camp. For a man so formidable and ambitious he was remarkably immune to rancor. For a man so devoted to his kinsmen, he was peculiarly lacking in sensitivity to suffering and in the capacity to love.

It is doubtful that Bonaparte possessed a shred of religious faith or ideology. He was a materialist, suspicious of the insubstantial, the ideal, the intangible. He had an unquenchable thirst for the factual and the knowable —for objective reality. Yet the visionary and subjective cast of his mind, distorting reality, was no less marked. That which distinguished him until near the end of his career was an intuitive capacity to reconcile objective reality and subjective vision and to wring advantage from both.

As a demagogue in an era sick of demagoguery, he was masterful. Egotism, magnetism, and the evocation of a vision planned down to the last objective detail constituted a formula for leadership so successful that he was never seriously threatened with the loss of French allegiance. Unlike other demagogues, Napoleon never deluded himself that his pronouncements represented the whole truth, but in his egotism he was unmoved by the prospect that the whole truth might catch up with him.

The most revealing personal quality of the man who would master Europe was devotion to family. It moved him to almost boundless generosity in titles and wealth to his mother (his father died in 1785), four brothers, and three sisters. At its height about 1810 the Grand Empire of Napoleon was run like a family chain store: holding thrones in Napoleon's satellite states were Joseph (Spain), Louis (Holland), Jerome (Westphalia), Maria (Tuscany), and Caroline and her husband Marshal Murat (Naples). Only his brother Lucien, of whose marriage Napoleon did not approve, received no more than ambassadorships. He endowed his mother Letitia, called "Madame Mother," with great wealth, much of which she thriftily hoarded, saying, "When it is all over, you will be glad of my savings." His uncle Joseph Fesch, who during the Revolution had temporarily given up his clerical calling for the more remunerative business of army contracts, became a cardinal and the chief religious figure of the empire.

THE RISE OF BONAPARTE

As a captain of artillery, he performed his first notable service to the Republic in 1793. Royalists, aided by British and Spanish troops, had seized the major French naval base of Toulon on the Mediterranean, and the Republican army laid siege to it. Bonaparte used with deadly effect the concentrated artillery fire that he was to perfect as a prime tactic in his campaigns. He was in the van of the storming column that took the enemy's main position and forced the retreat of the British and Spaniards. Promoted to brigadier general by the Committee of Public Safety, he became chief of artillery in the Italian campaign launched in 1794. Robespierre's fall put him under suspicion, and he was arrested. He was soon released, but the Italian campaign had been shelved. In 1795, after refusing a command on grounds of ill health, he was struck from the list of general officers, and it seemed that his military career was finished.

Then came the opportunity offered by the Vendémiaire Royalist uprising in Paris in October, 1795, in which Napoleon dispersed the mob by firing a "whiff of grapeshot." A grateful Directory approved his new plan for the conquest of Italy in January, 1796, where he covered himself with glory. Next came his expedition to conquer Egypt, then his return to France where he participated in the coup d'état of 18 Brumaire (November 19, 1799) that overthrew the Directory and established the Consulate with Bonaparte as First Consul.

The Domestic Reformer

On December 15, 1799, the First Consul, speaking for himself and his two fellow consuls, Abbé Sieyès and Roger Ducos, proclaimed the end of the French Revolution with the words, "Citizens, the Revolution is established upon the principles which began it. It is ended." Bonaparte did not propose to delude anyone when he said the Revolution was ended. It was. However, he intended to salvage from the Revolution substantial, material reforms, derived both from the Enlightenment's teachings and the Revolution's unfulfilled intentions.

The first task of the government was to draw up the Constitution of the Year VII (1799)—the fourth constitution in nine years. Drafted according to Bonaparte's wishes and heralded as based on the "true principles" of the Revolutionary past, the constitution established a thoroughgoing dictatorship in the guise of a democratic republic. It did not contain a declaration of the rights of citizens, nor did it guarantee freedom of speech and press. Bonaparte, as First Consul, was made chief executive for ten years, aided by two other consuls and by a Council of State chosen by him. A bicameral legislature lacked any real power. All men over twenty-one could vote, but only for electors and by a procedure guaranteed to filter out the voters' will. In each commune the voters were to select one-tenth of their number as a "communal list"; members of all the communal lists in a department chose one-tenth of their number for a "departmental list"; those in the departmental lists then selected one-tenth of their number for the "national list." The men in the national list, called the "Notables of France," numbered about ten thousand—considerably fewer qualified electors than under the constitutions of 1791 (about fifty thousand) and 1793 (about twenty thousand). The members of the two legislative bodies, the chief judges, and the higher government officials were all selected from the Notables.

The new constitution was a mockery of both the democratic process and the principles of the Revolution. Yet when it was submitted to the people for their approval in December, 1799, 3,001,007 voted for it, and only 1,526 voted against it. Having voted away its freedom, France received for a time the most efficient, honest, and vigorous government in its history. Dominated by Bonaparte, who in the years of the Consulate was at the height of his creative powers, the new regime restored internal order and created or reshaped institutions that long survived Bonaparte's fall.

RELIGIOUS, FISCAL, AND ADMINISTRATIVE REFORMS

The most pressing need was to restore order. Within months Bonaparte suppressed the Royalist rebellion that had been raging in the Vendée since 1793, and wiped out the bands of brigands that had terrorized many parts of France. More significant, he ended the constant threat to internal order that the Catholic clergy's discontent with the Civil Constitution of the Clergy had posed. For this purpose, and also to obtain the papacy's good will preparatory to conquering Catholic states, he reached a settlement with Pope Pius VII on terms highly favorable to the French government. By the Concordat of 1801 the Pope agreed to give up all claims to Church property confiscated in the Revolution and to confirm French bishops nominated by

Napoleon. The bishops were to name the lower clergy, subject to approval by the government; and the clergy, to be paid by the state, were to swear allegiance to the state. Bonaparte agreed to papal deposition of French bishops who fell under papal disapproval, reopening of the seminaries, and public Catholic worship, such as street processions. The Concordat of 1801 remained in force for over a century. If Pius VII had hoped that it would return France, "the eldest daughter of the Church," fully to the fold, he was soon disabused. Clerical privilege was not re-established, and to show that Catholicism was not the only recognized religion in France, Bonaparte subsidized Protestant sects and in 1809 after conferences with Jewish leaders devised a scheme of local government for Jewish communities.

The Consulate remedied the state's financial feebleness, which had precipitated the Revolution and continued during the 1790's. The Bank of France, established in 1800 for the purpose of lending money to the government, freed the state from reliance on private financiers and the necessity to float loans at extortionate interest rates. Bonaparte did what perhaps only the travail of the previous decade could have permitted anyone to do: he reorganized the entire fiscal structure. Tax collection was systematized and its efficiency increased enormously. Strict auditing of collectors' accounts reduced corruption and embezzlement. For the first time in over a century the French government rested on a sound financial base.

At the local administrative level elected officials were replaced by appointees of the central government, from prefects in charge of each department down to mayors and town councils. Thus Bonaparte completed the work of administrative centralization begun long before by Richelieu. Much of his system of local government still persists in France.

CODE NAPOLÉON

Bonaparte's most important domestic accomplishment was the codification of the law. Successive monarchs since the fifteenth century had talked of codification, and during the 1790's the revolutionary governments had taken the first steps in this direction. Although the actual codification was done by a committee of legal experts, Bonaparte took a deep personal interest in the work. Comprising five codes that were compact enough to fit in one volume, the *Code Napoléon* was a fusion and refinement of Roman law, the remnants of the numerous customary laws of France, and legislation of the Revolution. The first of the five, the civil code, governed marital and familial relations and went into effect in March, 1804. It was followed by the code of civil procedure and the commercial code in 1807, the code of criminal procedure in 1808, and the penal code in 1810. The great merits of the Code Napoléon were its clarity, comprehensiveness (even though it lacked precision in detail), equitableness, and applicability to a bourgeois and secular social order. The code remains in force in France today, its original frame still discernible through the mass of subsequent additions and amendments that have enabled it to grow apace with industrialism and the modern state. Its merits were recognized elsewhere, and it was either adopted as, or greatly influenced, the codes of Belgium, Holland, Luxemburg, Italy, Spain, Portugal, Switzerland, Germany, Rumania, Egypt, a number of Latin American states, and Japan. It was deservedly the pride of Bonaparte among his domestic achievements.

EDUCATIONAL REFORM

Napoleon's reform of French education was a mixed blessing. Although it laid the foundation for a system of uniform excellence, it put French education in a straitjacket from which it has not yet emerged. Successive *Indoctrination* revolutionary governments had planned a national educational system but had never implemented the plans. Bonaparte appropriated a large amount of money for public education, and in 1802 he made provision for a network of primary and secondary schools and institutions of higher learning maintained at public expense. It was the first full-scale public school system in Europe. He left the primary and some secondary schools under local control, but placed other secondary schools, called *lycées,* and the higher institutions under the supervision of the central government. This centralizing tendency culminated in 1808 with the creation of the University of France, which was not a teaching institution but an administrative and supervisory organization for controlling all French educational institutions. It persists to this day.

Another creation of the First Consul that has survived is the Order of the Legion of Honor. All titles of nobility had been abolished in 1790, but Bonaparte recognized the deep appeal of special distinctions and honors. In 1802, over the strong protests of the legislature, who feared a restoration of special privileges, he established the Legion with himself as Supreme Commander. Persons who distinguished themselves in any field might be appointed to it. Initially limited to six thousand, within a few years its membership grew to over thirty thousand, and today its recipients are, indeed, legion.

The Legion of Honor represented one pole of the system of incentives that Napoleon introduced to replace the Republic's egalitarianism; merit brought its reward, and honors were generously showered upon the capable and the loyal. Demerit brought its deserts, too, and the other pole of Napoleonic incentives was represented by the efficient, inexorable, and harsh secret police headed by Joseph Fouché. Equality before the law meant equal application of censorship to the press, equal repression of dissent in speech, equal punishment for acts against the state, and equal surveillance by Fouché's agents. It was a society of equality, but it was not a free society.

The Empire Builder

Domestic achievement was not Napoleon Bonaparte's commanding ambition. He had read too much Roman history—not of Republican but of Imperial Rome—at school and on lonely garrison duty as a young lieutenant; he had seen too much of the world at the head of columns of French Republican soldiers; he had tasted too often the sweetness of victory. In his passion for the concrete and the tangible he found gratification not only in reshaping France. He found it, too, in the shattering destruction of salvo after salvo of well-aimed cannonade, in marching long columns of disciplined troops to the farthest reaches of a continent, in redrawing the boundaries of states and modeling new nations as if the terrain of Europe were potter's clay.

THE FIRST STEPS

He began his quest for imperial glory with a brilliant maneuver. French reverses at the hands of the Second Coalition (Britain, Russia, Austria, and Turkey) had contributed to the destruction of the Directory. The First Consul bowed to France's desire for an end to the war, which had been going on since 1792. With a characteristic flourish on Christmas Day, 1799, he wrote a personal letter to the king of England and the emperor of Austria (Russia had quarreled with her allies and withdrawn from active participation in the war) indicating his desire for peace. He knew that neither power would accept his offer so long as France controlled Belgium and the Rhine and threatened Italy, but he convinced Frenchmen that he wanted to end the war and that the enemy was responsible for its continuation.

After the British and Austrians had reacted as he expected, Bonaparte led his troops into Italy through the St. Bernard Pass while it was still under snow and smashed the Austrian army at Marengo in June, 1800. His victory aroused tremendous enthusiasm in France and thwarted opponents there who had plotted a Bourbon restoration in the event of his defeat. In December the French invaded Austria, and Emperor Francis sued for peace. The Treaty of Lunéville in 1801 confirmed the provisions of Campo Formio (1797), and France regained the territories lost during the war with the Second Coalition.

With Austria retired, Bonaparte turned to Great Britain. Of all the powers, he most detested and most feared Britain. Its navy had inflicted upon him his most humiliating defeat at Abukir Bay. For a brief while he thought he could persuade Russia to join him against the hated island kingdom, for Tsar Paul had become violently anti-British. Paul's murder in March, 1801, the accession of Alexander I, who favored England, and the British ambassador's judicious bribing of Alexander's advisers closed this avenue. A few

Napolean → Louis XIV

months later the French army in Egypt surrendered to the British. The war was at a stalemate, with France dominant on the Continent and Britain in control of the seas. In March, 1802, the two powers signed the Peace of Amiens. It was highly favorable to France, for Britain recognized nearly all French conquests in Europe and overseas. In return Britain gained little, for Bonaparte refused to reopen to British trade Continental countries controlled by France.

For the first and only time between 1792 and 1814 France was at peace with the other European powers. It was a brief interlude. Unable to stomach France's domination of so much of the Continent, the powers also knew that Bonaparte would seek further conquests. Britain was especially apprehensive. French control of Belgium was "a pistol pointed at the heart of England." Bonaparte had never hidden his appetite for British territory in the Western Hemisphere, the Near East, and India. Deeply resentful of the exclusion of British commerce from French-controlled lands, British merchants feared that unless Bonaparte was checked, their trade losses would become still greater.

The disappointment of the British with the Treaty of Amiens contrasted with the joy with which the French greeted it. Peace had come at last, and with it victory. Bonaparte gave the French a chance to show their gratitude by arranging a plebiscite in May, 1802, to make him sole consul for life. The vote was 3,564,885 for him, 8,374 against him.

THE NEW CAESAR

The overwhelming vote of confidence told Bonaparte that he need stop at nothing. He made changes in the constitution to put almost all power in his hands. He assumed the trappings of royalty—using his first name only in official documents, holding court at the Tuileries, and minting coins with his portrait. France became an absolute monarchy in everything but name. A more dramatic stage set was required before he could declare himself emperor. A royalist plot to assassinate him and restore the Bourbons supplied it. The conspirators implicated an unnamed member of the Bourbon family as the prime mover in the scheme. Napoleon's suspicions fell upon the youthful Duke d'Enghien, a relative of the king, who had emigrated to Baden, close to the French border. In March, 1804, d'Enghien was kidnapped, brought to Paris, tried hastily by a military tribunal, and shot within four days of his arrest, although it was apparent at the trial that he was innocent.

The illegality and brutality of this incident awakened widespread revulsion, but it also put a premium on Bonaparte's survival and the continuation of his line if France was to be spared chaos. The simple—and popular—solution was the creation of a hereditary empire, so that if Napoleon was killed, his heir would be the recognized ruler. In May, 1804, the legislative bodies of the Consulate accepted the Consul's new constitution making him emperor. Even then the fiction of a republic was preserved —as it had been in Rome—for the Constitution of the Year XII commenced, "The government of the Republic is entrusted to an emperor, who takes the title Emperor of the French." Again Bonaparte asked the people to ratify his act; this time the vote was 3,572,329 in favor, and only 2,569 opposed.

Bonaparte turned to an ancient imperial tradition for his dramatic coronation on December 2, 1804. Pope Pius VII agreed to preside at the crowning of the new Charlemagne, whose dreams of ruling over the Latin and Teutonic peoples already had a semblance of reality. In the Cathedral of Notre Dame de Paris, amid imperial splendor, the pontiff raised an imperial crown, paused, and Bonaparte took it from his hands and crowned himself. The prearranged self-crowning went flawlessly, and the Emperor of the French, though he might be said to rule under God, did not rule under God's Vicar on Earth. The Pope's reward for his self-abnegation was France's abandonment of the Revolutionary calendar and return to the traditional one with its Sundays and religious holidays.

THE WAR OF THE THIRD COALITION

The Peace of Amiens of 1802 proved to be only a truce. Peaceful coexistence of Napoleonic France and the other powers was impossible, for the ambitions of Napoleon came into conflict everywhere with the interests of the other nations. In May, 1803, after little more than a year of peace, England declared war on France and her ally, Spain. In 1804 William Pitt became prime minister again after three years out of office. By offering large subsidies to powers that would join Britain, Pitt created another coalition in 1805, the third since 1792, comprising Britain, Austria, Russia, and Sweden. Spain, allied with France in the wars of the First and Second Coalitions, once more made common cause with her northern neighbor.

In 1803 Napoleon assembled a large army on the French coast at Boulogne, ostensibly to invade England. For two years the expeditionary force waited for French naval mastery of the Channel so that it might cross. That mastery was never established. In 1805, as a result of Austria's and Russia's alliance with Britain, Napoleon suddenly marched the Boulogne army eastward to meet the Austrians. After a series of brilliant and lightning moves in Bavaria Napoleon encircled and shattered an Austrian army of eighty thousand at Ulm in October, 1805. The French captured nearly forty thousand prisoners, including eighteen generals. French losses were insignificant. The Austrians fell back to join their Russian allies. In November Napoleon led his soldiers into Vienna and established headquarters in Schönbrunn, a palace of Emperor Francis.

In Vienna Napoleon learned that the day after his great victory at Ulm he had lost his last chance of wresting control of the seas from Britain. On October 21, 1805, the combined French-Spanish fleet under Admiral Villeneuve had been annihilated off Cape Trafalgar by a British squadron commanded by Admiral Horatio Nelson. After five hours of fighting marked by great courage on both sides, Villeneuve had lost twenty of his thirty-three ships, and the remaining thirteen were in full flight. The British had lost not a single one of their twenty-seven vessels. Their only major casualty was Nelson himself. Mortally wounded, he lived just long enough to know that his fleet had triumphed.

The sole official reference that Napoleon made to the French defeat at Trafalgar was in a speech in 1806: "Storms caused us to lose some ships of the line after unwisely engaging in a fight." That "unwise" fight off the Spanish coast was one of the most important naval battles in history. It shattered Napoleon's chances of invading England, brought to an end the long struggle between England and France for mastery of the seas, and established British naval supremacy for the next century. It compelled Napoleon to change his strategy from direct attack upon the British Isles to an attempt to strangle Britain by economic means—a change in strategy that led to Napoleon's downfall.

AUSTERLITZ

Upon receiving news of the defeat at Trafalgar, Napoleon attempted to open peace negotiations with Russia and Austria. His advances rebuffed, he marched from Vienna into the Austrian province of Moravia and on December 2, 1805, at the small town of Austerlitz crushed the combined Austrian and Russian armies. The battle was called the Battle of the Three Emperors, for the emperors of Austria and Russia commanded the armies that faced the troops of Emperor Napoleon. Bonaparte recognized it as his most brilliant victory—"the battle of Austerlitz is the most splendid of all I have fought."

On the very night of the battle Emperor Francis sued for peace. It was the third time that he had been humbled by Napoleon, the first two times being the Treaty of Campo Formio in 1797 and the Treaty of Lunéville in 1801. By the Treaty of Pressburg in December, 1805, Francis surrendered his remaining Italian possessions (Venetia, Istria, and Dalmatia) to Napoleon, recognized Napoleon as king of Italy, and surrendered his German possessions and the Austrian provinces of Tyrol and Vorarlberg to France's German allies—Baden, Bavaria, and Württemberg.

Before Austerlitz Prussia had been on the point of joining the alliance against France. Now Napoleon persuaded Frederick William III to sign a treaty agreeing to turn over some of Prussia's West German possessions to Bavaria and France and to keep British ships from the northwest coast of

Germany. In return Napoleon gave Hanover, the ancestral home of Britain's kings, to Prussia. England stood firm, but William Pitt, broken in health and spirit by the collapse of the Third Coalition, died in January, 1806.

NAPOLEON'S PINNACLE

Napoleon then proceeded to reorganize his conquests according to his own wishes. He transformed the Batavian Republic into the Kingdom of Holland, with his brother Louis as king. He grouped together sixteen states in southern and central Germany into the Confederation of the Rhine (July, 1806), with himself as "Protector"—or dictator. The Confederation adopted the Code Napoléon and agreed to furnish sixty-three thousand soldiers for his army. Subsequently all German states except Prussia, Brunswick, and Hesse joined the Confederation, so that a large part of Germany was under Napoleon's scepter. Under French pressure further territorial consolidations were made, reducing still more the number of individual German states. Napoleon then announced that he no longer recognized the existence of the Holy Roman Empire. Emperor Francis accepted the inevitable and in 1806 gave up the title of Holy Roman Emperor that his family had held for centuries, and with it relinquished the Hapsburg claim to the domination of Germany. Thus perished the last reminder of the great but unfulfilled dream of a united Christendom, and the Corsican phoenix rising from its ashes might in truth claim to be the successor of Charlemagne.

Napoleon controlled the Continent from the English Channel to the Elbe River, from the North Sea to the Mediterranean. His domination did not go uncontested. Prussia, stung by the Napoleonic humiliations, declared war late in 1806 and was joined by Russia. Within a month Bonaparte had defeated Prussian forces in the dual victories of Jena and Auerstedt (October, 1807) and occupied Berlin. From there he marched into East Prussia. In February, 1807, at Eylau he fought a one-day draw against a combined Russian-Prussian army in one of the bloodiest battles in history: fifty thousand casualties, or one-third of the total number of troops engaged on both sides. Though even Napoleon was moved by the horrors of Eylau, he was not dissuaded from continuing the war. In June, 1807, at Friedland in East Prussia, the Russians went down to defeat and sued for peace.

The next month Napoleon, Tsar Alexander I, and King Frederick William III of Prussia came together at Tilsit on the Niemen River to discuss peace terms. Napoleon and Alexander got along famously, the young tsar mesmerized by the master of Europe. While the two conversed on a raft moored in the river between the two armies, the Prussian king paced along the bank in anxiety about what was being decided on the raft. His worries were well founded. The two emperors arranged a peace at Prussia's expense: Prussia's territory was halved, its ports were closed to British ships and goods, limitations were placed on the size of its army, a heavy war indemnity

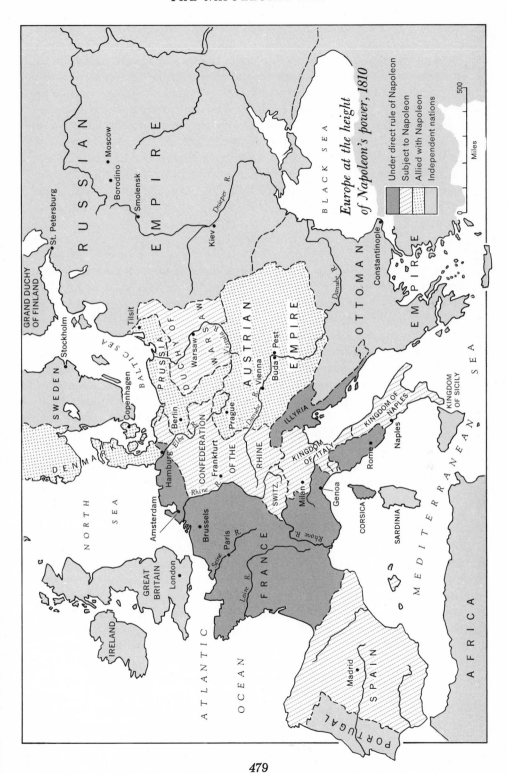

Europe at the height
of Napoleon's power, 1810

Under direct rule of Napoleon
Subject to Napoleon
Allied with Napoleon
Independent nations

500

Miles

0

BLACK SEA

RUSSIAN EMPIRE

Moscow
Borodino
Smolensk

St. Petersburg

Kiev

Dnieper R.

GRAND DUCHY
OF FINLAND

SWEDEN

Stockholm

BALTIC SEA

Tilsit

PRUSSIA

DUCHY OF WARSAW

Warsaw

Vistula R.

AUSTRIAN EMPIRE

Buda
Pest

Danube R.

OTTOMAN EMPIRE

Constantinople

Copenhagen

DENMARK

Berlin

Elbe R.

Prague

Danube R.

Vienna

ILLYRIA

CONFEDERATION OF THE RHINE

Frankfurt

Rhine R.

Hamburg

NORTH SEA

Amsterdam

Brussels

Paris

Seine R.

SWITZ.

Milan

Genoa

KINGDOM OF ITALY

Rome

KINGDOM OF NAPLES

Naples

KINGDOM OF SICILY

MEDITERRANEAN SEA

CORSICA

SARDINIA

FRANCE

Rhône R.

Loire R.

ATLANTIC OCEAN

GREAT BRITAIN

London

IRELAND

Madrid

SPAIN

PORTUGAL

AFRICA

was levied, and maintenance of a French army of occupation was required until the indemnity was paid. Prussia's Polish possessions became the Grand Duchy of Warsaw, a French satellite under the king of Saxony. The western Prussian provinces, together with several West German states, were fused into a new Kingdom of Westphalia, with Napoleon's youngest brother Jerome as king. The tsar recognized all Napoleon's conquests and the new states he had created and consented to serve as mediator in bringing about peace between Britain and France. In secret articles Alexander agreed to ally with Napoleon if the British refused to make peace, and to aid Napoleon in compelling Austria, Denmark, Sweden, and Portugal to join them against England. In return Napoleon agreed to assist Alexander in his war against the Turks.

THE CONTINENTAL SYSTEM

Only Britain remained at war with France, and only Britain stood in the way of still greater conquests for Napoleon in the Near East and India. Britain had to be defeated. British naval supremacy made it impossible to invade the island kingdom, but there were other ways to humble the persistent foe. If Britain, heavily dependent on its export trade to the Continent, could be shut out of Europe, the ruin of its business community and resultant mass unemployment, discontent, and perhaps revolt against the government would so weaken it internally that it would have to sue for peace. Napoleon did not have the sea power to accomplish this end by a naval blockade of Great Britain, but he could use his military power to blockade the Continent. He would compel the Continental nations to refuse to trade with England.

Economic warfare against England was not a new idea. The Revolutionary government had considered it in 1793, and it had been applied sporadically since then. Napoleon's domination of the Continent enabled him to apply the policy to a far greater area than had his predecessors, indeed, to so large an area that his strategy was named the Continental System. By excluding British goods he hoped to establish Continental production of those goods and create an integrated economic system, revolving around France, which would make the Continent nearly self-sufficient.

In November, 1806, in a decree issued at Berlin Napoleon forbade the importation of British goods into states controlled by or allied with France. At Tilsit Russia and Prussia were bound to the Continental System, and subsequently other nations were compelled to join. The British replied in 1807 with "orders in council" (orders given by the king on the advice of his ministers) declaring that neutral vessels trading with Continental ports must put in first at British ports, in the hope that the neutral ships would load with British goods and carry them to the Continent. Napoleon countered with the Milan Decree of December, 1807, threatening confiscation upon arrival on the Continent of any neutral ship that stopped in England or submitted to search at sea by British warships.

For Britain the most onerous result of the Continental System was a side effect. American shippers were caught in the cross fire of economic warfare: whichever course they chose, they risked capture and confiscation. President Thomas Jefferson attempted to steer a neutral course with the Embargo Act of 1807, forbidding all American exports to foreign nations, but it proved so harmful to the American economy that it was abandoned in 1810. America offered to resume trade with either France or England if either nation would annul its decrees against neutral shipping. Napoleon offered to do so if the United States would compel England to respect American rights on the high seas. Napoleon's offer appealed to expansionists in America who wanted to annex British territory in North America and who believed that Britain's involvement in war with France gave the United States that opportunity. In 1812 Congress declared war. Although Britain revoked the orders in council five days after the war began, the conflict dragged on for over two years, ending in a draw. The Anglo-American war came too late to do Napoleon any good. In June, 1812, the same month that the United States declared war on Britain, French troops invaded Russia.

It was impossible to seal the Continent against smugglers, who brought in great quantities of English goods. Napoleon also had to grant licenses to import certain English products, such as wool cloth for army overcoats, and on occasion he allowed the export of grain and wine from the Continent to England. Britain more than balanced the trade losses to the Continent by increasing trade with non-European lands, particularly Latin America. Although the Continental System was awkward for the British economy, it never seriously threatened it. At the same time, the sea commerce of the Continental states dwindled. British control of the coastal waters made it necessary to ship goods overland, and the cost of land transport pushed up prices. Most significant, the Continental states were unwilling to make the sacrifices involved in excluding such imported wares as cane sugar and tobacco.

THE PENINSULAR WAR

The most dire consequence of the Continental System came as a result of Napoleon's unyielding determination to bludgeon the states of Europe into maintaining the embargo on British goods. The first step on the road to Napoleon's ruin was his invasion of Portugal in 1807; that country, faithful to its alliance with England, had rejected the Continental System. Next, a French army moved in to guard the Spanish coasts in 1808. Though allied with France since 1796, the Spanish had not enforced the Continental System. Napoleon forced the Bourbon king, Charles IV, to abdicate and transferred his brother Joseph from the throne of Naples to that of Spain;

General Murat, Napoleon's brother-in-law, became king of Naples. A mass insurrection of Spaniards, led by aristocrats and inspired by priests, provoked the French to practice cruelties that only produced further resistance. Courageous and elusive Spanish guerrillas tied down an enormous French army. A small British force commanded by Arthur Wellesley, later Duke of Wellington, landed in Portugal, forced the French to evacuate, and marched into Spain. From 1808 to 1814 Napoleon was engaged in a long and costly struggle known as the Peninsular War.

In his efforts to enforce the Continental System in Italy Napoleon occupied the Papal States in 1808. In the next year he annexed the States to France. When Pius VII excommunicated him, Napoleon arrested the pontiff and interned him away from Rome. Catholic Europe was shocked by this affront to the pope—a second "Babylonian Captivity"—and it heightened the resistance of the devout Spaniards.

The successes of the Spanish against the French persuaded the Austrians that Napoleon was not invincible. In April, 1809, they declared war. Rushing from Spain to take personal command, Napoleon in a swift and brilliant campaign defeated the Austrians at Wagram in July. For the fourth time Emperor Francis sued for peace. By the Treaty of Schönbrunn in October, 1809, Austria surrendered 32,000 square miles and 3,500,000 people to France and her allies and entered into an alliance with Napoleon.

The Continental System brought Napoleon into conflict with even his own dearest brother. Louis Bonaparte, king of Holland since 1806, recognized that because his realm was primarily dependent on seaborne commerce, it would suffer too much from the system. He therefore did not enforce it. Napoleon, indignant at this disloyalty, annexed part of Holland to France in 1810 and sent French troops to guard Dutch harbors. Louis refused to remain king under these humiliating circumstances and abdicated. Holland was incorporated into France.

THE GRAND EMPIRE

In 1810 Napoleon's hegemony included all Europe. His own domain was the French Empire stretching from Rome to the North Sea. Subject to his command under a barely veiled dictatorship were the satellite states: the Kingdom of Italy, the Kingdom of Naples, the Kingdom of Spain, the Confederation of the Rhine, the Illyrian Provinces, and the Grand Duchy of Warsaw. These, together with the French Empire, made up the "Grand Empire." Austria, Prussia, Russia, Denmark, and Sweden were still ruled by their old governments but were allied with Napoleon.

Napoleon sought to strengthen the Austrian alliance through marriage. In 1809 he had secured an annulment from his first wife, Josephine de Beauharnais, whom he had married in 1796, because she had not presented him with an heir. She struck a hard bargain for her consent to the annulment: a large income and retention of the title of empress. After considering the merits of eighteen eligible ladies, Napoleon married Marie Louise, daughter of Emperor Francis of Austria. The marriage was neither a great diplomatic nor a marital success, but she bore him a son in 1811, upon whom Napoleon bestowed the title of King of Rome.

As a thoroughgoing materialist who saw the benefits of the French Revolution in essentially utilitarian terms, Napoleon sought stability for the Grand Empire in the fundamental uniformity of social institutions. Equal rights, equal opportunity, abolition of privileges, abolition of serfdom, universal obligation to pay taxes, religious freedom, and the Code Napoléon were introduced into his subject lands. The curbing of the Roman Catholic Church was the corollary of the exaltation of the secular state. Napoleon summed up his program in a letter to his brother Jerome upon the latter's coronation as king of Westphalia in 1807: "What is above all desired in Germany is that you will grant to those who are not nobles but have ability an equal claim to offices, and that all vestiges of serfdom and of barriers between the sovereign and the lowest class of the people should be abolished. The benefits of the Code Napoléon, legal procedure in open court, the jury, these are the points by which your monarchy should be distinguished. . . . Your people must enjoy a liberty, an equality, a prosperity, unknown in the rest of Germany."

Italy was the most deeply influenced by Napoleon's governance. Although he plundered its museums and galleries, levied heavy taxes and military conscriptions, and mercilessly repressed resistance, to the Italians "Buonaparte" was looked upon as a fellow Italian whose exploits recreated the greatness of Imperial Rome. His achievements and reforms—driving out the old oppressive governments; introducing the Napoleonic law codes and civil equality; constructing badly needed roads, canals, bridges, and a school system; and improving the administration of taxes—became the starting point for the Italian nationalist movement or Risorgimento (revival), which led to the unification of Italy a half-century later. Bonaparte, however, was interested in only a partial unification of Italy, for a divided Italy was more easily dominated than a united one. In 1805 he changed the satellite Italian Republic (successor to the Cisalpine Republic) comprising the northern third of Italy, into the Kingdom of Italy with himself as king. The next year he packed off the Bourbon king of Naples and rather than annexing Naples to his northern kingdom placed his brother Joseph on the Neapolitan throne. The remaining Italian states, including Piedmont, Genoa, and the Papal States, were annexed to France between 1801 and 1810.

In Germany Napoleon's domination led to a territorial reconstruction of Germany that drastically reduced the number of states there. The Treaties of Campo Formio (1797) and of Lunéville (1801) had ordered that German hereditary rulers whose lands on the Rhine's west bank had been annexed to France should be compensated with German territory east of the Rhine that belonged to the Church, free imperial cities, and imperial knights. The arrangements for distribution of land among the hereditary princes took place in Paris, where the rulers and their emissaries flocked to beg Napoleon for concessions and to bribe and wheedle French officials. Talleyrand, Napoleon's foreign secretary, is said to have taken ten million francs from the fawning Germans. The compensation program resulted in the disappearance of a myriad of small states. In 1815, after Napoleon's defeat, the statesmen of the victorious powers accepted his surgery by which the number of German states had been reduced from 360 to 39.

Despite his gigantic hegemony, rivaling Imperial Rome's, Napoleon's position had weakened measurably by 1810. The Peninsular War was a drain and the Continental System was a sieve. Tsar Alexander I no longer stood in sophomoric awe of the master of Europe. Fearful of Napoleon's unquenchable thirst for conquest and indignant at the harm done Russian trade by the Continental System, the tsar formally withdrew from the Continental System and in 1811 opened Russian ports to neutrals and levied a prohibitively high tariff on silks, wines and brandies, the chief exports of France to Russia.

Napoleon decided that he must invade Russia and crush the tsar. After extensive preparation he led 680,000 men into Alexander's empire in June, 1812. The Grand Army was probably the largest military force yet assembled under a single command. Only one-third was French, for Napoleon had drawn heavily on the troops of his allies and satellites. The Russians, whose forces totaled about 180,000 men, followed their traditional strategy of avoiding battle and drawing the invader ever deeper into the vast Russian plain. By the time Napoleon reached Smolensk, halfway to Moscow, he had lost 100,000 men. Only when he reached Borodino, seventy miles from Moscow, did he meet the Russians in force. He drove them back at a terrible cost to both sides and marched into Moscow in September, 1812. He found a deserted city, for most of its 300,000 people had fled. The day after the French entered the city caught fire, whether by accident or design, and four days of raging flames destroyed three-quarters of Moscow. It was impossible for the French to remain without cover through a Moscow winter. Convinced that his occupation of Moscow had forced Russia to its knees Napoleon three times offered to end the war. Alexander ignored his proposals. With winter approaching, Napoleon had no choice but retreat. Russian troops harassed the French columns as they moved westward. Winter set in unusually early. The retreat became a desperate rout. In December about 100,000 ragged and starving men crossed the Niemen River into the Grand Duchy of Warsaw. They were the entire remnant of the Grand Army; over 400,000 had perished, and 100,000 had been taken prisoner in the retreat.

THE WAR OF LIBERATION

The myth of Napoleonic invincibility, already shaken by French reverses in Spain, was shattered. In Prussia pressure from the Junker generals, smarting under the earlier defeats, and a popular rising compelled King Frederick William in 1813 to renounce his alliance with France and ally with Russia. A few months later Austria joined the coalition. The Swedes promised 30,000 troops, the Confederation of the Rhine began to disintegrate, anti-French riots broke out in Italy, and the Duke of Wellington rolled back the French in Spain and led his soldiers across the Pyrenees into southern France. Britain poured a fortune into the Continent to subsidize the enemies of Napoleon: 32,000,000 pounds sterling between 1813 and 1815.

The Prussians had been preparing for this "War of Liberation" ever since their calamitous defeat in 1807. Jena, Auerstedt, and Eylau, instead of crushing Prussia, had inspired an amazing revival of nationalist fervor. In spite of the French army of occupation the Prussians made ready for the struggle to throw off the Napoleonic yoke. Zealous government ministers carried through a broad program of reform to quicken the people's sense of loyalty and identification with the state. Under the guidance of Baron vom Stein and his successor Prince Hardenberg serfdom was abolished and the people were given a greater voice in local government. General Scharnhorst and Count Gneisenau revamped the army to make it an efficient fighting force. Baron K. W. von Humboldt reorganized the school system and in 1811 persuaded the king to establish the University of Berlin. Johann Gottlieb Fichte, professor of philosophy at the new university, held his youthful audiences spellbound as he spoke of the *Volksgeist*, the national spirit peculiar to the German people, finer than the *Volksgeist* of other peoples, and a precious heritage to be preserved from contamination by foreign influences. Moritz Arndt popularized nationalistic ideas in songs and poems. Friedrich Ludwig Jahn, or Father Jahn, as his devoted followers called him, organized young men into gymnastic societies, where he taught them the superiority of the Germans and hatred for foreigners and Jews while preparing them physically for war against the French. The Prussian renaissance awakened a new nationalistic spirit all over Germany. Thousands of new patriots, looking to Prussia for leadership in the struggle against French domination, formed Free Corps to aid Prussia in the war for liberation.

Napoleon—supremely self-confident, undaunted by his reversals, and contemptuous of the enemy—now carried through one of his greatest feats. In the first four months of 1813 he raised and equipped an army of 250,000 to replace the army he had lost in Russia. With his demagogic masterfulness he rallied the French people to his support, and with his energy and genius he organized and guided this great national endeavor.

The new troops were brave—and green. They were often poorly led as

Napoleon at Bautzen, May 21, 1813, by Auguste Raffet

"Napoleon is the first and only man who could have provided Europe with the equilibrium for which she had sought in vain for many centuries, and which today is farther away than ever. . . . With this real equilibrium Napoleon could have given to the peoples of Europe an organization conforming to true moral law. . . . Napoleon could have done these things, but did not. If he had done them, gratitude would have raised statues to him everywhere . . . Instead . . . posterity will say of him: that man was gifted with a very great intellectual force; but he did not understand true glory. His moral force was too small or entirely lacking. He could not endure prosperity with moderation, nor misfortune with dignity; and it is because he lacked moral force that he brought about the ruin of Europe and of himself." Talleyrand, MÉMOIRES (Paris, 1891), Vol. VI.

Courtesy of the Museum of Fine Arts, Boston

well, for Napoleon had lost many experienced officers. Napoleon himself seemed to have lost some of his own tactical skill. His ambitions in the field outran his means. After a number of reverses, the Allies defeated him in October, 1813, at Leipzig in a three-day battle, called by the Germans the Battle of the Nations. The French army, reduced to 80,000, retreated home. Once again Napoleon set about building up a new army, but the miracle could not be repeated. He could raise only 110,000 troops, many of them young boys. They fought a series of magnificently desperate actions, but the weight of enemy numbers overwhelmed him.

END OF THE EMPIRE

As the Allies pushed the French westward they began a discussion of the peace settlement. By offers of large subsidies Viscount Castlereagh, the British foreign minister, persuaded Austria, Russia, and Prussia to join Britain in a security pact. The Treaty of Chaumont in March, 1814, bound the four powers to protect one another against France for the next twenty years, each to provide 150,000 men to enforce the peace terms. Three weeks later the Allies marched into Paris. Napoleon abdicated in favor of his infant son. The victors, however, gave the French throne to the Count of Provence, brother of the executed Louis XVI, who acceded as King Louis XVIII.

In May, 1814, the Allies signed the First Treaty of Paris with the restored Bourbon monarch. It reduced France to its pre-1792 boundaries. The victors were generous, demanding no indemnities, restoring some of France's overseas possessions, and even permitting the French to keep the art treasures Napoleon had taken from the lands he conquered. Napoleon himself had already been sent into exile on the small island of Elba, lying between Italy and Corsica. The Allies granted him Elba as his sovereign principality—eighty-six square miles—provided him with a sizable income, and allowed him to keep his title of emperor. His empress Marie Louise was also permitted to retain her title and received the duchies of Parma, Piacenza, and Guastalla, in Italy.

THE HUNDRED DAYS

With the war over, old suspicions and jealousies cropped up among the Allies. Unable to agree on the distribution of the territories taken from Napoleon, they decided to meet in Vienna in the autumn and to postpone decisions until then. In September, 1814, the Congress of Vienna was convened and lasted until the following June. In the midst of its negotiations in rearranging the Napoleonic map the Congress was stunned by the news that Napoleon had returned to France and received a tumultuous and frenzied display of affection and loyalty at every step of his trip to Paris. Frenchmen, not least the emperor's soldiers, who were used to the excitement and grandeur of Napoleon's time, had quickly tired of the colorless and cautious Louis XVIII; more important, they feared that the returning aristocrats and high churchmen would claim their old privileges. Napoleon hoped to capitalize on this discontent in France and by the shock of his return sunder the Allies and re-establish himself. He landed in southern France on March 1, 1815, with about one thousand men from the small guard force allowed him in exile, and reached Paris on March 13. Louis had already fled to Belgium. Napoleon rallied Louis XVIII's army—his old soldiers—to his banner and was once more Emperor of the French.

His reign lasted one hundred days. The news of his return ended the bickering at Vienna. A mighty army assembled under the supreme command of the Duke of Wellington. On June 18, 1815, near the Belgian village of Waterloo, a combined force of Germans, Dutchmen, and Englishmen crushed the new army that Napoleon had raised. The Hundred Days were over.

The final trip of the man who had crossed Europe at the head of armies was a voyage on a British warship carrying him as prisoner of war to the

British-owned St. Helena, a bleak rock in the South Atlantic. There, 4,500 miles from Paris, Napoleon existed with a few faithful followers for six bitter years. Clearheaded and exhibiting the greatest demagogic masterfulness of his career, he fashioned his own legend for posterity in writing his memoirs. Although the Imperial Eagle chained to the rock lives on as the most brilliant man-myth of the European world, the man himself was mortal. On May 5, 1821, Napoleon died of cancer of the stomach. He was fifty-one.

The Napoleonic Legacy

May 5, 1821, was the thirty-second anniversary of the convention of the Estates-General at Versailles. The man who died that day on St. Helena had been a subaltern on garrison duty in the old fortress town of Auxonne in eastern France that day thirty-two years before when the French Revolution began. He had ended the Revolution, but in two important ways it also reached out to finish him.

The British, who had had their revolution a century and a half before, saw Revolutionary France as the devil incarnate. Their implacable enmity to Napoleon Bonaparte had a bitter edge to it because he seemed to represent that Revolution on the march. More than any other factor, Britain's relentless pursuit of Napoleon undid him.

The other means by which the French Revolution finished Napoleon was the nationalism that it unleashed throughout Continental Europe. Patriotic fervor was the most exportable article of the Revolutionary faith. Jacobinism, republicanism, even liberty and equality, varied in their relevancy to the conditions and aspirations of the Germans, Italians, Russians, Poles, Dutchmen, Belgians, Spaniards, and Portuguese. But patriotic nationalism had universal appeal. Germans from states that had been archrivals for centuries fought side by side at the Battle of the Nations, as Germans. Napoleon's foes, despots as well as democrats, rallied their countrymen to oppose and overthrow him by appeals to the national spirit.

Although it is impossible to disengage the French Revolution's impact from Napoleon's—he had, after all, used the Revolution's slogans and sometimes its doctrines as weapons of war and tools to build his empire—his contribution was in four spheres clear and unique. First, the Grand Empire had erected in Germany and Italy, if only for a few years, single entities out of the three-hundred-odd principalities of Germany and the dozen-odd states of Italy. Those historically divided peoples were granted a vision of unity that would in the future become a reality for both.

Second, Napoleon's armies, rather than native revolutionaries, overthrew privilege within the Grand Empire's reaches. For all its shallowness in practice, the conqueror's show of establishing representative government, equality before the law, individual liberty, and religious freedom provided peoples unused to them with a fleeting experience of a new and better order. Napoleon planted the seeds of aspiration for representative government and liberal constitutions, and he gave the middle classes of Europe a priceless moment of freedom from the arrogant repression of privilege.

Third, the Napoleonic era fixed upon France a legend of glory and grandeur that has affected French political life ever since. Although much of the legend was created by Napoleon in exile, its essentials were not; ephemeral though it was, the Grand Empire was not chimerical. Within a few years of his downfall Frenchmen forgot the heavy drain of men and wealth that were the price of his victories and remembered only the grandeur of his conquests.

Finally, Napoleon Bonaparte taught all authoritarian leaders who have followed him the essentials of dictatorship: propaganda, an effective and inexorable secret police forming a state within the state, the use of such democratic devices as the plebiscite to rally popular support behind the regime, state bureaucratization of the critical institutions of education and religion so that they might become instruments of indoctrination, and the value of foreign adventures to make domestic repression bearable. Napoleon originated none of these tools of authoritarianism; his contribution was to weave them together into the instrument of the modern authoritarian state and to prove how effective internally that instrument can be.

The last word will be Napoleon Bonaparte's. In 1813 he summed up to Metternich his beginning and what he wished to be his end as a sovereign. Knowing well how uncertain was his future, and how slender his hold on the allegiance of his people, he told Metternich: "I shall know how to die, but never to yield an inch of territory. Your sovereigns who were born to the throne may get beaten twenty times and still return to their capitals. I cannot. For I rose to power through the camp."

A Reading List

THIS READING LIST is designed to provide the interested student with suggestions for further reading and the titles of books with which he can begin research for course papers and independent work. With these purposes in mind we have restricted our recommendations to books in English. Most of the works listed contain bibliographical information that will provide the student with detailed assistance in further reading or research in the subject that interests him.

An asterisk before the title indicates that the book is available in a paperback edition.

BIBLIOGRAPHIES

The titles and authors of important works in every field of historical research, often with valuable critical comments, are contained in G. M. Dutcher and others, *A Guide to Historical Literature* (1931) and *The American Historical Association's Guide to Historical Literature* (1961). The annual *International Bibliography of the Historical Sciences* should also be consulted. There are many specialized bibliographies. Their titles can be found in T. Besterman, *A World Bibliography of Bibliographies* (4 vols., 1955–56), and C. M. Winchell, *Guide to Reference Books* (7th ed., 1951).

In 1957 the Service Center for Teachers of History of the American Historical Association began the publication of a series of pamphlets, each written by a specialist, that present concise summaries of publications reflecting recent research and new interpretations in a particular field of history. Historical periodicals, such as the *American Historical Review,* the *Journal of Modern History, Speculum,* and many others, contain book reviews and lists of new books and recently published articles.

REFERENCE WORKS

Useful reference works include W. L. Langer, ed., *An Encyclopedia of World History* (rev. ed., 1952), an amazingly detailed and annotated collection of important events and dates from the beginning of recorded history; *The Columbia Encyclopedia* (3rd ed., 1963), the best of the one-volume encyclopedias. W. R. Shepherd, *Historical Atlas* (new ed., 1965) and R. R. Palmer, ed., *Atlas of World History* (1957) are helpful aids, as is *Lippincott's Pronouncing Gazetteer* (1962). Most important nations have their own multi-volume biographical dictionaries; in English the major ones are the *Dictionary of National Biography* (1885–1960) for Great Britain and the *Dictionary of American Biography* (1928–36).

The *Encyclopaedia Britannica* is still the most useful of the general encyclopedias; regrettably, its quality has declined in recent years. The *Encyclopedia of the Social Sciences* (1930–35) is helpful, though many of its articles need revision to bring them up to date. The *Catholic Encyclopaedia,* the *Jewish Encyclopedia,* and the *Encyclopaedia of Islam* are among the most valuable of the specialized encyclopedias.

GENERAL HISTORIES

Historians have often joined together to write comprehensive histories that are published either as collaborative volumes, with each chapter written by a different author, or as individual volumes each by a single author. These works are of an uneven quality. The best known of the collaborative works in English are *The Cambridge Ancient History* (8 vols., 1923–39), *The Cambridge Mediaeval History* (8 vols., 1911–36), *The Cambridge Modern History* (13 vols., 1902–12), *The New Cambridge Modern History* (1957–   ), and *The Cambridge Economic History of Europe* (1941–   ). The last two are still incomplete. W. L. Langer is editing a series called *The Rise of Modern Europe,* in which each volume is written by a single historian. Nearly all of the projected twenty volumes have appeared. Many of them are listed in the following pages. E. Eyre, ed., *European Civilization, Its Origin and Development* (7 vols., 1934–39), is an often overlooked but useful collaborative work.

There are many general histories, in both single and multi-volume form, of the countries and of the institutions, ideas, economic life, and culture discussed in this book. A number of them are mentioned in the reading lists for the individual chapters. A useful beginning guide to general histories with excellent critical comments is provided in M. Faisler, *Key to the Past* (3rd ed., 1965), a publication of the Service Center for Teachers of History.

CHAPTER 1: THE HERITAGE OF THE EUROPEAN WORLD

The Legacy of Ancient Civilization

* W. F. Albright, *From the Stone Age to Christianity: Monotheism and the Historical Process* (1940). A thoughtful and informative inquiry into the development of man's ideas about God.

A. E. R. Boak, *A History of Rome to 565 A.D.* (4th ed., 1955). A clear and well organized survey.

J. H. Breasted, *A History of Egypt from the Earliest Times to the Persian Conquest* (1905). Remains the standard work.

H. Breuil, *Four Hundred Centuries of Cave Art* (1952). The classic work on this subject.

J. B. Bury, *History of Greece to the Time of Alexander the Great* (3rd ed., 1951). One of the best one-volume surveys.

* V. G. Childe, *The Dawn of European Civilization* (5th ed., 1951). An imaginative reconstruction of the story of European man before recorded history.

L. Duchesne, *Early History of the Church* (2 vols., 1902–15). A valuable treatment of the spread of Christianity.

W. Jaeger, *Paedeia: The Ideals of Greek Culture* (3 vols., 1939–44). A masterly interpretation of Greek intellectual and spiritual life.

The Birth of Europe

* J. Brønsted, *The Vikings* (1960). An outstanding account of the civilization of the Norsemen.

A. Dopsch, *The Economic and Social Foundations of European Civilization* (1937). Argues that Roman civilization provided the basis for the revival of Western civilization in the eleventh century.

* H. Fichtenau, *The Carolingian Empire* (1957). A balanced estimate of Charlemagne's achievements.

* H. A. R. Gibb, *Mohammedanism: An Historical Survey* (2nd ed., 1953). The best introduction.

A. H. M. Jones, *The Later Roman Empire, 284–602* (2 vols., 1964). An outstanding work.

* F. Lot, *The End of the Ancient World and the Beginnings of the Middle Ages* (1931). Stresses the continuity of Roman institutions in the Germanic kingdoms.

G. Ostrogorsky, *History of the Byzantine State* (1956). The most authoritative study.

F. W. Walbank, *The Decline of the Roman Empire in the West* (1946). A useful summary of the theories explaining the end of the classical world.

Medieval Civilization in Its Prime

* G. Barraclough, *The Origins of Modern Germany* (1949). The best book in English on medieval Germany.

* M. Bloch, *Feudal Society* (1961). A brilliant analysis of the evolution and spread of feudalism and manorialism by a renowned French scholar.

The Cambridge Economic History, vols. I–III (1941–1963). Essays on medieval agrarian life, commerce, industry, and economic organization and policies.

R. H. C. Davis, *A History of Medieval Europe from Constantine to St. Louis* (1957). Especially valuable for its treatment of religious history.

P. Frankl, *Gothic: Literary Sources and Interpretations* (1960). A magnificent study of the Gothic style.

C. H. Haskins, *The Normans in European History* (1915). Deals with the role of the Normans in the establishment of European states.

* ——, *The Renaissance of the Twelfth Century* (1927). The classic study of the revival of learning in medieval Europe.

E. Kantorowicz, *Frederick II* (1931). A penetrating analysis of relations between the papacy and the Hohenstaufen emperors.

* C. Petit-Dutaillis, *The Feudal Monarchy in France and England* (1936). The best comparative treatment of the Western feudal monarchies.

* H. Pirenne, *Medieval Cities* (1925) and *Economic and Social History of Medieval Europe* (1937). Ground-breaking reinterpretations by the famed Belgian scholar.

* S. Runciman, *A History of the Crusades* (3 vols., 1951–54). A fascinating account.

H. O. Taylor, *The Medieval Mind* (new ed., 2 vols., 1949). Valuable, though scholars have pointed out many inadequacies in it.

The Crisis of the Medieval Order

F. G. Heymann, *John Žižka and the Hussite Revolution* (1955) and *George of Bohemia, King of Heretics* (1965). Major contributions to the history of the religious troubles in Bohemia.

* K. B. McFarlane, *John Wycliffe and the Beginnings of English Non-Conformity* (1953). A useful brief account.

W. Ullman, *Origins of the Great Schism* (1948). The best study in English.

CHAPTER 2: ECONOMIC CHANGE AND THE EXPANSION OF EUROPE

The Great Depression of the Later Middle Ages

W. Kirchner, *The Rise of the Baltic Question* (1954). A well written scholarly study of an important area of Hanseatic activity.

P. Lindsay and R. Groves, *The Peasants' Revolt, 1381* (1950). A popular account of the English rural disturbances.

M. M. Postan and E. E. Rich, eds., *Trade and Industry in the Middle Ages* (1952), vol. II of *The Cambridge Economic History*. Provides the now generally accepted view of the economic history of the later Middle Ages.

B. H. Slicher van Bath, *The Agrarian History of Western Europe* A.D. *500–1850* (1963). Contains a useful section on the agricultural depression of the fourteenth and fifteenth centuries.

J. W. Thompson, *Economic and Social History of Europe in the Later Middle Ages, 1300–1530* (1931). Research since its appearance has dated much of the interpretation, but still useful for factual material.

The Rise of Modern Capitalism

* M. Dobb, *Studies in the Development of Capitalism* (rev. ed., 1964). A sophisticated Marxist analysis.

R. Ehrenburg, *Capital and Finance in the Age of the Renaissance* (1928). Informative about the activities of the Fugger banking family.

F. C. Lane, *Andrea Barberigo, Merchant of Venice, 1418–1449* (1944). A detailed study.

B. N. Nelson, *The Idea of Usury: From Tribal Brotherhood to Universal Otherhood* (1949). Analysis of the religious, social, and psychological background of the prohibition against usury.

I. Origo, *The Merchant of Prato: Francesco di Marco Datini, 1335–1410* (1957). A warm and intimate account.

R. A. de Roover, *The Rise and Decline of the Medici Bank, 1307–1494* (1963) and *Money, Banking and Credit in Medieval Bruges* (1948). Two superb studies, based on intensive archival research.

H. See, *Modern Capitalism* (1926). A useful introduction.

The Great Discoveries

S. E. Morison, *Admiral of the Ocean Sea* (1942). By far the best book on Columbus.

A. P. Newton, ed., *The Great Age of Discovery* (1932). Account of the discoveries and early colonial policies of the European states.

J. H. Parry, *Europe and a Wider World* (1949) and *The Age of Reconnaissance, 1415–1650* (1963). Useful for an understanding of the organization and effects on Europe of European overseas expansion.

* B. Penrose, *Travel and Discovery in the Renaissance* (2nd ed., 1955). Scholarly account of exploration, navigation, and mapmaking.

E. Prestage, *The Portuguese Pioneers* (1933). The standard work covering Portuguese explorations up to the early sixteenth century.

R. L. Reynolds, *Europe Emerges* (1961). A thoughtful analysis of the emergence and growth of Europe and its expansion beyond its borders.

Overseas Expansion and the Feedback to Europe

E. J. Hamilton, *American Treasure and the Price Revolution in Spain, 1501–1650* (1934). A detailed analysis of the effects of American bullion on Spanish economic life.

* L. Hanke, *The Spanish Struggle for Justice in the Conquest of America* (1949). An objective study of the treatment accorded the Indians by the Spanish conquerors.

* F. A. Kirkpatrick, *The Spanish Conquistadores* (1934). A colorful account.

495

G. Masselman, *The Cradle of Colonialism* (1963). A study of Dutch colonialism from the 1590's to 1630, with special emphasis on the work of Jan Pieterszoon Coen.

R. B. Merriam, *The Rise of the Spanish Empire in the Old World and the New* (4 vols., 1918–34). A magisterial survey.

J. H. Parry, *The Spanish Theory of Empire in the Sixteenth Century* (1940). Traces the evolution of ideas about colonial government and the impact upon the Spanish government of the colonial forms of government.

W. H. Prescott, *History of the Conquest of Mexico* (3 vols., 1843) and *History of the Conquest of Peru* (2 vols., 1847). Historical classics.

H. R. Wagner, *The Rise of Hernando Cortés* (1944). A carefully done history of the conquest of Mexico.

CHAPTER 3: THE RENAISSANCE

The Renaissance in Italy

H. Baron, *The Crisis of the Early Italian Renaissance* (2 vols., 1955). Shows the shift in humanism in Florence from a medieval orientation to a realization of the value of freedom and of participation in civic life.

* J. C. Burckhardt, *The Civilization of the Renaissance* (1860). Still the point of departure for study of the Renaissance.

W. K. Ferguson, *The Renaissance in Historical Thought* (1948). A presentation of the concept of the Renaissance from the humanists to the mid-twentieth century.

* M. P. Gilmore, *The World of Humanism 1453–1517* (1952). A useful general survey.

D. Hay, *The Italian Renaissance in its Historical Background* (1961). Places the Renaissance in the stream of general historical development.

A. W. O. von Martin, *Sociology of the Renaissance* (1944). An attempt to show humanism as part of a bourgeois revolt against the medieval social order.

G. R. Potter, ed., *The Renaissance, 1493–1520* (1957), vol. I of *The New Cambridge Modern History*. Contains valuable essays by outstanding scholars on aspects of the era.

Italian Humanism

P. O. Kristeller, *The Classics and Renaissance Thought* (1955) and *Studies in Renaissance Thought and Letters* (1956). Lucid and stimulating discussions of the philosophical thought of the Renaissance.

L. Martines, *The Social World of the Florentine Humanists 1390–1460* (1963). Shows that Florentine humanists came from the ruling classes and had independent means.

L. Olschki, *The Genius of Italy* (1949). Presents humanism as a movement supported by most of Italian lay society.

G. Toffanin, *History of Humanism* (1954). Views humanism as an orthodox Catholic movement rather than an irreligious break with the Middle Ages.

R. Weiss, *The Dawn of Humanism in Italy* (1947). A discussion of humanism before Petrarch.

J. H. Whitfield, *Petrarch and the Renaissance* (1943). A brief introduction.

Italian Art

* B. Berenson, *The Italian Painters of the Renaissance* (rev. ed., 1952). A widely accepted interpretation of Renaissance painting.

K. M. Clark, *Leonardo da Vinci: An Account of His Development as an Artist* (2nd ed., 1952). A useful work.

E. Panofsky,* *Studies in Iconology: Humanistic Themes in the Art of the Renaissance* (1939) and *Renaissance and Renascences in Western Art* (2 vols., 1959). Works of great erudition and brilliant insights into the philosophical meaning of works of art.

C. de Tolnay, *Michelangelo* (5 vols., 1943–60). A monumental study.

R. Wittkower, *Architectural Principles in the Age of Humanism* (2nd ed., 1952). Discusses the relationships between architecture and philosophical ideas.

H. Wölfflin, *Classic Art: An Introduction to the Italian Renaissance* (new ed., 1952). Long-time standard work on the High Renaissance.

The Northern Renaissance

O. Benesch, *The Art of the Renaissance in Northern Europe* (1945). Studies the connections between art and religious and philosophical thought.

* R. W. Chambers, *Thomas More* (1935). The best biography.

* E. H. Harbison, *The Christian Scholar in the Age of the Reformation* (1956). A penetrating analysis of the effort to reconcile Christianity and learning.

* J. H. Hexter, *More's Utopia: The Biography of an Idea* (1952). Important for an understanding of More's famous book.

* J. Huizinga, *The Waning of the Middle Ages* (1924). A vivid assessment of French and Burgundian culture in the fourteenth and fifteenth centuries.

E. Panofsky, *Early Netherlandish Painting* (2 vols., 1953) and *Albrecht Dürer* (2 vols., 1948). The standard works on their respective subjects.

* M. M. Phillips, *Erasmus and the Northern Renaissance* (1950). A brief treatment.

* P. Smith, *Erasmus* (1923). A sympathetic biography.

L. W. Spitz, *Conrad Celtis: The German Arch-Humanist* (1957). A carefully done study.

Renaissance Science

M. Boas, *The Scientific Renaissance 1450–1630* (1962). A valuable survey that stresses the relationship between humanism and the development of science.

* A. C. Crombie, *Medieval and Early Modern Science* (1958). An authoritative and comprehensive survey.

G. Sarton, *Six Wings: Men of Science in the Renaissance* (1957). A reversal of Sarton's earlier claim that science lagged during the Renaissance.

CHAPTER 4: THE POLITICS OF THE RENAISSANCE

Political Theory

* F. Chabod, *Machiavelli and the Renaissance* (1958). Shows the influence of Italian political history upon Machiavelli's thought. Has a remarkable bibliographical essay.

* J. N. Figgis, *Studies of Political Thought from Gerson to Grotius, 1414–1625* (2nd ed., 1916). The long-time standard work.

F. Gilbert, *Machiavelli and Guicciardini* (1965). A study of historical and political ideas in sixteenth-century Florence.

* J. R. Hale, *Machiavelli and Renaissance Italy* (1960). A short, skilfully done study.

* D. L. Jensen, *Machiavelli: Cynic, Patriot, or Political Scientist?* (1960). A selection of views of Machiavelli over four centuries, with a useful bibliography.

* F. Meinecke, *Machiavellism* (1957). Shows the contribution of Machiavelli's philosophy to the modern concept of the supremacy of the state's interests over moral law.

G. H. Sabine, *A History of Political Theory* (3rd ed., 1961). The appropriate sections in this outstanding book provide the best brief survey.

J. C. Whitfield, *Machiavelli* (1947). A sympathetic view of Machiavelli as a misunderstood and really moral philosopher.

Italian Politics

* C. M. Ady, *Lorenzo de' Medici and Renaissance Italy* (1952). A useful short survey.

W. M. Bowsky, *Henry VII in Italy: The Conflict of Empire and City-State* (1960). A careful analysis of Italian politics at the start of the Renaissance.

G. A. Brucker, *Florentine Politics and Society, 1343–1378* (1962). An important study of a critical period in Florentine history.

C. S. Gutkind, *Cosimo de' Medici, Pater Patriae* (1938). A good biography, with valuable appendices on Florentine government and economic life.

D. Herlihy, *Pisa in the Early Renaissance: A Study in Urban Growth* (1958). A major contribution to the understanding of social and economic factors determining Italian city development.

* G. Mattingly, *Renaissance Diplomacy* (1955). Discusses the theory and practice of medieval and Renaissance diplomacy.

* F. Schevil, *History of Florence from the Founding of the City through the Renaissance* (1936). The best general history in English.

The Rise of the Nation-States

P. Champion, *Louis XI* (1929). A popular biography.

* E. P. Cheyney, *The Dawn of a New Era, 1250–1453* (1936). Useful, though seriously dated in a number of respects, especially in economic and social history.

J. H. Elliott, *Imperial Spain, 1469–1716* (1964). An outstanding book.

* G. R. Elton, *The Tudor Revolution in Government* (1953). Disputes the view that a new kind of monarchy began with the Tudors.

* M. P. Gilmore, *The World of Humanism, 1453–1517* (1952). A good general survey, with an extensive bibliographical essay.

H. Holborn, *A History of Modern Germany*, vol. I, *The Reformation* (1959). The first volume of a three-volume history; shows the transformation of medieval Germany.

J. D. Mackie, *The Early Tudors, 1485–1559* (1952). A volume in *The Oxford History of England*.

J. R. Major, *Representative Institutions in Renaissance France, 1421–1559* (1960) and *The Deputies to the Estates General in Renaissance France* (1960). Shows the close working relationship between the monarch and popular assemblies.

* A. R. Myers, *England in the Later Middle Ages, 1307–1536* (1952). A short and very readable volume in the *Pelican History of England*.

CHAPTER 5: REFORMATIONS, PROTESTANT AND CATHOLIC

General Accounts

H. J. Grimm, *The Reformation Era* (1954). Especially good on Luther, and also has a lengthy critical bibliography.

* G. Mosse, *The Reformation* (rev. ed., 1963). The best short survey.

* P. Smith, *The Age of the Reformation* (1920). Still useful, though many sections need revision as the result of subsequent scholarly research.

The Eleventh Hour of the Medieval Church

A. C. Flick, *The Decline of the Medieval Church* (2 vols., 1930). An informative and impressive presentation.

P. Hughes, *A History of the Church* (3 vols., 1947–49). Volume III provides a modern Catholic view on conditions in the Church on the eve of the Reformation.

J. Mackinnon, *The Origins of the Reformation* (1939). A useful survey.

L. Pastor, *The History of the Popes from the Close of the Middle Ages* (40 vols., 1891–1953). The standard work.

Luther and the German Reformation

* R. H. Bainton, *Here I Stand: A Life of Martin Luther* (1950). The best biography in English.

* E. H. Erikson, *Young Man Luther: A Study in Psychoanalysis and History* (1958). Attempts to explain Luther by means of modern psychoanalytical techniques, using Luther's own writings.

* H. Grisar, *Martin Luther* (1950). An unfavorable biography by a Jesuit scholar.

F. H. Littell, *The Anabaptist View of the Church* (1952) and *The Free Church* (1958). Useful for the Anabaptist movement.

C. L. Manschreck, *Melanchthon, the Quiet Reformer* (1958). A sensitive study of Luther's friend and fellow reformer.

E. G. Schwiebert, *Luther and his Times: The Reformation from a New Perspective* (1950). Stresses the influence of the University of Wittenberg in the spread of the Reformation.

G. Williams, *The Radical Reformation* (1962). A general survey of the left wing of the Reformation.

The Swiss Reformation and the Rise of Calvinism

* R. W. Green, *Protestantism and Capitalism. The Weber Thesis and Its Critics* (1959). Extracts from the major contributions to the debate, with a critical bibliography.

J. Mackinnon, *Calvin and the Reformation* (1936). A critical evaluation.

J. T. McNeill, *The History and Character of Calvinism* (1954). Discusses the diffusion of Calvinism.

* K. Samuelsson, *Religion and Economic Action* (1961). A sometimes overstated refutation of the Weber thesis.

* R. H. Tawney, *Religion and the Rise of Capitalism* (1926). Agrees with the essentials of Weber's thesis.

W. Walker, *John Calvin* (1906). Still the best biography.

* M. Weber, *The Protestant Ethic and the Spirit of Capitalism* (transl., 1930). The seminal study in the debate over the relationship between Protestantism and capitalism.

The Reformation in England

P. Hughes, *The Reformation in England* (3 vols., 1950–54). An excellent work by a Catholic historian.

——, *Rome and the Counter Reformation in England* (1944). Includes a valuable analysis of Queen Mary's efforts to restore Catholicism.

M. M. Knappen, *Tudor Puritanism* (1939). Carefully works out the beginnings of English puritanism.

D. Knowles, *The Religious Orders in England* (3 vols., 1948–59). Volume III, *The Tudor Age*, is the most authoritative treatment of the dissolution of the monasteries.

T. M. Parker, *The English Reformation to 1558* (1950). A good general account.

A. F. Pollard, *Henry VIII* (1951). The best scholarly biography.

H. M. Smith, *Henry VIII and the Reformation* (1948). Stresses the importance of state policy and minimizes the influence of the religious reformers.

The Catholic Reformation

H. Boehmer, *The Jesuits* (1928). The best study by a Protestant.

J. Brodrick, *The Economic Morals of the Jesuits* (1934); * *The Origins of the Jesuits* (1940); *The Progress of the Jesuits* (1947). Interesting studies by a Jesuit scholar.

* H. Daniel-Rops, *The Catholic Reformation* (transl., 2 vols., 1961). An outstanding work.

P. Dudon, *St. Ignatius of Loyola* (1949). A good biography.

CHAPTER 6: THE AGE OF THE REFORMATION

The Empire of Charles V

K. Brandi, *The Emperor Charles V* (1939). The best biography.

B. Chudoba, *Spain and the Empire 1519–1643* (1952). An able analysis of Spanish imperialism on the Continent, particularly in Central Europe.

R. B. Merriman, *The Rise of the Spanish Empire in the Old World and the New* (4 vols., 1918–34), and J. H. Elliott, *Imperial Spain, 1494–1716* (1964) are the best works to consult; Elliott's book emphasizes social and economic development.

The Wars of Religion in France

W. F. Church, *Constitutional Thought in Sixteenth Century France* (1941). A treatment of the conflict between medieval and modern ideas of government.

A. J. Grant, *The Huguenots* (1934). A useful study.

* J. E. Neale, *The Age of Catherine de' Medici* (1943). A valuable study.

H. Noguères, *The Massacre of St. Bartholomew* (1962). A very readable account.

F. C. Palm, *Calvinism and the Religious Wars* (1932). An excellent brief analysis.

H. Pearson, *Henry of Navarre* (1963). A good biography.

The Spanish Predominance

See the books by Merriman, Elliott, and Chudoba listed above.

P. Geyl, *The Revolt of the Netherlands, 1555–1609* (1937). A major reinterpretation.

E. J. Hamilton, *American Treasure and the Price Revolution in Spain 1501–1650* (1934).

J. Klein, *The Mesta* (1920). The outstanding work on Spanish agricultural history.

* G. Mattingly, *The Armada* (1959). A brilliantly done account of international relations during the Anglo-Spanish war.

C. W. Oman, *A History of the Art of War in the Sixteenth Century* (1937). Study of the conduct of the wars of the era.

W. H. Prescott, *History of the Reign of Philip II* (1874). Still not superseded in comprehensive coverage.

R. S. Smith, *The Spanish Guild Merchant* (1940). A study of the social and economic life of the mercantile class.

C. V. Wedgewood, *William the Silent* (1944). Well written, though marred by excessive adulation of William.

Elizabethan England

* S. I. Bindoff, *Tudor England* (1959). An excellent brief survey.

J. B. Black, *The Reign of Elizabeth, 1558–1603* (2nd ed., 1959). An outstanding work.

E. Lipson, *Economic History of England* (3 vols., 1956). Volume II presents the best overall treatment of economic life in Elizabethan England.

* J. E. Neale, *Queen Elizabeth I* (2nd ed., 1952). The best biography.

J. U. Nef, *The Rise of the British Coal Industry* (2 vols., 1932). An important study, though it tends to overstate the extent of industrialization in sixteenth–seventeenth century England.

C. Read, *Mr. Secretary Walsingham* (3 vols., 1925), *Mr. Secretary Cecil and Queen Elizabeth* (1955), *Lord Burghley and Queen Elizabeth* (1960). Thorough studies of English governmental policy.

H. L. Rowse, *The Elizabethan Age* (2 vols., 1950–55). Captures the color and excitement of the era.

R. H. Tawney, *The Agrarian Problem in the Sixteenth Century* (1912). A study of the effects of the growing commercialization of agriculture on noncapitalistic landowners.

CHAPTER 7: THE BORDERLANDS OF EUROPE

Russia, 1533–1682

J. H. Billington, *The Icon and the Axe* (1966). A history of Russian culture written with imagination and verve.

* J. Blum, *Lord and Peasant in Russia from the Ninth to the Nineteenth Century* (1961). Deals with agrarian developments.

G. N. Lantzeff, *Siberia in the Seventeenth Century* (1943). An outstanding work on Russian expansion eastward.

P. I. Liashchenko, *History of the National Economy in Russia to the 1917 Revolution* (1949). A Soviet work of prime importance.

W. K. Medlin, *Moscow and East Rome* (1952). First-rate study of relations between church and state.

G. Vernadsky, *The Mongols and Russia* (1953) and *Russia at the Dawn of the Modern Age* (1959). Scholarly and well written volumes.

R. I. Wipper, *Ivan Grozny* (1947). The official Soviet view of Ivan the Terrible as a great national hero.

Poland to 1660

O. Halecki, *Borderlands of Western Civilization: A History of East Central Europe* (1952). A political history of the region lying between Germany and Russia.

——, *A History of Poland* (1956). Has a strong Polish nationalistic bias.

W. F. Reddaway et al., eds., *The Cambridge History of Poland* (2 vols., 1941–50). A useful collaborative work.

Scandinavia to 1660

N. G. Ahnlund, *Gustaf Adolf, the Great* (1940). A competent biography.

I. Andersson, *A History of Sweden* (1956). The standard general history in English.

J. H. S. Birch, *Denmark in History* (1938). A rather elementary survey.

E. F. Heckscher, *An Economic History of Sweden* (1954). Contains a brief treatment of the economic development of the era.

C. de Lannoy, *A History of Swedish Colonial Expansion* (1938). Deals with the Swedish Empire and its impact on Swedish domestic history.

K. Larsen, *A History of Norway* (1948). Competent and well written.

P. Lauring, *A History of the Kingdom of Denmark* (1960). A mediocre survey.

M. Roberts, *Gustavus Adolphus: A History of Sweden 1611–1632* (2 vols., 1953–58). A major contribution.

The Ottoman Empire to 1656

A. D. Alderson, *The Structure of the Ottoman Dynasty* (1956). A careful study of the institution of the sultanate.

* C. Brockelman, *History of the Islamic Peoples* (1947). An attempt at a comprehensive history of the Middle East.

W. H. McNeill, *Europe's Steppe Frontier, 1500–1800* (1964). Sketches the history of the great eastern European plainland that was divided among the Ottoman, Austrian, and Russian empires.

R. B. Merriman, *Suleiman the Magnificent* (1944). Biography of the greatest Ottoman ruler.

A. Pallis, *In the Days of the Janissaries* (1951). An interesting account of Ottoman social history.

L. Stavrianos, *The Balkans Since 1453* (1958). An indispensable work.

D. M. Vaughan, *Europe and the Turk: A Pattern of Alliances, 1350–1700* (1954). Treats Turkey's role in international affairs.

P. Wittlek, *The Rise of the Ottoman Empire* (1958). An outstanding brief account.

CHAPTER 8: SOCIAL, INTELLECTUAL, AND CULTURAL
DYNAMISM, 1500–1660

Society and Social Dynamics

M. Campbell, *The English Yeoman under Elizabeth and the Early Stuarts* (1942). An important study of the role of the yeomanry in English society.

F. L. Carsten, *The Origins of Prussia* (1954). Traces the main social and political developments in the history of Brandenburg-Prussia to the mid-seventeenth century.

* G. N. Clark, *The Seventeenth Century* (1931). Analytical essays on aspects of the life of the period, including economic development, population, and cultural life.

J. C. Davis, *The Decline of the Venetian Nobility as a Ruling Class* (1962). Follows the fortunes of the Venetian aristocracy from the mid-sixteenth to the end of the eighteenth century.

* C. J. Friedrich, *The Age of the Baroque, 1610–1660* (1952). An effort to relate politics to other aspects of life during this era.

* J. H. Hexter, *Reappraisals in History* (1961). Includes sparkling essays on Tudor and Stuart social history.

W. K. Jordan, *Philanthropy in England, 1480–1660* (1960). Traces with great skill the changes in social attitudes and aspirations as revealed by bequests to charity.

* J. U. Nef, *Industry and Government in France and England, 1540–1640* (1940). Shows the contrast in the relationships between government and business in the two countries, and helps explain why their forms of government differed.

A. Simpson, *The Wealth of the Gentry, 1540–1640* (1961). A careful analysis based on the records of individuals and families.

L. Stone, *The Crisis of the Aristocracy, 1558–1641* (1965). A monumental study of the long-term changes in the prestige and wealth of the English nobility.

The Scientific Revolution

* H. Butterfield, *The Origins of Modern Science, 1300–1800* (1949). Well written essays for the general reader on selected topics.

M. Kaspar, *Kepler* (1959). A superb biography, translated from German.

* A. Koyré, *From the Closed World to the Infinite Universe* (1957). A brilliant discussion of the effects of the Scientific Revolution upon man's thoughts about God and the universe.

* T. S. Kuhn, *The Copernican Revolution* (1956). A vivid and illuminating analysis that makes difficult concepts understandable to the nonspecialist.

* G. de Santillana, *The Crime of Galileo* (1955). Fascinating account of Galileo's trial.

A. Wolf, *A History of Science, Technology, and Philosophy in the 16th and 17th Centuries* (1939). A storehouse of information.

Scientific Method and Political Theory

W. A. Dunning, *A History of Political Theories from Luther to Montesquieu* (1905). Long the standard work, and still very useful.

C. C. Gillispie, *The Edge of Objectivity* (1960). A masterly study of the advance in science since Galileo through the use of mathematical logic and experiment.

* T. S. Kuhn, *The Structure of Scientific Revolutions* (1962). A philosophically oriented explanation of the process by which accepted scientific concepts are replaced by new concepts.

G. H. Sabine, *A History of Political Theory* (3rd ed., 1961). The best general account.

* P. Smith, *A History of Modern Culture* (2 vols., 1930–34). The first volume of this now somewhat outdated but still very useful detailed account of European thought covers the period from 1543 to 1687.

* A. N. Whitehead, *Science and the Modern World* (1930). Places the scientific revolution in the context of Western culture.

The Baroque

M. F. Bukofzer, *Music in the Baroque Era* (1947). Valuable critical account of the musical styles and ideas of the period.

F. Haskell, *Patrons and Painters* (1963). Gracefully written study of the relationships between the art and society of Italy in the age of the baroque.

A. Hausser, *Mannerism* (2 vols., 1965). A controversial effort to identify mannerism as the starting point for modern art.

* W. Sypher, *Four Stages of Renaissance Style* (1955). Considers baroque as later stage of Renaissance style.

V. L. Tapié, *The Age of Grandeur* (1960). Surveys the art, architecture, and civilization of the seventeenth century.

* H. Wölfflin, *Principles of Art History* (1932). Defines baroque and contrasts it with the classical Renaissance style.

CHAPTER 9: AGE OF CRISIS, 1600–1660: ABSOLUTIST SOLUTION

Age of Crisis

E. Barker et al., eds., *The European Inheritance* (3 vols., 1954). Volume II contains a valuable interpretive essay by Sir George Clark.

Crisis in Europe 1560–1660 (1965), T. Aston, ed. An anthology of articles from the English journal *Past and Present*.

* C. J. Friedrich and C. Blitzer, *The Age of Power* (1957). A survey focused on the search for power in political and intellectual life.

* D. Ogg, *Europe in the Seventeenth Century* (6th ed., 1954). A general survey, useful for political history.

The Thirty Years' War

* H. J. C. von Grimmelshausen, *The Adventurous Simplicissimus* (transl., 1912). Contemporary German novel that tells much about life during the war.

H. Holborn, *A History of Modern Germany: the Reformation* (1959). The third part of this useful study deals with the origins of the war and the war itself.

* T. K. Rabb, *The Thirty Years' War* (1964). Readings presenting differing points of view on the causes, nature, and effects of the war.

M. Roberts, *Gustavus Adolphus: A History of Sweden 1611–1632* (2 vols., 1953–58). A definitive study.

——, *The Military Revolution 1560–1660* (1956). A brief, stimulating reassessment.

F. Watson, *Wallenstein: Soldier under Saturn* (1938). A sometimes inaccurate account, but the best biography in English.

* C. V. Wedgewood, *The Thirty Years' War* (1938). The best general account in English.

The Decline of Spain, 1598–1665

B. Chudoba, *Spain and the Empire, 1519–1643* (1952). An excellent study of the connections between the Spanish and Austrian Hapsburgs.

R. Trevor Davies, *Spain in Decline, 1621–1700* (1957). A useful survey, though lacking in analytical depth.

J. H. Elliott, *Imperial Spain, 1469–1716* (New York, 1964). The best survey of Spanish history of the era.

J. H. Elliott, *The Revolt of the Catalans* (1963). A superb analysis of the causes of Spanish decline after Philip II's death.

L. Goldscheider, *El Greco* (1954). A magnificently illustrated study.

C. H. Haring, *Trade and Navigation between Spain and the Indies* (1918). The standard study of Spain's Atlantic trade during the era of the Spanish Hapsburgs.

M. A. S. Hume, *The Court of Philip IV* (1907). An account of the fantastic atmosphere of the royal court.

J. Lassaigne, *Spanish Painting* (2 vols., 1952). Excellent reproductions and a scholarly text.

The Reconstruction of France

* J. Boulenger, *The Seventeenth Century in France* (1963). Translation of an old standard French work.

* C. J. Burckhardt, *Richelieu: His Rise to Power* (1964). Translation of an excellent German study.

P. R. Doolin, *The Fronde* (1935). A study of the revolt and the power of the monarchy.

Q. Hurst, *Henry of Navarre* (1938). A useful account.

* A. Huxley, *Grey Eminence* (1941). A stimulating if not scholarly biography of Richelieu's associate, the Capuchin Father Joseph.

* C. V. Wedgewood, *Richelieu and the French Monarchy* (1949). A brief, easily read study.

CHAPTER 10: ABSOLUTISM VERSUS OLIGARCHY: ENGLAND AND THE DUTCH REPUBLIC

England's Constitutional Crisis, 1603–1640

G. E. Aylmer, *The King's Servants* (1961). A detailed analysis of the social and economic status and political views of the men in the administration of Charles I.

* C. D. Bowen, *The Lion and the Throne* (1957). Well written biography of Sir Edward Coke, lord chief justice.

G. Davies, *The Early Stuarts, 1603–1660* (2nd ed., 1959). A useful survey of the politics of the era.

S. R. Gardiner, *The History of England from the Accession of James I to the Outbreak of the Civil War 1603–1642* (10 vols., 1899–1901). An endlessly detailed account, year by year.

* W. Haller, *The Rise of Puritanism* (1938). Examination of the teachings of Puritanism up to the revolution.

J. H. Hexter, *The Rule of King Pym* (1941). A study of the political opposition to King Charles I.

C. Hill, *The Century of Revolution, 1603–1714* (1961). The first two parts of this valuable survey cover the period from James I to the Revolution.

——, *Intellectual Origins of the English Revolution* (1965). A study of the intellectual forces that helped prepare the way for revolution.

M. A. Judson, *The Crisis of the Constitution* (1949). A valuable analysis of the conflicting political ideologies.

H. F. Kearney, *Strafford in Ireland* (1959). Revises some long-held views about Strafford's lord deputyship.

G. L. Mosse, *The Struggle for Sovereignty in England* (1950). Skilfully traces the evolution of constitutional ideas from the reign of Elizabeth to the Petition of Right (1628).

* W. Notestein, *The English People on the Eve of Colonization, 1603–1660* (1954). Provides a survey of social life and institutions.

R. H. Tawney, *Business and Politics under James I* (1958). A brilliant study of economic life shown through the career of Lionel Cranfield, merchant and high government official.

H. R. Trevor-Roper, *Archbishop Laud* (2nd ed., 1962). A careful, objective work.

M. Walzer, *The Revolution of the Saints* (1965). Portrays Puritanism as a by-product of the social dislocation of the era.

D. H. Willson, *King James VI and I* (1956). An outstanding biography.

"Another Protestant Republic"

C. H. Firth, *Oliver Cromwell and the Rule of the Puritans* (1900). Still regarded as the best scholarly biography of Cromwell.

* W. Haller, *Liberty and Reformation in the Puritan Revolution* (1955). Recounts the development of Puritanism during the 1640's.

C. V. Wedgewood, *The King's Peace* (1955), *The King's War* (1959), *A Coffin for King Charles* (1964). Successive volumes in a well written but traditional account of the history of the rebellion.

——, *Oliver Cromwell* (1939). A very readable biography.

P. Zagorin, *History of Political Thought in the English Revolution* (1954). A provocative survey.

The Rise of the Dutch Republic

* V. Barbour, *Capitalism in Amsterdam in the Seventeenth Century* (1959). A valuable study of the most important business center of the seventeenth century.

P. J. Blok, *History of the People of the Netherlands* (5 vols., 1898–1912). The standard general history. Volume III and the first part of volume IV cover the era from 1559 to 1660.

W. Bode, *Great Masters of Dutch and Flemish Painting* (1909). A useful general survey.

P. Geyl, *The Netherlands in the Seventeenth Century* (2 vols., 1961–64). A magisterial work by the great Dutch historian. Volume I goes to 1648.

J. Rosenberg, *Rembrandt* (2 vols., 1948). The outstanding treatment.

CHAPTER 11: THE PINNACLE OF FRENCH ABSOLUTISM

The Age of Louis XIV

* M. Ashley, *Louis XIV and the Greatness of France* (1946). An introductory survey.

* W. F. Church, ed., *The Greatness of Louis XIV. Myth or Reality* (1959). Well chosen selection of differing views of Louis XIV.

J. E. King, *Science and Rationalism in the Government of Louis XIV, 1661–1683* (1949). Explains the technique of government as a reflection of Cartesian rationalism.

* W. H. Lewis, *The Splendid Century* (1953). A well written popular account of aspects of French social life.

H. Martin, *The Age of Louis XIV* (2 vols., 1865). Translated from French, this old work is still of prime importance.

The New Cambridge Modern History, vol. V, *The Ascendancy of France 1648–88* (1961). Useful essays by leading scholars on various aspects of the period.

* F. L. Nussbaum, *The Triumph of Science and Reason, 1660–1685* (1953). A good survey of European history pivoting around Louis XIV's France.

D. Ogg, *Louis XIV* (1933). A good biography.

L. B. Packard, *The Age of Louis XIV* (1929). A very brief, good account.

F. Steegmuller, *The Grand Madamoiselle* (1956). A delightful biography based on the memoirs of Louis XIV's cousin who lived at the court.

Absolutism in Economics and Religion

C. W. Cole, *Colbert and a Century of French Mercantilism* (2 vols., 1939) and *French Mercantilism, 1683–1700* (1943). Scholarly studies crammed with data.

E. Lodge, *Sully, Colbert and Turgot* (1931). A very general comparative treatment, presenting Colbert's mercantilism as a failure.

W. C. Scoville, *The Persecution of the Huguenots and French Economic Development, 1680–1720* (1960). Shows that Louis' anti-Huguenot policies were not responsible for French economic decline.

A. P. Usher, *The History of the Grain Trade in France, 1400–1710* (1913). Valuable chapter on the seventeenth century.

The French Predominance

R. B. Mowat, *A History of European Diplomacy, 1451–1789* (1928). A standard work.

* J. B. Wolf, *The Emergence of the Great Powers, 1685–1715* (1951). A valuable synthesis, especially good for the international diplomacy and wars of the era.

French Culture

E. B. O. Borgerhoff, *The Freedom of French Classicism* (1950). An excellent study of seventeenth-century authors.

H. Brown, *Scientific Organizations in Seventeenth Century France* (1934). Shows the relationships between the government and the scientific community.

* A. Guérard, *The Life and Death of an Ideal* (1928). A scintillating analysis of the culture of seventeenth-century France.

J. Lough, *An Introduction to Seventeenth Century France* (1954). Shows the connections between literature and economic, social, and political life.

H. D. MacPherson, *Censorship under Louis XIV* (1929). Efforts at government control of literature.

CHAPTER 12: ABSOLUTISM IN AUSTRIA, SPAIN, AND PRUSSIA

For sketches of the history of these three countries from 1660 to 1705 see the volumes by Nussbaum and Wolf cited in the reading list for Chapter Eleven. For the years from 1715 to the 1740's see the appropriate sections in the following general works:

M. S. Anderson, *Europe in the Eighteenth Century* (1961). A very good survey of comparative history.

* M. Beloff, *The Age of Absolutism* (1954). A brief, well handled survey.

The New Cambridge Modern History, vol. VII, *The Old Regime, 1713–1763* (1957).

* P. Roberts, *The Quest for Security, 1715–1740* (1947). An uneven treatment.

The Rise of the Austrian Hapsburgs

P. Frischauer, *The Imperial Crown* (1939). A history of the Hapsburgs to 1792.

——, *Prince Eugene, 1663–1736* (1934). The only biography in English of the great Austrian statesman and general.

R. A. Kann, *A Study in Austrian Intellectual History from Late Baroque to Romanticism* (1960). A skilful analysis.

L. P. Léger, *History of Austria-Hungary* (1889). Translated from French, this antiquated work is the only general history in English.

C. A. Macartney, *Hungary: A Short History* (1962). The best account in English.

H. F. Schwarz, *The Imperial Privy Council in the Seventeenth Century* (1943). A scholarly study of the chief administrative agency of Hapsburg centralization.

The Rise of the Spanish Bourbons

R. Altamira, *A History of Spain* (1949). An impressionistic short history, translated from Spanish.

R. Herr, *The Eighteenth Century Revolution in Spain* (1958). An important study of changes in Spanish life and thought under Bourbon rule.

* H. V. Livermore, *A History of Spain* (1958). Informative but uninspired.

The Rise of Hohenzollern Prussia

W. H. Bruford, *Germany in the Eighteenth Century* (1935). A useful study of German society.

F. L. Carsten, *Princes and Parliaments in Germany from the Fifteenth to the Nineteenth Century* (1959). A study of the increase in princely power at the expense of the nobility and townsmen.

* G. A. Craig, *The Politics of the Prussian Army* (1955). Early chapters of this important book discuss the seventeenth and eighteenth centuries.

R. A. Dorwart, *The Administrative Reforms of Frederick William I of Prussia* (1953). A scholarly, valuable study.

R. R. Ergang, *The Potsdam Führer* (1941). A well done biography of the unpleasant Frederick William I.

S. B. Fay, *The Rise of Brandenburg-Prussia* (1937). A short, readable introduction.

G. P. Gooch, *Frederick the Great* (1947). A critical but still favorable treatment, told in large part through Frederick's own writings.

H. Holborn, *A History of Modern Germany: 1648–1840* (1964). The first section covers the confusing period in German history after 1648.

W. F. Reddaway, *Frederick the Great and the Rise of Prussia* (1904). A well written, favorable biography.

H. Rosenberg, *Bureaucracy, Aristocracy and Autocracy* (1958). A remarkable analysis of the emergence of the Prussian state bureaucracy and its impact on the Prussian social structure.

F. Schevill, *The Great Elector* (1947). A highly favorable and uncritical popular biography.

CHAPTER 13: ABSOLUTISM AND OLIGARCHY IN THE EAST

Russia Becomes a Great Power

See the appropriate chapters in the books cited in the reading list for Chapter Seven.

G. P. Gooch, *Catherine the Great and Other Studies* (1954). An urbane and fascinating portrait of the empress and her influence.

V. Kliuchevsky, *Peter the Great* (1958). A good translation of a famed pre-Soviet treatment.

J. A. R. Marriott, *Anglo-Russian Relations 1689–1943* (1944). A useful survey.

H. Rogger, *National Consciousness in Eighteenth-Century Russia* (1960). An important monograph showing the development of national feeling as part of Westernization.

* B. H. Sumner, *Peter the Great and the Emergence of Russia* (1951). An excellent brief survey.

——, *Peter the Great and the Ottoman Empire* (1950). The beginnings of Russian imperialism in the Near East.

* G. S. Thomson, *Catherine the Great and the Expansion of Russia* (1950). A well written brief survey.

The Decline and Disappearance of Poland

See the appropriate chapters in the books by Halecki cited in the reading list for Chapter Seven.

H. H. Kaplan, *The First Partition of Poland* (1962). A careful study showing the links between Poland's internal troubles and the intrigues of its powerful neighbors.

M. Kridl, *A Survey of Polish Literature and Culture* (1956). The first quarter of the book covers the period up to the end of the eighteenth century.

R. H. Lord, *The Second Partition of Poland* (1915). Long the standard work.

The Ottoman Empire, 1656–1792

See the appropriate chapters in the books cited in the readings for Chapter Seven.

H. A. R. Gibb and H. Bowen, *Islamic Society and the West* (2 vols., 1950–57). A detailed and comprehensive analysis of Ottoman governmental and religious institutions.

J. A. R. Marriott, *The Eastern Question* (4th ed., 1940). A survey of the Ottoman decline and the resulting effects in European international relations.

W. L. Wright, *Ottoman Statecraft: A Book of Counsel for Viziers and Governors* (1935). The long introduction is an excellent analysis of the Ottoman machinery of government.

CHAPTER 14: CONSTITUTIONALISM AND OLIGARCHY IN THE WEST

The Dutch Oligarchy, 1660–1766

P. Geyl, *The Netherlands in the Seventeenth Century, 1609–1715* (1961). Essential for an understanding of the era.

D. Ogg, *William III* (1956). An excellent biography.

H. H. Rowen, *The Ambassador Prepares for War: The Dutch Embassy of Arnauld de Pomponne, 1669–1671* (1957). Provides information about the Netherlands in De Witt's last years.

C. H. Wilson, *Profit and Power: A Study of England and the Dutch Wars* (1957) and *Anglo-Dutch Commerce and Finance in the Eighteenth Century* (1941). Important studies of economic aspects of Dutch-English relations.

Triumph of the English Oligarchy, 1660–1689

G. Davies, *The Restoration of Charles II, 1658–1660* (1955). A scholarly analysis of the background for the restoration of the English monarchy.

J. Locke, *Two Treatises on Government*, ed. by P. Laslett (1960). The lengthy introductory essay by the editor is of major importance for understanding Locke's political theory.

D. Ogg, *England in the Reign of Charles II* (2 vols., 1934) and *England in the Reigns of James II and William III* (1955). The best detailed surveys of the Restoration era.

G. M. Trevelyan, *The English Revolution, 1688–1689* (1939). A defense of the Revolution as the critical turning point in modern English history.

F. C. Turner, *James II* (1948). A good biography.

The Augustan Age of English Oligarchy, 1689–1760

E. Eyck, *Pitt versus Fox: Father and Son, 1735–1806* (1950). An authoritative study.

M. D. George, *London Life in the Eighteenth Century* (1925). An excellent social history.

D. Marshall, *English People in the Eighteenth Century* (1956). A study of the social structure of England.

J. H. Plumb, *Chatham* (1953). A readable and effective brief biography of the elder Pitt.

* ——, *England in the Eighteenth Century* (1951). An outstanding brief account.

——, *The First Four Georges* (1956). A very readable sketch of the first Hanoverian monarchs of Great Britain.

G. M. Trevelyan, *England Under Queen Anne* (3 vols., 1930–34). An exhaustive examination of the period.

R. Walcott, *English Politics in the Early Eighteenth Century* (1956). A careful study of the major groups within the Whig and Tory parties.

B. Williams, *The Whig Supremacy, 1714–1760* (1939). A detailed survey.

Dutch and British Oligarchy Beset, 1760–1790

C. Cone, *Burke and the Nature of Politics* (2 vols., 1957–64). A useful study.

S. Maccoby, *English Radicalism, 1762–1785* (1955). An exhaustive survey.

L. B. Namier, *The Structure of Politics at the Accession of George III* (2nd' ed., 1957), and *England in the Age of the American Revolution* (2nd ed., 1961). Major studies that revise long-held views of English political history of the era.

R. Pares, *King George III and the Politicians* (1953). An outstanding analysis of the operations of politics.

G. Rudé, *Wilkes and Liberty: A Social Study of 1763 to 1774* (1962). Studies the social background of the times and the political movements associated with Wilkes.

J. S. Watson, *The Reign of George III, 1760–1815* (1960). The best general study.

CHAPTER 15: WEALTH, WAR, AND EMPIRE

General Surveys

M. S. Anderson, *Europe in the Eighteenth Century* (1961). A very good survey of comparative history.

* W. L. Dorn, *Competition for Empire, 1740–1763* (1940). An extremely able synthesis.

* L. Gershoy, *From Despotism to Revolution* (1944). Well written and authoritative.

H. Heaton, *Economic History of Europe* (1948). An outstanding textbook, providing a sketch of economic development of the period.

Power and Plenty

G. N. Clark, *The Wealth of England, 1496–1760* (1946). A brief, informative study.

E. Heckscher, *Mercantilism* (rev. ed., 2 vols., 1955). The standard work.

E. A. J. Johnson, *Predecessors of Adam Smith* (1937). A well written study of the shift from mercantilistic theory.

K. E. Knorr, *British Colonial Theories, 1570–1850* (1944). A clear, useful analysis.

Europe Overseas: Colonies and Commerce

R. G. Albion, *Forests and Sea Power* (1926). A pioneering work showing the importance of naval stores in British colonial policy.

P. Bamford, *Forests and French Sea Power, 1660–1789* (1956). A first-rate study analyzing the rise and decline of French naval power.

The Cambridge History of the British Empire (9 vols., 1929–59). Volume I of this collaborative work provides a detailed study of the empire in the seventeenth and eighteenth centuries.

C. E. Carrington, *The British Overseas* (1950). A thousand-page comprehensive survey of British expansion.

K. Feiling, *Warren Hastings* (1954). A valuable account of the work of the first British governor-general of India, showing the confusion and corruption of British rule in the eighteenth century.

H. Furber, *John Company at Work* (1948). An account of the activities of the British East India Company and other companies in the second half of the eighteenth century.

* C. H. Haring, *The Spanish Empire in America* (1947). The best modern work on Spanish colonialism.

J. J. van Klaveren, *The Dutch Colonial System in the East Indies* (1953). A survey from the early seventeenth-century to 1939.

S. L. Mims, *Colbert's West Indian Policy* (1912). Shows the importance of Colbert's colonial policies in shaping the development of French colonialism.

* S. E. Morison, ed., *The Parkman Reader* (1955). Well chosen selections from the famed nineteenth-century multi-volume *France and England in North America*.

H. I. Priestley, *France Overseas through the Old Regime* (1939). Covers the history of the French Empire up to 1815.

* C. G. Robertson, *Chatham and the British Empire* (1948). An excellent brief survey of the work of the elder Pitt in building the empire.

* F. Tannenbaum, *Slave and Citizen: the Negro in the Americas* (1940). Maintains that the Spaniards were more considerate of their Negro slaves than were the English in North America.

B. H. M. Vlekke, *Nusantara: A History of the East Indian Archipelago* (1943). A useful survey.

G. M. Wrong, *The Rise and Fall of New France* (2 vols., 1928). A readable account.

Dynastic and Imperial Statecraft, 1700–1763

A. H. Buffington, *The Second Hundred Years' War, 1689–1815* (1929). A brief survey of French-British relations.

R. B. Mowat, *A History of European Diplomacy, 1451–1789* (1928). A useful survey.

* A. Sorel, *Europe under the Old Regime* (1947). Translation of a famed French study of the balance of power in the eighteenth century.

The American Revolution, 1763–1783

* J. R. Alden, *The American Revolution* (1954). An excellent presentation.

* S. F. Bemis, *The Diplomacy of the American Revolution* (1935). A detailed and precise study.

* O. M. Dickerson, *The Navigation Acts and the American Revolution* (1951). Questions the old view of the harmful effect of the Navigation Acts on colonial America.

M. Kraus, *The Atlantic Civilization* (1949). Demonstrates the influence of European colonies in America upon European thought and political life.

* E. S. Morgan, *The Birth of the Republic* (1956). A masterful brief survey that incorporates new interpretations.

CHAPTER 16: THE AGE OF SCIENCE

The Scientific Community of Intellect

H. Brown, *Scientific Organization in Seventeenth Century France* (1934). Shows the relationships between the government and the scientific community.

* M. Nicolson, *Science and the Imagination* (1956). A study of the impact of the new science on literature.

M. Ornstein, *The Role of Scientific Societies in the Seventeenth Century* (3rd ed., 1938). The best and most thorough study.

D. Stimson, *Scientists and Amateurs* (1948). A well written history of the Royal Society, emphasizing the seventeenth century.

* B. Willey, *The Seventeenth Century Background* (1934). Indicates the influence of the scientific revolution on writers and philosophers.

The Physical World

For general treatments see the works by Butterfield, Gillispie, and Wolf cited in the readings for Chapter Eight.

* E. N. daC. Andrade, *Sir Isaac Newton* (1950). The best brief biography.

A. E. Bell, *Christian Huygens and the Development of Science in the Seventeenth Century* (1947). A study of the Dutch scientist and his times.

M. Boas, *Robert Boyle and Seventeenth Century Chemistry* (1958). An important re-evaluation of Boyle's contribution.

A. R. Hall, *Galileo to Newton* (1963). A useful survey.

——, *The Scientific Revolution* (2nd ed., 1962). A closely reasoned analysis of scientific advance in the seventeenth and eighteenth centuries.

G. Holton and D. H. D. Roller, *Foundations of Modern Physical Science* (1958). An unusual textbook that combines physics and history, written by a physicist and an historian of science.

The Psychic World

R. I. Aaron, *John Locke* (2nd ed., 1955). A biography and detailed analysis of Locke's political theory, moral philosophy, and teachings on education and religion.

* J. Bronowski and B. Mazlish, *The Western Intellectual Tradition* (1960). A stimulating survey; Part II covers the period of this chapter.
M. Cranston, *John Locke* (1957). An excellent biography.

The World of Faith

F. L. Baumer, *Religion and the Rise of Scepticism* (1960). The development of scepticism from the seventeenth century to the present.
M. Bishop, *Pascal, the Life of Genius* (1936). A beautifully written scholarly biography.
* S. Hampshire, *Spinoza* (1951). A first-rate introduction.
* P. Hazard, *The European Mind: the Critical Years, 1680–1715* (1935). A famous work, showing the conflict between Christian dogma and science and rationalism.
R. S. Westfall, *Science and Religion in 17th Century England* (1958). A study of the interaction of science and religion as shown in the writings of the scientists.

The Social World

E. Beller and M. duP. Lee, Jr., *Selections from Bayle's Dictionary* (1952). Has a useful introduction.
M. A. Fitzsimons, A. G. Pundt, C. E. Nowell, eds., *The Development of Historiography* (1954). An encyclopedic survey of the development of historical writing.
R. F. Jones, *Ancients and Moderns* (1936). Treats the debates on the effect of increased scientific knowledge on human intellectual progress.
H. Robinson, *Bayle the Sceptic* (1931). The best work in English.
E. Roll, *A History of Economic Thought* (rev. ed., 1946). Contains a useful section on the early economists.
* P. Smith, *History of Modern Culture* (2 vols., 1930–34). A storehouse of information.

CHAPTER 17: THE ENLIGHTENMENT

The Philosophes

* C. Becker, *The Heavenly City of the Eighteenth Century Philosophers* (1932). Argues that the Age of Reason was really an age of faith.
D. D. Bien, *The Calas Affair* (1960). A well written and perceptive study of this famed episode in the history of toleration.
* H. N. Brailsford, *Voltaire* (1935). The best short biography in English.
* E. Cassirer, *The Philosophy of the Enlightenment* (1951). A major study of the basic philosophical ideas of the eighteenth century.
A. Cobban, *In Search of Humanity* (1960). A stimulating reassessment of the Enlightenment in relation to the present.
G. R. Cragg, *Reason and Authority in the Eighteenth Century* (1964). An excellent study of the Enlightenment in England.
* P. Gay, *Voltaire's Politics: the Poet as Realist* (1959). Shows that Voltaire's political ideas were pragmatic and not doctrinaire.

* G. R. Havens, *The Age of Ideas: From Reaction to Revolution in Eighteenth-Century France* (1955). Uses the biographical approach to explain the ideas of the Enlightenment.

* P. Hazard, *European Thought in the Eighteenth Century* (1954). A treatment of the conflict between Christian doctrine and the Enlightenment.

* F. E. Manuel, *The Age of Reason* (1951). A very good introductory survey.

* K. Martin, *French Liberal Thought in the Eighteenth Century* (rev. ed., 1954). A study of political ideas from Bayle to Condorcet.

R. O. Rockwood, ed., *Carl Becker's Heavenly City Revisited* (1958). A symposium of differing views on Becker's thesis about the Age of Reason.

R. V. Sampson, *Progress in the Age of Reason* (1956). A treatment of the philosophies of history of the Enlightenment.

H. Vyverberg, *Historical Pessimism in the French Enlightenment* (1958). Argues that there was an undercurrent of pessimism in eighteenth-century thought hostile to the belief in progress.

The Encyclopedists and the Progress of Science

A. and N. Clow, *The Chemical Revolution* (1952). A study of the chemical trade in eighteenth-century Scotland.

I. B. Cohen, *Franklin and Newton* (1956). An authoritative study of Franklin's work in electricity.

H. Guerlac, *Lavoisier, the Crucial Year* (1961). Explains the background and origin of Lavoisier's experiments in combustion in 1772.

* A. R. Hall, *The Scientific Revolution* (2nd ed., 1962). See the chapters on the eighteenth century.

A. Wilson, *Diderot, the Testing Years, 1713–1759* (1957). First of a planned two-volume biography.

A. Wolf, *A History of Science, Technology and Philosophy in the Eighteenth Century* (1939). A useful work of reference.

Counter-Enlightenment

* E. Cassirer, *The Question of Jean Jacques Rousseau* (1954). An effort to show the essential unity of Rousseau's thought.

C. W. Hendel, *Jean Jacques Rousseau* (2nd ed., 1934). Traces the development of Rousseau's philosophy.

A. D. Lindsay, *Kant* (1934). A good introduction to Kant's philosophy.

N. K. Smith, *The Philosophy of David Hume* (1941). A useful study.

J. L. Talmon, *The Rise of Totalitarian Democracy* (1952). Finds the origins of modern totalitarianism in Rousseau's political thought.

CHAPTER 18: THE CRISIS OF ABSOLUTISM

Enlightened Despotism

For general surveys see the books by Dorn, Gershoy, and Anderson listed in the suggested readings for Chapter Fifteen.

J. F. Bright, *Maria Theresa* (1897). Emphasizes political and international affairs.

G. Bruun, *The Enlightened Despots* (1929). A good brief account.

G. P. Gooch, *Maria Theresa and Other Studies* (1951). Ably shows the qualities of character and judgment of the Empress.

R. Herr, *The Eighteenth Century in Spain* (1958). Excellent for enlightened despotism in Spain.

F. Hertz, *The Development of the German Public Mind*, vol. II (1962). An important study, especially valuable for Frederick II and his political ideas.

R. J. Kerner, *Bohemia in the Eighteenth Century* (1932). Deals chiefly with the reigns of Joseph II and Leopold II.

The New Cambridge Modern History, vol. VII, *The Old Regime, 1713–1763* (1957). Contains useful chapters on all aspects of this period.

S. K. Padover, *The Revolutionary Emperor: Joseph the Second, 1741–1790* (1934). A useful biography, although uncritical at times.

Louis XV and Fleury

* A. Cobban, *A History of Modern France* (2 vols., 1960). Volume I covers the eighteenth century.

P. Gaxotte, *Louis XV and his Times* (1934). A defense of the king.

G. P. Gooch, *Louis XV; the Monarchy in Decline* (1956). A condemnation of Louis' political ineptitude.

E. J. Lowell, *France under Louis XV* (2 vols., 1897). An old but still useful general treatment.

The Failure to Renovate France

M. Beer, *An Inquiry into Physiocracy* (1939). A very competent brief survey.

P. Beik, *A Judgment of the Old Regime* (1944). A survey of economic and fiscal policies at the end of the Seven Years' War.

A. Bourde, *The Influence of England on the French Agronomes, 1750–1789* (1953). A study of French agricultural developments.

G. T. Mathews, *The Royal General Farms in Eighteenth Century France* (1958). A careful study of the institution of tax farming.

W. Scoville, *Capitalism and French Glassmaking 1640–1789* (1950). An exemplary monograph, showing the transition to large-scale manufacturing.

H. See, *Economic and Social Conditions in France during the Eighteenth Century* (1927). A good survey.

France on the Eve of Revolution

E. Barber, *The Bourgeoisie in Eighteenth Century France* (1955). A study of the ideals and motivations of the middle classes.

D. Dakin, *Turgot and the Ancien Régime in France* (1939). Offers good description and analysis of the system of government.

F. L. Ford, *The Robe and the Sword* (1953). An analysis of the aristocratic resurgence.

R. Forster, *The Nobility of Toulouse in the Eighteenth Century* (1960). An excellent study of the economic and social activity of the nobility.

* G. Lefebvre, *The Coming of the French Revolution* (1947). A translation of the best survey of the social and economic history of the Old Regime.
* A. de Tocqueville, *The Old Regime and the French Revolution* (1955). A classic.
A. Young, *Travels in France during the Years 1787, 1788, 1789* (1929). An invaluable contemporary account by an observant Englishman.

CHAPTER 19: THE FRENCH REVOLUTION

General Accounts

* C. C. Brinton, *The Anatomy of Revolution* (1938). A comparative study of revolutions with emphasis on the French Revolution.
* ——, *A Decade of Revolution, 1789–1799* (1934). A well written survey, somewhat critical of the Revolution.
P. Farmer, *France Reviews its Revolutionary Origins* (1944). A survey of the changes in the interpretations of the Revolution.
N. Hampson, *A Social History of the French Revolution* (1963). A perceptive analysis of the interaction between social structure and political action.
G. Lefebvre, *The French Revolution* (2 vols., 1963–64). The best account, by a great French scholar.

The Coming of the Revolution and the Constitutional Monarchy

R. M. Brace, *Bordeaux and the Gironde, 1789–1794* (1947). A study of middle-class involvement in the revolutionary movement.
C. C. Brinton, *The Jacobins* (1930). Portrays Jacobinism as a kind of religious movement.
R. K. Gooch, *Parliamentary Government in France: Revolutionary Origins, 1789–1791* (1960). A study of the abortive attempt to introduce parliamentary government.
* G. Lefebvre, *The Coming of the French Revolution* (1947). The best brief account of the background of the revolution through October, 1789.
* A. Mathiez, *The French Revolution* (1928). A strong defense of the revolution by a famous authority.
R. W. Phipps, *The Armies of the First French Republic and the Rise of the Marshals of Napoleon* (5 vols., 1926–39). An exhaustive account.
C. B. Rogers, *The Spirit of Revolution in 1789* (1949). Shows the unrest among the masses.
* G. Rudé, *The Crowd in the French Revolution* (1959). An examination of the composition and motives of the revolutionary mobs.
M. J. Sydenham, *The Girondins* (1961). A revisionist study that claims that there was no real difference between the policies of the Girondins and the Montagnards.

The Republic of Virtue, 1792–1794

* J. D. Godfrey, *Revolutionary Justice* (1951). Deals with the organization and procedures of the revolutionary tribunals.

D. Greer, *The Incidence of the Terror: A Statistical Interpretation* (1935) and *The Incidence of Emigration during the French Revolution* (1951). These studies show that members of all classes, not just nobles, suffered from the excesses of the Revolution.

W. F. Shepherd, *Price Control and the Reign of Terror* (1953). A careful, detailed monograph.

A. Soboul, *The Parisian Sans-Culottes and the French Revolution 1793–1794* (1964). An important study.

J. M. Thompson, *Robespierre* (2 vols., 1935). The best biography.

* ——, *Robespierre and the French Revolution* (1953). An excellent brief survey.

Reaction and Irresolution, 1794–1799

J. C. Herold, *Bonaparte in Egypt* (1963). An exciting account, treated in depth.

G. Lefebvre, *The Thermidoreans and the Directory* (1964). A balanced treatment.

* A. Mathiez, *After Robespierre; the Thermidorean Reaction* (1931). An important study, especially valuable for the account of political retaliations.

B. Morton, *Brumaire, the Rise of Bonaparte* (1948). A well done, popular account.

D. Thomson, *The Babeuf Plot: The Making of a Republican Legend* (1947). A careful study of the leftist group.

The Impact of the French Revolution

* P. Amann, ed., *The Eighteenth-Century Revolution, French or Western?* (1963). Selections from writings reappraising the French Revolution as part of a Western revolution.

G. P. Gooch, *Germany and the French Revolution* (1920). A standard work.

R. R. Palmer, *The Age of the Democratic Revolution* (2 vols., 1959–64). Views the French Revolution as part of a revolution of the Western world.

E. Wangerman, *From Joseph II to the Jacobin Trials* (1959). Studies the impact of the French Revolution in Austria up to 1794.

CHAPTER 20: THE NAPOLEONIC ERA

Napoleon Bonaparte

* G. Bruun, *Europe and the French Imperium 1799–1814* (rev. ed., 1957). The best one-volume survey, with an excellent bibliographical essay.

W. Greer, *Napoleon and his Family; the Story of a Corsican Clan* (3 vols., 1927–29). Informative; drawn in large part from a thirteen-volume work in French.

* F. Markham, *Napoleon and the Awakening of Europe* (1954). The best brief survey.

——, *Napoleon* (1964). An excellent brief biography.

F. Pratt, *The Road to Power* (1939) and *The Empire and the Glory: Napoleon Bonaparte, 1800–1806* (1949). Popular accounts by an outstanding American military historian.

J. H. Rose, *Life of Napoleon I* (2 vols., 1902). A detailed study.

S. Wilkinson, *Rise of General Bonaparte* (1930). An able discussion of Napoleon's military training and early career.

The Domestic Reformer

J. B. Brissard, *History of French Private Law* (1912) and *History of French Public Law* (1915). For detailed discussion of Napoleon's legal reforms.

R. B. Holtman, *Napoleonic Propaganda* (1950). A study of methods of "thought-control."

B. C. Poland, *French Protestantism and the French Revolution, 1685–1815* (1957). A useful study.

H. H. Walsh, *The Concordat of 1801* (1933). A study of Napoleon's agreement with the pope.

The Empire Builder

E. N. Anderson, *Nationalism and the Cultural Crisis in Prussia, 1806–1815* (1939). The growth of the idea of nationalism based on a study of seven leading figures.

* C. C. Brinton, *The Lives of Talleyrand* (1936). A very readable biography of Napoleon's foreign minister.

A. Bryant, *The Years of Endurance, 1793–1802* (1942); *The Years of Victory, 1802–1812* (1944); *The Age of Elegance, 1812–1822* (1950). Studies of Great Britain during the Revolutionary and Napoleonic eras.

H. C. Deutsch, *The Genesis of Napoleonic Imperialism* (1938). A valuable study, going up to 1805.

E. Heckscher, *The Continental System: an Economic Interpretation* (1922). Deals with effects of the system on both the French and British economies.

E. F. Kraehe, *Metternich's German Policy*, vol. I, *The Contest with Napoleon* (1963). A work of prime importance.

C. N. Parkinson, *The Trade Winds. A Study of British Overseas Trade during the French Wars, 1793–1815* (1948). A study in fluctuations and changing patterns in commerce.

R. J. Rath, *The Fall of the Napoleonic Kingdom of Italy* (1941). A superior study of the forces leading to the collapse of the Napoleonic Italian state.

W. O. Shanahan, *Prussian Military Reforms, 1786–1813* (1945). A careful and detailed study.

W. M. Simon, *The Failure of the Prussian Reform Movement, 1807–1819* (1955). A superior analysis of the obstacles to reform and the triumph of Prussian authoritarianism.

E. Tarlé, *Napoleon's Invasion of Russia, 1812* (1942). Written by a Soviet historian.

The Napoleonic Legacy

* P. Geyl, *Napoleon: For and Against* (1949). A fascinating analysis of the changes in judgments of Napoleon since 1815.

A. L. Guérard, *Reflections on the Napoleonic Legend* (1923). A detached judgment of Napoleon and a study of the genesis and growth of his legend.

R. Korngold, *The Last Years of Napoleon* (1950). A sympathetic account.

Index

Fedor, Tsar, 164
Ferdinand of Aragon, 98
Ferdinand, Emperor (Holy Roman Empire),
207, 208, 209; and Wallenstein, 210
Ferdinand III (Holy Roman Empire), 281
Ferdinand (Hungary), 139; and Turkish ag-
gression, 144; elected emperor, 144
Ferdinand and Isabella (Spain), 103-105;
and Columbus, 49; and unruly nobility,
105; church-state relationship, 114; In-
quisition, 130
Ferdinand VI (Spain), 187, 189
Fesch, Joseph, 470
Feudal law, 31
Feudalism, 20; in England, 30; in Germany,
32; peasant revolt, 37; 15th century, 106
Fichte, Johann Gottlieb, 485
Ficino, Marsilio, 86
Finland, and Russian wars, 313; loss of
territory, 327
First Estate, 443, 446-447
First French Republic, 464
First Northern War, 177; Denmark and, 323
First Treaty of Paris (1814), 487
Fiume, 285
Five Great Farms (France), 265
Five Hundred, Council of (France), 462
Flanders, 25; manufacturing in, 23; trade,
60; decline of, 61; art in, 80
Flemish school of painting, 80
Fleury, Cardinal, 374, 432-433
Florence, workers uprising, 37; Black
Death, 37; economic warfare, 38; woolen
industry, 44; Platonic Academy, 70, 86;
art in, 74; architectural center, 78; bal-
ance of power, 93; city-state, 94-95
Florentine Academy, 75
Florentine Republic, 94
Formosa, Dutch trade with, 361
Fouché, Joseph, 473
Fouquet, Nicholas, 258
France, 7; paleolithic age, 9; Burgundians,
15; conquered by Franks, 16; formation
of, 17; and Vikings, 19; growth of towns,
24; monarchy in, 30-31; war with England, 32; Black Death, 37; Hundred
Years' War, 37; economy, 44; Mongol
representatives, 47; explores North America, 53; slave trade, 57; decline of, 60;
and Spanish decline, 62; invasion of Italy,
79, 81; and Italian culture, 79; Renaissance architecture, 81; humanism in, 82;
monarchy, 97-98; under Louis XI, 99; war
with Italy, 101, 107-110, 141; hold of
Church on, 101; Turks as allies, 108; Protestant Reformation, 111; Lutheranism in,
113; church-state relationship, 115;
Calvinism in, 125, 145; Jesuits in, 132;
Protestants allied with, 140; religious
wars in, 144-147; influence of, in Scotland, 158; relations with England under
Elizabeth I, 159; reformation in, 183; absolutism in, 206, 253, 255-277; and Thirty
Years' War, 211; and Peace of Westphalia,
213; and Peace of the Pyrenees, 213;
reconstruction of, 219-225; nobility in,
222, 445-446; war with England, 235;

subjugation of nobility, 259; income tax,
259; East India trade, 265; throne to control Church, 266; predominance of, under
Louis XIV, 269-273; War of Devolution,
271; war with Dutch, 271-272; culture,
273-277; alliance against Spain, 284; and
partition of Poland, 320; Sweden an ally,
327; invades Holland, 335, 368; North
American empire, 346, 364-365, 375; economic policy, 358; influence of, in India,
373-374; Treaty of Paris, 376; despotism
in, 431-439; regal interregnum, 435-436;
single tax structure, 436; pre-revolutionary, 436-442; noble assertion, 438;
Assembly of Notables, 440; aristocratic
rebellion, 441; Estates-General summoned, 441; peasantry in, 444; constituent assembly, 452; Catholicism in, 452-
453, 471; Church property confiscated,
452-453; Pope denounces, 453; Constitutional Monarchy, 453; war with Austria,
455; end of monarchy, 455; a republic,
456; reforms under Napoleon, 471; Jews
in, 472; Protestantism in, 472; Second
Coalition, 473, 476; Peace of Amiens,
475; Third Coalition, 476; war with U.S.,
481; loss of Napoleonic empire, 485-487.
See also French Revolution, Huguenots,
Napoleon.
Franche-Comté, 99; and War of Devolution,
271
Francis of Assisi, Saint, 27
Francis I (Austria), 405
Francis II (Austria), 455
Francis I (France), 101; and Italian culture,
79; church-state relationships, 115; and
Holy Roman Empire, 141
Francis II (France), 145, 153
Francis II (Holy Roman Empire), and
Napoleon, 478
Francis, Duke of Guise, 145-146
Franciscans, 27, 112; and Savonarola, 95
Franco-Dutch War (1672-1679), 264, 271-
272; Sweden and, 324
Franklin, Benjamin, 404, 410, 415; and
French *philosophes*, 382; and electrical
experiments, 414
Franks, 15-16
Frederick, Elector (Palitinate), 208, 209
Frederick, Elector (the Wise, of Saxony),
118, 119; supports Luther, 117
Frederick I (Denmark), 121
Frederick I (Prussia), 294
Frederick II (the Great, of Prussia), 297,
298-302, 405; War of the Austrian Succes-
sion, 284; averts Russo-Austrian War,
317; Seven Years' War, 376; and Voltaire,
408; despotic rule, 422-423
Frederick Henry (Denmark), 332
Frederick Henry (of Orange), 246
Frederick William I (Great Elector of Bran-
denburg), 291-294
Frederick William I (Prussia), 294-297, 372
Frederick William II (Prussia), and French
Revolution, 454
Frederick William III (Prussia), and Napo-
leon, 477-478; allies with Russia, 485

NORTH

SEA

IRELAND

DENMARK

S W

Cope

GREAT
BRITAIN

Amsterdam

Hamburg

Elbe R.

Berlin

ATLANTIC

Brussels

Rhine R.

CONFEDERATION

Frankfurt

OCEAN

Seine R.

Paris

OF THE

Prague

Loire R.

Danube

FRANCE

RHINE

SWITZ.

KINGDOM

ILLYRIA

PORTUGAL

Rhone R.

Milan

OF ITALY

Madrid

Genoa

SPAIN

CORSICA

KINGDOM

Rome

NAPL

SARDINIA

Naples

M E D I T E R R A N E A N

KI
O

A F R I C A